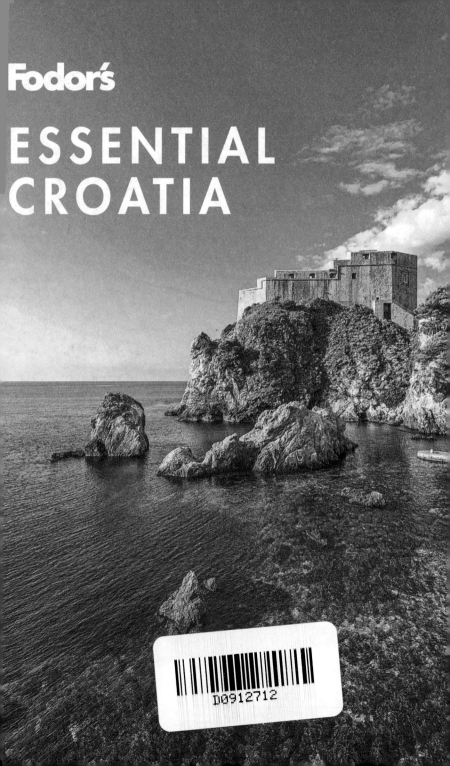

Fodor's
ESSENTIAL CROATIA

D0912712

Welcome to Croatia

Croatia's splendors extend from the deep-blue waters of the Adriatic coastline to the waterfall-laced mountains of the Dinaric Alps and throughout its medieval towns. From Dubrovnik's walled city where baroque buildings are surrounded by centuries-old forts to the lively islands of Brač and Hvar, this Central European country is an exciting blend of glamour and tradition. This book was produced in the middle of the COVID-19 pandemic. As you plan your upcoming travels to Croatia, please confirm that places are still open and let us know when we need to make updates by writing to us at editors@fodors.com.

TOP REASONS TO GO

★ **History:** Dubrovnik's walled Old Town, Split's Diocletian palace.

★ **Cool Cities:** Zagreb's museums and café culture, Rovinj's old city charm.

★ **Beaches:** From secluded hideaways to ocean-side party spots, each beach is unique.

★ **Natural Parks:** Plitvice Lakes, Brijuni Islands, Mljet.

★ **Wine:** From Istria to Korčula, vineyards and wineries abound.

★ **Sailing:** Southern Dalmatia's dramatic coastline is paradise for boating enthusiasts.

Contents

Chapter 1

EXPERIENCE CROATIA

20 ULTIMATE EXPERIENCES

Croatia offers terrific experiences that should be on every traveler's list. Here are Fodor's top picks for a memorable trip.

1 Dubrovnik

Few sights in Croatia are as impressive or popular as this medieval wonder of a city. With its ancient walls and bell towers set high above the blue waters of the Adriatic, Dubrovnik commands a spectacular location. *(Ch. 3)*

2 Sailing

A 1,100-mile coastline studded with stunning islands, emerald inlets, unspoiled beaches, and lively towns makes the country a paradise for avid boating enthusiasts. *(Ch. 1)*

3 Diocletian's Palace, Split

The city's main attraction, the Roman emperor Diocletian's summer palace, dates to the 3rd century AD; its spectacular walls surround the old town. *(Ch. 4)*

4 Hvar

The seaside town of Hvar is the country's nightlife capital and a favorite destination of yachting revelers and nature enthusiasts alike. *(Ch. 4)*

5 Seafood

Croatians delight in trying fresh fish, sardines, oysters, mussels, and octopus, often taken from the sea right beside your dining location. *(Ch. 3-7)*

6 Plitvice National Park

One of eight national parks in the country (and perhaps the most spectacular), Plitvice National Park has 16 magnificent lakes connected by cascades. *(Ch. 8)*

7 Zagreb

With a thriving café culture, the country's best museums, great shopping, and plenty of green space, underrated Zagreb offers the rare chance to experience a living European city without the crowds. *(Ch. 8)*

8 Wine

Sometimes touted as "the new Tuscany," Istria is known for its white Malvazija and red Teran. Vineyards produce excellent wines, many from villages like Motovun. *(Ch. 7)*

9 Café Culture

Coffee drinking is a favorite national pastime. Do it the local way: linger at a café, watch the world go by, and practice ordering a *bijela kav* ("white coffee"). *(Ch. 3-9)*

10 Beaches

Lovely pebble beaches abound in Croatia, but Zlatni Rat, a spit of land on Brač Island, is particularly stunning with its white sand, lush pine groves, and intensely blue water. *(Ch. 3–6)*

11 Biking

Exploring towns, islands, and the countryside by bike is both fun and smart. The inland region of Slavonia is made for cycling with its flat roads, miles of bike lanes, and well-traveled routes. *(Ch. 9)*

12 Old Wine Cellars in Ilok

Croatia's easternmost town also offers one the country's most unique wine experiences in the form of its historic wine cellars. *(Ch. 9)*

13 Vukovar

A visit to this Slavonian city is both a sobering reminder of the tragedies that unfolded here in the last half century and an inspiring vision of a city rebuilt. *(Ch. 9)*

14 Istria's Hill Towns

Perhaps the most perfect road trip in Croatia involves visiting medieval towns like Grožnjan and Motovun, sampling wine, olive oil, and truffles along the way. *(Ch. 7)*

15 Kvarner Bay Islands

Four of Croatia's largest, wildest islands—Cres, Rab, Krk and Lošinj—offer dramatic views, diverse landscapes, sandy beaches, and excellent island-hopping opportunities. *(Ch. 6)*

16 Korčula

This pine-covered island is steeped in history, from its reputation as the birthplace of Marco Polo to the legendary sea battles that were waged along its shores. *(Ch. 3)*

17 Opatija Resorts

Genteel Opatija has been a resort town since the 1840s, fashionable among the high society who came to stay in its elegant spas and grand villas. *(Ch. 6)*

18 Varazdin

A town of castles, ornate cemeteries, and thermal springs, Varazdin makes a wonderful day trip from Zagreb. *(Ch. 8)*

19 Kornati National Park

This archipelago with more than 100 uninhabited islands, islets, and reefs is a nautical paradise in Northern Dalmatia. *(Ch. 5)*

20 Roman Ruins in Pula

Pula boasts one of the largest and best-preserved ancient Roman arenas in the world; today, it makes a stunning backdrop to concerts and the annual Pula Film Festival. *(Ch. 7)*

WHAT'S WHERE

1 Dubrovnik and Southern Dalmatia. Few cities in the world impress as Dubrovnik does, with its ancient walls and towers perched above the deep blue waters of the Adriatic. If you need to escape the crowds, cruise to the lush Elafiti islands, Korčula, or Mljet, or head south to the bucolic Konavle region.

2 Split and Central Dalmatia. With the remains of the 2,000-year old Diocletian's Palace that dominate its Old Town, Split makes a fascinating jumping-off point to the islands of Vis, Brač, or Hvar.

3 Zadar and Northern Dalmatia. Low-key Zadar offers a pleasant seaside atmosphere and easy access to four beautiful national parks.

4 Kvarner Bay and the Northern Adriatic Islands. Protected by mountain ranges on three sides, Kvarner enjoys a particularly mild climate, with Opatija, Rijeka, and nearby islands beckoning visitors to explore.

5 Istria. On Croatia's western peninsula, distinct Roman and Venetian influences blend into a vibrant café scene and the best cuisine in the country.

6 Zagreb and Inland Croatia. Croatia's interior capital is a charming, well-kept city that evokes a distant Habsburg past and features a host of excellent museums. Well-maintained roads lead to Plitvice National Park, a spectacular series of 16 cascading lakes nestled in a wild forest.

7 Slavonia. The country's largest region offers charming Pannonian villages, centuries-old wineries, and quiet rural life.

8 Montenegro. This tiny country lies on the Adriatic coast, just south of Dubrovnik and its beautiful coastline makes for a popular side trip.

9 Slovenia. Located just past Croatia's northwest border, Slovenia is filled with stunning natural beauty and a distinctive culture all its own.

Croatia Today

After centuries of being a part of larger political entities, Croatia's three decades of independence have been anything but steady. Coming out of the former Yugoslavia into a messy civil war, Croatia very swiftly traveled the long and winding road from a war zone to one of the world's must-see travel destinations. Few European countries have seen such highs and lows.

TOURISM (AND OVERTOURISM)

Croatian territory encompasses some of the most stunning locations on the Mediterranean. From the truffle-bearing forests of Istria to the gleaming limestone cities of Dalmatia, Croatia is a singularly beautiful country. Although it has been a popular destination for European travelers for years (some of its busiest seasons were between World War II and 1991, when Europeans flocked to the resorts and hotels in Istria and Dalmatia), as little as ten years ago it still stood out as the "best buy" spot on the Mediterranean, with history, sights, service, and safety at reasonable rates. But due to the migrant crisis that affected Turkey and Greece and aided by an increasing number of cruise ships and a proliferation of private accommodations, Croatia has seen an unprecedented tourism boom in the last few years, with tourism now accounting for up to 20% of its GDP. Destinations like Hvar, Plitvice National Park, and Dubrovnik became poster children for the blight of overtourism, where the pressure of so many visitors put a massive strain on the infrastructure and quality of life for locals, and severely impacted the experience for visitors.

After recording its highest tourist numbers ever between 2017 and 2019, the COVID-19 crisis hit Croatia hard, particularly Dubrovnik, where tourist numbers fell up to 80%, ravaging the local economy and highlighting the danger of relying too heavily on one sector. Local officials saw it as an opportunity to rebuild from the ground up, putting sustainability at the core of its tourism plan moving forward. The challenge for the entire country in the years to come is how to manage growth while maintaing its beautiful nature and authentic culture.

POST-WAR CROATIA

The war ended 30 years ago, and you could theoretically visit today and not realize that anything untoward happened here. Croatia is a remarkably safe country with one of the lowest violent crime rates in Europe. But scratch the surface and you will find remnants of the physical damage that remains: in Dalmatia, many of the grand Communist-era hotels lay in ruins, having been abandoned during the war. It is still a significant part of the national psyche, and in most conversations with a Croatian person that goes beyond the basic pleasantries, the war will almost inevitably come up. If you're interested in learning more, there are museums and memorials in many towns, including the Homeland War Museum in Dubrovnik and the entire city of Vukovar in Slavonia, which is akin to a living war museum.

FAMILY

Like in many European countries, family is everything to Croatians. It isn't uncommon to see multiple generations living in the same house, and children tend to remain under their parents' roof until they get married. Often in family restaurants or hotels, grandparents are in the kitchen cooking while the kids are running around outside school hours. The older generation is an active part of society; you'll find them swimming in the sea, shopping in the markets, sitting in the cafe-bars, and taking care of their grandchildren. By the same token, kids are very much a part of daily life; you'll see them in restaurants, playgrounds, and around town much later than you might consider their bedtime. Few differences are as apparent as the schism in customer service and attitude between the generation that grew up in communist Yugoslavia and the younger generation that has been exposed to Western influence. Perhaps the most pragmatic difference is of linguistic nature: older people will be more likely to speak German, Italian, or Russian, while younger people lean towards English, which they speak very well.

AUTHENTICALLY CROATIAN

Even with the increasing number of tourists, there's something that feels authentic about Croatia. Destinations that might be packed with chain hotels and tourist-trap restaurants in other countries still retain a natural, local vibe here. Only the most modern of restaurants play anything other than very traditional *klapa* music, and folk festivals are still enthusiastically celebrated by all ages. Nature, particularly the sea, is cherished, and you won't find many eyesores blighting the landscape. Croatians, especially the older generation, won't go far out of their way to accommodate tourists; they live their lives, and you're welcome to take part or not. No one is in a hurry here, and the best way to make friends is to sit down for a drink and have a conversation.

LOOKING AHEAD

Corruption in politics and bureaucracy has not changed much since the country's Communist days, and it can be discouraging to start a business in Croatia. The long-awaited accession into the European Union in 2013 opened the door for a freer movement of capital and people, but many people, especially young Croats seeking a more secure future, still left for places like Germany and Ireland. However, there is hope for the future as young entrepreneurs try to cut through the red tape to open new ventures such as wineries, craft breweries, art galleries, IT companies, and start-ups. There is also a burgeoning music festival scene here that rivals any in Europe, cutting-edge museums, and a culinary movement that is gaining international renown. There are also many Croatians who left during the Communist years or during the war who are now coming back with the means and brains to re-establish themselves and breathe new life into the country.

What to Eat and Drink in Croatia

SEAFOOD

From locally caught fish like sea bass and tuna to dishes like black risotto (made with cuttlefish or squid) and the oysters of Mali Ston, seafood is the star of most the dishes served along the Adriatic coast.

CURED MEATS AND CHEESES

Most Croatian meals begin with a platter of local charcuterie. In Zagreb and Slavonia, you are likely to come across *kulen*, a pork sausage richly seasoned with pepper and paprika (leading to its bright red color). *Pršut* is very popular along the coast in Dalmatia and Istria; Dalmatians smoke and cure it longer and with more spices than the Istrians, and both leave it out to dry in the famous northeastern *bura* wind. That same wind is responsible for flavoring the country's most celebrated cheese, *paški sir*; the bura sprinkles the entire island of Pag with salt water, flavoring the herbs (like fennel and sage) on which the sheeps graze, making for a salty, dry, and crumbly cheese. Rounding out your charcuterie platter will likely be some type of *pašteta*, (a fish or meat pâté), a few olives, perhaps marinated anchovies, fresh bread, and a glass of local wine.

BUREK

You can barely walk a city block in a Croatian city, most notably Zagreb, without stumbling upon a bakery overflowing with everything from pizza to salty bread rolls to beloved *burek*, a flaky filo pastry filled with cheese (similar to cottage cheese), meat, spinach, or potatoes. It's the most popular type of street food, typically eaten by locals for breakfast, but can be enjoyed any time of day.

TRUFFLES

The rolling hills of inland Istria are home to highly prized truffles. The black truffle season conveniently peaks at the same time as the tourist season, from May until October, so it's relatively easy (if not inexpensive) to find this rare mushroom on the menus of Istrian restaurants. The white truffle, on the other hand, grows in the winter months and may be harder to come by. The secretive, flavorful truffles are rooted out in forests by specially trained dogs or pigs and incorporated into a variety of dishes.

PEKA

A traditional way of cooking meat (usually lamb or beef), seafood (usually octopus), or even bread, is *ispod peke*, meaning "under the bell". The *peka*, a clay or wrought-iron cooking vessel, is buried under a pile of hot coals so that the meat (together with potatoes, carrots, rosemary, sage, and other Mediterranean herbs) stews slowly in its own juice until it falls off the bone. It's a must when visiting Dalmatia, but be warned that advance notice is usually required to order it.

WINE

Croatia's wine-making renaissance continues with many France-, Napa Valley–, or Italy-educated winemakers returning to make the best of some

Wine

truly exceptional terroirs. Croatian wine is quite difficult to find at international wine shops, which is all the more reason to delve into these craftily revisited local vintages during your stay. The four main wine-growing regions are Istria, renowned for the Malvaija white and Teran red; Dalmatia, the home of some excellent reds like Plavac Mali and Vranac; Zagorje, which produces small quantities of very crisp dessert wines and Rieslings; and Eastern Slavonia, with its millennia-long tradition of producing the Graševina white varietal. If you want to be really local about it (especially in hot weather), add some sparkling water to your white wine to make a *gemišt*, or still water to your red wine to make a *bevanda*.

BEER
Croatian beer is very common, affordable, and easy to drink. The leading brands are *Ožujsko* (produced in Zagreb) and *Karlovačko* (brewed in the town of Karlovac). Lagers are most typical, but you can also find quality dark ales and a growing craft beer scene.

RAKIJA
You won't be in Croatia long before you're introduced to your first taste of *rakija*, a distilled herbal or fruit spirit that makes up an important part of Croatian culture. All across the country, business deals are sealed, friendships are cemented, and journeys are begun to the clink of a few shot glasses of the fiery schnapps. It's used as a cure for everything, from a sore throat to a sea urchin sting. Croatians often brew rakija themselves at home, using everything from plums (*šljivovica*)

to walnuts (*orahovica*) to herbs (*travarica*). In the countryside, you can often find roadside stands selling the family blend out of plastic bottles. It's a gesture of welcome and friendship, so if you're offered a glass, accept politely and have a sip.

DESSERTS
The most common dessert in Croatia is *palačinke*, a thin pancake stuffed with Nutella or marmalade. *Fritule*, Croatia's rakija-spiked version of a doughnut hole, is made with lemon zest and raisins and sprinkled with powdered sugar; it originated in Dalmatia and is traditionally served at holidays. Another of the most traditional dishes of Dubrovnik is *rožata*, a custard pudding flavored with rose liqueur and topped with caramel sauce.

What to Buy in Croatia

HANDCRAFTED PAG LACE
Handcrafted by women from the island of Pag since the 15th century, the method of making these intricate lace patterns has been passed down through generations and each piece is unique to the individual who crochets it.

WOODEN TOYS OF HRVATSKO ZAGORJE
Dating back to the 19th century, these toys were traditionally carved by hand out of local wood (willow, beech, maple, and lime), painted in bright yellow, red, and blue patterns, and then passed down through generations.

LAVENDER
As soon as you arrive on the Croatian coast, particularly the island of Hvar, you will pick up the fresh scent of lavender. It is used in cooking, cosmetics, and even to treat sunburn and mosquito bites. You can buy all manner of lavender souvenirs, including sachets of the dried herb.

CRAVATS
In the 17th century, Croatian military uniforms featured patterned scarves knotted around the neck. French soldiers appreciated the style, introduced them to Parisian society with the name *cravat* (a play on the word Croat), and the rest is sartorial history. You can pick up an "original Croatian tie" in shops around the country, including the chain boutique Croata.

ŠIBENIK BUTON JEWELRY
Originally part of the traditional folk costume worn by men in Šibenik, the Šibenik Button was proclaimed the most original Croatian souvenir in 2007. Originally made with silver, today you can find these round, intricate buttons in different materials and different sizes adorning earrings, rings, and other jewelry.

OLIVE OIL
Croatians have been making oil olive for two millenia, most notably in Istria, which has been named the top olive oil region in the world for several years running. You'll find excellent products elsewhere along the coast too, notably the islands of Cres, Krk, and Korčula. Croatian olive oil is distinctive for its bright green color and particularly pungent, peppery taste.

LICITAR HEART
These heart-shaped biscuits, handmade with honey dough and painted red with intricate swirls

Licitar heart

and hearts, have been given as romantic gifts since the 16th century. They are typical of Central Europe, particularly Zagreb, where they are used to decorate Christmas trees, including the thousands put up around the city during the Advent Market each December.

ŠESTINE UMBRELLAS

This bright red umbrella with colorful stripes was a part of the traditional folk costume of the Šestine neighborhood in Zagreb. While these days it is most often worn only at special events, it has become the most famous emblem of Zagreb thanks to its use as a sun shade by the vendors at the Dolac Market.

BRAČ WHITE STONE

Pure white stone has been excavated from quarries on Brač, the largest Dalmatian island, since ancient times, and has been used to build some of the most famous structures in the world. The center of stone masonry on the island is Pučišća, where students come to learn stone masonry at quarries that date back to Roman times. You can take a piece home with you in the form of candleholders, pestles and mortars, or sculptures.

STON SEA SALT

In the unassuming town of Ston on the Pelješac Peninsula, you'll find Europe's oldest salt pans, dating back 4,000 years. You can take a short tour to see how the salt is still gathered using mostly ancient tools—sun, sea, and wind—and take home a small bag of the tasty, all-natural sea salt.

SAMOBOR CRYSTAL

A worthwhile day trip from Zagreb, the quaint town of Samobor is known for two things: their exquisite cream cake and their crystalware. Hand-carved here using the same method since 1839, you can find beautifully crafted jugs, glasses, and vases in factories and shops around town.

Best Islands in Croatia

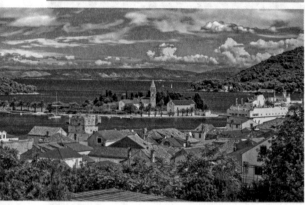

LASTOVO
One of the most remote inhabited islands in the country, Lastovo has only one hotel and a handful of other accommodation options, plus it takes several hours to reach by ferry from both Split and Dubrovnik so there are no day-trippers. Come to enjoy the walking trails, empty beaches, fresh shrimp on skewers, and complete solitude.

VIS
Vis is an off-the-beaten-path destination with a wonderfully remote ambience, fragrant citrus orchards, and few tourists. Plan to spend a couple of days exploring the main town of Vis, ancient ruins, Renaissance churches, and the famous blue cave on the nearby island of Biševo.

MLJET
If you're looking for a quiet escape to a natural paradise, consider Mljet, Croatia's greenest island. It's just a ferry ride away from Dubrovnik, and is cloaked in dense pine forests, secret coves, and olive groves. Housed within a national park on one side of the island are two salt lakes, *Veliko* and *Malo Jezero*, with a Benedictine monastery on a small islet in the former.

BRAČ
On the island of Brač, you'll find Zlatni Rat, touted as the most beautiful beach in Croatia; Vidova Gora, the highest peak in the Adriatic; and the alluring towns of Pučišća and Supetar, where you can buy souvenirs made of the famous white Brač stone.

PAG
With its barren expanses, wind-whipped jagged peaks, and the occasional patch of shrubs, Pag offers something totally unique to the rest of verdant Dalmatia. Trek to the mysterious Pag Triangle and make lots of time to sample the country's most celebrated cheese, *paški sir*.

RAB

If you're looking for a sandy beach, the island of Rab in Kvarner Bay has more than 30 to choose from. Perfect for anyone who just wants to leave their water shoes behind and lounge on the sand, Rab offers a respite from Croatia's typically rocky shores.

HVAR

Hvar is famous for its nightlife so if you're looking to enjoy a bit of glitz and glamor with the party boat crowds, this is your place. Sun-splashed Hvar Town showcases a sparkling marina filled with envy-inducing yachts, trendy beach bars, and bumping nightclubs. Hvar Town also has heritage-rich landmarks, including the hilltop Spanish Fortress.

KRK

There's no shortage of delightful things to see and do on Croatia's largest island. The varied terrain means you can tour vineyards, traipse through pine forests, and test your acrophobia on the jaw-dropping limestone cliffs of Vrbnik—all before lunch.

KORČULA

Korčula often earns top billing as the best island to visit in Croatia. With miles of perfect mountain biking roads, islands to discover by sail or motorboat, perfect white beaches with turquoise water, boutique wine, plenty of olive oil and honey to sample, and an Old Town that is rivaled only by Dubrovnik itself in beauty and history, you can spend weeks here and never see it all.

ZLARIN

Home to just 300 permanent residents, Zlarin remains a refuge of peace, quiet, and unspoiled splendor. This tiny treasure features a lone village with narrow lanes, old stone buildings, and a handful of shops selling coral trinkets.

Sailing and Cruising in Croatia

The Croatian Adriatic has almost 2,000 km (around 1,200 miles) of mainland coast, with more than 1,000 islands and islets (about 50 of which are inhabited). The country's captivating islands are peppered next to to the mainland coast, which means easy island-hopping in the protected waters.

Besides picturesque coastal towns, Croatia has three national parks on the sea: Brijuni National Park (a cluster of 14 verdant islands by the Istrian Peninsula), Kornati National Park (an archipelago of 89 otherwordly, cliff-adorned islands in North Dalmatia), and Mljet National Park (a lush island adorned by Mediterranean greenery in South Dalmatia). Krka National Park (a spectacular series of waterfalls, winding rivers, and karst canyons in Central Dalmatia) can also be approached by sailboat; simply sail up the Šibenik Channel to Skradin Bay.

SAILING 101

A holiday aboard a sailboat is a fabulous option for anyone seeking to explore Croatia in style. You can get a taste of the array of Adriatic islands and coastal sights here, with your hotel being whichever cove you decide to anchor in for the night.

If you are already an experienced sailor, you can charter a so-called bareboat yacht and sail independently. By Croatian law at least one crew member needs to have an international sailing license considered valid by the Croatian Ministry of the Sea, Transport, and Infrastructure, plus a VHF radio certificate if it is not included in your license. To check whether your licenses are acceptable, head to the ministry's website.

If you have never sailed before, or have little experience, then you will need a skipper. Generally, skippers do much more than navigate the boat; most are

from the region and, therefore know the local waters, weather conditions, history, culture, the best secret coves for putting down anchor, the local gastronomic hideouts, and the best diving spots.

The third option is sailing in a flotilla. A flotilla is a group of yachts, with people of mixed levels of sailing experience, led by a qualified expert.

A typical one-week sailing itinerary in Central Dalmatia could run as follows. On the first day, you can set sail from Split to Maslinica on the island of Šolta. Then, from Maslinica to Vis Town on the island of Vis. Next, there's Vis Town to Komiža, also on Vis, with a can't-miss pit stop on Biševo en route. For Day 4, you can travel from Komiža to Hvar Town on the island of Hvar. Next, Hvar Town to Bol on the island of Brač, followed by Bol to Milna on the island of Brač. On your last day, depart from Milna and head back to Split.

CHARTER COMPANIES

On the Croatian Adriatic there are dozens of charter companies operating tens of thousands of boats of all sizes, making this one of the busiest charter areas in the world. As a rough guide to prices, in the summer 2020 high season, Sail Croatia offered a 2018 eleven-berth Bavaria Cruiser 51 sailboat for €2,200 per week, though this price does not include food, fuel, or mooring fees.

The high season runs from May through October, with demand and prices peaking in July and August. Summer on the Croatian coast is typically hot, dry, and sunny, with windier periods usually happening on the polar ends of the high season. However, an experienced skipper, who knows which areas of the sea tend to be windy and which are calm, will be able to cater to your wishes, whether you want to crank it up a notch and go diagonal, or just take it easy and smooth sail. During peak season, many charter rentals begin at 5 pm Saturday and end at 9 am the following Saturday, but times and lengths can vary depending on the company and your needs.

Adriatic Nautical Academy Based in the town of Jezera on the island of Murter in Central Dalmatia, the Adriatic Nautical Academy (ANA) is an international sailing school and certified RYA training center. ANA's offerings include basic sailing courses, advanced sailing lessons, and leisure sailing for those who just want to kick their feet up and enjoy the views. ⊕ www.anasail.com/en.

Activity Yachting The sailing programs offered by Activity Yachting operate along the roughly 160-km (100-mile) stretch of coastline between Split and Zadar. Flotilla holidays (with or without an educational "Learn to Sail" program during which you can get your own skipper certification) are available along with bareboat rentals. The company offers an array of sailboats and catamarans ranging in size from 30 to 55 feet. ☎ 1243/641–304 from UK ⊕ www.activityyachting.com.

Euromarine With bases in Pula, Split, and Dubrovnik, Euromarine charters more than 100 sailing boats, motorboats, and catamarans. You can choose from bareboat, skippered, and crewed options. ☎ 1/555–2222 ⊕ www.charter.euromarine.com.hr.

Nautilus This company bareboat, skippered, and crewed yachts, catamarans, and motorboats at beautiful bases in Pula, Zadar, Biograd, Trogir, Split, and Dubrovnik. Flotilla sailing is also available from Trogir and Dubrovnik. ☎ 01732/867–445 ⊕ www.nautilusyachting.com.

Sail Croatia Offering cruises and yachts with diverse itinerary options to suit everyone, with Sail Croatia you can pick from party, adventure, relaxation,

or luxury-focused experiences. While itineraries are flexible, departures are generally from Split. Boats can also be chartered on a bareboat, skippered, or crewed basis. ✉ Split ☎ 866/601–3187 from the U.S. ⊕ www.sail-croatia.com.

Ultra Sailing Founded by former members of the Croatian Olympic Team who now work as instructors, Ultra Sailing offers a variety of courses with a main school office and base in the ACI Marina Split. The company also offers yacht charters from Pula, Trogir, Split, and Dubrovnik, plus an organized regatta center in Kaštela. ✉ Split ☎ 21/398–578 ⊕ www.ultra-sailing.hr.

The Yacht Week This company offers flexible routes along the Croatian coast, all of which are focused on having a good time. The "Original Route," which operates all summer long, leaves from Trogir, and includes the islands of Brač, Hvar, and Vis, with a range of activities like a flotilla party, food tastings, and water sports. The "Ultra Festival Route" is centered on the music festival of the same name that takes place in Split and Hvar each summer. Join solo or with a group, opt for an on-board host to cook for you, and let your skipper take care of the rest. ☎ 1389/656–005 ⊕ www.theyachtweek.com.

Zizoo From luxury to affordable, Zizoo offers yacht, catamaran, gulet, sailboat, and speedboat charters at every price point. You can sail bareboat or with an expert skipper from Pula, Šibenik, Trogir, Split, and Dubrovnik. ☎ 727/258–5406 from the U.S. ⊕ www.zizoo.com.

Latin culture | Greek culture
Roman Cathol. | Orth. Christianity

A Short History of Croatia

THE EARLY HISTORY OF THE CROATIAN LANDS

The three main regions that form Croatia today are known as Slavonia, Dalmatia, and Croatia proper. These have also been called the "Triune Kingdom." In addition, the ethnically mixed Istrian peninsula is now considered Croatian territory. Bosnia-Herzegovina has a mixed population and once had a pronounced regional identity, but some Croat nationalists consider it their territory.

Even before the influx of the Slavs between AD 500 and 800, the region of Croatia had a long history. The Illyrians and Thracians were originally at home there, and traces of Hellenistic and Celtic influences can also be seen. From the 3rd century BC to the 1st century AD, Rome controlled the Balkans; indeed, at times Croatian history was closely tied to Roman politics, even though it was hardly a central province of the far-flung empire. For instance, the well-known Emperor Diocletian (AD 284–305) was from Dalmatia, as were four other emperors. After his reign, Diocletian returned to his native Split, where he built a large palace. The city of Pula also contains many important Roman sites dating from this time.

Rome's influence on the Croatian lands has been far-reaching. The Romans developed the region's basic infrastructure and industries related to mining and metallurgy. The Croatian coast was established as an outpost of European high culture; this connection was soon strengthened by the Croats' conversion to Christianity and later by ties to the Renaissance city-states of Italy, especially Venice. The Italian influence can be felt even today, particularly in the Istrian peninsula and on some of the islands.

As the Empire was divided into its eastern and western halves, the internal frontier came to symbolize for many the "fault line" between Latin culture and Roman Catholicism, on the one hand, and Greek culture and Orthodox Christianity, on the other. The division was actually always quite porous and inexact, but its nature changed during the Ottoman Turkish invasions starting in the 14th century. Islam again became one of the major religions of Europe, and new ethnic groups arrived or were created in the former Byzantine lands.

Despite the fact that the Croatian lands clearly belonged to Rome's sphere of influence, the Croatian culture went through some complicated developments after the fall of the western portion of the Roman Empire in AD 476. First, many Croats—like their neighbors, the Slovenes—had been converted to Christianity by Frankish (or "German") missionaries from Charlemagne's Holy Roman Empire. Second, Croatian monks working in Dalmatia developed a unique alphabet, known as Glagolitic, from contact with Orthodox missionaries. Croatia remained Catholic after the official religious break between Rome and Constantinople in 1054, but the Glagolitic alphabet was used in some places into the 19th century, serving to reinforce Croatian identity amidst various political and ethnic rivalries. Finally, the Ottoman occupation of the Balkans made much of Croatia into a contested region of population flux and the new cultural norms associated with being a "bulwark of Christendom."

The first independent Croatian state was formed by the leader Tomislav. In 924 he was crowned king of Croatia and recognized by the pope. Although historians disagree over the exact extent of his territory, Tomislav did set another important precedent as well: he united many regions of the former Roman provinces of Dalmatia and Pannonia (central Croatia and Slavonia). The national symbols of the kuna (currency denomination) and šahovnica (red-and-white checkerboard coat of arms) originated at this time.

CROATIA IN THE HIGH MIDDLE AGES

By 1102 the royal line had died out, and the Sabor (assembly of nobles) accepted Hungarian rule. Croatia preserved its own laws and customs through the Pacta Conventa, which seems to have been essentially a personal union between the countries, not an annexation. Medieval Croatia also achieved considerable cultural heights. The first known writing in Croatian dates from around 1100, on a stone tablet from the island of Krk, known as the Bašćanska Ploča. In the 16th century, Dubrovnik dramatist and poet Ivan Gundulić (1555–1638) wrote *Osman* in the Croatian language to inspire resistance to the Turks. Croatia's unique literary history had begun. Dubrovnik also boasted major scientists and composers. Soon there were three major outside forces contending for Croatian territory: the Ottoman Empire, the Kingdom of Hungary, and the Venetian Republic. The Venetians quickly displaced rivals such as the Byzantine Empire and the kingdoms of Serbia and Bosnia. A major blow came in 1202, when Venice directed the Fourth Crusade to sack the important port of Zadar.

The Ottoman expansion into Europe reached Hungary in 1526; Sultan Suleiman defeated Hungary's King Lajos at Mohacs. The Croatian nobles had already been defeated at Udbina in 1493. Ottoman rule would last for 150 years, but the Hungarian and Croatian nobility quickly opted for personal union with the royal Habsburg family in Vienna. In 1593 the Croats stemmed the tide of Turkish invasion by the successful defense of the fortress-city of Sisak, but intense fighting

in the area continued until the Treaty of Karlowitz in 1699. That momentous agreement removed most of Croatia and Hungary from Ottoman sovereignty, and Habsburg rule continued.

The wealthy city-state of Dubrovnik retained its independence until Napoléon's invasion of 1797. Bosnia-Herzegovina, home to many Croats and other groups, would remain under Ottoman rule until 1878. As central Croatia was liberated by the crusading Habsburgs, they created a military frontier zone that is often known by its Croatian (and Serbian) name of Vojna Krajina. The frontier included the Lika region south of Zagreb and stretched all along the southern periphery of the Empire from Italy to Romania. The Austrians recruited Serbs and other groups into the area, adding new minority groups to the Croatian lands.

The nobility, or landowning class, of Croatia played the key role in developments over the next several centuries. Croatia's basic feudal structure was preserved by the Habsburgs, although some nobles from the Zrinski and Frankapan families were executed for plotting against Vienna. The country also remained overwhelmingly Catholic; Catholic scholars working in Venice and Rome also produced the earliest dictionaries and grammars of the Croatian language. These trends stand in sharp contrast to the neighboring Serb lands, where Ottoman rule removed nearly all traces of the traditional elites. The Croat nobles resented Vienna for its attempts at centralization and its territorial compromises with the Ottomans. At times the Croats gravitated, culturally and politically, toward outside powers that could provide leverage in their struggle against Vienna: Russia, France, and even at times their own erstwhile foes the Venetians and the Ottomans.

THE CROATIAN NATIONAL REVIVAL

The remaining Croatian nobility was revived as a political "nation" by the enlightened despotism of one of the most iconoclastic of the Habsburg emperors, Joseph II (r. 1780–90). Joseph's modernizing vision involved centralization of power in Vienna and, to some extent, Germanization. Both of these processes elicited strong negative reactions around the Empire, where traditional autonomy existed in many areas. In Croatia it was the nobility who responded with alarm both to Joseph and to the excesses of the French Revolution. Many in the Croatian elite chose to strengthen ties with Hungary, forming a political party known as the Unionists, or Magyarones, a term corresponding basically to "Hungarophiles."

In 1809 the invading Napoléon created a short-lived satellite state out of conquered Habsburg lands called the Illyrian Provinces. This state abolished feudalism and turned local administration, including language policy, over to the Croats and Slovenes. These actions increased popular awareness of Croatian nationality. It was from these two starting points—both of them reactions to external events—that the tortured development of modern, mass nationalism in Croatia began.

The Magyarone solution soon became problematic as Hungary gradually increased its control over the Croatian lands decade by decade. Croats, now alienated from both Vienna and Budapest, began to react in various new ways. Of considerable importance was the Illyrian Movement, which was at once a Croatian national movement and a kind of supra-national forerunner of Yugoslavism. Its chief exponent was the writer and editor Ljudevit Gaj, who helped establish the basis for the modern Croatian language. The Illyrians espoused political cooperation among the Slovenes, Serbs, and Croats within the framework of the Habsburg Empire; they were basically federalists and did not seek an independent nation-state just for Croats. The National Party, led by Bishop Josip Strossmayer, revived Illyrianism in the form of Yugoslavism and also greatly enriched Croatian cultural life by founding the Yugoslav Academy of Sciences and the modern University of Zagreb.

In 1848, nationalism and liberalism brought major insurrections across Europe. Although Hungary rebelled, the Croats remained loyal to Vienna. In the middle of the 19th century, the Croatian political scene was dominated by an important figure named Josip Jelačić (1801–59), an Austrian military officer and a convinced Illyrianist. In 1848 the Habsburgs turned to him to help defeat the nationalist uprising in Hungary. He succeeded and managed to unite nearly all Croatian territory under Austrian rule. He also abolished feudalism and promoted Croatian interests on major cultural issues. Although Jelačić is a Croatian hero today, he also propounded a progressive version of nationality based on regional rather than ethnic identity. The long-reigning Emperor Franz Josef tried to placate the Hungarians by issuing the Ausgleich (Compromise) in 1867, breaking the empire in two and renaming it "Austria-Hungary." The Croats wisely negotiated their own version of the Ausgleich, known as the Nagodba, in 1868.

INTO THE GREAT WAR: FROM HABSBURGS TO YUGOSLAVS

This arrangement gave the Croats, at last, a considerable degree of internal autonomy, and Croatia even had representatives in the Hungarian parliament and cabinet and also in Vienna. But it also provided for the Croatian territories to be split up again, with control over Dalmatia and Istria going to Vienna while Slavonia and central Croatia were under the Hungarian crown.

These final Habsburg decades were turbulent. Territorial divisions wounded Croatian pride and hindered economic development. Hungarian manipulation of the political scene and attempts at Magyarization continued. Count Károly Khuen-Héderváry ruled from 1883 to 1903 and became notorious for setting Croatia's Serbian and ethnic Croatian populations against each other. Despite his tactics and the turmoil of World War I, the Serbs and Croats of Croatia actually achieved a considerable level of political cooperation.

In 1918, with the Habsburg Empire vanquished, a combination of factors induced Croatian politicians to lead their country into the new Kingdom of Serbs, Croats, and Slovenes (called Yugoslavia after 1929). By 1921 many Croats grew suspicious of the new state, run from Belgrade by the Serbian king. Many political parties, as well as the *ban* (viceroys) and the Sabor, were suppressed. Royal legitimacy was shaky: Serbs dominated the police, military, and economy; agriculture, the mainstay of the economy, languished; and Italy retained possession of large amounts of Croatian territory in Istria and Dalmatia. Stjepan Radić, the leader of the powerful Croatian Peasant Party, alternately boycotted and negotiated with the central government; his murder in 1928 fueled radicalism in Croatia.

As World War II approached, Belgrade grew more willing to compromise with Croatia. A 1939 arrangement known as the Sporazum restored the ban and Sabor and combined many Croatian lands into one autonomous unit. But war broke out just weeks later.

WORLD WAR II AND THE SECOND YUGOSLAVIA

The darkest chapter in Croatian history took place amidst the chaos of World War II. An interwar political agitator on the fascist right, Ante Pavelić (1889–1959) rose to power and ruled the "Independent State of Croatia" for 49 bloody months.

Pavelić, who founded the Ustaša (insurrectionist) movement in 1929, originally developed his ideas within the tradition of the Croatian Party of Right. This group, founded by Ante Starčević (1823–96) in 1861, advocated the creation of a greater Croatia, including Bosnia-Herzegovina. They believed that Bosnian Muslims (today's Bosniaks) and Serbs were ethnic Croats who had been forced to adopt other faiths. Pavelić developed ties with similar movements in Nazi Germany, Bulgaria, Hungary, and especially Mussolini's Italy. The Ustaša helped assassinate King Aleksandar in 1934. The most revolutionary aspects of the Ustaša movement were their willingness to use terror and genocide against minorities in order to form an ethnically "pure" Croatian state and their desire to create a mass political movement that displaced the established elites in the country. Mussolini's army installed Pavelić's government in Zagreb after the Axis invasion of 1941, and the Nazis agreed to let Pavelić rule. Croatia was immediately split into two spheres of influence. The Ustaša were unpopular, but they ruled by terror over a population that included vast numbers of non-Croatians, especially Serbs. The Germans were increasingly disconcerted by the Ustaša's murderous policies, which spawned significant resistance movements. The main German goal in the region was simply the extraction of mineral and agricultural wealth. In all, the Ustaša government killed more than 300,000 Serbs, along with tens of thousands of Jews and Roma (Gypsies).

In addition to a number of concentration camps like the notorious Jasenovac east of Zagreb—where about 85,000 people, mostly Serbs, were killed—many horrific rural massacres occurred. Pavelić's state was a failure; the communist Partisans and the Chetniks (Serbian royalists) actually controlled much of its territory. Yugoslavia was reconstituted after World War II, this time under the rule of Josip Broz Tito (1892–1980), a communist born in Croatia. The trauma of World War II was the main reason for decades of "Croatian silence" in Yugoslavia. In 1967, leading cultural and academic figures broke ranks with the party and publicly asserted the distinctiveness and legitimacy of the Croatian language. This was divisive, because it ran counter to the official embrace of a common "Croato-Serbian" or "Serbo-Croatian" language and culture.

A period of dissent and crackdown known as the "Croatian Spring" followed. There were demonstrations, strikes, and many debates in print about Yugoslavia's political discrimination and economic exploitation. This lasted until 1972, and resulted in Tito's sidelining numerous prominent Croatian communists, including many who could have provided cosmopolitan, intelligent alternatives to both communism and what came after. This repression belies the fact that Tito's regime became, after 1952, the most liberal socialist state in Eastern Europe; in addition, the LCY (League of Communists of Yugoslavia) was not averse to using the nationalism of some Yugoslav peoples (such as the Bosnians, the Macedonians, and the Albanians of Kosovo) to further its agenda—just not Croatian nationalism.

Despite significant grievances, Croatia underwent considerable modernization under communist rule. There were increases in industrialization, urbanization, life expectancy, standard of living, and literacy. New universities were founded in Split, Rijeka, and Osijek. Croatia's beaches became famous across Europe. The economy was also helped by the large numbers of Croats who worked abroad as *Gastarbeiter* (guest workers), but heavy emmigration and low birth rates left many worried about the country's demographic future.

Both Serbia and Croatia felt the heavy hand of Tito's rule; as the most powerful traditional nations in Yugoslavia, Tito neutralized their ability to rock the federal boat. The LCY encouraged nation-building, however, in Bosnia, Macedonia, Montenegro, and among the Albanians of Kosovo both as a counterweight to Croatian and Serbian ambitions and as a developmental strategy.

FROM TITO TO TUĐMAN AND BEYOND: SOVEREIGN CROATIA

Historians disagree over when Yugoslavia passed the point of no return. At some point in the decade between Tito's death in 1980 and the momentous political changes in Slovenia and Croatia by 1991, the breakup actually began. In 1990, Slovenia and Croatia held free, multiparty elections, declared their sovereignty, and held referenda in which they overwhelmingly approved the idea of independence. But even then the eventual violence was not inevitable. Two highly regarded Croatian reformist politicians, Ante Marković and Stjepan Mesić, were stymied in their efforts to place the Yugoslav federation on a new foundation. What soon exploded were not the so-called ancient ethnic hatreds but rather the aggressive and conflicting aims of various political factions competing in a superheated environment. This violence was furthered by the egoism of conniving politicians, sensationalism in the media, and mixed signals from Western Europe and the United States.

The 1980s had been extremely tense across the country. Serbs and Albanians clashed in Kosovo; hyperinflation, unemployment, public debt, and strikes characterized a ruined economy; and the fall of the Berlin Wall marked the end of other European socialist states. The rise of the dictator Slobodan Milošević in Serbia brought new levels of confrontation to politics and revealed gross Serbian manipulation of the economy. Croats and Slovenes gradually realized that Yugoslavia was unworkable as a country. The Serbian population, incited by ambitious politicians, lashed out at Croat police in the spring of 1991. Thus, even before Croatia's declaration of independence on June 25, 1991, the villages of Pakrac and Borovo Selo became scenes of bitter bloodshed, as did the famed Plitvice Lakes National Park and other areas in central Croatia. There were about 600,000 Serbs living in Croatia, over 12% of the population. The new Croatian government, led by the now-nationalist Tuđman, was brash in its treatment of minorities and irresponsible in its handling of the legacy of World War II, and these approaches greatly increased Serbs' anxiety.

After secession, full-scale fighting broke out. The autumn of 1991 saw two shocking sieges: the bloody street-fighting and massacres at Vukovar in Slavonia and the weeks-long shelling of venerable Dubrovnik for no legitimate military purpose. The contemporary Croatian poet Slavko Mihalić described this era as one in which the Serbian leader—"the one who sends the bombs"—grimly and accurately promised to turn Croatia into a "national park of death." In fact Milošević was willing to let Croatia secede but without its Serb-inhabited regions; later, he and Tuđman agreed on how to partition Bosnia-Herzegovina as well. In May 1992 the war spread to independence-minded Bosnia, where 200,000 people died, many of them civilians, and 2 million were made homeless. In Croatia, 10,000 people were killed and over a fourth of the country fell to the Serbs. Large numbers of Croats and Bosnians were driven from their homes with terror campaigns of "ethnic cleansing." With American aid, Croatian forces rallied in the summer of 1995 and recaptured Slavonia and the Krajina region. Many thousands of Serbs fled and property issues remain unresolved. Croatian forces also committed atrocities in Bosnia-Herzegovina, but most of the international community finally recognized that the lion's share of guilt for the wars themselves belonged to the Serbian government. The Dayton Peace Agreement of late 1995, backed by NATO's military might, paved the way for Serbian withdrawal from Croatia and Bosnia.

President Tuđman was roundly criticized internationally for his authoritarian tendencies and overzealous nationalism. Internal opposition grew as well, especially over his censorship and policies in Bosnia. Tuđman allowed political parties other than the HDZ (Croatian Democratic Union), but they were weak until his death in December 1999. Since Tuđman's death, Croatia has begun serious cooperation with The Hague war-crimes tribunal. Many other reforms have also succeeded, but open questions include the quest for autonomy by the ethnically and historically distinct region of Istria and Croatia's ability to cooperate on a variety of issues with its neighbors.

Wine in Croatia

You will be forgiven if you've never heard of Croatian wine. While it has a winemaking history that dates back to the Illyrian tribes in the 11th century BC, with input from the Romans, Greeks, and Austrians over the centuries, the 20th century was bad for the wine business here. The insect pest phylloxera, war, and crippling economic policies ravaged Croatian wineries; under Communism, private wineries were abolished and only a select few state-run winemakers were allowed to produce wine, with a major focus on quantity over quality. The war from 1990-1995 wiped out what remained. Many vintners fled to the United States, New Zealand, Australia, South Africa, and South America, taking their knowledge with them and leaving Croatia's vineyards virtually deserted.

But a wine renaissance is occuring in Croatia today. Blessed with a unique, mineral-rich terroir that's ideal for grape-growing, Croatia currently grows more than 130 indigenous grapes and its wines are once again finding a special place in the hearts of oenophiles everywhere. Many who left have come back to reclaim their family land and revive their winemaking traditions.

WINE-MAKING AND ITS DEEP ROOTS

The Delmati, an Illyrian tribe, were the first to cultivate the vine in modern-day Croatia, as early as the 11th century BC. When the Romans invaded the Dalmatian Coast in the 3rd century BC, they discovered an entire wine industry. The Greeks, who'd been sharing the region with the Illyrians, had not failed to exploit *Vitis sylvestris* (the wild grapevine), which was plentiful there, merging it with the strains of the cultivated vines they brought from their own country. The conquering Roman soldiers also brought

new varietals with them as a way of expanding their culture; the vine itself was a symbol of their power.

By the 9th century, Croatian princes had a cup bearer as part of their court staff. When Venice subjugated much of Dalmatia and Istria in the 14th century, the planting of new vineyards was restricted to the areas around Split. It was in this period that noble families, after building their vineyards, built fortresses in the middle of their estates for protection, perhaps anticipating the destruction of the coming Venetian-Turkish wars. By the time the Habsburgs had ousted the Ottomans, the Austrians were already well on their way to introducing new varietals to the area, capitalizing on the superior wine-producing capacity of their newly acquired resources.

Modern developments in cloning techniques and the use of industrial machinery brought wine-making in Croatia to the economic position it occupies today, where 10% of the population derives income from the industry.

THE NAPA VALLEY CONNECTION

Croatia has had some world-class help in reestablishing its wine-making industry. Miljenko "Mike" Grgić, one of the founding fathers of the Napa Valley wine industry, is at the forefront of the race to realize the potential of Croatia's indigenous varietals. Born in Dalmatia in 1923, he left for California in 1954 and went on to become one of its most renowned wine producers. He was one of the first to notice that the ubiquitous Zinfandel grape of California (also known as primitivo in Italy)—whose origin had long been guessed at but remained shrouded in mystery—had similarities to the Plavac Mali grape that he had cultivated in his youth back in Dalmatia.

In 1998, Professor Carole Meredith, a renowned grapevine geneticist who had previously uncovered the origins of Chardonnay, Cabernet Sauvignon, and Petit Syrah, began a similar search for Zinfandel's origin. The exciting four-year project, known as the "Zinquest", entailed the collection of leaf samples from indigenous varieties of southern Dalmatia, DNA fingerprinting analyses of samples' cultivars, and comparisons with Zinfandel cuttings from California. The team of scientists eventually discovered an old vineyard in Kaštel Novi, where a few additional "suspects" were discovered, and the DNA analysis confirmed that a wine locally known as Crljenak Kaštelanski, or Tribidrag—completely forgotten and virtually eradicated from Dalmatian vineyards—is the long-sought Croatian corollary of Zinfandel.

REGIONS AND WINERIES

Almost 70% of wine produced in Croatia is white, coming mainly from the country's interior, while 30% are reds, mainly produced along the coast. The four most important wine producing regions are: Slavonia, home to the country's principal white variety, Graševina; Central and Southern Dalmatia, where the hearty Plavac Mali flourishes on the Pelješac Peninsula; Istria, known for its Malvazija (white) and Teran (red); and increasingly Zagorje, which produces small quantities of very crisp dessert wines and Rieslings.

Kids and Families

Croatia is one of the best countries in Europe to travel with children. Distances between towns are short so you're never stuck in the car or on public transport for long. Most restaurants welcome little ones and have kid-friendly options on the menu like spaghetti or hamburgers while pizzerias, markets, and bakeries are plentiful so you can always grab a quick bite to stave off hunger (and it won't break the bank). There are national parks to explore, medieval towns to spark imagination, playgrounds aplenty, interactive museums, and when you're ready for a swim, you can jump into the sea from just about anywhere.

Where to Stay. Private accommodations, or self-catering apartments, are your best option when traveling with kids, as they can fit the whole family at a fraction of what a hotel would cost and you'll have facilities that will come in handy, such as a kitchen, laundry, separate bedrooms and bathrooms, more room to play, and sometimes even a private pool. There are also many campsites along the Adriatic where accommodations range from tents to bungalows with all modern amenities. Or if you want to treat yourselves to a hotel or resort, there are many excellent options with water parks, pools, kids clubs, and playgrounds on-site.

Outdoor Activities. The crystal-clear Adriatic is an instant magnet for almost any little one, but make sure to pack a pair of water shoes; most of the coast is rocky and sea urchins also tend to enjoy the clear shallow waters. If you're traveling with a toddler, you might consider visiting some of the sandy beaches scattered around the islands, which are easier on little feet; Rab is a great choice or further south opt for Saplunara Beach on Mljet. The islands are wonderful places for kids to enjoy the sea, nature, and life's simple pleasures: don't miss Lokrum, just off Dubrovnik, where they can wander through old botanical gardens spotting peacocks and bunnies along the way. Croatian national parks are also great spots to spend a day hiking, climbing, and admiring nature; Brijuni National Park in Istria might be particularly interesting with its history of dinosaurs and the exotic animals at the safari park.

Cities Croatian cities are extremely easy to maneuver with kids. They're safe, walkable, and compact. The Old Towns in cities like Dubrovnik and Split are car-free, so you can let them run around without worry. Even the capital city, Zagreb, is extremely child-friendly. There's a fun funicular to shuttle you between the Upper and Lower Towns, interactive museums, the biggest and best playgrounds in the country, and a myriad of parks to wander. If you're in Šibenik in June and July, the International Children's Festival takes over the streets for two weeks with fun workshops, games, concerts, and performances geared to kids.

Culture and History. Croatian culture and history is so evocative and entertaining that it will delight kids just as much as adults. They can watch a thrilling live sword dance on the island of Korčula, look at the cavemen at the Museum of the Krapina Neanderthal, or get lost in the Museum of Illusions in Zagreb.

Chapter 2

TRAVEL SMART

Updated by
Andrea MacDonald

★ **CAPITAL:**
Zagreb

👫 **POPULATION:**
4,100,788

💬 **LANGUAGE:**
Croatian

$ **CURRENCY:**
Kuna (Kn)

☎ **COUNTRY CODE:**
385

⚠ **EMERGENCIES:**
112

🚗 **DRIVING:**
On the right

⚡ **ELECTRICITY:**
200v/50 cycles; electrical plugs have two round prongs

🕐 **TIME:**
Six hours ahead of New York

🌐 **WEB RESOURCES:**
www.croatia.hr

Know Before You Go

A beautiful and diverse country, Croatia can be overwhelming for a first-time visitor. Here are some key tips to help you navigate your trip, whether it's your first time visiting or your twentieth.

WHEN TO GO

Although most famous for its summertime activities along the Adriatic coast, Croatia makes for a perfect year-round destination. In fact, the best time to visit is arguably the shoulder seasons (May and June and September and October), when the weather is still warm enough to swim, the coastal cities aren't crowded with tourists, hotel prices are reasonable, and locals are relaxed with time to chat. Spring is a wonderful time to see Zagreb and Plitvice National Park burst to life, while fall is the season for truffle-hunting in Istria, the harvest in Slavonia, and autumnal colors in the national parks. Winter offers skiing, the world-renowned Advent Market in Zagreb, soaking in baroque thermal springs, and the chance to experience a more local way of life along the coast. But beware that many establishments close for the winter, and public transport options (particularly ferries to the islands) might have reduced service. Of course, if your ideal vacation involves festivals, fresh seafood, and fun in the sun, there's simply no better place to be than the Croatia in the summer.

REGIONAL DIFFERENCES

The same can be said of many European countries, but the differences between the regions in Croatia are stark. Their bordering countries, allegiances throughout the years, and the influence ruling forces have had over the centuries has left a lasting impact on the country. Along the coast, for example, where Italy is just across the sea (or, in the case of Istria, just down the road), you'll find Italian influence in everything from food and architecture to the language; in Istria, which was part of Italy until 1947, you'll even still find many official signs and documents translated into Italian. Further inland, you'll find a more prominent Austro-Hungarian influence, stemming from centuries under Habsburg rule. Cities such as Zagreb and Osijek resemble Vienna more than they resemble Split, and culinary traditions harken back to Hungary. Though extremely proud of Croatia as a whole, Croats have a particularly strong allegiance to their regions, and most identify by their regional name (Istrian, Dalmatian, etc) first, then Croatian.

SPORTS

For a relatively small country, Croatia has had enormous sporting success. Their football (that's soccer to the Americans) team made it to the semi-finals of the World Cup in 1998—the first time they participated!—almost knocking out the hosts, and favorites to win, France. Fast forward to 2018, when they squared off (and lost) against the same team, but this time in the final. And it's not just football; Croatia can boast among the best teams in the world at handball, water polo, basketball, and tennis, and they fare extremely well at many Olympic disciplines, despite a smaller population and lower funding than many other countries. Talking about sports, and maybe dropping a name or two, is a fantastic ice-breaker with any Croatian person. Just don't dare mention Hajduk Split to a Dinamo Zagreb fan, or vice versa.

CROATIAN BEACHES

If you've been dreaming about a vacation spent lounging on a sandy Croatian beach, you might be surprised to learn that there are only a handful in the entire country. Croatian beaches are mostly stony, and many of them involve a simple ladder leading straight from the rocks into the sea. That's exactly what makes the Croatian Adriatic coast so special: the water is impossibly clear with no sand to muddy it up, and you can dive into the sea from just about anywhere. Make sure to pack water shoes, and beware of sea urchins attached to the rocks—you can usually spot their round, spiky black form from a distance, but sometimes they are hidden.

In addition, there's a long history of naturism here and Croatia has been one of the most progressive countries in pioneering the nude resort. Naturist campsites, beaches, and even sailing charters abound in certain parts of the coast (mainly Istria), and hundreds of thousands come here each year to enjoy some fun in the sun au naturel. Naturism in Croatia began in 1936 when British King Edward VII and Wallis Simpson went skinny-dipping at a beach on the island of Rab. That beach became one of Europe's first official nude beaches, and since then, a thriving culture has taken root, mainly among European enthusiasts, especially Germans and Austrians. Today, you can find naturist "camps" and "villages" all along the Adriatic, particularly in Istria, as well as officially designated "free naturist beaches" where going au naturel is welcome. Croatians themselves don't make up the bulk of the clientele at these beaches, but they graciously make visitors feel welcome.

COFFEE CULTURE

Croatians don't often go to restaurants for a meal unless it's a special occasion, preferring to eat at home with their families. In fact, outside of tourist areas, there are towns where you might not find a restaurant at all other than a bakery or small pizzeria. But no matter where you are, you will always be able to find a cafe-bar because Croatians like to meet, chat, and have business meetings over coffee. They never order their kava to take-away; they always sit for a few minutes to enjoy. Coffee here is affordable, delicious, and sitting in one of the many cafe-bars is a great immersion into the local culture. If you like your coffee strong, order an espresso; if you prefer something milkier, practice ordering a bijela kava. Be aware that smoking is still permitted in many establishments, so a seat outside on the terrace might be more comfortable.

HOLIDAYS

In Croatia, national holidays include the following: January 1 (New Year's Day); January 6 (Epiphany); Easter Sunday and Monday; May 1 (May Day); Corpus Christi (40 days after Easter); June 22 (Anti-Fascist Day); June 25 (Statehood Day); August 5 (National Thanksgiving Day); August 15 (Assumption), October 8 (Independence Day); November 1 (All Saints' Day); and December 25 and 26 (Christmas).

AVOIDING THE CROWDS

In the past decade, Croatia has gained a firm spot on the list of must-see European destinations, and many places within the country, especially Dubrovnik, Hvar, and Plitvice National Park, can get severely overcrowded during the high season (July and August). If possible, schedule your trip for the shoulder seasons (May/June and September/October) for a much more relaxed and enjoyable experience. If you must visit in the summer, plan your sightseeing for the early morning or late afternoon when the cruise ships crowds and day-trippers have left. Or consider staying in quieter destinations and doing day trips; Pelješac Peninsula and Cavtat are great bases from which to visit Dubrovnik, while less-visited islands such as Mljet, Korčula, and Vis make great alternatives to Hvar. Another option is to skip the hot spots altogether because just as Croatia has some of the continent's busiest destinations, it rewards intrepid travelers with other places that feel completely untouched by tourism, including Slavonia, parts of Istria, and Zagreb, one of the least crowded and most authentic capital cities in Europe.

Getting Here and Around

Air

In 2019, the first direct flight between the United States and Croatia finally took off from Philadelphia to Dubrovnik via American Airlines, although it's since been grounded due to COVID-19 and its future is still undetermined. Usually, travelers from the U.S. must fly into a European hub first—the best options are London, Munich, Frankfurt, Madrid, or Vienna—and then transfer to a flight to Croatia. Croatia Airlines has many affordable options, or you can check budget airlines such as EasyJet, Ryanair, or WizzAir; just keep in mind that they have stringent baggage limits, offer few free in-flight services, and you'll likely have to reclaim and recheck your bags at the airport, so make sure to leave plenty of time between flights.

Italy is another great choice for a stopover because there are many direct flights, buses, and ferries connecting to Croatia. If you're traveling to Istria or Kvarner, consider a flight to nearby Venice (2½ hours to Rijeka by car) or Trieste (1½ hours by car), and then arranging a car rental or bus. Or if you're going to Dalmatia, you can take an overnight ferry across the Adriatic from either Bari or Ancona.

Within Croatia, flights are very affordable in the low season. You can travel between Dubrovnik and Zagreb, for example, for under $100, which is a comparable price to taking the bus but much quicker. In the high season, it's worth looking at domestic flight options if you want to save some time and cover more ground, although buses or a car rental will likely be cheaper then.

AIRPORTS
There are airports in Dubrovnik (DBV), Osijek (OSI), Pula (PUY), Rijeka (RJK), Split (SPU), Zadar (ZAD), and Zagreb (ZAG). You can fly direct to all of them year-round from international destinations, although in winter most international flights go to Zagreb.

GROUND TRANSPORTATION
Ground transportation to major cities from airports in Croatia is well organized and user-friendly; shuttle buses and taxis operate at all airports year-round. Tickets can be purchased online, at the airport, in the city center or from the bus driver.

🛥 Boat and Ferry

Several companies run ferries between Italy and Croatia throughout the summer, the largest being the national carrier, Jadrolinija. The most popular route is Ancona to Split (11 hours), with up to eight crossings weekly in the summer (twice weekly in the low season) from Jadrolinija and the Italian-based company SNAV. The Ancona to Zadar ferry (9 hours) travels five times weekly in the summer (no service in the low season), while further south, there is a daily ferry between Bari and Dubrovnik (11 hours). Up the coast, Trieste Lines operates a high-speed ferry in the summer between Trieste and ports in Istria, including Rovinj (1 hour, 30 minutes), Pula (2 hours, 15 minutes), and Porec (1 hour), while Venezia Lines and Adriatic Lines connect those same Istrian ports with Venice (3–4 hours).

If you're traveling with a car or other vehicle, you only have three options: the route from Ancona-Split, Ancona-Zadar, or Bari-Dubrovnik.

Within Croatia, regular ferries connect all islands to the mainland, and slightly fewer connect the islands to each other. Jadrolinija operates all car ferries, while a few private companies operate passenger ferries. Keep in mind that local ferries are quick and cheap for foot passengers (you can usually show up at the port, buy a ticket, and jump onboard), whereas car passengers should reserve in advance, and still might end up waiting hours for a spot in high season.

Bus

Bus travel in Croatia is inexpensive, efficient, and the best way to travel long distances. You can reach even the smallest towns by public bus, while larger cities are connected by regular, comfortable, and usually air-conditioned coaches. On most routes you can purchase a ticket at the station or from the driver, but for the major routes (between Zagreb and the coast or between Dubrovnik and Split), it's safer to buy tickets at least a few days in advance. Seating is assigned if you book in advance, but not if you buy your ticket on the spot; however, apart from fully booked buses, seat allocations are not usually adhered to. Carry some coins in case you have to pay to put luggage in the hold (about 7 Kn per bag) or for the washroom at the station.

GetByBus is an excellent resource for checking routes and timetables and buying tickets in advance. Flixbus is a German bus company that operates many routes to Croatia from abroad, and within Croatia, which can easily be booked online and combined with international bus passes.

Car

GASOLINE
Most gas stations are open daily from 6 am to 8 pm; from June through September, many stations are open until 10 pm. In the bigger cities and on main international roads, stations offer 24-hour service. All pumps sell Eurosuper 95, Eurosuper 98, and Eurodiesel.

PARKING
Most towns mark parking spaces with a blue line and a sign denoting time restrictions. Buy a ticket at the closest parking machine and leave it in the front window; make sure to carry coins because not all parking machines take bills or cards. The historic centers of walled towns along the coast (Split, Trogir, Hvar Town, Korčula, and Dubrovnik) are completely closed to traffic, putting heavy pressure on the number of parking spaces outside the fortifications (and since parking is limited, it is also expensive).

ROAD CONDITIONS
The A1 highway that links Zagreb with Rijeka, Zadar, and Split is fast and has frequent, well-maintained rest stops. Construction has been underway for years to connect Dubrovnik to the highway, but for now it stretches only to Ploče, while the remaining 100 km (62 miles) to Dubrovnik is done by winding coastal road. It's not advisable to take a car to the islands as it can add hours to your itinerary when trying to board a car ferry, plus parking is usually limited. But if you decide to drive, remember that the roads are narrow, twisty, and unevenly maintained. During winter, driving through the inland regions of Gorski Kotar and Lika is occasionally made hazardous by heavy snow. Roads in Slavonia are typically flat, well marked, and well maintained.

RULES OF THE ROAD
Croatians drive on the right and follow rules similar to those in other European countries. Speed limits are 50 kph (30 mph) in urban areas, 90 kph (55 mph) in the outskirts, 110 kph (68 mph) on main roads, and 130 kph (80 mph) on motorways. Seatbelts are compulsory. The permitted blood-alcohol limit is 0.05%; drunk driving is punishable and can lead

Getting Here and Around

to severe fines. Talking on the phone while driving is prohibited unless the driver is using a hands-free device.

DRIVING TIMES

The A1 Highway connecting Zagreb to Rijeka, Zadar, and Split is the fastest route to Kvarner and Central Dalmatia. If traveling farther south to Dubrovnik, you will switch to the coastal road that passes through a 22 km (13 miles) section of Bosnia and Herzegovina, which can mean delays at the border; have your passport handy for this stretch.

CAR RENTALS

It is possible to rent a car quite cheaply in Croatia, for as little as €5 a day (excluding extras such as child seats, GPS, and insurance). Most major car rental companies are represented in the main tourist areas and airports, but you'll find the best rates online; check the website Auto Europe for the best deals.

In Croatia an International Driver's Permit is desirable but not necessary to rent a car from a major agency; a valid driver's license is all you need. The minimum age required for renting is usually 23 or older, and some companies also have maximum ages; be sure to inquire when making your arrangements.

If you intend to drive across a border, ask about restrictions on driving into other countries. Also, when you reserve a car, ask about cancellation penalties, taxes, drop-off charges (if you're planning to pick up the car in one city and leave it in another), and surcharges (for being under or over a certain age, for additional drivers, or for driving across state or country borders or beyond a specific distance from your point of rental). All these things can add substantially to your costs. Request car seats and extras such as GPS when you book.

Travel Times from Zagreb by Car

Zadar	3 hours	285 km (177 miles)
Pula	3½ hours	264 km (164 miles)
Rijeka	2 hours	160 km (99 miles)
Split	4 hours	408 km (253 miles)
Dubrovnik	7½ hours	550 km (341 miles)
Osijek	2½ hours	283 km (175 miles)
Kotor	8 hours	690 km (428 miles)

Finally, make sure that a confirmed reservation guarantees you a car; agencies sometimes overbook, particularly for busy weekends and holiday periods.

Cruise

Dubrovnik, Split, Hvar, and Korčula are common port calls for Eastern Mediterranean cruises. Small ships cruise up and down the country's coastline.

Train

The train is a great option for getting to Croatia from abroad, with direct international connections to Zagreb from Austria, Germany, Hungary, Slovenia, and Switzerland. However, within Croatia, trains are typically slower than buses and there are far fewer of them. Train travel is a viable alternative to the bus if you're traveling around the north or east to Slavonia. If you're going to Istria, you'll travel as far as Rijeka before switching to a bus. There are no trains that travel the coastal route south to Dalmatia.

Essentials

 Lodging

You can find any type of accommodation you like in Croatia, including five-star hotels, hostels, private villas, or a room in a family home, plus resorts, more than 500 campsites, and a handful of boutique wineries. In Zagreb, Istria, and Dalmatia, standards (and prices) are high, while in less busy regions, such as Slavonia, you might not be spoiled for choice but you can always find something suitable and reasonably priced.

On the coast, prices are at their highest in July and August and hotels are often fully booked far in advance. Outside of the high season, you can usually find a good bargain for places that might be out of your budget through the summer (another reason to consider traveling to Croatia in the shoulder season).

All foreign guests have to pay a tourist tax for each night they stay in a hotel or private accommodation. It's a negligible amount, between 2 Kn and 7 Kn per night depending on the hotel category and the season, and it's most often just added to your bill.

APARTMENT AND VILLA RENTALS

Until a decade or so ago, the best way to find local accommodations was to show up at the bus station, where a local person would wait with faded photos of their room for rent. In recent years the number of private beds has skyrocketed; you can now find everything from a single bed in a family home to a deluxe five-star apartment online. They vary greatly in size, standard, and amenities, but are generally a safe and unique way to stay in a quiet neighbourhood and interact with locals. Private villas are also very popular in Istria and Dalmatia, and a great option if you're traveling in a group or as a family since they have more space and facilities than a hotel room.

Dining

You won't find many restaurants in Croatia buzzing with local people, as locals prefer to eat their main meals at home with family and meet their friends for a drink at a cafe-bar. But that doesn't mean that there is a shortage of great places to eat; on the contrary, the dining scenes in places like Zagreb, Istria, and Dalmatia get more diverse and sophisticated every year. Some of the most renowned restaurants in the country (and in some towns, the only restaurants available) are found in hotels, including half of all the Michelin-starred restaurants in Croatia. And while you might not be dining with many local people, you can certainly try some excellent local dishes; the best Croatian restaurants focus on using fresh, locally sourced ingredients in a modern take on traditional recipes. In general, fish dominates along the coast and meat rules the interior. That said, one of the most popular dishes in Dalmatia is lamb *peka* while the must-try dish in Slavonia is fish *paprikaš*.

MEALS AND MEALTIMES

As the working day begins early here (with some offices opening as early as 7:30 am on weekdays), you'll find cafés open early as well. Lunch is usually served between noon and 3 in restaurants, and dinner is most often served after 7. In the height of the tourist season along the coast, restaurants may stay open later (after 10 pm) to handle the volume.

RESERVATIONS

Regardless of where you are, it's a good idea to make a reservation if you really want to eat at a particular restaurant. Reviews mention them specifically only when reservations are essential or when they are not accepted. Large parties should always call ahead to check the reservations policy.

Essentials

⊕ Health

Water is safe to drink throughout Croatia. EU countries have reciprocal health-care agreements with Croatia, entitling those nationals to medical consultation for a basic minimum fee. Citizens from outside the EU have to pay in accordance with listed prices. Most doctors speak English.

COVID-19

The emergence of COVID-19 brought all travel to a virtual standstill in the first half of 2020, and interruptions to travel have continued through 2020 and into 2021. Although the illness is mild in most people, some experience severe and even life-threatening complications. Once travel started up again, albeit slowly and cautiously, travelers were asked to be particularly careful about hygiene and to avoid any unnecessary travel, especially if they are sick.

Older adults, especially those over 65, have a greater chance of having severe complications from COVID-19. The same is true for people with weaker immune systems or those living with some types of medical conditions, including diabetes, asthma, heart disease, cancer, HIV/AIDS, kidney disease, and liver disease. Starting two weeks before a trip, anyone planning to travel should be on the lookout for some of the following symptoms: cough, fever, chills, trouble breathing, muscle pain, sore throat, new loss of smell or taste. If you experience any of these symptoms, you should not travel at all.

And to protect yourself during travel, do your best to avoid contact with people showing symptoms. Wash your hands often with soap and water. Limit your time in public places, and, when you are out and about, wear a face mask that

covers your nose and mouth. Indeed, a mask may be required in some places, such as on an airplane or in a confined space like a theater, where you share the space with a lot of people.

You may wish to bring extra supplies, such as disinfecting wipes, hand sanitizer (12-ounce bottles were allowed in carry-on luggage at this writing), and a first-aid kit with a thermometer.

OVER-THE-COUNTER REMEDIES

In Croatia, over-the-counter medications are sold in pharmacies, which are open until 6 or 7 pm on weekdays and 1 or 2 pm on Saturday. In each town there is usually a 24-hour pharmacy for emergencies. Most European pharmacists speak a word or two of English, but you're better off asking for a remedy by its medical name (e.g., ibuprofen) than its brand name (e.g., Advil). Pharmacies don't have a lot of open shelf space for goods, so you will have to ask the pharmacist for what you want. In both countries paracetemol (and its brand name Panadol) is more recognized than acetaminophen (and the brand name Tylenol) for basic pain relief. Claritin, the allergy relief medication, is sold in Croatia by that name at the pharmacy. Many products that Americans would normally find in their local drugstore—cough syrup, diaper cream, cough drops, muscle cream, and vitamins, to name a few—must be bought in the pharmacy in Croatia. While this system is inconvenient, if you get an allergy attack in the middle of the night, the upside is that prices are kept down by the government, so many things will be a fraction of the cost at home. The word for pharmacy in Croatia is *ljekarna*, but stick to the equally understood *apoteka*.

✚ Safety

Croatia is one of the safest countries in Europe; violent crime is very rare and there are no particular local scams that visitors should be aware of. Take the normal precautions: be on guard for pickpockets in crowded markets and don't wander alone down dark streets at night.

$ Taxes

Foreigners who spend over 740 Kn in one store on a single day can reclaim the V.A.T. (value added tax) upon leaving the country. To do this, you need to present the receipts and the goods bought at the *carina* (customs) desk at the airport, ferry port, or border crossing on your way out of the country.

When making a purchase, ask for a V.A.T. refund form and find out whether the merchant gives refunds—not all stores do, nor are they required to. Have the form stamped like any customs form by customs officials when you leave the country or, if you're visiting several European Union countries, when you leave the EU. After you're through passport control, take the form to a refund-service counter for an on-the-spot refund (which is usually the quickest and easiest option), or mail it to the address on the form (or the envelope with it) after you arrive home. You receive the total refund stated on the form, but the processing time can be long, especially if you request a credit-card adjustment.

Global Blue is a Europe-wide service with 225,000 affiliated stores and more than 700 refund counters at major airports and border crossings. Its refund form, called a Tax Free Check, is the most common across the European continent. The service issues refunds in the form of cash, check, or credit-card adjustment.

💵 Tipping

When eating out in Croatia, if you have enjoyed your meal and are satisfied with the service, it is customary to leave a 10% to 15% tip. It is not usual to tip in cafés or bars. Housekeepers and taxi drivers are not usually tipped. Tour guides do receive a tip, especially if they are particularly good. For porters on trains and bellhops at hotels, 5 Kn to 10 Kn per bag will be appreciated.

📍 Visitor Information

The first place to start planning your trip to Croatia (after this book, of course) is the Croatian National Tourist Board's website. In addition to a general overview of the culture and history of the country, it has lots of practical information on accommodations, travel agencies, and events. Then you can consult regional tourist board websites to narrow your trip focus even further.

Helpful Croatian Phrases

BASICS

Hello	Zdravo/Halo	zdrah-voh/ha-lo
Yes/No	Da/Ne	dah/neh
Please	Molim	moh-leem
Thank you	Hvala	hvah-lah
You're welcome	Nema na čemu/molim	nema na chemoo/moh-leem
I'm Sorry (apology)	Žao mi je	jhao mee yeh
Sorry (Excuse me)	Oprostite	oh-pro-stee-teh
Good morning	Dobro jutro	doh-bro yoo-tro
Good day	Dobar dan	doh-bar dan
Good evening	Dobro veče	doh-bro ve-che
Goodbye	Doviđenja	doh-vee-jen-ya
Mr. (Sir)	Gospodin	gos-poh-deen
Mrs.	Gospođa	gos-poh-ja
Miss	Gospođica	gos-poh-jee-tsa
Pleased to meet you	Drago mi je	drago-mee-yeh
How are you?	Kako ste?	ka-ko steh

NUMBERS

one-half	pola	po-la
one	jedan	yeh-dan
two	dva	dvah
three	tri	tree
four	četiri	cheh-tee-ree
five	pet	pet
six	šest	shest
seven	sedam	seh-dam
eight	osam	oh-sam
nine	devet	deh-vet
ten	deset	deh-set
eleven	dedanaest	yeh-dana-est
twelve	dvanaest	dvana-est
thirteen	trinaest	treena-est
fourteen	četrnaest	cheh-terna-est
fifteen	petnaest	petna-est
sixteen	šesnaest	shesna-est
seventeen	sedamnaest	seh-damna-est
eighteen	osamnaest	oh-samna-est
nineteen	devetnaest	deh-vetna-est
twenty	dvadeset	dva-deh-set
twenty-one	dvadeset jedan	dva-deh-set yeh-dan
thirty	trideset	tree-deh-set
forty	četrdeset	cheh-ter deh-set
fifty	pedeset	peh-deh-set
sixty	šezdeset	shez-deh-set
seventy	sedamdeset	seh-dam-deh-set
eighty	osamdeset	oh-sam-deh-set
ninety	devedeset	deh-veh-deh-set
one hundred	sto	stoh
one thousand	tisuća	tee-soo-chah
one million	milijun	mee-lee-yoon

COLORS

black	crn	tsern
blue	plav	plav
brown	smeđ	smej
green	zelen	ze-len
orange	narančast	na-ran-chast
red	crven	tser-ven
white	bijel	bee-ell
yellow	žut	jhoot

DAYS

Sunday	nedjelja	ned-yelya
Monday	ponedjeljak	poh-ned-yelyak
Tuesday	utorak	oo-torak
Wednesday	srijeda	sree-yed-ah
Thursday	četvrtak	chet-ver-tak
Friday	petak	peh-tak
Saturday	subota	soo-bota

MONTHS

January	siječanj	see-yeh-chan
February	veljača	vel-ya-cha
March	ožujak	oh-jhoo-yak
April	travanj	tra-van
May	svibanj	svee-ban
June	lipanj	lee-pan
July	srpanj	ser-pan
August	kolovoz	koh-loh-voz
September	rujan	roo-yan
October	listopad	lee-sto-pad
November	studeni	stoo-den-ee
December	prosinac	pro-see-nats

USEFUL PHRASES

Do you speak English?	Govorite li engleski?	goh-vo-ree-teh lee Eng-les-kee
I don't speak Croatian	Ne govorim Hrvatski	neh goh-vo-reem Her-vat-skee
I don't understand.	Ne razumijem	Neh rah-zoo-mee-yem
I don't know.	Ne znam	ne znam
I understand.	Razumijem	rah-zoo-mee-yem
I'm American.	Ja sam Amerikanac/Americanka	ya sam ameree-ka-nats/ameree-kan-ka
I'm British.	Ja sam Britanac/Britanka	ya sam Bree-tan-ats/Bree-tan-ka
What's your name?	Kako se zovete?	ka-ko seh zo-veh-teh
My name is ...	Zovem se...	zo-vem seh
What time is it?	Koliko je sati?	ko-lee-ko yeh sa-tee
How?	Kako?	ka-ko

When?	Kada?	**ka**-da
Yesterday	Jučer	**yoo**-cher
Today	Danas	**dah**-nas
Tomorrow	Sutra	**soo**-tra
This morning	Jutros	**yoo**-tros
This afternoon	Danas poslije podne	**dah**-nas **pos**-lee-yeh **pod**-neh
Tonight	Večeras	vech-**air**-as
What?	Što?	shto
What is it?	Što je?	shto yeh
Why?	Zašto?	**za**-shto
Who?	Tko?	tko
Where is ...	Gdje je...	gd-yeh yeh
... the train station?	...željeznički kolodvor?	**jhel**-yez-neetch-kee **ko**-lod-vor
... the subway station?	...podzemna željeznica?	**pod**-zem-na **jhel**-yez-neetsa
... the bus stop?	...autobusna postaja?	a-ooto-busna po-sta-ya
... the airport?	...zračna luka?	**zra**-chna **loo**-ka
... the post office?	...pošta?	po-shta
... the bank?	...banka?	**ban**-ka
... the hotel?	...hotel?	**ho**-tel
... the museum?	...muzej?	**moo**-zay
... the hospital?	...bolnica?	**bol**-neetsa
... the elevator?	...dizalo?	**dee**-zalo
Where are the restrooms?	Gdje su zahodi?	gd-yeh soo **za**-hod-ee
Here/there	Ovdje/tamo	ov-dyeh/**ta**-mo
Left/right	Lijevo/Desno	lee-**yeh**-voh/**deh**-sno
Is it near/far?	Je li blizu/daleko?	yeh lee **blee**-zoo/**dah**-lecko
I'd like ...	Želio/Željela bih...	**jhel**-eeo/**jhel**-yell-ah bee
... a room	...soba	**so**-ba
... the key	...ključ	klyooch
... a newspaper	...novine	**no**-vee-neh
... a stamp	...marka	**mar**-ka
I'd like to buy ...	Želio/Željela bih kupiti	**jhel**-eeo/**jhel**-yell-ah bee **koo**-pee-tee
... a city map	...karta grada	**karta gra**-da
... a road map	...autokarta	ah-ooto-karta
... a magazine	...magazin	**mah**-ga-zeen
... envelopes	...koverta	ko-**ver**-ta
... writing paper	...papir za pisanje	pa-peer za pee-**san**-yeh
... a postcard	...razglednica	raz-gled-neetsa
... a ticket	...karta	**kar**-ta
How much is it?	Koliko je to?	**koh**-lee-ko
It's expensive/cheap	Skupo/Jeftino je	**skoo**-po/**yef**-teeno yeh
A little/a lot	Malo/mnogo	**ma**-lo/mn-**oh**-goh
More/less	Više/manje	**vee**-shay/**man**-yeh

Enough/too (much)	Dovoljno/previše	**do**-vol-eeno/**preh**-vee-sheh
I am ill/sick	Osjećam se bolesno	**os**-yecham seh **bo**-lesno
Call a doctor	Zovite liječnika	**zoh**-vee-teh lee-**yech**-neeka
Help!	Upomoć!	**oo**-po-moch
Stop!	Prestani!	**pre**-stan-ee

DINING OUT

A bottle of ...	Boca...	**bo**-tsa
A cup of ...	Šalica ...	**sha**-leetsa
A glass of ...	Čaša....	**cha**-sha
Beer	Pivo	**pee**-voh
Bill/check	Račun	**rah**-chun
Bread	Kruh	krooh
Breakfast	Doručak	**doh**-roo-chak
Butter	Maslac	**mas**-lats
Cocktail/aperatif	Koktel	**kok**-tel
Coffee	Kava	**ka**-va
Dinner	Večera	**ve**-cher-ah
Fixed-price menu	Meni	**me**-nee
Fork	Vilica	**vee**-leetsa
I am a vegetarian/I don't eat meat	Jja sam vegetarijanac/Ne jedem meso	ya sam vegetaree-**yan**-ats/neh **yeh**-dem **meh**-so
I cannot eat ...	Ne mogu jesti...	neh **mo**-goo **yeh**-stee
I'd like to order ...	Želio bih naručiti	**jhel**-ee-oh bee nah-**roo**-chee-tee
Is service included?	Je li napojnica uključena?	yeh lee **nah**-poy-neetsa ook-lee-**oo**-chen-ah
I'm hungry/thirsty	Gladan/žedan sam	**gla**-dan/**jhe**-dan sam
It's good/bad	Dobro je/to je loše	**doh**-bro yeh/toh yeh **lo**-sheh
It's hot/cold	To je vruće/hladno	toh yeh **vroo**-cheh/**hlad**-no
Knife	Nož	nojh
Lunch	Ručak	**roo**-chak
Menu	Jelovnik	yeh-**lov**-neek
Napkin	Salveta	sal-**vet**-ah
Pepper	Bbiber	**bee**-ber
Plate	Tanjur	tan-**yoor**
Please give me ...	Možete li mi dati...	**mo**-jhe-teh lee mee **dah**-tee
Salt	Sol	sol
Spoon	Žlica	**jhlee**-tsa
Tea	Čaj	chy
Water	Voda	**voh**-da
Wine	Vino	**vee**-no

Great Itineraries

Dubrovnik, Southern Dalmatia, and Montenegro

The Jewel of the Adriatic is the perfect starting point for excursions to the wine and gastronomic pleasures of the Pelješac Peninsula, Korčula, and Montenegro. Dubrovnik has an international airport that is well connected to all European hubs during the summer season.

DAY 1: DUBROVNIK

If arriving by sea or air, you'll see one of the prettiest fortified cities in the world, and you are likely to immediately fall in love with it. From this view, you can tell why Dubrovnik (formerly Ragusa) was once the master of all Dalmatia. Check into your hotel and head straight to the Old Town. Most of the day-trippers depart by the late afternoon, making it the best time to walk the circuit of the City Walls without the crowds. Have dinner at an outdoor terrace, then stroll along the *Stradun* after dark, popping into a wine bar or grabbing an ice cream along the way.

DAY 2: THE PELJEŠAC PENINSULA

Pick up your rental car early and drive straight out of town. Stop to admire the gardens at Trsteno before reaching the Pelješac Peninsula. Just before you reach Mali Ston, there is a small shack on the right-hand side: pull over and order a couple of oysters, which are grown right beside you in the channel. Indulge in more at one of the waterfront restaurants in Mali Ston, and if it's not too hot, take a walk on the defensive walls that stretch between Mali Ston and Ston, or take a tour of the famed salt pans. Pelješac is

Dalmatia's best red wine–growing region, producing the famed Dingač and Postup from the Plavac Mali grape. There's one 60-km (37-mile) road that leads from Mali Ston to Orebič, and along the way you can stop off at family-owned wineries to sample the goods. If you are traveling by bus from Dubrovnik, get off in Mali Ston for lunch, or continue all the way to Orebič; make sure to consult the bus timetables as service is not super frequent. Spend the night in Orebič or take the short 15-minute ferry ride to Korčula.

DAYS 3 AND 4: KORČULA

Enjoy two full days on Korčula, where you'll find some of the best accommodations, restaurants, and beaches in the region. If you have a car, you can drive to the island's secluded coves, rural villages, and wineries. If you've come by passenger ferry, you can rent a mountain bike or arrange a sightseeing tour of the island. Alternatively, take a day trip from Korčula to Mljet for the day, returning to Korčula Town for dinner; if you're there on the right day, you might be able to see a performance of the Moreška sword dance.

DAY 5: PERAST, MONTENEGRO

Take the morning ferry back to Dubrovnik and head straight down the coast by car or bus to the sparkling Bay of Kotor in Montenegro. Plan on spending your first night in the tiny waterfront village of Perast, which is best known for a pair of tiny islets, each topped with a church. See the Roman mosaics at Risan and stay at one of the town's charming boutique hotels.

DAY 6: KOTOR, MONTENEGRO

Continue on to the UNESCO World Heritage town of Kotor, which sits on Europe's most southerly ria (a coastal inlet commonly confused with a fjord). Spend the day exploring its churches, markets, and wandering the Old Town's labyrinth of winding cobbled streets. Have lunch in one of the splendid marble piazzas. Don't miss hiking up to St. John's Fortress, following the medieval walls for breathtaking views.

DAY 7: CAVTAT

Return to Croatia, stopping in Cavtat for lunch and a stroll along the waterfront, or visit one of the rural agritourism properties in the Konavle region. Cavtat is near the airport, so you might consider spending your final night here. Otherwise, return to Dubrovnik and catch the cable car to the top of Mt. Srd for your final spectacular sunset of the trip.

Tips

■ This itinerary is best done by car, allowing you the freedom to stop at wineries, oyster shacks, and beaches along the way. However, in the height of the tourist season a car can add hours to your itinerary, with heavy traffic in Dubrovnik and often hours-long waits for car ferries. If it's particularly busy in the region during your visit, it might be quicker to take public buses and passenger ferries, though you won't be able to cover as much ground. If you're flexible, you can wait until you arrive to make your decision as buses, ferries, and car rentals can usually be booked at the last minute.

■ There are excellent organized tour options in this region, so if neither a car rental nor public transport suits you, consider basing yourself in Dubrovnik, Korčula, and/or Kotor, and taking day trips from there.

Great Itineraries

Island Hopping and National Parks: Central and Northern Dalmatia

If you want to immerse yourself in the natural landscapes of Croatia, this itinerary will take you to three national parks, several strikingly diverse islands, and a couple of ancient towns thrown in for good measure. Plan for a combination of car and boat travel, and try to schedule car trips on weekdays as the roads, particularly the A1 highway, can get busy on weekends. Both Split and Zadar have international airports, so you can start this itinerary from either one.

DAY 1: SPLIT
Though many people use Split as the jumping-off point for nearby islands, it's definitely worth spending at least one day exploring the Meštrović Gallery and the Archaeological Museum, strolling the waterfront Riva, and getting lost in the streets of Diocletian's Palace. In the early evening, sit in the Palace's open peristyle and admire the Imperial quarters, the Cathedral of St. Domnius, and the Egyptian sphinx before having dinner.

DAYS 2 AND 3: ISLAND HOPPING
The three closest islands to Split offer very different attractions, so choose your getaway based on what type of vacation you're looking for. Brač, home to the famous Zlatni Rat beach, is best for families and wholesome seaside fun. Hvar is known for the beach clubs and nightlife of its main settlement, Hvar Town,

although you'll find lavender fields, wineries, and beautiful Old Towns beyond the glitz and glamour. And if you're looking to get away from it all, Vis, a former Yugoslavian military base, is the least developed of all the islands and offers a wonderful respite from the crowds.

DAY 4: KORNATI NATIONAL PARK
Take a ferry back to Split and from there make your way up the stunning coastline, stopping off at Primošten and Šibenik for sights and food along the way. At Vodice, board one of the many boats offering day trips to Kornati National Park, the largest archipelago in the Adriatic with over 100 privately owned islands. This bare and beautiful archipelago's bone-white-to-ochre colors are in striking contrast to the shockingly blue sea. If possible, take a boat that will drop you off at Zadar on the way back. Alternatively, drive from Vodice to Zadar to spend the night.

DAYS 5 AND 6: ZADAR AND PAKLENICA NATIONAL PARK
Zadar has fast emerged as one of Croatia's top tourist destinations, and for good reason. Zadar's Old Town is bustling and beautiful, with marble pedestrian streets, Roman ruins, medieval churches, palaces, and museums. Be sure to visit the St. Donatus Church, a massive cylindrical structure that is one of the largest early Byzantine churches in Croatia; don't miss the sea organ and the Greeting to the Sun either. Drive or take a bus to neighboring Nin to see the former seat of the Dalmatian royal family as well as a quaint little salt museum.

The following day, venture out to Paklenica National Park, an imposing canyon in the Velebit Mountains. This rugged limestone canyon offers some great hiking and the ultimate challenge for cliff climbers. Also check out the old A-bomb shelter that Marshal Tito had built in the 1950s in case Stalin got a little too aggressive.

DAY 7: KRKA NATIONAL PARK, TROGIR, AND SPLIT

Head back toward Split and stop along the way at Krka National Park, which challenges Plitvice for cascading water and amazing turquoise waterfalls. From there it is an easy drive to Split via Trogir, a UNESCO World Heritage Site. This small island is a pristinely preserved medieval town that's attached to the mainland by one bridge. The town's jewel is the mighty Cathedral of St. Lawrence, a superb example of Romanesque architecture.

Tips

■ Avoid taking a car to the islands. Ferry reservations for cars must be made well in advance, and you won't need one once you arrive.

■ Bring an umbrella or waterproof jacket in case of summer showers near the Velebit Mountains.

Great Itineraries

Western Croatia in a Week: Zagreb, Istria, and Kvarner

If you only have a week but want to get a sense of all that Croatia has to offer, this itinerary is a good place to start. You'll get the mountains, the seaside, the city, the countryside, a stunning national park, and a first-class Roman ruin.

DAY 1: ZAGREB

Zagreb is a compact city that begs to be explored on foot. Start your morning with a visit to the Cathedral and the Dolac Market, then take the funicular to the Upper Town to explore the museums; the Croatian Historical Museum and the Museum of Broken Relationships are both worth a visit. Spend the afternoon wandering around the Lower Town; stop for a drink on the pedestrian street Ul. Tkalčića, do some shopping along Ilica (Zagreb's modern high street), and have dinner at one of the city's excellent restaurants.

DAY 2: PLITVICE LAKES

The next morning head south toward the coast, exiting the highway in Karlovac in the direction of Plitvice National Park. Plitvice is a naturally occurring water world, with 19 crystal-clear pools connected by cascades and waterfalls. A UNESCO World Heritage Site, this is one of Croatia's most popular tourist sites and has been for years, so the park is well-protected and visits are well-organized. No matter what time of year you visit, the colors here are spectacular and you'll spend hours wandering the trails. Spend the night in either of the nearby towns, Mukinje or Jezerce, both a nice walking distance from the park.

DAY 3: RAB ISLAND

Enjoy the journey to Rab Island from Plitvice, which involves driving down the country's largest mountain range, Velebit, to the eastern Kvarner coast. Then catch a ferry to Rab, one of the bay's most beautiful islands. The northeastern side of the island is mostly barren, while the southwestern side is covered by one of the last oak forests of the Mediterranean. Once there, take in the sights of the medieval stone town of Rab, or head straight to one of the island's many sandy beaches. Spend the night in Rab, or if you still have the energy, take a ferry from Rab to the island of Krk and enjoy the cliff-top town of Valbiska, home of Zlahtina white wine.

DAY 4: OPATIJA

Take the ferry from Rab or the bridge from Krk to Opatija where you can spend time relaxing, Habsburg-style. Check into one of the atmospheric, turn-of-the-century hotels for a little slice of nostalgia, then head out for a stroll along the 12-km (7½-mile-long) promenade that zigzags along the sea. If you get antsy for more seaside diversity, catch the Istrian side ferry to the islands of Cres or Lošinj.

DAY 5: PULA

From Opatija or Lošinj head south or west, respectively, to Pula and spend the morning exploring its incredible amphitheater, one of the best-preserved sites in the Roman world. After lunch, take a boat to the Brijuni Islands for the afternoon to visit the Tito-designed zoo and tropical gardens. Drive the short distance to Rovinj for the night.

DAY 6: ROVINJ AND POREC

Have breakfast and a morning stroll through the limestone architecture and Venetian houses of Rovinj. Set out for Poreč, stopping at some of the many fine Istrian wineries along the way. Upon arrival in Poreč, check out the St. Euphrasius Basilica, one of the most important remnants of Byzantine art on the Adriatic. Spend the night at any of the fine hotels in town.

DAY 7: MOTOVUN AND ZAGREB

Head back to Zagreb via the Istrian interior. Drive east toward Pazin, stopping in the medieval hill towns of Motovun or Grožnjan for lunch and breathtaking views. These medieval villages are in the heart of truffle country, so keep your eyes open for some fresh goods to bring home. Continue northeast toward Zagreb, possibly stopping at the mountain town of Fužine for its famous cherry strudel with views of Lake Bajer.

Tips

■ This itinerary can be done by bus, but it is easier with a car. The main highway connecting Zagreb to Istria (the A6) is well maintained and offers beautiful views of Gorski Kotar. Tolls can be paid in cash or by card.

■ Consider planning your visit to Plitvice on a weekday, when travel on the main highway between Zagreb and Zadar is lighter.

■ The closest ferry crossing from Opatija to Cres and Lošinj is at Brestova in Istria. If you plan to take your car in the height of summer, count on a wait.

On the Calendar

For exact dates and further information about events in Croatia, check the Croatian National Tourist Board website (⊕ *www.croatia.hr*).

January

On the last Friday of the month, most of the country's top museums and galleries offer free entrance from 6 pm to 1 am during the **Night of Museums** (⊕ *www. nocmuzeja.hr*). The event, which has increased from 6 participating museums in Zagreb when it started in 2005 to more than 200 institutions (and counting) today, is a fun way for visitors and locals alike to spend the night exploring new spots around the city.

February

Carnival is celebrated across the country, but the biggest and best party is the **Rijeka Carnival** (⊕ *www.rijecki-karneval.hr*). Held from mid-January to early February, it is considered one of the most vibrant festivals in the world, attracting hundreds of thousands of revelers who come to enjoy the costumes, street parties, masked balls, and parades.

March

For two days in March, the small towns of Ston and Mali Ston on the Pelješac Peninsula celebrate the Feast of St. Joseph with the **Festival of Oysters** (⊕ *www.ston.hr*). You can enjoy Dalmatian music along the waterfront and taste the renowned oysters at their very best, as well as Pelješac wines and other local products.

April

Zagreb hosts **Biennale** (⊕ *www.mbz.hr*), an international festival of contemporary music every spring. It's attended by the heavy hitters of the classical world as well as groundbreaking pioneers.

June

The island of Korčula celebrates **Half New Year** on June 30, with a masquerade parade followed by music, dancing, and fireworks on the streets of its medieval Old Town. Elsewhere, Croatia hosts some of the top dance music festivals in the world in June; the season kicks off on the island of Pag with **Hideout** (⊕ *www. hideoutfestival.com*), a five-day party on Zrce Beach.

July and August

Practically every island and town up and down the coast hosts some kind of festival in July and/or August. The largest of the EDM festivals, **Ultra Europe** (⊕ *www. ultraeurope.com*), takes place in Split while Croatia's largest and most prestigious cultural event, the **Dubrovnik Summer Festival** (⊕ *www.dubrovnik-festival.hr*), draws international artists and musicians and features drama, ballet, concerts, and opera, all performed on open-air stages within Old Town. Similarly, the **Split Summer Festival** (⊕ *www.splitsko-ljeto.hr*) hosts opera, theater, and dance events at open-air venues within the walls of Diocletian's Palace.

There are also several international film festivals that take place in impressive locations across the country, including the oldest one in Croatia, the **Pula Film Festival** (⊕ www.pulafilmfestival.hr), where films are screened against the stunning backdrop of the Roman Arena, and the **Motovun Film Festival** (⊕ motovunfilmfestival.com), which highlights international independent films in a rustic medieval setting.

September

The **Epidaurus Festival** (⊕ www.epidaurus-festival.com) brings a variety of concerts, mostly classical and jazz, as well as an excellent selection of hands-on workshops to the town of Cavtat, while up north, **Varaždin Baroque Evenings** (⊕ www.vbv.hr) see eminent soloists and orchestras from Croatia and abroad perform Baroque music recitals in the city's most beautiful churches.

October

October is high season for the elusive white truffle in Istria, and it is celebrated during the **Zigante Truffle Days** (⊕ www.trufflefair.com). The fair takes place across nine weekends from September through November in the Motovun Forest, where you can attend culinary workshops, watch demonstrations of truffle hunting, and sample truffles and other Istrian delicacies.

November

In Zagorje, **Martinje (St. Martin's Day)**, November 11, sees the blessing of the season's new wine, accompanied by a hearty goose feast and endless toasts.

December

Zagreb comes to life in December with its **Advent Market** (⊕ www.adventzagreb.hr), heralded the best Christmas market in Europe many times over. The capital dazzles with thousands of Christmas lights, ice skating rinks, outdoor concerts, food stalls, and, of course, mulled wine.

Best Tours in Croatia

Guided tours are a great option when you don't want to plan your whole trip yourself. These days you can find a tour to suit whatever your interests may be, whether you're in Croatia for the food, wine, biking, sea, history, or *Game of Thrones*.

Backroads. Cycling tours are extremely popular in Croatia, and this company that combines island-hopping and cycling is one of the originals. ⊕ *www.backroads. com.*

Culinary Croatia. Run by the folks at Secret Dalmatia, Culinary Croatia focuses on cooking classes, wine tours, and personalized foodie experiences of Dalmatia and Istria. ⊕ *www.culinary-croatia.com.*

Dubrovnik Walking Tours. Anyone who has watched and loved *Game of Thrones* will be curious to learn more about how and where the show was filmed in Dubrovnik. This company mixes *GoT* tidbits with real history. ⊕ *www.dubrovnik-walking-tours.com.*

Exodus Travels. With 500 itineraries across over 90 countries, Exodus is one of the largest and best international travel companies for active travelers. They organize sustainable cycling, walking, and trekking tours of Croatia and the Balkans for travelers ages 12 and up. ⊕ *www. exodustravels.com.*

Intrepid Travel. This well-respected Australian company comes with a strong emphasis on sustainable travel around the world. They specialize in small-group tours and cover a wide range of activities in Croatia, from sailing and cycling the islands to visiting the inland national parks. They use local guides and focus on authentic, off-the-beaten-track experiences. ⊕ *www.intrepidtravel.com.*

The North Way Travel. One of the only companies specializing in Slavonian travel, the helpful folks at the North Way Travel organize tailor-made, guided, and self-guided tours of the region with a focus on food, wine, and sustainable local experiences. ⊕ *www.thenorthwaytravel.com.*

Piknik. For a unique perspective on Dubrovnik, order a Piknik: you'll get an insulated backpack stocked with homemade dishes, using all local ingredients, and plenty of tips on where to go to enjoy them. Guided sunset hikes of Konavle and Mount Srđ can also be arranged. ⊕ *www.piknikdubrovnik.com.*

Secret Dalmatia. Croatia-based Secret Dalmatia excels at creating bespoke tours of Dalmatia, specializing in off-the-beaten track destinations and a premium, personalized experience. ⊕ *www. secretdalmatia.com.*

Tureta Travel. This boutique Zagreb-based company specializes in tailor-made tours to all corners of Croatia. ⊕ *www.tureta-travel.com.*

Zagreb Bites. This company offers a fun, fresh way to explore the capital and surrounding area through its food, craft beer, and wine scenes. They also organize guided food tours of Zagreb's Advent Market. ⊕ *www.zagrebites.com.*

Contacts

Air

AIRPORT CONTACTS
Dubrovnik Airport.
☎ *020/773–100* ⊕ *www.
airport-dubrovnik.hr.* **Osijek
Airport.** ☎ *031/284–611*
⊕ *www.osijek-airport.hr.*
Pula Airport. ☎ *060/308–
308* ⊕ *www.airport-pu-
la.hr.* **Rijeka Airport.**
☎ *099/525–8911* ⊕ *www.
rijeka-airport.hr.* **Split
Airport.** ☎ *021/203–555*
⊕ *www.split-airport.hr.*
Zadar Airport. ☎ *023/205–
917* ⊕ *www.zadar-air-
port.hr.* **Zagreb Airport.**
☎ *060/320–320* ⊕ *www.
zagreb-airport.hr.*

🚢 Boat and Ferry

**CONTACTS Croatia
Ferries.** ⊕ *www.croatia-
ferries.com.* **Jadrolinija.**
☎ *051/666–111* ⊕ *www.
jadrolinija.hr.* **SNAV.**
☎ *081/428–5555* ⊕ *www.
snav.it.* **Venezia Lines.**
☎ *052/422–896* ⊕ *www.
venezialines.com.*

🚌 Bus

CONTACTS FlixBus.
⊕ *www.flixbus.com.* **Get-
ByBus.** ⊕ *www.getbybus.
com.*

🛏 Lodging

CROATIA SPECIALISTS
Croatian Villas. ⊕ *www.cro-
atianvillas.com.* **Dominium
Accommodation and Tours.**
☎ *095/131–3142* ⊕ *www.
book-dubrovnik.com.*

📍 Visitor Information

**CONTACTS Croatia National
Tourist Board.** ⊕ *www.
croatia.hr.* **Dalmatia Region.**
⊕ *www.dalmatia.hr.* **Istria
Region.** ⊕ *www.istra.hr.*
Kvarner Region. ⊕ *www.
kvarner.hr.* **Zagreb.** ⊕ *www.
infozagreb.hr.*

Chapter 3

DUBROVNIK AND SOUTHERN DALMATIA

Updated by
Andrea MacDonald

◉ Sights	🍴 Restaurants	🛏 Hotels	🛍 Shopping	🍸 Nightlife
★★★★★	★★★★★	★★★★★	★★★★☆	★★★★☆

WELCOME TO DUBROVNIK AND SOUTHERN DALMATIA

TOP REASONS TO GO

★ **Wall walking:** Walk the entire circuit of Dubrovnik's medieval city walls—which date back to the 13th century—for splendid views. Then take the cable car up Mt. Srd for the postcard-perfect views of the walls, the city, and the sea together in all their glory.

★ **World's best oysters:** Feast on fresh oysters straight out of the sea and local wine at a waterside restaurant in the Pelješac Peninsula's Mali Ston. The oysters are justifiably famous and served year round.

★ **Sword dancing:** Watch an incredibly entertaining, centuries-old sword dance in Korčula Town, the stunning city where Marco Polo was born.

★ **Secluded swimming:** Swim in Mljet's pristine Veliko Jezero surrounded by dense pine forests, then take a kayak to the Benedictine monastery on an island in the middle of the lake.

★ **Chilling out:** Spend a day hiking, biking, or just lounging on the relaxed, sun-drenched Elafiti Islands.

Occupying the tail end of Croatia before it trails off into Montenegro and the Gulf of Kotor, Southern Dalmatia is bordered to the east by Bosnia-Herzegovina and to the west by the Adriatic Sea. Heading out across the water you will hit Korčula, Mljet, and the Elafiti Islands. On the other side is Italy.

1 Dubrovnik. A historic walled city and Croatia's crown jewel.

2 Elafiti Islands. Laidback islands that make great day trips from Dubrovnik.

3 Cavtat. An easy-going seaside retreat.

4 The Pelješac Peninsula. Home to the walled city Ston (famous for its oysters) and the resort city Orebić (famous for its wine).

5 Korčula. The alleged birthplace of Marco Polo.

6 Mljet. A beautiful island home to a gorgeous national park.

A region would be lucky to have just one sight as majestic as Dubrovnik. In Southern Dalmatia, the walled city is only the beginning.

Head south to pine-scented hiking trails in Cavtat, or up the coast to a garden full of exotic trees in Trsteno. Tour an ancient salt factory, feast on world-class oysters and superb red wine from the Pelješac Peninsula, then head out to sea to explore Marco Polo's birthplace on Korčula and Odysseus's mythical cave on Mljet. Along the way you'll find some of the best windsurfing and sailing in Europe, kayak trips to citrus and sage-covered islands, centuries-old houses, millennia-old caves, fresh seafood, and always, everywhere, that big blue sea.

The highlight of Southern Dalmatia is undoubtedly the stunning walled city of Dubrovnik, from 1358 to 1808 a rich and powerful independent republic that exerted its economic and cultural influence over almost the entire region. Today it is one of Croatia's most sophisticated and upmarket destinations, and one of the world's most beautiful cities.

Dubrovnik is busy in the high season, but somehow the destinations around it have remained remarkably untouched by mass tourism. Moving down the mainland coast you come to bucolic Konavle, the breadbasket of the region. Full of family farms, folk festivals, and wineries, it offers a wonderful glimpse into rural life. The gateway to Konavle is Cavtat, a town founded by the ancient Greeks as Epidaurum. Dubrovnik was actually founded by residents of Epidaurum after the town was destroyed in the early 7th century. Today's Cavtat is a cheerful holiday resort with a palm-lined seaside promenade,

several sights of cultural note, and a laid-back vibe.

Back up the coast, northwest of Dubrovnik, one arrives at the Pelješac Peninsula, famed locally for its excellent red wines and shellfish. The main towns here are Mali Ston, known for its oysters, salt pans, and 14th-century walls, and Orebić, a low-key resort with a lovely beach and water-sports facilities, backed by a majestic hillside monastery. From Orebić there are regular ferry crossings to Korčula, one of the most sophisticated of the Croatian islands. Further away, the sparsely populated island of Mljet offers little in the way of architectural sites, but with coniferous forests, lagoons, sandy beaches, and two emerald-green saltwater lakes in Mljet National Park, it is a haven for hiking, mountain biking, swimming, and kayaking.

Planning

When to Go

Southern Dalmatia works for half the year and sleeps for the other as much of the region shuts down through the winter. Dubrovnik is the exception; sightseeing is just as important as swimming here, so even in winter you will find many restaurants and attractions still open, plus serious deals on accommodations and a chance to tune into the local way of life.

But the best times to visit the region are the shoulder seasons: May through

June and September through October. The days are still warm enough to swim but not too hot for sightseeing, there are many festivals to enjoy, less crowds, and the locals are more relaxed.

July and August is when everything happens at full speed; the prices are high, the hotels fully booked, the harbors are full of boats, and the small streets full of people. The pay-off of a summer visit is that you're guaranteed hot, sunny weather and plenty of entertainment. If you plan to visit during this period, make sure to book accommodations well in advance and make dinner reservations a day or two ahead.

Getting Here and Around

AIR
Southern Dalmatia is served by Dubrovnik Airport (DBV) at Čilipi, 18 km (11 miles) southeast of the city.

The national carrier, Croatia Airlines, operates direct internal flights between Dubrovnik and Zagreb year-round. Through summer, there are regular direct flights between Dubrovnik and many European destinations with Croatia Airlines and other budget airlines, including easyJet. British Airways operates flights year-round between Dubrovnik and London. It is also possible to fly direct to Barcelona, Istanbul, and Rome throughout the winter.

The Platanus shuttle bus travels several times per day between the airport and the main bus station in Gruž (55 Kn one way; 80 Kn return). It also drops people off at the Pile Gate on the way from the airport, and picks up from a stop near the cable car so if you're staying in the Old Town, these are your more convenient options. The shuttle meets all incoming flights upon arrival, while the trip back to the airport is usually scheduled for two hours before flight departure times.

Consult the website for exact timing as it changes daily.

AIRPORT CONTACTS Dubrovnik Airport. ☎ 020/773–100 ⊕ www.airport-dubrovnik.hr.

AIRPORT TRANSFER CONTACTS Platanus Shuttle Bus. ✉ Ulica od Batale 2A, Dubrovnik ☎ 099/275–1145 ⊕ www.platanus.hr.

BOAT AND FERRY
Jadrolinija runs a regular ferry service between Dubrovnik and Bari (Italy), departing from Bari late in the evening and arriving in Dubrovnik early the next morning, with a similar schedule in the other direction. Throughour the summer, there are several Jadrolinija passenger ferries per day from Dubrovnik to the Elafiti Islands (Koločep, Lopud) and car ferries that stop in Mljet and Korčula before carrying on to Split.

Krilo's faster, more comfortable catamaran, *Kapetan Luka,* travels twice daily between Split and Dubrovnik, stopping in Korčula and Mljet en route. You can also take a high-speed catamaran operated by G&V Line that runs daily from Dubrovnik to Šipan, Sobra, Polače on Mljet, Korčula, and Lastovo. In addition, there are five daily Jadrolinija ferries between Mljet and Prapratno on the Pelješac Peninsula.

Tickets can be purchased at the individual ferry companies' offices at the harbor in each destination.

CONTACTS G&V Line. ✉ Vukovarska 34, Gruž ☎ 020/313–119 ⊕ www.gv-line.hr. **Jadrolinija.** ✉ Obala Stjepana Radića 40, Dubrovnik ☎ 020/418–000 ⊕ www.jadrolinija.hr. **Krilo (Kapetan Luka).** ✉ Gruž ☎ 021/645–476 ⊕ www.krilo.hr.

BUS
There are regular bus routes between the main bus station in Dubrovnik and destinations all over mainland Croatia, including hourly buses to Split. Remember that if you're traveling between Central and Southern Dalmatia by road,

you'll pass through a narrow coastal strip called Neum, which belongs to Bosnia-Herzegovina, so have your passport at hand for the border checkpoint. Within the Southern Dalmatia region, there are regular buses that run from Dubrovnik down the coast to Cavtat, and up the coast to Ston and onward to Orebić on the Pelješac Peninsula.

CONTACTS Dubrovnik Bus Station. ⊠ *Obala Pape Ivana Pavla II 44A, Gruž* ☎ *060/305–070* ⊕ *libertasdubrovnik.hr.*

CAR

While visiting Dubrovnik and the islands, you are better off without a car as parking can be hard to find and expensive, and traffic can be a problem. Korčula and Mljet are the exceptions, as a car will allow you to explore more secluded parts of the islands. You may also consider renting a car if you are traveling up the coast to the Pelješac Peninsula or down the coast to Cavtat and Konavle, as these areas are not well served by public transport and having a car will allow you to explore farther than the bus will take you.

TAXI

In Dubrovnik, there are taxi ranks at the main bus station and the airport, just outside the city walls at Pile Gate and Ploče Gate, in front of Gruž harbor, and in Lapad. It isn't possible to hail a taxi on the street; you must go to the rank or call to order one. Most taxi stands post authorized prices; a taxi to the airport costs 280 Kn. Uber is also very popular in Dubrovnik.

Restaurants

Seafood lovers rejoice: fresh catch predominates throughout Southern Dalmatia. White fish, including sea bream and sea bass, is very common, often served with *blitva* (potatoes and swiss chard). The region's top venue for shellfish is the village of Mali Ston on the Pelješac Peninsula, where locally grown *ostrige* (oysters) and *dagnje* (mussels) attract diners from far and wide; you can try them in restaurants all across the region, but nothing beats eating them beside the channel where they are grown. Mljet is noted for its *jastog* (lobster), a culinary luxury highly appreciated by the sailing crowd.

And make sure to find a restaurant that serves food prepared *ispod peke* ("under the bell"): a terra-cotta casserole dish, usually containing either lamb or octopus, is buried in embers over which the *peka* (metal dome) is placed to ensure a long, slow cooking process—it usually needs to be ordered a day in advance but it's worth the wait. Another must-try for meat lovers is *pašticada*, a sweet, rich, slow-cooked beef dish typically served with gnocchi. Sweet tooths will be satisfied by the region's specialty *rožata* (a creamy custard pudding), and the abundance of dried fruit such as figs, apricots, candied almonds, and *arancini* (candied orange or lemon peels), which are often accompanied by a glass of *prošek* (sweet wine) or another excellent local wine; Plavac Mali, Pošip, and Malvasija are names you'll get to know if you're an oenophile. Most meals are washed down with a small glass of *rakija*, often made with carob, roses, honey, or herbs.

Hotels

You can find accommodations to suit any budget in Southern Dalmatia, from campsites and private rooms to Croatia's highest concentration of five-star hotels. The most luxurious lodgings are in Dubrovnik, but you'll find unique properties in Korčula, Pelješac, and Lopud as well. Private apartments and villas are a great choice for families or groups of friends as they often have kitchen facilities and more space. For most of the region, the high season runs from Easter through late October, peaking during July and August, when prices rise significantly. In

Dubrovnik, many properties stay open through the winter and you can find excellent deals on places that might normally be out of reach.

★ Dominium Travel

With so many private apartments throughout the region, choosing the right one can be overwhelming, not to mention a little risky. Do yourself a favor and contact Dominium Travel, one of the most helpful agencies in the region. A young, enthusiastic company that manages more than 500 private apartments in 20 destinations along the coast, they'll work to find the perfect apartment to suit your budget and style, and they can also organize transfers and tours. ⊠ *Pile* ☎ *095/131–3142* ⊕ *www.book-dubrovnik. com.*

Restaurant and hotel reviews have been shortened. For full information, visit Fodors.com. Restaurant prices are the average cost of a main course at dinner or, if dinner is not served, at lunch. Hotel prices are the lowest cost of a standard double room in high season.

What It Costs in Croatian kuna (Kn)			
$	$$	$$$	$$$$
RESTAURANTS			
under 65 Kn	65 Kn–125 Kn	126 Kn–200 Kn	over 200 Kn
HOTELS			
under 800 Kn	800 Kn–1,450 Kn	1451 Kn–2,000 Kn	over 2,000 Kn

Tours

Dubrovnik Day Tours

GUIDED TOURS | The friendly locals who operate this company bring more than a decade's worth of guiding experience, plus a lifetime of living in Dubrovnik, to their great-value private tours. They operate wine and oyster excursions to the Pelješac Peninsula as well as day trips to Konavle, Bosnia and Herzegovina, and Montenegro. They also do walking tours around Dubrovnik, including a fun Game of Thrones tour with swords and props. Highly recommended is the 3-hour Dubrovnik Above and Beyond tour, which includes a drive up Mt. Srđ for a viewpoint that rivals the Cable Car, and a comprehensive city tour that incorporates history, local knowledge, and personal experience. ⊠ *Obala Stjepana Radica 2, Dubrovnik* ☎ *098/175–1775* ⊕ *www.dubrovnikdaytours.net.*

Piknik

GUIDED TOURS | For a unique foodie experience, order a Piknik. You'll get an insulated backpack thoughtfully stocked with gourmet Croatian goodies, and a map to the best secret beaches or panoramic viewpoints where you can enjoy it. You can join in on a guided hike to the best trails around Konavle or up Mt. Srđ to watch the sunset. Keep in mind that twenty-four-hour notice is required for a Piknik. ⊕ *www.piknikdubrovnik.com.*

Secret Dalmatia

EXCURSIONS | One of the pioneers in custom-made tours in the region, Secret Dalmatia organizes upmarket itineraries around Southern Dalmatia and Montenegro with a focus on local experiences, food and wine tastings, and off-the-beaten-track destinations. Their superhelpful and friendly team can organize private or small-group tours. ⊕ *www.secretdalmatia.com.*

Visitor Information

CONTACTS Cavtat-Konavle Tourist Office. ⊠ *Zidine 6, Cavtat* ☎ *020/479–025* ⊕ *visit. cavtat-konavle.com.* Dubrovnik Tourist Office. ⊠ *Brsalje 5, Pile* ☎ *020/312–011* ⊕ *www.tzdubrovnik.hr.* Korčula Tourist Office. ⊠ *Ul. Plokata 19, Korcula* ☎ *020/715–701* ⊕ *www.visitkorcula.eu.* Lopud Tourist Office. ⊠ *Obala Iva Kuljevana 12, Lopud* ☎ *020/322–322.* Mljet Tourist

Office. ☎ 020/746–025 ⊕ www.mljet.hr.
Orebić Tourist Office. ✉ Zrinsko-frankopan-
ska 2, Orebić ☎ 020/713–718 ⊕ www.
visitorebic-croatia.hr. **Ston Tourist Office.**
✉ Pelješki put 1, Ston ☎ 020/754–452
⊕ www.ston.hr.

Dubrovnik

Nothing can prepare you for your first
sight of Dubrovnik. Completely encircled
by thick fortified walls, with a maze of
gleaming white streets within, it is truly
one of the world's most beautiful cities.
And it never gets old; whether you're
admiring it from the top of Mt. Srd, from
a kayak out at sea, or standing in the
middle of the Stradun looking around
you in awe, your imagination will run
wild picturing what it looked like when
the walls were built eight centuries ago,
without any suburbs or highways around
it, just this magnificent stone city rising
out of the sea.

In the 7th century AD, residents of the
Roman city Epidaurum (now Cavtat)
fled the Avars and Slavs of the north
and founded a new settlement on a
small rocky island, which they named
Laus, and later Ragusa. On the mainland
hillside opposite the island, the Slav
settlement called Dubrovnik grew up.
In the 12th century, the narrow channel
separating the two settlements was filled
in (now the main street through the Old
Town, called Stradun), and Ragusa and
Dubrovnik became one. The city was
surrounded by defensive walls during the
13th century, and these were reinforced
with towers and bastions in the late 15th
century.

From 1358 to 1808, the city thrived as a
powerful and remarkably sophisticated
independent republic, reaching its golden
age during the 16th century. In 1667
many of its splendid Gothic and Renaissance buildings were destroyed by an
earthquake. The defensive walls survived

the disaster, and the city was rebuilt in
Baroque style.

Dubrovnik lost its independence to
Napoléon in 1808, and in 1815 passed to
Austria-Hungary. During the 20th century,
as part of Yugoslavia, the city was a popular destination for European travelers,
and in 1979 it was listed as a UNESCO
World Heritage Site. During the Homeland War in 1991, it came under heavy
siege. Thanks to careful restoration, few
traces of damage remain. It's only when
you see Dubrovnik yourself that you can
understand what a treasure the world
nearly lost.

Naturally, as one of the world's most
beautiful cities, it has also become one
of the most popular with tourists. During
the past decade, the number of private
accommodation units exploded, and
an increasing number of cruise ships
brought massive crowds into the walled
city, negatively impacting not only the visitor experience, but the quality of life for
locals, many of whom simply moved out.
In 2019, Dubrovnik had its highest tourist
numbers ever and plans were in place
to address sustainability issues. But in
2020, COVID-19 brought everything to
a crashing halt. Cruise ships stopped
sailing, flights were grounded, and while
other regions survived on domestic
tourism, Dubrovnik, which is not well
connected to the rest of the country
by land, saw tourism drop by 80%. It
was devastating for the economy, but
also provided an opportunity for locals
to reclaim the city for a summer: kids
played soccer in the Old Town for the first
time in many years and seasonal workers
had the time to enjoy their beaches and
islands for themselves.

It's not the first time that Dubrovnik's
fortunes changed practically overnight. It
has rebuilt itself before and will undoubtedly rise again. But one thing is certain:
it will take a few years for numbers to
reach the heights of 2019, so if you were

ever planning to visit Dubrovnik, now is the time.

GETTING HERE AND AROUND

The city is not linked to the rest of the country by train, but there are regular bus routes to destinations all over mainland Croatia and beyond. The main bus station is located in Gruž, 20 minutes outside the Old Town, which is also where you'll find the main port. While the Old Town is car-free, the rest of the Dubrovnik is well-served by public transport; buses are regular and quick (but sometimes a little crowded) and tickets can be purchased from the driver or from red Tisak stands. If you're going to Lapad or Gruž, you can catch the bus from just outside the Pile Gate. If you're going south to Cavtat or the airport, catch the bus near the entrance to the Cable Car. If you must bring a car to Dubrovnik, there is a public parking garage on Zagrebačka Street leading to the Old Town, where you'll find the most reasonable prices.

◉ Sights

There are three main areas where you will spend most of your time in Dubrovnik. All of the major historical sites lie in Stari Grad (Old Town) within the city walls, a compact, car-free area. Lapad is located on a peninsula about 4 km (2½ miles) west of the Old Town; it is a family-friendly neighborhood with the city's most accessible beach. Gruž Harbor is about 3½ km (2 miles) from the Old Town, and it's where you'll find the main bus and ferry stations, as well as a bustling morning market popular with locals.

When planning your days, keep in mind that the Old Town can get very busy in the morning and early afternoon when the cruise ships are in town. If you're an early bird, take a walk around the city and the walls first thing in the morning before the crowds arrive, then spend the afternoon relaxing at the beach or taking

Dubrovnik Card

If you plan to do a bit of sightseeing, it's worthwhile to buy the Dubrovnik Card, which includes entry to nine cultural sights around town (including the city walls), plus free public transportation and a return bus ticket to Cavtat. You can buy a card for 1-Day (250 Kn), 3-Days (300 Kn) or 7-Days (350 Kn). Purchase the card online for an extra 10% discount ⊕ *www. dubrovnikcard.com* and pick it up at any of the Tourist Offices around the city.

a boat trip to Lokrum Island. Alternatively, you can spend the morning and afternoon at the beach, and head into the city once the cruise ship crowds return to their ships, usually around sunset. Enjoy dinner in Old Town or take the cable car to the top of Mt. Srđ for incredible sunset views.

Bell Tower

BUILDING | All walks down the Stradun lead to one point: the bell tower, the centerpiece of Luža Square. The bright white structure from 1444 is one of the main symbols of the city, reaching 31 meters high and featuring a moon dial and the original bell from 1506. Look a little closer to see Dubrovnik's two favorite mascots tolling the hours on either side of the bell; known as Maro and Baro, the current figures are made of bronze, while the original wooden men are now found in the Rector's Palace. ⊠ *Luža, Stari Grad.*

★ City Walls (*Gradske Zidine*)

LOCAL INTEREST | **FAMILY** | Dubrovnik's city walls define the Old Town and are one of the world's most stunning architectural achievements. A walk along the top is the ultimate Dubrovnik must-do for

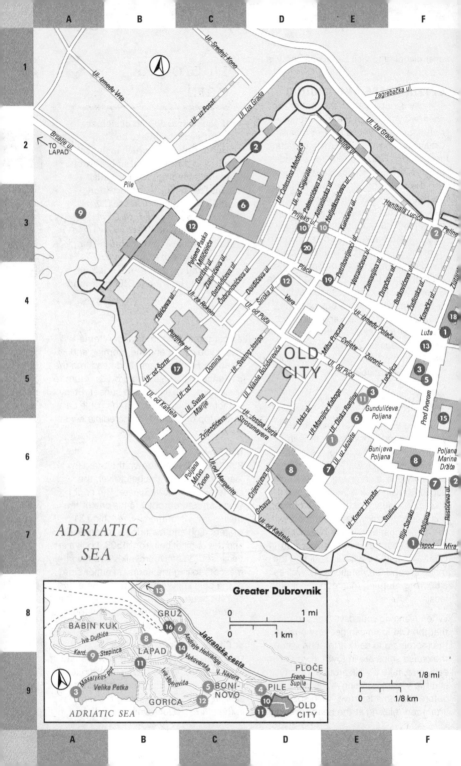

Dubrovnik

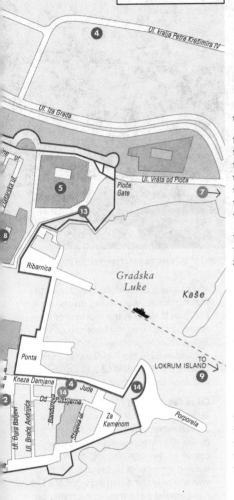

Ploče Gate

Gradska Luke

Kaše

TO LOKRUM ISLAND

Ribarnica

Ponta

Kneza Damjana

Jude

Od Pustijerne

Za Kamenom

Porporela

Ul. kralja Petra Krešimira IV

Ul. Iza Grada

Ul. Vrata od Ploča

Sights ▼

1 Bell Tower **F4**
2 City Walls **D2**
3 Crkva Svetog Vlaha **F5**
4 Dubrovnik Cable Car ... **H2**
5 Dominican Monastery............... **G4**
6 Franciscan Monastery................ **C3**
7 Jesuit Steps **D6**
8 Katedrala Velika Gospa **F6**
9 Lokrum Island **I6**
10 Love Stories Museum **D9**
11 Lovrijenac Fortress **D9**
12 Onofrio Fountain **C3**
13 Orlando's Column **F5**
14 Maritime Museum...... **H6**
15 Rector's Palace **F5**
16 Red History Museum... **B8**
17 Rupe Ethnographic Museum **C5**
18 Sponza Palace **F4**
19 Stradun **E4**
20 War Photo Limited...... **D3**

Restaurants ▼

1 Azur **F7**
2 Bota Šare Oyster & Sushi Bar **F6**
3 Café Royal **E5**
4 Gianni **G6**
5 Gradska Kavana **F5**
6 Kamenice................. **E5**
7 Konoba Amoret **F6**
8 Kopun **D6**
9 Nautika Restaurant..... **A3**
10 Nishta **D3**
11 Pantarul................. **B9**
12 Proto **D4**
13 Restaurant 360 .... **H4**
14 Urban and Veggie **C8**

Hotels ▼

1 Amoret Apartments **D6**
2 Apartments Paviša **F3**
3 Dubrovnik Palace....... **A9**
4 Hilton Imperial Dubrovnik................ **D9**
5 Hotel Bellevue **C9**
6 Hotel Berkeley **C8**
7 Hotel Excelsior............ **I4**
8 Hotel Kazbek **B8**
9 Hotel More **A9**
10 Prijeko Palace............ **E3**
11 Pucić Palace **E5**
12 Rixos Libertas **C9**
13 Sun Gardens **B8**
14 Van Bloemen Apartments.............. **G6**

KEY

1 *Exploring Sights*
1 *Restaurants*
1 *Hotels*

The Dubrovnik Cable Car gives you a bird's-eye view from Mt. Srđ over the iconic red rooftops of the city.

the magnificent views of the sea and Lokrum Island outside the walls and the terracotta rooftops within. Most of the original construction took place during the 13th century, though the walls were further reinforced with towers and bastions over the next 400 years. The walls completely encircle the Old Town as part of a fortification system that also includes four gates, including the **Pile** and **Ploče Gates** (the main entrances and exits to the Old Town), and four towers, including the freestanding Lovrijenac Fortress to the west and the Minčeta Tower toward the land. On average, the walls are 80 feet high and 2 km (1¼ miles) long, 10 feet thick on the seaward side, 20 feet thick on the inland side; the inland walls are thicker because when they were constructed, the largest threat came from the Turks who might attack from that direction (ironically they got the direction right, but not the source: it was Napoléon, attacking from the inland fortress atop Mt. Srd, who finally conquered the Republic). The entire circuit takes a couple of hours if you stop for photos

and maybe a drink along the way; note that it involves many stairs up and down, and is best done in the morning or late afternoon to avoid the heat and crowds. Tickets can be purchased at the main entrance inside the Pile Gate. ⊠ *Stari Grad* ☎ *020/638–800* 🌐 *200 Kn, includes entrance to Lovrijenac Fortress.*

Crkva Svetog Vlaha (*Church of St. Blaise*) **RELIGIOUS SITE** | This 18th-century Baroque church replaced an earlier one destroyed by fire. Of particular note is the silver statue on the high altar of St. Blaise holding a model of Dubrovnik, which was the only thing that survived the fire. It is paraded around town each year on February 3, the Day of St. Blaise. ⊠ *Luža 3, Stari Grad* 🌐 *Free.*

★ **Dubrovnik Cable Car**
VIEWPOINT | **FAMILY** | Reopened in July 2010 after being destroyed in the siege of Dubrovnik, the ultramodern cable car whisks you up Mt. Srd for the best view of the city and the islands. At the top, you can join an hour-long buggy tour of the area, go for a hike, or have a cocktail

at the smart Panorama Restaurant. The Imperial Fort, built between 1806 and 1812 by Napoléon during his short rule of the city, now hosts the Homeland War Museum, where you can learn about the siege. To reach the cable car from the Old Town, go up the stairs from the Stradun (toward the mountain) and exit via the Buža Gate; tickets can be purchased at the station.' ■ TIP➔ **Plan your visit for sunset, when the views are magnificent, and the line is shorter.** ✉ *Lower station, Petra Krešimira IV, Ploce* ☎ *020/414–355* ⊕ *www.dubrovnikcablecar.com* ✆ *90 Kn one-way, 160 Kn return* ⊗ *Closed Feb.*

Dominican Monastery (*Dominikanski samostan*)

RELIGIOUS SITE | With a splendid, late-15th-century floral Gothic cloister as its centerpiece, the monastery is best known for its museum, which houses a rich collection of religious paintings by the Dubrovnik School from the 15th and 16th centuries. Look out for works by Titian, Božidarević, Hamzić, and Dobričević, as well as gold and silver ecclesiastical artifacts crafted by local goldsmiths. ✉ *Sv. Dominika 4, Stari Grad* ☎ *020/321–423* ✆ *30 Kn.*

Franciscan Monastery (*Franjevačka samostan*)

RELIGIOUS SITE | This monastery's chief claim to fame is its pharmacy, which was founded in 1318 and is still in existence today, making it one of the oldest in Europe. There's also a delightful cloistered garden, framed by Romanesque arcades supported by double columns, each crowned with a set of grotesque figures. In the Treasury a painting shows what Dubrovnik looked like before the disastrous earthquake of 1667. ■ TIP➔ **Watch for locals (mostly young men) jumping up on a small gargoyle's head attached to the outer wall of the monastery along the Stradun. Legend has it that if you can stand on the head facing the wall and take off your shirt off without falling down, you will find love. Yes, it's harder than it**

looks. ✉ *Placa 2, Stari Grad* ☎ *020/321–410* ✆ *40 Kn.*

★ Jesuit Steps

PLAZA | Find this monumental Baroque staircase, Dubrovnik's very own version of the Spanish Steps, at the south side of Gundulićeva Poljana. At the top is the lovely Jesuit Church of St. Ignatius of Loyola, built 1699–1725. This staircase will be particularly familiar to *Game of Thrones* fans for a certain "shameful" scene. ✉ *Poljana Ruđera Boškovića 6, Stari Grad* ✆ *Free.*

Katedrala Velika Gospa (*Assumption of the Virgin Mary Cathedral*)

RELIGIOUS SITE | The present structure was completed in 1713 in Baroque style after the original was destroyed in the 1667 earthquake. Legend says that when Richard the Lionheart was shipwrecked on Lokrum Island, he vowed to show his thanks to God for saving his life by building a cathedral on the spot; locals convinced him to move his plans to Dubrovnik instead. The interior contains a number of notable paintings, including a large polyptych above the main altar depicting the *Assumption of Our Lady*, attributed to Titian. The treasury displays 138 gold and silver reliquaries, including the skull of St. Blaise in the form of a bejeweled Byzantine crown and also an arm and leg of the saint, likewise encased in decorated gold plating. ✉ *Držićeva Poljana, Stari Grad* ✆ *Cathedral free, Treasury 20 Kn.*

★ Lokrum Island

ISLAND | **FAMILY** | Some of Dubrovnik's most natural and peaceful beaches can be found on Lokrum, a short distance southeast of the Old Town. Lush and fertile, this tiny island is home to the ruins of an abandoned 11th-century monastery, set in exotic botanical gardens. Lokrum has swirled with legend and mystery ever since Richard the Lionheart was supposedly cast ashore there in 1191 upon returning from the Crusades. The story goes that when the Benedictine

Monks were expelled from the island to make room for aristocrats in the 19th century, they left behind a curse on any future owners of the land, including Habsburg Emperor Maximilian, who turned the monastery into his summer residence eight years before he was executed in Mexico. To this day, it is considered bad luck to stay overnight on the island, though many a pair of romantics have tried.

At the top of the island is a star-shaped fortress built by Napoléon's troops during French occupation and later used by the Austrian army. A network of footpaths leads down to the rocky shoreline, past the "dead sea" lake, where it's possible to swim. There are cliffs to jump from, coves to bathe in, and a small stretch of coast reserved for nudists. There's also a small *Game of Thrones* museum with the original Iron Throne (Lokrum was one of many filming locations around town). One of the most popular side trips from Dubrovnik, it's a wonderful place to spend a day spotting the peacocks (a Habsburg legacy), feeding the wild rabbits, or just enjoying the fresh air among the pines. To reach Lokrum, take a taxi-boat from the old port (100 Kn); they run every half hour during the summer and take approximately 15 minutes. ⊠ *Dubrovnik* ✛ *1 km (½ mile) from Old Port* ⊕ *www.lokrum.hr* ☾ *Closed Nov.–Apr.*

★ **Love Stories Museum**

MUSEUM | FAMILY | Similar to the Museum of Broken Relationships in Zagreb except with happy endings, this delightful museum outside the Pile Gate is a simple, life-affirming celebration of romance spread over four floors. Each room has a different theme, from Croatia-specific tales and local lore to celebrity love stories to an exhibit about the movies and series filmed in Dubrovnik (yes, *Game of Thrones* is represented). The top floors are perhaps the most moving with items sent in from real people and notes scribbled on heart-shaped Post-its tacked all over the "love wall". ⊠ *Od Tabakarije 2, Pile* ☎ *095/3555–145* ⊕ *www.lovestoriesmuseum.com* ☞ *50 Kn.*

★ **Lovrijenac Fortress**

BUILDING | The only freestanding part of Dubrovnik's fortification system, this impressive tower stands on a 37-meter-high sheer rock overlooking the sea outside the Pile Gate. Construction began sometime in the 11th century; the story goes that the Venetians planned to build a fortress atop the rock from which to conquer Dubrovnik, but the Republic learned of their plans in advance and beat them to it. The seaward walls are 12 meters thick while the walls facing Dubrovnik are only 60 centimeters thick, so that in the event the fortress was captured it could easily be destroyed from within the city walls. Above the entrance a latin enscription reads: "*Non bene pro toto libertas venditur auro*": "Freedom is not sold for all the gold in the world". The fortress makes a particularly memorable venue during the Dubrovnik Summer Festival when it is the setting for Hamlet, and it is also recognizable to *Game of Thrones* fans as the Red Keep (with slightly less CGI-added towers). ⊠ *Ul. od Tabakarije 29, Stari Grad* ☞ *200 Kn, includes City Walls.*

Onofrio Fountain

FOUNTAIN | Built between 1438 and 1440, the Onofrio Fountain is one of the most iconic sites in Dubrovnik and the first thing you see upon entering the Pile Gate. The 16-sided stone fountain is topped by a large dome and was designed by architect Onofrio Giordano della Cava. Along with the Small Onofrio Fountain at the other end of the Stradun, it was part of a complex water-supply system designed to bring water into the Old Town from a well 12 km (7½ miles) away. The water is still cold and drinkable, and the fountain is a nice place to rest and refuel. ⊠ *Pred Dvorom, Stari Grad.*

A walk along Dubrovnik's city walls is one of the best ways to get a sense of the city.

Orlando's Column

MEMORIAL | Dating back to 1418, Orlando's Column, located at the end of the Stradun and serving as a popular meeting point, is dedicated to legendary 8th-century knight Roland, who is said to have saved Dubrovnik from a Saracen attack near Lokrum. The white stone column has become a symbol of freedom for the city, and the white Libertas flag is traditionally flown from the top during important events, such as the opening ceremony of the Dubrovnik Summer Festival. ⊠ *Luža, Stari Grad.*

Maritime Museum (*Pomorski Muzej*)

MUSEUM | Above the aquarium, located on the first and second floors of St. John's Fortress, this museum's exhibits illustrate how rich and powerful Dubrovnik became one of the world's most important seafaring cities. On display are intricately detailed models of ships as well as engine-room equipment, sailors' uniforms, paintings, and maps. ⊠ *St. John's Fort, Damjana Jude 2, Stari Grad* ☎ *020/323–904* 💲 *100 Kn* 🕙 *Closed Mon.*

★ Rector's Palace (*Knežev Dvor*)

BUILDING | One of the most significant buildings along the Croatian Coast, this was the administrative center of the Dubrovnik Republic. It's where the Grand Council and Senate held their meetings and the chief citizen, the Rector, lived and did business during his one-month term. It also held a courtroom, prisons, meeting halls, and a gunpowder room, which exploded twice in the 15th century. The explosions, plus the earthquake of 1667, required the building to be reconstructed over the years in varying Baroque, Renaissance, and Gothic styles. The palace is now home to the Cultural Historical Museum, containing exhibits that give a picture of life in Dubrovnik from early days until the fall of the republic. ⊠ *Pred Dvorom 3, Stari Grad* ☎ *020/321–422* 💲 *100 Kn.*

★ Red History Museum

MUSEUM | Located in an industrial factory in Gruž, the Red History Museum tells the story of the rise and fall of communism in Croatia. Founded by a young

Game of Thrones fans love flocking to the Jesuit Steps to snap a photo where Queen Cersei did her walk of shame.

group of entrepreneurs in 2019, among them a designer, a historian, and a couple who worked on film sets, it is fun and fresh museum designed to be touched and explored. Taking a steadfastly neutral approach, the exhibits focus largely on everyday life under communism, from the clothing of the era to the kitchen sets to sex education, with historical information weaved effortlessly throughout the colorful displays. In a city that tends to rest on the laurels of its illustrious past, it's nice to see a new museum dedicated to something other than the Republic of Dubrovnik. ⊠ *Svetog Kriza 3, Gruž* ☎ *020/091–540* ⊕ *www.redhistorymuseum.com* 🖂 *50 Kn.*

Rupe Ethnographic Museum

MUSEUM | This charming museum is worth the visit for both the building itself (built in 1590, it was used as a grain storage during the time of the Republic) as well as the collection of 6,000 heritage pieces from Dalmatia, other parts of Croatia, and neighboring countries, including tools, folk costumes, lace, and other

handiwork. Rupe means "holes," which refer to the underground grain storage pits carved out of tufa below the building. ⊠ *Od rupa 3, Stari Grad* ☎ *020/323–056* 🖂 *130 Kn* ⊘ *Closed Tues.*

Sponza Palace

HISTORIC SITE | Originally the location where all trade goods coming into Dubrovnik went to be taxed, this 16th-century Gothic Renaissance palace served as the mint, an arsenal, and eventually a place for the Republic's most educated citizens, called the "Academy of the Learned," to discuss cultural matters. It now contains the city's archives, some of the most important documents in Dubrovnik's history. There's not much to see inside except the occasional art exhibition, but the shady, arcaded interior is a lovely spot to escape the heat and crowds. Turn left as you enter to find the "Memorial Room for the Defenders of Dubrovnik," a heart-wrenching little gallery with photographs of those who died defending the city, along with remnants of the flag that once flew atop Mount

Game of Thrones

Perhaps no film setting is as evocative as Dubrovnik, or as *Game of Thrones* fans know it better, King's Landing. For seven of its eight seasons, the popular HBO show was filmed in the walled city, on Lokrum Island (where you'll find a small museum and the "original" Iron Throne), and in Trsteno. Many locals have great stories about their experiences with the show, including tales of cast members winding up on their hostel's couch after a big night out or the lengths to which the production went to protect the secrecy of the final season. Some CGI was used in the show, but there are many sites around town that will be immediately recognizable to fans, including Lovrijenac Fort, the "shame steps", and the abandoned Hotel Belvedere which was the setting for the battle between Oberyn and The Mountain. There are many *Game of Thrones* tours to choose from, most of which follow a similar structure: a walking tour of the main filming spots where the guide holds up a still shot of the scene so you can compare the set to reality. More broadly appealing are tours that combine details of Dubrovnik history with the stories and legends of King's Landing. A great option is **Dubrovnik Day Tours** (⊕ *www.tourthegameofthrones.com*), which offers a fun tour experience with real swords and props.

Srd. ⊠ *Placa bb, Stari Grad* ☎ *020/321–032* 🗺 *25 Kn, Memorial Room free.*

★ **Stradun** (*Placa*)

NEIGHBORHOOD | The Placa, commonly known as the Stradun, is the main street in Dubrovnik's Old Town, stretching 300 meters from the Pile Gate to Luža Square and the Bell Tower. It is paved with limestone and polished by regular use; in the middle of summer, when the street is being walked upon by thousands of people, it shines like glass and is particularly impressive at night, when it reflects the light from the street lamps. It was once the shallow sea channel separating the island of Laus from the mainland. Although it was filled in during the 12th century, it continued to divide the city socially for several centuries, with the nobility living in the area south of Placa and the commoners living on the hillside to the north. The Stradun is the best people-watching promenade in town, but beware that prices at the bars and restaurants lining it reflect its popularity. ⊠ *Stari Grad.*

War Photo Limited

MUSEUM | Shocking and impressive, this modern gallery run by New Zealand photo journalist Wade Goddard, who drove from London to Croatia in 1992 to document the war and never left, devotes two floors to war photojournalism. The permanent exhibition showcases photos and video from former Yugoslavia, while recent exhibitions have been dedicated to conflicts in Iraq, Myanmar, and Vietnam. It's a sobering, illuminating, and extremely worthwhile gallery. ⊠ *Antuninska 6, Stari Grad* ☎ *020/322–166* ⊕ *www.warphotoltd.com* 🗺 *50 Kn* ⊗ *Closed Nov.–Mar.*

🍴 Restaurants

As elsewhere along the coast, seafood dominates Dubrovnik's menus, but here it is being turned into sophisticated sushi, sashimi, and stir-fry. Dubrovnik dining is a mix of longstanding institutions, local favorites serving traditional cuisine, sophisticated modern establishments, and even one Michelin-starred eatery.

Dubrovnik Under Siege

From November 1991 to May 1992, Dubrovnik was intermittently shelled by the Yugoslav army and Serb and Montenegrin irregulars, who were stationed on the rugged hills behind the city. Electricity and water supplies were cut off, and the local population took refuge in basements, surviving on a slowly diminishing quantity of foodstuffs, fuel, and medical supplies. The city's massive medieval fortifications stood up well to the assault, though none of Dubrovnik's main monuments was targeted—apparently the Yugoslav army wanted to capture the city intact. Extensive media coverage whipped up a storm of international criticism over the wanton bombing of this historic city, which effectively turned world opinion against Belgrade and in favor of granting Croatia diplomatic recognition. Once hostilities ceased, the cleanup and rebuilding began. During the second half of the 1990s, money poured in from all over the world for the restoration and today, thanks to the work of highly skilled craftspeople, barely any traces of war damage remain. But there is still a subtle reminder of the damage wrought upon 68% of the buildings in the Old Town. Look closer at the clay roof tiles when you're walking the city walls; the brighter orange tiles are new, the faded tiles are the originals.

Yes, restaurants in Dubrovnik are more expensive than elsewhere in Croatia, and the Old Town is packed with touristy restaurants and waiters trolling for customers (particularly the narrow street Prijeko, which runs parallel to the Stradun). But go to the right places, where the quality matches the prices, and you won't mind paying a little extra.

★ Azur

$$$ | ASIAN FUSION | Spread over two shady terraces high up in the Old Town, just beneath the City Walls near Buža Bar, Azur is a great place to escape the crowds with a leisurely lunch of internationally inspired dishes that burst with flavor. The menu changes regularly but favorites include pork belly tacos and Szechuan chili garlic prawns. **Known for:** unique meals and tapas-style dishes to share; well-priced, high-quality food; quiet location under the City Walls. *$ Average main: 130 Kn* ⊠ *Pobijana 10, Stari Grad* 🕾 *020/324–806* ⊕ *www.azurvision. com.*

Bota Šare Oyster & Sushi Bar

$$ | JAPANESE | Tucked away on a small terrace near the cathedral, Bota Šare takes the best local produce and turns it into beautifully presented sushi, sashimi, carpaccio, and tartare. This is also a great place to try oysters from the nearby town of Ston; it's safe to say the Šare family, who also runs one of the best restaurants in Mali Ston, does them best. **Known for:** Dalmatian ingredients; Asian flair; excellent local oysters. *$ Average main: 120 Kn* ⊠ *Od Pustijerne bb, Stari Grad* 🕾 *020/324–034* ⊕ *www.bota-sare. hr.*

Café Royal

$$ | MEDITERRANEAN | One of the pleasures of staying at Pucić Palace is having breakfast at their adjoining restaurant, Café Royal that's thankfully open to the public as well. A classy and cool café with an art-splashed interior and large terrace on Gundulić Square, it offers the best breakfast in Dubrovnik, with scrumptious options like Caprese salad with burrata and eggs benedict with

Old Town's main street, the Stradun, is lined with historic buildings like the Rector's Palace.

truffle, or lighter options like coffee and cake. **Known for:** best breakfast in Dubrovnik; great location beside the morning market on Gundulić Square; classy interiors. [$] *Average main: 80 Kn* ✉ *Gundulićeva poljana 8, Stari Grad* ☎ *020/326–222* 🌐 *www.thepucicpalace.com.*

★ Gianni

$ | CAFÉ | When the former pastry chef at Restaurant 360 opens his own artisanal ice cream and cake shop in Dubrovnik, you know it's going to be good. Gianni serves up hands-down the best ice cream in the city, incorporating natural ingredients and some unusual flavors such as curry and chili, alongside traditional favorites like pistachio and chocolate. **Known for:** best ice cream in Dubrovnik; quiet location in the Old Town; excellent coffee. [$] *Average main: 30 Kn* ✉ *Kneza Damjana Jude, Stari Grad* ☎ *095/392–6323* 🌐 *www.gianni-dubrovnik.com.*

Gradska Kavana

$ | CAFÉ | Occuping the ornate Arsenal building right on Luža Square, Gradska Kavana remains Dubrovnik's favorite meeting place for morning coffee and cake or an evening aperitif. The grand café has an ample summer terrace and is a perfect spot for people-watching and admiring the sites that surround it, including Rector's Palace, Sponza Palace, and the cathedral. **Known for:** place to see-and-be seen; one of Dubrovnik's best-known addresses; great aperitif cocktails. [$] *Average main: 30 Kn* ✉ *Pred Dvorom 1, Stari Grad* 🌐 *www.nautikarestaurants.com.*

Kamenice

$$ | SEAFOOD | Overlooking the morning market in the Old Town, Kamenice remains popular for the fresh oysters for which it is named, plus generous platters of *girice* (small fried fish) and *pržene ligne* (fried squid). It's cheap and cheerful, offers unbeatable value for the location, and is much-loved by locals and tourists alike. **Known for:** cheap prices;

Old Town is filled with charming restaurants where you can dine outside right on the cobblestones.

large portions; high turnover means dishes are fresh and good. [$] *Average main: 80 Kn* ✉ *Gundulićeva poljana 8, Stari Grad* ☎ *020/323–682.*

Konoba Amoret

$$ | **SEAFOOD** | A great choice for traditional food in the Old Town, this restaurant right beside the cathedral serves quality meals with an unbeatable ambience. It's open late, great for people-watching under the stars, and live musicians often set up on the cathedral steps. **Known for:** traditional Dalmatian food; central Old Town location; romantic atmosphere. [$] *Average main: 110 Kn* ✉ *Od Pustijerne, Stari Grad* ☎ *020/323–739* 🌐 *www.amoret-dubrovnik.com* 🕓 *Closed Nov.–Apr.*

Kopun

$$ | **MEDITERRANEAN** | Kopun refers to *capon*, the rooster that was a delicacy during the time of the Republic. It's just one of the old-fashioned dishes you can find at this charming local favorite that, with its modern aesthetic, manages to make the most traditional of Dubrovnik recipes seem avant-garde. **Known for:** traditional capon dishes; great place to try Dubrovnik specialties like šporki makaruli; reservations recommended for dinner. [$] *Average main: 120 Kn* ✉ *Poljana Ruđera Boškovića 7, Stari Grad* ☎ *020/323–969* 🌐 *www.restaurantkopun.com.*

Nautika Restaurant

$$$$ | **SEAFOOD** | With two terraces overlooking the Lovrijenac Fort and a solid reputation as Dubrovnik's smartest fine dining restaurant, Nautika is a reliable choice for a formal meal. It is known for its local shellfish, lobster, and fresh fish, but also serves meat and vegetarian dishes, and has an excellent wine list. **Known for:** longstanding Dubrovnik institution; five-course tasting menu and à la carte options available; very expensive. [$] *Average main: 350 Kn* ✉ *Brsalje 3, Pile* ☎ *020/442–526* 🌐 *www.nautikarestaurants.com* 🕓 *Closed Oct.–Mar.*

St. Blaise

If you've noticed the statue of a bearded man holding a model of Dubrovnik in various spots around the city, that's St. Blaise, the patron saint of Dubrovnik. The former Bishop of Sebaste in Turkey, Blaise lost his life in AD 316 during a Roman-led anti-Christian campaign. He was made Dubrovnik's protector in 972, having appeared to the parish priest in a dream warning of an imminent Venetian attack and thus saving the city. He was featured on the Republic's coins and flags, and his figure can still be seen along the walls, entrances, and towers of the Old City. The grand Baroque church on Luža Square is named in his honor, and every Febuary 3rd, Dubrovnik celebrates St. Blaise's Day.

Nishta

$$ | VEGETARIAN | Specializing in vegan fare, this playful eatery on Prijeko Street has just a dozen tables and is deservedly popular; for years it was the only veggie option in town. Their menu changes regularly, but you can expect soups, salads, and international dishes like falafel, curry, and moussaka. **Known for:** some of the best—and only—vegan food in Dubrovnik; the best restaurant on busy Prijeko street; playful vibe. $ *Average main: 80 Kn* ⊠ *Prijeko bb, Stari Grad* ☎ *020/322–088* ⊕ *www.nishtarestaurant. com* ☽ *Closed Sun.*

★ Pantarul

$$$ | MEDITERRANEAN | A local favorite, a little off the beaten track but worth the trek, Pantarul is a fun bistro with a uniquely Dubrovnik feel—even the name means "fork" in local dialect. A love of traditional dishes comes through here; the menu changes weekly but there are a few mainstays like sea bream, foie gras, and super tender ox cheek. **Known for:** Dubrovnik comfort food; local favorite; dinner reservations required. $ *Average main: 130 Kn* ⊠ *Kralja Tomisla- va 1, Lapad* ☎ *020/333–486* ⊕ *www. pantarul.com.*

★ Proto

$$$$ | SEAFOOD | Located right in the heart of the Old Town, longstanding Dubrovnik institution Proto dates back to 1886 and most locals will respectfully acknowl- edge that it's still one of the best in town. It has hosted everyone from King Edward VIII and Wallis Simpson to modern-day celebs and sports figures who come to try its menu of reliably prepared tradition- al Dalmatian dishes using simple local ingredients and premium local seafood such as lobster and shrimp. **Known for:** longstanding Dubrovnik institution; five- course tasting menu option; reservations required. $ *Average main: 266 Kn* ⊠ *Širo- ka 1, Stari Grad* ☎ *020/323–234* ⊕ *www. esculaprestaurants.com.*

★ Restaurant 360

$$$$ | MEDITERRANEAN | Michelin-starred Restaurant 360 offers an impeccable fine dining experience, from the unbeatably romantic view overlooking the old port to the friendly, unpretentious service. The extraordinary food will surprise and delight you with its sophistication and simplicity in equal measures, and the five-course tasting menu is worth the splurge; settle in for a few hours and enjoy the ride. **Known for:** beautiful pan- oramic outdoor terrace; need to reserve at least 1 month in advance; fine-dining tasting menu and 2- or 3-course à la carte options. $ *Average main: 600 Kn* ⊠ *Sv. Dominka bb, Stari Grad* ☎ *020/322–222* ⊕ *www.360dubrovnik.com* ☽ *Closed Mon. and Oct.–Apr.; no lunch.*

Urban and Veggie

$$ | **VEGETARIAN** | This colorful little bistro has a young, passionate team and a creative female chef; together they have created a plant-based menu using local, seasonal produce from farms in Southern Dalmatia, Konavle, and the open market just around the corner. The menu changes seasonally but highlights include "Mac 'n Tease" (pasta with truffle "cheese" sauce) and pizza made with sweet potato crust. **Known for:** one of the only vegan options in Dubrovnik; spacious back terrace; local, seasonal ingredients. [$] *Average main: 70 Kn* ✉ *Obala Stjepana Radića 13, Gruž* ☎ *099/266–7590* 🌐 *www.urbanveggie.restaurant* 🕓 *Closed Oct.–May.*

🛏 Hotels

There are a plethora of excellent hotel choices all around Dubrovnik. The Old Town offers the chance to sleep in historical quarters, with charming restored palaces and apartments right in the center of the action. The more exclusive establishments line the coastal road east of the center, offering five-star luxury, private beaches, and stunning views of the Old Town. You'll find more modern (and slightly cheaper) hotels in Lapad, which has a summer resort vibe with live music by night, a busy bar-lined promenade, and a recently renovated beach. The port area of Gruž makes a practical and affordable base. There are also private rooms and apartments scattered around the city, which vary in quality and price. If you visit in the off-season, you can find bargain deals at the best addresses in town, sometimes down to a quarter of the price of the high season—yet another reason to consider a winter visit to Dubrovnik.

Amoret Apartments

$$ | **RENTAL** | In the heart of the Old Town, these tastefully furnished studios, with heavy antiques and traditional Dubrovnik decor, are an excellent value. **Pros:** Old Town location; homey, atmospheric rooms with antique furniture; inexpensive by Dubrovnik standards. **Cons:** rooms can be noisy at night; some amenities need updating; no owners or staff on-site. [$] *Rooms from: 985 Kn* ✉ *Dinka Ranjine 5, Stari Grad* ☎ *020/638-194* 🌐 *www.dubrovnik-amoret.com* 🛏 *14 apartments* 🍴 *No meals.*

Apartments Paviša

$$ | **RENTAL** | These five well-established apartments, equipped with kitchenettes, televisions, and simple furniture, are some of the best budget accommodations you'll find in Dubrovnik. **Pros:** friendly service from owner Pero; excellent value for money; perfect Old Town location. **Cons:** up several flights of steps from the Stradun; room decor is dated; basic amenities. [$] *Rooms from: 910 Kn* ✉ *Žudioska 19, Stari Grad* ☎ *098/427–399* 🌐 *www.apartmentspavisa.com* 💳 *No credit cards* 🛏 *5 apartments* 🍴 *No meals.*

Dubrovnik Palace

$$$$ | **HOTEL** | Located at a secluded tip of the Lapad peninsula, this vast five-star hotel is undeniably chic, with indoor and outdoor pools plus a swim-up bar, shady walking and jogging trails on the grounds, and an excellent restaurant (the truffle risotto is a must-try). **Pros:** great buffet breakfast; seafront location with private beach; public bus stops right outside the entrance. **Cons:** distant from the other parts of the city; vast with somewhat impersonal service; decor feels more like a business than a luxury hotel. [$] *Rooms from: 3000 Kn* ✉ *Masarykov put 20, Lapad* ☎ *020/300–300* 🌐 *www.adriaticluxuryhotels.com* 🕓 *Closed Dec.–Mar.* 🛏 *308 rooms* 🍴 *Free breakfast.*

★ Hilton Imperial Dubrovnik

$$$$ | **HOTEL** | The Grand Hotel Imperial was Dubrovnik's first modern hotel when it opened in 1897, and through the years it has played a part in the city's most memorable events, attracting high-class visitors from Viennese Counts to King

Edward VII and Wallis Simpson, who danced in the garden in 1936. **Pros:** perfect location close to Pile Gate; tranquil, spacious, and stylish rooms and common areas; great facilities. **Cons:** room decor is slightly generic; chain hotels are not for everyone; small pool. [$] *Rooms from: 2680 Kn* ✉ *Marijana Blazica 2, Pile* ☎ *020/320–320* 🌐 *www.hilton.com* 🛏 *149 rooms* 🍴 *Free breakfast.*

★ Hotel Bellevue

$$$$ | HOTEL | Nestled on a fairy-tale stretch of the Adriatic Sea, Hotel Bellevue is a luxury property with both style and soul, thanks to the dedicated staff devoted to customer service. **Pros:** cliff-top location overlooking the sea; chic interiors; excellent dining. **Cons:** expensive; not in Old Town; not all rooms have balconies. [$] *Rooms from: 3000 Kn* ✉ *Pera Čingrije 7* ☎ *020/330–000* 🌐 *www.adriaticluxuryhotels.com* 🛏 *94 rooms* 🍴 *Free breakfast.*

★ Hotel Berkeley

$$ | HOTEL | Located on a quiet street just a five-minute walk from Gruž harbor, this welcoming hotel run by a Croatian-Australian family is the best value property in town and will greatly exceed the discerning traveler's expectations. **Pros:** excellent cooked-to-order breakfast; outdoor pool and jacuzzi; well-priced spa on-site. **Cons:** distance from Old Town; slightly isolated location; restaurant is not open for dinner. [$] *Rooms from: 1200 Kn* ✉ *Andrije Hebranga 116A, Gruž* ☎ *020/494–160* 🌐 *www.berkeleyhotel.hr* ⏲ *Closed Jan. and Feb.* 🛏 *24 rooms* 🍴 *Free breakfast.*

★ Hotel Excelsior

$$$$ | HOTEL | On the coastal road east of the center, this prestigious hotel was the first five-star property in Dubrovnik, dating back to 1913—everyone from Queen Elizabeth II to Francis Ford Coppola has come to stay. **Pros:** seafront location with incredible views of the Old Town; luxurious indoor pool, sauna, and spa; most rooms have balconies or terraces. **Cons:** somewhat impersonal service; distance from the Old Town; slightly stuffy atmosphere. [$] *Rooms from: 3550 Kn* ✉ *Put Frane Supila 12, Ploce* ☎ *020/300–300* 🌐 *www.adriaticluxuryhotels.com* 🛏 *158 rooms* 🍴 *Free breakfast.*

★ Hotel Kazbek

$$$$ | HOTEL | The boutique, top-notch Hotel Kazbek offers a more intimate experience than the larger five-star hotels in Dubrovnik, with receptionists who know your name, a platter of sweets waiting in your room, and a spectacular courtyard pool that you'll never want to leave. **Pros:** personalized service; made-to-order gourmet breakfast; beautiful, peaceful pool. **Cons:** not many other services nearby; quite expensive; bus or taxi is necessary to reach Old Town. [$] *Rooms from: 2350 Kn* ✉ *Lapadska Obala 25, Lapad* ☎ *020/362–999* 🌐 *www.kazbekdubrovnik.com* ⏲ *Closed Nov.–Apr.* 🛏 *13 rooms* 🍴 *Free breakfast.*

Hotel More

$$$ | HOTEL | Rising from a seaside walkway up a forested cliff on Lapad Peninsula just a few minutes walk from the pebble beach, this five-star property boasts one of the most peaceful locations in Dubrovnik, the best spots for swimming, and the city's most unique venue for a cocktail. **Pros:** accessible swimming spots; two swimming pools; most affordable of the five-star hotels in Dubrovnik. **Cons:** distance from town; hotel layout is large and confusing; room decor is slightly dated. [$] *Rooms from: 1590 Kn* ✉ *Kardinala Stepinca 33, Lapad* ☎ *020/494–200* 🌐 *hotel-more.hr* 🛏 *85 rooms* 🍴 *Free breakfast.*

Prijeko Palace

$$$ | HOTEL | This quirky design property in the center of the Old Town merges an impeccably restored 15th-century palace with a fantastical art gallery, where each room is a unique creation with explosions of photography, Murano chandeliers, collages, lavish prints, and everything draped in silk. **Pros:** central location; excellent dining on-site, including one of the only rooftop terraces within the Old Town; unique experience for art and history lovers. **Cons:** design is not for everyone; some rooms can be noisy at night; no pool or spa facilities. $ *Rooms from: 1700 Kn* ✉ *Prijeko 22, Stari Grad* ☎ *020/321–145* ⊕ *www.prijekopalace. com* ⟿ *9 rooms* ⏹ *Free breakfast.*

★ Pucić Palace

$$$$ | HOTEL | Occupying a beautifully-re-stored Renaissance-style palace, the boutique Pucić Palace is ideally situated on Gundulić Square and offers the sort of aristocratic delights that its location suggests. **Pros:** prime location in Old Town; warm, personal service; unique chance to stay in a historic palace. **Cons:** very expensive; no coffee-making facil-ities in room; no pool or spa. $ *Rooms from: 3000 Kn* ✉ *Ul od Puča 1, Stari Grad* ☎ *020/326–222* ⊕ *www.thepucicpalace. com* ⟿ *19 rooms* ⏹ *Free breakfast.*

Rixos Libertas

$$$ | RESORT | The resort that you can see from pretty much any vantage point in Dubrovnik, the Rixos Libertas makes great use of its large size with three res-taurants, four bars, one indoor pool, and one huge outdoor pool beside the private beach and sprawling sundeck, plus plen-ty of inviting indoor and outdoor seating areas. **Pros:** great for couples with lots of activities and romantic corners; one of the best spas in Dubrovnik; excellent choice for a winter stay with indoor facilities and great discounts. **Cons:** huge layout means a lot of walking; lacks a distinctly Croatian vibe; no facilities or activities for young kids. $ *Rooms from: 1900 Kn* ✉ *Liechtensteinov put 3, Lapad* ☎ *020/200–000* ⊕ *www.rixos.com* ⟿ *310 rooms* ⏹ *Free breakfast.*

Sun Gardens

$$$ | RESORT | FAMILY | Eleven kilometers (7 miles) up the coast from Dubrovnik in the village of Orašac, you'll find one of the city's classiest hotels, set on 54 acres of sprawling gardens and walking trails beside the sea. **Pros:** beautifully

furnished rooms; wide range of facilities for the whole family; one of Dubrovnik's best spas. **Cons:** breakfast buffet is large but disappointing; some distance from Dubrovnik; isolated location. $ *Rooms from: 1700 Kn* ✉ *Na Moru 1* ☎ *020/361–500* ⊕ *www.dubrovniksungardens. com* ☾ *Closed Oct.–May* ⟿ *201 rooms* ⏹ *Free breakfast.*

Van Bloemen Apartments

$ | RENTAL | Formerly known as Karmen Apartments, these eclectic apartments are an excellent budget choice in the Old Town, with high ceilings, well-stocked kitchenettes, colorful furniture, and books and relics collected from all around the world. **Pros:** central location in Old Town; best value for money; friendly owners. **Cons:** space can feel cluttered; can be noisy at night; no breakfast. $ *Rooms from: 720 Kn* ✉ *Bandureva 1, Stari Grad* ☎ *020/323–433* ⊕ *www. vanbloemen.com* ⟿ *4 apartments* ⏹ *No meals.*

☷ Nightlife

Throughout the summer, there's no better place to be than Dubrovnik's Old Town at night. From wine bars to jazz cafés, English pubs to beach clubs, there is something for every nocturnal taste. Terraces spill onto the streets, musicians set up in squares, and you can grab a seat anywhere to have a drink or an ice cream and enjoy the show.

BARS
★ Buža

BARS/PUBS | Walk through an 800-year-old wall to find a secret swimming spot across the sea from a cursed island. Sounds like a fairy tale, but in Dubrovnik such places actually exist, and there are two of them. One of the *Buža* (hole-in-the-wall) bars is marked by a wooden sign pointing toward "cold drinks." The other has no signage at all; you just walk through a doorway in the city walls. With tables arranged on a series of terraces

The Republic of Dubrovnik

As an independent republic from 1358 to 1808, Dubrovnik kept its freedom not through military power, but thanks to diplomatic cunning. Would-be aggressors, including Hungary and the Ottoman Turks, were paid an annual fee in return for peaceful relations, and Dubrovnik avoided involvement in international conflicts between Christians and Muslims, preferring to remain neutral.

The republic's economy was based on shipping and trading goods between Europe and the Middle East, and by the 16th century the republic had consulates in some 50 foreign ports, along with a merchant fleet of 200 ships on the Mediterranean. By this time its territory had also extended to include 120 km (75 miles) of mainland coast (from Neum to the Bay of Kotor) plus the islands of Lastovo and Mljet.

The chief citizen was the Rector, who had to be over 50; he was elected for only a month at a time to share management of the republic's business with the Great Council (composed of members of the local nobility) and the Senate (a consultative body made up of 45 "wise men," all over the age of 40). Most of the military and naval commands were held by members of the nobility, while lower-ranking soldiers were mercenaries from the regions that are now Germany and the Czech Republic. The increasingly prosperous middle class carried on trade. The Archbishop of Dubrovnik had to be a foreigner (usually an Italian), a law intended to keep politics and religion apart.

Outstandingly sophisticated for its time, Dubrovnik was very socially conscious: the first pharmacy opened in 1317; the first nursing home was founded in 1347; slave trading was abolished in 1418; and the first orphan-age opened in 1432.

built into the rocks and jazzy soundtracks to go along with stunning vistas, both bars make a great place to stop for a drink or a swim; you can jump right off the rocks in front of the bar into the sea. ⊠ *Stari Grad* ⊹ *The only bars on the seaside of the city walls—look for "cold drinks" sign.*

★ Cave Bar More

CAFES—NIGHTLIFE | When the Hotel More was being built, a piece of machinery fell through the ground; it was only then that an 8,000-year-old cave was discovered underneath. It has been carefully convert-ed into a three-story bar, with twinkling lights and stalactites, making it a great place for a light bite during the day and an unforgettable setting for a cocktail by night. Outside, their seaside terrace is a fabulous place to lounge with a coffee or cocktail and have a swim. ⊠ *Kardina-la Stepinca 33, Lapad* ☎ *020/494–200* ⊕ *cavebar-more.com.*

Dubrovnik Beer Company

BREWPUBS/BEER GARDENS | Dubrovnik's only craft brewery (and one of only a handful in Croatia), Dubrovnik Beer Company produces four main beers: an IPA, a milk stout, a lager, and a pale ale. Located in a former salt storage building in Gruž, it's a popular hangout for both locals and tourists, with regular concerts, pub quizzes, and other events taking place. Hour-long brewery tours, which include samples and snacks, are offered daily. ⊠ *Obala Pape Ivana Pavla II 15, Gruž* ☎ *095/356–9620* ⊕ *www.dubrovack-apivovara.hr.*

★ D'Vino Wine Bar

WINE BARS—NIGHTLIFE | A cozy, candle-lit wine bar that spills onto the street outside in summer, D'Vino is a great place to spend an evening, chatting and people-watching with the fun, knowledgeable staff. They have an impressive selection of 60 wines by the glass and bottle, including many Croatian options, plus tasting menus and wine flights accompanied by gourmet cheese and antipasto platters. ⊠ *Palmotićeva 4a, Stari Grad* ☎ *020/321–130* ⊕ *www.dvino. net.*

DANCE CLUBS

★ Culture Club Revelin

DANCE CLUBS | Surely one of the most unique places in the world to party, Culture Club Revelin is the best nightclub in Dubrovnik, with big-name DJs and theme nights throughout the summer. Find it located in the 500-year-old Revelin Fort, part of the Old Town's fortification system, near the Ploče Gate. ⊠ *Svetog Dominika 3, Ploce* ✛ *100 meters from Ploče Gate* ☎ *020/436–010* ⊕ *www. clubrevelin.com.*

Banje Beach Club

DANCE CLUBS | Located on the only sandy beach near the Old Town, Banje Beach is a chilled-out lounge bar and restaurant by day where you can relax on plush couches and beach beds, and a sleek dance club by night. You can't beat watching the sunset over the city from the terrace, and dancing on the sand with a view of the City Walls is a great way to spend an evening in Dubrovnik. You'll find it a five-minute walk east of the Ploče Gate. ⊠ *Frana Supila 10b, Banje Beach* ☎ *099/314–6485* ⊕ *www.banjebeach. com.*

🎭 Performing Arts

FESTIVALS

★ Dubrovnik Summer Festival

ARTS FESTIVALS | The city's cultural highlight is the annual Dubrovnik Summer Festival, which runs from mid-July to late August and attracts thousands of artists from around the world. A variety of open-air classical concerts, ballet, and theatrical performances are held at various venues within the walls, and the city becomes a riot of folklore, traditional dresses, midnight performances, and music. Tickets, ranging from 30 Kn to 500 Kn, can be purchased online or at the festival box office. ⊠ *Od Sigurate 1, Stari Grad* ☎ *020/326–100* ⊕ *www. dubrovnik-festival.hr.*

FILM

★ Kino Slavica

FILM | Watch a movie outdoors with either the city walls or the Adriatic Sea as your backdrop at Dubrovnik's two open-air cinemas, which show predominantly English-language films in their original version nightly throughout the summer. Kino Slavica is located in a walled garden on the main road between the Old Town and Lapad, while Kino Jadran is right in the Old Town, completely hidden from sight. ■ **TIP→ They sell drinks on-site but you are welcome to bring your own.** ⊠ *Branitelja Dubrovnika 42, Pile* ☎ *020/638–640* ⊕ *www.kinematografi. org* 💰 *25 Kn.*

🛍 Shopping

It's getting harder to find quality souvenirs in Dubrovnik as more and more shops cater to the cruise ship crowds looking for candy and *Game of Thrones* paraphernalia. Here are a few places where you can pick up souvenirs and authentic products, including olive oil, Dalmatian wine, and rakija.

Bonbonnière Kraš

FOOD/CANDY | If you're looking for a sweet treat with history, keep an eye out for the brand Kraš. Named after an anti-fascist war hero from World War II, Kraš produced the first chocolate bars in Southeast Europe in 1911 and has been making Croatia's favorite chocolate goodies ever since. From the beloved Bajadera (chocolate-covered almond and hazelnut nougat) and Domaćica (choc-olate-covered tea biscuits) to simple Dorina chocolate bars and Bananko (chocolate-covered confectionery banan-as), you'll find Kraš products everywhere: on your pillow in a hotel, on the shelves at the grocery store, and in the flagship Bonbonnière shop in cities around the country, including this one at the end of the Stradun in Luža Square. ✉ *Luža 1, Stari Grad* ⊕ *www.kras.hr.*

Dubrovačka Kuća
LOCAL SPECIALTIES | This tastefully deco-rated shop near the Ploče Gate stocks a fine selection of regional Croatian wines and sweets, rakija, olive oil, and handmade jewelry, plus works of art by contemporary local artists on the upper two levels. ✉ *Svetog Dominika bb, Stari Grad* ☎ *020/322–092.*

Dubrovnik Treasures
JEWELRY/ACCESSORIES | You'll find this lovely oasis of a shop just steps from the bustling Pile Gate (and a second location farther down the Stradun). The jewlery is handmade by local artists who use quality sterling silver, coral, and semipre-cious stones to turn traditional designs into beautiful modern pieces. ✉ *Celestina Medovića 2, Stari Grad* ☎ *020/321–098* ⊕ *www.dubrovniktreasures.com.*

★ Life According to Kawa
GIFTS/SOUVENIRS | Everything in this well-curated shop just outside the Ploče Gate is local, artisanal, hipster, and fun, from jewelry and clothing to homewares and craft beer and wine. Pop in for some shopping or just hang out on the couch and chat with the staff who are happy to share local tips and help plan your stay. ✉ *Hvarska 2, Ploce* ☎ *020/696–958.*

★ Open Markets
OUTDOOR/FLEA/GREEN MARKETS | At two open markets in Dubrovnik, you can get a wonderful glimpse into local life, as well as pick up a few goodies. The market in

Gundulićeva Poljana (Gundulić Square), beside Pucić Palace, is a great place to try local delicacies from Dubrovnik and Konavle such as dried figs, liqueurs, and delicious candied fruit peels. Plan your visit for noon to see the local man who feeds the pigeons—it's quite the specta-cle to see hundreds of pigeons flock to the square in anticipation. Across town at the market in Gruž, you'll find even more fresh produce and you're likely to be the only tourist around; every morning from around 6 am, locals come to pick up fruits, vegetables, fish, and flowers. It's easy to forget that Dubrovnik is a living, working city; this market and the café-bars around it are an excellent reminder. ✉ *Dubrovnik.*

Suveniri Bačan
TEXTILES/SEWING | The streets of the Old Town are filled with older women selling hand-stitched embroidery and needlecraft products created using traditional methods and materials. The best storefront is Bačan, which sells decorative fabric in a variety of sizes and designs, all inspired by tradtional Croatian folk costumes. The store is run by a husband-and-wife team, with the wife handcrafting all the items sold in the store. ✉ *Prijeko 6* ☎ *20/321–121* ⊕ *www. facebook.com/souvenirs.bachan.*

🏃 Activities

BEACHES
Closest to the Old Town, **Banje Beach** is a small sandy beach just beyond the Ploče Gate where you can grab a drink at Banje Beach Club and swim with fantastic views. For more family-friendly beaches, head to Sunset Beach in **Lapad,** where the kids can enjoy water sports and inflat-able toys. A 20-minute walk east brings you to **Sveti Jakov** beach, a bright white sliver at the bottom of a steep staircase. The most natural and peaceful beaches lie on the tiny island of **Lokrum,** popular with rock-jumpers and nudists. For the most unique Dubrovnik experience,

Dubrovnik and Southern Dalmatia

BOSNIA-HERZEGOVINA

MONTENEGRO

Imotski
Zagvozd
Makarska
Zaostrog
Al
Metković
Drvenik Gradac
BRAČ
Sućuraj Ploče
The Pelješac Peninsula
Doli
Slano
Trpanj
Trsteno
Kamani Dvori
Korta Katarina Winery
Stpn
ŠIPAN LOPUD
Orebić
Cavtat
Čilipi
HVAR
Korčula
Mljet
Elafiti Islands
Sobra
KORČULA
Odysseus Cave
Dubrovnik see detail map
Nacionalni Park Mljeta
TO SPLIT
LASTOVO
SUŠAC
ADRIATIC SEA

0   30 miles
0   30 kilometers

head to either of the Buža bars to swim directly under the city walls, or to local favorite **Šulić** beach in the shadow of the Lovrijenac Fortress.

SEA KAYAKING
Adriatic Kayak Tours
KAYAKING | FAMILY | There is literally a sea full of kayaking companies in Dubrovnik, but the best is Adriatic Kayak Tours. Besides introductory half-day sea-kayaking tours around Zaton Bay, they offer day trips, some of which include biking and hiking components, to the Elafiti Islands and even farther to the Konavle region and Montenegro. ⊠ *Zrinsko Frankopanska 6, Ploce* ☎ *020/312–770* ⊕ *www. adriatickayaktours.com.*

Elafiti Islands

Lopud is 7 nautical miles northwest of Dubrovnik, Šipan is 15 nautical miles northwest of Dubrovnik.

Sometimes you need a break from the city crowds, and the lush, laid-back Elafiti Islands are happy to provide a retreat. Historically, the 13 tiny islets have always been under Dubrovnik's control; the local aristocracy kept summer villas here (which are now scattered in various states of ruin around the islands). Today only the three larger ones—Koločep, Lopud, and Šipan—are inhabited, with a total population of around 1,000.

Lopud is best equipped to deal with visitors, with one main settlement made up of old stone houses built around a sheltered bay, plus a handful of shops and restaurants. The main sights are a 15th-century Franciscan monastery which has been converted into a luxury villa, the ruins of 30 chapels built during the golden age of the Republic, the 16th-century Sutvrac Fortress located on the highest point of the island, and family-friendly Šunj, one of Croatia's rare sandy beaches. Lopud is a wonderful place for hiking along the herb-scented paths that crisscross the island.

Šipan is the largest of the three islands and the only one with cars, although the best way to experience it is to ride a bicycle along the 5 km (3 mile) long road between the two main settlements (Suđurađ and Šipanska Luka), enjoying the views of the olive groves and vineyards along the way. If it's a slower pace of life you're after, Šipan is most likely to be your favorite.

GETTING HERE AND AROUND
Jadrolinija runs four or five passenger ferries per day between Gruž and the Elafiti Islands, stopping at Koločep (30 minutes) and Lopud (1 hour). Šipan is connected to Dubrovnik and Mljet by G&V Line (45 minutes). You can also book an island-hopping day trip from Dubrovnik to visit all three in one afternoon (with lunch included). Only the island of Šipan has cars, while Lopud is best explored on foot or by golf cart.

 Sights

Lopud 1483
HOUSE | As you round the bend into Lopud by sea, the first thing you notice is the imposing Franciscan Monastery on the tip of the island. Dating back to 1483 (hence the name), it was abandoned for 200 years before being rescued by an unlikely patron: Francesca Thyssen-Bornemisza. The daughter of the Swiss baron who founded the Thyssen-Bornemisza Museum in Madrid and former wife of the heir to the Habsburg dynasty, Francesca gained fame in her

own right as a London "It Girl" in the 1980s. But it is likely her work as a patron of the arts that will be her legacy, and one of her defining works will surely be Lopud 1483. After a meticulous 20-year refurbishment, it is now one of the most unique, elegant properties in Croatia which defies categorization: it is part villa, part art gallery, and part historical site. The property retains the contemplative atmosphere of the monastery and infuses it with furniture and art—everything from the Old Masters to modern photography—from the family's private collection, which was once second only to the collection of the Queen of England. The property is surrounded by botanical gardens that were designed by a shaman, meditation spots, a yoga studio, and supremely modern touches like a giant outdoor screen that can be mounted on the old fortress wall for movie nights. The entire property, which sleeps 10 people, can be rented for the night, and tours of the monastery can be arranged (100 Kn). ⊠ *Franciscan Monastery of Our Lady of the Cave, Dubrovnik* ☎ *020/322–123* ⊕ *www.lopud1483.com.*

★ Šunj Beach
BEACH—SIGHT | FAMILY | A swath of white sand backed by pine forests, with a couple of unobtrusive bars and restaurants, it's worth the 2½ km (1½ mile) trek across the island to reach one of Croatia's only sandy beaches. The path is quite hilly in both directions, so you might want to hail a golf cart to get there or back—you'll see them driving around the main promenade or parked just above the beach. ⊠ *Lopud.*

Your Black Horizon Art Pavilion
PUBLIC ART | Another interesting project by Francesca Thyssen-Bornemisza's organization, albeit a slightly less imposing one, is this modern art light installation on Lopud, inaugurated at the 2005 Venice Biennale. A play on light and perspective, you'll find it hidden away in the

middle of the island. ✉ *Lopud* 🌐 *www.TBA21.org/lopud* ⏲ *Closed Oct.–May.*

🍴 Restaurants

★ BOWA

$$$$ | MEDITERRANEAN | For the ultimate exclusive island dining experience, head to BOWA, nestled on its own secluded beach on Šipan. With raised cabanas right over the water that can be booked for groups of up to 12 (with a minimum spend), it is an ideal place to spend the day swimming and sunbathing between courses. **Known for:** beautiful cabanas over the water; exclusive dining on a private beach; reservations recommended. [$] *Average main: 490 Kn* ✉ *Pakljena 3, Šipan* ☎ *091/636–6111* 🌐 *www.bowa-dubrovnik.com* ⏲ *Closed Oct.–May.*

Konoba Kod Marka

$$ | SEAFOOD | An island that belongs to local fishers and the cats who await them on the dock is naturally going to be home to one of the best seafood restaurants in all of Southern Dalmatia. With its prime location overlooking the harbor in Šipanska Luka, opposite the bay from the ferry pier, Kod Marka is very popular with sailors and yacht guests. **Known for:** fresh catch of the day; seaside location; reservations required. [$] *Average main: 120 Kn* ✉ *Šipanska Luka* ☎ *020/758–007* ⏲ *Closed Oct.–May.*

Restoran Obala

$$$ | SEAFOOD | This smart restaurant has offered fine dining on Lopud's seafront promenade since 1939, with idyllic sunset views across the bay and wonderfully formal waiters. The house specialty is *školjke na buzaru* (mixed shellfish cooked in wine and garlic), and they also do an excellent prawn and truffle risotto. **Known for:** local seafood; seaside location; formal service. [$] *Average main: 150 Kn* ✉ *Obala Iva Kuljevana 18* ☎ *020/759–170* 🌐 *www.obalalopud.com* ⏲ *Closed Nov.–Apr.*

🛏 Hotels

Hotel Božica

$$ | HOTEL | One of the most welcoming and relaxing hotels in the region, Hotel Božica on the bay of Suđurađ makes a great base for exploring Šipan and beyond. **Pros:** private beach; close to ferry dock; wonderful pool. **Cons:** rooms are a little small and outdated; not many services nearby; on-site restaurant is expensive. [$] *Rooms from: 1400 Kn* ✉ *Suđurađ 13 1d, Šipan* ☎ *020/325–400* 🌐 *www.hotel-bozica.hr* ⏲ *Closed Nov.–Apr.* 🛏 *33 rooms* 🍽 *Free breakfast.*

Lafodia Sea Resort

$$$ | HOTEL | The luxurious Lafodia rises up a hillside overlooking the harbor and bay with sleek rooms and terraces, four restaurants, a bakery, and a gorgeous infinity pool. **Pros:** seafront location with views over the bay; wonderful spa; modern amenities. **Cons:** big and rather impersonal; distance from the ferry; day trip boats from Dubrovnik dock just outside. [$] *Rooms from: 1500 Kn* ✉ *Obala Iva Kuljevana 35* ☎ *020/450–300* 🌐 *www.lafodiahotel.com* ⏲ *Closed Oct.–Apr.* 🛏 *182 rooms* 🍽 *Free breakfast.*

Cavtat

17 km (10½ miles) southeast of Dubrovnik.

While Dubrovnik's streets are being polished under the shoes of thousands of visitors per day, Cavtat's pine-covered trails seem comparatively tourist-free. There are secluded swimming spots, quiet walking paths, and park benches waiting for you to sit and enjoy the beauty and tranquility that you came to Croatia to find.

Founded by the ancient Greeks as Epidauros, then taken by the Romans and renamed Epidaurum, the original settlement on the site of Cavtat was subsequently destroyed by tribes of

The seaside resort of Cavtat is filled with pine-shaded paths and lacks Dubrovnik's tourists.

Avars and Slavs in the early 7th century. The Romans fleeing Epidaurum founded Dubrovnik.

Today's Cavtat, which developed during the 15th century under the Republic of Dubrovnik, is an easygoing seaside resort and the gateway to the bucolic Konavle region. The medieval stone buildings of the Old Town occupy a small peninsula with a natural bay to each side. A palm-lined seaside promenade with open-air cafés and restaurants curves around the main bay, while the second bay is overlooked by a beach backed by several socialist-era hotels.

GETTING HERE AND AROUND

The drive to Cavtat, whether by car or bus from Dubrovnik (departing half-hourly from the main bus station and the stop near the cable car), offers some of the best views over the Old Town. Another option is a taxi boat along the coast from Dubrovnik's Old Harbor (1 hour; 60 Kn one-way). Once in Cavtat, all sights are within walking distance, although a car is useful for exploring further into Konavle.

 Sights

★ Kameni Dvori

LOCAL INTEREST | FAMILY | In an area famous for its seaside, Konavle, at the southernmost tip of Southern Dalmatia before it trails off into Montenegro, is a rare green, bucolic region, known for its rural agriculture, traditional crafts and festivals, and burgeoning wineries which primarily produce white Malvasia. The best place to get a sense of Konavle life is Kameni Dvori, a wonderfully rustic villa and konoba in the settlement of Lovorno, 14 km (9 miles) south of Cavtat. They have lovely rooms to rent which include access to the pool, or you can partake in a traditional cooking class with the exceptionally friendly family who owns the property. You'll try their homemade wine and rakija, get your hands dirty in the garden choosing vegetables for the soup, and make fresh bread and their specialty, Livorno skewers. You might even find yourself holding a turtle or milking a goat. It's a great excursion from Dubrovnik or Cavtat; contact Tureta Travel to organize a visit if you don't have your own car. ☒ *Lovorno 11* ☎ *020/797–056* ⊕ *www.holiday-village-konavle.com.*

Kuća Bukovac (*Vlaho Bukovac Home*)
MUSEUM | The former home of local son Vlaho Bukovac (1855–1922), one of Croatia's greatest artists, has been beautifully converted into a gallery of his life and work. The two floors feature family and self-portraits and oil paintings from the periods he spent in Paris, Zagreb, Prague, and Cavtat. The house—with walls covered in murals Bukovac painted as a young man, period furniture, and personal items, plus the gardens surrounding it—is a lovely place to spend a quiet afternoon. ☒ *Bukovćeva 5* ☎ *020/478–646* ⊕ *www.kuca-bukovac. hr* ☒ *30 Kn* ⊙ *Closed Mon.*

Mauzolej Obitelji Račić (*Račić Mausoleum*)
CEMETERY | The peaceful cemetery St. Rocco sits atop the highest point of the peninsula overlooking the city and surrounding area. Its centerpiece is the mausoleum, sculpted from white Brač stone by beloved Croatian sculptor Ivan Meštrović for the Račić family in 1921. It is octagonal in plan, and the main entrance is guarded by two art nouveau caryatids. ☒ *Cavtat* ✛ *On the highest point of the peninsula* ☎ ☒ *10 Kn* ⊙ *Closed Nov.–Mar.*

Župa Dubrovačka (*Dubrovnik Riviera*)
BEACH—SIGHT | When traveling between Dubrovnik and Cavtat, you'll pass a string of cheerful seaside resorts collectively known as the Župa Dubrovačka, or the Dubrovnik Riviera. The villages of **Srebreno, Mlini,** and **Plat** each have a handful of seasonal hotels and restaurants and family-friendly beaches. The most interesting village to explore is **Kupari,** the first one you reach from Dubrovnik. During the time of the Dubrovnik Republic, clay tiles were made in a factory here (*kupa* means tile in Croatian). Between the two world wars, the village was one of the pioneers of tourism in the area. In

the 1960s, it became a resort for the Yugoslav army and their families, but when war broke out in 1991, the army fled and the hotels were looted, bombed, and abandoned. Today, as the backdrop to a stunning beach, the crumbling hotels remain and can be explored freely (but cautiously), a spooky and rare reminder of war in a once-again prosperous region. ☒ *Dubrovnik.*

 Restaurants

★ **Bugenvila**
$$$ | SEAFOOD | This eatery is vibrant in every sense, from the flowers climbing the sides of the terrace to the happy patrons tucking into dishes that wouldn't be out of place on the menu of a fine dining restaurant in Dubrovnik. The menu changes regularly but you can expect lobster, octopus, pork belly, and other local ingredients prepared in fresh and exciting ways. **Known for:** top-quality local food; waterfront location in the center of Cavtat; laid-back atmosphere. Ⓢ *Average main: 170 Kn* ☒ *Obala A. Starcevica 9* ☎ *020/479–949* ⊕ *bugenvila.eu* ⊙ *Closed Nov.–Mar.*

Konoba Kolona
$$ | SEAFOOD | Located one street behind Tiha Bay, Konoba Kolona is a firm favorite among locals. It has two large covered terraces plus indoor seating and reasonable prices for popular dishes such as lobster by the kilo, mussels *buzara* (tomato and white wine sauce), and octopus carpaccio. **Known for:** fresh seafood; popularity with locals; friendly service. Ⓢ *Average main: 110 Kn* ☒ *Put Tihe 2* ☎ *020/478–787.*

🛏 **Hotels**

★ **Castelletto**
$ | HOTEL | With bougainvillea-strewn terraces, cheerful rooms, a small pool, and wonderful staff, family-run Castelletto is a perfect place to unwind and peacefully enjoy the view. **Pros:** very friendly

owners; excellent buffet breakfast; private bar on-site. **Cons:** 10-minute uphill walk from center; often fully booked; some rooms are a little noisy. *Rooms from: 650 Kn* ✉ *Jurja Dalmatinca 9* ☎ *020/479–547* 🌐 *www.dubrovnikexperience.com* ⏲ *closed Nov.–Apr.* *13 rooms* *Free breakfast.*

Hotel Cavtat

$$ | HOTEL | FAMILY | This spot represents a nice middle ground between the big resorts in Cavtat and the smaller villas. **Pros:** close to beach and center of town; on-site spa; made-to-order breakfast in waterfront restaurant. **Cons:** hotel layout can be confusing; decor is dated; some rooms have no view. *Rooms from: 1050 Kn* ✉ *Tiha 8* ☎ *020/202–000* 🌐 *www.hotel-cavtat.hr* ⏲ *Closed Nov.–Apr.* *140 rooms* *Free breakfast.*

Hotel Croatia

$$$ | HOTEL | Sprawling across its own rocky, pine-studded peninsula, with quiet walking trails through the property, this vast hotel offers guests the chance to find their own place in the sun or shade, seemingly miles away from the rest of the world. **Pros:** two private beaches; five restaurants on-site; lovely spa and sauna. **Cons:** large property with an impersonal atmosphere; distance from center of town; expensive by Cavtat standards. *Rooms from: 2000 Kn* ✉ *Frankopanska 10* ☎ *020/475–555* 🌐 *www.adriaticluxuryhotels.com* ⏲ *Closed Nov.–Mar.* *487 rooms* *Free breakfast.*

Shopping

Škatulica

GIFTS/SOUVENIRS | Find this little treasure trove tucked away in an old stone storage building on the promenade. Items come from all over Croatia but the majority are handmade in South Dalmatia. You'll find wine, liqueurs, their own candied almonds, and *arancini*, plus items made with Brač stone, jewelry, artwork, and natural cosmetics. Between the lovely interior and the friendly owner Nives, this is a perfect place to pick up great quality, well-priced gifts and souvenirs. ✉ *Obala Ante Starčevića 36* ☎ *020/773–505* 🌐 *www.skatulica.weebly.com.*

Activities

The beaches east of the center, near **Uvala Tiha** (Tiha Bay), are where you'll find the large modern hotels and family-friendly beaches. Take a walk around the peninsula to find smaller beaches and a more peaceful spot to swim.

DIVING

Epidaurum Diving and Water Sports Center

DIVING/SNORKELING | There are some excellent underwater sights around Cavtat, including shipwrecks and amforas. Epidaurum Diving and Water Center organizes certification and dive trips, as well as Jet-Skiing, parasailing, and other types of water fun. ✉ *Šetalište Žal 31* ☎ *098/427–550* 🌐 *www.epidaurum.com.*

The Pelješac Peninsula

54 km (34 miles) northwest of Dubrovnik; 2 nautical miles from Korčula.

The Pelješac Peninsula is Croatia at its best. You know that red wine you've been drinking since you got to Dalmatia? It comes from the vineyards here. Those secret beaches you've been trying to find? The peninsula is surrounded by them. And those famous oysters you've been eating in Dubrovnik? They pull them out of the channel right in front of you and serve them with a slice of lemon. A wild, unexplored region full of secluded coves, stone villages, vineyards, and breathtaking views, it's a rare, undiscovered gem just an hour away from Dubrovnik.

There are two main towns that make a great base from which to explore the Peninsula. **Mali Ston** is the first town you come to when driving from Dubrovnik, famous for its fortified walls, salt pans, and oysters. On the other end of the Peninsula, **Orebić** straggles along the coast, facing across a narrow sea channel to the island of Korčula. Historically, the town spent several centuries under the Republic of Dubrovnik, supplying many able seamen to the republic's merchant navy. From 1865 to 1887, the town even had its own shipping company; today, you can see a string of villas and their gardens overlooking the coastal promenade, built by wealthy local sea captains.

GETTING HERE AND AROUND

The Pelješac Peninsula is 65 km (50 miles) in length, with one main road stretching from Mali Ston at one end to the small seaside town of Lovište at the other. Several public buses drive this route daily in both directions, but they are not frequent; the best way to explore the Peninsula is by car, which will allow you to visit wineries, villages, and beaches off the main road. There are also several organized tours from Dubrovnik or Korčula; **Secret Dalmatia** and **Dubrovnik Day Tours** are two of the best. A passenger and car ferry connects Orebić with Korčula (15 minutes) and another connects Prapratno with the island of Mljet (45 minutes).

 # Sights

Franjevački Samostan (*Franciscan Monastery of Our Lady of the Angels*)
MUSEUM | A 20-minute walk up the hill above Orebić brings you to the 15th-century Franciscan monastery, perched 492 feet above sea level. The view across the channel to Korčula is spectacular; the view, in fact, explains the monastery's prime location. During the heyday of the Dubrovnik Republic, Pelješac was under Dubrovnik control, while Korčula was ruled by their archrival, Venice. From this privileged vantage point, the Franciscan monks would spy upon their island neighbors, under strict orders to send a messenger to Dubrovnik if trouble looked likely. Today the monastery is a

most welcoming retreat, with a lovely cloister and a small museum displaying scale models of the ships that local sea captains sailed across the oceans; there's also an array of votive pictures dedicated to the Virgin, commissioned and donated by sailors who had been saved from trouble on the high seas. Before leaving, check out the cemetery, where gray marble tombstones shaded by cypress trees mark the final resting places of many a local seafarer. ⊠ *Orebić* ☎ *020/713–075* 🖂 *20 Kn.*

★ Korta Katarina Winery

WINERY/DISTILLERY | Perched on a hill overlooking Trstenica Beach, award-winning Korta Katarina is a beautiful place to try Pelješac wines and the most accessible winery from Orebić. *Korta* is the name for the typical courtyards outside sea captains' homes around town, while *Katarina* is the daughter of the American couple, Lee and Penny Anderson, who traveled to Croatia in 2001 while on a rebuilding mission in Bosnia, fell in love with it, and opened the winery. Korta Katerina now produces eight wines: six red and rosé made from Plavac Mali, one Rukatac, and one Pošip. A winery visit, tasting, and optional pairings, which range from wine and chocolate to a full gastronomical experience, can be arranged in advance. In addition, after nearly a decade of no-expenses spared renovations to the former Rivijera Hotel next-door, the five-star Relais & Chateaux Villa Korta Katerina opened to guests with eight luxury rooms available to rent. ⊠ *Bana J. Jelacica 3, Orebić* ☎ *099/525–7955* ⊕ *www.kortakatarina.com.*

★ Solana Ston (*Salt Pans*)

HISTORIC SITE | There are records of salt being collected by Romans in this area dating back to 167 B.C, but it was the Republic of Dubrovnik that fully recognized the economic potential of the salt pans. In 1333, it founded the towns of Ston and Mali Ston, built a fortified wall to protect them, and eventually the sea

Wines of Pelješac

The Pelješac Peninsula is a rare Southern Dalmatian region that relies not only on tourism but also agriculture, thanks mainly to its vineyards producing two types of red wine from the hearty Plavac Mali grape: **Postup** and **Dingač**. Both are full-bodied, but Dingač is particularly robust with an alcohol content that may reach as high as 17.6%, owing to the conditions of its terroir. The grapes are grown on a 45° "Dingač Slope", with the sun reflecting on the vines from three different surfaces—the sky, the sea, and the white karst stone—which increases the sugar content. Working conditions on the slope are notoriously difficult, and before 1976 (when local winemakers excavated a 400 meter long tunnel by hand to make it more accessible), donkeys were used to help carry harvested grapes over the mountain and into the wineries. The donkey found on some bottles of Dingač is a symbol of the hearty, stubborn vine that reaches its full potential in this very limited region. In 1961, Dingač became the first protected wine region in Croatia, followed by Postup.

There are many family-owned wineries along the Peninsula where you can sample and buy wine. An organized tour will take in three or four, or if you're driving yourself, you might consider the following route. Coming from Dubrovnik, make your first stop at **Vinarija Miloš** (⊕ *www.milos.hr*) near Ston, renowned for its award-winning stagnum wines and family atmosphere. Next up is the village of Trstenik, where California wine lovers might recognize the name Mike Grgich, who was born in Dalmatia but gained fame in the Napa Valley; his winery, **Grgić Vina** (⊕ *www.grgic-vina. com)*, is one of the most sophisticated on the peninsula. Next, you'll reach the village of Potomje, where you'll find a cluster of wineries; just beyond the village is **Vinarija Bartulović** (⊕ *www.vinarijabartulovic.hr*). The Bartulović family has been making wine on Pelješac for some 480 years, and today it's the young, energetic winemaker Mario who will tell you all about the wine-making process, his experiences on the Dingač slopes, and his family's traditions. This winery is especially popular with visitors thanks to its authentic Dalmatian konoba, located in the former wine cellar, where you can combine wine tasting with a meal (call ahead to reserve). Return to Potomje and drive through the Dingač Tunnel to continue along the coastal road for gorgeous views. Your final winery of the day is the luxurious **Korta Katerina** in Orebić.

salt became its most valuable product, generating one-third of its wealth. Today you can take a tour of the massive salt pans, the oldest in Europe, to learn about the ancient collecting process using just sun, sea, and wind, which are still employed today. If the salt pans are closed when you arrive, ask at Vila Koruna in Mali Ston (which also owns the salt pans) about organizing a tour. You can also buy souvenir bags of the organic sea salt around town. ⊠ *Pelješki put 1* ☏ *020/754–027* ⊕ *www.solanaston.hr* 🎫 *15 Kn* ⊘ *Closed Oct.–Apr.*

Ston Walls
BUILDING | In order to protect the early settlement, particularly the enormously valuable Ston salt pans, in 1333 the Republic of Dubrovnik built a 7-km (4½-mile) fortified wall, effectively controlling

From the city walls of Ston, you can get a glimpse of the town's famous salt pans.

land access to the peninsula. Today the wall stretches 5½ km (3 miles) and locals will tell you it's second in length only to the Great Wall of China; a disputable claim, but nevertheless it is an impressive sight. There is a Ston Wall marathon every September, and throughout the year, you can take a slightly strenuous walk atop a section between Ston and Mali Ston (40 minutes) for incredible views of the channel and the salt pans. ⊠ Ston ✛ Follow signs to the entrance from Ston or Mali Ston ✇ 70 Kn.

Trsteno Arboretum

GARDEN | The area around Dubrovnik has many fine examples of summer villas built by noble families, but the one in Trsteno is something special. Within the grounds of a small Renaissance villa is an arboretum set up during the 16th century by the Gučetić family. Laid out on a geometric plan, the garden is filled with hundreds of exotic species of trees and shrubs, most of which were brought home from distant voyages by local sailors. An original aqueduct is still in use, and a Baroque fountain of Neptune and two nymphs dates from 1736. The site has been continuously developed for five centuries, acquiring Renaissance, Baroque, and Romantic forms along the way. The surroundings are breathtaking, with the grounds running down toward a cliff overlooking the sea. Buses run regularly to Trsteno from Dubrovnik, and it makes a great stopover on the way to the Pelješac Peninsula. ■ TIP→ For something a little different, organize a cooking class at a local house within the grounds of the Arboretum. Katja's family has lived in the house for four generations, and together you will prepare a feast which might include black risotto, peka, or pašticada. Tour price includes admission to the arboretum, and Katja will also take you on a walking tour of the grounds. The cooking class can be booked through Secret Dalmatia. ⊠ Potok 20, Trsteno ☎ 020/751–019 ✇ 50 Kn.

Mali Ston Oysters

Ston is renowned throughout Croatia, and increasingly internationally, for the oysters grown in Mali Ston Bay. Their high quality is due to the perfect brackish conditions of the bay; salty sea water mixed with the fresh, mineral-laden water that flows in from the nearby Neretva River. They have been farmed since Roman times, and appreciated by nobles from the Dubrovnik Republic to the Habsburgs. But as famous as these oysters are, oyster farming in Ston is still a small-scale operation; only a handful of local families have permits. While you can try them in the best restaurants in the country, nothing beats an oyster straight out of the bay with just a slice of lemon and a glass of wine to wash it down. Mali Ston has several great restaurants, foremost among them Bota, plus a handful of oyster stands along the road for a quick taste. They are said to be at their best in March, around the time of the Festival of Oysters celebrating the feast of St. Joseph, where you can try oysters, wine, and other local products alongside concerts and folk festivals in Ston and Mali Ston.

🍴 Restaurants

★ Bota

$$$ | SEAFOOD | Occupying a 14th-century salt warehouse, Bota (part of the Šare family empire) is known for its menu of outstanding, locally caught seafood—it's the best place to try Ston's famous oysters. If raw oysters make you squeamish, try oyster soup or *pohane oštrige* (deep-fried oysters), and don't leave without trying the unusual *stonski makaruli,* a cake made from pasta, nuts, sugar, and cinnamon, unique to Ston. **Known for:** local oysters; lovely terrace seating; boat trips to try oysters right from the Mali Ston channel. $ *Average main: 140 Kn* ⊠ *Mali Ston* ☎ *020/754–482* ⊕ *www. bota-sare.hr.*

Croccantino

$ | CAFÉ | FAMILY | It's getting harder and harder to find quality ice cream in Southern Dalmatia, so you'll be relieved to find Croccantino, a fun, colorful little café on the waterfront promenade in Orebić. It serves exquisite homemade gelato, artisan cakes, and cupcakes, as well as excellent smoothies, coffee, and milkshakes. **Known for:** homemade gelato and cakes; waterfront location; one of the best gelaterias in Southern Dalmatia. $ *Average main: 15 Kn* ⊠ *Obala Pomoraca 30, Orebić* ☎ *020/714–416.*

Estravaganca

$$$ | SEAFOOD | FAMILY | The epitome of a hidden gem, there is no menu or prices at Estravaganca, just a chalkboard with the catch of the day, and the owner who will rush out to grab your boat ropes, show you to your table, bring out the fish for you to choose from, then light the fire, and grill it right in front of you. Most days there are mussels and oysters kept in the sea and pulled out just minutes before they're put on your plate; same goes for the lobster, which is then cooked in a spicy red sauce with home-made pasta. **Known for:** fresh seafood pulled out of the sea and cooked in front of you; reachable by steep, narrow road or by boat; secluded location right on the beach. $ *Average main: 150 Kn* ⊠ *Lovište* ☎ *098/944–7099* ⊕ *www.estravaganca. com* 🕐 *No dinner* 🚫 *No credit cards.*

Kapetanova Kuća

$$ | SEAFOOD | Known throughout Croatia, this longstanding favorite is synonymous with Ston and fresh oysters. Slightly

more upscale than the other restaurants in Mali Ston, people come from far and wide to feast on the shellfish here, as well as the black risotto, prepared by owner and cook Lidija Kralj. **Known for:** local oysters, mussels, and clams; excellent black risotto; family-run restaurant. $ *Average main: 90 Kn* ⊠ *Mali Ston* ☎ *020/754–555* ⊕ *www.ostrea.hr.*

Stari Kapetan

$$ | **SEAFOOD** | Designed to look like an actual ship with a life-size captain at the helm, what at first glance might seem like a tourist trap is actually one of the best restaurants in town. Try the seafood platter for two, with tuna steak, grilled squid, mussels, scampi, and extraordinary sea bream, plus a glass of local wine. **Known for:** fresh seafood; al fresco seaside dining; fun design. $ *Average main: 100 Kn* ⊠ *Šetalište Kneza Domagoja 8, Orebić* ☎ *020/714–488* ⊕ *www. hoteladriaticorebic.com.*

 ## Hotels

Aminess Grand Azur Hotel

$$ | **RESORT** | **FAMILY** | Set on a pebbly beach 10 minutes from the center of Orebić, this is a perfect base for the whole family. **Pros:** perfect for families with children; beachfront location; generous buffet and all-inclusive service. **Cons:** can be hectic in the high season; not enough beach chairs; distance from center of town. $ *Rooms from: 980 Kn* ⊠ *Petra Kresimira IV 107, Orebić* ☎ *052/858–600* ⊕ *www.aminess. com* ۞ *Closed Nov.–Apr.* ↙ *185 rooms* ⦿ *All-inclusive.*

Boutique Hotel Adriatic

$$ | **HOTEL** | Locals are proud of their sea history in Orebić, but the Mikulić family has gone the extra mile and turned their hotel—easily one of the most elegant, charming, and classy hotels on Pelješac—into an unofficial seafaring museum. **Pros:** beautifully restored rooms with stone walls; close to town center and

beach; excellent restaurant. **Cons:** often fully booked; no elevator; online booking options are limited. $ *Rooms from: 1250 Kn* ⊠ *Šetalište Kneza Domagoja 8, Orebić* ☎ *020/714–488* ⊕ *www.hoteladriaticorebic.com* ↙ *6 rooms* ⦿ *Free breakfast.*

★ Waterfront Oasis Mali Ston

$$$ | **RENTAL** | **FAMILY** | Occupying its own peninsula in the Mali Ston channel, with wonderful views across to the village and the fortified walls above, Waterfront Oasis is one of the nicest, most private accommodation options in the region. **Pros:** peaceful location on a private peninsula; well-stocked, stylish, and spacious apartments; very friendly and helpful owners. **Cons:** not many services within walking distance; no meals included; rocky beach not ideal for young kids. $ *Rooms from: 1500 Kn* ⊠ *Put od Siga 10* ☎ *0915/885–478* ⊕ *www.waterfrontoasismaliston.com* ↙ *4 rooms* ⦿ *No meals.*

 ## Activities

BEACHES

There are wild beaches and coves all around the Pelješac Peninsula, almost all of which need to be reached via private transport. The most accessible beach is **Trstenica**, a family-friendly 1½-km (1-mile) stretch of sand and pebbles in Orebić just below Korta Katerina winery. Just a few kilometers up the road, **Viganj** is regarded as one of the top windsurfing locations in Croatia and beyond. It hosts the Croatian surfing championship annually and has held both the European and world championships as well. Closer to Ston, there is a lovely pebble beach in **Prapratno**, where you can also catch a ferry to Mljet.

WINDSURFING

Water Donkey Windsurfing and Kitesurfing Center

WINDSURFING | You can rent wind and kitesurfing equipment and take lessons from the friendly staff here in Viganj. They also rent kayaks, bikes, and stand-up paddle boards. ✉ *Ponta Beach, Viganj* ☎ *091/152–0258* ⊕ *www.windsurf-ing-kitesurfing-viganj.com.*

Korčula

49 nautical miles northwest of Dubrovnik; 57 nautical miles southeast of Split.

Southern Dalmatia's largest island, Korčula is quietly emerging as the most sophisticated and alluring island in the region. First settled by the ancient Greeks around 4 B.C. —who named it Kerkyra Melaina, or "Black Corfu," for its dark Aleppo pine trees—it spent several periods under Venetian rule between the 10th and 18th centuries, much to the frustration of Dubrovnik, which considered the Italian city-state its archrival. Venetian influence can still be seen in **Korčula Town**, one of the best preserved medieval island towns in the Mediterranean. It resembles a mini-Dubrovnik with its high fortified walls and circular fortresses jutting out into a sparkling sea; the main difference lies in the design of the streets, which are laid out in a fishbone pattern to prevent cold winter winds from whistling unimpeded through town. Within you'll find a treasure trove of Gothic and Renaissance churches, palaces, and piazzas, all built from fine local stone. Today Korčula Town is known for its traditional sword dances, and its main, though disputed, claim to fame as the birthplace of Marco Polo.

Beyond the capital, the island is made up of stone villages, miles of mountainous roads perfect for biking, secluded beaches, boutique wine, honey and olive oil producers, and proud, welcoming locals. Just 4 km (2½ miles) above Korčula Town you'll find **Žrnovo**, with its sleepy hamlets and walking trails past centuries-old cypresses, vineyards, and stone houses, plus some of the most traditional restaurants in the area. **Lumbarda**, 6 km (4 miles) southeast of Korčula Town with around 1,000 inhabitants, is where you'll find the nearest family-friendly sandy beaches and a handful of family wineries producing white wine from the indigenous grape *Grk*. The other main wine producing centers of **Čara** and **Smokvica** are inland, as is the smallest and oldest settlement on the island, picturesque **Pupnat**. To the west is the port town of **Vela Luka**, where you'll find beautiful beaches, and lovely **Proizd**, one of the many islets of the Korčula Archipelago.

GETTING HERE AND AROUND

The Krilo Jet fast catamaran travels daily between Dubrovnik and Split, stopping at Mljet, Korčula Town, Hvar, and Brač along the way, while in July and August, the Nona Ana catamaran travels to Korčula Town from Dubrovnik and Split. If coming by car or bus, you'll drive across the Pelješac Peninsula and board a ferry at Orebić for a 15-minute crossing to Korčula Town. Keep in mind that if traveling with a car, you might have to wait hours in the high season for a space on the ferry, whereas if you're traveling by foot, you'll likely be able to buy a ticket and jump right on. The Old Town is car-free and compact, while the rest of the island is fairly well connected by public buses and taxis, though best explored with private transportation.

TOURS

Korčula Outdoor

ADVENTURE TOURS | For more active tours around the island, this bohemian company will take you mountain biking, kayaking, rock climbing, and sailing to secret beaches, wineries, and the more hidden corners of Korčula. ✉ *Korcula* ☎ *091/6224–566* ⊕ *www.korcula-out-door.com.*

Korkyra Info

This travel agency with an office just outside the Old Town organizes shuttle buses to and from Dubrovnik Airport (240 Kn), as well as excursions around

Korčula and the islands, Dubrovnik, and Pelješac. They also offer car, boat, and scooter rental. ✉ *Trg Petra Šegedina 3a* ☎ *020/711-750* 🌐 *www.korkyra.info.*

Sights

Gradski Muzej Korčula (*Town Museum*)
MUSEUM | Located in a 16th-century stone palace on the main square, this charming museum contains items from all eras of the island's history, from Neolithic stone knives to vessels excavated from Greek and Roman shipwrecks to wooden ships models built in the 1960s. Check out the quirky objects in the original kitchen in the attic, such as gadgets for making macaroni or kneading bread. ✉ *Trg Sv. Marka* ☎ *091/262–3002* 🌐 *www.gm-korcula.com* 🎫 *20 Kn* 🕑 *Closed weekends unless by appointment.*

Katedrala sv. Marka (*St. Mark's Cathedral*)
RELIGIOUS SITE | On the main square, the splendid Gothic-Renaissance cathedral is built from a wheat-colored stone that turns pale gold in sunlight, amber at sunset. Enter through the beautifully carved Romanesque main portal, which is guarded by Adam and Eve standing underneath twin lions. **■ TIP→ Make sure to climb the bell tower for the best view in town; it's steep and awkward, but worthwhile.** ✉ *Trg Sv. Marka* 🌐 *www.gm-korcula.com* 🎫 *25 Kn, bell tower 25 Kn* 🕑 *Cathedral closed Sun.*

Kopnena Vrata (*Land Gate*)
BUILDING | This gate, the main entrance into the Old Town, is topped by the 15th-century Revelin Tower, housing an exhibition connected with the Moreška sword dance and offering panoramic views over the Old Town. Like the other towers around town, it features a winged lion—the symbol of Venice—and the seal of the Rector of Korčula. ✉ *Kopnena Vrata* 🎫 *20 Kn* 🕑 *Closed Nov.–Apr.*

Kuća Marca Pola (*Marco Polo House*)
BUILDING | A couple of blocks east of the main square is the place where the legendary 13th-century explorer is said to have been born, when Korčula was part of the Venetian Empire. The house itself is nearly in ruins but the tower next door is open, with a very modest exhibit about Polo's life on the first floor and a belvedere up top offering panoramic views. ✉ *Ul. Depolo* ☎ *091/262–3002* 🌐 *www.gm-korcula.com* 🎫 *20 Kn* 🕑 *Closed Sept.–June.*

Marco Polo Museum
MUSEUM | **FAMILY** | Meticulously researched, a little cheesy, but undeniably charming, this multimedia, multistory exhibition, complete with life-size figures in medieval costumes, leads visitors through seven stages of the explorer's life, from setting sail from Korčula for the first time, through serving the Kublai Khan, and back home again. The kids will love it, and you will learn a thing or two as well. ✉ *Plokata 19, travnja 33* ☎ *098/970–5334* 🎫 *60 Kn* 🕑 *Closed Oct.–May.*

Restaurants

Aterina
$$ | **MEDITERRANEAN** | Follow the scent of fresh basil—Chef Maja's favorite herb—to Aterina, a playful restaurant occupying a square on the periphery of the Old Town, with views to the palm-lined promenade and sea below. Making use of great local produce, it offers a refreshing change from typically heavy Dalmatian dishes with a lighter take on local favorites. **Known for:** excellent vegetarian options; extensive Korčula-focused wine list; breezy Old Town location. [$] *Average main: 110 Kn* ✉ *Trg korčulanskih klesara i kipara 2* ☎ *091/9861–856* 🕑 *Closed Oct.–June.*

★ Eko Škoj
$$$ | **MEDITERRANEAN** | Head to the hills around Žrnovo to a tiny stone konoba, rustically strung with lavender and bouquets of elderflower, where the Marović family has set up a tasting room where you can try homemade liqueurs,

The sword dancers of Korčula are the island's most famous sight.

marmalades, and award-winning olive oil. Call ahead to book a tasting or lunch which might include platters of grilled vegetables pulled from their garden, charcuterie, traditional Korčula macaroni, and homemade ice cream. **Known for:** best agritourism on the island; exquisite homemade and organic lunch menu; call ahead to book a visit or lunch. $ *Average main: 200 Kn* ⊠ *Žrnovo 96, Prvo Selo* ☎ *099/685–6301* ⊗ *No dinner.*

★ Konoba Belin

$$ | **MEDITERRANEAN** | **FAMILY** | Plan to relax for a couple of hours at this old stone home in the village of Žrnovo over a glass of wine and a platter of authentic, delicious food; try grilled seafood or traditional *Žrnovski makaruni* (fresh handmade pasta). Call ahead to arrange a short walking tour of the village and a sweet lesson on how to roll macaroni with the patriarch of the family. **Known for:** traditional macaroni; excellent seafood; family atmosphere. $ *Average main: 100 Kn* ⊠ *Žrnovo 50* ☎ *091/503–9258* ⊟ *No credit cards* ⊗ *Closed Sept.–May. No lunch.*

Konoba Feral

$$ | **SEAFOOD** | The village of Lumbarda is known for two things: beaches and Grk wine, and you can enjoy them both at this beachside konoba, where you'll tuck into uberfresh octopus while sipping Grk made by the charming local brothers who own the restaurant. Great for a lazy lunch or a romantic dinner, this is one of the best and most reliable spots on Korčula. **Known for:** fresh seafood; family atmosphere; seaside location. $ *Average main: 105 Kn* ⊠ *Lumbarda 63, Lumbarda* ☎ *020/712–090* ⊗ *Closed Oct.–May.*

★ Konoba Mate

$$ | **MEDITERRANEAN** | **FAMILY** | In the courtyard of an old stone cottage in the tiny village of Pupnat (34 km [21 miles] west of Korčula Town), this welcoming restaurant is a firm favorite serving gourmet fare prepared from the family's own farm. The menu changes seasonally, but look out for the house specialty; a platter of homemade *pršut* (prosciutto), goat's cheese, olives, and eggplant pâté, in which the owner says you can see

their entire history. **Known for:** organic vegetables from family garden; great local wine list; traditional meals with a twist. $ *Average main: 100 Kn* ✉ *Pupnat 28* ☎ *020/717–109* 🌐 *www.konobamate.com* 🕘 *Closed Oct.–Apr. No lunch.*

LD Restaurant

$$$$ | **MEDITERRANEAN** | Doing for the dining scene what Lešic Dimitri Palace did for accommodation on Korčula, LD Restaurant has brought a whole new level of sophistication to the island along with its first Michelin star. The menu elevates exclusively local, seasonal produce—think wild asparagus in spring, wild strawberries in the summer, truffles and root vegetables in the fall—and seasonal seafood such as lobster, Ston oysters, and scorpion fish, into fine dining creations. **Known for:** charming terrace with excellent views; tasting menu and a la carte options available; reservations required. $ *Average main: 300 Kn* ✉ *Don Pavla Poše 1-6* ☎ *020/601–726* 🌐 *www.ldrestaurant.com* 🕘 *Closed Oct.–June.*

Hotels

Hotel Korčula de la Ville

$$$ | **HOTEL** | Built in 1871, when the area was a part of Austria-Hungary, the building was converted to become Korčula's first hotel in 1912. **Pros:** best location of all Korčula's hotels (on the seafront in the Old Town); pleasant terrace overlooking sea; old-world charm. **Cons:** basic and decor very dated; front rooms can be noisy; limited facilities. $ *Rooms from: 1500 Kn* ✉ *Obala Dr Franje Tuđmana 5* ☎ *020/726–900* 🌐 *www.korcula-hotels.com* 🕘 *Closed Jan.–Mar.* 🛏 *20 rooms* 🍴 *Free breakfast.*

★ Korčula Waterfront Accommodation

$ | **RENTAL** | Located in a quiet bay a 10-minute walk from Korčula Town, on a large private dock perfect for sunbathing and impromptu barbecues, these homey, well-equipped rooms are run by Paulina and Antonio, the most helpful couple you could hope to meet on holiday. **Pros:** helpful and very friendly hosts; quiet location with private dock for swiming and sunbathing; excellent value for money. **Cons:** no breakfast; few shops or other facilities nearby; distance from the Old Town. $ *Rooms from: 530 Kn* ✉ *Šetalište Tina Ujevića 33* ☎ *098/937–0463* 🌐 *korcula-waterfront-accommodation.com* 🛏 *4 rooms* 🍴 *No meals.*

★ Lešić Dimitri Palace

$$$$ | **HOTEL** | A cluster of stone buildings woven into the fabric of the Old Town, this 18th-century palace has been thoughtfully restored into five individual apartments, each representing a stop along Marco Polo's silk route with inspired designs, chic furniture, luscious fabrics, and high-quality amenities. **Pros:** stunning, unique interior design; location in the Old Town; gourmet made-to-order breakfast served in a Michelin-starred restaurant. **Cons:** very expensive; no pool; no common areas or extra services. $ *Rooms from: 3370 Kn* ✉ *Don Pavla Poše 1–6* ☎ *020/715–560* 🌐 *www.ldpalace.com* 🕘 *Closed Nov.–Apr.* 🛏 *5 apartments* 🍴 *Free breakfast.*

Port 9 Resort

$$ | **RESORT** | **FAMILY** | Named after the nine defensive towers around the Old Town, Port 9 offers the best of both worlds: it's just a 30-minute walk or short taxi boat ride to Korčula Town where you can shop, dine, and wander whenever you like, but with enough resort amenities to entertain the whole family if you prefer to just hang out. **Pros:** excellent amenities and activities organized for kids; four lovely pools, including infinity pool overlooking private beach; well-connected to the rest of the island. **Cons:** food at the buffet is disappointing; service is warm, but a little tired; decor is a bit bland. $ *Rooms from: 1130 Kn* ✉ *Dubrovačka cesta 19* ☎ *020/726–880* 🌐 *www.port9resort.com* 🕘 *Closed Oct.–Apr.* 🛏 *271 rooms* 🍴 *Free breakfast.*

Nightlife

BARS

Cocktail Bar Massimo

BARS/PUBS | Surely among the world's most impressive venues, Cocktail Bar Massimo is located inside one of the turrets of the fortified town walls and offers wonderful sunset views over the peninsula. Drinks are raised up the turret on a pulley, and you have to climb a steep ladder to get to the top (fair warning to anyone wearing a dress). ⊠ *Šetalište Petra Kanavelića* ☎ *099/214–4568* ⏱ *Closed Oct.–May.*

 Performing Arts

DANCE

★ Moreška

DANCE | For one of the most entertaining cultural performances you'll see in Croatia, catch a performance of the Moreška, a colorful medieval sword dance—with real swords—that has been performed in Korčula for more than 400 years. The word Moreška means "Moorish" and is said to celebrate the victory of the Christians over the Moors in Spain, told through the story of a clash between the Black King and the White King over a young maiden. The dance itself is not native to Croatia and was once performed in many Mediterranean countries, but the tradition has disappeared elsewhere and nowadays remains only here. The hour-long performance involves traditional a cappella singing, a live brass band, and the energetic sword dance, performed only by males from local families. Performances take place at 9 pm Monday and Thursday in July and August and Thursday in May, June, September and October. They happen on an open-air stage just outside the city walls next to the Land Gate, with a spectacular performance held on July 29, the feast day of Korčula's protector, St. Theodore.

⊠ *Kopnena Vrata* ⊕ *www.moreska.hr* 🎫 *100 Kn.*

Shopping

Korčula Town is renowned for its shopping, particularly artwork, local white stone items, and handmade jewelry. It's the best destination in the region to stock up on unique souvenirs and quality gifts. Elsewhere on the island, Korčula's wealth of homemade products, such as wine, olive oil, and honey can be purchased right where they are made, and you can usually sample the goods first.

Cukarin

FOOD/CANDY | This family-run shop is renowned as the best place to try Korčula's most traditional goodies, particularly the delicious handmade biscuit *cukarin*, and *klašun*, a walnut pastry. ⊠ *Hrvatska Bratske Zajednice bb* ☎ *020/711–055* ⊕ *www.cukarin.hr.*

Galerija Vapor

ART GALLERIES | Funky jewelry, colorful sculptures, and paintings with pop-art twists by more than 60 contemporary Croatian artists adorn the walls of this cavernous gallery inside the Sea Gate. ⊠ *Kula morska vrata* ☎ ⊕ *www.vapor-gallery.com.*

Tommy

SHOPPING CENTERS/MALLS | The largest supermarket near Korčula Town is the Tommy, located in a shopping mall up the hill about a 15-minute walk from the main bus station. There are a couple of other shops in the same mall, and be sure sure to stop for lunch or a coffee on the spacious terrace of Kavana No. 1 restaurant, where you'll be treated to excellent views of Korčula Town from above. ⊠ *Ulica Ante Starčevića 6* ☎ *020/400–557.*

Activities

BEACHES

The sea around Korčula is so clean and clear you can swim anywhere (and the locals do), including jumping right off the rocks outside the Old Town walls and beside the harbor. The closest beach for a quick swim is **Banje**, a small pebble beach about 10 minutes on foot east of the town walls. The best beaches near Korčula Town are 6 km (4 miles) away in the village of **Lumbarda**: sandy **Przina**, 2 km (1 mile) south of Lumbarda, and smooth-white-stoned **Bili Žal**, a short distance east. Further away, **Pupnatska Luka**, 15 km (9 miles) southwest of Korčula Town, is a perfect wedge of shingle beach backed by steep hills where you can have lunch or a cold drink at the very inviting Beach Bar Mate, owned by the same family who run Konoba Mate. **Vaja Beach**, near the lovely limestone fishing village of **Račišće** 13 km (8 miles) away, is a secret bay that involves a steep downhill hike, but you're rewarded with an isolated, perfect white pebble beach. If driving, make sure to stop where the tarmac ends, about 150 meters before your GPS tells you to stop; park your car and walk the rest of the way, as the road quickly becomes treacherously steep and unsuitable for cars.

Of course, being an island surrounded by little islets, the best way to enjoy the sea around Korčula is taking a boat into the archipelago. The three most popular islets to visit from Korčula Town are **Badija**, the largest in the archipelago, with walking trails and a 14th-century Franciscan monastery; **Stupe**, where you can spend the day sipping cocktails at flashy Moro Beach Bar; and **Vrnik**, where you can see Roman-era stone quarries.

 Mljet

Polače is 18 nautical miles west of Dubrovnik.

Mljet is a long, thin island—37 km (23 miles) long and an average of 3 km (2 miles) wide—of steep, rocky slopes and dense pine forests, more than a third of which is contained within Mljet National Park. It is the southernmost of the Dalmatian islands, and one of the most peaceful and natural. There is one main road that runs the length of the island from the national park in the west to the sandy beaches and lagoons in the east. In the middle are olive groves, sleepy stone towns, and magnificent views. For a small island of 1,100 inhabitants, it has two significant historical claims to fame. The first is being the Biblical island of Melita, where the apostle Paul was shipwrecked. The second is being home to the cave where Greek legend Odysseus spent seven years with the nymph Calyspo. Whether either claim is true is up for debate (most Biblical scholars place Melita as modern-day Malta), but what is undoubtable is that Mljet has a magic that pulls people in and you, like Odysseus, will not want to leave.

GETTING HERE AND AROUND

Sobra is the main port on the island, while Polače and Pomena are the most convenient ports for the national park. The Nona Ana passenger ferry (operated by G&V Line) connects Dubrovnik and Mljet with a stop in Šipan along the way, while Krilo Jet travels from Dubrovnik and Korčula. A Jadrolinija car ferry departs several times daily from the port of Prapratno (on the Pelješac Peninsula) to Sobra. Once on Mljet, public buses connect points across the island, or you can rent scooters or cars for the day in the main settlements. If you are short on time, consider taking an organized day trip from Dubrovnik or Korčula.

A gorgeous national park covers the entire western part of the island of Mljet.

Sights

★ Mljet National Park (*Nacionalni Park Mljeta*)

NATIONAL/STATE PARK | FAMILY | Most people come to Mljet to visit the peaceful national park that covers the entire western part of the island and encompasses the towns of Pomena and Polače, plus miles of dense pine forests, biking and walking trails, and two interconnected aquamarine saltwater lakes—**Malo Jezero** (Little Lake) and **Veliko Jezero** (Big Lake)—which are ideal for swimming from spring to autumn. The Benedictine monks who owned the island between 1191 and 1410 left a significant footprint; they dug a transport channel to the coast through the lakes, which turned them from freshwater to saltwater. In the middle of Veliko Jezero is the **Isle of St. Mary**, with its charming 12th-century monastery, which now houses a small restaurant. You can reach the Isle of St. Mary by boat (30 Kn return) or kayak (80 Kn per hour) from the small bridge Mali Most. Mountain bikes are also available to rent at Mali Most or from Hotel Odisej in Pomena. The park is within walking distance from the port in Polače or Pomena, or if you arrive to the port in Sobra you can catch a local bus. ⊠ *Pristanište 2, Govedari* ☎ *020/744–041* ⊕ *www. np-mljet.hr* ✉ *June–Sept., 125 Kn; Oct.– May, 70 Kn.*

★ Odysseus Cave

CAVE | There are wonderful places to swim all around Mljet, but the village of Babino Polje, in the center of the island, is home to the most magical spot of all. Greek legend has it that when the hero Odysseus was shipwrecked off the island known as Ogygia, he swam into a cave where he was met by a nymph called Calypso; he was so bewitched by her that he stayed for the next seven years. The cave isn't easy to reach so there are never any crowds, which adds to its mystique. You can get there directly by boat, or if you're traveling by car, bike, or scooter, park at the Tommy market in Babino Polje and follow the signs and trails through the olive groves on foot. The walk takes around an hour, and includes a steep downhill section and uneven rocks, so make sure to wear decent shoes and bring water. Once you arrive, you can jump off the rocks and swim through a short tunnel into the cave; aim to arrive around noon when the sun is high and the water is aquamarine. There is a makeshift café perched on the rocks above the cave; there may or may not be someone working there, but it makes a great place to stop for a break. ✉ *Babino Polje.*

🍴 Restaurants

★ Ante's Place
$$$$ | **MEDITERRANEAN** | **FAMILY** | Run by the same wonderful family who owns Boutique Pine Tree Apartments, Ante's Place, with its breezy terrace right on the water, is so good you'll likely eat all of your meals there. It's the best place to taste all of the traditional Dalmatian dishes you've been wanting to try, from peka to octopus salad to seafood platters. **Known for:** excellent seafood platters; great place to try peka; seaside location. [$] *Average main: 220 Kn* ✉ *Saplunara 17* ☎ *99/591–0024* 🌐 *www.pinetreemljet.com* 🕒 *Closed Oct.–May.*

🛏 Hotels

★ Boutique Pine Tree Resort
$$ | **RENTAL** | **FAMILY** | All of Mljet is peaceful, but Saplunara is where you go to really get away from it all, and this boutique property just steps from the sandy beach, with its light, airy feel, spacious rooms, infinity pool, and excellent amenities, represents relaxation at its best. **Pros:** owners and staff who feel like family; lovely infinity pool; 50 meters from sandy beach. **Cons:** not many services nearby; far from the national park; car or taxi necessary to explore other parts of the island. [$] *Rooms from: 1360 Kn* ✉ *Saplunara 17* ☎ *098/266–007* 🌐 *www.pinetreemljet.com* 🕒 *Closed Oct.–May* 🛎 *12 rooms* 🍽 *Free breakfast.*

Hotel Odisej
$ | **HOTEL** | Located in the village of Pomena, just a 15-minute walk from the lakes, the Odisej's main appeal is its proximity to the national park. **Pros:** seafront location near the national park; beautiful views; only official hotel on Mljet. **Cons:** large and rather impersonal; food is disappointing; decor and amenities need updating. [$] *Rooms from: 740 Kn* ✉ *Pomena bb, Pomena* ☎ *020/362–111* 🌐 *www.adriaticluxuryhotels.com* 🕒 *Closed Nov.–Mar.* 🛎 *157 rooms* 🍽 *Free breakfast.*

🏃 Activities

BEACHES

One of Croatia's few sandy beaches, **Saplunara** lies at the southeastern tip of the island, outside the national park. Happily, it remains relatively wild and untended, and you will find several seasonal restaurants and beach bars in the tiny nearby settlement of the same name.

DIVING

Aquatica Mljet
DIVING/SNORKELING | Jacques Cousteau once called Mljet one of the best diving destinations in the world, and divers will love the reefs, wrecks, and caves around the island. This outfitter in Pomena will show you some of the best spots. ✉ *Pomena bb* ☎ *098/479–916* 🌐 *www.aquatica-mljet.hr.*

Chapter 4

SPLIT AND CENTRAL DALMATIA

Updated by
Lara Rasin

⊙ Sights	🍴 Restaurants	🛏 Hotels	🛍 Shopping	🍸 Nightlife
★★★★☆	★★★☆☆	★★★☆☆	★★★☆☆	★★★★★

WELCOME TO SPLIT AND CENTRAL DALMATIA

TOP REASONS TO GO

★ **Roman splendor:** Explore Diocletian's Palace, a massive 3rd-century Roman palace complex. Arrange to take a tour in the early morning hours before the buzz of daily life drowns out the voices of the past in this amazing historical location.

★ **Island hopping:** Hire a taxi boat or a one-day sailing charter to take you across to one of central Dalmatia's most enchanting islands, Hvar. Here, among endless lavender fields and olive tree groves, you can experience the delight of island life.

★ **Hiking and swimming:** Plunge into the clear waters of Sutivan on Brač after climbing to Vidova Gora, the highest point on all the Croatian islands, or walking the Dolce Vita trail through the island's vineyards, where the some of Dalmatia's best wine varieties are produced.

★ **Sailing adventures:** Sail into Komiža harbor on Vis Island aboard a yacht after a long day on the water, perhaps having visited Modra Špilja (the Blue Cave) on the nearby islet of Biševo.

Split is the main jumping-off point for exploring all of Dalmatia, not just Central Dalmatia. From there it is easy to catch a bus, boat, train, or rental car in any direction to see everything Dalmatia offers, on and off the beaten path. Directly south of Split are the islands of Brač and Šolta, both easily accessed by ferry in about an hour. Southeast of Split is Omiš and the Cetina River Valley, and directly west from Split is the ancient walled city of Trogir, which can be reached in 20 minutes by taxi boat. Northeast of Split and a 30-minute drive away are the Klis Fortress and the Vranjača Cave, both spectacular sights which are often overlooked by tourists. Southwest toward Dubrovnik is the Makarska Riviera with its plethora of hidden cove beaches that can be reached in about one hour by car from Split. Head in the opposite direction to discover Krka National Park. about a one-hour scenic drive or two-hour boat ride from Split.

1 Split. An ancient city with one of Croatia's most exciting dining scenes.

2 Šibenik. A cobblestoned city home to the UNESCO-protected Cathedral of St. James.

3 Prvić. A charming island dotted with secret swimming coves.

4 Krka National Park. A national park with a stunning collection of turquoise waterfalls.

5 Trogir. A marvelous medieval city with an Old Town nestled between stunningly preserved walls from the 3rd century BC.

6 Omiš and the Cetina River Valley. A town where one of the country's prettiest rivers meets the Adriatic Sea.

7 Brač. A gorgeous island with historic gems like a hidden 16th-century monastery reachable only by foot.

8 Hvar. One of the Adriatic's most popular islands, with a happening party scene and cultural wonders to boot.

9 Vis. An untouched island with a craggy, cave-dotted coastline popular with yachters.

10 Makarska. A buzzing and beautiful seaside town.

11 Lastovo. An off-the-beaten-track island with scenic hiking opportunities galore.

Central Dalmatia's untamed natural beauty encompasses rocky coastal beaches, steep mountains, and a terrain dotted by olive groves, vineyards, and wild Mediterranean herbs. The wonder elicited by these landscapes is matched only by the area's unique culture and lifestyle.

Here, you can take in everything from ancient ruins and Renaissance-era architectural masterpieces to the exciting entertainment, buzzing art, and cutting-edge gastro scenes of today. For many, the one-of-a-kind journey around Central Dalmatia begins from Croatia's second-largest city and Dalmatia's de facto capital, Split.

Within the last decade, Split has blossomed into one of the Mediterranean's most popular coastal hotspots. The layers of history contained within its Old Town walls (including the UNESCO-listed Diocletian's Palace) are worth more than a quick walk-through and a few photos. Take your time as you stroll through the city's labyrinth-like stone streets. While you're in town, channel your inner Dalmatian by going *laganini*—laid-back and without rushing—as you savor each bite of fresh seafood and enjoy each sip of sun-ripened local wine.

From Split you can hop on a ferry or catamaran to one of the nearby islands that offer paradise just two hours or less away. Split is also the region's main base for boat charter companies operating routes throughout the Adriatic. A 60-minute drive up the coast, northwest of Split, you'll find the stunning city of Šibenik, home to the UNESCO-designated Gothic-Renaissance Cathedral of St. James. Šibenik, with its medieval-era old town and grand fortresses of St. Michael and St. Nicholas, is more than worthy of a couple days of your time. The city also makes a splendid base for visiting the nearby cascading waterfalls of Krka National Park, and the peaceful riverside town of Skradin.

On the way back from Šibenik toward Split is the historic city of Trogir. The city's Old Town is a remarkable conglomeration of Roman, Greek, and Venetian ancient stone architecture all contained on a tiny island that residents call their living museum. On the other end, a 30-minute drive down the coast south from Split brings you to Omiš and the mouth of the Cetina River. The river forms a steep-sided valley renowned as an adventure sport hotspot with activities ranging from rafting to rock climbing.

But what makes Central Dalmatia truly special are its islands. One of the nearest, Brač, often recognized for its famous Zlatni Rat (Golden Cape) Beach, is an island of exceptional beauty and enchanting traditions, including a world-renowned stonemasonry school. West of Brač is the island of Šolta, a natural refuge which has been home to royalty, artists, pirates, and farmers alike throughout its unique history. Along the south side of Šolta, you will find several idyllic bays that are accessible only by sea. South of Brač rises the island of Hvar, home to one of Central Dalmatia's most exclusive party destinations, Hvar Town. Sixteenth-century Venetian buildings ring three sides of the Hvar Town harbor and its magnificent main square, home to the a Renaissance bell tower and the Cathedral of St. Stephen, dating back to the 6th century. The proud hilltop Fortica Fortress to the left of the main square beckons visitors to take in the view from higher ground.

Even farther out to sea lies wild, windswept Vis, Croatia's most distant inhabited island. There are two major settlements here: Vis Town and Komiža, the latter making the best starting point for a day trip to Modra Špilja (Blue Cave) on the islet of Biševo. Back on the mainland, a two-hour drive down the coast south of Split brings you to Makarska, a bustling seaside city built around a bay filled with fishing boats and backed by the stunningly rugged silhouette of Biokovo Mountain. Biokovo, with its St. George Peak soaring about 5,770 feet, is the third highest of Croatia's mountains and offers stunning views over the entire region.

Finally, Lastovo, Croatia's second–most distant inhabited island, remains firmly off the beaten track. Although it is geographically part of Southern Dalmatia, Lastovo's only public ferry and catamaran services to and from the mainland connect to Split.

Planning

When to Go

High season runs from July through August, when tourists from all over the world flock to the region and the weather averages from the mid-80s to the mid-90s Fahrenheit. Split Airport is connected to over 100 locations during this time, and dozens of different airlines have scheduled flights into Split, making it one of Croatia's most accessible destinations. Prices at this time can rise significantly, restaurant visits may require reservations, main beaches can be crowded, and it can be difficult to find a place to sleep if you haven't reserved in advance. Because of all this, local tourism ramps things up even more to provide the best experiences for its guests: museums and churches have extended hours, open-air bars and clubs bring nightlife to the fore, and numerous cultural festivals host performances starring international musicians, dancers, and actors.

Low season runs from November through April, when some hotels and restaurants close completely. Exceptions during these slower months are around Christmas and the New Year, when Advent markets pop up with food stands and live music galore, among other events organized to celebrate the holidays. The weather can be unreliable during this time, but if you're lucky, you can find yourself drinking morning coffee in the sunshine below a deep blue sky, against a backdrop of snowcapped mountains.

However, many tout mid-season, May through June and September through October, as the best time to visit the region. During these periods you'll miss the crowds, the weather is most often sunny and dry, and the sea is still warm enough for swimming. The region's hotels and restaurants will still be open, but their pace is slow enough to lend an air of true relaxation.

Getting Here and Around

AIR

Split is served by Split Airport (SPU) at Kaštela, 25 km (16 miles) northwest of the city center. The island of Brač is served by Brač Airport (BWK) at Gornji Humac, 13 km (8 miles) northeast of Bol. Pleso Transport is a shuttle service that takes passengers to and from the Split Airport and the main Split bus station. A one-way ticket is 30 Kn and the trip takes around 30 minutes. The shuttle usually runs hourly between 5 am and 7:30 pm every day.

Croatia's national carrier, Croatia Airlines, operates domestic flights from Split to Zagreb, Dubrovnik, Pula, Rijeka, and Osijek. During the summer high season, Croatia Airlines also flies directly between Split and Amsterdam, Athens, Barcelona, Belgrade, Berlin, Brussels, Bucharest, Copenhagen, Dusseldorf, Frankfurt, Hamburg, Istanbul, Lisbon, London (LHR and LGW), Lyon, Milan, Munich, Oslo, Paris, Prague, Rome, Stockholm, Vienna, Warsaw, and Zurich. Also through summer, Croatia Airlines flies nonstop from the island of Brač to Zagreb. Several major international carriers also fly to Split. Low-budget operators EasyJet, Jet2, Ryanair, and Wizz Air operate there as well. Keep in mind that flights and timetables are subject to change, so it is best to double-check all booking details directly with airlines.

AIRPORT CONTACTS Split Airport. ⊠ *Dr. Franje Tuđmana 1270, Kaštel Štafilic* ☎ *021/203–589* ⊕ *www.split-airport.hr.* **Brač Airport.** ⊠ *Brač Airport, Gornji Humac 145, Supetar* ☎ *021/559–701* ⊕ *www. airport-brac.hr.*

AIRPORT TRANSFER CONTACTS Pleso Transport. (*Pleso Prijevoz*) ☎ *21/203–1190* ⊕ *www.plesoprijevoz.hr.*

BOAT AND FERRY

From June through September, Jadro-linija, Croatia's largest boat transport company, usually runs services multiple times a week to Ancona, Italy, departing at 8 pm from Split and arriving in Ancona at 7 am the following day. The same vessels depart at 8 pm from Ancona to arrive in Split at 7 am. The journey time is approximately 11 hours in either direction. During winter, route frequency can be reduced. From April to October, Italian company SNAV runs services between Ancona and Split mutiple times a week as well. Departure times vary depending on the month and day of travel. The journey time is between nine and 13 hours in either direction.

Jadrolinija also operates domestic coastal routes that run all the way from Rijeka to Dubrovnik. Split has direct connections with Vis (journey time is approximately 150 minutes), Stari Grad on Hvar (journey time approximately 120 minutes), Hvar Town on Hvar (journey time approximately 100 minutes), Rogač on Šolta (journey time approximately 60 minutes), and Supetar on Brač (journey time approximately 60 minutes). From Sumartin on Brač, there's a daily, year-round (excluding some holidays) line with Makarska as well. Most Jadrolinija routes offer car transport too. Purchase your ticket online in advance whenever possible, especially during the high season when waiting until the last minute could mean waiting an extra day to travel.

CONTACTS Jadrolinija. ☎ *021/338–333* ⊕ *www.jadrolinija.hr.* **SNAV.** ☎ *021/322–252* ⊕ *www.snav.it.*

BUS

International buses arrive daily or weekly to Split from Belgrade, Berlin, Bled, Bologna, Bonn, Bratislava, Budapest, Dortmund, Dusseldorf, Frankfurt,

Geneve, Graz, Hamburg, Hannover, Kassel, Krakow, Ljubljana, Munich, Padua, Salzburg, Sarajevo, Stuttgart, Tuzla, Vienna, Villach, and Verona, among other cities. Timetables are subject to change, so before planning your trip, check with the Split Bus Station directly.

There are regular bus connections to destinations all over Croatia. There are approximately 25 buses per day to Zagreb, 10 to Dubrovnik, 10 to Zadar, and 10 to Rijeka. Some buses traveling south to Dubrovnik stop at Makarska en route while others going north to Zadar stop at Šibenik. In addition, regular local buses run multiple times a day to Trogir and down the coast to Omiš. Timetable information is available from the Split Bus Station or from their website.

CONTACTS Split Bus Station. ✉ *Obala Kneza Domogoja 12, Split* ☎ *021/329–180* ⊕ *www.ak-split.hr.*

CAR
You can certainly enjoy the delights of Split and the nearby islands of Brač, Hvar, and Vis without a car. However, you may wish to rent a vehicle for more flexibility in driving up the coast to Šibenik and Krka National Park, or down the coast to Omiš and Makarska, although these destinations are also well served by buses. Renting a car once you arrive on the islands is also an affordable option to see the entire island at your own pace.

While on the islands, you can also rent a bright-colored convertible VW Beetle, scooter, van, or beach buggy for the day and explore in style and at your own pace. Rapidus has a fleet of quirky cars that can be picked up and dropped off in Hvar Town, Stari Grad, Jelsa, and Vrboska on Hvar.

CONTACTS Rapidus Rent-a-Car.
✉ *Dubrovačka 61, Split* ☎ *095/922–9884* 🚗 ⊕ *www.rapidus.hr.*

TAXI
In Split the main taxi ranks lie at each end of the Riva (Obala Hrvatskog narodnog preporoda), in front of the *glavni pazar* (main open-air market), and in front of Hotel Bellevue. You will also find taxis waiting outside the Split train station. You can also call for a taxi in Split, or order an Uber or Bolt.

TRAIN
There are multiple day and night trains daily between Split and Zagreb (journey time between five and nine hours). In addition, there are multiple trains that travel daily between Split and Šibenik (journey times are approximately between one and five hours).

CONTACTS Split Train Station. ✉ *Domagojeva obala 9, Split* ☎ *1/3782–583* ⊕ *www.hzpp.hr/en.*

Restaurants

Eateries fall into two main categories here: you can eat in a *restoran* (restaurant) or *konoba* (tavern). Restaurants are more formal affairs, and often offer Croatian cuisine plus a choice of international dishes. In contrast, a konoba usually serves typical local dishes; many offer an authentic *marenda* (the equivalant of affordable lunch specials), often consisting of fish, vegetables, and a glass of wine. Central Dalmatian specialties are mainly seafood-based. *Rižot* (risotto)—especially the kind with fresh squid ink—and *brodet* (fish stewed in a rich tomato, onion, and wine sauce) are often featured on menus. Fish are often divided into two categories: "white" fish, including *brancin* (sea bass) and *kovač* (John Dory), are more expensive, while "blue" fish, including *srdele* (sardines) and *skuša* (mackerel), are cheaper. In restaurants, be aware that fresh fish is often priced by the kilogram, so prices can vary dramatically depending on how big your fish is. Another popular trend is eating at a charming Dalmatian wine bar, featuring the region's best local wines, cheeses, and prosciutto. Some offer a wide selection of original tapas, and all are eager to educate their clientele about local wines and provide suggestions on pairings.

Hotels

Central Dalmatia's best and most expensive hotels are in Split and Hvar Town on the island of Hvar. The region has accommodation options to suit all needs and budgets, including big-name upscale hotels, smaller boutique luxury hotels, and exclusive private villas. However, many visitors still prefer to rent a private room or apartment, a choice that offers value for money, direct contact with the locals, and (if you are lucky) an authentic stone cottage or apartment opening onto a terrace lined with potted geraniums and a blissful sea view. The high season runs from Easter to late October, and peaks during July and August, when prices rise significantly and when it may be difficult to find a place to sleep if you have not booked in advance.

Restaurant and hotel reviews have been shortened. For full information, visit Fodors.com. Restaurant prices are the average cost of a main course at dinner or, if dinner is not served, at lunch. Hotel prices are the lowest cost of a standard double room in high season.

What It Costs in Croatian kuna (Kn)			
$	$$	$$$	$$$$
RESTAURANTS			
under 65 Kn	65 Kn–125 Kn	126 Kn–200 Kn	over 200 Kn
HOTELS			
under 800 Kn	800 Kn–1,450 Kn	1,451 Kn–2,000 Kn	over 2,000 Kn

Tours

There are many tour options to choose from in Split. New agencies and itineraries pop up every year offering different options to explore the region. Many companies are committed to preserving the natural beauty, culture, and traditions of Dalmatia, seeking to provide tourists with authentic and personalized experiences.

★ Secret Dalmatia

These luxury tours are the best choice for adventurous foodies who want to experience Dalmatia's cultural heritage in an authentic way. Secret Dalmatia offers culinary tours, sailing, and biking trips that showcase not only great food, wine, and chefs, but also Croatia's blue seas, rolling hills, and forests in the hinterlands. Top-notch accommodation and transportation are arranged, too. ✉ *Ulica Marina Držića 15, Split* ☎ *091/567–1604* ⊕ *www. secretdalmatia.com.*

OH!SO

GUIDED TOURS | This company offers a number of all-inclusive road trips full of adventure and off-the-beaten-path explorations. Itineraries leave from and end in Split, or leave from Split and end in Dubrovnik. Think sunrise hikes to hidden waterfalls followed by yoga sessions, private glamping under views of the Milky Way, partying on Hvar, and more. ☎ *091/760–0018* ⊕ *www.ohso.co.*

Portal Day Tours

GUIDED TOURS | This company offers tours both of Split and the surrounding area, including Plitvice National Park. ✉ *Trg Republike 1, Split* ☎ *021/360–061* ⊕ *www.split-excursions.com.*

Visitor Information

CONTACTS Bol Tourist Board. ✉ *Porat bolskih pomoraca bb, Bol* ☎ *021/635–638* ⊕ *www.bol.hr/en.* **Hvar Tourist Board.** ✉ *Trg sv. Stjepana 42, Hvar* ☎ *021/741–059* ⊕ *www.visithvar.hr.* **Lastovo Tourist**

Board. ✉ *Pjevor 7, Lastovo* ☎ *020/801–018* ⊕ *www.tz-lastovo.hr.* **Makarska Tourist Board.** ✉ *Franjevački put 2, Makarska* ☎ *021/612–002* ⊕ *www.makarska-info.hr.* **Šibenik Tourist Board.** ✉ *Fausta Vrančića 18, Šibenik* ☎ *022/214–075* ⊕ *www.sibenik-tourism.hr.* **Split Tourist Board.** ✉ *Obala Hrv. narodnog preporoda 9, Split* ☎ *021/348–600* ⊕ *www.visitsplit.com.* **Trogir Tourist Board.** ✉ *Trg Ivana Pavla II/1, Trogir* ☎ *021/885–628* ⊕ *www.visittrogir.hr.* **Vis Tourist Board.** ✉ *Šetalište Stare Isse 5, Vis Town* ☎ *021/717–017* ⊕ *www.tz-vis.hr.*

Split

230 km (143 miles) north of Dubrovnik.

Split's ancient core and its centuries of history are spectacular. This is a city whose heritage dates back to prehistoric times and across the pre-Roman Illyrian period. The very heart of the city lies within the walls of Roman emperor Diocletian's palace, which was built in the 3rd century AD. Diocletian, born in the nearby Roman settlement of Salona around AD 245, achieved a successful career as a soldier and became emperor at the age of 40. It's thought that in 295, he ordered a vast palace complex to be built in his native Dalmatia, and when it was completed he stepped down from the throne and retired to his beloved homeland. Upon his death, he was laid to rest in an octagonal mausoleum, around which Split's magnificent cathedral was built.

Centuries later, Eurasian nomads migrated from the north, clashing with local inhabitants around the 7th century AD. Some locals found refuge within the palace walls. Over the years, the palace complex and its vast imperial apartments were divided up and expanded into living quarters. During the 10th century, Croatia got its first king, and the area developed into an important urban center for the new kindgom; by the 11th century, the small original settlement had expanded beyond the ancient walls.

From the 15th through 19th centuries, Split saw Venetian and Hapsburg rule. In the early Middle Ages, the city became one of the Adriatic's main trading ports and saw a blossoming of splendid Renaissance buildings, art, and literature. During the 19th century, an overland connection to Central Europe was established by the construction of the Split–Zagreb–Vienna railway line.

After World War II, Split saw a period of rapid urban expansion; industrialization accelerated, and the suburbs extended to accommodate high-rise apartment blocks. Today the historic center of Split is included on UNESCO's list of World Heritage Sites.

GETTING HERE AND AROUND
Central Dalmatia's coastal capital is easy to get around and offers ferries to popular tourist spots like the islands of Brač and Hvar. There are also local buses available to visit nearby towns like Šibenik and Trogir.

 Sights

The Old Town (locally referred to as *Grad*, meaning town), where many stunning architectural monuments are found, lies within the walls of Diocletian's Palace, which fronts the seafront promenade, also known as the Riva. West of the center, Varoš is a conglomeration of stone fishermen's cottages built into a hillside, behind which rises 585-foot-tall Marjan Hill, a 3½-km-long (2-mile-long) peninsula covered with pinewoods and Mediterranean shrubbery. Southeast of the center, the ferry port, bus station, and train station are grouped close together on Obala Kneza Domagoja. A waterfront continuation of the Riva, known as West Coast, is dotted with cool cafés; it's a three-minute walk from the center of

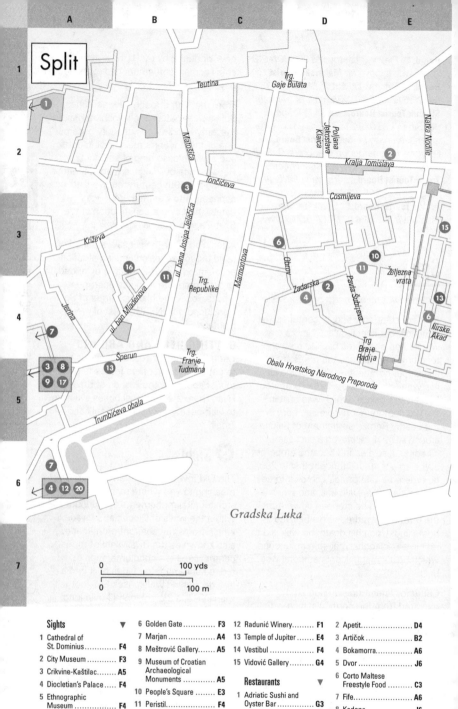

Split

| A | B | C | D | E |

Gradska Luka

0   100 yds
0   100 m

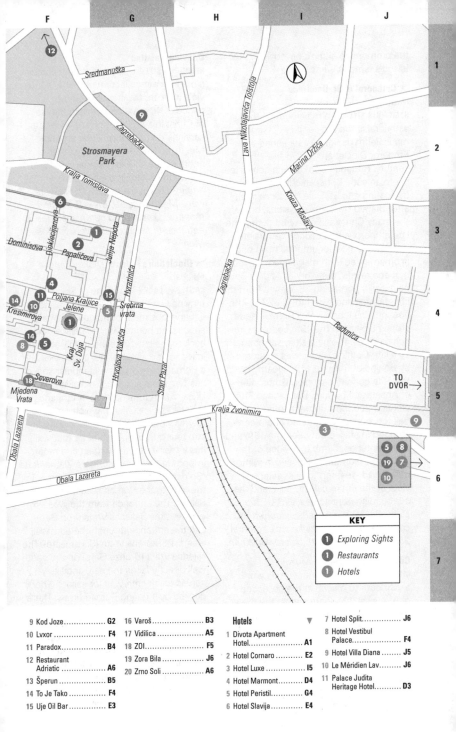

the promenade and it's paved with Brač Island's famous white stone.

★ Cathedral of St. Dominius
(*Katedrala sv. Duje*)
RELIGIOUS SITE | The main body of this cathedral is the 3rd-century octagonal mausoleum designed as a shrine to Emperor Diocletian. During the 7th century, refugees from Salona converted it into an early Christian church, ironically dedicating it to St. Duje (St. Domnius), after Bishop Domnius of Salona, one of the many Christians martyred during the late emperor's persecution campaign. The cathedral's monumental main door is ornamented with magnificent carved wooden reliefs, the work of Andrija Buvina of Split, portraying 28 scenes from the life of Christ and dated to 1214. The interior contains a hexagonal Romanesque stone pulpit from the 13th century with rich carvings. The high altar, surmounted by a late-Gothic canopy, was executed by Bonino of Milan in 1427. Nearby is the 15th-century canopied Gothic altar of Anastasius by Juraj Dalmatinac. The elegant, 200-foot, Romanesque-Gothic bell tower was constructed and reconstructed in stages between the 13th and 20th centuries. Climb to the top of the bell tower (sometimes closed in winter during bad weather) for a spectacular view of the entire palace, Split, and the surrounding Adriatic Sea. ⊠ *3 Ul. Kraj Sv. Duje, Grad* ⊕ *www.visitsplit.com/en/527/cathedral-of-saint-domnius* ⊠ *Cathedral 25 Kn (including crypt); bell tower 20 Kn.*

City Museum (*Gradski Muzej*)
MUSEUM | Split's city museum is worth a visit both to marvel at the collection of medieval weaponry and to see the interior of this splendid 15th-century town house. The dining room, on the first floor, is furnished just as it would have been when the Papalić family owned the house, giving some idea of how the aristocracy of that time lived. ⊠ *Papalićeva 1, Grad* ☎ *021/360–171* ⊕ *www.mgst.net* ⊠ *25 Kn* ☾ *Closed Sun.*

Crikvine-Kaštilac
RELIGIOUS SITE | This small chapel contains a magnificent collection of Ivan Meštrović's work that was produced over a period of 40 years and depicts the life of Christ in a series of bas-relief wood carvings that many consider among Meštrović's finest work. Viewing the entire series should not be rushed and it's worth visiting in conjunction with his other works in the gallery. ⊠ *Šetalište Ivana Meštrovića 39, Meje* ⊕ *mdc.hr/mestrovic/kastelet* ⊠ *50 Kn, includes entrance to Meštrović Gallery* ☾ *Closed Mon.*

★ Diocletian's Palace (*Dioklecijanova Palača*)
CASTLE/PALACE | The home of Split's thriving Old Town, Diocletian's Palace is a marvelous maze of restaurants, cafés, shops, and boutiques. The palace dates back to the late 3rd century AD, and originally served as both a luxurious villa and a Roman garrison. Its rectangular shape has two main streets: Dioklecijanova Ulica, which runs north to south, and Poljana Krajlice Jelene, which runs east to west, that divide the palace complex into four quarters. Each of its four walls has a main gate, the largest and most important being the northern Zlatna Vrata (Golden Gate), which once opened onto the road to the Roman settlement of Salona. The entrance from the western wall was the Željezna Vrata (Iron Gate), and the entrance through the east wall was the Srebrena Vrata (Silver Gate). The Mjedna Vrata (Bronze Gate) on the south wall directly faces the sea, and likely served as an entryway for sailors who docked by it during Roman times. There are still more than 1,000 people living within the walls today. ■TIP→ Hire an experienced private guide that can give you a walking tour in the early morning hours in order to experience the true history of the palace walls without the crowds. ⊠ *Obala Hrvatskog Narodnog Preporoda, Grad* ⊕ *www.diocletianspalace.org.*

Split's Old Town is actually located within the historic walls of Diocletian's Palace.

Ethnographic Museum (*Etnografski Muzej*)
MUSEUM | Occupying a splendid location within the walls of Diocletian's Palace, this museum displays traditional Dalmatian folk costumes and local antique furniture among other objects that give visitors a look into everyday life in historic Dalmatia. ■ TIP→ **If you are staying in Split for more than a day, be sure to pick up your free SplitCard, which gives you free entry to certain museums and galleries and reduced rates at other establishment, including some restaurants and cafés. Just ask the staff at your hotel or go to the nearest Tourist Information Center to pick one up.** ✉ *Iza Vestibula 4, Grad* ☎ *021/344–161* ⊕ *www.etnografski-muzej-split.hr* 🖭 *20 Kn, free if you have the SplitCard* ☉ *Closed Sun.*

Golden Gate (*Zlatna Vrata*)
LOCAL INTEREST | Formerly the main entrance into the palace, the northern Zlatna Vrata is the most visited of the four gates—two guards in Roman costume stand here throughout the summer. Just outside the Zlatna Vrata stands Meštrović's gigantic bronze **statue**

of **Grgur Ninski** (Bishop Gregory of Nin). During the 10th century, the bishop campaigned for the use of the Slav language in the Croatian Church, as opposed to Latin, and found himself at odds with Rome. This statue was created in 1929 and first placed on Peristil, then moved here in 1954. Note the big toe on the left foot, which is considered to be a good luck charm and has been worn gold and smooth through years of rubbing. ✉ *Zlatna Vrata, Grad.*

Marjan (*Marjan Hill*)
CITY PARK | Situated on a 3½-km-long (2-mile-long) peninsula covered with pine trees and Mediterranean shrubs, 585-foot-tall Marjan Hill has been a protected nature reserve since 1964. It is known as the "lungs of the city" because of all its greenery and the fact that locals flock to it on weekends as a nearby recreational area. There are stunning views from the top and rocky beach areas circling the peninsula. Paths crisscrossing the grounds are suitable for biking and jogging. There are 13 small churches and

Emperor Diocletian

Many powerful state leaders tend toward eccentricity, and Roman emperor Diocletian was no exception. Born to a humble family in Dalmatia, he went on to govern the empire for 20 years, proving to be an astute and innovative leader. However, he was also something of a megalomaniac. Believing himself to be Jupiter's representative on Earth, he set about persecuting Christians, ordering religious scriptures to be burnt, churches destroyed, and thousands of believers executed. He dressed in robes of satin and gold, along with a crown embedded with pearls and shoes studded with precious stones. His imperial apartments were guarded by eunuchs, and it's said that anyone who came into his presence was obliged to fall prostrate on the ground out of respect. Among his many well-known building schemes are the Baths of Diocletian in Rome, a vast complex of marble and mosaics, constructed by 10,000 Christian prisoners for the pleasure of some 3,000 bathers.

chapels throughout the park, including St. Jerome (sv. Jeronim), which was built in the 15th century into a rock face and includes Renaissance-style stone reliefs on the walls. The beaches on this side are more relaxed and offer shade, but there is limited access for cars, which helps to preserve the wilderness of the park. There are bikes to rent and water sports available too. ⊠ *Marjan Hill, Marjan* ⊕ *www.marjan-parksuma.hr.*

★ **Meštrović Gallery** (*Galerija Meštrović*)
MUSEUM | A short walk from the Riva, this must-see gallery is in a tranquil location overlooking the sea, surrounded by extensive gardens. Ivan Meštrović (1883-1962), one of Europe's greatest 20th-century sculptors, originally designed this building as his summer residence during the 1920s and '30s. Some 200 of his sculptural works in wood, marble, stone, and bronze are on display, both indoors and out. The gallery is a green oasis in the center of the city with an open-air café that is frequented by children and families during the day and young locals in the evening. It's a great place to escape the crowded city streets and enjoy a refreshing drink surrounded by a stunning collection of a master's work.

⊠ *Šetalište Ivana Meštrovicá 46, Meje* ☏ *021/340–800* ⊕ *www.mestrovic.hr/ en/museum/mestrovic-gallery* ⊠ *50 Kn, includes entrance to Crikvine-Kaštilac* ☉ *Closed Mon.*

Museum of Croatian Archaeological Monuments (*Muzej Hrvatskih Arheološki Spomenika*)
MUSEUM | One of the oldest Croatian museums, it houses more than 20,000 Croatian archaeological artifacts, only a quarter of which are regularly on display. Among the most interesting exhibits are fine stone carvings decorated with traditional plaitwork designs. In the garden are several *stećci,* medieval monolithic tombstones. The museum also conducts archaeological excavations in the southern Croatian regions between the Cetina and Zrmanja rivers and has a large collection of cultural and historical guidebooks on early medieval monuments in Croatia. ⊠ *Šetalište Ivana Meštrovića 18, Meje* ☏ *021/323–901* ⊕ *www.mhas-split. hr* ⊠ *20 Kn.*

People's Square (*Narodni Trg*)
PLAZA | This is the main city square (locally known as a *pjaca*) and can be accessed from Diocletian's Palace through the

western or Iron Gate. Historically this was an important gathering place for Splićani (people from Split), and remains so today. In the 15th century, several major public buildings were constructed here: the Town Hall (that today houses a contemporary art gallery), plus the Rector's Palace and a theater. The latter two were sadly demolished by the Habsburgs in the 19th century. A Secessionist building at the west end of the square stands as a testament to that era. Once the city center of administration, it is now a prime location for kicking your feet up and indulging in one of the many restaurants and cafés that line the white marble square. ✉ *Narodni trg, Grad.*

Peristil (*Peristyle*)

HISTORIC SITE | From Roman times to the present day, this has been the main public meeting place within the palace walls. The spacious central courtyard is flanked by marble columns topped with Corinthian capitals and richly ornamented cornices linked by arches. There are six columns on both the east and west sides and four more at the south end, which mark the monumental entrance to the Vestibul. During summer, occasional live concerts are held here. ✉ *Peristil, Grad.*

Radunić Winery

WINERY/DISTILLERY | After an extensive DNA quest for the European sort from which Zinfandel originates, a group of scientists from UC Davis and University of Zagreb finally found the match in an almost extinct Croatian vine called Crljenak Kaštelanski. The small vineyard where Crljenak Kaštelanski was found belongs to a local firefighter, Ivica Radunić. His family's wine-growing tradition goes back several generations, but their operation is still informal; this isn't your usual tasting-and-tour winery. Ivica and his wife make a small amount of highly prestigious, award-winning wine bottles a year, and are happy to show any true wine lovers around their minute, no-frills Radunić Winery. It is recommended to call ahead to make sure they have time to prepare for your visit. ✉ *Narodnog Preporoda 46-Brce, Kaštel Novi* ☎ *021/231–138* 🖃 *ivicaradunic@vip.hr.*

Temple of Jupiter (*Jupiterov Hram*)

ARCHAEOLOGICAL SITE | Roman Emperor Diocletian ordered the construction of this temple to worship the god Jupiter. It was eventually converted into a baptistery by Christians, who were greatly persecuted during the emperor's reign. The entrance is guarded by a black-granite sphinx that stands in front of the cathedral. The sphinx, brought to the palace from Egypt by Diocletian, was partially destroyed by Christians as revenge for the persecution they suffered during his rule. Inside, beneath the coffered barrel vault and ornamented cornice, the 11th-century baptismal font is adorned with a stone relief showing a medieval Croatian king on his throne. Directly behind it stands the bronze statue of St. John the Baptist, a work from Meštrović. ✉ *Kraj sv. Ivana 2, Grad* 🖃 *15 Kn.*

Vestibul

BUILDING | The cupola of this domed space would once have been decorated with marble and mosaics. Today there's only a round hole in the top of the dome, but it produces a stunning effect: picture the dark interior, the blue sky or a star-lit night above, and the tip of the cathedral's bell tower framed in the opening. ✉ *Peristil, Grad.*

Vidović Gallery (*Galerija Vidović*)

MUSEUM | Emanuel Vidović (1870–1953) is acknowledged as one of Split's greatest painters and in this gallery, you can see 69 of his original works, bought by the city from his family. Large, bold canvases depict local landmarks cast in hazy light, while the sketches done outdoors before returning to his studio to paint are playful and colorful. ✉ *Poljana kraljice Jelene bb, Grad* ☎ *021/360–155* ⊕ *www.galerija-vidovic.com* 🖃 *10 Kn; guided tours in English 100 Kn* ⊗ *Closed Mon.*

🍴 Restaurants

Adriatic Sushi and Oyster Bar

$$ | **JAPANESE FUSION** | Eighty percent of this restaurant's menu comes directly from the Adriatic Sea and, to take it a step further, most of the ingredients in general are sourced within a 50-km (30-mile) radius of the premises from the yellowfin tuna to sheep's cheese and Dalmatian prosciutto. The atmosphere is relaxed and the wine menu has been well researched to pair well with sushi. **Known for:** locally sourced ingredients; superfresh seafood and sushi; good wine list. [$] *Average main: 100 Kn* ✉ *Carrarina Poljana, 4, Grad* ☎ *099/360–7777* 🌐 *www.adriatic-sushi.com.*

Apetit

$$$ | **MEDITERRANEAN** | A small, low-key restaurant, tucked away on the second floor of a 15th-century palazzo just off the main square, Apetit serves traditional dishes that are made with fresh, locally sourced, high-quality ingredients. Some favorites to look out for are *Jadranska lignja sa žara* (Adriatic grilled squid) or a house specialty, *rezanci s kozicama* (homemade tagliatelle with prawn). **Known for:** delicious tuna; homemade tagliatelle; romantic setting. [$] *Average main: 140 Kn* ✉ *Šubićeva 5, Grad* ☎ *021/332–549* 🌐 *www.apetit-split.hr.*

Artičok

$$ | **FUSION** | This funky restaurant serves exciting food with well-selected ingredients. The owner is a designer and has taken great care to ensure that an enjoyable dining experience is accompanied by an equally satisfying visual experience. **Known for:** fish tacos; super fresh ingredients; hip decor. [$] *Average main: 75 Kn* ✉ *Bana Josipa Jelačića 19* ☎ *021/819–324* 🌐 *www.facebook.com/articoksplit.*

Bokamorra (*Bokamorra Pizzaurant & Cocktails*)

$$ | **PIZZA** | **FAMILY** | You'll find some of the best pizza in Split at Bokamorra, thanks to its dough that is handmade and aged for 48 hours. Pizzas are topped with locally sourced ingredients, from smoked meats to truffles. **Known for:** best pizza in town; unique house cocktails; fun and family-friendly atmosphere. [$] *Average main: 80 Kn* ✉ *Obala Ante Trumbića 16* ☎ *099/4177–191* 🌐 *www.facebook.com/bokamorra.*

Dvor

$$ | **MEDITERRANEAN** | Located in a quiet area a few miles out of town, Dvor offers up a superior rendition of Croatian seafood, professional service, and a broad selection of local and international wines, all with garden seating and outstanding views over the sea. There's an outdoor grill as well as parking, which is a luxury in Split. **Known for:** stunning outdoor location; superb tasting menu; nice selection of wine. [$] *Average main: 120 Kn* ✉ *Put Firula 14* ☎ *021/571–513* 🌐 *www.facebook.com/dvor.split.*

Corto Maltese Freestyle Food

$$ | **MEDITERRANEAN** | **FAMILY** | Decorated with a bit of the wit and themes from the beloved Italian comic strip of Corto Maltese, this restaurant offers traditional Croatian ingredients prepared in a healthy way and explained on a funny, irreverent menu. With lots of seafood and salad options, the presentation of food is eclipsed only by the flavor. **Known for:** quirky menu descriptions; healthy cooking techniques; open kitchen setting. [$] *Average main: 100 Kn* ✉ *Obrov 7, near fish market* ☎ *021/587–201* 🌐 *www.cortomaltese.rocks.*

★ Fife

$ | **MEDITERRANEAN** | This local hangout, one of Split's most popular restaurants for years, offers traditional dishes commonly found on Dalmatian dinner tables. The food is hearty, filling, and affordable, with a daily selection of local specialties and plenty of fish dishes that include sardines, mackerel, and mullet. **Known for:** affordable fish dishes; tasty chicken tomato stew; longstanding local favorite.

[$] *Average main: 65 Kn* ✉ *Trubičeva Obala 11, Matejuška* ☎ *021/345–223* 🌐 *www.facebook.com/buffetfife* 💳 *No credit cards.*

Kadena

$$$$ | MEDITERRANEAN | Spearheaded by renowned head chef Damir Sertić, Kadena serves Mediterranean fare with a contemporary twist in a modern and sleek interior space. Don't miss the *salata od hobotnice* (octopus salad), a trademark dish of Dalmatia. **Known for:** traditional Dalmatian dishes; modern, sleek atmosphere; renowned chefs. [$] *Average main: 170 Kn* ✉ *Ivana pl. Zajca 4* ☎ *021/389–400* 🌐 *www.restorankadena.com/en.*

Kod Joze

$$ | MEDITERRANEAN | This typical Dalmatian restaurant is relaxed and romantic, with exposed stone walls and heavy wooden furniture illuminated by candlelight. Located just outside the palace walls, a five-minute walk from Zlatna Vrata (Golden Gate), it is slightly hidden and easy to miss. **Known for:** romantic ambience; excellent seafood risotto; al fresco dining on the open-air terrace. [$] *Average main: 120 Kn* ✉ *Sredmanuška 4, Manuš* ☎ *021/347–397.*

Lvxor

$$ | SEAFOOD | This is a perfect place to sit over coffee or a glass of local wine and absorb the 2,000 years of magnificent architecture that surround you. The morning-to-night restaurant serves Mediterranean-style breakfast, lunch, and dinner. **Known for:** views of surrounding architecture; Adriatic cuisine options; nice spot to get a drink. [$] *Average main: Kn75* ✉ *Kraj sv. Ivana 11, Grad* ☎ *021/341–082* 🌐 *www.lvxor.hr/en.*

★ Paradox

$$$ | WINE BAR | Split's top tapas and wine bar is *the* place to gather for wine aficionados. The superb waitstaff are well-versed in their craft and eager to share their knowledge of more than 120 different wine labels and the foods with which to pair them. **Known for:** happening atmosphere; snazzy rooftop location; live music and local artwork. [$] *Average main: 150 Kn* ✉ *Ulica bana Josipa Jelačića 3, Grad* ☎ *021/787–778* 🌐 *www.paradox.hr* ⏲ *Closed Mon.*

Restaurant Adriatic

$$$ | SEAFOOD | Above the ACI Marina, at the foot of Marjan Hill and close to the gardens of Sveti Stipan, this seafood restaurant has a light and airy minimalist interior, plus a summer terrace where you can watch the yachts sail in and out of port. In the vein of "slow food," the kitchen gives great care to seasonal ingredients and presentation. **Known for:** fabulous views; classic Croatian fine dining; spot for local celebrities. [$] *Average main: 170 Kn* ✉ *Sustipanski put 2, Zvoncac* ☎ *021/398–560* 🌐 *www.restaurantadriatic.com.*

Šperun

$$ | SEAFOOD | This cozy restaurant has become popular because of its reasonably priced menu and quaint atmosphere. The Italo-Dalmatian menu features pasta dishes, seafood risottos, and old-fashioned local fish specialties such as *bakalar na crveno* (dried cod cooked in a rich tomato and onion sauce) and *brudet* (fish stew). **Known for:** classic Croatian fare; hearty fish stew for lunch; small dining room. [$] *Average main: 100 Kn* ✉ *Šperun 3, Varoš* ☎ *021/346–999.*

To Je Tako

$ | MEXICAN | Located in a narrow back alley, this cozy little space attracts a young, fun crowd with their tasty muddled drinks and Dalmatian take on Latin American street food, including tacos, burritos, and empanadas. To Je Tako offers breakfast, lunch, and dinner, as well as a good craft beer selection and gluten-free options, all at great prices. **Known for:** good food at great prices; unusual cuisine for Croatia; delicious tacos and empanadas. [$] *Average main: 60 Kn* ✉ *Ulica Kraj Svetog Ivana*

5 ☎ 021/553–021 ⊕ www.tojetako.com
🖃 No credit cards.

★ Uje Oil Bar

$$ | **MEDITERRANEAN** | Stop in at Uje and
sample some of the region's best olive
oil, as well as a choice selection of
Croatia's best cheese, prosciutto, and
wine. The quaint back-alley tapas (locally
known as *pikulece*) bar showcases
popular local chefs during the off-season,
changes its menu regularly, and sources
many ingredients from local organic
family farms. **Known for:** good selection
of olive oils for sale; delicious tapas;
lots of crowds so get here early or late
in the evening. $ *Average main: 90 Kn*
🖂 Dominisova 6, Grad ☎ 095/200–8009
⊕ www.oilbar.hr.

Varoš

$$$ | **EASTERN EUROPEAN** | The dining-room
walls here are hung with seascapes and
fishing nets, and the waiters wear traditional Dalmatian waistcoats. The fresh
fish and *pržene lignje* (fried squid) are
excellent, and there's also a reasonable
choice of Croatian meat dishes. **Known
for:** fresh seafood dishes; authentic
atmosphere with traditional decor;
location close to city center. $ *Average
main: 140 Kn* 🖂 Ban Mladenova 9, Varoš
☎ 021/396–138.

Vidilica (*Teraca Vidilica*)

$$ | **CAFÉ** | This lounge-style café terrace
with breathtaking views is a good spot
for lunch or a sunset dinner. They're
also open for breakfast starting at 8 am.
Known for: quick bites; panoramic sea
views; beautiful sunsets. $ *Average
main: 90 Kn* 🖂 Prilaz Vladimira Nazora 1,
Marjan ☎ 095/871–8792.

ZOI

$$$$ | **MEDITERRANEAN** | This restaurant is
located right by Diocletian's Palace on
the Riva, and has the fabulous views to
prove it. Grab a seat on the terrace under
the palm trees and enjoy high quality
Adriatic cuisine. **Known for:** sea-to-table
dishes; central location; pretty terrace

with views. $ *Average main: 190 Kn*
🖂 Obala hrvatskog narodnog preporoda
23 ☎ 021/637–491 ⊕ www.zoi.hr.

★ Zora Bila

$$$ | **MEDITERRANEAN** | This seaside Med-
iterranean restaurant is spearheaded by
two of the area's most celebrated chefs,
Sandra and Dane Tahirović. Their haute,
edgy takes on classic Adriatic cuisine
include dishes like tuna tartare served in
a sea urchin (with the spines on). **Known
for:** haute Adriatic cuisine; good selection
of seafood; location right by the sea.
$ *Average main: 180 Kn* 🖂 Setaliste Pet-
ra Preradovica 2 ☎ 021/782–711 ⊕ www.
facebook.com/ZoraBilabySandraiDane.

Zrno Soli

$$$$ | **MEDITERRANEAN** | Located right
on the ACI Marina in Split, "Zrno Soli"
means "grain of salt". This hot spot
serves Mediterranean cuisine such as
crni jakov, scallops with Adriatic prawns
and cuttlefish ink-blackened gnocchi.
Known for: great location for on-boat visitors; views of ACI Marina; fresh Adriatic
fish. $ *Average main: 200 Kn* 🖂 Uvala
baluni 8 ☎ 021/399–333 ⊕ www.zrnosoli.
hr.

 Hotels

★ Divota Apartment Hotel

$$ | **B&B/INN** | **FAMILY** | Set in row of 13
ancient stone houses in the charming
neighborhood of Veli Varoš, these 29
beautifully renovated apartments and
rooms have been lovingly re-imagined to
create a clean, bright, modern accommo-
dation that preserves historic elements,
like the steep tiled roofs and tiny shut-
tered windows. **Pros:** spa and concierge
services available; unique hotel experi-
ence; great location. **Cons:** apartments
are close together; reception is located
in a separate nearby office; kitchenettes
in some apartments are basic. $ *Rooms
from: 1,200 Kn* 🖂 Plinarska 75, Varoš
☎ 021/782–700 ⊕ www.divota.hr 🛏 29
rooms ⊙ *Free breakfast.*

Hotel Cornaro

$$$$ | HOTEL | This sleek four-star hotel is a short walk from the city's car-free city center and close to all the main attractions. **Pros:** hearty buffet breakfast; spa and rooftop bar; alfresco dining with great views. **Cons:** parking is expensive; spa not included in all room rates; some rooms can be a little noisy. $ *Rooms from: 2000 Kn* ✉ *Sinjska 6 and Kralja Tomislava 9* ☎ *021/644–200* ⊕ *www.cornarohotel.com* ⇌ *156 rooms* ⦿ *Free breakfast.*

Hotel Luxe

$$$ | HOTEL | FAMILY | Located just outside the palace walls and close to the port, this contemporary boutique hotel makes a great base for exploring the city. **Pros:** nearby free parking; a well organized and functional fitness and wellness area; generous breakfast buffet. **Cons:** additional meals must be catered by a nearby restaurant; some rooms on first floor have no sea view; not in a quiet neighborhood. $ *Rooms from: 1900 Kn* ✉ *Kralja Zvonimira 6, Grad* ☎ *021/314–444* ⊕ *www.hotelluxesplit.com* ⇌ *30 rooms* ⦿ *Free breakfast.*

Hotel Marmont

$$$ | HOTEL | This beautifully refurbished, 15th-century stone building is in the heart of the city and offers guests a quiet retreat from the hustle and bustle of Split's Old Town. **Pros:** 10% discount for hotel guests in restaurant; rooftop terrace with a view; comfortable and smartly designed rooms. **Cons:** no parking nearby; some rooms have unattractive views of adjacent walls or windows; rooms can feel small. $ *Rooms from: 1500 Kn* ✉ *Zadarska 13-21, Grad* ☎ *021/308–060* ⊕ *www.marmonthotel.com* ⇌ *22 rooms* ⦿ *Free breakfast.*

Hotel Peristil

$$ | HOTEL | One of only a handful of hotels within the palace walls, Hotel Peristil is located behind the cathedral and just inside Srebrena Vrata, the city gate leading to the open-air market. **Pros:** good value for money based on location; friendly, attentive staff; lovely open-air restaurant terrace. **Cons:** often fully booked; nearby parking difficult; limited facilities. $ *Rooms from: 1350 Kn* ✉ *Poljana kraljice Jelene 5, Grad* ☎ *021/329–070* ⊕ *www.hotelperistil.com* ⇌ *12 rooms* ⦿ *Free breakfast.*

Hotel Slavija

$$$ | HOTEL | Split's longest continuously working hotel since it opened in 1900, Slavija occupies a historic building within the Diocletian's Palace walls that dates back to the 16th century. **Pros:** cool historic building; great nightlife nearby; comfortable rooms. **Cons:** no restaurant; parking is not convenient; can get loud during high season. $ *Rooms from: 1575 Kn* ✉ *Buvinina 2, Grad* ☎ *021/323–840* ⊕ *www.hotelslavija.hr* ⇌ *25 rooms* ⦿ *Free breakfast.*

Hotel Split

$$$$ | HOTEL | Located on the outskirts of the city, Hotel Split offers every guest a comfortable, eco-friendly room with sea views and quality furnishings. **Pros:** spa and fitness facilities; panoramic elevator; easy access into city. **Cons:** on-site parking on the pricier side; crowded breakfast area during peak season; located outside of Old Town. $ *Rooms from: 2100 Kn* ✉ *Strožanačka 20, Podstrana* ☎ *021/420–420* ⊕ *www.hotelsplit.hr* ⇌ *40 rooms* ⦿ *All-inclusive.*

★ Hotel Vestibul Palace

$$$$ | B&B/INN | Three palaces from different eras have been combined to form this intimate Old Town standout with interiors that have been carefully renovated to expose Roman stone- and brick-work, along with more modern, minimalist designer details. **Pros:** cool history and standout architecture; superb concierge service; private boat available for excursions. **Cons:** expensive for most of the season; often fully booked; not great if you have trouble with stairs.

[$] *Rooms from: 3000 Kn* ✉ *Iza Vestibula 4, Grad* ☎ *021/329–329* 🌐 *www.vestibulpalace.com* 🛏 *11 rooms* 🍴 *Free breakfast.*

Hotel Villa Diana

$$ | **B&B/INN** | **FAMILY** | On a peaceful side street just a five-minute walk east of the Old Town, Villa Diana is a traditional Dalmatian stone building with green wooden shutters. **Pros:** close to Old Town; more affordable alternative to nearby larger, more expensive hotels; intimate setting that provides individual attention. **Cons:** often fully booked; located on a busy road leading into Split; parking costs extra. [$] *Rooms from: 1125 Kn* ✉ *Kuzmanića 3, Radunica* ☎ *021/482–460* 🌐 *www.villadiana.hr* 🛏 *6 rooms* 🍴 *Free breakfast.*

Le Méridien Lav

$$$$ | **RESORT** | **FAMILY** | A world unto its own, this vast, self-contained complex was Split's first five-star hotel. **Pros:** beautifully designed modern interior; excellent sports facilities; luxurious spa. **Cons:** far from the center of Split; expensive; large and impersonal. [$] *Rooms from: 2000 Kn* ✉ *Grljevačka 2A, Podstrana* ☎ *021/500–500* 🌐 *www.marriott.com/hotels/travel/spumd-le-meridien-lav-split* 🛏 *381 rooms* 🍴 *Free breakfast.*

Palace Judita Heritage Hotel

$$$$ | **B&B/INN** | Only a couple of steps away from the Diocletian Palace, the Palace Judita is quite possibly the best lodging in the city. **Pros:** beyond comfortable and spacious rooms; perfect location; excellent rooftop terrace, library, and bar. **Cons:** the hotel is small, so it's always full; parking not included; in the pedestrian-only area of Split so can be hard to get to with baggage. [$] *Rooms from: 2260 Kn* ✉ *Narodni trg 4, Grad* ☎ *021/420–220* 🌐 *www.juditapalace.com* 🛏 *11 rooms* 🍴 *Free breakfast.*

Nightlife

Split is much livelier at night during the summer season, when bars stay open late and discos hold open-air parties by the sea. Throughout the summer, many bars and clubs have extended licenses and stay open well into the early morning hours. You'll often see posters around town announcing special events. On the doorstep of the Riva sits one of the best starting points for a night out in Split: Matejuška. The small bay has been used as a dock by fishermen for centuries, and today the rocks surrounding the dock are a BYOB hang-out spot for locals and tourists (mainly young people). You're likely to make new friends here while gazing out at the sea, and probably hearing a few guitar twangs from among the crowd before heading to a bar or club in town.

BARS

Academia Club Ghetto

BARS/PUBS | With a colorful, bohemian interior and a courtyard garden lit with flaming torches, Academia pulls in the cool, young, artsy crowd and hosts occasional exhibitions and concerts. ✉ *Dosud 10, Grad* ☎ *021/346–879* 🌐 *www.facebook.com/academiaclubghetto.*

Splash

BARS/PUBS | This is a rock music, biker-style bar that regularly offers live music performances by up-and-coming bands from the region. Expect a fun, welcoming atmosphere, plus a solid selection of beer at affordable prices. ✉ *Vicka Andrića, Manuš* 🌐 *www.facebook.com/splash.caffebar.*

Teak

BARS/PUBS | Close to Zlatna Vrata, Teak is a small café with an exposed-stonework-and-wood interior plus tables outside throughout summer. It's popular with highbrow locals who come here to leaf through the piles of international newspapers and magazines. ✉ *Majstora Jurja 11, Grad* ☎ *021/362–596.*

⭐ To Je To

CAFES—NIGHTLIFE | This happening café-bar showcases a careful selection of Croatian craft beers and locally roasted organic coffee beans. The owners are passionate about their coffee and beer and keep things fun with karaoke, live music, quiz nights, and other specialty events. The bar's name translates as "That's It," and that is exactly how you feel once you get here. The fun vibe of To Je To is sure to leave you with a smile. ✉ *Pistura 3, Grad* ☎ *021/413–139* ⊕ *www.facebook.com/ tojetocaffe.*

⭐ Tortuga

BARS/PUBS | A barbecue-centered restaurant during the day, Tortuga turns into one of Split's hottest bars come midnight, when the kitchen closes. Expect themed live DJ parties on the weekends. Tortuga is one of the spots dotting Split's biggest nightlife hub, the beach stretch of Bačvice Bay. ✉ *Bačvice, Bacvica* ☎ *021/488–490* ⊕ *www.facebook.com/ tortuga.grill.pub.*

CLUBS AND DISCOS

Club Bačvice (*Caffe-Club Bačvice*)
DANCE CLUBS | At the center of Split's mini-Ibiza-like stretch of beach, you'll find Club Bačvice, but there is a whole slew of venues along the way with pulsating music until the wee hours of the night. By day, you can sip coffee at this café. ✉ *Preradovićevo šetalište 2, Bacvica* ☎ *095/510–2271.*

Gaga

CAFES—NIGHTLIFE | Just behind the main pjaca, Gaga is one of the primary evening hang-out joints within the palace walls. The cocktails are comparatively less expensive than in other bars and the music is funky, with themed and karaoke nights organized on occassion, too. In summer it is frequented mostly by young tourists sharing their Croatian experiences. ✉ *Iza lože 5, Grad* ☎ *021/348–257* ⊕ *www.facebook.com/cocktailbargaga.*

Kocka

MUSIC CLUBS | Run by a coalition of local youth organizations, Kocka is the primary underground alternative club in Split. Over the past 20 years, they have hosted thousands of bands and artists from the region and from around the world with shows, exhibits, and other events. The club is located within a complex hosting its own independent library, studio, gallery, two stages, bar, and offices. It attracts hordes of young people year-round seeking to listen to everything from dub and trip-hop to ska and metal. ✉ *Ulica Slobode 28* ☎ *021/540–537* ⊕ *www.kum-split.hr.*

Vanilla

DANCE CLUBS | In summer Vanilla hosts pool parties for "Yacht Week" partygoers with international DJs every Friday night. Located about a 20-minute walk from the center of town near the public pools, there's a great terrace and a rotating bar. During the year, it is a trendy place for fans of all sorts of music from international hip-hop and rock to turbofolk and Croatian pop. ✉ *Mediteranskih igara 21* ☎ *099/831–3050* ⊕ *www.club-vanilla.hr.*

🎭 Performing Arts

FESTIVALS

Split Summer Festival (*Splitsko ljeto*)
CULTURAL FESTIVALS | FAMILY | Usually running annually from mid-July to mid-August, the Split Summer Festival includes a variety of open-air opera, classical music concerts, dance, and theatrical performances. One of the highlights is opera on Prokurative (Republic Square). ■TIP➔ **Tickets can be purchased online or from the theater box office. Book your accommodation in advance, as hotel rates and occupancies go up during the festival.** ✉ *Croatian National Theater , Trg Gaje Bulata 1, Grad* ☎ *021/306–908 For ticket sales* ⊕ *www.splitsko-ljeto.hr* ▨ *From 75 Kn.*

FILM

Bačvice Open Air Cinema (*Ljetno kino Bačvice*)

FILM | This is an open-air summer cinema located in the pine woods above Bačvice Bay. The Bačvice location is one of three movie theaters that operate as one complex. Predominantly English-language, big-picture films are shown in their original versions with subtitles. Special movie event nights that feature different foreign and local films are mostly shown at the Bačvice location. Discount seats are available on Mondays. ⊠ *Šetalište Petra Preradovića 6, Bacvica* ⊕ *www.kinomediteran.hr/en/cities/split-bacvice-open-air-cinema* 🎟 *30 Kn.*

💼 Shopping

Croatian women—and those from Split in particular—are renowned for their sense of style. You'll find a good number of exclusive boutiques selling original women's clothes, jewelry, and housewares, not to mention numerous shoe and dress shops with goods imported from Italy all throughout the city. Art galleries will often feature some unique handmade products you can't find elsewhere because of the difficulty local artists and crafters have in distributing their work. The city's most memorable shopping venue remains the *pjaca,* the colorful open-air market held each morning just outside the palace walls, where you can find everything from lavender and Brač stone souvenirs to fresh vegetables and Dalmatian delicacies. Dalmatia is known for producing some of the country's best wine, olive oil, and *pršut* (prosciutto), all of which can be found in the market in Split.

Art Studio Naranča

ART GALLERIES | Founded in 1983, Art Studio Naranča is a design studio showcasing and selling work by local artists. Here, you'll find everything from graphic art and paintings to books and small handicrafts.

⊠ *Majstora Jurja 5, Varoš* ☎ *021/344–118* ⊕ *www.facebook.com/studionaranca.*

City Marketplaces

OUTDOOR/FLEA/GREEN MARKETS | From the central Green Market (*Pazar*) and the main Pjaca on the eastern side of Diocletian's Palace, which sell everything from vegtables to clothes, to the basement of Diocletian's Palace, full of stands selling jewelry, wood carvings, and other creative artisan handicrafts, Split is home to an array of open-air marketplaces selling all sorts of goods. Split's fish market (*ribarnica*) is also known as one of the best in the country; you'll find it on the pedestrian Marmontova.

Croata

CLOTHING | Overlooking Trg Brace Radića, close to the seafront, Croata specializes in a wide range of specialty designed and handcrafted ties. Each tie is stylishly presented in fine boxes. ⊠ *Mihovilova Širina 7, Grad* ☎ *021/346–336* ⊕ *www.croata.hr.*

Kraš

FOOD/CANDY | One of Croatia's most famous brands of all time, Kraš has delicious products to boot. The company has been producing high-quality chocolate, wafers, cocoa, and more for over a century. One of the most popular gifts to give in Croatia is a Kraš Bajadera, a chocolate box comprised of gold-package-wrapped nutty chocolates. ⊠ *Narodni trg 6* ☎ *021/346–138* ⊕ *www.kras.hr/en.*

Mall of Split

SHOPPING CENTERS/MALLS | This is the largest shopping center in Dalmatia, home to a range of affordable and high-end brands, including Mango, Tommy Hilfiger, and Pepe Jeans. Also in the mall are a range of dietary and technology stores, as well as a casino and food court. ⊠ *Split* ✢ *At the crossing on Domovinskog rata, Zbor Narodne Garde, and Vukovarska streets* ☎ *021/444–397* ⊕ *www.mallofsplit.hr.*

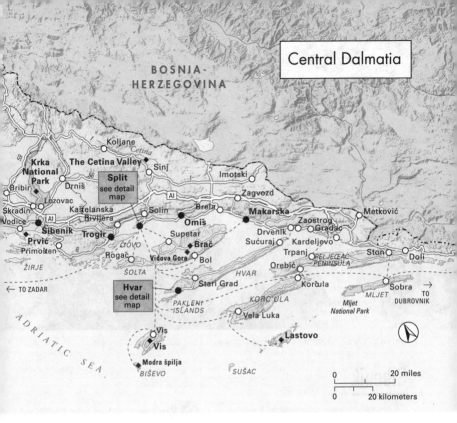

Central Dalmatia

BOSNIA-HERZEGOVINA

ADRIATIC SEA

← TO ZADAR

TO DUBROVNIK →

0   20 miles
0   20 kilometers

 Activities

BEACHES

Bačvice Beach

BEACHES | FAMILY | The largest beach area in Split is a 10-minute walk east of the Old Town. If you don't mind the crowds, you can rent beach chairs and umbrellas, and there's a string of cafés and bars along this stretch of coast. It's one of the few sandy beaches on the Dalmatian coast, with a shallow swimming area. By night, you'll find a thriving club complex here. ⊠ *Plaža Bačvice, Bacvica.*

Bene Beach

BEACHES | This is is a quieter cove located west of Split's Old Town, on the north side of Marjan Hill. Here you can engage in a number of sports such as kayaking or tennis (there are courts). Along with Bene, you'll find a whole string of other beaches and coves dotting the Marjan Hill's peninsula. ⊠ *Bene Beach, Marjan.*

SAILING

Well-connected to the rest of Europe by air, land, and sea—and within just a few hours' sailing of several of the Adriatic's most beautiful islands—Split is a major hub of the yacht-charter business in Dalmatia.

ACI Marina Split

SAILING | The 348-berth ACI Marina is southwest of the city center. It stays open all year and is a base for dozens of charter companies organizing sailing on the Adriatic. Prices for berth rental and amenities can be found on their website. It also features wonderful views of Old Town Split and the surrounding Adriatic, plus a full range of amenities. ⊠ *Uvala Baluni 8, Zvoncac* ☎ *098/398–850* ⊕ *www.aci-marinas.com.*

Šibenik's Gothic-Renaissance Cathedral of St. James is a UNESCO World Heritage Site.

Šibenik

75 km (47 miles) northwest of Split.

The trademark of Šibenik is its Gothic-Renaissance cathedral, built of pale-gray Dalmatian stone and designated a UNESCO World Heritage Site, which stands on a raised piazza close to the seafront promenade. From here a network of narrow, cobbled streets leads through the medieval quarter of tightly packed, terra-cotta-roof houses, and up to the ruins of a 16th-century hilltop fortress. The city is worth at least a day of exploring, if only to get lost wandering through its time-smoothed cobblestone streets and wowing at its medieval architecture. More underrated—and therefore more peaceful—than some larger coastal towns, Šibenik is the perfect location for a romantic and peaceful getaway.

GETTING HERE AND AROUND

The narrow cobblestone streets of the city's Old Town are easily walkable. Šibenik also makes for a fantastic base for visiting the nearby waterfalls of Krka National Park.

Sights

Cathedral of St. James (*Katedrala sv. Jakova*)

RELIGIOUS SITE | Šibenik's most famous piece of architecture, the Cathedral of St. James was built in several distinct stages and styles between 1431 and 1535, and it's been a UNESCO World Heritage Site since 2000. The lower level is the work of Venetian architects who contributed the finely carved Venetian-Gothic portals, whereas the rest of the building follows plans drawn up by local architect Juraj Dalmatinac, who proposed the Renaissance cupola. Note the frieze running around the outer wall, with 74 faces carved in stone from the island of Brač. One of the cathedral's highlights, the tiny baptistery with minutely chiseled stone decorations, was designed by Dalmatinac but executed by Andrija Aleši. ■TIP→ As you leave, take a look at the bronze statue just outside the main door: that's Dalmatinac himself, his likeness sculpted by legendary 20th-century sculptor Ivan Meštrović. ⊠ *Cathedral of Saint James, Trg Republike Hrvatske* 🖭 *Free.*

Fortress of St. Michael (*Tvrđava sv. Mihovila*)

MILITARY SITE | This fortress guards the city below from atop a steep, rocky hill. Dating back to the 11th century and re-fortified over the years, it was once the city's main point of defense. Today, a climb to the top grants you vistas of the sea, surrounding islands, and the medieval town. On occassion, special events and concerts are held on an open-air stage on the fortress. ⊠ *Zagrađe 21* ⊕ *www.tvrdjava-kulture.hr/en/home.*

Fortress of St. Nicholas (*Tvrđava sv. Nikole*)

MILITARY SITE | Standing at the entrance of Šibenik's St. Anthony's Channel, the Fortress of St. Nicholas sits on the islet of Ljuljevac and showcases a Renaissance-era Venetian-style building. Constructed in 1540, the fortress was added to the UNESCO World Heritage List in 2017. It is definitely worth a visit from land, or better yet, from the sea via kayak. ⊠ *Šibenik* ⊕ *www.kanal-svetog-ante.com/en.*

Vinoplod Winery (*Vinoplod vinarija*)

WINERY/DISTILLERY | The award-winning makers of the famous Babić wine variety (today a symbol of Primošten, Šibenik, and all of Croatia), Vinoplod-Vinarija can be contacted for tours and tastings. ⊠ *Velimira Škorpika 2* ☎ *022/334–011* ⊕ *www.vinoplod-vinarija.hr.*

🍴 Restaurants

★ Pelegrini

$$$$ | **MEDITERRANEAN** | In a carefully restored 14th-century palazzo opposite the historic St. James Cathedral in Šibenik sits Pelegrini, one of seven restaurants in Croatia to hold a Michelin star—and the only one in Central Dalmatia to do so. Pelegrini's menu features traditional Dalmatian cuisine that is innovatively prepared, with exquisite flavor being the restaurant's guiding principle. **Known for:** excellent Dalmatian cuisine; extensive wine list; four-course minimum for dinner. 💲 *Average main: 850 Kn* ⊠ *Jurja Dalmatinca 1* ☎ *022/213–701* ⊕ *www.pelegrini.hr/en.*

Vino&Ino

$ | **MEDITERRANEAN** | It's hard to pass the inviting Vino&Ino in the center of Šibenik and not stop in, either for a coffee or a glass of wine and tapas. There's outdoor seating and always a balanced mix of locals and visitors enjoying the small-plates menu. **Known for:** live music in the summer; excellent coffee; tapas and small plates. 💲 *Average main: 20 Kn* ⊠ *Fausta Vrančića bb* ☎ *091/250–6022* ⊕ *www.vinoiino.hr.*

Hotels

Agroturizam Kalpić

$$ | **B&B/INN** | **FAMILY** | Experience the peacefulness of the Croatian countryside at the Kalpić family estate while exploring both Šibenik and Krka National Park. **Pros:** shady garden for kids to play; nice break from the city; traditional dishes from the restaurant. **Cons:** must have a car to reach it; too rural for city folk; nightlife options a bit far away. 💲 *Rooms from: Kn1350* ⊠ *Kalpići 4, Lozovac* ☎ *091/584–5520* ⊕ *www.kalpic.com* 🛏 *13 rooms* 🍽 *Free breakfast.*

Hotel Bellevue

$$$ | **HOTEL** | Sitting on the city waterfront, right next to the historic center, this four-star hotel offers a range of elegant rooms and suites, most of which have sea views. **Pros:** excellent views; nice wellness center; tasty free breakfast. **Cons:** can be expensive; waterfront but 10 minutes walk from a beach; no restaurant on-site. 💲 *Rooms from: 1500 Kn* ⊠ *Obala hrvatske mornarice 1* ☎ *022/646–400* ⊕ *www.bellevuehotel.hr* 🛏 *49 rooms* 🍽 *Free breakfast.*

Mare

$ | **B&B/INN** | Šibenik's first hostel, Mare is nestled within a courtyard in the city's medieval center. **Pros:** location in city center; modern and airy rooms; offers laundry services. **Cons:** no breakfast; parking can be a challenge; lack of privacy. $ *Rooms from: 750 Kn* ⊠ *Kralja Zvonimira 40* ☎ *022/215–269* ⊕ *www. facebook.com/hostel.mare* ⤸ *40 beds* ○ *No meals.*

Nightlife

Azimut

BARS/PUBS | Found on the city's waterfront, Azimut is an underground bar located within the otherwise mostly peaceful walls of historic Šibenik. Here, you'll find alternative music covering genres from rock to techno playing (often live) all night. With a spacious dance floor and a number of courtyard tables, Azimut is a hidden gem and offers delicious cocktails to boot. ⊠ *Obala palih omladinaca 2* ⊕ *www.instagram.com/klub_azimut.*

En Vogue Beach Club

MUSIC CLUBS | While you can also stay at the adjacent all-inclusive Solaris Resort, many people visit En Vogue Beach Club just to party poolside and seaside at the same time. The pool complex is right next to the sea and dotted with bars, restaurants, and snack stands, all of which you can enjoy while you dip your feet into the water. All-day, all-night DJ parties happen often. The trip outside of the city center (about 6 miles) is worth it for partiers. ⊠ *Hoteli Solaris 86* ☎ *022/362–963* ⊕ *www.en.campingsolaris.com* ☞ *En Vogue Beach Club is only open during the summer months.*

Prvić

4.5 nautical miles west of Šibenik by ferry.

Beyond Šibenik Bay lie the splendidly scattered islands of the Šibenik archipelago, five of which—Zlarin, Prvić, Kaprije, Obonjan, and Žirje—are accessible by ferry from Šibenik. For a quick taste of island life, the nearest, Zlarin and Prvić, can be visited as day trips, but if you intend to stay overnight, Prvić is the better equipped, with a lovely, small hotel, rooms to rent, and about half a dozen rustic eateries. Tiny, car-free Prvić is just 3 km (2 miles) long and has a year-round population of around 540. Its two main villages, Prvić Luka and Šepurine, are made up of centuries-old traditional stone cottages (built from the UNESCO-designated art of dry stone walling) and connected by a lovely footpath leading through a stand of pine trees that takes about 15 minutes to walk. Though some of the locals work in Šibenik, others still make a living on the island by cultivating figs, olives, and vines and by fishing. There are no large, overcrowded beaches, but plenty of small, secluded pebble coves with crystal-clean water that is perfect for swimming.

GETTING HERE AND AROUND

Through high season, there are four ferries per day from Šibenik, calling at Zlarin (30 minutes), Prvić Luka (45 minutes), Šepurine (1 hour), and Vodice (1 hour 10 minutes). All four then return to Šibenik, doing the same journey in reverse. Alternatively, you can take a water taxi from the Šibenik seafront to Prvić Luka (expect to pay a hefty sum, as much as 1000 Kn, as opposed to the ferry, which charges under 20 Kn).

🍴 Restaurants

Nanini

$$ | PIZZA | This down-to-earth, family-run eatery occupying an old stone building furnished with heavy wooden tables offers a decent selection of Dalmatian dishes and pizzas, with an emphasis on fresh seafood. It stays open all year and is a popular spot for local wedding receptions. **Known for:** decent pizza; fresh seafood; popular with wedding parties. [$] *Average main: 113 Kn* ✉ *IX. Ulica 56* ☎ *091/212–0684* 🌐 *www.facebook.com/konobaapartmaninaniniotokprvic.*

🛏 Hotels

Hotel Maestral

$ | HOTEL | FAMILY | On the seafront in Prvić Luka, this 19th-century stone building was once the village school, and after a careful restoration it reopened as a boutique hotel. **Pros:** delightful island location; small (so guests receive individual attention); good restaurant. **Cons:** if you miss the ferry, you could end up stranded; often fully booked; limited nightlife possibilities. [$] *Rooms from: 600 Kn* ✉ *Ulica IX br. 1* ☎ *022/448–300* 🌐 *www.hotelmaestral.com* 🛏 *15 rooms* 🍴 *Free breakfast.*

🏃 Activities

SWIMMING

Swim Trek

BEACHES | This Britain-based agency has a pretty straightforward motto: "Ferries are for wimps—let's swim." The company offers a challenging and unusual one-week holiday, including swimming around the islands of the Šibenik archipelago. Participants cover an average of 4 km (2½ miles) per day, including the stretch between the islands of Zlarin and Prvić. Overnight accommodation is in the Hotel Maestral in Prvić Luka. ☎ *1273/739–713 in U.K.* 🌐 *www.swimtrek.com.*

Krka National Park

20 km (13 miles) north of Šibenik.

The Krka River cuts its way through a gorge shaded by limestone cliffs and dense woodland, tumbling down toward the Adriatic in a series of spectacular pools and waterfalls. The most beautiful stretch has been designated as the Krka National Park.

GETTING HERE AND AROUND

Drive from Šibenik to the town of Skradin, then take a 25-minute boat ride up the Krka River on a national-park ferry. Alternatively, skip the boat ride and hike your way through the waterfalls.

👁 Sights

★ Krka National Park (*Nacionalni Park Krka*)

NATIONAL/STATE PARK | FAMILY | A series of seven waterfalls are the main attraction here, the most spectacular being Skradinski Buk, where 17 cascades of water fall 40 meters into an emerald-green pool. Moving upriver, a trail of wooden walkways and bridges crisscrosses its way through the woods and along the river to the Roški Slap waterfall, passing by the tiny island of Visovac, which is home to a Franciscan monastery that can be visited by boat. On the islet, there is also an old mill with a museum that demonstrates the different ways the mill was used centuries ago. From here, one can better understand how the power of these waters inspired Nikola Tesla, whose boyhood home is not far from the national park. In 1895 the first hydroelectric plant became operational here, only two days after Tesla's hydroelectric plant on Niagara Falls. This made the residents of Skradin the first Eastern European citizens to have electricity.

A series of seven waterfalls are the main attraction here, the most spectacular being Skradinski Buk, where 17 cascades

Within Krka National Park is the island of Visovac, home to a Franciscan monastery.

of water fall 40 meters into an emerald-green pool. Moving upriver, a trail of wooden walkways and bridges crisscrosses its way through the woods and along the river to the Roški Slap waterfall, passing by the tiny island of Visovac, which is home to a Franciscan monastery that can be visited by boat. On the islet, there is also an old mill with a museum that demonstrates the different ways the mill was used centuries ago. From here, one can better understand how the power of these waters inspired Nikola Tesla, whose boyhood home is not far from the national park. In 1895 the first hydroelectric plant became operational here, only two days after Tesla's hydroelectric plant on Niagara Falls. This made the residents of Skradin the first Eastern European citizens to have electricity.

More than 860 species of plant life have been identified throughout the park and more than 200 bird species live there, making it one of the most valuable ornithological areas in Europe. Something many visitors miss is a hawk training center where you can observe birds of prey being trained by ornithological experts. For bird enthusiasts there is also the Guduća Nature Reserve, where various species are closely studied and can be observed from boats. The Krka National Park office is located in Šibenik. ■TIP➜ **For more active travelers, there is a 8½-km (5-mile) hiking trail, going Sitnice–Roški Slap–Ozidana Cave, that takes about 2½ hours and has educational panels along the way that explain plant and animal life, geological phenomena, and historic sites.** ✉ *Krka National Park, Lozovac* ☎ *022/201–777* ⊕ *www.np-krka.hr* 💰 *200 Kn June–Sept., 100 Kn Oct. and Apr.–May, 30 Kn Dec.–Mar.*

Restaurants

Cantinetta

$$ | **MEDITERRANEAN** | **FAMILY** | Hidden away in the Skradin Bay, in a quiet location where the fresh waters from Krka National Park flow into the sea, Cantinetta is well recognized among local residents as the best place to eat in Skradin.

From a humble family *konoba* to a serious culinary destination, this restaurant takes great pride in its well-preserved old recipes that have been passed on from generation to generation. **Known for:** best dining in Skradin; family recipes, including excellent veal risotto; reasonable prices. [$] *Average main: 113 Kn* ✉ *Aleja skradinskih svilara 7, Skradin* ☎ *091/150–6434* 🌐 *www.cantinetta.hr/en.*

Zlatne Školjke

$$ | SEAFOOD | FAMILY | A favorite among the yachting crowd, due in part to its location near the ACI Marina Skradin, Zlatne Školjke occupies a natural stone building with a terrace overlooking the water. The restaurant is aptly named Zlatne Školjke, which means golden shells, because of the plethora of shellfish farms nearby. **Known for:** superfresh shellfish; terrace overlooking the water; lovely wine list. [$] *Average main: 100 Kn* ✉ *Grgura Ninskog 9, Skradin* ☎ *022/771–022* 🌐 *www.zlatne-skoljke.com.*

Hotels

Hotel Skradinski Buk

$ | HOTEL | FAMILY | A friendly, family-run hotel in a refurbished stone town house in the center of Skradin is also the only hotel in town. **Pros:** great location in pretty village close to the entrance of Krka National Park; comfortable rooms; good breakfast. **Cons:** only hotel in town and often fully booked; limited nightlife in Skradin; prices can spike during high season. [$] *Rooms from: 680 Kn* ✉ *Burinovac 2, Skradin* ☎ *022/771–771* 🌐 *skradinskibuk.hr* 🛏 *29 rooms* 🍴 *Free breakfast.*

Shopping

Vinoteka Bedrica

WINE/SPIRITS | While in Skradin, pay a visit to Vinoteka Bedrica, an old-fashioned family-run wine cellar where you can taste and buy bottles of locally produced wine and *rakija* (fruit brandy). Be sure to try their delicious rakija made with rose petals. ✉ *Fra Luje Maruna 14, Skradin* ☎ *022/771–270.*

Trogir

27 km (17 miles) west of Split.

On a small island no more than a few city blocks in length, the beautifully preserved medieval Old Town of Trogir is connected to the mainland by one bridge and tied to the outlying island of Čiovo by a second. The settlement dates back to the 3rd century BC, when it was colonized by the Greeks, who named it Tragurion. It later flourished as a Roman port. With the fall of the Western Roman Empire, it became part of Byzantium and then followed the shifting rulers of the Adriatic. In 1420 the Venetians moved in and stayed until 1797. Today, it is a UNESCO World Heritage Site, and survives principally from tourism. You can explore the Old Town in about an hour on foot. A labyrinth of narrow, cobbled streets centers on Narodni trg, the main square, where the most notable buildings are located, including the 15th-century loggia and clock tower, the Venetian-Gothic Ćipiko Palace, and the splendid cathedral, with its elegant bell tower. The south-facing seafront promenade is lined with cafés, ice-cream parlors, and restaurants, and there are also several small, old-fashioned hotels that offer a reasonable alternative to accommodations in Split.

GETTING HERE AND AROUND

It can be more convenient and affordable to take a short boat ride from Split to Trogir if visiting for a day, as parking is limited and expensive during high season.

Sights

★ **Cathedral of St. Lawrence** (*Katedrala Sveti Lovrijenac*)

RELIGIOUS SITE | FAMILY | The Cathedral of St. Lawrence, whose first construction dates back to the early 13th century, is a remarkable example of Romanesque architecture. The most striking detail is the main (west) portal, adorned with superb Romanesque sculpture by the Croatian master known as Radovan. The great door, flanked by a pair of imperious lions that form pedestals for figures of Adam and Eve, is framed by a fascinating series illustrating the daily life of peasants in a kind of medieval comic strip. In the dimly lit Romanesque interior, the 15th-century chapel of Sveti Ivan Orsini (St. John Orsini) of Trogir features statues of saints and apostles in niches facing the sarcophagus, on which lies the figure of St. John. The bell tower, built in successive stages—the first two stories Gothic, the third Renaissance—offers stunning views across the ancient rooftops. An entrance ticket includes a visit to the cathedral, treasury, and the bell tower. **■ TIP→ Be sure to also look down as you stroll through and gaze at the amazing structures at eye level and below—the marble sculptures and checkerboard floors make for a memorable view.** ✉ *Trg Ivana Pavla II* ☎ *021/885–628* 🌐 *www.visittrogir.hr/st-lawrence-cathedral* 🎫 *Free.*

🍴 Restaurants

Calebotta
$$ | MEDITERRANEAN | FAMILY | Retreat to a quiet closed-in courtyard, where the Trogir cinema once sat, and allow the Calebotta family to wow you with their first-class service and menu of fresh ingredients expertly prepared like no other restaurant in Trogir. The sea platter, which includes tuna steak tartare, octopus carpaccio, and scampi with grapefruit and pistachio, is a perfect way to start a meal on a hot summer afternoon. **Known for:** quiet courtyard location; fine dining experience; delicious desserts. [$] *Average main: 98 Kn* ✉ *Gradska 23* ☎ *091/738–0454* 🌐 *www.calebotta.com.*

Konoba TRS
$$$$ | MEDITERRANEAN | With a tremendous sense of style, TRS combines traditional food with modern ingredients that are freshly sourced from the owner's family farm in a nearby village. These unusual combinations, like chickpea puree and fried octupus, are a welcome change and still subtle enough to allow the strength of the traditional Dalmatian food to dominate. **Known for:** family farm-to-table cuisine; traditional dishes with twist, like cauliflower soup with sheep's cheese and pancetta chips; excellent fish. [$] *Average main: 225 Kn* ✉ *Ulica Matije Gupca 14* ☎ *021/796–956* 🌐 *www.konoba-trs.com.*

Vanjaka
$$ | MEDITERRANEAN | FAMILY | In an elegant 17th-century stone building in the Old Town, close to the cathedral, this welcoming family-run restaurant serves Dalmatian specialties such as black risotto, gnocchi, and fresh fish, as well as a good choice of local wines. Sit outside on the open-air terrace, or take a table in the intimate air-conditioned dining room. **Known for:** Dalmatian cuisine; al fresco dining; local wines. [$] *Average main: 100 Kn* ✉ *Radovanov trg 9* ☎ *021/884–061* 🌐 *www.vanjaka.hr.*

🛏 Hotels

Domus Maritima
$ | B&B/INN | This small family-run bed-and-breakfast is perfectly located a few minutes' walk from bustling Trogir and just across the street from the ACI Marina. **Pros:** relaxing garden; free parking close by; handy location near ACI Marina Trogir. **Cons:** meals must be ordered in advance; noisy at night; expensive during high season. [$] *Rooms from: 750 Kn* ✉ *Put Cumbrijana 10* ☎ *091/513–7802* 🛏 *8 rooms* 🍴 *Free breakfast.*

Hotel Fontana

$$ | HOTEL | Located in Old Town overlooking the Trogir Channel, Hotel Fontana is in an old stone building that's been been tastefully refurbished into a small family-run hotel above a popular restaurant. **Pros:** location on seafront promenade in the Old Town; breakfast served on charming seafront terrace; some rooms have jacuzzis. **Cons:** rooms rather small; basic furnishings; Wi-Fi does not work at times. $ *Rooms from: 1130 Kn ⊠ Obrov 1* ☎ *098/911–8650* ⊕ *www.fontana-trogir. com* ⇆ *14 rooms* ❑ *Free breakfast.*

Hotel Pašike

$$ | B&B/INN | In a typical Dalmatian stone building in the heart of Old Town, this charming hotel is filled with inherited and restored antique furniture. **Pros:** great Old Town location; free airport transfers; fun restaurant. **Cons:** some rooms are dark; no elevator; parking is paid and must be reserved ahead of time. $ *Rooms from: 1430 Kn ⊠ Splitska 4* ☎ *021/885–185* ⊕ *www.hotelpasike.com* ⇆ *14 rooms* ❑ *Free breakfast.*

Tragos

$$ | HOTEL | Occupying an 18th-century Baroque palace in the heart of the Old Town, two blocks from the cathedral, Tragos has 12 simply furnished, modern rooms, decorated in warm hues of cream, yellow, and orange, each with a modern, spacious tiled bathroom. **Pros:** located in Old Town; friendly and helpful staff; good restaurant. **Cons:** rooms can be noisy from downstairs restaurant; no elevator could be a problem for some visitors; parking can be challenging. $ *Rooms from: 1130 Kn ⊠ Budislavićeva 3* ☎ *021/884–729* ⊕ *www.tragos.hr* ⇆ *12 rooms* ❑ *Free breakfast.*

Vila Sikaa Hotel

$$ | B&B/INN | This 18th-century villa on Čiovo Island has been converted into a small, family-run hotel overlooking the Trogir Channel. **Pros:** seafront location with great views of Trogir's Old Town; friendly and helpful staff; beautiful old building with modern facilities. **Cons:** front rooms can be noisy (think loud music and motorbikes); two hotels are in the same building (which can be confusing); parking can be difficult. $ *Rooms from: 980 Kn ⊠ Obala kralja Zvonimira 13* ☎ *021/881–223* ⊕ *www.vila-sikaa-r.com* ⇆ *10 rooms* ❑ *Free breakfast.*

Omiš and the Cetina Valley

28 km (17½ miles) southeast of Split.

An easy day trip from Split, Omiš is a pleasant seaside town with a colorful open-air market and a conglomeration of old stone houses backed by a medieval hilltop fortress. What also makes it special is its location at the mouth of a dramatic gorge, where the Cetina River meets the Adriatic Sea. The river carves a spectacular canyon with the fertile, green Cetina Valley at the bottom, surrounded by sheer limestone cliffs. The river, tumbling its way down toward the sea over a series of rapids, is a popular and challenging site for rafting and rock climbing. An asphalt road follows the course of the river upstream from Omiš, leading to a couple of pleasant waterside restaurants. Omiš is also the location of the annual Festival of Dalmatian Klapa, which attracts singers of the UNESCO-protected music style from all over Croatia.

GETTING HERE AND AROUND

Omiš is an easy day trip from Split by rental car or bus (a few buses run between the cities daily).

🍴 Restaurants

Radmanove Mlinice

$$ | EASTERN EUROPEAN | FAMILY | This renovated water mill is well known for miles around for its fresh *pastrva* (trout) and *peč ena janjetina* (roast lamb), served at tables under trees in a riverside garden. Throughout July and August, on Wednesday evenings, the dreamy spot also stages live folk music and dancing from 8 pm onward. **Known for:** classic Croatian cuisine; live music in summer; beautiful natural surroundings. [$] *Average main: 90 Kn* ✉ *Cetina Valley regional road, in the direction of Zadvarje, Omiš* ☎ *021/862–238* 🌐 *www.radmanove-mlinice.hr* 🕒 *Closed Nov.–Mar.*

Hotels

★ Hotel Villa Dvor

$$ | **HOTEL** | **FAMILY** | Built into a sheer cliff face overlooking the Cetina River, this hotel is reached through a tunnel and then via a glass elevator. **Pros:** hillside location offers stunning view across river to Old Town and sea; eco-friendly ethos; rooftop Jacuzzi. **Cons:** the location/view outshines the hotel itself; limited nightlife in area; might be difficult to reach for some. [$] *Rooms from: 1130 Kn* ✉ *Mosorska Cesta 13, Omiš* ☎ *021/863–444* 🌐 *www.hotel-villadvor.hr* 🛏 *23 rooms* 🍴 *Free breakfast.*

Performing Arts

FESTIVALS

Dalmatian Klapa Festival

FESTIVALS | Klapa singing, which is an integral part of Dalmatian, and Croatian, culture, is widely celebrated all summer long with festivals devoted specifically to the cherished musical tradition. The Dalmatian Klapa Festival brings together the best klapa performers from the region; it usually occurs for three weeks every July. Performances are staged in the parish church and on the main square, where you can enjoy the UNESCO-protected melodies alfresco. ✉ *Ivana Katušića 5, Omiš* ☎ *021/861–015* 🌐 *fdk.hr/festival-in-omis.*

Dalmatian Klapa

When visiting towns and villages along the Dalmatian coast, you might be lucky enough to come across a group of locals giving an impromptu *klapa* (Dalmatian acapella) performance. Traditionally, klapa groups are formed by men (though there are also amazing all-female groups), who sing hauntingly beautiful melodies and harmonies about themes like the sea, love, and family life. The music was added to UNESCO's Intangible Cultural Heritage of Humanity list in 2012.

Activities

The Cetina Valley is a destination for adventure sports lovers of all kinds, from white-water rafters to rock climbers, who all appreciate getting their adrenaline rush with a side of sheer natural beauty. Several adventure-tour companies arrange Cetina Valley trips through the limestone cliffs of the canyon, leaving from both Split and Omiš.

Active Holidays

WATER SPORTS | This company offers ziplining, rafting, canyoning, canoeing, and rock climbing in the Cetina Valley, as well as windsurfing and sea kayaking off the coast at Omiš. ✉ *Knezova Kačića bb, Omiš* ☎ *021/756–708* 🌐 *www.activeholidays-croatia.com.*

Brač

9 nautical miles south of Split by ferry.

Well-connected to Split by ferry and catamaran services, the island of Brač makes for the perfect offshore escape. While

Blaca Hermitage was built by monks who also grew vineyards and olive groves in the area.

it makes for a delightful day trip from Split, you will see why opting to stay a few nights is a no-brainer as soon as you step foot on the island. Think craggy seascapes, rosy bougainvillea crawling over sun-drenched stone houses, and calming cricket songs ringing out from the pine trees. Despite its proximity to the mainland, the slow pace of island life pervades many of Brač's main attractions, from the Blaca Hermitage and the Dragon's Cave to the Pučišća Stonemasonry School. While you're on the island, try a walking tour through the Dolce Vita trail to see, touch, and taste where the country's best olive oil comes from. Or hook up with one of the many outdoor adventure–sports companies for heart-pumping kayaking, climbing, wind-surfing, or sailing. Although a visit to the famous Zlatni Rat (Golden Cape) beach, which is also a prime windsurfing spot, can seem a bit overcrowded, exploring the more hidden sides of the island like Bobovisće or Sutivan will reveal some of the most crystal-clear water in the entire Adriatic.

GETTING HERE AND AROUND

Brač is accessible by ferry, catamaran, and boat. To get there, either catch an early-morning Jadrolinija ferry from Split to Supetar (9 nautical miles) and then take a bus across the island to the south coast, or catch the mid-afternoon Jadrolinija catamaran from Split to Bol (24 nautical miles), which then continues to Jelsa on the island of Hvar.

◉ Sights

★ **Blaca Hermitage** (*Pustinja Blaca*)
RELIGIOUS SITE | FAMILY | Built into a cliff face overlooking the sea by Glagolitic monks fleeing Ottoman invaders in the 16th century, the Blaca Hermitage is one of Brač's most serene sights. From the bay below the complex, it's a 2-km (1-mile) hike uphill and well off the beaten path as it's only reachable by foot. The hike is well worth the experience to understand the sacrifice the monks made in constructing the site without modern amenities. You can also arrive by car from Nerežišća over Vidova Gora

to Dragovoda and then walk about 30 minutes up to the monastery (either way, don your hiking shoes). The monks who built the hermitage also grew rich vineyards and lush olive groves, despite the wild and arid landscape. Inside, visitors can see a fine collection of period furniture including a piano and telescope which belonged to Father Nikola Miličević (1887-1963), Blaca's last hermit and an avid astronomer. In its heyday, the hermitage had a printing press, a school, and an observatory. There are no longer any monks living there; today, it functions as a museum, where a guided tour is well worth the expense. ⊠ *Pustinja Blaca* ☎ *091/516–4671* ⊕ *www.czk-brac.hr/index.php/o-pustinji-blaca* 🎫 *40 Kn.*

Branislav Dešković Art Gallery (*Galerija Branislav Dešković*)

MUSEUM | FAMILY | In a fine Baroque building on the seafront, the Branislav Dešković Art Gallery displays over 300 paintings and sculptures by big-name 20th-century Croatian artists who were inspired by the sea and landscapes of Dalmatia. The gallery was named after Brač-born sculptor Branislav Dešković (1883-1939), whose works are on display along with those of Ivan Meštović, Ivan Rendić, and more. ⊠ *Bolskih Pomoraca 7, Bol* ☎ *091/635–2700* ⊕ *www.czk-brac.hr/index.php/o-galeriji-branimir-deskovic-bol* 🎫 *20 Kn.*

Dominican Monastery (*Dominikanski Samostan*)

RELIGIOUS SITE | With its beautiful gardens overlooking the sea, the Dominican Monastery on the western edge of Bol was founded in 1475. The monastery church is home to a valuable 16th-century painting by Jacopo Tintoretto, and the small on-site museum displays ancient Greek coins and amphorae found on the nearby islands of Hvar and Vis. In addition to maintaining the museum and church, the Dominican Monastery's priests actively study and carry out the Dominican mission throughout Croatia

and Europe. ⊠ *Anđelka Rabadana 4, Bol* ☎ *021/778–000* ⊕ *www.dominikanci.hr/index.php/samostani/bol.*

Island of Brač Museum, Škrip (*Muzej otoka Brača, Škrip*)

MUSEUM | This is the island's regional museum and, as such, it's located within the oldest settlement on the island, called Škrip. "Škrip" come from the Latin *scrupus*, referring to large, sharp stones. The area was inhabited by the ancient Illyrians around 1400 BC and later a Roman community. Today at the museum you'll find artifacts from both of these eras, and much more. ⊠ *Škrip, Pjaca 15* ☎ *091/637–0920* ⊕ *www.czk-brac.hr/index.php/muzej.*

Sutivan Nature Park (*Park Prirode Sutivan*)

CITY PARK | FAMILY | After spending a few days swimming and lying on the beach, Sutivan Nature Park is a great place to make an afternoon picnic with kids. There is a small animal park that shelters a wide variety of domestic animals including ducks, pigs, goats, turtles, peacocks, parrots, and cows. There are even donkeys and horses available for riding with a professional guide. The park is located about 3 km (2 miles) from Sutivan toward Mlin and has a large playground, a barbecue area, and a botanical garden with a fountain, as well as an amphitheater for performances and events. The restaurant only serves drinks, but meals can be prepared if you make a reservation ahead of time. ⊠ *Park Prirode Sutivan, Krtine bb, Sutivan* ☎ *098/133–7345.*

Vidova Gora

MOUNTAIN—SIGHT | The village of Bol is backed by the highest peak on all the Croatian islands, Vidova Gora. From here, at a height of 2,552 feet above sea level, the Adriatic Sea and the islands of Hvar and Vis spread out before you like a map. It's possible to reach the top following a clearly marked footpath from Bol, but be sure to wear good hiking boots, take plenty of water, and expect to walk at least two and a half hours to reach the summit. Alternatively, rent a mountain bike from Big Blue and cycle up—note that you need to be pretty fit to face the challenge. ■**TIP→ If you have a headlamp and are relatively fit, wake early and hike up before sunrise, or go in the late afternoon and watch the sun set from Croatia's highest island peak.** ✉ *4 km (2½ miles) north of the town center, Bol.*

Restaurants

Arguola

$ | **DELI** | If you're looking for a quick bite for lunch on your way to the beach or after a late night out partying, this sandwich bar will do the trick. The salads and bread are made fresh and the portions are perfect. **Known for:** quick sandwiches; lunches to go; late-night snacks. Ⓢ *Average main: 30 Kn* ✉ *Vladimir Nazora 6, Bol* ☎ *091/518–8295* ▭ *No credit cards* ⊘ *Closed Nov.–Apr.*

Kaštil Gospodnetić

$$ | **MEDITERRANEAN** | Sitting above village of Dol, this konoba not only offers an amazing view of the valley all the way to the sea, but also offers guests a chance to step back in time with a tour though its historic 19th-century building before sitting down to a home-cooked meal. Order a grilled fish if you pop in unannounced and do not have the inclination to wait for the *peka*-cooked meals, or just take in the views over a slice of the local sweet cake, *hrapaćuša*. Meals can be paired with tours of the village too, and you can even add on an authentic cooking class. **Known for:** Dalmatian farm-fresh food; reservations required in May and October; amazing views. Ⓢ *Average main: 120 Kn* ✉ *Dol bb, Dol* ☎ *091/799–7182* ⊕ *www.konobadol.com* ⊘ *Closed from Nov.–Apr.*

Konoba Kopačina

$$ | **MEDITERRANEAN** | **FAMILY** | It is hard to spend more than a day on the island of Brač without giving in to the succulent aromas of roasted lamb, and many

Brač Stone

The island of Brač is well known for its fine white stone, quarried across the island but particularly represented in the village of Pučišća, on the north coast. Through the centuries, Brač stone has been used for world-famous buildings, including Diocletian's Palace in Split and the Cathedral of St. James in Šibenik. There are rumors that it is what was used for the U.S. White House and the parliament building in Budapest. Today, the prized stone is used by sculptors and for the reconstruction of historic monuments.

people claim Konoba Kopačina is the best place to enjoy the island delicacy. While waiting for your lamb, consider trying Konoba Kopačina's *vitalac,* an island delicacy that includes the sheeps' innards wrapped in gauze or membrane and roasted on a spit. **Known for:** expertly grilled lamb; caramelized sheep cheese; good selection of local wines. Ⓢ *Average main: 120 Kn* ✉ *Donji Humac 7, Donji Humac* ☎ *021/647–707* ⊕ *www.konoba-kopacina.com.*

Ribarska Kučica

$$$ | **SEAFOOD** | On the waterside footpath near the Dominican Monastery, with romantic nighttime views over the open sea, this friendly eatery serves seafood dishes, or pizza or pasta as a cheaper option. Look for the delicious gnocchi with Gorgonzola and prosciutto. **Known for:** beachside location; adjoining cocktail bar; slow service when busy. Ⓢ *Average main: 135 Kn* ✉ *Šetalište Anđelka Rabadana 2d, Bol* ☎ *095/902–9844* ⊘ *Closed Oct.–May.*

Hotels

Bluesun Hotel Borak

$$ | HOTEL | FAMILY | Set amid pine trees on the path to Zlatni Rat beach—and just a 10-minute walk from Bol's Old Town—this hotel occupies a modern, three-story white building with a restaurant terrace and a pool out front. **Pros:** proximity to Zlatni Rat beach; good sports facilities; family rooms available for those with kids. **Cons:** large and slightly impersonal; popular with large tour groups; spa is located in another hotel. $ *Rooms from: 975 Kn* ⊠ *Bračka Cesta 13* ☎ *021/306–202* ⊕ *www.brachotelborak. com* ☾ *Closed Nov.–Apr.* ⇋ *184 rooms* ❙○❙ *Free breakfast.*

Hotel Osam

$$ | HOTEL | This sleek adults-only hotel with rooftop bar and swimming pool offers something not found in many places on Brač: an urban-style island retreat. **Pros:** excellent buffet breakfast and restaurant; extremely convenient location; unique former schoolhouse building. **Cons:** rooms are not soundproof; swimming pool is small; adults-only policy might not suit families. $ *Rooms from: 1210 Kn* ⊠ *Vlačica 3, Supetar* ☎ *021/552–333* ⊕ *www.hotel-osam.com* ⇋ *27 rooms* ❙○❙ *All meals.*

★ Villa Giardino (*Villa Giardino Heritage Boutique Hotel*)

$$ | B&B/INN | Set in a quiet garden full of Mediterranean greenery, this hotel is just a five-minute walk from the harbor. **Pros:** attentive staff; peaceful yet centrally located; breakfast served in lovely garden. **Cons:** often fully booked; limited facilities; on the expensive side. $ *Rooms from: 1285 Kn* ⊠ *Novi put 2* ☎ *021/635–900* ⊕ *www.villagiardinobol. com* ☾ *Closed Nov.–Apr.* ⇋ *5 rooms* ❙○❙ *Free breakfast.*

 Activities

ADVENTURE TOURS

Aldura Sport

TOUR—SPORTS | FAMILY | If you want to explore the island of Brač with local outdoor enthusiasts committed to preserving the traditions and beauty of the island, the experts at Aldura Sport have you covered. From beginner to experienced adventurers, everyone will enjoy the company's unparalleled excursions and tours in walking, sailing, biking, kayaking, and hiking. ⊠ *Porat BB, Sutivan* ☎ *098/423–689* ⊕ *www.aldura-sport.hr.*

BEACHES

★ Zlatni Rat (*Golden Horn*)

BEACHES | FAMILY | The obvious spot for swimming and sunning here is the glorious Zlatni Rat (Golden Horn or Golden Cape) beach, complete with a café and snack bar, plus sun beds and parasols along with paddleboats and jet skis for rent through peak season. To the west of Zlatni Rat lies a small beach reserved for nudists. Regular taxi-boats run from the Old Town harbor to Zlatni Rat beach; walking distance is 20 minutes. **Amenities**: food and drink; showers; toilets; water sports. **Best for**: snorkeling; sunrise; sunset; swimming; windsurfing. ⊠ *Zlatni Rat* ⊕ *www.bol.hr/ experience-bol/zlatni-rat-en1204.*

WATER SPORTS

Big Blue Sport

BEACHES | FAMILY | For windsurfing and scuba-diving training, stand-up paddleboarding, and equipment rentals, this well-established local company also rents sea kayaks and mountain bikes. ⊠ *Podan Glavice 2, Bol* ☎ *091/449–7087* ⊕ *www. bigbluesport.com.*

Hvar

23 nautical miles south of Split by ferry.

The island of Hvar bills itself as the "sunniest island in the Adriatic." And it even has the figures to back up this claim—an annual average of 2,760 hours of sunshine with a maximum of two foggy days a year.

GETTING HERE AND AROUND

The easiest way to reach Hvar Town is to catch a mid-afternoon Jadrolinija catamaran from Split, which stops at Hvar Town (23 nautical miles) before continuing to the South Dalmatian islands of Korčula and Lastovo. Alternatively, take an early morning Jadrolinija ferry from Split to Stari Grad (23 nautical miles) and then catch a local bus across the island.

 ## Sights

Hvar is both the name of the island and the name of the capital (Hvar Town), which sits near the island's western tip. Hvar Town rises like an amphitheater from its harbor, backed by a hilltop fortress and protected from the open sea by a scattering of small islands known as Pakleni Otoci ("hellish islands", although paradise islands would be a more fitting name). Along the palm-lined quay, a string of cafés and restaurants is shaded by colorful awnings and umbrellas. A few steps away, the magnificent main square, St. Stephen's Square (Trg sv. Stjepana), the largest piazza in Dalmatia, is backed by the 16th-century Cathedral of St. Stephen (Katedrala sv. Stjepana). Other notable sights in town include the Fortica Fortress and the Franciscan Monastery (Franjevački samostan). In addition, partiers and explorers from all over the world flock to Hvar Town en masse so expect it to be crowded and expensive through peak season. Celebrity visitors have included King Abdullah of Jordan and his wife, Queen Rania, Italian clothing entrepreneur Luciano Benetton, Prince Harry of England, Beyoncé and her husband Jay Z, and many, many more.

★ **Fortica Fortress** (*Španjola*)
VIEWPOINT | This 16th-century hilltop fortress is a symbol of Hvar Town. Climbing to the top takes about 25 minutes, and you get to take in the amazing Mediterranean plant garden as you go. Once you're at the top, you can explore the fortress's stone walls and behold breathtaking views of the city below, along with the sea and islands stretching over the horizon as far as the eye can see. ⊠ *Fortica Fortress.*

Franciscan Monastery (*Franjevački samostan*)
RELIGIOUS SITE | **FAMILY** | A short walk east of town, along the quay past the Arsenal, lies Hvar Town's Franciscan Monastery. Within its walls, a pretty 15th-century Renaissance cloister leads to the former refectory, now housing a small museum with several notable artworks, including a beautiful fresco of the Last Supper, while the grounds outside make a relaxing place for a stroll among centuries-old cypress trees. ⊠ *Križa bb* 🚇 *30 Kn.*

Jelsa
TOWN | **FAMILY** | Hvar's third main town is often overlooked, but that makes it all the more delightful once you do discover it as a more peaceful alternative to Hvar Town. On the northern coast of the island you will see many structures from the Renaissance and Baroque periods, though St. Mary's Church dates back to the early 1300s. A tower built by the ancient Greeks overlooks the harbor; it dates to the 3rd or 4th century BC. About 1 km (0.6 mile) east of the modern town is the older Grad, with the original fortified area that was protected by the fortress called Galešnik, and now stands in ruins. This small town is surrounded by a thick forest of pine trees, several resorts, and many swimmable beaches—including some of the island's most popular nude beaches. The town is also famous for its annual Za Križen procession,

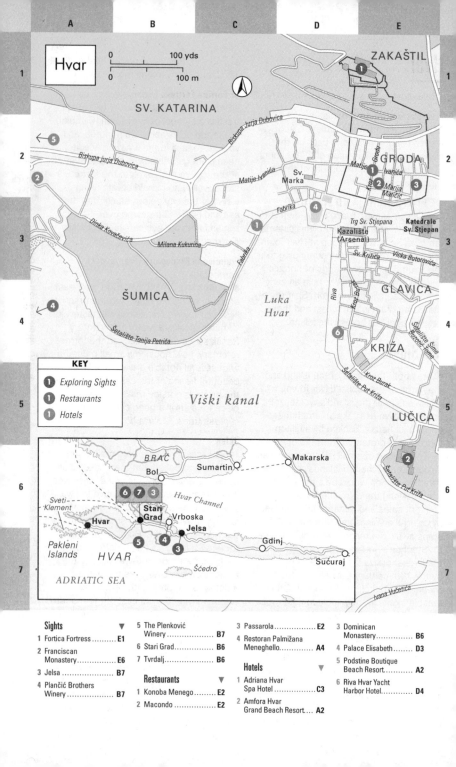

Hvar

0 ——— 100 yds
0 ——— 100 m

SV. KATARINA

Biskupa Jurja Dubovica

Biskupa jurja Dubovica

Matije Ivaniča

Dinka Kovačevića

Milana Kukurina

ŠUMICA

Šetalište Tonija Petrića

Fabrika

Sv. Marka

ZAKAŠTIL

GRODA

Matije Ivaniča

Trg Sv. Stjepana

Kazalište
(Arsenal)

Sv. Križica

Vicka Butorovica

Katedrale
Sv. Stjepan

Marija
Matičić

Luka
Hvar

Riva

Kroz Burak

GLAVICA

Šetalište Sime
Buconić-Tome

KRIŽA

Šetalište Put Križa

Kroz Burak

Šetalište Put Križa

LUČICA

KEY

- Exploring Sights
- Restaurants
- Hotels

Viški kanal

BRAČ

Bol

Sumartin

Makarska

Sveti-
Klement

Hvar Channel

Stari
Grad

Vrboska

Jelsa

Gdinj

Sućuraj

Pakleni
Islands

HVAR

Ščedro

ADRIATIC SEA

Ivana Vučetića

a 500-year-old, UNESCO-protected Easter tradition during which a shoeless cross-bearer and a crowd embark on a 25 km (16 mile) overnight walk. Carrying the cross is considered very prestigious, and the wait time to do so can last decades. ⊠ *20 km (13 miles) east of Hvar Town.*

Plančić Brothers Winery (*Vinarija Braća Plančić*)

WINERY/DISTILLERY | On the beautiful, vineyard-strewn island of Hvar you can visit Plančić Winery, where the Plančić family has been producing a variety of top-quality wines, including rosé and dessert wines, as well as local rakija, since 1919. Look out for Bogdanuša (dry white wine) or Ivan Dolać (a select red). ⊠ *Vrbanj 191* ☎ *091/973–2025* ⊕ *www.facebook.com/vinaplancic.*

The Plenković Winery

WINERY/DISTILLERY | The award-winning Plenković Winery on the island of Hvar, along with its restaurant and hotel, are also well worth a visit. In fact, in the past few years the Zlatan Plavac (a dry red) made by Zlatan Plenković has continually won prestigious awards at local and international wine fairs. ⊠ *Stari Grad* ☎ *021/745–709* ⊕ *www.zlatanotok.hr.*

★ Stari Grad

TOWN | **FAMILY** | As its name suggests, Stari Grad, or Old Town, is one of the oldest towns in Europe, with some locals claiming it to be the oldest. Founded in the fourth century BC, this is the site of the original Greek settlement on Hvar, called Pharos by the Greeks. While much of the attraction in Stari Grad focuses on its ancient history, the city is still very much alive throughout the year. It is the entry point to the island for bus transportation from the mainland, as well as the car ferry terminal. It features a beautiful, walkable riviera and forest path, as well as a number of cultural attractions, such as the 15th-century Dominican Monastery of St. Peter the Martyr. The town is about 23 km (14 miles) east of Hvar Town. ⊠ *Stari Grad* ⊕ *www.stari-grad.hr.*

Wine in Central Dalmatia

The island of Hvar makes some of Croatia's top wines. On the south coast, the steep, rugged, seaward-facing slopes between the villages of Sveti Nedelja and Ivan Dolac focus on full-bodied reds, made predominantly from the Plavac Mali grape. In contrast, the vineyards in the flat valley between Stari Grad and Jelsa on the north side produce mostly whites, such as the greenish-yellow Bogdanuša.

Tvrdalj

HOUSE | Stari Grad's *trvdalj*, or fortress, is the palace of renowned local poet Petar Hektorović (1487-1572). The Tvrdalj was first renovated in 18th-century Baroque style, and a partial restoration was completed in the 19th century. Hektorović originally attempted to create a "model universe" to be embodied in his home. To that end, a large fish pond on-site is stocked with gray mullet, as it was in the poet's own time, representing the sea; and above the fish pond in a tower is a dovecote, representing the air. Ivy was allowed to cover the walls to tie the home to the land. Quotations from Hektorović's striking poetry are inscribed on many walls. The home is not open to visitors, but the garden is worth a visit, and there is also a display of ancient agricultural equipment. ⊠ *8 Ul. Molo Njiva* ☎ *021/765–068* ⊞ *20 Kn.*

🍴 Restaurants

Konoba Menego

$$ | **MEDITERRANEAN** | **FAMILY** | On the steps between the main square and the fortress, this authentic stone-walled konoba has candlelit tables and *pršut* hanging from the raftered ceiling. Come

Hvar's Stari Grad is a frequent entryway for those arriving to the island via boat.

here to share platters of locally produced, cold Dalmatian specialties such as *kožji sir* (goat cheese), *salata od hobotnice* (octopus salad), and *masline* (olives), or feast on wild boar and traditional pašticada. **Known for:** small plates and "drunken" (brandy-marinated) figs; no reservations so waits are possible; cash only. $ *Average main: 120 Kn* ⊠ *Kroz Grodu 26* ☎ *021/717–411* ⊕ *www.menego.hr* ▤ *No credit cards* ☉ *Closed Dec.–Mar.*

Macondo

$$$ | **SEAFOOD** | **FAMILY** | Fresh fish takes center stage at this superb restaurant hidden away on a narrow, cobbled street of Hvar Town. The dining room is simply furnished with wooden tables, discreet modern art, and a large open fire, and the food and service are practically faultless. **Known for:** superfresh seafood; well-versed waitstaff; great place to try gregada (fish stew). $ *Average main: 150 Kn* ⊠ *Marije Maričić 7* ☎ *021/742–850* ⊕ *www.macondo.com.hr* ▤ *No credit cards* ☉ *Closed Dec.–Mar.*

Passarola

$$$$ | **MEDITERRANEAN** | Tucked away in a picturesque courtyard off the main square, great care is taken at this sophisticated restaurant to select and focus on the best local, organic ingredients. The wine list is impressive and includes local standouts and a wide international selection. **Known for:** traditional dishes; beautiful presentation and flavors; impressive wine list. $ *Average main: 225 Kn* ⊠ *Dr. Mate Miličića 10* ☎ *021/717–374* ⊕ *restaurant-passarola.eu* ☉ *Closed Nov.–Apr.*

★ Restoran Palmižana Meneghello

$$$ | **SEAFOOD** | On the tiny island of Sveti Klement, a 20-minute taxi-boat ride from Hvar Town, this terrace restaurant is backed by a romantic wilderness of Mediterranean flora and offers stunning views over the open sea. Besides wonderfully fresh seafood, dishes include *kožji sir sa rukolom* (goat cheese with arugula), and *pašticada* (beef stewed in sweet wine and prunes). **Known for:** exquisite view and heavenly surroundings; upscale Croatian dishes; Croatian art decor and

Sunday morning classical music recitals. $ *Average main: 150 Kn* ✉ *Vinogradišće Uvala, Sveti Klement* ☎ *091/478–3111* ⊕ *www.palmizana.com* ▤ *No credit cards* ☾ *Closed Nov.–Mar.*

Hotels

Adriana Hvar Spa Hotel

$$$$ | **HOTEL** | This well-appointed hotel has a rooftop pool and sophisticated cocktail bar, affording stunning views onto the sea and Old Town, and a chic ground-floor restaurant serving Mediter-ranean cuisine on the harborfront. **Pros:** prime location on seafront promenade; beautifully designed interiors; luxuri-ous spa. **Cons:** very expensive; most bathrooms have a big shower but no tub; not always up to five-star standards. $ *Rooms from: 2260 Kn* ✉ *Obala Fabrika 28* ☎ *021/750–555* ⊕ *www.suncanihvar. com/adriana-hvar-spa-hotel.html* ⇄ *62 rooms* ⦿| *Free breakfast.*

Amfora Hvar Grand Beach Resort

$$$$ | **HOTEL** | **FAMILY** | This colossal white, modern structure sits in its own bay with a pinewood backdrop, and is a 10-minute walk along the coastal path from the center of town. **Pros:** beautiful pool; chic modern design; private beach cabins. **Cons:** inconsistent service; large and somewhat impersonal; on the expensive side. $ *Rooms from: 2080 Kn* ✉ *Bisku-pa Jurja Dubokovica 5* ☎ *021/750–300* ⊕ *www.suncanihvar.com/amfora-hvar-grand-beach-resort.html* ⇄ *324 rooms* ⦿| *Free breakfast.*

Dominican Monastery

$ | **B&B/INN** | If you're looking for some-thing different than the usual accom-modations, Stari Grad's 15th-century Dominican Monastery is among the first monasteries in Croatia to open their historic doors to guests. **Pros:** total relax-ation and peace; gorgeous courtyard gar-den; two minutes by foot from the town center and beaches. **Cons:** amenities

are more humble; no on-site restaurant; limited hours for service and reception. $ *Rooms from: 450 Kn* ✉ *Kod Svetog Petra 1P, Stari Grad* ☎ *021/765–442* ⊕ *www.monastays.com/accommodation/ otokhvar* ⇄ *15 rooms* ⦿| *Free breakfast.*

Palace Elisabeth

$$$$ | **HOTEL** | **FAMILY** | Commanding a prime site on the edge of the main square and overlooking the harbor, the Palace remains open most of the year, offering much lower prices during the off-season. **Pros:** centrally located; use of Hotel Amfora pool is free; very reasonable price given the location. **Cons:** rooms are dated; no air-conditioning in rooms; can be loud during high season. $ *Rooms from: 2650 Kn* ✉ *Trg sv. Stjep-ana* ☎ *021/741–966* ⊕ *www.suncanihvar. com/palace-elisabeth-hvar-heritage-hotel. html* ☾ *Closed Dec.–Mar.* ⇄ *73 rooms* ⦿| *Free breakfast.*

Podstine Boutique Beach Resort

$$$ | **HOTEL** | With cool, peaceful rooms—most with sea views and balconies, and spacious marble bathrooms—this peaceful, family-run boutique resort lies on the coast, a 20-minute walk west of the town center. **Pros:** peaceful seafront location; beautiful gardens; small beach out front with sun beds and umbrellas. **Cons:** far from Old Town; no nightlife near-by (the hotel's bar shuts at 11 pm even in summer); standard rooms have no views. $ *Rooms from: 1565 Kn* ✉ *Put Podstina 11* ☎ *021/740–400* ⊕ *www.podstine. com* ☾ *Closed Nov.–Mar.* ⇄ *50 rooms* ⦿| *All-inclusive.*

★ Riva Hvar Yacht Harbor Hotel

$$$ | **HOTEL** | Located on the palm-lined waterfront, opposite the ferry landing station, Hotel Riva is considered one of Hvar's hippest hotels. **Pros:** prime location on seafront promenade; cool, eclectic atmosphere; excellent bar and restaurant. **Cons:** showers are visible in rooms; rooms in front are very noisy; small rooms. $ *Rooms from: 1815 Kn*

✉ *Obala Riva 27* ☎ *021/750–100* ⊕ *www.suncanihvar.com/riva-hvar-yacht-harbour-hotel.html* ⚓ *54 rooms* ❍ *Free breakfast.*

Nightlife

Over the past few years, Hvar has become one of the hottest party destinations for the young and well-to-do. This phenomenon has led to a lot of crowding and rowdiness during the high season, which can can be off-putting for those looking to enjoy the island's natural and traditional attractions. But if you are looking for a good time, you're sure to find it here: several stylish cocktail bars and clubs cater to the annual influx of summer visitors, including those that arrive with Yacht Week and the Ultra Music Festival that starts in Split and celebrates its last night with a beach party on Hvar. For the more discerning traveler, there are a number of elegant evening events too.

BARS

★ Carpe Diem Bar

BARS/PUBS | A legendary harborside cocktail bar popular with twentysomethings, Carpe Diem has been Hvar's top party destination for years. Go during the day for a more relaxed vibe, great views, and the best people-watching. To reach this beach bar (located on an island off the coast of Hvar), you can simply catch a taxi boat from the harbor. ✉ *Hvar* ☎ *099/377–6776* ⊕ *www.carpe-diem-hvar.com.*

Hula Hula

BARS/PUBS | This wooden beach bar, built into the rocks overlooking the sea, attracts bathers through daytime with its chill music, lounge chairs, VIP tables, and massages. Many stay for the sunset as the beach club transforms into a dance party with DJ music and cocktails. Even Beyoncé has been spotted here. ✉ *Petrićevo šetalište 10* ☎ *095/911–1871* ⊕ *www.hulahulahvar.com.*

Pink Champagne

DANCE CLUBS | A staple nightclub in Hvar, large-scale Pink Champagne is known for its extravagance, break-the-dial blasting music, and tasty house cocktails. ✉ *Ive Miličića 4* ☎ *021/742–283* ⊕ *www.facebook.com/PinkChampagneHvar.*

Performing Arts

FESTIVALS

Hvar Summer Festival

MUSIC FESTIVALS | Classical-music recitals in the cloisters of the Franciscan Monastery have long been the highlight of the Hvar Summer Festival. Also look out for theater, folklore, and jazz at various open-air locations around town. The annual festival usually runs for a month sometime between June and September. ✉ *Hvar* ☎ *021/718–336* ⊕ *www.hvarsummerfestival.hr/en.*

☄ Activities

BEACHES

Although there are several pretty beaches within walking distance of Hvar Town—the best-equipped being the Hotel Amfora's pebble beach, 10 minutes west of the main square—sun worshippers in the know head for the nearby Pakleni Otoci, which can be reached by taxi-boats that depart regularly (in peak season, every hour, from 8 to 8) from the town harbor. The best known and best served are Sveti Jerolim (on the island of the same name, partially a nudist beach), Stipanska (on the island of Marinkovac, clothing-optional), and Palmižana (on the island of Sveti Klement, also clothing-optional).

Carpe Diem Beach

BEACHES | Doubling as a daytime beach club and an after-dark party venue, Carpe Diem Beach lies on the tiny pine-scented island of Stipanska, a 10-minute taxi-boat ride from Hvar Town's harbor. It has two pebble beaches complete with wooden sun-beds and big parasols, an outdoor pool, and an open-air massage pavilion. There's also a lounge-bar and restaurant, and from mid-July to mid-August it hosts international DJs, playing till sunrise. By night, free taxi boats depart from outside Carpe Diem Bar. **Amenities:** food and drink; showers; toilets. **Best for:** partiers; swimming. ⊠ *Stipanska* ☎ *099/446–8468* ⊕ *www.carpe-diem-beach-hvar.com.*

DIVING
Diving Center Viking
SCUBA DIVING | Those with a taste for underwater adventure might have a go at scuba diving. The seabed is scattered with pieces of broken Greek amphorae, while the area's biggest underwater attraction is the Stambedar seawall, home to red and violet gorgonians (a type of coral), which is close to the Pakleni Islands. For courses at all levels, try Diving Center Viking. ⊠ *Put Podstine 7* ☎ *091/6205–847* ⊕ *www.viking-diving. com.*

SAILING
Hvar Town is a popular port of call for those sailing on the Adriatic; the town harbor is packed with flashy yachts through peak season and beyond.

ACI Marina Palmižana
SAILING | This 180-berth marina is open from April through October, and is served by regular taxi boats from Hvar Town through peak season. Located on Palmižana Bay on the island of Sveti Klement, one of the Pakleni Otoci, it lies just 2½ nautical miles from Hvar Town. ⊠ *Palmižana Bay, Sveti Klement* ☎ *021/744–995* ⊕ *www.aci-marinas.com/ marina/aci-palmizana.*

Hvar Adventure
DIVING/SNORKELING | FAMILY | This company arranges sea kayaking tours from Hvar Town to the Pakleni islets, as well as one-day sailing trips, hiking, cycling, rock climbing, and more. ⊠ *Jurja Matijevića 20* ☎ *091/228–0088* ⊕ *www.hvar-adventure. com.*

★ **Sunburst Sailing**
SAILING | Here, you can rent out a 42-foot sailing yacht called Nera, based in Split, that is available for fully catered day charters and evening cruises. ⊠ *Hrvatske mornarice 1* ☎ *091/185–4559* ⊕ *www. sunburstsailing.com.*

YOGA
Suncokret Body & Soul Retreat
AEROBICS/YOGA | Founded by a New Yorker and her Dalmatia-born partner, Suncokret offers holistic wellness retreats that combine yoga, nature walks, Reiki, life-path workshops, and painting. Guests are accommodated in private cottages in the village, and typical Dalmatian meals are provided. Most courses last one week, but visitors are also welcome to drop in for a session. Dol lies 6 km (4 miles) from Stari Grad and 26 km (16 miles) from Hvar Town. ⊠ *Gojava 7 Sveta Ana, Postira* ☎ *091/519–8717* ⊕ *www. suncokretdream.net.*

Vis

34 nautical miles southwest of Split by ferry.

Closed to foreigners until 1989 due to its use as a military base, the distant island of Vis is relatively wild and unspoiled. Built around wide harbors, the main towns are popular among yachters, who appreciate the island's rugged nature, unpretentious fish restaurants, and excellent locally produced wine.

The pretty fishing village of Komiža is 11 km (7 miles) from Vis Town. Here you're just a 40-minute boat ride away from the Modra špilja (Blue Cave), often compared to the Blue Grotto on Italy's Capri.

GETTING HERE AND AROUND
To get here from Split, you can take a 2½-hour Jadrolinija ferry ride to arrive in Vis Town, or you can stop in at your own pace if you're sailing.

Vis is well known for its low-key vineyards and wineries.

Sights

★ **Modra špilja** (*Blue Cave*)
CAVE | FAMILY | Hidden away on the islet of Biševo (5 nautical miles southwest of Komiža), the Blue Cave is 78 feet long and 39 feet wide. Sunlight enters through the water, reflects off the seabed, and casts the interior in a fantastic shade of blue. Throughout the summer, local fishermen and agencies take tourists (some coming from Split and Hvar by speedboat) into the caverns..It can be a long wait in summer when there's a line of small boats waiting to enter the cave. Ask at the marina or the tourist information office to see who is offering trips. Sometimes, small boat operators will wait at the entrance of the cave for visitors arriving on sailboat or yacht (which are too large to enter the cave). ✉ *Biševo island* 🎫 *50 Kn; extra for a dock if you're sailing.*

Restaurants

Fabrika
$$ | ECLECTIC | The cool atmosphere, bohemian furniture, and original jewelry sold on-site, all add up to a funky little place to go for a burger and a drink. Don't miss out on their delicious prawn burger. **Known for:** great location; good breakfast menu; fashionable owners. [$] *Average main: 75 Kn* ✉ *Riva Sv. Mikule 12, Komiža* ☎ *021/713–155* 🌐 *www.fabrikavis.hr* 💳 *No credit cards* 🕒 *Closed Oct.–Apr.*

Jastožera
$$$$ | SEAFOOD | FAMILY | Originally opened in 1883 as a lobster house, this cleverly converted restaurant has platforms with tables built out above the water, and small boats can drive right under the platforms and into the central dining room. The house specialty is *jastog sa špagetima* (lobster with spaghetti). **Known for:** access to main dining room via the water; slow service; grilled fish. [$] *Average main: 225 Kn* ✉ *Gundulićeva*

6, Komiža ☎ 099/670–7755 ⊕ www. jastozera.eu ☉ Closed Nov.–Mar.

Konoba Bako

$$$$ | **SEAFOOD** | **FAMILY** | Popular with locals and visitors alike, this excellent fish restaurant overlooks a tiny bay in Komiža. Outdoors, tables are set right up to the water's edge, and inside there's a small pool with lobsters and amphorae. **Known for:** good seafood; unbeatable views and location; scampi risotto and barbecued fish. $ *Average main: 225 Kn ⊠ Gundulićeva 1, Komiža ☎ 098/360–469 ⊕ www.konobabako.hr/en ☉ No lunch.*

★ Konoba & Bar Lola

$$$ | **MEDITERRANEAN** | **FAMILY** | A funky garden restaurant, Konoba & bar Lola offers something refreshingly different on the island of Vis. The atmosphere is relaxed, the food is fresh, and most of the vegetables come from Lola's own garden on the mainland. **Known for:** romantic garden setting; impressive cocktails and desserts; excellent steak. $ *Average main: 150 Kn ⊠ Matije Gupca 12, Vis Town ☎ 095/563–3247 ⊕ www. lolavisisland.com ☉ Closed Nov.–Mar.*

Pojoda

$$$$ | **SEAFOOD** | **FAMILY** | A modern glass-and-wood conservatory that looks onto a courtyard garden of orange and lemon trees, Pojoda makes for a popular spot among the sailing crowd that won't disappoint a food-savvy traveler either. The dishes are named in local dialect: check out the *manistra na brudet* (bean and pasta soup) and *luc u verudi* (tuna stewed with vegetables), or try the *pojorski bronzinić,* a thick brodetto of squid with lentils and barley. **Known for:** grilled fresh fish; family-friendly atmosphere; brilliantly flavored lobster brudet. $ *Average main: 225 Kn ⊠ Don Cvjetka Marasovića 8, Vis Town ☎ 021/711–575 ☉ Closed for dinner in winter.*

Villa Kaliopa

$$$$ | **SEAFOOD** | With tables set under the trees in the romantic walled garden of a 16th-century villa, dinner at this restaurant in Vis Town is an unforgettable experience. The menu changes daily depending on what fresh fish and shellfish are available. **Known for:** excellent setting and location; catering to the high-end crowd; fish priced by weight. $ *Average main: 300 Kn ⊠ Vladimira Nazora 32, Vis Town ☎ 091/271–1755 ▭ No credit cards ☉ Closed Nov.–Mar.*

 ## Hotels

Hotel San Giorgio

$$ | **HOTEL** | **FAMILY** | In Vis Town, east of the ferry quay, this chic little hotel is hidden away between stone cottages in a quiet, cobbled side street. **Pros:** yoga vacations offered; modern and comfortable rooms; good restaurant. **Cons:** a couple of blocks in from the seafront (only the top-floor suite has a sea view); often fully booked; 20-minute walk from ferry landing can be difficult for visitors with heavy luggage. $ *Rooms from: 1285 Kn ⊠ Petra Hektorovića 2, Vis Town ☎ 021/607–630 ⊕ www.hotelsangiorgio-vis.com ⇲ 10 rooms ⊙ Free breakfast.*

Tamaris

$$ | **HOTEL** | **FAMILY** | Overlooking the harbor and seafront promenade in Vis Town, Tamaris occupies a late-19th-century building. **Pros:** on seafront promenade in center of town; most rooms have sea views; cheerful café terrace out front. **Cons:** rooms very basic; service rather indifferent; some rooms do not have views. $ *Rooms from: 1050 Kn ⊠ Obala sv. Jurja 30, Vis Town ☎ 021/711–350 ⊕ www.hotelsvis.com/en ⇲ 25 rooms ⊙ Free breakfast.*

 ## Activities

DIVING
ISSA Diving Center

SCUBA DIVING | Scuba-diving enthusiasts will find underwater attractions including several underwater caves, at least half a dozen shipwrecks, and some spectacular coral reefs. Beginners and those with previous experience should contact this center for organized diving trips and training at all levels with expert instructors. ✉ *Ribarska 91, Komiža* ☎ *021/713–651* 🌐 *www.scubadiving.hr.*

Makarska

67 km (42 miles) southeast of Split.

This city's seafront promenade, lined with palm trees and cheerful open-air cafés, looks onto a protected bay dotted with wooden fishing boats. From here one enters the Old Town, a warren of stone buildings and cobbled streets surrounding the main square, which is backed by the parish church and a small open-air market off to one side. The atmosphere is relaxed and easygoing. The only drama you'll likely see is created by the limestone heights of Biokovo Mountain, which seems to alternate between protecting and threatening the town, depending on the color of the sky and the cloud formations that ride over its rugged peaks.

Makarska is the center of the area known as the "Makarska Riviera", a 60 km (38 mile) stretch of coastline from Brela to Gradac.

GETTING HERE AND AROUND

The cobblestone streets of this small bayside town are fully walkable, and best experienced on foot.

Sights

Biokovo Nature Park (*Park Prirode Biokovo*)

NATURE PRESERVE | FAMILY | Behind Makarska, a large area of the rocky heights that form the majestic Biokovo Mountain have been designated as a nature park. Part of the Dinaric Alps, which run from Slovenia down to Montenegro, Biokovo abounds in rare indigenous plant species, and is primarily limestone with little green coverage. It's possible to reach the highest peak, Sveti Jure (5,781 feet) in five and a half hours from Makarska. However, this is a strenuous hike, especially in summer, for which you will need good boots and plenty of water. It is not recommended to hike it alone. It is best to organize an excursion through Biokovo Active Holidays, a company that offers fun organized trips up the mountain, traveling part of the way by jeep. ✉ *Biokovo Nature Park* ☎ *021/616–924* 🌐 *www.pp-biokovo.hr.*

Restaurants

★ Jeny

$$$$ | **MODERN EUROPEAN** | One of the best fine dining restaurants on the Makarska Riviera, it's clear that time and care has gone into creating the wine pairing menu at Jeny and the expertise of the food preparation can hold a candle to many of Croatia's most awarded restaurants. A tasting menu, at 830 Kn per person, includes 7 plates and 6 wines. **Known for:** delectable scallops; sophisticated wine pairing menu; beautiful views. [$] *Average main: 225 Kn* ✉ *Čovići 1, Tucepi* ☎ *091/587–8078* 🌐 *www.restaurant-jeny.hr.*

Konoba Ranč

$$$ | **MEDITERRANEAN** | **FAMILY** | Surrounded on all four sides by the shade of an olive grove, this restaurant is the perfect place to wind down a day of sun and sightseeing. It's known for the steak and lamb from the peka and fish prepared traditionally *na gradele* (on the grill). **Known for:** outdoor area for kids to run around; hearty food; al fresco dining. [$] *Average main: 150 Kn* ✉ *Kamena 62, Tucepi* ☎ *021/623–563* 🌐 *www.ranc-tucepi.hr.*

Stari Mlin

$$$ | **ECLECTIC** | Hanging plants, funky paintings, and colorful canvases set the mood inside this old stone building, where the interior garden is draped with vines and decorated with pots of herbs and cherry tomatoes. Barbecued seafood

tops the menu, but there's also a select choice of Thai dishes. **Known for:** quality Croatian fare; excellent mojitos; waitstaff that tends to upsell. $ *Average main: 165 Kn* ✉ *Prvosvibanska 43* ☎ *021/611–509.*

Hotels

★ Boutique Hotel Marco Polo
$$ | **B&B/INN** | From the luxurious accommodations to the fine food to the individualized excursions, Boutique Hotel Marco Polo stands out on the Makarska Riviera as *the* place to make your summer holiday. **Pros:** excellent restaurant, rooftop terrace, pool, and spa; intimate and comfortable atmosphere; devoted owners who personally research and arrange guest excursions. **Cons:** can get crowded; hard to find a spot on the beach; can be expensive. $ *Rooms from: 1170 Kn* ✉ *Obala 15, Gradac* ☎ *021/695–060* ⊕ *www.hotel-marcopolo.com* ⇥ *25 rooms.*

Hotel Biokovo
$ | **HOTEL** | In the center of Makarska, on the palm-lined seafront promenade, this old-fashioned hotel is perfectly lovely. **Pros:** centrally located; friendly and helpful staff; pleasant café and decent restaurant. **Cons:** limited facilities; parking can be a problem; might be too old-school for modern decor lovers. $ *Rooms from: 430 Kn* ✉ *Obala Kralja Tomislava 14* ☎ *021/615–244* ⊕ *www.sol.hr/hr/hotel-biokovo* ⇥ *56 rooms* ⦿ *Free breakfast.*

Activities

BEACHES
The main town beach, a lovely 1½-km (1-mile) stretch of pebbles backed by pine woods, lies northwest of the center and close to a string of big modern hotels. Alternatively, walk along the narrow coastal path southeast of town to find rocks and a series of secluded coves perfect for a swimming base. Farther afield, the Makarska Riviera is a 60-km (38-mile) stretch of coast running from Brela to Gradac. The Makarska Riviera's lovely Adriatic views, paired with the stunningly beautiful backdrop of the Biokovo Mountain, rival the French Riviera. Several easily accessed islands are also at its doorstep, along with an assortment of small coved private beaches and villages that are each islands unto themselves.

DIVING
Local underwater attractions include a nearby reef, known as **Kraljev Gaj,** which is populated by sponges, coral, octopi, and scorpion fish, while farther out from the coast you can visit the *Dubrovnik,* an old steam boat that sank in 1917.

More Sub Makarska
SCUBA DIVING | **FAMILY** | Scuba-diving enthusiasts, as well as complete beginners, can head to More Sub for organized diving trips and training at all levels. ✉ *Kralja Petra Krešimira IV 43* ☎ *098/173–9926* ⊕ *www.more-sub-makarska.hr.*

Lastovo

80 km (50 nautical miles) southeast of Split (daily direct ferry connection).

Very few Croatians have visited Lastovo, though they will all tell you that it's beautiful. Like Vis, Lastovo was a Yugoslav military naval base during the Tito years, and was therefore closed to foreigners, so commercial tourism never developed. Today, there is still just one hotel.

Lying far out to sea, Lastovo is an island of green, fertile valleys and is practically self-sufficient: locally caught seafood—not least the delicious lobster—and homegrown vegetables are the staple diet. The main settlement, Lastovo Town, is made up of stone houses built amphitheater-style into a hillside, crisscrossed by cobbled alleys and flights of steps; they're renowned for tall chimneys resembling minarets. The only other settlement on the island is the small port of Ubli, which is 10 km (6 miles) from Lastovo Town.

GETTING HERE AND AROUND

Although it is officially in South Dalmatia, Lastovo only has direct transport links with Split in Central Dalmatia rather than Dubrovnik. To get to the idyllic island, take the Jadrolinija daily ferry service from Split to Ubli, stopping at Hvar Town and Vela Luka (on Korčula) en route. Jadrolinija also runs a daily catamaran from Split covering the same route; it's faster but a little more expensive.

 Restaurants

Konoba Bačvara

$$ | SEAFOOD | Traditional home-cooked Dalmatian fare is served at this family-run eatery in an old stone building in Lastovo Town. Barbecued seafood predominates, and you'll also have the chance to try homegrown vegetables and local wine. **Known for:** affordable meals; refreshing escape; homegrown veggies. $ *Average main: 70 Kn* ⌂ *Počuvalo* ☎ *020/801–131* ⊕ *www.tz-lastovo.hr/vodic-po-lastovu/ gastronomija/objekt/konoba-bacvara* ⊟ *No credit cards* ⊘ *Closed Nov.–May.*

Konoba Triton

$$$$ | SEAFOOD | Widely acknowledged to be the best restaurant on the island, Triton is particularly popular with those traveling by sailboat, who can moor up on a small quay out front. The owners catch and cook the fish themselves; they also produce the wine, olive oil, and vegetables. **Known for:** good antipasto; free mooring for those arriving by boat; freshly caught fish. $ *Average main: 250 Kn* ⌂ *Zaklopatica 15* ☎ *020/801–161* ⊕ *www.facebook.com/tritonlastovo* ⊟ *No credit cards* ⊘ *Closed Nov.–Mar.*

 Hotels

Hotel Solitudo

$ | HOTEL | FAMILY | The only hotel on the island, Hotel Solitudo (confusingly sometimes referred to as Hotel Ladesta) is a modern white building on a peaceful bay backed by pines, 3 km (2 miles) north of Ubli. **Pros:** sea and forest views; peaceful off-the-beaten-path island; on-site dive shop. **Cons:** basic breakfast; spotty service; not very many nightlife options. $ *Rooms from: 775 Kn* ⌂ *Pasadur bb* ☎ *020/802–100* ⊕ *www.hotel-solitudo. com/en* ⇆ *72 rooms* ⦿ *Free breakfast.*

 Activities

BEACHES

Lastovo has no shortage of phenomenal beaches, but the best ones might just be slightly offshore; see for yourself by heading to **Saplun,** one of the tiny unpopulated **Lastovnjaci Islands,** which are a short distance northeast of Lastovo and are served by taxi-boats through high season.

DIVING

Paradise Diving Center

SCUBA DIVING | FAMILY | Just a five-minute boat ride from this scuba-diving center based in the Hotel Solitudo and at a depth of 49 feet lies a reef of red, yellow, and violet gorgonias. Farther afield, experienced divers can expect to explore sea caves and sunken ships. ⌂ *Pasadur bb* ☎ *020/805–179* ⊕ *www.tz-lastovo. hr/en/korisne-info/zute-stranice/objekt/ diving-paradise.*

SAILING

Marina Lastovo

SAILING | This 30-berth marina is attached to Hotel Solitudo. ⌂ *Pasadur bb* ☎ *020/802–100* ⊕ *www.hotel-solitudo. com/en/facilities.*

ZADAR AND NORTHERN DALMATIA

Updated by
John Bills

⊙ Sights	🍴 Restaurants	🛏 Hotels	🛍 Shopping	🍸 Nightlife
★★★☆☆	★★☆☆☆	★★☆☆☆	★★☆☆☆	★★☆☆☆

WELCOME TO ZADAR AND NORTHERN DALMATIA

TOP REASONS TO GO

★ **Zadar's historical center:** A history of trade and faith is embellished by a youthful populace and curious modern attractions.

★ **National and nature parks:** Croatia's natural beauty is at its most endearing here, thanks to the stunning landscapes of places like Telašćica Nature Park and Paklenica National Park.

★ **Island-hopping:** You'll find adventure and calm in equal measure, just off the Adriatic coast's northern reaches, from the peaceful Kornati Islands to fun-filled Pag, with its cheese and lace.

★ **Beaches:** Northern Dalmatia is a mecca for sun-worshippers of all shapes and sizes.

Getting to Zadar is easiest by car. Be it on the A1 highway from Zagreb, down a winding coastal road from Rijeka or from nearby Split, the roads are good and there are signs aplenty.

1 Zadar. The former capital of Dalmatia.

2 Nin. A peaceful town with rare sandy beaches.

3 Sali and Telašćica Nature Park. A charming fishing village that serves as the gateway to a lush nature park.

4 Murter and the Kornati Islands. The gateway to the largest archipelago in the Adriatic.

5 Paklenica National Park. A national park home to two fantastic gorges and other geological features.

6 Pag Island. An island famous for partying, cheese, and lace.

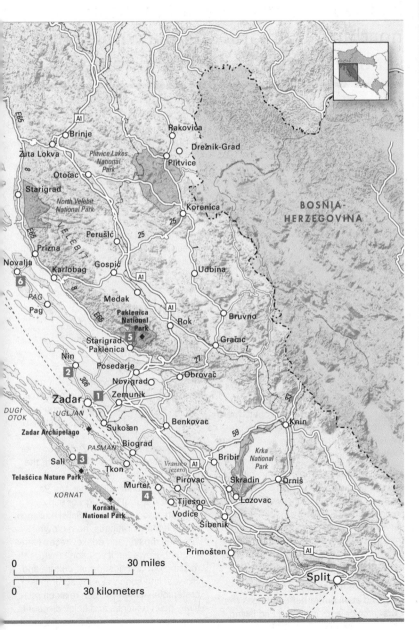

E65
A1
Brinje
Žuta Lokva
Rakovica
Drežnik-Grad
Plitvice Lakes National Park
Plitvice
Otočac
Starigrad
North Velebit National Park
Korenica
BOSNIA-HERZEGOVINA
25
V E L E B I T
Perušić
25
E65
Prizna
Gospić
Udbina
Novalja
Karlobag
A1
PAG
Medak
Pag
E65
Paklenica National Park
Starigrad-Paklenica
A1
Rok
Bruvno
Gračac
Nin
Posedarje
21
1
Novigrad
Obrovac
Zadar
Zemunik
306
DUGI OTOK
UGLJAN
Sukošan
Benkovac
Knin
Zadar Archipelago
PASMAN
Biograd
59
Sali
Tkon
Vransko jezero
A1
Bribir
Krka National Park
Telašćica Nature Park
Murter
Pirovac
Skradin
Drniš
KORNAT
Kornati National Park
Tijesno
Lozovac
Vodice
Šibenik
Primošten
A1
Split

0   30 miles

0   30 kilometers

Safely protected from the northern Adriatic shore and continental Croatia by the imposing Velebit Mountain, northern Dalmatia offers a whole new set of aesthetic and cultural values.

The islands get smaller and more abundant and the architecture, which varies between Roman, Venetian, socialist and modern influences, still carries the elegance of locally quarried limestone. Make Zadar, a fast-growing historical city, the focal point of your sojourn, but do not overlook Nin and the islands, especially Kornati and Telašćica. Admirers of intact, rough nature will revel in the beauty of Paklenica National Park.

Where exactly does Northern Dalmatia begin? Zadar may be the region's cultural and urban capital—it is, after all, the first sizable city you encounter in Dalmatia on your way south from Zagreb or Rijeka—but it is not where the region begins, either culturally or geographically. Look instead to the southern reaches of Velebit Mountain, where that coastal range gives way to the flat, sandy coastline of Nin and environs. Practically speaking, though, you enter Dalmatia proper when you cross the long, bright-red span of the Maslenica Bridge going south on the route from Zagreb to Zadar.

Though it's easy enough to drive on straight to Zadar, you won't regret stopping for a visit in Nin. While today it's an unassuming little town with well-preserved 17th-century architecture, more than 1,000 years ago—and for centuries afterward—it was one of the most important Croatian towns of all.

Much of the region is not on the mainland at all but rather comprises the Zadar archipelago, including Pag Island, and, farther south, the Adriatic's largest archipelago, Kornati National Park. Farther inland, only miles from the coast, is a sweeping expanse of countryside still visibly recovering from the Yugoslav war of the 1990s, where tourists rarely tread. Zadar itself, with its mix of Roman, Venetian, communist-era, and modern architecture, has a bustling and beautiful historic center and is also the main point of access by ferry to the islands, which include the beautiful Telašćica Nature Park.

Planning

When to Go

If you don't mind crowds, midsummer is a good time to visit Northern Dalmatia—when the Adriatic is at its optimal temperature for beachgoing, and when you can also delight in the varied music, dance, and drama of the Zadar Summer Theatre (late June to early August), the Full Moon Festival (late July or early August) in and around Zadar, the Pag Summer Carnival (late July or early August), and Sali's annual Saljske užance, which features raucous, horn-blown "donkey music" and donkey races (early August). However, if you don't mind missing out on midsummer culture and crowds, late spring to early autumn is preferable—when you can relax on relatively quiet beaches and enjoy discounts of up to 20% on accommodations relative to high season prices.

Getting Here and Around

If you're driving or taking a bus from the north, you can stop for an excursion to Pag Island and at Paklenica National Park before arriving in Zadar. The pretty little town of Nin, meanwhile, is just a half-hour north of Zadar and most easily done as a day trip (or even a half-day trip). Though many daily ferries can take you to the Zadar archipelago, Sali (two hours from Zadar by ferry) is a good place to base yourself for a night or two if you want to explore the outer reaches and have the best access to Telašćica Nature Park. A drive or bus trip to Murter will get you within a short boat ride of the spectacular Kornati National Park.

AIR

Zadar's airport is in Zemunik Donji, 9 km (5½ miles) southeast of the city. Croatia Airlines, which offers service between Zadar and Zagreb as well as Paris and other European cities, runs buses (25 Kn one-way) between the airport, the city bus station, and the harborside near the ferry port on the Old Town's peninsula.

BOAT AND FERRY

Jadrolinija's local ferries (*trajektne linije*) and passenger boats (*brodske linije*) run daily routes that connect Zadar not only with the surrounding islands but also with Southern Dalmatia and Italy. The offices are by the Harbor Gate in the city walls, across from the ferry port.

Jadrolinija runs ferry routes from the port of Zadar, just outside the city walls on the western side of the Old Town, to Sali. The trip, which takes about two hours and costs 40 Kn, takes you initially south in the Zadarski kanal, then through a narrow strait between Ugljan and Pašman islands before proceeding to the island of Dugi Otok, where you stop briefly in Zaglav before heading on to Sali. If you

don't want to base yourself in Murter, you can take a cruise straight from the Borik marina just outside Zadar all the way to Kornati National Park, that almost mythical archipelago even farther south. The *Zadar Archipelago*, which holds 12 passengers, will take you on a full-day journey (9 am to 7 pm) to the national park, including stops at Telašćica Nature Reserve, Vrulje bay, Sali, and the islands of Mana and Levrnaka.

CONTACTS Jadrolinija. ✉ *Liburnska obala 7, Zadar* ☎ *051/666–111* ⊕ *www. jadrolinija.hr.*

BUS

Though sometimes crowded in midsummer, Zadar's bus station will almost certainly figure prominently in your travel plans unless you're driving or flying directly here. The trip to or from Zagreb takes around 3½ hours, and the one-way cost is between 56 Kn and 120 Kn, depending on the company. Timetables are available at the station.

Getting to Nin from Zadar is easy by bus. The half-hour trip follows the coastal road north; the fare is around 20 Kn one-way, with buses running daily out of Zadar's station every 45 minutes or so.

Getting to Murter—to its tiny main square, Trg Rudina, which is where you're dropped off and picked up—from Zadar is certainly doable, if a bit complicated. You can transfer either at Šibenik or at Vodice. Although the former option looks longer on the map, given the crowded confusion at Vodice's small station, Šibenik—around 12 buses daily from Zadar—may be a less trying experience (and a surer way of getting a seat) even if it might take a bit longer; about nine buses go on from Šibenik to Murter (via Vodice). Travel time via Šibenik is 2½ hours or more (i.e., 90 minutes from Zadar to Šibenik, up to an hour of waiting time, then another 45 minutes to Murter via Vodice). The total cost is around 70 Kn via Šibenik and around 55 Kn if you go straight to Vodice (travel time is less than two hours, plus an even harder-to-predict wait time, because the bus from Šibenik might be contending with heavy traffic).

Numerous buses ply the one-hour route daily between Zadar and Starigrad for access to Paklenica National Park. The one-way cost to or from Starigrad—via the Zadar–Rijeka bus—is between 26 Kn and 38 Kn, depending on the company. There are two stops in Starigrad; the national park information office is between the two, and the access road to the park is near the first stop (if you're coming from Zadar).

Around half a dozen buses daily ply the one-hour route from Zadar to Pag Town, on Pag Island (52 Kn).

Last but not least, the easiest way to get either from the bus station to Zadar's town center, or from the center to the Borik complex (with its beaches, hotels, and restaurants) on the northern outskirts, is by any of several, user-friendly local buses. You can buy tickets at news kiosks for 8 Kn (single ride) or for 10 Kn from the driver; be sure to validate your ticket on boarding by inserting it into the stamping device.

CONTACTS Zadar Bus Station. ✉ *Ante Starčevića 1, Zadar* ☎ *023/316–915* ⊕ *www.liburnija-zadar.hr.*

CAR

Zadar is the first major stop on the A1 highway between Zagreb and Dalmatia, which proceeds south toward Split. Barring traffic congestion, especially on weekends, the trip between Zagreb and Zadar is doable in 2½ hours. That said, you can also easily get to Zadar by bus, whether from Zagreb, Rijeka, or Split, and rent a car there if necessary. As the Zadar bus station can be a chaotic place at times, especially in midsummer, you might want to rent a car for some excursions—to Murter, for example, which otherwise involves a somewhat complicated, time-consuming trip to or

toward Šibenik with a transfer. But you'll be just fine without a car in and immediately around Zadar, as bus service is both good and affordable. To get to Pag Island by the Pag Bridge route, Pag Town (at the island's center) is within a one-hour drive from Zadar. One good option is to spend two nights and take in Paklenica National Park, then drive another 25 minutes or so north along the coastal road toward Rab Island and Rijeka, and take the ferry from the village of Prizna—roughly midway between Rijeka and Zadar, just south of Rab Island—to Žigljen, in the north of the island (17 Kn per person, 96 Kn for a car in midsummer); or do the same in reverse.

TRAIN

Zadar and Zagreb do not have direct train connections, but there is the option of taking the bus from Zadar to Knin (in just over two hours with almost 20 stops in between), and from Knin you can transfer to a train that gets you to Zagreb in around four-and-a-half hours—so that's roughly seven hours in all from Zadar to Zagreb, for about 190 Kn one-way. Unless you want to see some relatively war-wearied parts of the interior, though, you'll do well to simply hop aboard one of the many daily Zagreb-bound buses at Zadar's bus station, which get you to the capital in less time and for less money (in between 56 Kn and 120 Kn). Trains also run between Knin and Split, and service and travel times are improving yearly on all these routes.

Restaurants

Fresh seafood is the cuisine of choice in Northern Dalmatia, as it is elsewhere on Croatia's coast. Beyond standard coastal fare, look for Dalmatian specialties including Pag Island lamb and *Paški sir* (Pag cheese); *pršut* (prosciutto), and *šokol* (smoked pork neck) from Posedarje; and sheep's cheese and peppery meat dishes from inner Dalmatia. And of course, there's Zadar's famous maraschino liqueur—compliments of the area's uniquely zesty cherry and the Maraska company, whose facility is just across the town's pedestrian bridge and whose brand name graces the bottles of the best maraschino.

Hotels

As elsewhere along practically every populated area of the Croatian coast, package-hotel resorts are easy to find, in particular in the Borik complex on the northern outskirts of Zadar. Top-notch pensions and intimate, elegant small hotels are in somewhat short supply, though a whole host of private rooms and apartments can be found, often for half the price of larger, more established accommodations, either through the local tourist-information office or through private travel agencies. And, as is the practice in other parts of Croatia, short stays (i.e., fewer than three days) often mean a surcharge of around 20%.

Restaurant and hotel reviews have been shortened. For full information, visit Fodors.com. Restaurant prices are the average cost of a main course at dinner or, if dinner is not served, at lunch. Hotel prices are the lowest cost of a standard double room in high season.

What It Costs in Croatian kuna (Kn)			
$	$$	$$$	$$$$
RESTAURANTS			
under 65 Kn	65 Kn–125 Kn	126 Kn–200 Kn	over 200 Kn
HOTELS			
under 800 Kn	800 Kn–1450 Kn	1451 Kn–2,000 Kn	over 2,000 Kn

Visitor Information

If there's no English speaker at the office you happen to contact, try the Zadar County Tourist Information office or the city of Zadar's corresponding office.

CONTACTS Zadar County Tourist Information. ⊠ *Jurja Barakovića 5, Zadar* ☎ *023/315–316* ⊕ *www.zadar.hr.* **Zadar Tourist Information.** ⊠ *Jurja Barakovića 5., Zadar* ☎ *023/315–316* ⊕ *www.zadar.hr.*

Zadar

158 km (98 miles) northeast of Split.

Dalmatia's capital for more than 1,000 years, Zadar is all too often passed over by travelers on their way to Split or Dubrovnik. What they miss out on is a city of more than 73,000 that is remarkably lovely and lively despite—and, in some measure, because of—its tumultuous history. The Old Town, separated from the rest of the city on a peninsula some 4 km (2½ miles) long and just 1,640 feet wide, is bustling and beautiful: the marble pedestrian streets are replete with Roman ruins, medieval churches, palaces, museums, archives, and libraries. Parts of the new town are comparatively dreary, a testament to what a world war followed by decades of communism, not to mention a civil war, can do to the architecture of a city that is 3,000 years old.

A settlement had already existed on the site of the present-day city for some 2,000 years when Rome finally conquered Zadar in the 1st century BC; the foundations of the Forum can be seen today. Before the Romans came, the Liburnians had made it a key center for trade with the Greeks and Romans for 800 years. In the 3rd century BC the Romans began to seriously pester the Liburnians, but required two centuries to bring the area under their control.

St. Donatus Church is named after an Irish bishop who lived in the area in the early 800s.

During the Byzantine era, Zadar became the capital of Dalmatia, and this period saw the construction of its most famous church, the 9th-century St. Donat's Basilica. It remained the region's foremost city through the ensuing centuries. The city then experienced successive onslaughts and occupations—both long and short— by the Ostrogoths, the Croatian-Hungarian kings, the Venetians, the Turks, the Habsburgs, the French, the Habsburgs again, and finally the Italians before becoming part of Yugoslavia and, in 1991, the independent republic of Croatia.

Zadar was for centuries an Italian-speaking city, and Italian is still spoken widely, especially older people. Indeed, it was ceded to Italy in 1921 under the Treaty of Rapallo (and reverted to its Italian name of Zara). However, its occupation by the Germans in 1943 led to intense bombing by the Allies during World War II, which left most of the city in ruins. Zadar became part of Tito's Yugoslavia in 1947, prompting many Italian residents to leave. Zadar's more recent ravages occurred during a three-month siege by Serb forces and months more of bombardment during the Croatian-Serbian war between 1991 and 1995. But you'd be hard-pressed to find outward signs of this today in what is a city to behold.

GETTING HERE AND AROUND
Zadar is the only sizable city in Northern Dalmatia and quite likely your first destination in the area. It has an international airport that connects it to Europe during the summer season (mostly via budget airlines) and to Zagreb and Pula year-round. You can also drive in via the A1 highway or the Adriatic "magistrala" road, but a car will be of little use in the city itself, where narrow alleys are best explored on foot. There are ample regular bus lines from Zagreb, Rijeka, and Split, but be advised that the bus station is not in walking distance from the old city. Zadar's port is very busy with lines serving local islands and a daily international line to Ancona, Italy.

TOURS

Malik Adventures

ADVENTURE TOURS | FAMILY | Discover remote islands, sheltered coves, and steep cliffs only a short catamaran sail from Zadar with the energetic crew of Malik Adventures. The juxtaposition of intense adventure activities during the day with a night of slowly paced, exquisite local cuisine and island life may be the defining point of your vacation. This serene island is a rejuvenating break between touring cities. ⊠ *Molat 40* ☏ *091/784–7547* ⊕ *www.malikadventures.com.*

Secret Dalmatia

Not the biggest, but certainly one of the best organized companies, Secret Dalmatia specializes in showing you parts of Dalmatia that might not be on the tourist map. The owner, Alan, is very outgoing and reliable, and his team have Dalmatia well covered, from hidden little wineries to sailboats. Young and professional, their English is excellent. ⊠ *Turanj 426* ☏ *091/567–1604* ⊕ *www.secretdalmatia.com.*

◉ Sights

There are helpful interpretive signs in English all around the Old Town, so you certainly won't feel lost when trying to make sense of the wide variety of architectural sites you might otherwise pass by with only a cursory look.

★ Archaeological Museum

MUSEUM | Founded in 1832, Zadar's archaeological museum is one of the oldest museums in this part of Europe. It occupies a plain but pleasant modern building beside the convent complex of Crkva Sv. Marije (St. Mary's Church). It is home to numerous artifacts from Zadar's past, from prehistoric times to the first Croatian settlements. The third floor focuses on ceramics, weaponry, and other items the seafaring Liburnians brought home from Greece and Italy, whereas the second floor covers the classical period, including a model of the Forum square as it would have looked back then; a smaller exhibit addresses the development of Christianity in Northern Dalmatia and contains rare artifacts from the invasion of the Goths. On the first floor you'll find an exhibit from the early Middle Ages, taking you to the 12th century. ⊠ *Trg Opatice Čike 1* ☏ *023/250–613* ⊕ *www.amzd.hr* ⌑ *30 Kn* ☉ *Closed Sun. Nov.– May.*

Bibich Winery

WINERY/DISTILLERY | This winery, which operates a wine boutique in Zadar, produces wine both from native Dalmatian varieties, including Babić, Plavina, Lašina, and Debit, and nonnative grapes, including Grenache and Shiraz. The winery itself is located just outside of Skradin. ⊠ *Plastovo* ☏ *091/323–5279.*

★ Crkva Sv. Donata (*St. Donatus Church*)

RELIGIOUS SITE | Zadar's star attraction, this huge cylindrical structure is the most monumental early Byzantine church in Croatia. Originally called Church of the Holy Trinity, it was probably inspired by plans set forth in a book by the Byzantine emperor Constantine Porphyrogenitus, *On Ruling the Empire*. Centuries later it was rededicated to St. Donatus, the bishop here from 801 to 814. Legend has it that Donatus, an Irishman, was the one who had it built, using stone from the adjacent Forum. The stark, round interior features a circular center surrounded by an annular passageway; a sanctuary consisting of three apses attached to the lofty mantle of the church walls, set off from the center by two columns; and a gallery reached by a circular stairway. Although the church no longer holds services, its fine acoustics make it a regular concert venue. During the off-season (November to March), when the church is closed, someone at the Archaeological Museum next door may have a key to let you in. ⊠ *Šimuna Kožičića Benje* ☏ *023/250–613* ⊕ *www.amzd.hr* ⌑ *20 Kn* ☉ *Closed Nov.–Mar.*

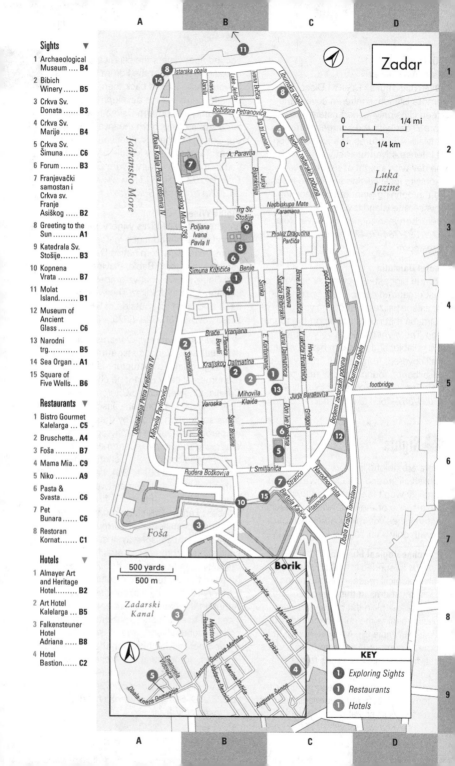

Zadar

Crkva Sv. Marije (*St. Mary's Church*)
RELIGIOUS SITE | Legend has it that a local noblewoman founded a Benedictine convent on this site in 1066, and the adjoining St. Mary's Church in 1091. Rebuilt in the 16th century, the church was supposed to incorporate a new Renaissance look into the remnants of its earlier style: its rounded gables remained, continuing to express a certain Dalmatian touch; early Romanesque frescoes are still evident amid the largely Baroque interior; and your eyes will discover 18th-century rococo above the original columns. Most noteworthy for modern-day visitors, however, is the adjoining convent complex, two wings of which house one of Zadar's most treasured museums. The **Permanent Exhibition of Religious Art**, whose highlight is commonly called "The Gold and Silver of Zadar," is a remarkable collection of work from centuries past by local gold- and silversmiths (including Italians and Venetians who lived here), from reliquaries for saints and crucifixes to vestments interwoven with gold and silver thread. ⊠ *Poljana Opatice Čike* 🕾 ⊠ *Museum 30 Kn.*

Crkva Sv. Šimuna (*St. Simeon's Church*)
RELIGIOUS SITE | Built in the 5th century as a three-nave basilica, it was later reconstructed in Gothic style, and again in Baroque style, though the terra-cotta and white exterior pales in comparison to some of the city's other churches. St. Simeon's Church is best known for housing the gilded silver sarcophagus of Zadar's most popular patron saint. The chest, which depicts intricately detailed scenes from St. Simeon's life and the city's history, was commissioned in 1381 by Elizabeth, wife of Croat-Hungarian King Ludwig I of Anjou, and made by Francesco De Sesto of Milan, one of Zadar's best silversmiths. As for St. Simeon, legend has it that his body wound up here while being transported from the Holy Land to Venice by a merchant who got caught in a storm, took refuge here, fell ill, and died—but not before drawing attention to the saintliness of the body he'd brought with him. Palm trees outside the church lend the site a pleasant, Mediterranean touch. ⊠ *Crkva Sv. Šime, Trg Petra Zoranića 7* 🕾 *023/211–705* ⊠ *Free.*

Forum
ARCHAEOLOGICAL SITE | Established in the 1st century BC by the first emperor Augustus, the Roman Forum is, more than 2,000 years later, pretty much a wide empty space with some scattered ruins. However, since it was rediscovered in the 1930s and restored to its present condition in the 1960s, the Forum has been one of Zadar's most important public spaces. A raised area on the western flank indicates the site of a onetime temple dedicated to Jupiter, Juno, and Minerva, and if you look closely you will notice what remains of its altars that served as venues for blood sacrifices. The only surviving column was used in the Middle Ages as a "Pillar of Shame," to which wayward individuals were chained. Fragments of a second column were removed from the Forum in 1729 and put back together again near the Square of Five Wells, where the column still stands today. ⊠ *Zeleni trg.*

Franjevački samostan i Crkva sv. Franje Asiškog (*St. Francis Church & Franciscan Monastery*)
RELIGIOUS SITE | Dalmatia's oldest Gothic church, consecrated in 1280, is a stellar example of a so-called Gothic monastic church, characterized by a single nave with a raised shrine. Although the church underwent extensive reconstruction in the 18th century, behind the main altar is a shrine dating to 1672; inside the shrine you can see choir stalls in the floral Gothic style that date to 1394. In 1358 a peace treaty was signed in this very sacristy under which the Venetian Republic ended centuries of attack and handed Zadar over to the protection of the Croat-Hungarian kingdom. ■ **TIP**➔ **You can walk around the atmospheric inner**

courtyard for free, but you pay a fee to enter the church itself. From mid-October through March or April, the church may keep irregular hours. ⊠ *Samostan Sv. Franje, Trg Sv. Frane 1* ☎ *01/481–1125* 🎫 *15 Kn.*

Greeting to the Sun (*Pozdrav Suncu*)
LOCAL INTEREST | The whimsically named Greeting to the Sun is a 22-meter circle of multilayered glass plates set into the stone-paved waterfront. Under the glass, light-sensitive solar modules soak up the sun's energy during daylight hours, turning it into electrical energy. Just after sunset, it puts on an impressive light show, illuminating the waterfront in shades of blue, green, red, and yellow. It was installed in 2008 and was created by local architect Nikola Bašić, who also made the nearby sound art project, the Sea Organ. ⊠ *Obala Kralja Petra Krešimira IV* ✛ *toward the western tip of the peninsula.*

Katedrala Sv. Stošije (*St. Anastasia's Cathedral*)
RELIGIOUS SITE | Dalmatia's largest basilica was shaped into its magnificent Romanesque form in the 12th and 13th centuries from an earlier church; though it was damaged severely during World War II, it was later reconstructed. The front portal is adorned with striking Gothic reliefs and a dedication to the archbishop Ivan from the year 1324. The interior includes not only a high, spacious nave but also a Gothic stone ciborium from 1332 covering the 9th-century altar; intricately carved 15th-century choir stalls by the Venetian artist Matej Morozon; and, in the sacristy, an early Christian mosaic. St. Anastasia is buried in the altar's left apse; according to legend, she was the wife of a patrician in Rome but was eventually burned at the stake. Bishop Donatus of Zadar obtained the remains in 804 from Byzantine Emperor Niceforos.
■ TIP→ **The late-19th-century belfry, which is separate from the main church building, offers a sweeping view to those who climb** to the top for a fee, but even the 20 steps up to the ticket desk rewards you with a decent view of the square below. ⊠ *Trg Sv. Stošije 2* 🏛🎫 *Church free, belfry 10 Kn* ⊗ *Closed Sun.*

Kopnena Vrata (*The Land Gate*)
ARCHAEOLOGICAL SITE | A walk around the walls of Zadar's Old Town is a walk around what was, once, the largest city-fortress in the Venetian Republic. One of the finest Venetian-era monuments in Dalmatia, the Land Gate was built in 1543 by the small Foša harbor as the main entrance to the city. It takes the form of a triumphal arch, with a large, central passage for vehicles and two side entrances for pedestrians, and is decorated with reliefs of St. Chrysogonus (Zadar's main patron saint) on his horse and a winged lion (the symbol of the Venetian Republic). ⊠ *Ul. Među bedemima.*

Molat Island
ISLAND | Many of Croatia's islands like to emphasize their serenity, but only one island gets the status of a true hermit heaven. Fewer than 200 people live on magnificent Molat, a verdant island covered in maquis and pine and a tranquil place that has fought for its survival over the centuries and lived to tell the tale. There isn't much to do on the island but that is sort of the point; this is an island for those in search of space and peace. One ferry heads this way daily from Zadar (sometimes two in summer, but there is no concrete schedule), with the journey taking an hour or so. Tickets are 40Kn for foot passengers.

Museum of Ancient Glass
MUSEUM | Occupying the 19th-century Cosmacendi Palace, on the edge of the Old Town, this museum displays one of the world's finest collections of Roman glassware outside Italy, with a vast array of ancient pieces unearthed from archaeological sites across Dalmatia. Highlights include the delicate vessels used by Roman ladies to keep their

Take a walk along Zadar's Riva promenade to hear the melodic tunes of the Sea Organ.

perfumes, skin creams, essential oils, as well as sacred goblets used to celebrate Mass. ■**TIP→ The museum shop offers a fine choice of replicas of Roman glassware, which make great gifts to bring home.** ✉ *Poljana Zemaljskog odbora 1* ☎ *023/363–831* ⊕ *www.mas-zadar.hr* ✉ *30 kn* ⊙ *Closed Sun. Nov.– Apr.*

Narodni trg (*People's Square*)
PLAZA | FAMILY | One of the Old Town's two main public spaces, the ever bustling Narodni trg is home of the Gradska Straža (City Sentinel), which was designed by a Venetian architect in late-Renaissance style with a large central clock tower. The sentinel's stone barrier and railing, complete with holes for cannons, were added later. This impressive tower once housed the ethnographic section of the National Museum and is today a venue for various regular cultural exhibits. ✉ *Narodni trg.*

★ Sea Organ
LOCAL INTEREST | Comprising 35 pipes under the quay stretching along a 230-foot stretch of Zadar's atmospheric

Riva promenade, the Sea Organ yields a never-ending (and ever free) concert that delights one and all. Designed by architect Nikola Bašić with the help of other experts, the organ's sound resembles a whale song, but it is in fact the sea itself. It's hard not to be in awe as the sound of the sea undulates in rhythm and volume with the waves. ✉ *Obala kralja Petra Krešimira IV, toward the end of the western tip of the peninsula.*

Square of Five Wells
PLAZA | The square is the site of a large cistern built by the Venetians in the 1570s to help Zadar endure sieges by the Turks. The cistern itself has five wells that still look quite serviceable, even though they have long been sealed shut. Much later, in 1829, Baron Franz Ludwig von Welden, a passionate botanist, established a park above an adjacent pentagonal bastion that was also built to keep the Turks at bay. ✉ *Trg Pet Bunara 1.*

🍴 Restaurants

Bistro Gourmet Kalelarga

$$ | MEDITERRANEAN | Located within the Art Hotel Kalelarga just off the square, sleek Bistro Gourmet Kalelarga serves up authentic local specialties complemented by a carefully arranged wine list and best enjoyed on the charming outdoor terrace. Be sure to ask your server to help you take advantage of seasonal dishes, especially if you find yourself here during asparagus season in early spring. **Known for:** Zadar orange and Maraška—sour cherry cakes; chic design; creative tasting plates. $ *Average main: 70 Kn* ✉ *Art Hotel Kalelarga, Ul. Majke Margarite 3, 23000, Zadar* ☎ *023/233–000* ⊕ *www.arthotel-kalelarga.com/en/gourmet.*

Bruschetta

$$ | MEDITERRANEAN | With outdoor tables on a lovely terrace, overlooking the sea in the Old Town, Bruschetta serves reasonably priced and well-presented Mediterranean cuisine. Popular with locals and visitors alike, it's especially known for its pizzas and pasta dishes, but it also does excellent steaks and fresh fish, as well as an irresistible tiramisu. **Known for:** local seafood; view of the water; late night eats. $ *Average main: 100 Kn* ✉ *Mihovila Pavlinovica 12* ☎ *023/312–915* ⊕ *www.bruschetta.hr.*

★ Foša

$$$$ | SEAFOOD | Boasting an appealing outdoor terrace overlooking a quiet little harbor, Foša is a combination of age-old Dalmatian style and modern trends, in architecture, design, and gastronomy. It's old-world tastes give foundation to creative modern dishes, such as the tuna carpaccio beautifully complemented by a dab of wasabi cream or the sea bass marinated in a potent emulsion of local fennel root, citrus, and honey. **Known for:** terrace views of the town walls; tasting menus; local tuna. $ *Average main: 500 Kn* ✉ *Kralja Dimitra Zvonimira 2* ☎ *023/314–421* ⊕ *www.fosa.hr.*

Zadar's Cherry Liqueur

Zadar's famous maraschino cherry liqueur, one of the world's few liqueurs produced by distillation, manages to be subtly sweet and robustly dry at the same time. Look for bottles labeled Maraska, the Zadar company that produces this transparent spirit from the area's zesty sour cherries. It is typically enjoyed as either an aperitif or digestif.

Mama Mia

$$ | PIZZA | This is a popular place for locals and tourists, and with good reason: delicious, generous portions at fair prices and pizzas big enough to share (not that you'll want to). Pizza is definitely the star here, with an impressive spread of toppings to choose from, but if you're not a pizza fan the cuttlefish risotto and daily specials never disappoint. **Known for:** oversized dishes; wood-fired pizza; good value. $ *Average main: 80 Kn* ✉ *Put Dikla 54* ☎ *023/334–246.*

★ Niko

$$ | MEDITERRANEAN | Just across from a public beach and near the Borik resort complex, this distinguished restaurant has been serving up a delicious array of seafood, beef, veal, pork, and pasta dishes since 1963. You can choose between such lower-end fare as spaghetti with scampi or more expensive delights like scampi on the skewer. **Known for:** beachside location; historical ambience; something for everyone on the menu. $ *Average main: 120 Kn* ✉ *Obala Kneza Domagoja 9* ☎ *023/337–880* ⊕ *www.hotel-niko.hr.*

Pasta & Svasta

$$ | ITALIAN | Charming and cozy (with limited but coveted seating), this tucked-away spot offers a consistently pleasant experience, especially on a clear night when you can sit in the courtyard, enjoying a tasty house wine that complements both the lighter fare and pasta plates. Knowledgeable waiters will help you pair the fresh pastas and sauces; don't overlook the pillowy gnocchi. **Known for:** local aperitifs; lovely courtyard; secluded location. $ *Average main: 80 Kn* ⊠ *Poljana Šime Budinića 1* ☎ *023/317–401.*

★ Pet Bunara

$$$ | MEDITERRANEAN | For a break from the tourist bustle, head for the Pet Bunara, a slow food restaurant situated in a quiet little nook just off the Pet Bunara square. The fare is creative and changes weekly, if not daily, according to local produce available. **Known for:** secluded vibe; homemade fig jam; all local food. $ *Average main: 190 Kn* ⊠ *Stratico Street, near Trg pet Bunara* ☎ *023/224–010* ⊕ *www.petbunara.hr.*

Restoran Kornat

$$ | SEAFOOD | Just outside the city walls on the tip of the peninsula and on the ground floor of a four-story concrete-box building, the Kornat serves original, first-rate cuisine, with an emphasis on seafood—try the monkfish fillet with truffle sauce—plus a limited choice of hearty meat dishes, including leg of lamb with roasted potatoes. Desserts include melon with Champagne. **Known for:** excellent seafood; wide-ranging wine list; interesting desserts. $ *Average main: 120 Kn* ⊠ *Liburnska obala 6* ☎ *023/254–501* ⊕ *www.restaurant-kornat.com.*

Hotels

There are very few hotels in or near Zadar's Old Town. As you leave the center, you'll find either fairly expensive, top-end hotels or relatively simple, budget places, but not much in the middle price ranges. In midsummer, you can step off the ferry from Pula at midnight

and be reasonably assured that some relatively trustworthy person—more likely than not a pensioner who speaks more Italian than English—will offer you a room in a centrally located apartment for around 300 Kn for two people. But your best bet is to book a room—for a slightly higher cost—through a travel agency, which also offers excursions to nearby islands and national parks.

Almayer Art and Heritage Hotel

$$$ | HOTEL | Nestled into the historic Old Town, this family-owned boutique hotel in a 19th-century building both preserves its historical character and has a modern, open, and artistic feel. **Pros:** beautiful interior and courtyard; green space; close to attractions and the beach. **Cons:** limited rooms so often fully booked in high season; parking can be problematic; blankets on the small size. $ *Rooms from: 1800 Kn* ⊠ *Braće Bersa 2* ☎ *023/335–357* ⊕ *www.almayer.hr* ➪ 9 rooms ⦿ No meals.

★ Art Hotel Kalelarga

$$$ | HOTEL | Carefully curated modern furnishings create a cool relief after a day of hustling through Zadar's narrow streets. **Pros:** excellent restaurant; one of the few hotels in the Old Town; good off-season packages. **Cons:** atmosphere can be stuffy; pricey; busy in summer. $ *Rooms from: 1960 Kn* ⊠ *Majke Margarite 3* ☎ *023/233–000* ⊕ *www.arthotel-kalelarga.com* ➪ 10 rooms ⦿ Free breakfast.

Falkensteuner Hotel Adriana

$$$$ | RESORT | Flanked beachside by a grove of tall pines and encircled by a security fence (more to keep nonguests from enjoying the hotel's outdoor pool than for the sake of safety), this is an appealing place to stay even if the long, narrow lobby does resemble an airport terminal. **Pros:** bright, spacious rooms; lovely private beach; substantial discounts for stays of three nights or more. **Cons:** pricey; in a huge, somewhat characterless complex; far from the town center. $ *Rooms from: 2130 Kn*

✉ *Majstora Radovana 7, Borik* ☎ *023/206–300* 🌐 *www.falkensteiner.com* 🛏 *48 rooms* 🍴 *Some meals.*

★ **Hotel Bastion**

$$$ | HOTEL | Elegant, with artistic decoration and a refined ambience, Hotel Bastion offers a chic respite for travelers with a taste for sophistication. **Pros:** perhaps the best slow-food restaurant in the country; location in the Old Town; stylish interiors. **Cons:** small, so often fully booked in high season; Old Town is pedestrian only and parking nearby can be problematic; guests pay to use the spa. [$] *Rooms from: 1650 Kn* ✉ *Bedem zadarskih pobuna 13* ☎ *023/494–950* 🌐 *www.hotel-bastion.hr* 🛏 *28 rooms* 🍴 *Free breakfast.*

Nightlife

Bamboo Caffe & Lounge Bar

BARS/PUBS | The big wooden deck clad with wooden benches, deck chairs, and grass umbrellas right on the beach certainly has its appeal. Bamboo Caffe & Lounge Bar overlooks the old city and outward to the islands. They know how to keep it simple, and their version of simple is pretty good. ✉ *Obala Kneza Domagoja bb* ☎ *098/756–998* 🌐 *www.restorani-zadar.hr/beach-bar-bamboo.*

Performing Arts

SUMMER FESTIVALS

Musical Evenings in Saint Donat

FESTIVALS | Despite its name, performances of this month-long series of classical music concerts and recitals, staged between early July and early August, are held in the Roman Forum, Saint Anastasia Cathedral, Saint Donat Church, and Marina Dalmacija, down the road in Bibinje. ✉ *Trg Petra Zoranića 1* 🌐 *www.donat-festival.com.*

Zadar Snova (*Zadar of Dreams*)

FESTIVALS | The eclectic Zadar Snova festival, held the first two weeks of August, welcomes everything from contemporary dance and films to comic strip exhibits and workshops to theatrical events to a rich array of music, and more. ✉ *I. Meštrovića 9* 🌐 *www.zadarsnova.hr.*

Zadar Summer Theatre

FESTIVALS | From late June to early August the annual Zadar Summer Theatre festival sees a whole range of music, dance, and drama performed in various squares, churches, and other buildings about town. ✉ *Zadar.*

Shopping

As hip as it otherwise is, Zadar is low on high fashion and has few outlets for quality souvenirs (as opposed to the usual kitsch, which there is plenty of). That said, those interested will be happy to know that jewelry stores are in no short supply. Also, one of the first shopping opportunities you will pass if you enter the Old Town via the main pedestrian bridge is a large enclosed hall with an antiques market inside; look for the open doorway to your right on Jurja Barakovića, just before you reach H. Vukšića Hrvatinića (9–2 and 5–10 daily).

★ **Arsenal**

SHOPPING CENTERS/MALLS | Where the Venetians repaired their galleys in the 18th century is today a multipurpose cultural space that hosts art exhibitions and concerts, as well as a lounge bar, a restaurant, and a wine shop. ✉ *Trg Tri Bunara 1* ☎ *023/253–821* 🌐 *www.arsenalzadar.com.*

★ **Boutique MAR&VAL**

CLOTHING | This boutique is a multibrand store full of unique pieces from prominent Croatian fashion designers. ✉ *Don Ivo Prodan 3* ☎ *023/213–239.*

Northern Dalmatia

| 0 | | 30 miles |
| 0 | | 30 kilometers |

BEACHES

Feel free to take a short dip off the quay in the Old Town—the most atmospheric place to do so being the **Riva** promenade and especially the tip of the peninsula directly over the Sea Organ, as nature's music accompanies your strokes. But for a more tranquil swim, head to the **Kolovare** district, just southeast of the Old Town, with its long stretch of park-flanked beach punctuated here and there by restaurants and cafés. There's also the resort complex in **Borik,** where relatively shallow waters and a sandy bottom may be more amenable to kids. Last but not least, by driving or taking a bus 30 minutes north along the coast you can reach the famously sandy beaches of

Zaton and **Nin.** For true peace and quiet, though, your best bet is an excursion by ferry and then on foot, by bicycle, or in a rental car out to some more isolated stretch of beach on an island of the Zadar archipelago.

BOATING

Zadar Archipelago

This Zadar-based company runs day trips by boat from Zadar to the islands of Kornati National Park. All tours have a maximum of 12 travelers, allowing for a more individual approach rather than the general tourist offering of uncomfortably packed boats. ✉ *Obala kneza Trpimira 2* ☎ *099/627-3333* ⊕ *www.zadar-archipelago.com.*

The small island of Nin holds only 1,700 residents.

Nin

14 km (9 miles) northeast of Zadar.

On a tiny, 1,640-foot-wide island in a shallow, sandy lagoon that affords a spectacular view of the Velebit range to the northeast, Nin is connected to the mainland by two small bridges. The peaceful town of 1,700, a compact gem whose present-day size and unassuming attitude belie a stormy history, is well worth a visit, whether on the way to Zadar or as a day trip from there, assuming that the beautiful sand beaches stretching for miles around Nin don't inspire you to stay a bit longer.

Nin was a major settlement of the Liburnians, an Illyrian people who also settled Zadar, hundreds of years before the Romans came, conquered, and named it Aenona. A vital harbor for centuries, it was the first seat of Croatia's royalty, and was long the region's episcopal see, whose bishop was responsible for the conversion to Christianity of all Croatian

territory. In 1382 the Venetians seized it and prospered from the trade in salt, livestock, and agriculture. However, the Venetian-Turkish wars eventually brought devastating onslaughts, including Nin's destruction in 1571; later, the Candian Wars of 1645–69 led to the decimation of Nin and the surrounding area yet again.

Aside from its historic buildings and monuments that testify to a rich past, Nin's draw also includes the only sandy beaches on this stretch of the Adriatic, not to mention the area's medicinal seaside mud. Since the sea here is shallow, water temperatures are warmer than in the rest of the Adriatic; moreover, the water is more saline, accounting for Nin's major export product—salt. But what would a Croatian coastal town be without the usual resort complex on its fringes? Holiday Village Zaton is a 15-minute walk from the Old Town.

If you're coming from Zadar, soon before you reach Nin proper, look to your left (your right if headed back toward Zadar) to see the squat, stony, 12th-century form of **St. Nicholas's Church** on a hillock out in the middle of a field, looking rather like a cake ornament, with a lone Scotch pine at the foot of the little hill keeping it company, as it were. You can enter Nin via one of two small bridges—the most likely of the two being the charming, pedestrian **Donja Most** (Lower Bridge), only yards from the tourist information office, which provides a helpful map that folds small enough to fit in your palm. If you're coming by car, you can park in a lot on the right just beyond the office and then cross the bridge, or else find a semi-legal spot along the road roughly opposite the lot, which plenty of enterprising visitors prefer.

GETTING HERE AND AROUND

The best way to Nin is a 15-km (9-mile) drive from Zadar, be it by car or one of the hourly regular buses. Once there, you can only get around on foot.

 # Sights

Arheološki Muzej (*Archaeological Museum*)

MUSEUM | Nin's shallow coast and centuries of sand deposits preserved numerous remains from prehistory to the Middle Ages under the sea. The Arheološki muzej has a rich collection for a town of this size, including replicas of two small, late-11th-century fishing boats discovered only in 1966 and carefully removed from the sea in 1974. One of these boats has been completely reconstructed, the other only to the extent to which it had been preserved underwater. The main themes in each room are elucidated in clear English translations. ⊠ *Trg Kraljevac 8, 23232, Nin* ☎ *023/264–160* ⊕ *www.nin. hr/en/cultural-heritage/museum-nin-antiquities* ☜ *20 Kn.*

Asseria

ARCHAEOLOGICAL SITE | Close to Nin in the town of Benkovac are the massive ruins of Asseria, an ancient city. First settled around 6 BC by Liburnians, who built it

into one of their most important towns before the Romans came, Asseria—which is nearly 1,640 feet long and roughly a third as wide, and is situated 6 km (3¾ miles) east of Benkovac, near the village of Podgrađe—was inhabited for more than 1,000 years before crumbling away along with the Roman Empire. ⊠ *Village Podgrađe.*

Crkva Sv. Anselma (*St. Anselm's Church*)

RELIGIOUS SITE | The 18th-century Crkva Sv. Anselma, dedicated to a 1st-century martyr believed to have been Nin's first bishop, was built on the site of Nin's former, 9th-century cathedral, the first cathedral of the medieval Croatian principality. To the right of the altar is a 15th-century statue of the Madonna of Zečevo, inspired by the appearance of the Virgin Mary to a woman on a nearby island. Though the church is plain—the ceiling is adorned with only a nice chandelier and a smoke detector—the foundations of the onetime cathedral are still much in evidence. Beside the church is the belfry, and next door is the treasury, which houses a stunning little collection of reliquaries containing various body parts of St. Anselm. ⊠ *Branimirova, near Višeslavov trg* ☎ *098/509–307* ⊕ *www. nin.hr/en/cultural-heritage/sv-anselmo* ☜ *Free.*

Crkva Sv. Križa (*Church of the Holy Cross*)

RELIGIOUS SITE | Croatia's oldest church, the 8th-century Crkva Sv. Križa is also known locally as the "world's smallest cathedral." Indeed, the unadorned, three-naved whitewashed structure—which has a solid, cylindrical top and a few tall, Romanesque windows (too high to peek inside)—has an unmistakable monumental quality to it even though it's no larger than a small house. There's little to see inside, though it is sometimes open, erratically, in summer; check with the tourist office or the Archaeological Museum. ⊠ *Petra Zoranića* ⊕ *www.nin.hr/en/ cultural-heritage/sv-kriz* ☜ *Free.*

Nin Saltworks

MUSEUM | Historically, Nin's riches came from an unlikely source: salt. Making the best of a rare geographical location with lots of sun, lots of wind, and shallow sea basins, Nin Saltworks produces salt in a traditional, ecological way to this date. To commemorate salt's vast influence on the development of the city, Nin opened up a small but charming salt museum that opens our eyes to how this common table adornment was produced back in the day. While there, make sure to pick up a bag of *fleur du sel*, or "flower of salt," ultrarich in minerals. For a fee, you can take a tour led by a professional guide (offered on the hour). ✉ *Ilirska cesta 7* ☎ *023/264–764* 🌐 *www.solananin.hr* 🎟 *Free; standard tour 65 Kn (ask about additional tours)* 🕒 *Closed weekends and public holidays.*

🍴 Restaurants

Bepo

$$ | **MEDITERRANEAN** | **FAMILY** | Even if you are not staying at Holiday Village Zaton, you might find yourself at Zaton's Konoba Bepo in search of a good meal because Nin does not have many worthy alternatives. Bepo's charming atmosphere is lively, and their menu is a good representation of local Mediterranean fare. **Known for:** excellent regional olive oil; favorite with locals; traditional desserts. [$] *Average main: 110 Kn* ✉ *Zaton Holiday Resort, Dražnikova 76t* ☎ *023/280–336* 🌐 *www.konoba-bepo.hr.*

Konoba Branimir

$$ | **EASTERN EUROPEAN** | Located yards away from the Church of the Holy Cross—indeed you might enter the restaurant by mistake, thinking you are proceeding to the churchyard from a back entrance—this pleasant spot's well-prepared fare ranges from fresh seafood to meats, and desserts such as pancakes with fig marmalade. Note that the spaghetti, though listed as a children's meal, makes for a hearty "light" (and budget) meal even for an adult. **Known for:** pancakes with local fig marmalade; hearty fare; beautiful location. [$] *Average main: 110 Kn* ✉ *Višeslavov trg 2* ☎ *023/264–145.*

🏃 Activities

With its long sandy **beaches,** the coastline in and around Nin, and Pag Island just to the north, is widely regarded as the most beautiful—and most swimmable—in Dalmatia.

Sali and Telašćica Nature Park

Sali is approximately 30 km (19 miles) southwest of Zadar; Telašćica Nature Park is 10 km (6 miles) southeast of Sali.

The largest and most westerly island of the Zadar archipelago, facing the open sea, Dugi Otok culminates at its southern end with a spectacular nature preserve in and around Telašćica Bay, the town of Sali being its ideal access point. Situated toward the southeastern tip of the 52-km-long (32-mile-long) island, which is no more than 4 km (2½ miles) wide, Sali is Dugi Otok's largest settlement—with around half of the island's 1,800 inhabitants, the rest of whom reside mostly in its 10 other villages—but it's an awfully peaceful little place to arrive in after the two-hour ferry ride from Zadar.

GETTING HERE AND AROUND

Sali is on Dugi Otok Island and functions as a gateway to Telašćica Nature Park. You can get to Sali via the regular ferry line from Zadar to Dugi Otok or hop on one of many organized tours leaving from the area. Telašćica is a special treat, of course, for those chartering their own boat.

Telašćica Nature Park is surrounded by high vertical cliffs to the west, with lovely views to the east.

Sights

Sali

TOWN | Once an out-of-the-way fishing village, Sali draws tourists these days due to its location in and near such natural splendors. It is home to several old churches, including the 12th-century **St. Mary's Church,** whose Baroque altar was carved in Venice. Adding to the village's appeal is its annual **Saljske užance** (Donkey Festival) during the first full weekend in August, which includes an evening ritual during which lantern-lit boats enter Sali harbor and there are donkey races and *tovareća muzika* (donkey music) produced by locals blowing or braying raucously into horns. Spending at least a night or two here can provide a relatively peaceful, nature-filled respite from the rigors of tourism on the mainland or, for that matter, on more tourist-trodden reaches of the Zadar archipelago. ⊠ *Sali.*

★ Telašćica Nature Park

NATIONAL/STATE PARK | This nature park encompasses Telašćica Bay, which cuts 7 km (4½ miles) into the southern tip of Dugi Otok with an inner coastline so indented that it is really a series of smaller bays and a handful of islands. Flanked by high vertical cliffs facing the open sea to the west, with low, peaceful bays on the other side, it has a variety of vegetation. Relatively lush alpine forests and flower-filled fields as well as vineyards, olive groves, and onetime cultivated fields give way, as you move south, to bare rocky ground of the sort that predominates on the Kornati Islands, whose northern boundary begins where Telašćica Nature Park ends.

Aside from Telašćica's other attractions, most of which are accessible only by boat, one of the park's key highlights—accessible by land on a 20-minute drive from Sali—is the salt lake **Jezero mir,** which was formed when a karst depression was filled by the sea. Small boats (generally with 8–12 passengers) bound for both Telašćica Nature Park and the northern fringes of Kornati National Park leave the east side of Sali's harbor (i.e., where the Zadar ferry arrives) at approximately 11:15 each morning and return by 6 or 6:30 in the evening. Verify ferry times at ⊕ *www.croatiaferries. com.* Expect to pay 200 Kn per person, sometimes less. The best way to arrange ferry passage is in person—by going to the harborside square near the post office around 8 pm on the day before you wish to leave (which means at least a one-night stay in Sali), when boat captains gather there looking for passengers for the next day's excursion. However, the tourist information office in Sali can put you in touch with operators by phone as well. ⊠ *Put Danijela Grbina, Sali* ☎ *023/377–096* ⊕ *www.telascica.hr.*

Zadar Archipelago

ISLAND | The Zadar archipelago is so close and yet so far away: Ugljan and Pašman are just two of the myriad islands comprising the lacelike islands, and yet they are among the largest and the easiest to reach from Zadar. More than 15 ferries a day run the 5-km (3-mile) distance between Zadar and Ugljan, a 19-km-long (12-mile-long) island whose narrow width of just a couple of kilometers runs parallel to the mainland, with its midway point across from Zadar. From the ferry landing on Ugljan, your best bet may be to head north along the seafront 10 minutes on foot to the heart of **Preko,** a fine access point to several worthwhile destinations (very) near and (not too) far. Going south will get you in roughly the same time to the unassuming fishing village of Kali. From Preko's harbor you can walk about 1 km (½ mile) farther north to a shallow bay locals like to swim in; or better yet, take a taxi-boat to **Galevac,** a charming wooded islet less than 100 yards from Preko that not only has splendid swimming but also a 15th-century Franciscan monastery set in a lush green park. And then there's the **Tvrđava Sv. Mihovila** (Fortress of St. Michael), a 13th-century landmark atop a hill roughly an hour's walk west of town. Though largely in ruins, the fortress offers spectacular views not

only of nearby Zadar, to the west, but on a cloudless day the Italian coast as well. Meanwhile, 10 km (6 miles) farther north is the quiet village of **Ugljan,** accessible from the ferry port by a handful of buses daily. For a somewhat sleepier island experience, hop aboard one of eight buses daily from Preko to the village of **Pašman.** Continuing on, you can eventually get to Tkon, Pašman island's largest village, from which some 10 ferries daily can get you back to the mainland south of Zadar. ⊠ *Zadar.*

🍴 Restaurants

Konoba Kod Sipe

$$ | EASTERN EUROPEAN | If you want to have a hearty meal well above the tourist fray in Sali, you'll have to do some climbing (over 100 steps!) to reach this rustic restaurant with tables on barrels, fishnets hanging from the ceiling's wooden beams, an enticing open hearth, and an outdoor terrace shaded by grapevines. Set in a villagelike atmosphere that feels very off the beaten path, Konoba Kod Sipe serves everything from grilled calamari and pork chops to cuttlefish spaghetti. **Known for:** octopus under a baking lid; rustic barrel-theme decor; favorite with locals. ⓢ *Average main: 110 Kn* ⊠ *Ulica Sv. Marije, Sali* ☎ *023/377–137* ⊟ *No credit cards.*

Konoba Trapula

$ | MEDITERRANEAN | Located in the cool shade of a stone alleyway behind Sali's harbor, Konoba Trapula has the charm of a place you can find only by word of mouth, as well as delicious, fresh seafood, such as *brudet* (seafood stew) and perfectly prepared tuna steak. The polished, dark wood tables and the nautical decor remind you of the restaurant's proximity to the sea. **Known for:** perfectly cooked seafood; nautical atmosphere; secluded location. ⓢ *Average main: 35 Kn* ⊠ *Sali II 74, Dugi otok, Sali* ☎ *095/713–7297.*

Hotels

The tourist information office can put you in touch with locals who rent private rooms, at around 220 Kn per night in high season. Large hotels will generally accept payment in either euros or kunas.

Murter and the Kornati Islands

70 km (44 miles) southeast of Zadar.

Built near the ruins of the 1st-century Roman settlement of Colentum, Murter has that unmistakable tourism-driven hustle and bustle in midsummer that Sali doesn't—both because it is the key gateway to one of Croatia's chief offshore natural splendors, Kornati National Park, and because it is easily accessible by road from Zadar.

GETTING HERE AND AROUND

Murter Island is serviced by a regular ferry line from the town of Tisno, halfway between Zadar and Šibenik. If you're visiting Kornati National Park only for a day, there are many daily boats leaving from Zadar (north of the park) and Vodice (south of the park).

◉ Sights

★ Kornati National Park

NATIONAL/STATE PARK | The largest archipelago in the Adriatic, Kornati National Park comprises more than 100 islands that are privately owned, mostly by residents of Murter, who purchased them more than a century ago from Zadar aristocrats. The new owners burned the forests to make room for sheep, which in turn ate much of the remaining vegetation. Although anything but lush today, the islands' almost mythical beauty is ironically synonymous with their barrenness: their bone-white-to-ochre colors represent a striking contrast to the azure sea.

However, owners tend vineyards and orchards on some, and there are quite a few small buildings scattered about, mostly stone cottages—many of them on **Kornat,** which is by far the largest island, at 35 km (22 miles) long and less than a tenth as wide. Indeed, some of these cottages are available for so-called *Robinson turizm* (ask at the Murter tourist office, or inquire around town).

In 1980 the archipelago became a national park. It was reportedly during a visit to Kornati in 1936 that King Edward of England decided between love for his throne and love for Wallis Simpson, the married woman who was to become his wife a year later. No public transport currently goes to Kornati, so visiting is only possible as part of an excursion or with a private boat, and tickets must be purchased beforehand. Pick up tickets from the official website or through the various tour groups in Zadar or Murter. ■TIP→ **The entrance ticket is included in the price of the excursion, departing from Zadar.** ✉ *An archipelago lying off the coast of North Dalmatia, between the mainland coastal cities of Zadar and Šibenik, Zadar* ☏ *022/435–740* ⊕ *www. np-kornati.hr.*

Murter

TOWN | However you go to Murter, you'll pass through Biograd-Na-Moru, a relatively big, bustling—but thoroughly tourist-trampled—town, where the resorts have long come to predominate in what was once a charming place; Biograd-Na-Moru also serves as another access point for ferries to the Kornati Islands.

Murter, a town of 2,000 on the island of the same name that lies just off the mainland, is accessible by road from the main coastal route that runs south from Zadar toward Split. As important as tourism is to its present-day economy, boatbuilding has, not surprisingly, long been vital to Murter as well. This is not to mention its olive oil, which was once so famous that it made its way to the imperial table in Vienna. ⊠ *Murter.*

 Restaurants

Konoba Boba

$$ | **MEDITERRANEAN** | **FAMILY** | Beyond its outstanding selection of seafood, Boba offers a variety of regional delicacies sure to please even finicky diners. The outdoor terrace and shaded gardens provide a quiet respite, and while the restaurant is very popular, it doesn't feel crowded. **Known for:** popular among locals; diverse regional dishes; charming garden terrace. $ *Average main: 110 Kn* ⊠ *Butina 22, Murter* ☎ *098/937–9181* ⊕ *www.konoba-boba.hr.*

Tic-Tac

$$$$ | **SEAFOOD** | In this elegant little restaurant near the main square, with tables lining the length of the narrow, historic alleyway, you can begin with an appetizer such as mussels in wine sauce and move on to monkfish tail or grilled scampi—both in wine sauce. The chef likes putting seafood in wine sauce here, to gratifyingly delicious effect. **Known for:** historic location; seafood in wine sauce; delightful family backstory. $ *Average main: 300 Kn* ⊠ *Hrokešina 5, Murter* ☎ *022/435–230* ⊕ *www.tictac-murter.com.*

Hotels

Check with local agencies, which can find you a private room for around 225 Kn for two people.

Performing Arts

FESTIVALS
Tisno Music Festivals

FESTIVALS | An array of music festivals come to the strait of Tisno every summer, including Garden Festival, Electric Elephant, Soundwave Croatia, SuncéBeat, and Stop Making Sense. Dates can vary, so check festival specific websites for up-to-date information. ⊠ *Tisno* ⊕ *www.tz-tisno.hr/en.*

Activities

DIVING

With its shipwrecks, reefs, and underwater cliffs, Kornati National Park is among Croatia's most popular diving destinations. You cannot dive alone here, so you must book your dive through a qualified center. The permit for diving in the park is 150 Kn, which includes the park entrance fee.

Aquanaut Diving Center

SCUBA DIVING | This company offers a small menu of choice courses and excursions (to more than 100 sites), including a daylong boat trip that includes two dives and a stopover in the Kornati Islands. Nondiving companions are also welcome to join at a reduced fee. ⊠ *Jurja Dalmatinca 1, Murter* ☎ *098/202–249* ⊕ *www.divingmurter.com.*

Najada Diving

SCUBA DIVING | Offering supervised shore dives as well as half-day group excursions that include two dives, Najada Diving features excursions to more than 30 sites. Among the highlights is a visit to the wreck of the World War II cargo ship *Francesca.* ⊠ *Put Jersan 17, Murter* ☎ *098/137–1565* ⊕ *www.najada.com.*

Paklenica National Park

50 km (31 miles) northeast of Zadar.

For mountain scenery at its most spectacular and mountain tourism at its most advanced, you need go no further from Zadar than Paklenica National Park.

Sights

★ Paklenica National Park

NATIONAL/STATE PARK | The Velebit mountain range stretches along the Croatian coast for more than 100 km (62 miles), but nowhere does it pack in as much to see and do as in this relatively small, 96-square-km (37-square-mile) park at the southern terminus of the range. Here, less than an hour from Zadar, is a wealth of extraordinary karst features—from fissures, crooks, and cliffs to pits and caves. The park comprises two lime-stone gorges, Velika Paklenica (which ends, near the sea, at the park entrance in Starigrad) and Mala Paklenica, a few kilometers to the south; trails through the former gorge are better marked (and more tourist-trodden).

All that dry rockiness visible from the seaward side of the range turns resplendently green as you cross over the mountains to the landward side. Named after the sap of the black pine, *paklina,* which was used long ago to prime boats, the park is in fact two-thirds forest, with beech and the indigenous black pine a key part of this picture; the remaining vegetation includes cliff-bound habitats featuring several types of blue-bells, and rocky areas abounding in sage and heather. The park is also home to 4,000 different species of fauna, includ-ing butterflies that have long vanished elsewhere in Europe. It is also the only mainland nesting ground in Croatia for the stately griffin vulture.

The park has more than 150 km (94 miles) of trails, from relatively easy ones leading from the Velika **Paklenica Canyon** (from the entrance in Starigrad) to the 1,640-foot-long complex of caverns called Manita Peć, to mountain huts situated strategically along the way to the Vel-ebit's highest peaks, Vaganski Vrh (5,768 feet) and Sveto brdo (5,751 feet). The most prominent of the park's large and spectacular caves, **Manita Peć** is acces-sible on foot from the park entrance in Starigrad; you can enter for 32 Kn, but remember to buy your ticket at the park entrance. Rock climbing is also a popular activity in the park. Meanwhile, mills and mountain villages scattered throughout

Paklenica evoke the life of mountain folk from the not-too-distant past.

About a half-mile down the park access road in Starigrad, you pass through the mostly abandoned hamlet of **Marasovići,** from which it's a few hundreds yards more downhill to the small building where you buy your tickets and enter the park (from this point on, only on foot). From here it's 45 minutes uphill to a side path to Anića kuk, a craggy peak, and from there it's not far to Manita Peć. However, if you don't have time or inclination for a substantial hike into the mountains, you will be happy to know that even the 45-minute walk to the entrance gate and back from the main road affords spectacular, close-up views of the Velebit range's craggy ridgeline and the gorge entrance. Also, be forewarned that if you are looking to escape the crowds, you will be hard-pressed to do so here in midsummer unless you head well into the mountains or, perhaps, opt for the park's less frequented entrance at Mala Paklenica; more likely than not, you will be sharing the sublimities of nature with thousands of other seaside revelers taking a brief respite from the coast.

A further point of interest at the park are the Bunkers, an intricate system of underground shelters built by Marshall Tito in the early 1950s. With relations between Yugoslavia and the USSR then at their worst, Tito used the geograph-ical benefits of the gorges to build an A-bomb shelter. All the work was done in complete secrecy and very few people knew of the Bunkers. After Stalin's death, they were closed down and only reopened in 1991.

Although the park headquarters is on the main coastal road in the middle of Starigrad, fees are payable where you actually enter the park on the access road. Beyond the basic park admission and the supplemental fee to enter Manita Peć cave, the park offers every imagina-ble service and presentation that might encourage you to part with your kunas, from half-day group tours (400 Kn) to presentations every half hour from 11 to noon and 4 to 7 on the park's birds of prey and on falconry. ✉ *Dr. Franje Tuđmana 14a, Starigrad* ☎ *023/369–202* 🌐 *www.paklenica.hr* 🎫 *60 Kn, three-day pass 120 Kn.*

🍴 Restaurants

Restaurant Dinko

$ | **MEDITERRANEAN** | With generous portions and a location just a short way down the road from Paklenica National Park, Restaurant Dinko is perfect for feeding hungry climbers, hikers, and park visitors. Dinko's sticks to the basics, serving fresh seafood and traditional Croatian dishes in a rustic outdoor setting. **Known for:** neighboring national park; outdoor rustic atmosphere; knowledgeable staff. [$] *Average main: 35 Kn* ✉ *Paklenicka 1, Starigrad-Paklenica, Zadar* ☎ *091/512–9455* 🌐 *www.dinko-paklenica.com.*

Taverna-Konoba Marasović

$$ | **EASTERN EUROPEAN** | An excellent choice for travelers looking to experience traditional Croatian-style architecture, this konoba is a transformed village house replete with period furniture and a customary front terrace. The kitchen prepares local, seasonal ingredients with care, producing meals that will satisfy the desire for an authentic Dalmatian experience. **Known for:** tasty regional dishes; rustic atmosphere; traditional architecture. [$] *Average main: 98 Kn* ✉ *Trg Marasovica, Starigrad* ☎ *091/218–7678.*

🛏 Hotels

Hotel Rajna

$ | **HOTEL** | On an isolated stretch of the main road just before you enter Starigrad from the south—and close to the national park access road—this friendly little hotel is a bit concrete-boxish in appearance, but offers not only a splendid view of the mountains to the east and clean, spacious (though not quite sparkling and modern) rooms, but also a restaurant with carefully prepared, scrumptious seafood fare. **Pros:** pleasantly isolated spot near park-access road; fine mountain views; good on-site dining. **Cons:** 15-minute walk from the village center; bland on the outside; rooms a tad worn. [$] *Rooms from: 300 Kn* ✉ *Dr. Franje Tuđmana, Starigrad* ☎ *023/359–121* 🌐 *www.hotel-rajna.com* 🛏 *10 rooms* 🍽 *Free breakfast.*

Pag Island

48 km (30 miles) northeast of Zadar.

Telling an urbane resident of architecturally well-endowed Zadar that you are headed to Pag Island for a night or two will make them think you want to wallow on a sandy beach all day and party all night. Indeed, Pag Island has developed a reputation in recent years as a place to sunbathe and live it up rather than visit historic sites. The town of Novalja, in the north, has quite a summertime population of easy-livin' revelers. But to be fair, this narrow island, one of Croatia's longest, stretching 63 km (40 miles) north to south, has long been famous for other reasons, among them its cheese, salt, and, not least, its lace. Moreover, Pag Town in particular has an attractive historic center, a surprising contrast to the modern, resortish feel of its outskirts, and a contrast to the breathtaking natural barrenness of so much of the island.

Inaccessible for centuries except by sea, Pag Island saw a dramatic boost in tourism starting in 1968 with the completion of the Paškog mosta (Pag Bridge), which linked it with the mainland and the Zagreb–Split motorway. The first thing you notice on crossing over the bridge onto the island is that practically all vegetation disappears. You are on a moonlike landscape of whitewashed rocks scattered with clumps of green hanging on for dear life. But, sure enough, soon you also notice the sheep so instrumental in producing both Pag cheese—that strong, hard, Parmesan-like product that results from the sheep munching all day long on the island's salty herbs—and, yes, Pag lamb. Then, five minutes or so apart, you pass through a couple of small villages and, finally, the huge salt flats stretching out along the road right before you pull into Pag Town.

GETTING HERE AND AROUND
Pag is easiest to reach by car or bus from Zadar via the toll-free Pag Bridge. There are 10 to 15 inexpensive bus connections a day. If driving along the magistrala from Rijeka, you will do well to take the ferry from Prizna, while nondrivers have the option of a daily fast boat connection from Rijeka to Novalja at the southern tip of the island.

Sights

Lest you think the modern vacation homes lining the bay are all there is to Pag Town, park your car (or get off the bus) for a walk into the historic center, the narrow streets of which provide not only a rich sense of centuries past but also a refuge of shade on a hot summer day. Pag Town was founded in 1443, when Juraj Dalmatinac of Šibenik, best known for designing Šibenik's magnificent cathedral, was commissioned by the Venetians to build a fortified island capital to replace its predecessor, which was ravaged by invaders in 1395. Today a few odd stretches remain of the 23-foot-high wall Dalmatinac built around the town, and a walk around the center reveals several Renaissance buildings and palaces from his era, as well as Baroque balconies and stone coats of arms from the 15th to 18th centuries. Pag Town's compact main square, **Trg Kralja Petra Krešimira IV,** is home to three of the town's key landmarks, two of them original buildings designed in the mid-14th century by Juraj Dalmatinac. The

Pag Cheese

Thanks to its many sheep, Pag Island is known as the home of one of Croatia's most esteemed cheeses: *Paški sir* (Pag cheese). You can buy some for around 250 Kn per kilogram, or 25 Kn for a decagram, which is a small piece indeed. If that sounds expensive, just try ordering a bit as an appetizer in a restaurant, where it's more than twice as much. You can easily find it on sale in private homes on some of the narrow streets off the main square. Celebrated local complements to the cheese include the lamb, an herb brandy called *travarica*, and Pag prosciutto.

bay stretches far, with sandy, shallow beaches aplenty—making Pag Island a great place to sunbathe and swim for a day or two, especially with children. The best and biggest beaches, amid pretty groves of pine and Dalmatian oak, are in Novalja.

Crkva Sveta Marija (*St. Mary's Church*)
RELIGIOUS SITE | This three-nave basilica's simple front is decorated with a Gothic portal, an appropriately lacelike Renaissance rosette, and unfinished figures of saints. A relief over the entrance depicts the Virgin Mary protecting the townsfolk of Pag. Begun in 1466 under Dalmatinac's direction, it was completed only decades later, after his death. Inside, note the elaborate, 18th-century Baroque altars, and the wood beams visible on the original stone walls. The church is open daily 9–noon and 5–7. ⊠ *Glavni Trg, 6 Ulica Jurja Dalmatinca, Pag.*

Knežev Dvor (*Duke's Palace*)
CASTLE/PALACE | Across the square is the imposing Knežev dvor with its magnificent, richly detailed portal, a sumptuous 15th-century edifice built to house the

Pag Lace

There was a time when *paške čipke* was passed off abroad as Greek, Austrian, or Italian. Those days are long over. Today an officially recognized "authentic Croatian product" that is sometimes called "white gold," Pag lace is the iconic souvenir to take home with you from a visit to Pag Island—unless you are confident that a hulking block of Pag cheese won't spoil. An integral component of the colorful folk costumes locals wear during festivals, this celebrated white lace is featured most saliently as the huge peaked head ornament ladies don on such occasions, which resembles a fastidiously folded, ultra-starched white cloth napkin.

Originating in the ancient Greek city of Mycenae, the Pag lace-making tradition endured for centuries before being popularized far and wide as a Pag product beginning in the late 19th century. A lace-making school was founded in Pag Town in 1906, drawing orders from royalty from distant lands. In 1938, Pag lace makers participated in the world exhibition in New York.

Pag lace differs from other types of lace in two key respects: a thin thread and exceptional durability. Using an ordinary mending needle against a solid background, and usually proceeding without a plan, the maker begins by creating a circle within which she (or he) makes tiny holes close together; the thread is then pulled through them. The completed lace has a starched quality and can even be washed without losing its firmness. It is best presented on a dark background and framed.

The process is painstaking, so Pag lace is not cheap: a typical small piece of around 20 centimeters in diameter costs at least 200 Kn from a maker or perhaps double that from a shop.

duke. Until the early 1990s, it housed a grocery store and a café; now it is a cultural and exhibition venue, hosting concerts, plays, and manifestations during the summer months. The upper floors have been converted into the City Hall. ⊠ *Glavni Trg, Pag.*

Stari Grad

TOWN | A mere 20-minute walk south of the present town center lie the ruins of the previous 9th-century town. You can wander around for free, taking in the Romanesque-style Crkva Sveta Marija (St. Mary's Church), first mentioned in historical records in 1192; the ruins of a Franciscan monastery; and a legendary, centuries-old well whose filling up with water after a drought was credited to the intervention of the Holy Virgin. On August 15, one of only two days St. Mary's Church is open to the public (the other is September 8), a procession of locals carries a statue of the Virgin Mary from here to the church of the same name on present-day Pag's main square. On September 8 they return. To get to Stari grad, walk across the bridge and keep left on Put Starog Grada, the road that runs south along the bay. ⊠ *Pag.*

🍴 Restaurants

★ Bistro Na Tale

$$$ | EASTERN EUROPEAN | An easy choice if you're looking to sample Pag's signature local lamb or specialty *Paški sir* (cheese produced by sheep consuming grass laced with salty sea water). While more unique eateries are to be had, Bistro Na Tale is nevertheless a popular spot that

serves quality dishes in a pleasant atmosphere. **Known for:** signature regional dishes; popular among locals; terrace overlooking the salt flats. ⓢ *Average main: 130 Kn* ✉ *Radiceva 2, Pag* ☎ *023/611–194* ⊙ *Closed late Dec.–early Feb.*

Hotels

★ **Boškinac**

$$ | B&B/INN | Nestled amid vineyards and olive groves, refined serenity awaits guests to Boškinac. **Pros:** phenomenal restaurant; great vineyard tour; luxurious everything. **Cons:** remote location; vehicle needed; overly formal staff. ⓢ *Rooms from: 1250 Kn* ✉ *Novaljsko Polje bb, Novalja* ☎ *053/663–500* ⊕ *www. boskinac.com* ⟳ *11 rooms* ⦿ *Free breakfast.*

 Performing Arts

FESTIVALS

Pag Music Festivals

FESTIVALS | An array of hip music festivals come to the island of Pag every summer. Some island festivals include Hideout Festival, Sonus Festival, and Fresh Island Festival. ✉ *Pag.*

Shopping

★ **Galerija Paške Čipke** (*Pag Lace Gallery*)

JEWELRY/ACCESSORIES | You needn't venture farther than the main square and surrounding narrow streets of Pag Town to find someone selling the famed Pag lace—whether an old lady or an equally enthusiastic child. Of course, you can also try Pag Town's very own Galerija Paške Čipke (mid-June through mid-September, daily 9–1) or any of several local shops that you are certain to encounter near the main square in Pag Town. ✉ *Trg Kralja Petra Krešimira IV, Pag* ☎ *091/534–0176* ⊕ *www.tzgpag.hr/ en/grad-i-otok-pag-en/kulturna-bastina/ paska-cipka-en.*

Activities

BEACHES

Deciding where to swim once you reach Pag Town is a no-brainer; you can pick practically anywhere in the huge, sheltered bay that stretches out from the short bridge in the town center. If you have kids, all that sand and shallow water is a real plus compared to Zadar and so many other stretches of Croatia's often deep, rocky coast. Most of the 27 km (17 miles) of public beaches in the bay are accessible by car. For even better swimming, if that is possible, try heading north to Novalja and environs. The tourist information office has a free map showing the locations of the best beaches.

Chapter 6

KVARNER BAY AND THE NORTHERN ADRIATIC ISLANDS

Updated by
Melissa Paul

👁 Sights	🍴 Restaurants	🛏 Hotels	🛍 Shopping	🍸 Nightlife
★★★☆☆	★★☆☆☆	★★☆☆☆	★☆☆☆☆	★☆☆☆☆

WELCOME TO KVARNER BAY AND THE NORTHERN ADRIATIC ISLANDS

TOP REASONS TO GO

★ **The ultimate waterfront path:** Opatija's Lungomare—an 11-km- (7-mile)-long seafront promenade between Lovran and Volosko—is ideal for an early morning walk to awaken all your senses to the wonders of the Kvarner bay.

★ **Beautiful remote beaches:** Take a taxi boat or join one of the many daily excursions to the remote beaches below the hilltop village of Lubenice on Cres Island. The famed Sv. Ivan beach is one of the prettiest in Croatia. Not far from it, at Žanja beach, you can visit a sea cave.

★ **Towering views:** Climb to the top of the Great Bell Tower in Rab Town and take in the bird's-eye view of the perfectly preserved medieval square and all four church towers.

★ **Dive deeper into the blue:** Get acquainted with the Blue World Institute on Mali Losinj that protects 180 dolphins in Kvarner, then visit the museum dedicated to the thousands-of-years-old Greek statue discovered in the seabed in 1999.

The Kvarner region includes a stretch of Adriatic coast dotted with some of the largest Croatian islands and more than three mountain ranges with over seven national parks. Croatia's main port city and Kvarner's administrative capital Rijeka is within a two- to five-hour drive of European hubs like Munich, Milan, Vienna, Budapest, Zagreb, and Ljubljana. Due to its complex history, Rijeka is Croatia's most diverse city, and its liberal population has always been well-connected to Europe thanks to its industrial, transport, and migratory roots. The seaside resort of Opatija was founded by the Habsburgs in the mid-19th century as a medicinal wellness retreat for Viennese royalty. The regional airport is found on the island of Krk.

1 Rijeka. Croatia's first city to hold the European title of the Capital of Culture.

2 Risnjak National Park. A national park dedicated to the endangered bobcat that roams the nature reserve.

3 Opatija. A center for wellness and healing that attracts visitors year-round.

4 Cres. The longest of all Croatian islands and where the sheep that roam the rocky hillsides graze on wild herbs and produce the most succulent lamb chops.

5 Lošinj. The "isle of wellness" founded in the 12th century that's dominated by the Osorčica Mountains.

6 Krk. Croatia's most popular and accessible island, connected to the mainland by a bridge.

7 Delnice. A mountainous region covered with hiking and biking trails that serves as a good base for exploring the mountains and rivers of Gorski Kotar.

8 Rab. A lush and romantic island with the only natural sand beaches in Croatia.

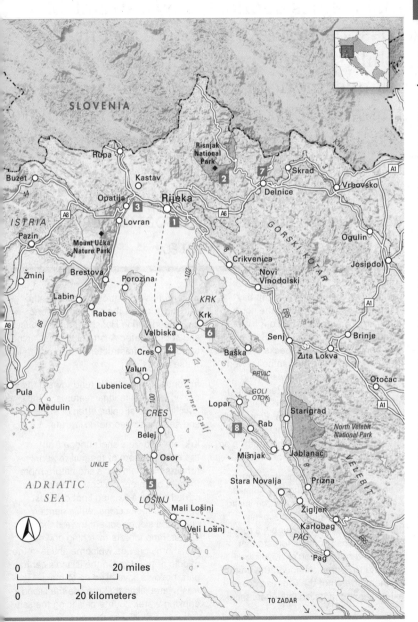

Majestic scenery and natural diversity characterize the Kvarner region: the mainland is dominated by a stretch of coast backed by high-rising mountains, while some of the largest Croatian islands fill the heart of Kvarner Bay. Hike the wild Gorski Kotar Mountains, explore Krk Island on two wheels, beach-hop on the island of Cres, enjoy the mild climate and abundant vegetation of Lošinj, and experience the best of Croatian cuisine along the Opatija Riviera.

The Kvarner Gulf is a large, deep bay with the Istrian peninsula to the north and Dalmatia to the south. Four major islands, Cres, Krk, Lošinj, and Rab, along with numerous smaller specks of land, fill the heart of the bay and can be viewed from the gentle resort towns strung around the coastal arc. The lush, rolling hills of this coastal strip wind their way around the gulf from Opatija. East of Rijeka, the scenic Magistrala costal highway cuts into the solid rock of the foothills on its way to the southern tip of Croatia.

The wild Gorski Kotar mountain district is on the mainland northeast of Rijeka. Across the narrow range sits the inland part of Primorsko-goranska županija (Primorje–Gorski Kotar county), a region of small towns and thick forests that you pass through if you're traveling overland to Zagreb. Although the entire northern stretch of the Croatian coast exhibits a strong Italian influence, thanks to centuries of control from across the Adriatic, most of the mainland resorts developed during Habsburg rule. Robust and sophisticated Austro-Hungarian architecture and infrastructure predominate in these towns.

In contrast, the islands tend toward the cozier, less aspirational features of Italy. Dwellings are simpler, often of stone, and set in less geometric layouts.

Krk, entered via a short bridge from the eastern shore of the gulf region, reflects the mainland's arid nature more than its brethren. On Cres, the northern stretches are a twisted knot of forest peaks and rocky crags, while gentler, cultivated slopes appear toward the center. Pine forests marching down to the shores provide welcome shade in the middle of the day. On the island's central part, hollows have filled up to make freshwater lakes that provide the island's drinking water, counterbalancing the salty sea that licks at the land just a hill crest away. At the foot of Cres, a hop across a narrow stretch of the Adriatic brings you to Lošinj. This lush oasis owes much of its charm to the gardens and villas that were built here during the seafaring heyday of the 19th century. As you approach from the north, the silhouette of Rab resembles the humped back of a diving sea monster. The high north of the island is dry and barren, almost a desert of rock and scrub, whereas the lower southern part is lush and fertile.

Planning

When to Go

The Kvarner region gets very busy in high summer, so don't even dream of heading, for instance, to Opatija or Krk in August without accommodations lined up. Late May through early June and September are ideal times to visit, since you can expect good weather, warm seas, and open facilities. Early May and October are good if you're looking for peace and quiet, but remember that there are fewer tourist-related activities on offer, and you still need to book accommodations in advance. Rijeka and Opatija have increasingly become an exciting place to visit during carnival season from late January through February, a time of year referred to as the "fifth season."

Getting Here and Around

AIR

Rijeka Airport is in Omišalj on Krk Island, with regular bus service provided by Autotrans to downtown Rijeka and the beach towns on Krk island as well as to Mali Lošinj and Cres (though not to Rab). The airport is served by Ryanair from London, Stockholm, and Brussels; Norwegian Air Shuttle from Oslo; Croatia

Airlines from Munich; and Eurowings from Cologne, Berlin, and from several other cities in Germany. ■TIP→ The list of new destinations and airlines changes every year, so always do your research.

CONTACTS Rijeka Airport. (RJK) ⊠ Hamec 1, Omišalj ☎ 051/842–040 ⊕ www. rijeka-airport.hr.

BOAT AND FERRY

The Jadrolinija ferries no longer travel between Dubrovnik and Rijeka, but ferries run daily from Rijeka to the islands of Cres, ILovik, Pag, Unije, Rab, and Susak. There is also a ferry from Brestova (several miles down the road from Lovran) that connects to Cres and Losinj. From June to September, as many as 13 ferries depart daily. Prices vary according to season, but expect to pay €2.50 a person (€16 if you have a car) during the summer; rates fall as much as 20% in the low season. Ferries also run between Valbiska on the island of Krk and Merag on the island of Cres.

Every day in high season, G&V Line has a fast passenger boat that travels from Rijeka to Krk, Rab, Silba, and Zadar. Meanwhile, a catamaran service heads out to Rab at 5 pm and drops into the northern Dalmatian island of Pag about 2½ hours later. Tourist boats and water taxis offering transport on shorter stretches are also abundant at many resorts.

CONTACTS Jadrolinija. ⊠ Riječki lukobran bb, Rijeka ✛ inside the building about 100 meters opposite from where the ferry docks ☎ 051/211–444 ⊕ www.jadrolinija. hr.

BUS

There's daily international bus service to Rijeka from Italy (Trieste), Slovenia (Ljubljana), Austria (Vienna), and Germany (Frankfurt, Munich, and Stuttgart). You can also reach destinations all over mainland Croatia from Rijeka. Timetable information is available at the Rijeka Bus Terminal. GetByBus, a Croatia-based company, offers instant online booking for many bus operators and lines in Croatia.

Buses travel from Rijeka to all the major towns on the mainland and the islands at least once a day. If you're traveling independently, you'll find that buses to the various islands are roughly scheduled to tie in with ferry services.

CONTACTS Autotrans (*Arriva*) ✉ *Rijeka Bus Terminal, Trg Žabica 2, Rijeka* ☎ *060/888-666* ⊕ *www.arriva.com. hr.* **GetByBus.** ⊕ *www.getbybus.com* . **Rijeka Bus Terminal.** ✉ *Žabica 1, Rijeka* ☎ *060/888-666* ⊕ *info@arriva.com.hr.*

CAR

Although local buses and ferries are an excellent, lower stress method of touring the region, touring the Kvarner by car does offer the opportunity to nose your way around some of the smaller and more remote villages on the islands and up in the mountains. In addition, despite a poor safety record and heavy traffic in high season, there are few roads more scenic than the Magistrala. A car is also useful if you plan to leave Kvarner and head for Istria (passing through the Učka Tunnel). However, good train and bus services to Zagreb, as well as bus service to Dalmatia, mean that a vehicle is not really essential for moving on to other areas.

TRAIN

There are three trains daily from Rijeka to Zagreb (journey time is approximately 4 hours) and two trains daily to Ljubljana (2½ hours).

CONTACTS Hrvatske Željeznice (Croatian Railways). ☎ *01/378–2583* ✐ *informacije@hzpp.hr* ⊕ *www.hzpp.hr.* **Rijeka Train Station.** (*Rijeka Glavni kolodvor*) ✉ *Trg kralja Tomislava 1, Rijeka* ☎ *051/211–304.*

Restaurants

In recent years, the Kvarner area, and all of Croatia, has experienced a renaissance in food that has had a delightful influence on restaurant offerings. Many Croatian restaurants have taken a refreshing new focus on high-quality locally grown foods that are woven together with traditional dishes and lighter, more modern fare. At the same time, a growing population of young Croatian designers is having an increasingly visible influence on the design of spaces and furniture in many wineries and restaurants. You can look for this influence not only in the newer places but also on the menus, in the management, and with chefs that are driving this process. More than one of the foodie famous has noticed, from the late Anthony Bourdain to Gordon Ramsay, who have explored Croatian heritage through its food. It is worth noting that while good fish lunches, pubs, and tapas-style eating are abundant in Rijeka, most of the higher quality eateries are generally found outside the city limits.

The quintessential traditional Croatian eating establishment known as a *konoba* still holds solid ground as the defining place for a Croatian meal. Originally, the konoba was the bottom floor of a family home, where fishermen and neighbors would gather after a day on the sea to raise a few glasses and grill the day's catch over a fire, serving it with homemade bread and copious amounts of locally produced *vino*. Ever present in most seaside towns, these rustically styled fish restaurants are often operated by the brothers, uncles, or cousins of the fishermen who spend the better part of the day either on the sea or in the small ports, sorting their fish nets.

While traveing in the Kvarner region be sure to try the famed Kvarner shrimp (*Kvarnerski skampi*) in a restaurant known for this specialty. Known for its size, light reddish color, thin and easy to peel shell, and delicate taste, this type of shrimp is best served on its own. (And it should not be confused with the scampi that is often served with pasta or risotto dishes.) Another popular way of serving shrimp in Croatia is *na buzaru* (cooked in wine with garlic and bread crumbs). In the mountainous region of Gorski Kotar, it is common to find hearty dishes like *jota*, a thick barley soup with sauerkraut, often served with cured meat. Frog legs, bear, wild boar, and wild mushrooms are common ingredients in stews prepared in the mountainous regions. *Palenta* and homemade pasta like gnocchi are often served with meat stews and are a specialty of Gorski Kotar, the hilly area between Rijeka and Karlovac.

On Krk try *Krk–Šurlice*, the local version of pasta; handmade on a spindle, it's often served with wild game, meat goulash, or shaved black truffles. Lamb from Cres is prized for its delicate flavor, which results from the harsh summers and winters on the island and the wild herbs the sheeps graze on. In Kvarner, *mrkač* is the local word for octopus (it's *hobotnica* in the rest of the country).

If you order white fish, either grilled (*na žaru*) or baked in salt (*u soli*), you'll be charged by the kilogram, whereas squid (either grilled or fried) and shrimp (often cooked in white wine, *na buzaru*) come in regular portions. The classic accompaniment to fish is chard (*blitva*) and potatoes (*krumpir*). In Croatia it is common to add a drizzle of local organic olive oil to a dish to enhance not only the flavor but the nutritional value. Most good restaurants partner with local olive growers and showcase a favorite brand, some will even offer a range of olive oils as the taste of the oil varies widely with the olive and the location it is grown. In fact, there is much to be said about the high quality of the olive oil grown in Croatia that there are tastings and tours devoted to this that will convince you to never buy a bottle of dubious Italian olive oil ever again. Krk is home to the most highly regarded wines from the region, with the dry white *Vrbnićka žlahtina* a

strong candidate for best. *Rakija* (fruit and herb brandies) are, of course, the common end to a meal and the start of a long night.

Hotels

Opatija, Krk, and Lošinj have a healthy selection of quality hotels that are generally part of a larger brand and managed as part of a group. Look for boutique-style and heritage villas that are owned and operated privately for a more personal experience. There is also an abundance of newly renovated homes and apartments equipped with swimming pools and other amenities available in most locations near the sea. Expect anything from a room in a block that shares a common kitchen, to private homes with bikes and other sports equipment. Terraces and outdoor spaces are standard and range from a simple tiled slab with metal rails to a beautifully appointed perch shaded by a vine-covered trellis with an open grill for alfresco cooking. If you want to save money, consider renting a room in a private home. This arrangement rarely involves food, so you'll have to get up and out in the morning for your breakfast. Croats are a house-proud people, so in general rented rooms are likely to be very clean and comfortable, with private bathrooms. Your welcome will probably be very warm, with drinks—especially strong coffee—thrust under your nose the moment you step across the threshold. There's no better way to get a real feel for how Croats live. *Restaurant and hotel reviews have been shortened. For full information, visit Fodors.com. Restaurant prices are the average cost of a main course at dinner or, if dinner is not served, at lunch. Hotel prices are the lowest cost of a standard double room in high season.*

What It Costs in Croatian kuna (Kn)			
$	$$	$$$	$$$$
RESTAURANTS			
under 35 Kn	35 Kn–60 Kn	61 Kn–80 Kn	over 80 Kn
HOTELS			
under 925 Kn	925 Kn–1,300 Kn	1,301 Kn–1,650 Kn	over 1,650 Kn

Visitor Information

Tourist information offices can help you with information about accommodations and activities and excursions like diving, windsurfing, and sightseeing. Most offices give out maps and ferry schedules for free.

CONTACTS Cres Tourist Information.
⊠ *Cons 10, Cres Town* ☎ *051/571–535* ⊕ *www.tzg-cres.hr.* **Krk Tourist Information.** ⊠ *Vela placa 1/1, Krk Town* ☎ *051/221–414* ⊕ *www.tz-krk.hr.* **Lošinj Tourist Information.** ⊠ *Priko 42, Mali Lošinj* ☎ *051/231–884* ⊕ *www.visitlosinj.hr.* **Opatija Tourist Information.** ⊠ *Maršala Tita 128, Opatija* ☎ *051/271–310* ⊕ *www. visitOpatija.com.* **Rab Tourist Information.** ⊠ *Trg Municipum Arba 8, Rab* ☎ *051/724–064* ⊕ *www.rab-visit.com.* **Rijeka Tourist Information.** ⊠ *Korzo 14, Rijeka* ☎ *051/335–882* ⊕ *www.visitrijeka.eu.*

Rijeka

165 km (103 miles) southwest of Zagreb.

Water is the essence of Kvarner, and the region's largest city expresses this simply. Whether in Croatian or Italian (Fiume) the translation of the name to English is the same: *river.* Although the history of Croatia's third city goes back to the days of Imperial Rome, modern Rijeka evolved under the rule of Austria-Hungary. The historic core retains vestiges of the old Habsburg monarchy from the time when Rijeka served as the empire's outlet to the Adriatic. During the 1960s, under Yugoslavia, the suburbs expanded rapidly. Rijeka is the country's largest port, with a huge shipyard, massive dry-dock facilities, refineries, and other heavy industries offering large-scale employment. Since the breakup of Yugoslavia, however, Rijeka's role as a shipping town has declined significantly, though local shipyards still repair many U.S. Navy ships and commercial cruisers.

At the city's core sits the Korzo, a pedestrian street of shops and cafés running parallel with the harbor and just to the south of where the land begins to rise toward the peaks of the mountains that back the bay. The high ground ensures that the suburbs stretch out to the east and the west, with little space to expand to the north. Rijeka holds an important location in the region, and thereby offers key rail, road, and sea access into Istria, Slovenia, and Italy. As such, many regard Rijeka as a transit location rather than a holiday destination. That limited view continues to change each year as more historical and cultural significance is recognized, such as Rijeka being awarded the prestigious title of European Capital of Culture 2020 for its "Port of Diversity" program.

Many visitors stay in the nearby seaside riviera of Opatija, and locals will often head that way in their free time as well. That said, Rijeka is a perfectly pleasant small city (approximately 130,000 people call it home). This makes it one of the more authentically Croatian spots in the region in summer. Those looking to avoid the hordes could do much worse than to stay in Rijeka and use the excellent network of ferries to explore the rest of Kvarner.

Rijeka is the home port of Jadrolinija, the coast's major ferry company. Local ferries connect with all the Kvarner islands and will take you farther afield as well.

Rijeka serves as the country's largest port, with many options for ferries and boat trips.

GETTING HERE AND AROUND

Rijeka is linked with Zagreb by the modern A6 motorway, which is clean and fast, though tolls add up on the journey. To reach the Dalmatian coast from Rijeka via the larger highway, you'll have to backtrack 75 km (47 miles) away from the coast and get on the motorway heading south toward Split and Dubrovnik. Rijeka is also the start of the Jadranska Magistrala (the scenic coastal highway), which follows the coast south, all the way to the Montenegro border.

Sights

City Market

MARKET | Bursting with color and the busyness of an open-air green market, this is the natural starting point for getting acquainted with this port city. It is housed in three large halls, each distinct in its architecture and also in what is sold under its roofs. The most interesting of these halls is the art-nouveau fish market, which includes crustacean sculptures on the walls and ceiling by Venetian artist Urbano Bottasso. Surrounding the market are a plethora of open-air stalls mostly manned by women eager to sell their locally grown fresh fruits, vegetables, and other Croatian delicacies. Come early for coffee and people-watching in one of the many surrounding cafés, or come later and have an early lunch or prix-fixe *marenda* (mid-morning snack) in one of the nearby local eateries, where most offerings come fresh from the market. ■ **TIP→ Before you leave the market, be sure to take a stroll through the small formal park in front of the magnificent Croatian National Theatre, which was built by Viennese architects Fellner and Helmer in 1885.** ✉ *Demetrova 3.*

Crkva Uznesenja Blažene Djevice Marije i Kosi toranj (*Church of St. Mary of the Assumption*)

RELIGIOUS SITE | Formerly the city's main church and dating back to the Middle Ages, St. Mary's is still known to locals as the "big church." However, many additions and changes now obscure much of the original architecture. The relatively

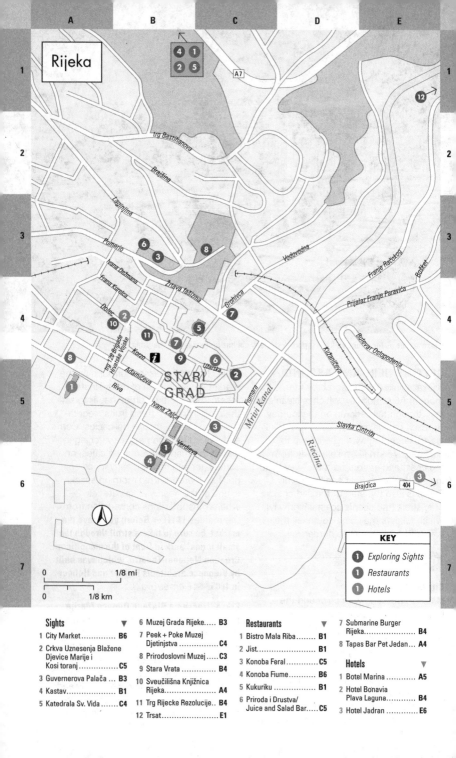

Rijeka

Sights ▼
1 City Market.............. **B6**
2 Crkva Uznesenja Blažene Djevice Marije i Kosi toranj................ **C5**
3 Guvernerova Palača ... **B3**
4 Kastav.................... **B1**
5 Katedrala Sv. Vida **C4**
6 Muzej Grada Rijeke..... **B3**
7 Peek + Poke Muzej Djetinjstva **C4**
8 Prirodoslovni Muzej..... **C3**
9 Stara Vrata **B4**
10 Sveučilišna Knjižnica Rijeka..................... **A4**
11 Trg Rijecke Rezolucije.. **B4**
12 Trsat...................... **E1**

Restaurants ▼
1 Bistro Mala Riba........ **B1**
2 Jist......................... **B1**
3 Konoba Feral **C5**
4 Konoba Fiume........... **B6**
5 Kukuriku **B1**
6 Priroda i Drustva/ Juice and Salad Bar..... **C5**
7 Submarine Burger Rijeka..................... **B4**
8 Tapas Bar Pet Jedan... **A4**

Hotels ▼
1 Botel Marina **A5**
2 Hotel Bonavia Plava Laguna............ **B4**
3 Hotel Jadran **E6**

KEY
- **1** Exploring Sights
- **1** Restaurants
- **1** Hotels

0   1/8 mi
0   1/8 km

recent updates have not imposed severe geometry, though: the bell tower remains leaning to one side by 40 centimeters or so. The church can be visited daily from 7 am to 12:30 pm. ✉ *Pavla Rittera Vitezovi-ca 3* ☎ *051/214–177.*

Guvernerova Palača (*The Governor's Palace*)

HOUSE | High on a hill facing the Mediter-ranean sun, and a short walk from the center of the city, the Governor's Palace affords a grand view over the harbor. Built in 1893 by Hungarian architect Alajos Hauszmann, who also designed Budapest's castle and Palace of Justice, it was done in High Renaissance style and now houses several exhibits and cul-tural events. The large columned facade communicates the self-confidence of the robust Habsburg empire, as do the numerous statues placed throughout the green area surrounding the palace. The **Maritime & Historical Museum of the Croatian Littoral,** which investigates Kvarner's seafaring traditions and cultural heritage is also housed here. After taking in one of the exhibits, enjoy the garden area surrounding the museum which sometimes hosts an outdoor summer theater and beer garden. ✉ *Muzejski trg 1* ☎ *051/213–578, 051/553–666* ⊕ *www.ppmhp.hr* 🎟 *20 Kn; guided tour 70 Kn.*

★ Kastav

TOWN | FAMILY | A fine spot from which to admire the splendors of the Kvarner bay, the Kastav, 11 km (7 miles) northwest of Rijeka, was originally a medieval fortress comprising nine defensive towers. The old hilltop village sits at 1,200 feet and is still home to some 900 residents. The backside of the hilltop village is blanketed by a forest area with biking, hiking, and horseback riding trails leading from the loggia to the woods. The town is a popular venue for regular events throughout the year from the monthly *Zeleni Kastav* organic green market, to the summer Kastav Blues and Cultur-al Festival, to the Bela Nedeja young

white wine festival in October and the traditional bell ringers during the carnival season in February. Having been home to wealthy and powerful clans in times past, the tiny town has many splendid—if not officially noted—buildings from through-out the ages. E-bike rentals are available at the forest entrance. ✉ *Kastav* ⊕ *www.kastav-touristinfo.hr.*

Katedrala Sv. Vida (*St. Vitus's Cathedral*)

RELIGIOUS SITE | This Romanesque cathe-dral is unusual in this part of the world because of its rotund and the semicircu-lar apse behind the altar. Fine Baroque statues are sheltered by Baroque and Gothic construction. Founded by the Jesuits in 1638, the cathedral was named for Rijeka's patron saint. An 18th-century gallery was reportedly built to protect young novice monks from the tempting sights presented when the local lovelies attended services. At the main entrance you can find a cannonball in the wall, apparently sent from a British ship during the Napoleonic wars. ✉ *Grivića 11* ☎ *051/330–879* ⊕ *www.tz-rijeka.hr.*

Muzej Grada Rijeke (*The Museum of the City of Rijeka*)

MUSEUM | In a cube-shaped building on the grounds of the Governor's Palace, the museum has more than a dozen different collections that capture the history of the city and the people who have left an indelible mark on it. The collections range from music to visual art and postage stamps as well as cultural and scientific displays representative of the heritage of this port city. The museum is likely to move in 2021 to expanded and improved facilities and will add Tito's yacht to its collection. ✉ *Muzejski trg 1/1* ☎ *051/336–711* ⊕ *www.muzej-rijeka.hr* 🎟 *15 Kn.*

Peek + Poke Muzej Djetinjstva (*Peek and Poke Computer Museum*)

MUSEUM | FAMILY | This museum was founded by computer enthusiasts interested in collecting vintage com-puters and technology from the early days of the technological revolution. The collection includes everything from Legos to computers, old game consoles, and calculators. A large part of the mission of the museum is to educate visitors in the areas of science and math as the foundation for understanding technology. The great thing about the museum is that they encourage visitors to peek and poke at the displays with not only their eyes but also with their hands and their minds. ⊠ *Ivana Grohovca 2* ☎ *091/780–5709* ⊕ *www.peekpoke.hr* ✉ *30 Kn* ⊙ *Closed Sun. May–Nov. Closed Sun.– Fri. Nov–May.*

Prirodoslovni Muzej (*Natural History Museum*)

MUSEUM | Exploring the geology and biology of the region invariably involves holding a sizable chunk of marine life up to the eyes. The shark and ray display here is predictably popular, starring a brigade of stuffed sharks swimming in strict formation while suspended from the ceiling. A multimedia center based on an aquarium adds to the extensive collection of non-mammalian species, which includes some 90,000 specimens in total, but includes rocks, plants, and other less animated elements of the locality. The botanical garden contributes more exotic plants to the array from the museum's grounds. Considering the fearsome appearance of some of the more fascinating inhabitants of the museum, it may be worth considering putting off a visit here until the end of your stay on the coast, lest your imagination get the better of you while bathing off the beaches. ⊠ *Lorenzov prolaz 1* ☎ *051/553–669* ⊕ *www.prirodoslovni.com* ✉ *10 Kn.*

Stara Vrata (*The Roman Gate*)

ARCHAEOLOGICAL SITE | This enormous stone arch—the oldest structure in the city—is an ancient town gate. Today it's partly engulfed by additions from more recent times, but it was from this site many centuries ago that the chain of mountain fortresses in the region was commanded by the Romans. These days,

the Roman elite's enthusiasm for comfort is catered to with a handful of park benches amid what is left of the ancient walls and columns. ⊠ *Ulica Stara Vrata.*

Sveučilišna Knjižnica Rijeka (*University Library*)

MUSEUM | The University Library now houses a permanent exhibition about the Glagolitic script. Stone tablets written in the ancient Slavic script, and more than 120 other items, are permanently exhibited here. Books, paintings, masonry, and frescoes are also displayed. Call in advance to view the exhibition, which is open by appointment only. ⊠ *Dolac 1* ☎ *051/336–129* ⊕ *www.svkri.uniri.hr* ✉ *20 Kn.*

Trg Rijecke Rezolucije (*Rijeka Resolution Square*)

PLAZA | The former **municipal palace** built in 1873 was originally part of an Augustinian monastery, and it connects to St. Jerome's Church. Named for the resolution that was drawn up here in 1905—and which contributed to the formation of Yugoslavia—the square's lemon-meringue buildings cluster around the foot of the city **flagpole,** erected on a high base in the 16th century and featuring a likeness of the city's patron saint, St. Vitus, holding a scale model of Rijeka protectively in his hand. Many outdoor events are staged here. ⊠ *Rijeka.*

★ Trsat (*Trsat Castle*)

CASTLE/PALACE | The medieval castle was built on the foundations of a prehistoric fort. In the early 1800s, it was bought by an Austrian general of Irish descent, who converted it to include a Greek temple with Doric columns. Today it hosts a popular café, offering stunning views of the Kvarner Bay; throughout the summer, open-air theater performances and concerts take place. Across the street, the pilgrimage church of **Sveta Marija** (St. Mary) was constructed in 1453 to commemorate the Miracle of Trsat, when angels carrying the humble

Medieval Trast Castle is surrounded by nature and offers stunning views.

house of the Virgin Mary are said to have landed here. Although the angels later moved the house to Loreto in Italy, Trsat has remained a place of pilgrimage. The path up to Trsat from the city center takes you close to Titov trg, at a bridge across the Rječina. It passes through a stone gateway, then makes a long, steep climb up 538 steps. Local Bus 2 will get you here, too. ⊠ Petra Zrinskog bb ☎ 051/217–714 castle, 051/452–900 church 🎫 Church free; castle free; castle exhibits 10 Kn ⊗ No church visits during religious services.

🍴 Restaurants

Bistro Mala Riba
$$$$ | SEAFOOD | Located on the Matulji–Kastav main road, this cozy tavern offers a delicious line-up of Kvarner-style tapas that are best enjoyed on the pleasant outdoor terrace that sits under a shady glen of pine trees. Seafood lovers will have a hard time choosing between menu items—fish marinated in lemon juice, sea-snail salad, fried olives, barley and squid stew—and will definitely find themselves coming back for more. **Known for:** Kvarner-style seafood tapas; cozy atmosphere; friendly service. $ Average main: 90 Kn ⊠ Tometići 33a, Kastav ☎ 051/277–945 ⊕ www.mala-riba.com.

Jist
$$$$ | STEAKHOUSE | This is the best and perhaps the only place to have steak in the entire Kvarner region. Not only is it rare to find T-bone steak on a menu in these parts, but the high-quality and sophisticated menu offerings here are highly worthy of the extra effort it requires to find the restaurant. **Known for:** steak tartare; degustation menu with wine pairings; duck prosciutto salad. $ Average main: 100 Kn ⊠ Siroli 27 ☎ 051/374–597 ⊕ jist.hr.

Konoba Feral
$$$ | SEAFOOD | Frequented by locals (especially at lunch), this excellent informal seafood restaurant lies on a side road conveniently close to the City

Market. House specialties are *crni rižot* (cuttlefish-ink risotto), seafood tagliatelle, and shellfish. **Known for:** affordable traditional dishes; popular with locals; cozy atmosphere. $ *Average main: 80 Kn* ✉ *Matije Gupca 5B* ☎ *051/212–274* ⊕ *www.konoba-feral.com* ☉ *No dinner Sun.; no dinner mid-Sept. to June.*

Konoba Fiume

$$$$ | **MEDITERRANEAN** | Tucked away in an alley right next to Rijeka's fish market, quaint Fiume fills with locals at lunchtime but closes early (by 6 pm). Unpretentious and friendly with a small streetside terrace, the tavern serves mostly seafood but also meat and pasta dishes. **Known for:** friendly atmosphere; fresh seafood; affordable prices. $ *Average main: 90 Kn* ✉ *Vatroslava Lisinskog 12* ☎ *051/312–108* ☉ *Closed Sun. No dinner.*

Kukuriku

$$$$ | **MEDITERRANEAN** | This restaurant is quaintly situated in the heart of the old city of Kastav, which sits on a hill that overlooks the entire Kvarner bay. It is attached to the Kukuriku boutique hotel and has a quiet terrace tucked into the back side of the historical hill top village. $ *Average main: 120 Kn* ✉ *Trg Lokvina 3, Kastav* ✛ *you must walk through the gate of the old town to get to the resaurant which is not on a road where cars can access.* ☎ *051/691–519* ⊕ *www.kukuriku.hr* ☉ *Closed Mon.*

★ Priroda i Drustva/Juice and Salad Bar

$ | **FAST FOOD** | This awesome juice bar is located off the korzo in a hidden corner that can be hard to find. For those that know, this is the healthiest quick lunch or breakfast spot in the city. **Known for:** decaffeinated soy latte; vitamin shots; flu fighter juice. $ *Average main: 25 Kn* ✉ *Užarska 14* ✛ *look for their signs pointing the way through the alley* ☎ *051/317–022* ⊕ *www.prirodaidrustvo.com* ☉ *Closed Sun. No dinner.*

Submarine Burger Rijeka

$$ | **VEGETARIAN** | **FAMILY** | Tucked in a corner just off the main walking area, this family-friendly spot is a great place to come for a healthier burger. Try the homemade fries with shaved grana padano cheese and tartufi sauce. **Known for:** sliders (3 mini-versions of their most popular burgers); ice cream with cookies; giving back to local community. $ *Average main: 50 Kn* ✉ *Ulica Marka Marulića 4* ☎ *051/581–363* ⊕ *submarineburger.com.*

Tapas Bar Pet Jedan

$$$ | **BURGER** | Located on the Riva just off the main walking area with a view of the port, this is a popular millennial meet-up spot for a drink and some good eats—a good place to come if you want to get the vibe of the city while enjoying a burger or a tuna steak that is one step above typical pub food. The menu features lighter tapas-style meals, but the entrees are equally inviting. **Known for:** tapas-style appetizers; great brunch; younger crowd. $ *Average main: 80 Kn* ✉ *Riva 14* ☎ *091/619–1182* ☉ *Closed Sun.*

Hotels

The selection of hotels in Rijeka reflects the city's humble status as a simple transit town with more accommodations desired in nearby Kastav, Opatija, and on Krk Island.

Botel Marina

$ | **HOTEL** | Docked at the pier in Rijeka, the first Croatian boat hotel features 35 modern rooms, from doubles to dorms, furnished with comfy beds and en suite bathrooms—a cool place to stay. **Pros:** centrally located; unique concept; friendly staff. **Cons:** no elevators, so carrying luggage to the rooms on lower decks can be inconvenient; smallish rooms; location is on a noisy working harbor. $ *Rooms from: 625 Kn* ✉ *Adamićev gat* ☎ *051/410–162* ⊕ *www.botel-marina.com* ⮌ *35 rooms* ⦿ *Free breakfast.*

Hotel Bonavia Plava Laguna

$$ | **HOTEL** | In the city center, one block back from the Korzo, this modern high-rise has comfortable rooms with specially designed furnishings and original oil paintings. **Pros:** spacious rooms; good service; excellent location. **Cons:** getting a bit outdated; also caters to business guests; not enough noise insulation. [$] *Rooms from: 950 Kn* ✉ *Dolac 4* ☎ *052/700–700* 🌐 *www.plavalaguna.com* 🛏 *121 rooms* 🍴 *Free breakfast.*

Hotel Jadran

$$ | **HOTEL** | A good 20-minute walk (or 10-minute bus ride) from central Rijeka, this pleasant hotel is situated right on the water, with incomparable views of the Gulf of Kvarner. **Pros:** substantial breakfast; unfettered sea views; city location with sea and Ucka mountain view. **Cons:** outdated decor; difficult parking; unremarkable food. [$] *Rooms from: 875 Kn* ✉ *Šetalište XIII divizije 46* ☎ *051/216–600* 🌐 *www.jadran-hoteli.hr* 🛏 *69 rooms* 🍴 *Free breakfast.*

Nightlife

BARS

Celtic Cafe Bard

BARS/PUBS | A hangout spot for locals in their twenties and thirties, and for beer lovers and coffee drinkers alike. The bar is located on a small town square next to St. Vitus Cathedral and the local jail. This cozy spot offers an excellent choice of Croatian and international beers in a friendly, low-key atmosphere. Local bands are often featured on weekends here, and occasionally you might actually hear some Irish music. Closed Sunday. ✉ *Trg Grivica 6b* ☎ *051/215–235.*

Cukarikafe

BARS/PUBS | A popular bohemian daytime café-bar in Rijeka, this shabby chic spot is packed with unique decor. People from all walks of life come here for the excellent selection of wine by the glass, beer, local spirits, teas, and freshly squeezed juices. ✉ *Trg Jurja Klovića 4* ☎ *099/583–8276.*

Karolina

BARS/PUBS | In an upmarket pavilion right on the quayside, Karolina serves cocktails and wine to the smart set as they watch the tide flow in and out of the bay. ✉ *Gat Karoline Riječke* ☎ *091/490–4042.*

Phanas Pub

BARS/PUBS | The best party place in town, this nautically themed pub is like an old sailboat with its dark wood, long bar, and maritime decorations. Music ranges from acoustic and R&B to dance, and you can enjoy it until 6 am from Thursday through Sunday. ✉ *Ivana Zajca 9.*

River Pub

BARS/PUBS | For those who might remember summer nights sitting on a terrace, drinking, dancing, chatting, and actually being able to hear what others are saying, the River Pub is the place to make it all come back. They have a regular pub quiz crowd on Wednesdays. ✉ *Frana Supila 12* ☎ *051/324–673* 🕒 *Closed Sun.*

Tunel

CAFES—NIGHTLIFE | In a real tunnel under the railway in the Skoljić area of town, one of Rijeka's favorite bars has a funky atmosphere, friendly staff, and cool crowd. Some nights jazz, rock, and funk bands take the small stage; other nights DJs play electronic music. ✉ *Školjić 12* 🕒 *Closed Sun.*

Performing Arts

ART VENUES

Palach

CONCERTS | The center of alternative and creative culture for youth in the city, Palach is a somewhat gritty urban space filled with exhibitions, workshops, performance, live music, and DJs, rotating on a regular basis. ✉ *Kružna ul 8* ☎ *051/215–063.*

FESTIVALS

★ Rijeka Carnival

CULTURAL FESTIVALS | Known as the "fifth season," Carnival lasts from the end of January until mid-February and awakens a specific kind of energy in the city only experienced during this time of year. The passion locals pour into carnival cannot be compared to neighboring Venice's big-city sophistication. Celebrations here have a village feel and are closely linked to local traditions that are safeguarded in each particular town and passed down through generations. The excitement in the streets as the city is taken over by crazy antics, colorful costumes, and masquerading revelers who poke fun at local politics to make Rijeka a worthy winter destination. The season kicks off with the Carnival Queen Pageant and continues with weeks of fun activities and masked parties all over town, and ends with the Children's Carnival Parade and the International Carnival Parade. ⊠ *Rijeka* ⊕ *www.rijecki-karneval.hr.*

Rijeka's Summer Nights

FESTIVALS | **FAMILY** | Beginning in late June, the four-week annual Rijeka's Summer Nights festival ensures that venues, streets, and squares are filled with cultural performances. Visitors can experience classical music, and theater, as well as contemporary music and performance art. Most of the venues are outdoors under the stars; smaller venues are in the various small squares throughout the city and add a charming intimacy to the atmosphere. ⊠ *Rijeka* ⊕ *www.rijeckeljet-nenoci.com.*

Summer on Gradina

ARTS FESTIVALS | **FAMILY** | From mid-July to the beginning of September, this cultural festival brings theater plays, live concerts, crafts, and conceptual and themed events from the Trsat Castle, which offers a beautiful hilltop view of the city. ⊠ *Trsat Fortress, Petar Zrinskog bb* ⊕ *www. trsatskagradina.com.*

Shopping

Appearance is of great importance to Croatians, and the local ladies will invariably be exhibiting style and glamour even as they sip coffee or shop for vegetables on any given weekday morning. To serve this fashion-conscious crowd, many hip little boutiques offer the latest styles in imported clothing and shoes (mostly from Italy and Germany). Prices are generally higher than what you'd pay in Italy, so unless you're caught short needing some posh clothes, it's better for your wallet to do your high-fashion shopping elsewhere. The Korzo, a pedestrian shopping street that snakes through the center of Rijeka, is the best place to go, should you be unable to contain your shopping urges. Modern, multilevel shopping malls are also available at both ends of the city center.

Fresh local produce, fish, cheeses, olive oils, wines, and rakijas are the items that should be on your Kvarner shopping list. The best place to buy these is the City Market on Verdijeva. Although there are "professional" traders present, many of the stallholders are still locals who bring their home-produced wares to sell. Noisy and colorful, Rijeka's central market is the place to haggle over fresh produce, swap gossip, and, of course, drink coffee. Pick up a picnic lunch of cheeses, salads, fruit, and nuts here, then pop into one of the multitude of bakeries for freshly baked *burek* (cheese and meat pies) to complete the feast. Although a little tricky to transport, homemade olive oil, apple-cider vinegar, and rakija—usually sold in recycled bottles—are good buys as well. Smaller containers of dried herbal tea leaves and seasonings like rosemary and oregano are a good alternative if your luggage is already tightly packed.

Mala Galerija Bruketa

ART GALLERIES | A family art gallery founded by sculptor Vladimir Bruketa with more than 40 years of experience producing specific art objects using media such as ceramics, wood, and glass. The various sculptures, ceramics, and paintings are all produced by Croatian artists including members of the Bruketa family. ⊠ *Užarska 25* ☎ *051/335–403* ⊕ *www. mala-galerija.hr* ☾ *Closed Sun.*

ZTC

SHOPPING CENTERS/MALLS | This mall right at the seafront is the favorite shopping destination of Rijeka residents. Shops include fashion brands like Benetton, H&M, and S'Oliver; Lush and L'Occitane cosmetics; and sport store Hervis. ⊠ *Zvonimirova 3* ☎ *051/561–014* ⊕ *www. ztc-shopping.hr.*

 Activities

BEACHES

Since it serves as the country's largest port, there aren't too many beautiful beaches in the middle of Rijeka. However, you don't imagine locals stay here the whole summer without having a few spots they try to keep secret from the tourists, do you? Favorite beaches easily accessible from the city include the **Bivio Cove,** near Kantrida to the west. In the opposite direction around the coast, **Uvala Žurkovo,** at Kostrena, is wonderful. Within the city itself, the popular place is **Pecine** to the east, where you can swim off rocky beaches and admire the local villas.

FISHING

The Croatian coast is well known for its population of bluefin tuna, as well as bass, sea bream, sardines, anchovies, mackerel, shrimp, squid, and other shellfish.

Ministry of Agriculture, Forestry & Water Management

FISHING | You need a fishing license to hunt for any marine life using a line or gun. Prices start from 60 Kn per day. In Rijeka licenses are available from the local office of the Ministry of Agriculture, Forestry & Water Management, or online through the ministry's website which is in English. ⊠ *Demetrova 3* ☎ *051/213– 626* ⊕ *www.ribarstvo.mps.hr.*

Risnjak National Park

40 km (25 miles) northeast of Rijeka.

The northern outpost of the forested and karst-peaked Gorski kotar region, Veliki Risnjak is the major peak in this national park, peering over Rijeka from 5,013 feet. The thick pine-forest meadows are covered with wildflowers in the spring, and limestone peaks, crevices, and caves cover around 60 square km (25 square miles).

 Sights

★ Risnjak National Park

NATIONAL/STATE PARK | Risnjak is a popular destination year-round. In winter you'll find a healthy contingent of snow aficionados desperately trying to avoid a trip up to Austria to sample the real thing. In summer, however, as the sun and the tourists beat down upon the coast, this is perhaps the best place to be. The cool mountain air—the average temperature in the region in July is around 16°C (60°F)—is a bonus to Risnjak's virtually unpopulated landscape.

You'll be free to commune with the locals, which include deer, bear, wildcat, and lynx (*ris*), from which the park takes its name. Geologic and botanical features are occasionally explained by English-language information points over which you may stumble on one of the more popular

Risnjak National Park is home to the mountain peak of Veliki Risnjak.

walking routes. Marked trails can occupy you for an hour's evening stroll to a full seven-day trek on the monstrous Rijeka Mountain Transversal from one side of Gorski kotar to the other. Hiking huts are strung across the peaks to accommodate such ambitious expeditions. More information regarding these multiday hiking trips is available from the Croatian Mountaineering Association.

The park information office is in the village of Crni Lug, at the eastern entrance to the park. Near the park entrance is a guesthouse and restaurant, Pension NP Risnjak, that is open year-round. You can easily explore the gentler trails on day trips from either Rijeka or Delnice. Paths from the villages of Razloge and Kupari lead up to the source of the wild Kupa River, which can then be followed down the slopes through the "Valley of the Butterflies." ⊠ *Bijela vodica 48, Crni Lug* ☎ *051/836–133* ⊕ *www.np-risnjak. hr* ⊠ *45 Kn* ☺ *Information office closed Oct.–Apr.*

Opatija

15 km (9 miles) southwest of Rijeka.

In the late 19th century, Opatija (Abbazia in Italian) was among the most elegant and fashionable resorts in Europe. Its history as a resort town dates from the 1840s, when villas were built for members of minor royalty. In 1873 the start of rail service from Vienna and Budapest, along with an aggressive publicity campaign, put Abbazia on the tourist map as a spa of the first magnitude. With the high mineral content of the sea water, iodine in the air, and an annual average of 2,230 hours of sunshine, it qualified as a top-rated climatic health resort, and emerged as a favorite wintering spot for Central European nobility and high society.

A hint of the formality that gilded Opatija in its heyday still survives; the narrow pines and grand buildings remind one of the Italian lakes. This means that many visitors from all over Europe continue to head to the Opatija Riviera in the summer. At the same time, this stretch of coast has not gone unnoticed by the locals. Until recent years the town was a weekend haunt for some younger, mobile Rijeka citizens. Thanks to these driving forces, the upmarket hotel guests still share the resort with some of the region's more upwardly mobile restaurants. However, their number is dwindling, while the town's once admirable nightlife has packed up and headed back to the cooler parts of Rijeka, leaving Opatija to wealthy and more elderly visitors from the surrounding countries. These guests seem more eager to sip the waters than wine and spirits.

The main street, ulica Maršala Tita, runs parallel to the coast for the length of town, and you can go from one end of town to the other on foot in about half an hour, passing numerous terrace cafés along the way. The best seafood restaurants are in the neighboring fishing village of Volosko, a 15-minute walk along the seafront. The mild climate year-round and resulting subtropical vegetation, frequently sunny skies, and shelter from cold north winds provided by Mt. Učka give Opatija pleasant weather for much of the year. In summer, fresh sea breezes tend to dispel any oppressive heat, making the city an ideal seaside resort.

 Sights

Croatian Museum of Tourism (*Villa Angiolina*)
MUSEUM | Visit this mini-museum to get a good understanding of Croatian (and particularly Opatija's) tourism in the 19th century. Set in the gorgeous pink Villa Angiolina and neighboring Swiss House, the museum's permanent collection includes postcards and photographs, souvenirs, and hotel inventory and equipment such as 19th-century hotel silverware and furniture. The villa's neoclassical design includes superb mosaic floors and frescoes. The park and green area in front of the museum are an attraction in and of themselves and a great place to make a small picnic on the grass. ⊠ *Park Angiolina 1* ☎ *051/603–636* ⊕ *www.hrmt.hr* ⊠ *10 Kn for Villa Angiolina, 15 kn for Villa Angiolina & Swiss House.*

Lovran
TOWN | Just 5 km (3 miles) southwest of Opatija, the lovely town of Lovran is home to good swimming coves, Habsburg villas, and paths up to Mount Učka Nature Park. Massive chestnut trees dot the medieval town, giving shady relief from the sun on long summer days. If the crowds of Opatija leave you no place for peace and quiet, walk along the Lungomare through Ičići and Ika (or take Bus No. 32) to Lovran, where you can take in the sea air that lured Austrian royalty to winter here. If you find yourself on the Opatija Riviera in October, don't miss Lovran's **Marunada,** or chestnut festival. Contact the Lovran Tourist Office (Trg Slobode 1, Opatija ☎ *051/291–740* ⊕ *www.tz-lovran.hr*) for information. ⊠ *Lovran.*

★ Lungomare
PROMENADE | If you enjoy walking by the sea, set off along the magnificent paved, waterfront Lungomare. Built in 1889, this 12-km (7½-mile) path leads from the fishing village of Volosko through Opatija—passing in front of old hotels, parks, and gardens and around yacht basins—and all the way past the villages of Ičići and Ika to Lovran. In the middle you'll find the popular town beach that fronts the center of Opatija. Close to many cafés, ice-cream shops, and other essentials, the beach also has a couple of protected sections of water for safe swimming. ⊠ *Obalno Šetalište Franza Josefa.*

★ Mount Učka Nature Park
NATURE PRESERVE | FAMILY | From gentle hiking to mountain biking, climbing and paragliding, all are available in the 160 square km (62 square miles) of Mount Učka Nature Park, a series of peaks that help shelter the Liburnia Riviera (the

official name for the stretch of coast centered on Opatija) and the islands from weather systems to the north. Hiking trails leading toward the summit on the Učka range start from all the resorts along the coast. A climb up to the highest peak, Vojak (4,596 feet), with a fine stone lookout tower at its summit, can be well worth it, it is not for the faint of heart nor inexperienced, out of shape hiking enthusiasts. On a clear day, the view offers a distant tour of the islands of Kvarner Bay, the Italian Alps, and perhaps even an indistinct view of Venice. Most routes up to the heights lead through forest, so you can make the trek in summer without overheating. Along the way you'll find natural springs from which to quench your thirst, along with ponds, tumbling waterfalls (in the wetter months), impressive natural stone columns and several hundred caves. The local inhabitants include deer, wild boar, and, in the northernmost sections of the park, bears. Humans have been living in these hills for centuries also, rearing cattle, farming, and working the forest; you'll come across numerous tiny villages and historic sites if you roam far enough. If you're running short of time, there are many mountain-biking tracks throughout the park offering the chance to expand your lungs on the way up and test your nerve rattling back down to the coast. There is also the possibility to drive to the top and take in the views from the stone tower. There is an information point with maps and souvenirs on the road leading to the summit, called Poklon. At Poklon hikers will find two great restaurants with accommodation and a mountain hiking hut that sleeps 18. A newly renovated modern educational center was built in 2020. ✉ *Liganj 42, Lovran* ☎ *051/293–753* 🌐 *www.pp-ucka.hr* 🎟 *Free.*

Park Angiolina

GARDEN | **FAMILY** | The grounds of Park Angiolina are a wonderful spread of palm-punctuated lawns with a botanical garden. The vegetation is strikingly lush, including cacti, bamboo, and magnolias, plus neatly kept beds of colorful flowers and sweet-scented shrubs. Indeed, Opatija as a whole is a town saturated with botanical splendor. Iginio Scarpa, an aristocrat from Rijeka and the first settler in Opatija, began importing exotic plants, and the tradition has survived into the present. The camellia is the symbol of the city. ✉ *Between Maršala Tita and the seafront* 🌐 *www.visitopatija.com* 🎟 *Free.*

🍴 Restaurants

Draga di Lovrana

$$$$ | **MODERN EUROPEAN** | Tucked in a forested green valley of the Ucka mountains with a gorgeous view of the island of Cres, this boutique hotel is also the proud holder of the first Michelin-starred restaurant in the Kvarner region. The peaceful nature of the surroundings that envelop the restaurant is enough reason to make the trek up from Lovran. **Known for:** first-class fine dining; tales that the hotel was once haunted; surroundings of wild beauty. [$] *Average main: 120 Kn* ✉ *Lovranska Draga 1, Lovran* ☎ *051/294–166* 🌐 *www.dragadilovrana.hr* 🕒 *Closed Mon. and Tues.*

★ Ganeum

$$$$ | **CONTEMPORARY** | This casual fine-dining experience is as relaxed and intimate as it is an enjoyable gourmet meal. When choosing the tasting menu, it is not hard to detect the passion for quality that has been invested into the selection of the produce and the selection of wines. **Known for:** tasting menu; engaging and welcoming wait staff; creative use of local products. [$] *Average main: 90 Kn* ✉ *Stari Grad 5, Lovran* ☎ *051/294–444* 🌐 *www.facebook.com/ganeumlovran.*

Istranka

$$$$ | **VENETIAN** | With a delightful covered terrace flanked by a twisting tree, this small restaurant is Opatija's best option for those who are not fans of seafood.

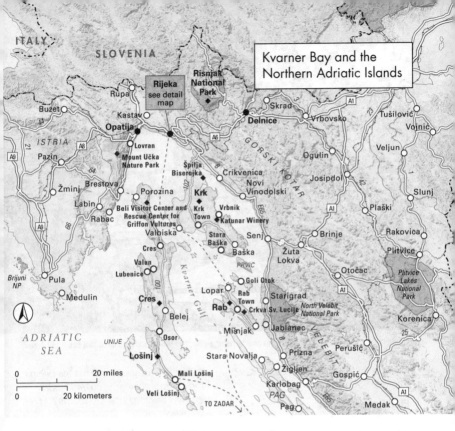

Kvarner Bay and the Northern Adriatic Islands

Taking its influence from the neighboring region of Istria, the menu concentrates more on landlubber food: hams, cheeses, and of course, the famous Istrian truffle! **Known for:** traditional Istrian cuisine; affordable prices; friendly service. $ *Average main: 90 Kn* ⊠ *Bože Milanoviča 2* ☎ *051/271–835* ⊗ *Closed Jan.*

Konoba Tramerka

$$$$ | **SEAFOOD** | Located in Volosko, just above more famed Plavi Podrum, this small seafood tavern offers fresh, creative seafood dishes in a cozy interior with exposed stone walls; a tiny streetside terrace has only a few tables. Locals rave about their bonito tartare, monkfish stew, and dirty calamari (baby calamari too small to be thoroughly cleaned before cooking, thus "dirty"). **Known for:** fish tapas; creative food; friendly atmosphere. $ *Average main: 100 Kn* ⊠ *Dr. Andrije Mohorovicica 15, Volosko* ☎ *051/701–707* ⊕ *www.konoba-tramerka.com* ⊗ *Closed Mon. and Jan.*

★ Konoba Valle Losca

$$$$ | **MEDITERRANEAN** | In the neighborly village of Volosko, where old stone houses are fixed precariously close to one another and give shape to the one road, this restaurant justifies spending an afternoon or evening in a setting that is something not to be missed. The intimate artistic atmosphere tells you everything you need to know about the owners and how sincere they are about sharing good food, much of which is produced on their family farm in Istria. **Known for:** intimate, communal dining experience; good food at a good price; homemade ice cream. $ *Average main: 90 Kn* ⊠ *Andrije Stangera 2, Volosko* ☎ *095 /580–3757* ⊕ *https://www.facebook.com/*

When in Opatija, make sure you visit the nearby fishing village of Volosko and its excellent seafood eateries.

Konoba-Valle-Losca-320105818028292/ ⏲ *Closed Sun. and Mon.*

Plavi Podrum

$$$$ | SEAFOOD | This is an upscale, traditional fine-dining fish restaurant in Volosko. The owner has won some wine awards and has, accordingly, inflated the costs for dining here, which results in unusually high expectations from diners. **Known for:** tasting menus; excellent wine list; pasta with shrimp, peaches, and black truffles. [$] *Average main: 180 Kn* ✉ *Obala Frana Supila 12, Volosko* ☎ *051/701–223* 🌐 *www.plavipodrum.com* ⏲ *Closed Jan.*

Hotels

★ Bevanda

$$$$ | HOTEL | With only 10 rooms—each with its own private view of the sea—this luxurious design hotel is one of Opatija's best. **Pros:** VIP saltwater pool; ideal for couples; offers concierge services. **Cons:** parking is tricky; not a place for families; pricey. [$] *Rooms from: 2385 Kn* ✉ *Zert 8* ✣ *located in the marina behind the outdoor theater* ☎ *051/493–888* 🌐 *www.bevanda.hr* 🛏 *10 rooms* 🍴 *Free breakfast.*

Hotel Astoria by OHM Group

$ | HOTEL | The modern interior here is more South Beach than "faded grandeur," and with its perks the Astoria is justifiably popular with young international travelers. **Pros:** convenient location to beach and restaurants; big breakfasts; stylish decor. **Cons:** superior rooms are on the small side; not directly on the seafront; difficult parking. [$] *Rooms from: 720 Kn* ✉ *Maršala Tita 174* ☎ *051/711–761* 🌐 *www.hotel-astoria.hr* 🛏 *50 rooms* 🍴 *Free Breakfast.*

Milenij Hotel Opatija

$$$$ | HOTEL | On the coastal promenade, this bright pink luxury villa is part old and part new; rooms are furnished accordingly, with either Louis XV–style antiques heavily striped in silk or modern designer pieces. **Pros:** centrally located luxury hotel on the seafront; outdoor breakfast area overlooking the sea and promenade occasionally has morning live music; excellent spa facilities. **Cons:** small pool with few lounge chairs; lack of parking spaces; service can be slow. *[$] Rooms from: 2264 Kn ✉ Maršala Tita 109 ☎ 051/202–000 🌐 www.milenijhoteli.hr 🛏 99 rooms 🍴 Free breakfast.*

Remisens Premium Hotel Ambasador
$$$ | **HOTEL** | This 10-floor skyscraper may not look appealing from the outside, but this luxurious hotel is surprisingly elegant on the inside, with an airy lobby area and floor-to-ceiling windows overlooking the sea. **Pros:** view from sea-facing rooms is gorgeous; luxurious pool area overlooking the beach; superior spa facilities. **Cons:** parking fees; hotel also caters to business travelers; only buffet-style dinners with half-board option. *[$] Rooms from: 1590 Kn ✉ Feliksa Peršića 5 ☎ 051/710–444 reservation center, 051/743–333 🌐 www.remisens.com 🛏 200 rooms 🍴 Free breakfast.*

Remisens Premium Hotel Kvarner
$$$ | **HOTEL** | The former summer residence of European royalty, Kvarner's oldest hotel first opened its doors to guests in 1884. **Pros:** Habsburg-era grandeur; spacious patio overlooking the sea; spa and fitness included in price of the room. **Cons:** noise from wedding parties sometimes hosted in the Crystal Ballroom; inconsistent food quality; stuffy atmosphere. *[$] Rooms from: 1510 Kn ✉ Pava Tomašica 2 ☎ 051/271–233, 051/710–444 reservation center 🌐 www.remisens.com ⏲ Closed Nov.–Mar. 🛏 58 rooms 🍴 Free breakfast.*

Nightlife

There was a time when folk from Rijeka used Opatija as their playground; then, the town offered superb nightlife options. These days, however, the big city along the coast is reclaiming its post as the cultural hot spot of the region, and Opatija has been busy transforming itself back into Central and Eastern Europe's health resort. The wealthy Italians and Austrians who dominate here enjoy nights out for live music, open-air movies, and regional theater.

Hemingway
BARS/PUBS | A Croatian chain of cocktail bars that also serves beach-style food like burgers and fries. The nightlife in Opatija is casual, as is the atmosphere here. This is a lounge setting where you can stop and enjoy a late-night drink as you stroll through the park and check out the happenings about the town. *✉ Zert 2 ☎ 051/711–333 🌐 www.hemingway.hr.*

Lounge and Beach Bar Colosseum
DANCE CLUBS | If there is nightlife to be found in Opatija, this is where it's at. The Colosseum has an actual disco and features DJs, dancers, and other performers with fun events geared toward a hip crowd. The club also has sun beds around a pool that looks out over the sea and is perfect for enjoying cocktails after salsa dancing. *✉ Marsala Tita 159 🌐 www.opatija-colosseum.com.*

Monokini
BARS/PUBS | Centrally located in Opatija, Monokini attracts a young crowd who enjoys lounging on the couches inside or in the glassed-in terrace as they listen to music and watch the passersby. You'll find good music, a young and mostly friendly staff, good drinks, cocktails, and a selection of teas—not to mention an enticing atmosphere that invites locals to meet up for a chat. *✉ Maršala Tita 96 ☎ 051/444–110.*

Performing Arts

Gervais Center
ARTS CENTERS | **FAMILY** | Since the 19th century, a live performance and musical theater has sat where the modern Gervais Center sits today. At the beginning of the 20th century the theater started showing films until it officially became the city cinema in the 1950s. In 2012, the original building was demolished,

then in 2017 the current contemporary performance house opened, now offering a vibrant year-round schedule of regional musical theater, plays, concerts, opera, festivals, and movie screenings. ⊠ *Ulica Nikole Tesle 5* ☏ *051/588–460* ⊕ *www. festivalopatija.hr/centargervais.*

Activities

Mount Učka Nature Park, accessible from virtually any point along the coast, offers the easiest opportunity for active exploring, including mountain-bike and hiking trails up through the forested slopes.

Marotti Windsurf Center

WINDSURFING | FAMILY | Marotti Windsurf Center in Volosko is the best place in the region to learn to windsurf. There is a Tramontana wind that blows down from the mountains every morning in Volosko, creating the perfect conditions for both beginners and experts. The team at Marotti are as friendly and relaxed as they are experienced. They also offer team building, stand-up paddleboarding tours, and equipment storage. ⊠ *Obala Frana Supila 2* ☏ *099/662–9546* ⊕ *www. marottiwindsurfing.hr.*

Cres

Brestova is 30 km (18 miles) southwest of Opatija, then a 20-minute ferry ride.

Twisting down the entire length of the Kvarner Bay on its western side is Cres, whose latest claim to fame is that it is the largest of all Croatian islands. For many years, squat neighbor Krk was awarded this distinction, but recent recalculations have rectified a long-standing error. Cres has been known as one of the most unspoiled islands in the Adriatic for a long time. More difficult to get to than Krk, and with a wilder and more rugged topography, Cres is quite frankly a delight. Its natural stretches are punctuated with olive groves and tiny towns and villages that remain authentic for the most part.

GETTING HERE AND AROUND
Ferries to Cres take about 20 minutes, embarking from Brestova, which is on the mainland southwest of Opatija, to Porozina; another ferry goes from Valbiska on Krk to Merag, on the east side of Cres.

Sights

★ Beli Visitor Centre and Rescue Centre for Griffon Vultures
NATURE PRESERVE | FAMILY | The northern end of Cres is mountainous and forested, harboring wildlife such as the rare griffin vulture. This rescue center helps protect and rescue these beasts, as well as preserve the environment and heritage of the island. The center houses rescued vultures before they are released back in to the wild and includes educational info on the biodiversity and history of northern Cres, and information on bird-watching, eco-trails, and volunteer opportunities. The naturalists that run the center are full of passion about their work and excited teachers. Visit this center with your kids to learn more about these protected birds, and then try to spot the griffins flying in their natural habitat around the cliffs of the island. From November to April, the center is open by appointment only, so call in advance during this period. ⊠ *Beli 4, Beli* ☏ *095/506–1116* ⊕ *www. belivisitorcentre.eu* ⊠ *Free (donations accepted).*

Cres Town
TOWN | Tucked into a well-protected bay, midway down the island, Cres Town is set around a lovely little fishing harbor, small but perfectly formed, with numerous Gothic and Renaissance churches, monasteries, and palaces. For the most part these are in the Old Town, which sits protected by winged Venetian lions atop three 16th-century gates, the only

On Cres, the small village of Lubenice is home to artists and music performances in the summer.

remains of a defensive wall. A small harbor (*Mandrać*), as well as a municipal loggia built in the 15th-century, remain the soul of the town.

The **town beach,** at Kovačine campsite, holds a Blue Flag award for cleanliness. To get there, follow the path around the harbor from the main road and keep going for at least 15 minutes along the promenade, where you'll find spots to jump into the water and the odd café or restaurant to keep you fueled. Although the seaside here is man-made, it somehow doesn't detract too much from the experience. ✉ *Cres Town* ⊕ *www.tzg-cres.hr.*

★ Lubenice

TOWN | One of the most tempting beaches on the island is on the western coast of Cres at the foot of a steep cliff, at the top of which is the tiny village of Lubenice, which offers great views out to sea and up the western coast. This picturesque collection of houses that surrounds the 15th-century Church of St. Anthony the Hermit has been clinging to its outcrop for around 4,000 years. The hamlet is popular among arty types and hosts exhibitions and music performances in the summer. From the beach below, a short walk through vineyards will bring you to Žanja Cove, which has a blue grotto, a cave at water level that enjoys brilliant blue light as strong sunlight filters through the azure water. ✉ *Lubenice* ⊕ *www.tzg-cres.hr.*

Osor

TOWN | At the southwestern tip of Cres is the town of Osor, whose strategic position on the channel between the islands of Cres and Lošinj ensured that wealth flowed into the town from trade ships. A wander through this well-preserved medieval town famous for its garden sculptures makes for a pleasant afternoon in an exceptionally tranquil location. Reflecting its former status, there's even a cathedral, and many important archaeological sites have been discovered in the vicinity. ✉ *Osor* ⊕ *www.visitlosinj.hr.*

As the largest of the Croatian islands, Cres has some of its best beaches.

Osor Archaeological Collection

MUSEUM | Housed in the former city hall near the cathedral, this museum contains one of the oldest archeological collections in Croatia, including artifacts from across the Roman empire. ✉ *Gradska vijecnica, Osor* ☎ *051/233–892* 🌐 *www.muzej.losinj.hr* 🎟 *35 Kn* 🕓 *Closed Mon. mid-Jun.–Aug.; by reservation only Oct.–mid-May.*

Valun

TOWN | Across the bay from Cres, the village of Valun has a nice beach. The town's claim to fame is the "Valun Tablet," a gravestone that is one of the oldest known examples of Glagolitic script. The tablet is now kept in the parish church, right on the waterfront. Get to Valun by car or by taking the wooden boat that sits just outside the Cres Harbor wall; it's easily spotted from the main square. ✉ *Valun.*

🍴 Restaurants

Konoba Belona

$$$$ | **MEDITERRANEAN** | This family-run restaurant understands the true meaning of making guests feel welcome. Meals are freshly prepared in a classic way that honors the treasures of Cres. **Known for:** pepper steak; pistachio semi-freddo; being away from the harbor crowds. [$] *Average main: 90 Kn* ✉ *Ul. Hrvatskih branitelja, Cres Town* ☎ *051/571–203* 🕓 *Closed Dec.–Mar.*

Konoba Bonifačić

$$$$ | **MEDITERRANEAN** | The subtitle on the road signs reads *nonina kuhinja* (granny's cooking), and you were a spoiled child indeed if your grandma turned out dishes of this standard for you. The shady garden in the heart of ancient Osor is a perfect setting in which to enjoy the typical plates of the konoba: meat, seafood, pasta, and salads. **Known for:** lovely garden terrace; traditional mediterranean dishes; idyllic location in Osor. [$] *Average main: 90 Kn* ✉ *Osor 64, Osor* ☎ *051/237–413*

⊕ *www.jazon.hr* ☉ *Closed Oct.–Easter. No lunch.*

★ Konoba Bukaleta

$$$$ | **MEDITERRANEAN** | Cres is famous for its lamb, and although the majority of restaurants have it on the menu, Bukaleta is *the* place for the best on the island. Located in the small village of Loznati, just 10 km (6 miles) south of Cres Town, Bukaleta has been run by the same family for over 30 years. **Known for:** lamb 13 different ways; lamb slow cooked in stone bread oven; traditional recipes passed down through generations. $ *Average main: 100 Kn* ⊠ *Loznati 9a, Loznati* ☎ *051/571–606* ☉ *Closed Oct.–Apr.*

Konoba Hibernicia

$$$ | **MEDITERRANEAN** | A nice little terrace right by the bell tower in the heart of the stone hilltop village of Lubenice is the perfect location for a light lunch of *pršut* (prosciutto), cheese, olives, and a glass of local wine. For a more hearty meal, order lamb-stew gnocchi or lamb liver with polenta, since lamb is a specialty on Cres. **Known for:** relaxed atmosphere; simple traditional food; not so friendly staff. $ *Average main: 80 Kn* ⊠ *Lubenice 17, Lubenice* ☎ *051/525–040* ▤ *No credit cards* ☉ *Closed Oct.–Apr.*

Riva

$$$$ | **SEAFOOD** | The colorful square on the edge of Cres Town harbor is lined with many restaurants serving seafood, pasta, and risotto, and Riva is an excellent choice. Tables edge out onto the flagstones of the square, meaning the steady stream of strollers through the town will eye your plate with appreciative glances. **Known for:** fresh seafood; harbor view terrace; dinner reservations necessary. $ *Average main: 130 Kn* ⊠ *Riva creskih kapetana 13, Cres Town* ☎ *051/571–107* ☉ *Closed Nov.–Easter.*

Hotels

Reflecting its splendid, undeveloped nature, Cres offers very few hotels, though there are plenty of apartments and guest rooms available for rent on the island.

Hotel Kimen

$$ | **HOTEL** | Tucked away in a shady pine forest just a stone's throw from the town beach and a 10-minute walk from the center, Kimen's four stories provide the only hotel accommodation in Cres Town. **Pros:** enviable position on an attractive cove; close to town center; kid- and dog-friendly. **Cons:** smallish rooms; a bit outdated; Wi-Fi not available in every room. $ *Rooms from: 985 Kn* ⊠ *Melin I 16, Cres Town* ☎ *051/573–305* ⊕ *www. hotel-kimen.com* ☉ *Closed mid-Oct.–Apr.* ⇥ *128 rooms* ⦿ *Free breakfast.*

Nightlife

The half-dozen or so bars around the main harbor are great for casual drinking and chatting while you sit outside on balmy evenings listening to the clinking chains of boats. Head inside for quicker quaffing and shouting above Croatian high-energy pop music, where you'll share the space with German yachtsmen. If you're looking for livelier options, unfortunately you're on the wrong island.

🏃 Activities

BIKING

Camp Kovačine

BICYCLING | The staff at Camp Kovačine, which is nicely set under shady pines and right on the main town beach, can rent you bikes and boats, organize diving trips, beach volleyball, and even paragliding. They have added a new pool and will extended their campground season until the end of October (it's closed from November to March). ⊠ *Melin I/20, Cres Town* ☎ *051/573–150 sales* *office, 051/571–423 front desk ⊕ www. camp-kovacine.com.*

DIVING

Diving Cres

SCUBA DIVING | If you prefer to explore beneath the waves, Diving Cres can be found in the Camp Kovačine, about a 10-minute walk from the harbor. A single-orientation dive can be tried for €69, or a ticket of 10 dives for €80. They also have a boat and rental equipment available in many sizes. The dive center is managed by a community of divers based in Germany and has been operating since 1996. ⊠ *Campsite Kovačine, Melin I/20, Cres Town* ☎ *051/571–706* ⊕ *www.diving.de.*

Lošinj

Mali Lošinj is 55 km (35 miles) from Cres Town.

As you approach the southern tip of Cres, you'll see the steep slopes of Osorčica Mountain on nearby Lošinj. Sheltered by the Alps to the North and Velebit to the east, the favorable island climate prompted the creation of a health resort here in 1892.

Blink and you might miss the bridge that connects Cres to Lošinj, unless you happen to arrive when the span is raised to allow a ship through the narrow channel that splits the two islands. In fact, until Roman times the two islands were one, connected near Osor. Mother Nature's inconsiderate arrangement did much to frustrate trade ships; entire vessels would be hauled across the few feet of land that blocked the route here rather than sail around the southern tip of the archipelago. Eventually, some bright spark decided to cut the present-day channel, opening the shipping lanes. Lošinj is an elongated, low-lying island covered with a pine forest. Viewed from the hills of Cres, the slim green outline of the main island and its surrounding islets,

with a backbone of hills in the middle, resembles a long frog splayed out in the water, basking in the sun and contrasting beautifully with the water. Lošinj's past and present are very much connected to the shipping industry. The sea captains who populated the towns of Veli and Mali Lošinj when the island reached its golden age in the 19th century are very much responsible for bringing exotic plant life here from around the world and for building the fine villas that have made this a colorful destination for vacationers, who contribute much more to the island's economy today. The smaller islands that make up the archipelago include Unije, Sušak, and Ilovik—all of which are large enough to provide some type of accommodation—and even smaller islands such as Vele and Male Srakane, Orjule, and Sveti Petar, which can be reached by tourist boats from the resorts on Lošinj.

 ## Sights

Church of St. Anthony the Hermit

RELIGIOUS SITE | The intimate harbor is the centerpiece of Veli Lošinj, at the entrance to which is the delightful Church of St. Anthony the Hermit, with a separate bell tower in pink and cream stone. Built on the site of a former church in 1774, the church has always had a congregation of seafarers, who have filled it with religious art and altars from spots such as Venice. ⊠ *On the Veli Lošinj waterfront* ⊙ *Closed Sun. and Sept.–July.*

Čikat Bay

BEACH—SIGHT | The road that runs along the Mali Lošinj harbor leads to Čikat Bay, a pine-covered area dotted with impressive Habsburg-era villas and pebbled beach coves. Nearby hotels and campsites, plus good parking, lots of cafés, and ice-cream stands make these beaches popular. There's a gracious promenade along the bay that's perfect for strolling, a windsurfing school for the adventurous, and paddleboat rentals. ⊠ *Mali Lošinj.*

The island of Lošinj has a past and present that are both very connected to the shipping industry.

Kula (*The Tower*)

MILITARY SITE | Opposite the harbor, but now hidden by a row of houses, are the battlements of a defensive tower that dates from the 15th century. The squat construction, known as the Tower, now houses a museum and an art gallery staging temporary exhibitions by notable Croatian artists. The permanent exhibition tracing the town's history includes a copy of a Greek statue of Apoksiomen, which was discovered on the seabed in 1999. ✉ *Kaštel bb, Veli Lošinj* ☎ *051/236–594* ⊕ *www.muzej.losinj.hr* 🖃 *35 Kn* 🕐 *Closed Mon. mid-June–mid-Sept.; Sun. and Mon. mid-Sept.–mid-Oct. and Easter–mid-June.*

★ Lošinj Marine Education Centre/Blue World Institute

LOCAL INTEREST | **FAMILY** | A community of around 180 bottlenose dolphins makes its home just off the coast of Lošinj, and the nonprofit Lošinj Marine Education Centre has made it their mission to protect the marine environment of the Adriatic sea. The center has a small number of engaging displays that use various media forms that invite visitors to take a deeper look at the amazing blue world that surrounds the island. The center is a great place for kids to learn more about the fascinating marine life that inhabit the Adriatic ocean. You may even end up "adopting" your own dolphin (although you can't take it home with you). But for €30 (about 225 Kn), you'll receive an adoption certificate, a photo of your adopted dolphin, membership for a year, and, of course, that warm fuzzy feeling of doing something good for the world. ✉ *Kaštel 24, Veli Lošinj* ☎ *051/604–666* ⊕ *www.blue-world.org* 🖃 *20 Kn* 🕐 *Closed Sun. in May, Jun., and Sept.; closed weekends Oct.–Apr.*

Mali Lošinj

TOWN | With 8,000 inhabitants sheltered around an inlet, Mali Lošinj is the largest island settlement in the Adriatic. In the 19th century, Mali and Veli Lošinj experienced a golden age, when many wealthy sea captains lived on the island. Brightening the waterfront, the mansions and villas they constructed contributed greatly to the towns' appeal. There are a handful of churches to wander into and take in the sense of history and time that has been well preserved by the island's faithful. The 15th-century **St. Martin's Church** was the original centerpiece around which the town was built but is now a bit decrepit, though its ominous presence with a tall square tower and pointed top are hard not to miss. At the base of the tower is a cemetery where the history of the town's past residents is collected. If you wish to dig a bit deeper, **The Church of Our Little Lady** (aka Church of the Nativity of Our Lord) houses many fine examples of religious art. ✉ *Mali Lošinj* 🌐 *www.visitlosinj.hr.*

Museum of Apoxyomenos

MUSEUM | **FAMILY** | This is an entire museum dedicated to telling the amazing story of a single ancient artifact found on the bottom of the sea near Mali Losinj in 1999. After six years of restoration, the bronze statue, which is presumed to date back to the 1st or 2nd BC, is an awesome piece of Greek work that is displayed in an artistic and mesmerizing way so that it is impossible to leave the museum without having a remarkable impression of what may have happened when the statue fell into the ocean thousands of years ago (but also about the process of its restoration). The building itself is reason enough to buy a ticket and enjoy a guided tour (offered twice-daily at 12 and 5). ✉ *Riva lošinjskih kapetana 13, Mali Lošinj* ☎ *051/734–260* 🌐 *www.muzejapoksiomena.hr* 🎫 *Nov.–Apr. 50 Kn.; May.–Oct. 75 Kn.* 🕓 *Closed Mon.*

Miomirisni otočki vrt/Losinj's Fragrant Garden (*Garden of Fine Scents*)

GARDEN | **FAMILY** | After a few days of dipping your toes in the water and basking in the sun, you might be itching for a diversionary outing. The Miomirisni otočki vrt is a pleasant place to spend the afternoon—rain or shine—sitting on the terrace admiring the sea of lavender on the hilltop. A donkey, a rabbit, and a small sheep delight visitors, especially children. A small shop in a wooden building sells organic products like soaps, marmalades, and of course, lavender oil. ✉ *Bukovica 6, Mali Lošinj* ☎ *098/326–519* 🌐 *www.miomirisni-vrt.hr* 🎫 *Free* 🕓 *Closed Jan. and Feb.*

Veli Lošinj

TOWN | The sea captains of Veli Lošinj evidently preferred to escape the harsh working condition of life on the sea while they were back on land, so they built their villas away from the waterfront, often surrounding themselves with gardens filled with exotic plants brought back from their travels. Archduke Karl Stephen built a winter residence in Veli Lošinj that is now a sanatorium surrounded by wonderful gardens, with a range of exotic plants and an arboretum. It's possible to spend the night in the sanatorium, even if you are healthy. A short walk beyond the main harbor is the quaint fishing cove of Rovenska. Beyond that, there's a pebble beach and several inviting restaurants. The breakwater was established by Habsburg archduke Maximilian. ✉ *Veli Lošinj* 🌐 *www.visitlosinj.hr.*

🍴 Restaurants

Artatore/Janje

$$$$ | **MEDITERRANEAN** | Ten km (6 miles) north of Mali Lošinj, in the small village of Artatore, you'll find the restaurant of the same name. Locals claim the restaurant, which they call *Kod Janje* (Chez Janje), is the best on the entire island. **Known for:** a seafood lover's paradise; longevity: the place has been open for 45 years; thick crab soup. [$] *Average main: 200 Kn* ✉ *Artatore 132, Mali Lošinj* ☎ *051/232–932* 🌐 *www.restaurant-artatore.hr* 🕓 *Closed Nov.–Easter.*

Slow Down: Islands of Lošinj

If the pace of life on the major islands is too hectic, knock your engine down to quarter-speed and head out to one of the tiny islands that pepper the seas around the coast of Lošinj. The island of **Unije** is by far the largest, managing to fit in a population of 90, although many of them are summer-only residents. The tiny town of the same name has a few restaurants settled around a large pebble bay, although exploring the northern coasts, by foot or by boat, should reveal many private swimming spots. **Ilovik** is the southernmost island of the group. Its nickname, "Island of Flowers," is accurate; oleanders and roses surround almost every home. Watch yachts at close quarters cutting through the channel between Ilovik and the islet of Sveti Petar, on which there was once a convent. The graveyard remains, and burial processions by fishing boat still take place. Paržine, on the southeastern coast, has a large sandy beach.

If you're from New Jersey, you may have a good chance of being related to one of the 188 people living on **Sušak** since many folk from here have settled in the Garden State. Sušak, flung farther out into the sea than any of the other islands, is a very different beast. First, while the rest of the Kvarner is composed of limestone karst, Sušak consists entirely of sand, so its coast is far gentler both in elevation and indentation. Not wanting to be outdone, the population retains a distinctive character and culture. The only wheeled transport on the island are wheelbarrows.

★ Baracuda

$$$$ | **SEAFOOD** | Many of the yachts that line the harbor unload their human cargo at this small restaurant, which enjoys a big reputation for fresh fish dinners. Tuna carpaccio, shark on the grill, and lobster *na buzaru* (cooked with wine) are all great. **Known for:** fresh fish and seafood; great location on the marina; friendly staff. $ *Average main: 130 Kn* ⊠ *Priko 31, Mali Lošinj* ☎ *051/233–309* ⏲ *Closed mid-Oct.–Apr.*

Bora Bar

$$$$ | **MEDITERRANEAN** | Creative Italian dishes like tuna carpaccio with celery root and truffles are what you'll find at this friendly restaurant in the Rovenska bay. The dynamic owners—part Croatian, part expat—bring a joie de vivre and an eclectic style to the place that attracts curious foodies to their tables. **Known for:** homemade pasta; truffle-infused dishes; homemade limoncello. $ *Average main: 130 Kn* ⊠ *Rovenska 3, Veli Lošinj* ☎ *051/867–544* ⊕ *www.borabar.net* ⏲ *Closed Oct.–Easter.*

Restaurant Matsunoki

$$$$ | **ASIAN FUSION** | This upscale restaurant combines the best of local, organic ingredients with Japanese cooking techniques and tastes. As good as Mediterranean food is, it can often leave your taste buds yearning for something more exotic, and the chef here introduces a masterful Japanese style to the menu. **Known for:** Japanese dumplings stuffed with lamb, fennel, and carrot; smoked oysters with unagi sauce; excellent selection of sake. $ *Average main: 195 Kn* ⊠ *Hotel Bellevue, Cikat 9* ☎ *051/679–0000* ⊕ *www.losinj-hotels.com/en/dining/restaurant-matsunoki/.*

Hotels

Hotel Apoksiomen

$$ | HOTEL | Named after a Greek statue that was recovered from the seabed near Mali Lošinj in 1999, this renovated villa imposes itself on the seafront close to the main square and is a model of a modern, small hotel. **Pros:** stunning views; central location right on the water; delicious pastries in the cafe. **Cons:** rooms don't match the gorgeous hotel exterior; parking is off-site and very expensive; can be noisy. $ *Rooms from: 1360 Kn* ✉ *Riva Lošinjskih kapetana 1, Mali Lošinj* ☎ *051/520–820* ⊕ *www.apoksiomen.com* ☽ *Closed Nov.–Apr.* ⇆ *25 rooms* ❍ *Free breakfast.*

Vitality Hotel Punta

$$$ | HOTEL | The attractive colored blocks of this newly renovated four-star property in Veli Lošinj line the seashore in a style that complements the island's traditional architecture surprisingly well. **Pros:** good on-site facilities; near both the sea and the town of Veli Lošinj; stunning views from some rooms. **Cons:** pool is on the small side for the size of the hotel; large hotel complex can feel a bit impersonal; inconsistent service. $ *Rooms from: 1510 Kn* ✉ *Šestavine 17, Veli Lošinj* ☎ *051/662–000* ⊕ *www.losinj-hotels. com* ☽ *Closed Nov.–Mar.* ⇆ *289 rooms* ❍ *Free breakfast.*

Nightlife

Both Mali and Vela Lošinj offer a healthy selection of bars, where you can sit outside on warm evenings, sip drinks, and chat. Those looking for brighter lights had better move on to Krk or the mainland.

Activities

BIKING

Rent-A-Bike Junior (*Rent-A-Bike Best Price*)

BICYCLING | You can rent bikes for 15 Kn per hour or 65 Kn per day, though

availability is limited (and you need to call ahead) from October through May. ✉ *Velopin 15, Mali Lošinj* ☎ *099/409–9943* ⊕ *http://www.losinjbike.com.*

DIVING AND SAILING

Sub Sea Son Scuba School

SCUBA DIVING | Sub Sea Son is run by Neno, an SSI diving instructor who is relaxed and experienced. The company has its own dive boat and offers a range of courses either for certification or advanced instruction. Take a test dive for €55 (about 400 Kn). ✉ *, Del Conte 1, Mali Lošinj* ☎ *098/ 294–887* ⊕ *www. subseason.com.*

FLIGHTSEEING

Airport Lošinj

FLYING/SKYDIVING/SOARING | To put it all in perspective, from Lošinj Airport you can take a panoramic 15-minute flight over the archipelago for about 500 Kn. The airport is open year-round, and from June to the end of September there are direct air taxi flights from Zagreb and Venice for a reasonable price. ✉ *Privlaka 19, Mali Lošinj* ☎ *051/231–666* ⊕ *www.airportmal-ilosinj.hr.*

Krk

Krk Town is 50 km (31 miles) southeast of Rijeka.

It's no surprise—since Krk is one of the largest Croatian islands, hosts the regional airport, and is connected to the mainland by a bridge—that the robust island is one of the most developed in the country. The dusty edges and agricultural interior get very busy during the high season, and if you visit then you will likely find yourself in traffic jams along the snaking routes between the resort towns. Add the sight of the oil refinery on the mainland near the bridge and the terminal for tankers near Omišalj on the northern coast of the island, and you may think twice about heading here. The sights aren't exactly what you'd call picturesque, but don't be put off so easily. Krk still offers many of the same delights found in the rest of the region: great beaches, interesting history, and pretty old towns. Although other islands may offer a slower pace, Krk compensates by offering more facilities and convenience. With numerous accommodation options and more entertainments, it may very well be the best choice for families with easily bored children in tow.

Sights

Baška
TOWN | On the southern end of the island, this town has a great beach as well as the conveniences of civilization. However, this means that you must sometimes fight to find a spot in season. The 2-km (1-mile) beach is fronted by colorfully painted houses (and hotels at the southern end) and adorned with interesting nooks and stairways, all lending a fun and slightly eccentric air to the town. Cute backstreets behind the houses offer a selection of cozy cafés and plethora of ice-cream shops. ⊠ *Baška* ⊕ *www. tz-baska.hr.*

Crkva Sv. Lucije (*Church of St. Lucy*)
RELIGIOUS SITE | Driving into Baška, you'll pass through Baščanska draga, and then find yourself in Jurandvor. While on this road, take the chance to visit the Church of St. Lucy, which has achieved cultlike status since the discovery of the glagolithic Baška Tablet on its grounds in 1851. ⊠ *Jurandvor* 🕾 *051/860–184* ⊕ *www.azjurandvor.com* 🎫 *25 Kn* ⊗ *Closed Nov.–Apr.*

Goli Otok
ISLAND | Like Communist history? Consider a day trip to this uninhabited island that was a Yugoslav prison, just off the coast of Rab. The name 'Goli Otok' means "naked island" and was aptly given for the lack of vegetation and inhabitable conditions on the island. After Tito broke ranks with Stalin in 1948, the island became known as the place where Yugoslav political prisoners were confined. Men were incarcerated here while women were taken to nearby Grgur island. The treatment of these prisoners is wholly unknown, as very few prisoners lived to tell of their experiences, but a stone quarry indicates that prisoners were forced to do hard labor quarrying stone. Conditions on Goli Otok were harsh, with blistering temperatures in the summer, and brutal *Bura* winds ripping across the barren island in the winter. Any mention of Goli Otok was strictly forbidden in Yugoslavia until after Tito's death. The prison was completely abandoned in 1989, but prison barracks remain there. You can make a short trip to this legendary gulag by taxi boat with one of the many charter companies in Baška or Punat on Krk island. ⊠ *Rab.*

Katunar Winery
WINERY/DISTILLERY | At Katunar winery on the island of Krk, you can sample the Žlatina varietal, which is indigenous to the island. Individual visits and group tours can be arranged to sample the dry white Žlahtina Katunar or the Černo Katunar (a dry red), or the "pearl wine" Biser Mora, a dessert wine produced from 100% Zlahtina grapes. This dry white wine is famous around the world. ⊠ *Sv. Nedilija, Krk Town* 🕾 *051/857–393* ⊕ *www.katunar.hr* 🎫 *100 kn for tasting (includes 7 wines, cheese, olives, bread, and olive oil).*

★ Krk Town
TOWN | In terms of its importance and the pride of the 4,000 locals, the island's capital could perhaps even be called a city. It's not completely clear when the old city walls were first built, but the oldest mention of the walls dates back to the 1st century BC. The present-day walls, however, date mainly to the Middle Ages. The city walls have four gates. The seafront has a pleasant green area that takes you past cafés and a fish market. The main square, **Vela Placa,** is just behind the first row of houses. There's a beach

Krk is one of the more developed of the Croatian islands, meaning more activities and entertainment options abound.

underneath the town walls with a lovely view of the town.

The **old town hall** on Vela Placa was built in the 15th century. Its clock shows all 24 hours: daytime on the upper part, nighttime on the lower. Krk Town has two well-known visual anchors. The first is the imposing **citadel** that sits on Trg Kamplin. The bell tower of **St. Quirinus** is the other, with its angular onion dome typical of Krk. ✉ *Krk Town.*

Stara Baška

TOWN | If you're looking for a more secluded, isolated spot, head to this town that sits just above the beaches that trim a wide cove and peninsula. The road here is a single track through the tiny village, so you may find yourself performing intricate maneuvers in your car should you be unlucky enough to meet the local water truck that keeps the houses supplied. Unless you arrive by boat, it is best to park in the first empty spot you see and walk in to the town or down the hill to the beach.

Špilja Biserujka (*Biserujka Cave*)

CAVE | North of Vrbnik, near Rudine, this cave is only one of many caverns on Krk; however, it's the only one open to the public. The stalactites, stalagmites, and calcine pillars inside are lighted for your pleasure. ✉ *½ km (1/3 mile) from Rudine* ✥ *parking is 150m from the entrance to the cave* ☎ *098/211–630, 051/852–203* ⊕ *www.spilja-biserujka.com.hr* 🖃 *30 Kn* ⊙ *Closed Nov.–Apr.*

Vrbnik

TOWN | This clifftop town on the northeast coast of the island offers majestic views of Velebit mountain and a bird's-eye view of the crystal clear waters far below. Clustered on a hilltop 157 feet above a small harbor, it's a mass of confusing, winding streets. As you traverse the town on foot you will find many corners where long staircases suddenly arise due to the steep terrain. As one of the oldest settlements on Krk, Vrbnik can feel a a little ramshackle, but this lends more to the charm than it distracts from it. The fragrance of old wine barrels is ubiquitous on Vrbnik and it is likely that they were once filled with Žlahtina, a local white wine that some claim as the best from the Kvarner region. The vineyards are but a short hop from town. ⊠ *Vrbnik.*

Restaurants

In the summer you'll be sharing tables with busloads of tourists at many of Krk's best restaurants, all of which tend to be outside the capital. However, Krk Town has many restaurants that will serve you perfectly reasonable renditions of less ambitious fare, such as fish, pasta, and pizza.

Nada

$$$$ | **MEDITERRANEAN** | Nada's terrace is considered by many islanders as the top place to sit for a glass of wine and cheese plate on a late summer afternoon. The konoba inside provides an authentic Croatian atmosphere and a welcome respite from the heat on a hot summer day. **Known for:** popular island restaurant; cheese platter, prosciutto, and wine; cliffside terrace. $ *Average main: 150 Kn* ⊠ *Glavača 22, Vrbnik* ☎ *051/857–065* ⊕ *www.nada-vrbnik.hr* ⊗ *Closed Nov.–Easter.*

Pod Prevolt

$$$$ | **MEDITERRANEAN** | **FAMILY** | Pod Prevolt, a small family-run tavern, located in the village of Milohnići, is a bit off the beaten path, but it's a place where you can get a real feel for the island's peaceful beauty and delicious traditional food. Find a seat on one of the large wooden tables under the fig trees and soak up the silence. **Known for:** baked octopus with veggies; housemade charcuterie and cheeses; simple but delicious desserts. $ *Average main: 90 Kn* ⊠ *Milohnići 21B, Malinska* ☎ *051/862–149* ⊗ *Closed Oct.–Apr.*

★ Rivica

$$$$ | **SEAFOOD** | Rivica is the kind of place that has a long tradition for superior service and sophisticated dishes but lacks much of the pretense attached to such accolades. This is not a restaurant that rests on its past laurels as is clear from the modern menu additions like the Tuna 2F, a fresh-fusion cold starter tuna tartare with sashimi and chips, or the duck mousse with caramelized onions on toast. **Known for:** grilled lobster and crayfish; foie gras and duck fillet; warm professional staff. $ *Average main: 130 Kn* ⊠ *Ribarska obala 13, Njivice* ☎ *051/846–101* ⊕ *www.rivica.hr* ⊗ *Closed Dec.–Mar.*

★ Žal

$$$$ | **SEAFOOD** | **FAMILY** | If you ask locals where to go on Krk island for incredible seafood in a scenic setting, you'll hear this restaurant recommended over and over again. Located right on the water in the small fishing village of Klimno (near Dobrinj), this family-run establishment combines delicious, traditional dishes like whole *brancin* (sea bass) slow-roasted *u soli* (under salt) and *šurlice* (homemade pasta) with Kvarner skampi, with gorgeous seaside views. **Known for:** fresh whole fish; quayside setting; traditional island specialties. $ *Average main: 150 Kn* ⊠ *Klimno 44, Dobrinj* ☎ *051/853–142* ⊕ *www.restaurant-zal.com.*

🛏 Hotels

Hotel Kanajt

$$ | **HOTEL** | **FAMILY** | A 16th-century building that once served as a bishop's summer residence, the resort hotel is on a large expanse of land that is surrounded by palm, pine, and olive trees. **Pros:** close to the marina; spa facilities; open all year. **Cons:** good beaches are a bit away from the hotel; not all rooms have a balcony; rooms need a little updating. $ *Rooms from: 1250 Kn* ⊠ *Kanajt 5, Punat* ☎ *051/654–340* ⊕ *www.kanajt.hr* ➪ *22 rooms* ⊚ *Free breakfast.*

Hotel Pinia

$$$ | **HOTEL** | Located in the small seaside village of Porat, just next to Malinska, this hotel is perfectly positioned close to the sea but also surrounded by greenery. **Pros:** great location by the sea; good on-site restaurant; spacious rooms. **Cons:** hotel beach can get very busy in July and August; a bit far from the center of Malinska; Wi-Fi connection not great. [$] *Rooms from: €1510* ✉ *Porat BB, Malinska* ☎ *051/866–333* 🌐 *www.hotel-pinia.hr* 🕒 *Closed Nov.–Apr.* 🛏 *45 rooms* 🍴 *Some meals.*

Valamar Atrium Baška Residence

$$$ | **HOTEL** | Located just a few steps away from the famed Baška beach, Atrium Residence has spacious, luxurious rooms and apartments. **Pros:** seafront location; great beach views; spacious rooms. **Cons:** standard rooms have French balconies; parking located at the sister hotel Corinthia; lack of in-hotel facilities (guests can use facilities of the nearby hotels). [$] *Rooms from: 1510 Kn* ✉ *Emila Geistlicha 39, Baška* ☎ *051/656–890 reception, 052/465–000 reservations* 🌐 *www.valamar.com* 🕒 *Closed Oct.–Apr.* 🛏 *64 rooms* 🍴 *Free breakfast.*

Valamar Koralj Hotel

$$ | **HOTEL** | **FAMILY** | For long days on the beach and all conveniences on tap, this hotel on the edge of Krk Town is a decent choice; half-board (breakfast and dinner) is included in all rates, though those who plan busy evenings may want to find somewhere closer to the center. **Pros:** great for families with kids in summer; good for couples off-season; peaceful location amid pine trees. **Cons:** small rooms; some rooms without balcony; better rooms quite pricey for the quality. [$] *Rooms from: 1250 Kn* ✉ *Ul. Vlade Tomašiča, Krk Town* ☎ *051/655–400 hotel, 052/465–000 reservations* 🌐 *www.valamar.com* 🕒 *Closed Oct.–Apr.* 🛏 *194 rooms* 🍴 *Free breakfast.*

Nightlife

Krk Town and Baška are the places to head for relatively low-key drinks in the evening. The center of the capital and the stretch of town above the beach at Baška offer numerous bars with music and tables out under the stars. A firm family favorite, Krk is definitely not the place for cutting-edge nightlife. However, if you really can't live without getting your club fix, there are a couple of large venues offering house DJs. Note that clubs are open only in the summer.

Cocktail Bar Volsonis

BARS/PUBS | One of the livelier nightspots in Krk Town, this bar has the appropriate, though somewhat mysterious, ruins of a wonderful sacrificial altar to love goddess Venus down in the basement. In fact, all of Volsonis is incorporated into a 2,000-year-old archaeological site that the owners, Maria Elena and Goran, found under the house. Electronic music plays on weekends in the underground Catacombs, or you can chill out with a glass of wine, beer, or coffee in their secret garden. The owners have expanded their offer with a menu that includes breakfast and lunch offerings that use many ingredients from their garden. This is likely the only place to have a substantial breakfast. ✉ *Vela Placa 8, Krk Town* ☎ *051/880–249* 🌐 *www.volsonis.hr.*

Shopping

Stanic

ART GALLERIES | This wonderful gallery is a comprehensive collection of works by local artists, as well as locally designed lamps, ceramics, mirrors, and other souvenirs. ✉ *Vela Placa 8, Krk Town* ☎ *051/220–052* 🌐 *www.helena.hr.*

Activities

BIKING
You can bike around the island for transportation or exercise.

Cycling Union Krk
BICYCLING | The best place to rent a bicycle is at the Cycling Union, either in Krk or at the Marina in Punat. ⊠ *Omišalja 14, Krk Town* ☎ *099/672-0424* ⊕ *www. cyclingunionkrk.info.*

DIVING
Dive Center Krk
SCUBA DIVING | The most interesting sights in Kvarner Bay are wrecks. At Dive Center Krk on the Bay of Punat, a full-day diving trip (two dives) sets you back about 450 Kn, plus 190 Kn for equipment rental, if you need it. ⊠ *Dunat 50, Kornic* ☎ *051/867–303* ⊕ *www.dive-center-krk. com.*

HIKING
There are many marked paths in the area around Baška. For a longer hike, consider visiting the splendid remote villages at Vela and Mala Luka; take this path as part of a group, and be aware that the section of the trail through the canyon may flood if there's rain. For some nice hikes around Baška; consider the path from Baška to Mjesec Hill (5½ km [3 miles], 2 hours). Offering spectacular views over the bay, this easy route passes by St. John's Church, where you can take a breather while you contemplate higher things. The route from Baška to Jurandvor (5 km [3 miles], 2 hours) takes you through the Baška Valley and leaves you with a visit to the Church of St. Lucy, home of the Baška Tablet. The short hike between Baška and Stara Baška will give you a little exercise; a delightful stretch of small, quiet beaches is the reward for a short hike.

Krk Tourist Office
HIKING/WALKING | For more hiking information and maps, contact the Krk Tourist Office. ⊠ *Trg Sv. Kvirina 1, Krk Town* ☎ *051/221–359* ⊕ *www.krk.hr.*

WATERSKIING
Cable Krk
WATER SPORTS | Always fancied spraying majestic jets of water across the aquamarine seas, but sorting out a boat and someone to drive just seems too much trouble? Well, the answer lies with Cable Krk, on a calm bay just outside the resort of Punat, toward Krk Town. A large wooden pier with a bar and restaurant to entertain your companions is the gateway to a cableway, which is not much different than a drag-lift at a ski resort. The cable pulls you around a short course, with instruction on hand to help you get your sea legs. One hour costs about 100 Kn, not including equipment. ⊠ *Dunat, Kornic* ☎ *091/262–7303* ⊕ *www.wakeboarder. hr.*

Delnice

50 km (31 miles) east of Rijeka.

Delnice, which sits on the road between Rijeka and Zagreb, is a breath of fresh mountain air, especially in summer after leaving the crowded hot seaside. It makes a good base for exploring the mountains of the Gorski kotar region that sit above Kvarner Bay. The region is covered with well-marked hiking and biking trails and mountain huts that offer refreshment and respite from the elements. In winter, Delnice is often blanketed in several feet of snow while cities along the sea are wet and gray. There is a full-size hockey rink, groomed cross-country ski trails, and popular sled-riding spots that make this a weekend winter escape for locals. It's also a convenient stopover if you're taking the slow route back to Zagreb on your way back to the airport. Take a day or two to swap the brilliant blue of the sea for a few nights in the peaceful and wild green forests and rivers of the Gorski kotar.

🍴 Restaurants

Volta

$$$ | **AUSTRIAN** | The small town of Fužine is very close to Delnice and is well known for its pine-bordered lake. This is typical mountain food that includes lots of wild game like boar, bear, deer stew, and frog legs. **Known for:** horse and game meat; local crowd; hearty meals. *[$] Average main: 80 Kn ✉ Franja Račkog 8, Fužine ☎ 051/830–030 ⏲ Closed Feb.*

🛏 Hotels

Mountain Center Petehovac

$ | **B&B/INN** | Come to Petehovac to escape the city and be surrounded by nature. **Pros:** location in nature; good and very affordable food; views over the surrounding area. **Cons:** basic facilities; rooms decor pretty unexciting; weak Wi-Fi connection. *[$] Rooms from: 450 Kn ✉ Polane 1a ☎ 051/814–901 🌐 www.petehovac.com.hr 🛏 18 rooms 🍴 Free breakfast.*

Hotel Risnjak

$ | **B&B/INNHOTEL** | This hunting lodge is a bare-bones, simple place to stay for hunters and hikers, and it's a worthwhile option if you need someplace cheap near Risnjak. **Pros:** near the entrance to Risnjak national park; the only place to stay in the surrounding area; great local food in the restaurant. **Cons:** basic amenities; does not feel very friendly; worn-out rooms. *[$] Rooms from: 350 Kn ✉ Lujzinska 36 ☎ 051/508–160 🌐 hotel-risnjak.hr 🛏 21 rooms 🍴 Free breakfast.*

🏃 Activities

HIKING

Delnice is a good base for hiking around Risnjak and the Gorski kotar range, which have many marked walking and hiking paths.

RAFTING AND CANOEING

Gorski Tok

WHITE-WATER RAFTING | **FAMILY** | On a super hot summer day, the cool refreshing waters of the Kupa River are a welcome change. Float down the river on an expedition organized by Gorski Tok, on either a canoe or a kayak depending on your skills and the water level. The company also runs canoe safari trips, in case the water level is low. *✉ Kralja Tomislava 11, Brod na Kupi ☎ 098/177-2585 🌐 www.gorski-tok.hr.*

Rab

120 km (75 miles) southeast of Rijeka.

Rab presents an utterly fascinating landscape. When you drive southward, down the Magistrala, you see that the island resembles the humped back of a diving sea monster. Once you've mounted this beast, via a short ferry ride from Stinica to Mišnjak, you travel along the center of its back, which is almost entirely bald to the north, letting all its hair hang out to the south. The high northern coast, which bears the brunt of the northern Bora winds, is dry, rocky, and barren. Crouching below this crusty ledge, the southern half of the island could hardly differ more, and has possibly the lushest terrain found on any Croatian island. Low, green hills dip into the seas, while the ancient Dundo forest grows so voraciously that it's almost impossible to walk in.

👁 Sights

Sitting on a narrow peninsula halfway up the island's southern coast, Rab Town, a compact, well-preserved medieval village, is best known for its distinctive skyline of four elegant bell towers, and its many churches. Author Rebecca West, who traveled through Yugoslavia in the 1930s, called Rab Town "one of the most beautiful cities of the world" in her

masterpiece, *Black Lamb and Grey Falcon.* Closed to traffic, the narrow cobbled streets of the Old Town, which are lined with Romanesque churches and patrician palaces, can be explored in an hour's leisurely stroll. The urban layout is simple: three longitudinal streets run parallel to the waterfront promenade and are linked together by steep passages traversing the hillside. The lower street is Donja ulica, the middle street Srednja ulica, and the upper street Gornja ulica.

Komrčar Park

CITY PARK | On the edge of town, the green expanse of Komrčar Park, laid out in the 19th century, offers avenues lined with pine trees for gentle strolling and access down to the sea. Although the Old Town and its immediate surroundings are Rab's chief treasures, this park is characteristic of the abundance of green areas on Rab island that are conducive for escaping the sun on hot days and are perfectly suited for laying a blanket down under one of the big trees and taking a nap. ✉ *Northwest of the Old Town, just behind the seafront promenade, Obala Kralja Petra Krešimira IV.*

Sveta Marija Velika (*Cathedral of St. Mary*)

RELIGIOUS SITE | The Romanesque Sveta Marija Velika, built in the 12th century and consecrated by the pope in 1177, is the biggest church in Rab Town, and was built on the site of Roman ruins. However, the only way to visit is to attend one of the masses, which are posted on the announcement board outside. ✉ *Ivana Rabljanina* 🌐 *www.rab-visit.com.*

★ **Veli Zvonik** (*Great Bell Tower*)

LOCAL INTEREST | The tallest and most beautiful of Rab's campaniles, the freestanding Veli Zvonik forms part of the former cathedral complex and dominates the southwest side of the peninsula. Built in the 12th century, it stands 85 feet high. ■ **TIP→ A climb to the top is well worth the effort since it affords breathtaking views over the town and sea.** ✉ *Gornja ulica* 🎟 *15 kn* 🕓 *Closed Oct.–May.*

🍴 Restaurants

Konoba Rab

$$$$ | **MEDITERRANEAN** | **FAMILY** | Tucked away in a narrow side street between Srednja ulica and Gornja ulica in Rab Town, this konoba is warm and inviting, with exposed-stone walls and rustic furniture. Grilled fish and meat are the house specialties, along with a good choice of pastas and risottos. **Known for:** welcoming staff and cozy atmosphere; traditional specialties slow cooked in the 'peka' over the fire; dried squid. [$] *Average main: 130 Kn* ✉ *Kneza Branimira 3* ☎ *051/725–666* 🕓 *Closed Nov. and Feb. No lunch Sun.*

Marco Polo

$$$$ | **MEDITERRANEAN** | With its superb food and convenient location in Banjol, this restaurant draws visitors from the nearby campground to its large outdoor terrace and small but elegant interior. Veggies are home-grown, seafood is local and always fresh, and meat dishes like Viennese schnitzel or beef tenderloin never disappoint. **Known for:** extensive classic menu; nice setting; good portions at affordable prices. [$] *Average main: 100 Kn* ✉ *Banjol 468, Banjol* ☎ *051/725–846* 🌐 *www.marcopolo-rab.com* 🕓 *Closed Oct.–Apr.*

Restaurant More

$$$$ | **MEDITERRANEAN** | This family-owned restaurant has an amazing location with seating right on the quay, especially attractive for those arriving by boat. The fish served here is caught by the owner, so the phrase "catch of the day" really means something. **Known for:** lovely waterfront location; grilled shellfish; romantic setting. [$] *Average main: 100 Kn* ✉ *Supetarska Draga 321, Supetarska Draga* ☎ *051/776–202* 🌐 *www.more-rab.com* 🕓 *Closed Oct.–Apr.*

Coffee and Quick Bites

Kuća Rapske Torte

$ | **CAFÉ** | **FAMILY** | Tucked away in the Old Town, this charming café-museum has a wonderful courtyard that's ideal for chilling out and enjoying a lemonade after exploring Rab Town. Sit inside and watch as they prepare the famed *rapska torta*, a traditional Croatian cake made of ground almonds, maraschino liqueur, lemon, and orange peel. **Known for:** traditional recipes; great small bites and sweets; charming location. $ *Average main: Kn65* ⊠ *Dinka Dokule 2* ☎ *051/771-122* ☉ *Closed Nov.–Apr.* ☰ *No credit cards.*

🛏 Hotels

Rab offers a variety of accommodation, from campgrounds on beaches to apartments and villa rentals, to chic boutique hotels, family resorts, and grand, adult-only hotels.

★ Arbiana Hotel

$$$ | **HOTEL** | It's hard to imagine a more romantic setting than this harborside inn that sits in a perfectly restored medieval villa with balconies and a gorgeous garden overlooking the Rab marina and the hills of Barbat in the distance. **Pros:** luxurious private setting; on-site parking; most rooms have beautiful seaviews. **Cons:** no pool or beach access; not all rooms have balconies; can be noisy during concerts. $ *Rooms from: 1510 Kn* ⊠ *Obala Kralja Petra Kresimira IV br.12* ☎ *051/725-563* ⊕ *www.arbianahotel.com* ☉ *Closed mid-Oct.–mid-Apr.* ⇋ *28 rooms* ⦿ *Free breakfast.*

San Marino Sunny Resort by Valamar

$$ | **HOTEL** | **FAMILY** | A complex of five hotels stretches across the peninsula at this family-friendly resort wrapping around the famous sandy Paradise Beach. **Pros:** access to Paradise Beach couldn't be better; good choice of on-site activities; free Wi-Fi. **Cons:** sprawling complex lacks personality; rooms are on the small side and lack luxuries; big and busy. $ *Rooms from: 1360 Kn* ⊠ *Lopar 608, Lopar* ☎ *051/667–700* ⊕ *www.valamar.com* ☉ *Closed Oct.–May* ⇋ *495 rooms* ⦿ *Free breakfast.*

Valamar Collection Imperial

$$ | **ALL-INCLUSIVE** | Amid the greenery of Komrčar Park, this peaceful 1930s-era heritage hotel is a stone's throw from the center of Rab Town. **Pros:** centrally located but removed from the crowds; tennis, indoor and outdoor pool, and spa facilities; heritage hotel. **Cons:** limited parking spaces in high season; double rooms a bit smallish; above a busy city park. $ *Rooms from: 1360 Kn* ⊠ *M. de Dominisa 9* ☎ *051/724–522* ⊕ *www.valamar.com* ⇋ *136 rooms* ⦿ *Free breakfast.*

Valamar Padova Hotel

$$$$ | **HOTEL** | **FAMILY** | As one of Valamar's "Maro" hotels, the Padova has thought of everything when it comes to family-friendly vacations, including a free on-site professional baby-sitting service that gives parents with young children a chance to get away for a few hours. **Pros:** 2 hours free professional babysitting either in-room or on-site day care center; well-organized animation program; walking distance to Rab town. **Cons:** soft beds; no a la carte restaurant for dinner; access to small public beach only. $ *Rooms from: €2200* ⊠ *Banjol 322* ☎ *051/724–544* ⊕ *www.valamar.com* ☉ *Closed Oct.–Apr.* ⇋ *175 rooms* ⦿ *All-inclusive.*

🍸 Nightlife

For such a small town, Rab has surprisingly active nightlife in the summer if you are not looking for techno discos. Trg Municipium Arbe on the waterfront is lined with bars and can get noisy as the night progresses. All-night house parties are found at Santos Beach Club on Puderica Beach, 2 km (1 mile) from Barbat toward the ferry terminal.

Forum

BARS/PUBS | A favorite among locals, Forum is short on luxury, but not on entertainment, beers, and great cocktails. ⊠ *Donja 9a.*

San Antonio

BARS/PUBS | Those after a little glitz to show off their suntan can head to the center of Rab Town for cocktails and music and some nightlife at San Antonio. ⊠ *Trg Municipium Arba 4* ☎ *051/724–145* ⊕ *www.sanantonio-club.com.*

Activities

DIVING

Aqua Sport

SCUBA DIVING | A single dive costs about 350 Kn including equipment; a full diving course costs 2,440 Kn. In addition, you can dive at various sites from their boat, and your nondiving companions are welcome to go along for the ride. ⊠ *Supetarska Draga 331, Supetarska Draga* ☎ *051/776–145* ⊕ *www.aquasport.hr.*

Chapter 7

ISTRIA

7

Updated by
Melissa Paul

⊙ Sights	🍴 Restaurants	🛏 Hotels	🛍 Shopping	🍸 Nightlife
★★★☆☆	★★★★★	★★★☆☆	★★★☆☆	★★☆☆☆

WELCOME TO ISTRIA

TOP REASONS TO GO

★ **Roman ruins:** Take a walk through the Roman area in Pula, where you will find one of the world's biggest and best-preserved amphitheaters (in fact, the sixth-largest in the world).

★ **Natural beauty:** Breathtaking beaches with crystal clear water, rolling vineyard-covered hills, and groves of ancient olive trees.

★ **Medieval hilltop towns:** A scenic drive through the medieval towns of Grožnjan, Oprtalj, and Motovun in the hilly interior is not to be missed; these are villages that time seems to have forgotten. Indulge in a wine- or olive-oil tasting at Kabola, Clai, or Chiavalon estates.

★ **Ancient churches:** Enjoy a tour of the amazing 6th-century Byzantine mosaics at St. Euphrasius Basilica in Poreč; St. Euphrasius is one of the best-preserved early Christian churches in Europe.

★ **Gourmet delights:** Indulge in delicious olive oil, wind-cured prosciutto, fresh seafood, earthy truffles, and boutique wines.

Sandwiched between Italy, Slovenia, and inland Croatia, the Istrian peninsula is located in the Northern Adriatic region, facing the Venetian lagoon to the west and Kvarner Bay to the southeast. Reaching Istria, Croatia's largest peninsula, is easy: many large European cities are less than a five-hour drive away. Pula is a seasonal airport, and airports in Venice, Trieste, Rijeka, and Zagreb are all within a three-hour drive.

1 Pula. A former Roman colony and now Istria's main city.

2 Vodnjan. A quiet town devoted to producing excellent olive oil.

3 Brijuni National Park. A group of small islands that is now a stunning national park.

4 Rovinj. The cultural heart and soul of Istria.

5 Poreč. A one-time Roman fort and current charming red-roofed city.

6 Novigrad. A pretty fisherman's village with a charming Old Town.

7 Umag. One of Istria's more low-key coastal towns.

8 Motovun. The highest medieval hilltop town in Istria.

9 Grožnjan. A quaint hilltop town filled with art and music.

10 Labin-Rabac. The charming hilltop town of Labin with its sister seaside resort of Rabac.

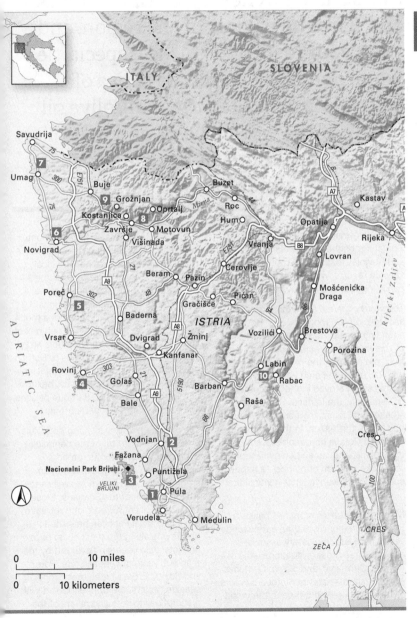

Discover a thousand years of rich Istrian history in the hilltop fortresses, early Christian churches, Byzantine mosaics, and Baroque palaces of the region, and treat your taste buds to local specialties: white and black truffles (a series of festivals is dedicated to them), olive oil (many of the world's best), and wine (crisp, fruity white Istarska Malvazija and light, harmonious red Teran).

Explore a remarkable 1,900-year-old Roman amphitheater in Pula. Visit Poreč and Rovinj, Croatia's two most popular seaside resorts, with Venetian-style campanili, loggias, and narrow stone streets.

The word conjures something magical as it rolls off the tongue: *Istria.* Beyond sounding poetic, however, the name of this region of Croatia is derived from the name of the Illyrian people who occupied the area well before the Romans first arrived in the 3rd century BC—namely, the Istrians, whose chief architectural legacy comprised numerous hilltop fortresses. In the northwest corner of Croatia bordering Slovenia, the triangular-shape Istrian peninsula looks rather like a bunch of grapes—a happy coincidence, given its strong viticultural heritage.

Much of Europe's history has passed through Istria for more than a thousand years, not least the history associated with three great civilizations—the Roman, Germanic, and Slavic. Centuries of Venetian rule, later reinforced by years of Italian occupation between the world wars, have left a sizable Italian minority here, and Italian influence is apparent in the architecture, cuisine, and local dialect. Here, even the effects of the concrete-box style of communist-era architecture seem relatively minimal compared to the overall sense of a much deeper past suggested by the rich mix of architectural styles—from a whole array of well-preserved Roman ruins to Romanesque basilicas; as well as breathtakingly well-preserved medieval towns, bell towers, fortifed town walls, Baroque palaces, and Austro-Hungarian battlements.

The region's principal city and port, Pula, is on the southern tip of the peninsula and is best known for its remarkably preserved 1,900-year-old Roman amphitheater and Forum as well as the Triumphal Arch of the Sergians. Close by, the beautifully nurtured island retreat of Brijuni National Park can be visited in a day. Towns along the west coast have an unmistakable Venetian flavor left by more than 500 years of Venetian rule. Poreč and Rovinj, Croatia's two most popular seaside resorts, are both endowed with graceful bell towers and reliefs of the winged Lion of St. Mark, patron saint of Venice. The effects of package tourism have long encroached—to varying degrees—on the outskirts of various Istrian towns, most notably Poreč and Vrsar. Rovinj, though likewise brimming with tourists in high season, retains more of its ravishing historic beauty and redolence than almost any other town in Croatia. A side trip to the romantic hilltop towns of Motovun, Oprtalj and Grožnjan will prove unforgettable, whether as a brief excursion from the sea in the warmer months or as a more substantial autumn journey. This inland area is particularly rich in truffles, mushrooms, grapes, and chestnuts and from mid-September to late October these local delicacies are celebrated with a series of gastronomic festivals.

Planning

When to Go

If you are partial to sun and the idea of swimming in the warm, clear aqua blue waters of the Adriatic, and you don't mind crowds and a bit of extra expense, by all means visit Istria in summer. Otherwise, this tourism-trampled region might be best saved for spring or fall (the water stays warm well into September), when you might save as much as 15% to 20% on lodging. The season in Istria for many restaurants and bars is Easter through the first week in November. While the region is always dramatically beautiful, you won't find much going on in the winter months.

Getting Here and Around

AIR

Croatia Airlines operates flights to Pula from Amsterdam, Frankfurt, Zadar, and Zagreb from April through October. Ryanair has service to Pula from London

Stansted, Berlin, Brussels, and Vienna. Jet2.com flies from Leeds, Manchester, Edinburgh, Birmingham, and London Stansted to Pula from May until late September. Many other airlines fly into Pula, including British Airways, Lufthansa, EasyJet, TUI, Edelweiss, Volotea, Transavia, Norwegian, Sedge, Air Serbia, Eurowings, Air Lingus, and Trade Air.

CONTACTS Croatia Airlines. ⊠ *Pula Airport, Valtursko polje 210, Ližnjan, Pula* ☏ *052/218–909* ⊕ *www.croatiaairlines. com.* **Jet2.com.** ⊕ *www.jet2.com.* **Ryanair.** ⊕ *www.ryanair.com.*

BOAT AND FERRY

From May to October, Venezia Lines runs a catamaran service from Venice to Rovinj, Pula, and Poreč. Tickets are available online.

CONTACTS Venezia Lines. ⊠ *Zagrebačka 7, Poreč* ☏ *052/422–896* ⊕ *www.venezial-ines.com.*

BUS

There are domestic connections all over mainland Croatia to and from Pula, Poreč, Labin, and Rovinj, and local services between these towns and smaller inland destinations such as Motovun and Vodnjan. International buses offer daily connections to Italy (Trieste) and Slovenia (Ljubljana, Koper, Piran, and Portorož). Bus stations in Pula, Rovinj, Labin, and Poreč, are run by one bus company, Autotrans. Additionally in summer, Flixbus, a Germany-based company offering low-cost bus travel throughout Europe, connects Istrian coastal towns with Germany (Munich), Italy (Venice, Padua, Brescia, Milano), and Austria (Villach, Vienna, Graz). Timetables are available at all bus stations. However, as elsewhere in Croatia, the sheer number of different companies offering bus service out of each station can be confusing; it's best to confirm at the information window what you might find posted on the wall.

BUS CONTACTS Autotrans. ☏ *060/888-612* ⊕ *https://www.arriva.com.hr/en-us/home.*

Great Itineraries

If You Have 3 Days

There is so much to see in Istria that three days is a must, though it may seem like a rush if that's all the time you have. Start in Pula, if you are coming from Zagreb; if from the north (Slovenia or Italy), start with Rovinj instead. Either way, do visit Rovinj. If you are interested in Istria's ecclesiastical heritage, you may want to prioritize Poreč over Pula; if Roman ruins are more your thing, by all means focus on Pula, whose architecture also gives you more of a sense of Istria's Austro-Hungarian past. On the first day, start off in **Pula**. Visit the Arena and at least take a stroll to the Forum. Plan to spend the night here. A short drive or bus ride toward the Verudela or Stoja resort area gets you to eminently swimmable, if rocky, stretches of shoreline. The next morning, head off to **Rovinj.** Visit the 18th-century Baroque Crkva Sv. Eufemije, and just revel in strolling about the most beautiful town on the Istrian coast. Plan to stay the night here. On the third day, spend some more time in or around Rovinj, whether strolling the Old Town or taking a dip in the sea. If you're up to it—particularly if you have a car—move on to **Poreč** to see the Eufrazijeva Basilica.

If You Have 5 Days

Spend your first day as above, but consider adding an excursion from Pula to **Vodnjan** or **Brijuni National Park,** depending on whether you're more interested in Vodnjan's olive oil producers, medieval atmosphere, mummies, and food, or in Brijuni's

natural splendors and luxurious, seaside ambience. Move on to **Rovinj** by the evening of Day 2 or the morning of Day 3, spending at least a full day or more there. On Day 4, it's on to **Poreč.** Perhaps go inland and spend the night in **Motovun.** On Day 5, if you're driving, take a look at **Grožnjan** as well before heading back. If you're getting around by bus, it's time to head back to a major town on the coast. Indeed, why not spend a few more hours in Rovinj or Pula before bidding *arrivederci* to Istria?

If You Have 7 Days

Spend your first four or five days as above, but be sure to supplement your time in Rovinj, Pula, and Poreč with a day in **Labin,** on the east coast of Istria. If you're driving from Zagreb, do it on the way to the other towns; if you're driving through the countryside that takes you through both **Motovun** and **Grožnjan,** spend a night in or near Motovun. Before going inland, you may want to pay a visit to Vrsar and the Limski kanal or, instead, Baredine Cave. If you have a car, you can do so as you go inland or on your way back to the coast; if traveling by bus, you can get to these places most easily on a group excursion from Poreč or Rovinj. You may want to visit **Novigrad,** too, especially if you're driving, but save Umag for a 10-day trip. Spend Day 6 in Grožnjan then go back to Poreč or, better yet, Rovinj for the night. On Day 7, proceed to **Pula,** with a stop in **Labin** if you haven't been there yet and will be going farther east. Perhaps spend your final night in Labin as well.

Flixbus. ⊕ *https://global.flixbus.com/bus/croatia.*

BUS STATIONS Poreč Bus Station. ✉ *Karla Huguesa 2, Poreč* ☎ *052/432-153.* **Pula Bus Station.** ✉ *Trg I. Istarske brigade 1, Pula* ☎ *052/356-532.* **Rovinj Bus Station.** ✉ *Trg na Lokvi 6, Rovinj* ☎ *060/888–611.*

CAR

While visiting Pula, Rovinj, and Poreč a car may be more of a hindrance than an asset: all three towns are served by good bus connections, and having your own vehicle only causes parking problems. The best way to see the Istrian interior and Eastern coast towns, however, is by car. The "sight" to see is the countryside itself and the small villages that dot it, so renting a car even for a day will give you much more satisfaction than trying to arrange a bus trip to one or another hilltop town. (And bus connections to the interior are infrequent or nonexistent.) If you are traveling from Zagreb, you can, of course, rent a car there, but major agencies have offices in Pula. Other towns along the coast all have one or more local agencies that generally offer better rates than the major chains without sacrificing quality of service; however, they may be less equipped than the major chains and have fewer cars on offer. (Some, such as Vetura, also rent bicycles, e-bicycles, and scooters [i.e., mopeds].) Lastly, bear in mind that finding an available car on short notice in midsummer can be tricky regardless of the agency involved and most are manual transmission.

CONTACTS Europcar. ✉ *Pula Airport, Valtursko polje 210, Pula* ☎ *098/475–346* ⊕ *www.europcar.com.* **Greenway Travel.** ✉ *Partizanska 5a, Poreč* ☎ *095/600–5500* ⊕ *www.greenway-travel.net.* **Hertz.** ✉ *Pula Airport, Valtursko polje 210, Pula* ☎ *052/550–968,* ⊕ *www.hertz.com.* **Inter-auto.** ✉ *Trgovačka 19, Umag* ☎ *052/743–111, 091/206-0483* ⊕ *www.inter-auto.hr.* **Sixt .** ✉ *Riva Mall, Ul. Rade Končara 1, Poreč* ☎ *095/438–2416* ⊕ *www.sixt.hr.* **Vetura.** ✉ *Trg Joakima Rakovca 2, Poreč* ☎ *052/434–700* ⊕ *www.vetura-rentacar.com.* **Vetura.** ✉ *Pula Airport, Valtursko polje 210, Pula* ☎ *091/49–49–627, 052/210–294* ⊕ *www.vetura-rentacar.com.* **Vetura.** ✉ *Šetalište Vjeća Europe bb, Rovinj* ☎ *052/815–209, 091/730–4408* ⊕ *www.vetura-rentacar.com.*

TRAIN

Istria is not well connected to the rest of Croatia—or neighboring Slovenia and Italy—by rail. To get to Zagreb or Split, you need to transit through Rijeka, partly by bus, but the train is an excellent way to move from Pula to Pazin if you don't have a car.

Restaurants

Food in Istria is more sophisticated and varied than in the rest of Croatia. Culinary tourism is one of the region's biggest draws, and you will get (for a price) a markedly better meal here than elsewhere in the country. The quaysides and old town squares have a plethora of touristy restaurants, and many new exceptional places have opened in recent years, helping to set the standard for the country's gastronomical identity. Istrian food today means fresh and simple seafood dishes, locally made *fuži* (egg noodles), elegant white or black truffle sauces and flavors, and earthy *pršut* (air-dried local ham), alongside the familiar Italian staples of pizza and pasta. Seafood is usually grilled, baked in sea salt, or served *crudo* (raw) with a dash of local extra virgin olive oil. Truffles are the superstars of the interior villages and work their way onto autumn menus in pastas, game dishes, grilled meats, frittatas, and on beds of homemade polenta. Keep your eyes peeled for traditional favorites like *supa*, a brew of red wine, sugar, olive oil, pepper, and warm, toasted bread; and *meneštra*, an Istrian bean soup, both popular in fall and winter. All these gourmet aspirations mean that dining in Istria can be costly relative to much of inland Croatia. Average prices for main courses start at 65 Kn for pasta and pizza, and move up to 85 Kn, or even twice that, for seafood (much of which is priced by the kilogram) and certain beef dishes. For a quick and cheap, albeit greasy, lunch, you can buy a *burek* (a cheese or meat-filled pastry) in a bakery for around 15 Kn.

Hotels

In Istria, as in most other reaches of the Croatian coast, it's basically a question of whether to stay at the big resorts on the beach, with a full range of services and activities available, or at smaller, boutique, sometimes family-run hotels and bed-and-breakfasts called *rezidenze*. Either way it's imperative to book ahead, as most places—big and small—book up fast for the summer months. Bear in mind that some smaller hotels and rezidenze may impose a surcharge—usually 20%—for stays of fewer than three nights in high season, since they cater primarily to tourists who stay a week or two. Hotels listed here are geared toward the traveler who is looking to stay fewer than seven nights in the same city.

VILLA RENTALS

Villa rentals are extremely popular in Istria, where many properties—from one-bedroom apartments to houses for 16—offer a high standard of accommodation. The medieval villages of the hilly interior are scenic and offer sweeping (and almost uninterrupted) views of vineyards and olive groves. Hunkering down in a stone farmhouse and exploring the rest of the peninsula from there is certainly a leisurely way to appreciate Istria. Istria is still not nearly as crowded as other parts of the Mediterranean, so you won't have to share your view with the hordes.

Kompas Travel

Kompas Travel offers a collection of luxury villa rentals and holiday homes

throughout Istria as well as daytime excursions across Istria, into other parts of Croatia; Slovenia; and Venice, Italy. Additional offices in Porec and Umag. ⊠ *Obala M. Tita 5, Rovinj* ☎ *052/813–211* ⊕ *kompas-travel.com.*

Restaurant and hotel reviews have been shortened. For full information, visit Fodors.com. Restaurant prices are the average cost of a main course at dinner or, if dinner is not served, at lunch. Hotel prices are the lowest cost of a standard double room in high season.

What It Costs in Croatian kuna (Kn)			
$	$$	$$$	$$$$
RESTAURANTS			
under 35 Kn	35 Kn–65Kn	61 Kn–80 Kn	over 80 Kn
HOTELS			
under 925 Kn	925 Kn–1,300 Kn	1,301 Kn–1,650 Kn	over 1,650 Kn

Tours

Self-guided cycling tours of Istria can be arranged by Fiore Tours, a Poreč-based cycling outfit. They also arrange gourmet tours, including wine-tasting tours of Istria.

Fiore Tours

BICYCLE TOURS | FAMILY | This Poreč-based agency specializing in outdoor tourism—cycling, kayaking and trekking— offers many fully guided and self-guided cycling and walking holidays in Istria, from half-day kayaking to week-long explorations. Their eight-day tour starts in historic Poreč and leads you through the Istrian countryside and on to the coast. Daily distances range from 47 km to 70 km (30 to 43 miles). Fiore tours arranges all accommodation, luggage transfers, and provides you with an itinerary. ⊠ *Mate Vlašića 6, Poreč* ☎ *052/431–397* ⊕ *www.fiore.hr* 🖃 *From 620 Kn.*

Travel Agencies

Kompas Travel can arrange daily excursions to Venice or Plitvice, as well as tours to inland Istria or Postojna Cave in Slovenia from either Poreč or Rovinj. Excursions Delfin arranges sunset cruises around Rovinj, dolphin watching boat rides, and tours to the Limski kanal, as do several other local companies and independent operators who happen to own boats and post flyers about their towns.

CONTACTS Excursions Delfin. ✉ *Obala Vladimira Nazora, Rovinj* ☎ *091/514–2169* ⊕ *www.excursion-delfin.com.* **Kompas Travel.** ✉ *Obala M. Tita 16, Poreč* ☎ *052/451–100* ⊕ *www.kompas-travel. com.*

Visitor Information

Although the official tourist offices listed here can provide you with every bit of information imaginable, they generally leave the booking of rooms, villas, and excursions to private tourist agencies and hotels.

CONTACTS Fažana Tourist Information. ✉ *Titova riva 2, Fažana* ☎ *052/383–727* ⊕ *www.infofazana.hr.* **Grožnjan Tourist Information.** ✉ *Umberta Gorjana 12, Grožnjan* ☎ *052/776–131, 052/776–064* ⊕ *www.tz-groznjan.hr.* **Istria Tourist Board.** ☎ *052/880–088* ⊕ *www.istra.hr.* **Labin & Rabac Tourist Information.** ✉ *A. Negri 20, Labin* ☎ *052/855–560 main office, 052/852–399 info point* ⊕ *www.rabac-labin.com.* **Novigrad Tourist Information.** ✉ *Mandrač 29a, Novigrad* ☎ *052/757–075* ⊕ *www.coloursofistria.com.* **Poreč Tourist Information.** ✉ *Zagrebačka 9, Poreč* ☎ *052/451–293* ⊕ *www.myporec.com.* **Rovinj Tourist Information.** ✉ *Trg na mostu 2, Rovinj* ☎ *052/811–566* ⊕ *https://www. rovinj-tourism.com/.* **Umag Tourist Information.** ✉ *Trgovačka 6, Umag* ☎ *052/741–363* ⊕ *www.coloursofistria.com.* **Vodnjan Tourist Information.** ✉ *Narodni trg 10, Vodnjan* ☎ *052/511–700* ⊕ *www.vodnjandignano.com.*

Pula

270 km (168 miles) southwest of Zagreb.

Today an industrial port town and Istria's chief administrative center (pop. 58,000), as well as a major tourist destination, Pula became a Roman colony in the 1st century BC. This came about a century after the decisive defeat by the Romans, in 177 BC, of the nearby Histrian stronghold of Nesactium, prompting the Histrian king Epulon to plunge a sword into his chest lest he fall into the hands of the victors, who indeed conquered all of Istria. Remains from Pula's ancient past have survived up to the present day: as you drive in on the coastal route toward its choice setting on a bay near the southern tip of the Istrian peninsula, the monumental Roman amphitheater blocks out the sky on your left. Under Venetian rule (1331–1797), Pula was architecturally neglected, even substantially dismantled. Many structures from the Roman era were pulled down, and stones and columns were carted off across the sea to Italy to be used for new buildings there. Pula's second great period of development took place in the late 19th century, under the Habsburgs, when it served as the chief base for the Imperial Austro-Hungarian Navy. Today it's as much working city as tourist town, where Roman ruins and Austro-Hungarian architecture serve as backdrop for the bustle of everyday life amid a bit of communist-era soot and socialist realism, too. James Joyce lived here for a short time, in 1904–05, before fleeing what he dismissed as a cultural backwater for Trieste. What's more, there are some outstanding restaurants and a number of pleasant family-run hotels, not to mention the nearby resort area of Verudela,

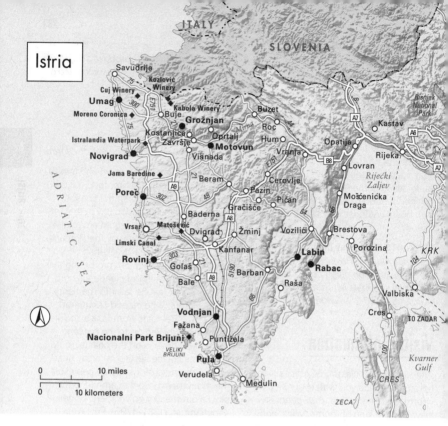

Istria

where seaside tourism thrives in all its soothing, sunny sameness.

GETTING HERE AND AROUND

Pula is Istria's main entry point as it's home to the only regional airport for commercial flights located 9 km (5½ miles) from the town center. There is a shuttle bus from the airport to Pula's main bus station (located downtown), but also to the resort areas of Verudela, Medulin, and Puntižela. The best way to get around Pula is on foot. However, buses run every 20 minutes to half an hour depending on the line.

VISITOR INFORMATION

CONTACTS Pula Tourist Information. ✉ Forum 3 P052/219–197 www.pulainfo.hr.

⊙ Sights

Pula's compact commercial and administrative center is on a small, semicircular protrusion of land in the Puljski Zaljev (Bay of Pula), which faces west into the Adriatic. Several ringlike streets radiate inward from the port, culminating in the small, fortress-capped hill at the center of this semicircle. Most of the cultural and historical sights are along this web of streets to the south, west, and north of the hill, with the huge Roman amphitheater on the northeastern fringes of this zone (accessible via Giardini and then Istarska ulica, on the landward side of the hill, a couple of blocks in from the bay); the bus station is another few minutes' walk from there. Meanwhile, a long walk (or a short drive) south of the city center are suburbs that culminate with the Verudela and Stoja peninsulas, home to

Pula is home to Croatia's largest collection of Roman ruins.

bustling tourist resorts, beaches, some excellent restaurants, and a modern shopping mall.

Aquarium Pula

ZOO | **FAMILY** | Located on the ground floor of the onetime Austro-Hungarian fortress in the resort complex of Verudela, a few kilometers from the city center, the aquarium also serves as a sea turtle rescue center. Its 35 pools offer a colorful look at hundreds of sea creatures from the Adriatic's underwater world, and include a touch pool with sea stars, sea urchin, crab, and sea squirt. ■**TIP**→ **Climb to the roof of the fort for great vistas over Pula.** ⊠ Verudela bb ☎ 052/381–402 ⊕ www.aquarium.hr ☞ 120 Kn.

★ Arena (Roman Amphitheater)

ARCHAEOLOGICAL SITE | Designed to accommodate 23,000 spectators, Pula's arena is the sixth-largest building of its type in the world (after the Colosseum in Rome and similar arenas in Verona, Catania, Capua, and Arles). Construction was completed in the 1st century AD under the reign of Emperor Vespasian,

and the Romans staged gladiator games here until such bloodthirsty sports were forbidden during the 5th century. It has remained more or less intact, except for the original tiers of stone seats and numerous columns that were hauled away for other buildings. Today it is used for summer concerts (by musicians including Sting, James Brown, and Jose Carreras), opera performances, and the annual film festival in mid-July. The underground halls house a museum with large wooden oil presses and amphorae. ⊠ Flavijevska ulica bb ☎ 052/219–028 ⊕ www.ami-pula.hr ☞ 70 Kn.

Crkvica Marije od Trstika (Chapel of St. Mary of Formosa)

RELIGIOUS SITE | Once part of a magnificent basilica built in the 6th century by Bishop Maximilian of Istria, the humble stone Chapel of St. Mary of Formosa can be found between Sigirijeva ulica and the port. Over the centuries, the chapel fell into ruin, especially during the 1242 fire at the time of the Venetian conquest of Pula. A large portion of its interior was

A Wreck of a Vacation

On August 13, 1914, the *Baron Gautsch*, a passenger ferry owned by Austria's royal family, was on its way from Kotor to Trieste when it collided with an undersea mine and sank 12½ km (8 miles) from Rovinj, claiming more than 240 lives.

Following the longstanding tradition of diving to shipwrecks, of which Istria's coastal waters hold several good examples, more than 100 years later the *Baron Gautsch* is considered one of the most beautiful dive sites in the world. With its upper deck at a depth of 28 meters, its lower deck at 36 meters, and its bottom at 40 meters, the site—now home to plenty of flora and fauna, including a whole lot of lobsters—caters to advanced divers while stirring the imaginations of many others.

From shipwrecks to caves and cliffs to coral reefs, Croatia has more than 100 officially registered dive sites. There are around twenty other shipwrecks off the Istrian coast that make for popular dives. Near Novigrad lies the *Coriolanus*, a suspected British spy ship that sank in 1945 after hitting a mine. And then there are the warships *Dezza*, *Rossarol*, and *Flamingo*, as well as the ships *Draga*, *Varese*, *Argo*, *Josephine*, and *John Gilmore*. Of course, Croatia's waters abound in shipwrecks well beyond Istria. For example, the waters off Krk Island are the resting place of the *Peltastis*, sunk in 1968 after smashing into rocks during a storm. At a depth of 16 to 32 meters, the ship is accessible to divers of all abilities.

For organized diving, you have to be a member of a diving center or a diving association that is registered in Croatia for underwater activities. For individual diving you have to get an approval for individual diving issued by the local Port Authority—local means that it has to be the one where you plan to dive, under its jurisdiction. Price for the approval or license is 2,400 Kn and is valid for one year from the issue date. Also, better be safe than sorry when it comes to licenses, and go straight to your local Port authority to get the license and info on zones where diving is not allowed.

Although diving in Istria is possible year-round, optimal sea temperatures are to be enjoyed from May to November. Locations must be marked by orange or red buoys or flags (and, at night, fitted with a yellow or white light visible from 300 meters); the maximum allowable diving depth, when using a compressed-air cylinder, is 40 meters. Diving is prohibited in protected areas, including Brijuni National Park and Krka National Park.

Dive centers can be found in all the major destinations in Istria, including Poreč and Rovinj.

The Forum has been Pula's central square for over 2,000 years.

shipped to Venice, where it was used in building the St. Mark's Library and the Sale delle Quattro Porte of the Doge's Palace. Usually closed to visitors, it's occasionally used as a gallery space, which will give you a chance to take a peek at the interior. ✉ *Between Sigirijeva ul and Flaciusova ul (left off Sigirijeva ul two blocks before the Forum).*

Floor Mosaic
ARCHAEOLOGICAL SITE | The central scene of this large and lovely 3rd-century mosaic—which otherwise features geometric patterns, animals, and plants aplenty—is of the punishment of Dirce, who, according to Greek legend, lies under the enraged bull to whose horns she is about to be fastened. Once part of a Roman house, the mosaic was unearthed after World War II bombings. ■**TIP→ The mosaic can be viewed for free by looking down through a grate beside an uninspiring apartment building a stone's throw from the Crkva Sv. Marije od Trstika (Chapel of St. Mary of Formosa).** ✉ *Between Sergijevaca ulica and Flaciusova ulica, left off Sergijevaca ulica, two blocks before the Forum.*

★ Forum
PLAZA | The Forum, the original central square, administrative hub, and marketplace of ancient and medieval Pula, is still the city's most important public meeting place after 2,000 years. Today, the forum is a spacious square ringed with bustling cafés, shops, and restaurants. There were once three temples here, only one of which remains: the Temple of Augustus. Perfectly preserved, the **Augustov Hram** was built between 2 BC and AD 14. Next to it stands the **Gradska Palača** (Town Hall), which was erected during the 13th century using part of another Roman temple as the back wall. The arcades on three sides of the forum square were added later during the Renaissance. ✉ *Pula* ✛ *10 meters (about 30 feet) past Kapitolinski trg from Kandlerova promenade* ⊕ *http://www. ami-pula.hr/* ✉ *Augustov Hram 10 Kn* ⊗ *Augustov Hram Closed Oct.–Apr.*

Kaštel (*Fortress*)

MILITARY SITE | FAMILY | Whether from the cathedral or elsewhere along Kandlerova ulica, a walk up the hill will lead you within minutes to the 17th-century Venetian fortress, the Kaštel, that towers over Pula's city center and houses the **Historical and Maritime Museum of Istria.** Built on the site of a pre-Roman fort, the preserved star-shaped fortress dates back to 1630 and has four bastions. Despite its 100,000 items of cultural, historical, political, military, and ethnographic character displayed across eighteen collections, the museum is somewhat lackluster. However, it does carry the value-added benefit of allowing you to wander around its ramparts. **■ TIP→ Simply walking around its perimeter ensures fine views of the city's extensive shipyard below and, if you look to the north, the steeple of Vodnjan's church 12 km (7½ miles) away.** ✉ *Gradinski uspon 6* ☎ *052/211–566* 🌐 *www.ppmi.hr* 🎟 *20 Kn.*

Katedrala Uznesenja Blazene Djevice Marije (*Cathedral of the Assumption of the Blessed Virgin Mary*)

RELIGIOUS SITE | FAMILY | Built originally in the 4th century, the Cathedral of the Assumption of the Blessed Virgin Mary, Pula's star ecclesiastical attraction—more often called simply St. Mary's Cathedral—was transformed in the second half of the 5th century into a three-nave basilica. Extensive reconstruction began in the 16th century, with the adjacent bell tower (campanile) constructed in the late 17th century from stones taken from the Arena. Note that the Roman-era mosaic on the floor of the central nave bears a 5th-century donor's inscription. ✉ *Kandlerova ulica 27* 🌐 *www.zupa-uznesenja-marijina-pula.hr/* 🕒 *Closed for tours Oct.–Apr. (open by appointment only).*

Narodni Trg (Market Square)

MARKET | For a lively and aromatic atmosphere in which to have a shot of espresso, buy a banana, or just wander about gazing at food stands, check out Pula's market square, Narodni trg. The Tržnica, or city market, sits in the center of the square. On one side of the stately, two-story market building—whose iron-and-glass construction was state-of-the-art when it opened to great fanfare in 1903—you'll find outdoor fruit and vegetable stands on stone tables under red umbrellas and, on the other side, cafés and small boutiques. Inside the Tržnica itself you will find the fish market (downstairs), meat and poultry butchers, bakeries, cheesemongers, fresh pasta, and several fast-food eateries (second floor). ✉ *Narodni trg 9* 🌐 *www.trznica-pula.hr.*

Slavoluk Sergijevaca (*Triumphal Arch of the Sergians*)

ARCHAEOLOGICAL SITE | Built by the Sergi family between 29 and 27 BC as a monument to three relatives who were great warriors, this striking monument features elaborate reliefs that inspired even Michelangelo to draw the arch during a 16th-century visit to Pula. The surrounding city gate and walls were removed in the 19th century to allow the city's expansion beyond the Old Town. Locals call it *Zlatna vrata*, or Golden Gate. ✉ *Between Giardini and Sergijevaca ulica.*

🍴 Restaurants

★ Alla Becaccia

$$$$ | EUROPEAN | FAMILY | Located in the village of Valbandon, close to Fažana, Alla Becaccia offers hearty meat dishes with an emphasis on game—the owner is a hunter. A huge fireplace dominates the dining room in the simple but tasteful interior, and the kitchen door is always open. **Known for:** meat and fish grilled on wood; wild game and steaks; quiet garden setting. [$] *Average main: 150 Kn* ✉ *Pineta 25, Fažana* ☎ *052/520–753* 🌐 *www.beccaccia.hr* 🕒 *Closed Tues. and Nov.*

Farabuto

$$$$ | **MEDITERRANEAN** | **FAMILY** | In residential Pula, far from tourist attractions, Farabuto has a short menu of fresh and tasty seafood and just few meat and vegetarian dishes, all based on what's available from Pula's green and fish market. The modern and innovative cuisine is well presented in Farabuto's small, cozy interior or on the terrace. **Known for:** local crowd; casual neighborhood vibe; fresh seafood. $ *Average main: 130 Kn* ✉ *Sisplac ulica 15* ☎ *052/386–074* ⊕ *www. farabuto.hr* ⏱ *Closed Sun.*

Jupiter

$$ | **PIZZA** | **FAMILY** | Located on a quiet street a couple of blocks' walk above the Forum, this is Pula's premier place for casual, budget-friendly Italian fare. Try any of its more than 20 types of wood-fired pizza, grilled meats like *Ćevapi* (small minced-meat sausages), or a plate of homestyle pasta as you sip a glass of house red wine at one of the rustic wooden tables on the rear terrace. **Known for:** pizzas from a wood-burning oven; good value for money; summer crowds. $ *Average main: 65 Kn* ✉ *Castropola 42* ☎ *052/214–333* ⊕ *www.pizzeriajupiter. com.*

★ Konoba Batelina

$$$$ | **SEAFOOD** | This quirky, innovative restaurant is considered by many locals—and foodies around the world—to be the best seafood restaurant in Croatia. Run by a family of fishermen, Batelina is popular for its fresh-caught but totally delicious appetizers, often created from what Anthony Bourdain, on his visit here, described as "trash fish." Specialties include fish tripe brodetto or scampi risotto, shark-liver pâté, bonito tartare, cuttlefish stew, and tuna carpaccio. **Known for:** owner David Skoko, one of the best chefs in Croatia; accepting cash only; being booked days in advance. $ *Average main: 150 Kn* ✉ *Čimulje 25* ☎ *052/573–767* ▭ *No credit cards*

⏱ *Closed Dec.–mid-Jan., and Sun. No lunch.*

Trattoria Vodnjanka

$$ | **VENETIAN** | **FAMILY** | One of the few restaurants in downtown Pula offering honest and authentic Croatian dishes, no-frills Vodnjanka is a short walk from the farmers' market. You'll find many chefs and restaurateurs in Istria make their way here for lunch before heading to their own restaurants. **Known for:** a reasonably priced home-cooked meal; cash only; small and cozy. $ *Average main: 65 Kn* ✉ *Vitezićeva ulica 4* ☎ *098/175–7343* ▭ *No credit cards* ⏱ *Closed Sun.*

Coffee and Quick Bites

Café Galerija Cvajner

$ | **CAFÉ** | Stop at the chic but unpretentious Café Galerija Cvajner for morning coffee or an evening aperitif. Inside, contemporary art and minimalist furniture play off frescoes uncovered during restoration, and outdoor tables offer great views onto the Forum square. **Known for:** outstanding location in ancient Roman square; art gallery interiors; indoor/outdoor seating. $ *Average main: 20 Kn* ✉ *Forum 2* ☎ *052/216–502.*

🛏 Hotels

Boutique Hotel Valsabbion

$$$$ | **HOTEL** | This stylish, waterfront boutique hotel is in Pjescana uvala, the posh seaside suburb just 3 km (2 miles) from Pula's city center. **Pros:** private beach; beautiful pool; stunning views of the bay. **Cons:** must drive to the City Center; no elevator to higher floors; breakfast is additional fee. $ *Rooms from: 2500 Kn* ✉ *Pješčana uvala IX/26* ☎ *052/218–003* ⊕ *www.valsabbion.hr* ⏱ *Closed Jan.– Mar.* ⌨ *Reservations essential* ↪ *10 rooms* ℺ *No meals.*

D&A Center Apartments

$ | **RENTAL** | **FAMILY** | These seven bright, modern, and clean apartments and studios are equipped with Wi-Fi, flat-screen TVs, air-conditioning, and kitchenettes. **Pros:** centrally located; modern and well-maintained; continental breakfast included. **Cons:** no parking; no views; no common areas. [$] *Rooms from: €750* ✉ *Giardini 3* ☎ *098/976–9586* 🌐 *dacenterapartments.com* 🛏 *7 units* 🍴 *Free breakfast.*

Hotel Amfiteatar

$ | **HOTEL** | **FAMILY** | This hotel in a converted three-story townhouse just two minutes from the Roman Arena and one block from the seafront has rooms with smart minimalist furniture, free Wi–Fi, and spacious, modern bathrooms. **Pros:** central location next to historic Roman ampitheater; good restaurant with open-air terrace; private parking. **Cons:** "sea views" really mean "port view"; only one room has a balcony; top-floor rooms have only skylights (i.e., no windows). [$] *Rooms from: €750* ✉ *Amfiteatarska 6* ☎ *052/375–600* 🌐 *www.hotelamfiteatar.com* 🛏 *18 rooms* 🍴 *Free breakfast.*

Hotel Scaletta

$ | **HOTEL** | **FAMILY** | Ideally situated close to the Roman Arena, this small, family-run boutique hotel occupies a tastefully refurbished old town house decorated in cheerful yellows and greens with simple modern furniture. **Pros:** friendly atmosphere; good central location; plenty of public parking nearby. **Cons:** popular but small, so books up quickly; no private parking; loud during concerts at the Arena. [$] *Rooms from: 750 Kn* ✉ *Flavijevska 26* ☎ *052/541–599, 052/541–025* 🌐 *www.hotel-scaletta.com* 🛏 *12 rooms* 🍴 *Free breakfast.*

★ Radisson Park Plaza Histria Pula

$$$ | **HOTEL** | **FAMILY** | With its superb location at the tip of the Verudela peninsula overlooking both the marina and the sea, this large Radisson hotel has stylish, modern rooms that are comfortable and well appointed with comfy beds, flat-screen TVs, Wi-Fi, and balconies. **Pros:** quiet seaside location; panoramic views from some rooms; good in-room and on-site facilities. **Cons:** can feel overcrowded and impersonal; a bit of a hike from town; disappointing sea views from some rooms. [$] *Rooms from: 1900 Kn* ✉ *Verudela 17* ☎ *052/590–000* 🌐 *www.radissonhotels.com* 🕒 *Closed Jan.–Mar.* 🛏 *368 rooms* 🍴 *Free breakfast.*

Ribarska Koliba Resort & Restaurant

$$$ | **HOTEL** | **FAMILY** | Formerly a fisherman's cottage, this 100-year-old waterfront hotel in Verudela offers stylish hotel rooms, a posh penthouse apartment, and an outdoor pool. **Pros:** excellent seafood restaurant on-site; rooftop lounge bar with great views; location is right on the marina. **Cons:** not walking distance to the city center; marina noise in the morning; small pool. [$] *Rooms from: 950 Kn* ✉ *Verudela 16* ☎ *091/600–1269* 🌐 *ribarskakoliba.com* 🛏 *18 rooms* 🍴 *Free breakfast.*

🍸 Nightlife

Club life in Pula tends to begin in early April and continue through late October or early November. Pubs and bars are open year round.

Beach Bar La Playa

CAFES—NIGHTLIFE | Just down the beach from Hotel Splendid, and a short walk through the forest, you'll find this casual waterfront bar and lounge. Tasty cocktails and cool live music can be found here on most summer nights. Three terraces and vibrant lighting mark this waterfront hot spot as the place to be after a long, lazy day on the beach. ✉ *Valsaline 29* ☎ *099/315–7020* 🌐 *www.facebook.com/beachbarlaplayapula.*

Club Uljanik

BARS/PUBS | Conveniently located in the city center, with posters announcing its various musical events posted all over town, Club Uljanik is an exceedingly popular counterculture haven with DJ nights all year and live music on its spacious terrace. ✉ *Dobrilina 2* ☎ *095/ 901–8811* 🌐 *www.clubuljanik.hr.*

E&D Lounge Bar

CAFES—NIGHTLIFE | Set in a landscaped garden with a small swimming pool surrounded by stylish lounge chairs, E&D "Day and Night" Lounge Bar is the perfect place to laze during the day with a leisurely coffee or beer as you enjoy the views over the sea and beaches below. At night in summer, the lounge comes alive with DJ dance parties. During the height of the summer season, the bar also serves light Mediterranean dishes, ice cream and other desserts. ⊠ *Verudela 22* ☎ *052/213–404.*

Pietas Julia

CAFES—NIGHTLIFE | This large, seafront lounge bar and dance club also features a coffee bar and pizzeria. This is the place to dance a night away in Pula, with DJs playing electronic, house, techno, and R&B music. A great selection of cocktails makes this sexy spot popular among Pula's hip crowd. ⊠ *Riva 20* ☎ *091/181–1855,* /⊕ *www.pietasjulia.com.*

Performing Arts

Being the most prominent place in town, the Arena hosts a fair share of the city's core art and music events.

Pula Film Festival

FESTIVALS | **FAMILY** | Dating back to 1954, this annual film festival is actually the oldest Croatian film festival and occurs around mid-July, before the more well-known Motovun International Film Festival. Screenings take place in the Pula Arena and feature both Croatian and international works. ⊠ *Kastel 2* ☎ *052/393-321* ⊕ *www.pulafilmfestival. hr.*

Visualia Festival

ARTS FESTIVALS | As the first festival of light in Croatia, Visualia has installed a variety of light, technology, performance, and multimedia installations all over the city for almost a decade now, usually geared to a single theme. In one of the most popular displays, "Lighting Giants," the illuminated cranes of Uljanik Shipyard struck a nerve and has become a consistent symbol of local pride. The Pulska Xica, a fun night run that starts at the Arena and past the Lighting Giants, takes place during Visualia. ⊠ *Gajeva 3* ☎ *099/233-8823* ⊕ *visualia-festival.com.*

Shopping

Pula continues to grow as a shopping destination, with several modern multilevel malls, stores with quality goods from Istria, as well as Croatian delicacies, wines, crafts, and more. On Monday and Tuesday evenings in July and August (from 8 to 11) the Forum hosts an open-air fair of Istrian handicrafts. A walk through the Triumphal Arch of the Sergians onto bustling Sergijevaca ulica will show you much of what the city has available, shopping-wise; the boutiques listed here are just a few of what's on offer. Most shops are closed on Sunday.

★ Hižica

GIFTS/SOUVENIRS | A curated collection of designer home accessories from architect and interior designers Ana Visković and Bernard and Sara Domniku is sold in the petite-but-stylish boutique. It sits right below their design studio and offices, all of which offer locally made, hand-crafted decorative pieces that double as wonderful take-home souvenirs. ⊠ *Veronska ul. 6* ☎ *052/204–320* ⊕ *hizica. business.site.*

Komo

CLOTHING | Komo is a designer concept store, where you can find everything you would put inside or on your own *komoda* (the Istrian word for "dresser" and an essential piece of furniture in every Istrian house), all created by Croatian designers. You'll find clothing, jewelry, beauty products, and other lifestyle collectibles. ⊠ *Istarska 22* ☎ *052/353–986* ⊕ *www. komodesignstore.com.*

Pula Green Market (Tržnica)

LOCAL SPECIALTIES | Join locals at the Tržnica as they stock up on their daily fresh produce, locally sourced meats, fresh-caught fish, and domestic cheeses. Although open most of the day, it's best to experience the market like the locals do, early in the morning. A couple of highlights include the **Jelenic charcuterie,** which offers homemade, traditional Istrian cured meat like cooked ham, prosciutto, and homemade sausages, as well as **Kumparicka Dairy, which** produces unpasteurized, fresh, and aged (up to 30 months) goat cheeses. ⊠ *Narodni trg 9* ☎ *052/218–122* ⊕ *trznica-pula.hr.*

Trapan Wine Station

WINE/SPIRITS | **FAMILY** | Don't miss a trip to Trapan Wine Station, in Šišan, less than 10 km (6 miles) from Pula. A visit to the trendy winery includes wine tasting and a tour, albeit by appointment only. Popular labels include Uroboros and Ponente, both white wines made of 100% Istrian Malvazija, and Che, a sparkling wine made of 100% Terrano. ⊠ *Giordano Dobran 63, Šišan* ☎ *091/581–7281* ⊕ *www.trapan.hr.*

 ## Activities

Unlike some smaller towns farther up the coast, such as Rovinj, downtown Pula can be a little more challenging to get that dip in the sea in between visits to cultural attractions. But the good news is that the **beaches** aren't far away. A short drive or bus ride to the Verudela or Stoja resort areas, each around 4 km (2½ miles) south of downtown, will provide the clear water (and rocky shores) Croatia has in no short supply. You might also try the long stretch of relatively isolated beach between the two, on the Lungomare. If you have a car or a bicycle, this lovely little stretch of undeveloped coast is close to town and popular with locals as well as tourists. Head south about 2 km (1½ miles) along the main road out of Pula and follow the signs to the right toward Stoja, a resort-cum-camping area. Once there, proceed left and then back north along the pine-fringed coastal road Lungomare as it makes its way to the Verudela resort area.

If you have a car at your disposal, drive 10 km (6¼ miles) southwest of central Pula to the Premantura peninsula. The relatively remote shoreline there, at the very southern tip of Istria, is even more scenic, punctuated by cliffs, caves, and coves, and the crowds are mercifully thinner.

Vodnjan

12 km (7½ miles) north of Pula.

Vodnjan may look a bit run-down at first glance, but there are five really good reasons to come here: its saintly mummies; its collection of award-winning olive oil producers; its quiet, narrow, centuries-old streets populated by Italian speakers; the more than 40 murals painted throughout the town; and the museum park devoted to the traditional stone hut. *Kažun.*

GETTING HERE AND AROUND

There are 10 buses daily between Pula and Vodnjan, at 15 Kn each way, payable directly to the driver.

 ## Sights

Chiavalon Olive Oil Tasting Room

STORE/MALL | Sandi Chiavalon was barely 13 years old when he planted his first olive trees and decided to become an olive-oil producer. Less than two decades later, Chiavalon's extra virgin olive oil was chosen among the 15 best olive oils in the world by the prestigious Flos Olei. A visit to the Chiavalon tasting room is well worth a detour; just call in advance to arrange the tasting and farm tour, some of which are accompanied by delicious Istrian fare like cheese, prosciutto, and sausages. Make sure to take or ship home their oils, as well as

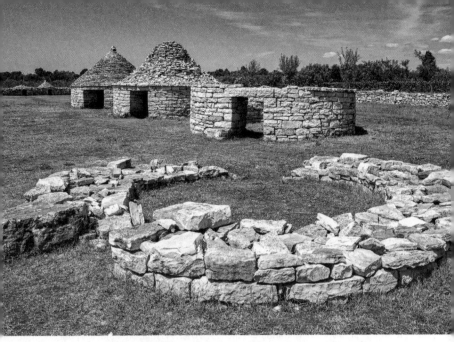

Kažun Park tells the story of the traditional structure known as a *kažun*.

their homemade tomato sauce and jams. ✉ *Vladimira Nazora 16* ☎ *052/511–906, 098/860–566* ⊕ *www.chiavalon.hr* ⊗ *Closed Sun.* ⌔ *Reservations essential.*

Crkva svetog Blaža (*St. Blaise's Church*)
RELIGIOUS SITE | FAMILY | From the tourist office on the main square, stroll down ulica Castello to Crkva svetog Blaža, an 18th-century structure built in the style of architect Palladio that not only has the highest campanile in all of Istria but is also the unlikely home of the mummies or mummified body parts of six saints impressively preserved without embalming. Among the best preserved are St. Nicolosa Bursa and Leon Bembo the Blessed. Nicolosa, whose relatively elastic skin and overall postmortem presentability make her one of the best-preserved human bodies in Europe, was born in Koper (Istria) in the 15th century and was a nun in Venice and elsewhere; she's the one with the garland of flowers still on her head. Leon Bembo the Blessed was a 12th-century Venetian priest who was tortured in religious riots while ambassador to Syria. And then there is St. Sebastian, a Roman officer-turned-Christian who was whipped and strangled around AD 288 in Rome after initially surviving torture by arrows. The head, spinal column, neck muscles, and related parts of this very famous saint are on display here. As for St. Barbara, from 3rd-century Nicomeda (in present-day Turkey), only her leg remains; she so disagreed with her father's pagan, slave-keeping lifestyle that he personally killed her with a sword. Admittance to the **mummy room**, behind the main altar, includes an English-language recording that sums up the saints' lives and roads to mummihood. Call to make an appointment to see the collection. ✉ *Župni ured Sv. Blaža, Sv. Roka 4* ☎ *052/511–420* ⊕ *www.zupavodnjan.com* 🎫 *€10* ⊗ *By appointment only. Closed Oct.–June.*

Kažun Park
MUSEUM VILLAGE | A *kažun* is a traditional, dry stone, round structure or hut built in ancient times, traditionally used as a shelter for farmers and shepherds in

remote fields. There are still more than 3,000 of these huts in the vicinity of Vodnjan. Kažun Park, an outdoor museum, demonstrates the four stages of the kažun construction, from its foundations, walls, and roofs to its final appearance. To many citizens of Vodnjan, the kažun is a part of their identity and serves as the pride of the people and the theme of their inexhaustible inspirations. ⊠ *Vodnjan* ☎ *052/511-522* ⊕ *www.vodnjan.hr/hr/ sto-posjetiti-u-vodnjanu-/park-kazuna.*

Murals

PUBLIC ART | Once a year, artists from around the world come to the ancient town of Vodnjan for the Boombarstick and Street Art Festival. They leave behind old stone walls and historic buildings completely covered with intriguing murals and creative graffiti designs. Art loving travelers will enjoy wandering the tiny streets of Vodnjan on the hunt for its more than 40 painted murals. ⊠ *Vodnjan* ⊹ *Murals can be found throughout the Old Town* ☎ *052/511–700.*

🍴 Restaurants

Vodnjanka

$$$$ | **VENETIAN** | **FAMILY** | This restaurant is the place to go for the most mouthwatering homemade pasta dishes you can imagine, not least *fuži* with wild asparagus and prosciutto, which is simply unforgettable. The inner of two small rooms, with its six tables and framed family-style photographs, is positively homey, while the outer room features bizarre but fantastic wall art by sculptor/painter Lilia Batel. **Known for:** Istrian cuisine; quirky decorations; roof terrace. $ *Average main: 140 Kn* ⊠ *Istarska 22* ☎ *052/511–435* ⊗ *Closed Jan. and Sun.*

🛏 Hotels

★ La Casa di Matiki

$ | **B&B/INN** | **FAMILY** | Located in the countryside near the village of Žminj, La Casa di Matiki may not be a fully working

farm, but you'll find donkeys, chickens, and three dogs here, and you can even opt to sleep on hay in the converted barn or in the more traditional apartments and a cottage. **Pros:** peaceful location far from the crowds; excellent breakfast with homemade and homegrown products (extra charge); swimming pool. **Cons:** remote location means a car is essential; no credit cards accepted; wake up call by rooster. $ *Rooms from: 750 Kn* ⊠ *Matiki 14, Žminj* ☎ *098/299–040* ⊕ *www.matiki. com* ▭ *No credit cards* ⤶ *8 rooms* ⦿ *No meals.*

Brijuni National Park

Ferry from Fažana, which is 15 km (9 miles) northwest of Pula.

When Austrian industrialist Paul Kupelwieser set off for Brijuni by boat from Fažana in 1885, the archipelago had long been a haven for the Austro-Hungarian military and for malaria. Kupelwieser was to change all that. In 1893 he bought the 14 islands and islets, eradicated the disease with the help of doctors, and fashioned parks from Mediterranean scrub. Thus arose a vacation retreat par excellence—not for rich Romans, as had been the case here 17 centuries earlier, but for fin-de-siècle Viennese and other European high-society sorts. Archduke Franz Ferdinand summered here, as did such literary lights as Thomas Mann and Arthur Schnitzler; James Joyce came here to celebrate his 23rd birthday. Two world wars ensued, however, and the islands' fate grew cloudy as they changed hands—coming under Italian rule and, later, Yugoslavian. From 1949 to 1979 the largest island, Veli Brijun, was the official summer residence of Marshal Josip Broz Tito, Yugoslavia's "president for life." Here he retreated to work, rest, and pursue his hobbies. World leaders, film and opera stars, artists, and writers were his frequent guests; and it was here that, together with Nasser of

In Brijuni National Park, you'll find many relics from the Roman and Byzantine eras.

Egypt and Nehru of India, Tito forged the Brioni Declaration, uniting the so-called nonaligned nations (countries adhering to neither NATO nor the Warsaw Pact). The archipelago was designated a national park in 1983 and opened to the public.

Sights

★ **Brijuni National Park** (*Nacionalni Park Brijuni*)

NATIONAL/STATE PARK | The Brijuni islands are a group of 14 small islands that were developed in the late 19th century. You'll need to pass through Fažana to get the boat, and pausing in the seaside town at one of its collection of touristy restaurants and charming cafés along its small harbor can be restorative. Fažana's main cultural attractions—all just a short walk from the harbor—are the 16th-century **Church of Saints Kosmas and Damian** and the smaller 14th-century **Church of Our Lady of Mount Carmel,** which you enter through an atmospheric loggia and whose ceiling features several layers of fascinating 15th-century Renaissance frescoes. But you are presumably here to visit the archipelago. Call or email the Brijuni National Park office in Fažana at least one day in advance to make a reservation; you can also do so in person, but especially in midsummer there is a substantial risk that there won't be space on the ferry. (Though various private tourist agencies in Fažana and Pula offer excursions, they do not generally measure up, in cost or quality, to making your arrangements directly with the national park. Some of the tourist agencies simply reserve you a spot on the "official" tour, adding their own commission when doing so.) After the 15-minute National Park ferry from Fažana; the entire tour of the park takes about four hours. Your first view is of a low-lying island with a dense canopy of evergreens over blue waters. Ashore on Veli Brijun, the largest island, a **tourist train** takes you past villas in the seaside forest and relics from the Roman and Byzantine eras. The network of roads on this 6½-km-long (4-mile-long) island was laid down by the Romans, and stretches of original Roman stonework remain. Rows of cypresses shade herds of deer, and peacocks strut along pathways. The train stops at the **Safari Park,** a piece of Africa transplanted to the Adriatic, its zebras, Indian holy cattle, llamas, and elephants all gifts from visitors from faraway lands. In the **museum,** an archaeological exhibition traces life on Brijuni through the centuries, and a photography exhibition, "Tito on Brijuni," focuses on Tito and his guests. **■ TIP→ The Brijuni Pocket Guide app is available to give you a self-guided tour by foot, bicycle, or electric car.** ✉ *Brionska 10, Fažana* ☎ *052/525–881, 052/525–882* 🌐 *www.np-brijuni.hr* 🎫 *July and Aug., 230 Kn; May and Jun.–Sept. 115 Kn* 🕓 *Closed Nov.–Apr.*

Hotels

You can save money by booking a room in Fažana and taking a day trip to the islands.

Heritage Hotel Chersin
$$ | **HOTEL** | Set in a beautifully restored old house in the center of Fažana, Heritage Hotel Chersin is a small and cozy family-run hotel perfect for couples. **Pros:** wonderful location; lovely design and ambience; tasty on-site restaurant. **Cons:** wooden floors; some village noise; beds a bit worn. [$] *Rooms from: 1135 Kn* ✉ *Piazza Grande 8, Fažana* ☎ *095/398–5350* 🌐 *www.hotel-chersin.com* 🕓 *Closed mid-Oct.–mid-Apr.* 🛏 *8 rooms* 🍴 *Free breakfast.*

Rovinj

35 km (22 miles) northwest of Pula.

It is hard to imagine how Rovinj could be more romantic than it is. In a fantastic setting, with centuries-old red-roofed houses clustered around the hill of a former island, Istria's cultural mecca is crowned by the monumental Baroque Crkva Sv. Eufemije (Church of St. Euphemia), which has a typical Venetian bell tower topped by a gleaming bronze figure of St. Euphemia. Far below, a wide harbor crowded with pleasure boats is rimmed with bright awnings and colorful café umbrellas. Artists, writers, musicians, and actors have long gravitated to this ravishing place to carve out apartments in historic houses. Throughout the summer, the winding cobbled streets are crowded with vacationers from all reaches of the world. South of the harbor lies the beautiful nature park of Zlatni Rt, planted with avenues of cedars, oaks, and cypresses for leisurely strolls and offering numerous secluded coves for bathing.

GETTING HERE AND AROUND

A shuttle bus runs from Pula airport to Rovinj. Buses travel daily between Pula central bus station and Rovinj and between Zagreb and Rovinj. The town is easily reachable by car, but the best way to get around Rovinj is on foot or bicycle, but due to stairs along almost all the steep streets, you cannot really cycle within the Old Town.

Sights

Practically all of Rovinj's key cultural and commercial attractions are packed into the compact one-time island and present-day peninsula that juts westward into the sea. The main square, Trg M. Tita, is at the southern juncture of this little peninsula with the mainland; from there you can either cut straight up the center of the peninsula (i.e., west) along Grisia toward the cathedral or walk around the outer edge of the peninsula, or you can go south along the harbor to some fine restaurants and the beaches of Zlatni Rt beyond.

★ **Crkva Sv. Eufemije** (*Church of St. Euphemia*)
RELIGIOUS SITE | Inside this 18th-century Baroque church, the remains of Rovinj's patron saint are said to lie within a 6th-century sarcophagus. Born near

Constantinople, Euphemia was martyred in her youth, on September 16 in AD 304, under the reign of Emperor Diocletian. The marble sarcophagus containing her remains mysteriously vanished in AD 800 when it was at risk of destruction by iconoclasts—and, legend has it, it somehow floated out to sea and washed up in faraway Rovinj. (Note the wall engraving just to the right of the entrance of St. Euphemia holding Rovinj in her arms.) On September 16 of each year many people gather to pray by her tomb. There is no better place to enjoy 360-degree sunset views of Rovinj than from the church bell tower. In summer, concerts and art shows take place in the piazza in front of the church. ⊠ *Trg Sv. Eufemije* ☎ *052/815–615* 🖃 *Church free, campanile 20 Kn* ⊙ *No tours Nov.–May.*

Dvigrad

TOWN | When its residents abandoned Dvigrad's "two towns" suddenly in the mid-17th century—fleeing the combined misfortune of plague and attacks by Uskok raiders—and established nearby Kanfanar, surely they didn't foresee that more than three centuries later tourists would delight in what they left behind. In any case, if exploring ruins is your (or your child's) thing, this is the place for you. Along an isolated road 23 km (14 miles) east of Rovinj, outside the sleepy town of Kanfanar (a short detour if you're headed north toward Poreč, Motovun, or Grožnjan), this huge maze of dirt paths surrounded by high stone walls makes for an adventuresome, imagination-stirring walk. Indeed, just enough restoration has been done to let your imagination "reconstruct" the rest: some of the walls are vine-covered, and much of the place is overgrown with vegetation. Nor is there a single explanatory sign, in any language. All this combines to give you the sense that you are discovering this eerie ghost town of a fortress city, even if a few other tourists are also wandering about. The battlements are impressively intact, and toward the center of the fortress you will find the remains of St. Sophia's Church, replete with depressions in the ground that contained the crypts of very important persons. To get here, take the main road east out of Rovinj toward Kanfanar. Just before you cross the railroad tracks and enter Kanfanar, you'll see a sign pointing to Dvigrad, which is to your left; from the sign the ruins are about 4 km (2½ miles) down an isolated, scrub-lined road. In May, a Medieval Fair takes place, complete with historical theater, music, jousting, food and drink. ⊠ *Kanfanar* 🖃 *Free.*

Galerija Sv. Toma (*St. Thomas Gallery*)
MUSEUM | Today a public art gallery, St. Thomas is a small, bright-yellow church dating to the Middle Ages but was rebuilt in 1722. It's on your way back down the hill from the main cathedral, and right after you pass by it, you will pass under a lovely, arched hall some 50 feet long and with a wooden-beamed ceiling. On your left, you'll notice a small courtyard, encircled by pastel painted houses with green and blue shutters and colorful flowers in the window. St. Thomas is part of the Heritage Museum of Rovinj. ⊠ *Bregovita ulica* ⊕ *www.muzej-rovinj.hr* 🖃 *Free* ⊙ *Closed Mon.–Tues. and Oct.–Jun.*

Kuća o Batani (*Batana Eco-museum*)
MUSEUM | Devoted to Rovinj's *batana* (traditional wooden boat), this small museum in a typical multistory house has a permanent exhibition of boats and fishing tools. It also hosts various cultural events and educational programs, and during the summer the museum organizes gourmet evenings on Tuesday and Thursday (220 Kn) in a *spacio*, a typical Rovinj tavern or wine cellar. These start with a batana ride from the Mali mol around Rovinj's Old Town to the tavern, where guests taste typical dishes like salted anchovies or marinated sardines and local wine. ⊠ *Obala Pinia Budicina 2* ☎ *052/812–593* ⊕ *www.batana.org* 🖃 *20 Kn* ⊙ *Closed Dec.–Mar.*

Matošević

WINERY/DISTILLERY | Matošević Winery, with vineyards in the northeast, welcomes visitors for a tour and tasting at their top-notch cellars in Krunčići, near Sv. Lovreč, a village not far from Rovinj. Their Malvazijas Rubina and Alba bear international renown and are served at many Michelin-starred restaurants. ✉ *Krunčići 2, Kruncici* ☎ *052/ 448–558* 🌐 *www.matosevic.com* 🕒 *Closed Sun.*

San Tommaso Winery

WINERY/DISTILLERY | **FAMILY** | This small family-run winery in Golaš, a small village in Bale, just 17 km (10½ miles) south of Rovinj, is housed in a beautifully restored 150 year-old farmhouse with exposed stones and large wooden beams. Relais and Wine San Tommaso features a wine cellar, tasting room with a big open fireplace, and a small ethnographic museum displaying old family photos and equipment that once was used in the wine-making process in Istria. Don't let their Malvazija Istarska fool you! Although the wine is fresh, easy to drink, and sweet, it is still 14% alcohol. They also produce a few reds, a rosé, and the sweet dessert wine Muscat Žuti. If the owner, Janja, happens to be there, ask her to let you taste her raisin wine, which isn't for sale. You can also stay in the winery's modern pension. ✉ *Golaš 13, Bale* ☎ *098/309–594* 🌐 *santommaso.hr* 🕒 *Closed Mon., and Nov.–Apr.*

Trg M. Tita

PLAZA | Standing on the Old Town's main square, you can't help but notice the **Balbi Arch,** which at one time was the gate to Rovinj's fish market. Notice the Venetian lion with an open book (a symbol of acceptance of Venetian rule without a fight) and a Venetian head on one side and a Turkish head on the other, the symbolism of which hasn't yet been explained. At the top, between the two Balbi coats of arms, is a Latin epigraph. Also quite prominent on the square is the city's pinkish-orange **watchtower,** whose base houses the tourist agency. Although it looks Venetian, the tower was erected in 1907. That said, the winged-lion relief on one side is indeed from the 16th century. ✉ *Trg Maršala Tita.*

Swimming in Rovinj

Swimming in the sea in Rovinj is a rocky business. There are no sandy beaches in the town itself; most of the swimming is done off the rocks or cement beaches (with ladders in some places) that jut into the sea. Head out to Crveni Otok (Red Island) or Uvala Lone (Lone Bay) for a pebble beach and a place to lay your towel or cushion, but don't forget to bring some rubber water sandals, as entering the water there, as in the rest of Istria, is a bit rough on tender feet.

🍴 Restaurants

★ Barba Danilo

$$$$ | **MEDITERRANEAN** | Don't let this restaurant's location—in a campsite outside of town—fool you: this fine-dining seafood restaurant is by far the best restaurant in Rovinj, and possibly in all Istria. Forget the standard starter-main-dessert kind of meal and instead indulge in a variety of innovative cold and warm appetizers made with the freshest local ingredients. **Known for:** upscale dining experience; imaginative dishes; a variety of cold and warm seafood starters. [$] *Average main: 150 Kn* ✉ *Polari 5* ☎ *052/830–002* 🌐 *barbadanilo.com* 🕒.

★ Bookeria

$$ | **MEDITERRANEAN** | Inventive Mediterranean food is served in an eye-catching, whimsically decorated garden dropped right on the stone square. You may not be seated on the sea but you'll feel the vibrant holiday vibe flowing from the minute you arrive. **Known for:** juicy burgers; hipster vibe and whimsical decor; friendly service. [$] *Average main: 110 Kn* ✉ *Trg G. Pignaton 7* ☎ *052/817–399, 091/219–0007* 🌐 *bookeria-rovinj.com* 🕓 *Closed Oct.–Apr.*

Giannino

$$$$ | **MEDITERRANEAN** | Tucked away on a small square in a residential area of the Old Town, Giannino is equally popular among locals and tourists for its fresh and delicious Mediterranean fare such as pan-fried squid with polenta, spicy boiled Adriatic shrimp, branzino al forno (baked slowly in the oven), cuttlefish ravioli, grilled rib-eye with roasted potatoes, and tagliatelle with lobster. Starched white and blue checkered tablecloths make the place look classy, but the atmosphere is convivial and relaxed with friendly staff. **Known for:** fresh fish and seafood; run by the same family since 1972; charming location in the center. [$] *Average main: 150 Kn* ✉ *Agusta Ferrija 38* ☎ *052/813–402* 🌐 *restoran-giannino.com* 🕓 *Closed Tues. and Nov.–Mar.*

Maestral

$$$$ | **MEDITERRANEAN** | You won't find a bad seat at this outdoor seafront restaurant with fantastic views of the Old Town. An extensive menu, the friendly staff, a laid-back vibe, and affordable prices draw crowds here all day. **Known for:** outstanding views; outdoor dining; fisherman's pie and squid stew. [$] *Average main: 100 Kn* ✉ *Obala V. Nazora 3* ☎ *052/830–565* 🕓 *Closed Oct.–Apr.*

★ Monte

$$$$ | **MEDITERRANEAN** | Dinner here promises upscale, out-of-this-world, creatively presented Italian-Istrian dishes served in a special garden terrace setting just below famous St. Euphemia's Church. Crisp white linen tablecloths on modern white wrought-iron patio tables dot the shady terrace. **Known for:** reservations essential; multicourse tasting menus; exceptional wine pairings. [$] *Average main: 300 Kn* ✉ *Montalbano 75* ☎ *052/830–203* 🌐 *www.monte.hr* 🕓 *Closed mid-Oct.–Easter. No lunch.*

Orca

$$$$ | **MEDITERRANEAN** | **FAMILY** | Local, fresh, traditional food makes this restaurant on the outskirts of town a favorite among locals. Its location on the main road may not draw visitors in, but the food is excellent and a great value. **Known for:** friendly staff; traditional restaurant with old-fashioned interior; big portions. [$] *Average main: 150 Kn* ✉ *Gripole 70* ☎ *052/816–851* 🌐 *www.orca-rovinj.com* 🕓 *Closed Nov., and Tues. Oct.–May.*

Pizzeria Da Sergio

$$ | **PIZZA** | **FAMILY** | With 50-plus varieties of delicious thin-crust pizzas, there's plenty to choose from at this conveniently located venue along the narrow road leading up to the main cathedral. Pizzas are all baked in a wood-burning oven and are so good locals come from all over Istria to get them. [$] *Average main: 65 Kn* ✉ *Grisia 11* ☎ *052/816–949* 💳 *No credit cards* 🕓 *Closed Mon. Nov.–Easter. No lunch Nov.–Easter.*

Hotels

★ Grand Park Hotel Rovinj

$$$$ | **HOTEL** | **FAMILY** | Emerging from the fragrant pine forest, this hotel has an unbelievably perfect location on the waterfront opposite Sv. Katarina Island and the charming Old Town of Rovinj, an excellent restaurant, a top spa, and luxurious accommodations. **Pros:** spectacular location overlooking Old Town Rovinj; exceptional Cap Aureo Restaurant; indoor and outdoor pools. **Cons:** shared beach with Katarina Hotel on island across; outdoor infinity pool can get crowded; some suites on lower floors do not have views. [$] *Rooms from: 3025 Kn* ✉ *Smareglijeva ulica 1A* ☎ *052/800–250* 🌐 *www.maistra.com/grand-park-hotel-rovinj* 🛏 *209 rooms* 🍴 *Free breakfast.*

Hotel Adriatic
$$$ | **HOTEL** | Founded in 1912, this harborside boutique hotel is the oldest (still functioning) one in town, and is modern, artsy, and as cosmopolitan as anything in New York or London. **Pros:** first-class view of Old Town square and harbor; breakfast served on the terrace; sophisticated design. **Cons:** no spa facilities; off-site parking; neither direct beach nor swimming pool. [$] *Rooms from: 2000 Kn* ✉ *P. Budicin 16* ☎ *052/803510, 052/800–250* 🌐 *www.maistra.com* 🛏 *18 rooms* 🍴 *Free breakfast.*

Hotel Angelo d'Oro
$$ | **HOTEL** | Rovinj's first boutique hotel is housed in a beautifully restored 16th-century building on a cobblestone street in the heart of the Old Town. **Pros:** beautiful Venetian building with wrought-iron and stone details; modern updates and recent renovations; secret courtyard garden for breakfast. **Cons:** some street noise; parking is outside Old Town; books up quickly. [$] *Rooms from: 1325 Kn* ✉ *Švalba 40* ☎ *052/853–920* 🌐 *www.angelodoro.com* 🛏 *27 rooms* 🍴 *Free breakfast.*

Hotel Lone
$$$$ | **HOTEL** | Superbly designed by an all-star Croatian team, the large Hotel Lone blends perfectly with its lush surroundings; rooms are modern, spacious, and comfortable, with sleek bathrooms and huge balconies. **Pros:** contemporary design; great balcony views; right on the beach in a wonderful forest park. **Cons:** pool is shared with nearby Eden Hotel; energy can feel a bit cold and distant; large hotel also caters to business travelers. [$] *Rooms from: 2500 Kn* ✉ *L. Adamovića 31* ☎ *052/800–250 reservation center, 052/632–000* 🌐 *www.maistra.com* 🛏 *248 rooms* 🍴 *Free breakfast.*

Hotel Monte Mulini
$$$$ | **HOTEL** | **FAMILY** | Considered one of the top luxury hotels in Croatia, the Hotel Monte Mulini has a stunning location just a 20-minute walk from Rovinj's Old Town, in a landscaped park next to the nature park Zlatni Rt and 164 feet from the sea. **Pros:** gorgeous location by the sea; within walking distance of town; spacious, elegantly appointed rooms. **Cons:** pricey; heated outdoor swimming pool sometimes too cold; not enough stools at the swim up bar. [$] *Rooms from: 3525 Kn* ✉ *A. Smareglia 3* ☎ *052/636000, 052/800–250 reservation center* 🌐 *www.maistra.com* 🕑 *Closed Nov.–Easter* 🛏 *113 rooms* 🍴 *Free breakfast.*

Island Hotel Katarina
$$ | **HOTEL** | Located on Santa Katarina Island, just a 15-minute boat ride from the Old Town, Island Hotel Katarina is partly housed in an old family castle from the early 20th century with basic and outdated but spacious rooms, some with breathtaking views over the Old Town. **Pros:** surrounded by beautiful parks; nice views; great amenities for families. **Cons:** dependent on a boat schedule; outdated decor in the rooms; pricey. [$] *Rooms from: 1250 Kn* ✉ *Otok Katarina 1* ☎ *052/800–250* 🌐 *www.maistra.com* 🕑 *Closed Oct.–May* 🛏 *120 rooms* 🍴 *Free Breakfast.*

🍸 Nightlife

Havana Club
BARS/PUBS | The Adriatic may not be quite as warm as the Caribbean, but at the Havana Club—a spacious, tropical-themed cocktail-bar-cum-café right on the harbor—you can sip a piña colada or a canchánchara (rum, lime, and honey). There's a great selection of over 100 Caribbean rums and premium gins plus nonalcoholic cocktails, as well as iced tea and coffee. Kick back and relax in a wicker chair under a bamboo umbrella while listening to reggae. That's not to mention the real Cuban cigars you can puff for anywhere between 60 Kn and 160 Kn. Ah, the life! ✉ *Obala Alda Negria* ☎ *091/588–3470* 🕑 *Closed Oct.–Apr.*

Rovinj is perhaps Istria's most picturesque city, thanks to its red-roof houses and beachside promenade.

★ Mediterraneo Bar

BARS/PUBS | With a lovely terrace literally on the sea's edge, with friendly staff at the ready but not hovering, a great selection of pretty cocktails, a relaxed atmosphere, and more affordable prices than similar bars in the vicinity, Mediterraneo is popular among locals and visitors alike. Pass through the low archway and head down a staircase to the fun terrace with colorful tables, stone benches, and cushions for those willing to have a drink sitting on the rocks. Even dolphins occasionally visit. The bar is closed from November to April. ✉ *Santa Croce 24* ☎ *091/532–8357.*

Piassa Granda da Miro

WINE BARS—NIGHTLIFE | Rovinj's must-visit bar for wine aficionados, Piassa Granda features over 70 white, red, rosé, dessert, and sparkling wines by the glass. Istrian vineyards dominate the list. Run by two sisters, both passionate oenophiles, this is a perfect place to taste, enjoy, and learn about Istrian wines and winemakers. Located at the small square right in the Old Town, Piassa Granda also serves simple food like bruschetta, salad, local cheeses, and cold cuts. It's closed November to April. ✉ *Veli trg 1* ☎ *098/762-6844.*

Puntulina Restaurant & Wine Bar

BARS/PUBS | Take the steps down to Puntulina's terrace, where you can enjoy a glass of Istrian or other Croatian wine in a pleasant atmosphere yards from the sea, with light pop music setting the tone, plus amazing sunsets. And, yes, you can take a few more steps down if you wish, to the rocks, and take a dip before or after being served—this is where Rovinj's free, public swimming area begins. There's also an excellent seafood restaurant on the upper level, which offers the same excellent views in one of the most romantic settings in Rovinj. ✉ *Sv. Križa 38* ☎ *052/813–186* ⊕ *www.puntulina.eu* ⊗ *Closed Nov.–Mar.*

Performing Arts

★ Croatian Summer Salsa Festival
ARTS FESTIVALS | FAMILY | During the last week of June, the Croatian Summer Salsa Festival offers eight days of dancing lessons in various town squares, gallery spaces, and even on the beach, as well as beach and pool parties, dance-life workshops, and best-practices on how to DJ and emcee dance parties. International salsa experts and professional DJs entertain, inspire, and encourge over 2,000 attendees. It's a real party you can't miss! ⊠ *Rovinj* ⊕ *www.crosalsafestival.com.*

Rovinj Photodays
ARTS FESTIVALS | Since 2008 Rovinj has hosted the largest photo festival and international competition of contemporary photography in southeastern Europe. Usually taking place during the first weekend in May, the festival activities include workshops, lectures, displays, presentations, gallery shows, and streets lined with artful and thought-provoking photography. ⊠ *Rovinj* ☎ *099/200–6666, 051/301–182* ⊕ *photodays-rovinj.com.*

Shopping

Rovinj is worth visiting for its outstanding beauty, not its boutiques. The souvenir market is very crowded with foreign-made trinkets that will help remind you of your stay. But for authentic, Istrian-made products, head to these boutiques and shops.

House of Batana
GIFTS/SOUVENIRS | Original souvenirs based on Rovinj's fishing heritage—including key-chains, T-shirts, and replicas of its traditional vessel, the batana—can be bought at the House of Batana museum. Besides batana-inspired souvenirs, you can pick up a small recipe book with old, almost-forgotten recipes from Rovinj fishermen, also available in English.

⊠ *Obala Pina Budicina 2* ☎ *052/812–593* ⊕ *www.batana.org.*

Profumo di Rovigno
PERFUME/COSMETICS | The Salvi family offers an intoxicating array of unique perfumes, sachets, bath gels, lotions, soaps, diffusers, cottom throws, silk wraps, and home fragrances under their Profumo di Rovigno brand. All products at their tiny store on the main shopping street are inspired by the flora and fauna found in the hills around Rovinj–from wild sage to lavendar, roses, lemon balm, and other herbals. All are beautifully packaged in elegant bottles and boxes, perfect to bring home as gifts or to enjoy in your own home. ⊠ *Carera 45-47* ☎ *052/813–419* ⊕ *www.profumodirovigno.com.*

Activities

SCUBA DIVING
As elsewhere along the coast, the Rovinj area has its share of places to kayak, boat, windsurf, jetski, parasail, stand-up paddle, cycle, and deep sea dive. In fact, several diving centers will take you by boat for supervised dives to shipwrecks and other fascinating spots, not least the famous wreck of the *Baron Gautsch,* an Austrian passenger ferry that sank in 1914 just nine nautical miles from Rovinj.

Diving Rovinj
DIVING/SNORKELING | This diving center offers shore dives, off-site island and wreck dives, and night diving (from 115 Kn). The *Baron Gautsch* shipwreck dive is the most popular around Rovinj, but at 570 Kn, it's also the most expensive. The center also offers diving courses, a two-hour discovery dive, and specialized courses for advanced divers. ⊠ *Hotel Istra, Otok Sveti Andrija* ☎ *095/902–5543* ⊕ *www.diving.de.*

Scuba-Rovinj Diving Center
DIVING/SNORKELING | Scuba-Rovinj Diving Center was founded in 1997 and offers diverse diving programs from shore, off the boat, and wreck dives, making it

suitable for inexperienced and experienced divers. The company also offers a complete range of diver education—from discovery dives to instructor seminars. ✉, *Camping Veštar Cocaletto* ☎ *098/212–360* ⊕ *www.diving-rovinj.com.*

Poreč

55 km (34 miles) northwest of Pula.

A chic, bustling little city founded as a Roman *castrum* (fort) in the 2nd century BC and swarming with tourists more than 2,000 years later, Poreč may not be quite as lovely as Rovinj—few places are—nor does it enjoy the benefits of a hilltop panorama, but it is nonetheless a pretty view of red-tiled roofs on a peninsula jutting out to sea. Within the historic center, the network of streets still follows the original urban layout. Dekumanova, the Roman *decumanus* (the main traverse street), has maintained its character as the principal thoroughfare. Today it is a worn flagstone passage lined with Romanesque and Gothic mansions and patrician palaces, some of which now house cafés and restaurants. Close by lies the magnificent UNESCO-listed Eufrazijeva Basilica (St. Euphrasius Basilica), Istria's prime ecclesiastical attraction and one of the coast's major artistic showpieces. Although the town itself is small, Poreč has ample capacity for overnight stays, thanks to the vast hotel complexes of Plava and Zelena Laguna, situated along the pine-rimmed shoreline a short distance from the center. Although you can cover the main sights in two or three hours, Poreč surely merits a one-night stay, or more if you figure in a day trip to a nearby attraction such as the Baredine Cave or the Limski kanal.

GETTING HERE AND AROUND

Getting to Poreč is easier straight from Pula than from Rovinj, as you simply take the main inland highway north for 42 km (26 miles) and then follow the signs before turning west onto the secondary road that leads you another 13 km (8 miles) to Poreč—a 45- to 60-minute drive in all, depending on the traffic and how much pressure you apply to the pedal.

CONTACTS Tourist Information Center Poreč. ✉ *Zagrebačka 9, Poreč* ☎ *052/451–293* ⊕ *www.myporec.com.*

VACATION RENTALS
FKK Naturist Park Koversada
Open from June through October, Koversada is Croatia's largest naturist (i.e., nudist), holiday resort area, offering campsites, modern tiny homes, and other accommodations to those wishing to enjoy beautiful beaches, pools, and other outdoor activities in their natural human form. ✉ *Koversada, Vrsar* ☎ *052/800–200* ⊕ *www.maistracamping.com/naturist-park-koversada-campsite-vrsar.*

 Sights

AgroLaguna Winery
WINERY/DISTILLERY | At AgroLaguna's tasting room it's possible to taste a number of their high-quality Istrian wines, olive oils, and cheeses. One white varietal, Malvazija, is well known throughout the Adriatic, dating back to the days of the Venetian city-states. Muškat ottonel is another high-quality native variety. Small, lovingly produced batches of barrique provide high-quality (red) wine are well-regarded in restaurants and hotels across Croatia. You can also get guided tastings, cellar tours, wine roads and vineyard tours, and the winery has the largest AgroLaguna single olive grove in Croatia. ✉ *Partizansko šetalište 2, Poreč* ☎ *052/431–921* ⊕ *www.agrolaguna.hr.*

Aquacolors Water Park Poreč
AMUSEMENT PARK/WATER PARK | **FAMILY** | Whether you're looking for an adrenaline-filled day or just a relaxing day by the pool, Aquacolors water park has you covered. With 12 slides and more than a full acre of pools, it's the largest water park in all Croatia. A looping, 61-meter-long

St. Euphrasius Basilica is decorated with stunning mosaics.

(200-foot-long) slide rockets you down at high speed, while a 204-meter-long (1/3-mile-long) lazy river eases you along on an inflatable tube. The park offers endless hours of fun for the whole family, as well as favorable family pricing. ✉ *Molindrio 18, Poreč* ☎ *052/219–671* ⊕ *www.aquacolors.eu* ✈ *135 Kn–230 Kn* 🕑 *Closed Oct.–Apr.*

★ Eufrazijeva Basilica (*St. Euphrasius Basilica*)

RELIGIOUS SITE | FAMILY | The magnificent Eufrazijeva Basilica is among the most perfectly preserved early Christian churches in Europe, and as a UNESCO World Heritage Site, one of the most important monuments of Byzantine art on the Adriatic. It was built by Bishop Euphrasius in the middle of the 6th century and consists of a delightful atrium, a church decorated with stunning mosaics, and an octagonal baptistery. Added in the 17th-century were a bell tower you can climb (for a modest fee) and a 17th-century Bishop's Palace, whose foundations date to the 6th century; the basement contains an exhibit of stone monuments and mosaics previously on the basilica floor. The church interior is dominated by biblical mosaics above, behind, and around the main apse. In the apsidal semidome, the Virgin holding the Christ child is seated in a celestial sphere on a golden throne, flanked by angels in flowing white robes. On the right side there are three martyrs, the patrons of Poreč; the mosaic on the left shows Bishop Euphrasius holding a model of the church, slightly askew. High above the main apse, just below the beamed ceiling, Christ holds an open book in his hands while apostles approach on both sides. Other luminous, shimmeringly intense mosaics portray further ecclesiastical themes. ✉ *Eufrazijeva 22, Poreč* ☎ *052/451–784* ⊕ *www.zupaporec. com/eufrazijeva-bazilika.html* ✈ *50 kn* 🕑 *Closed Sun.*

Jama Baredine (*Baredine Cave*)

CAVE | FAMILY | Far from sun and sea though it may be, the Baredine Cave has long been one of the Poreč area's top natural attractions. About 8 km (5 miles) northeast of town, near Nova Vas, this wonderful world of five limestone halls includes not only the miniature olm (known as the cave salamander) and insects but, of course, stalactites, stalagmites, and dripstone formations—from "curtains" 30 feet long to "statues" resembling the Virgin Mary, the Leaning Tower of Pisa, and the body of the 13th-century shepherdess Milka, who supposedly lost her way down here while looking for her lover Gabriel (who met the same fate). One of the halls includes a hatch some 70 yards deep that leads to underground lakes. Groups leave every half hour on a 40-minute guided tour. Those without car transport may wish to join an excursion to the cave from Poreč or another nearby town. ⊠ *Tar - Gedići 55, Nova Vas* ☎ *052/421–333, 095/421–4210* ⊕ *www.baredine.com* 🖅 *75 Kn.*

Limski Canal

BODY OF WATER | There's even a bit of Norwegian-style fjord in Croatia. The Limski *kanal* is a 13-km-long (8-mile-long) karst canyon, whose emerald-green waters are flanked by forested valley walls that rise gradually to heights of more than 300 feet inland. The canyon was formed in the last Ice Age, and it is Istria's most fertile breeding area for mussels and oysters—hence, you'll find the excellent Viking seafood restaurant on-site. Tours are available from both Poreč and Rovinj with various agencies and independent operators, whose stands and boats are impossible to miss. A reservation a day or two in advance can't hurt, though, particularly in midsummer. Expect to pay approximately 150 Kn for the four-hour tour or 250 Kn for a day-long tour that includes a "fish picnic." You can also visit the canal on your own by car. And hiking enthusiasts can take a trail to the Romualdova Cave, open daily from June to September. ⊠ *D21, halfway between Rovinj and Poreč, Kruncici.*

Romanička Kuća (*Romanesque House*)

HOUSE | Today housing an art gallery and the Ethnographic Heritage Collection, the Romanička kuća is one of the few preserved examples of residential architecture of the Romanesque period. It was built in the 13th century and has been renovated and extended several times, with the last major alterations, like the wooden balcony, made in the 18th century. ⊠ *Marafor 1, Poreč* ⊕ *www. muzejporec.hr* 🖅 *10 Kn (included with Regional Museum entry).*

Trg Marafor

PLAZA | This square is located toward the tip of the peninsula and was the site of Poreč's Roman forum, whose original stonework is visible in spots amid the present-day pavement. Beside it is a park containing the ruins of Roman temples dedicated to the gods Mars and Neptune. It's still an important meeting place, so you will find a variety of cafés, restaurants, and shops around the Marafor square. ⊠ *Poreč.*

★ Vrsar

TOWN | This pretty, waterfront medieval hilltop town just 10 km (6 miles) south of Poreč is situated near the fjord's northern juncture with the sea (and yet another place you can catch a tour of the fjord). Famous since Roman times for its high-quality stone, which helped build Venice, Vrsar is home to the 12th-century Romanesque church Sv. Marija Od Mora (St. Mary of the Sea), which has three naves. In his memoirs, the Venetian adventurer Casanova fondly recalled the local red wine, Teran. Just a couple of miles south, by the way, is Croatia's oldest and largest naturist resort, FKK Park Koversada. ⊕ *infovrsar.com.*

Zavičajni Muzej (*Regional Museum*)

MUSEUM | On the main pedestrian thoroughfare through town, between the aquarium and the basilica, is Istria's oldest museum, the Zavičajni muzej, which opened in 1884 in the 18th-century baroque Sinčić Palace. Presenting the history of Poreč and environs from ancient times through the 20th century, it features 2,000 exhibits, with highlights that include Roman tombstones, mosaics, and other archaeological fragments from antiquity, 16th-century portraits, and exhibits of baroque furniture; there's also a wonderful historical library with first editions of Diderot's 18th-century encyclopedia. ⊠ *Decumanus 9, Poreč* ☎ *052/431–585* ⊕ *muzejporec.hr* 🎫 *10 Kn.*

Beaches

Walk 10 minutes south of Poreč along the shore, past the marina, and you'll meet with the thoroughly swimmable, if typically rocky, pine-fringed beaches of the Brulo and Plava Laguna resort area. Keep walking until you're about 5 km (3 miles) south, and you'll be right in the center of the Zelena Laguna, which, though more concrete than rock, is one of the best-equipped tourist resorts on the Adriatic coast. Every day from May through September, two charming "tourist trains," tiny open-walled buses, run hourly from 9 am to 11 pm between the town center and the resort, as well as the Hotel Luna to the north—costing you 20 Kn but saving you the walk. Another option is the boat that runs between Zelena Laguna and the center May through September daily from 10 am to 11 pm, with stops at other resort areas in between. Tickets can be purchased on board.

Restaurants

Konoba Daniela
$$$$ | EUROPEAN | FAMILY | In the village of Veleniki just a few miles from Poreč, this rustic, family-run tavern has exposed stone walls, wooden beams, and an outdoor terrace in an enclosed courtyard. With its simple and honest food, friendly staff, and huge portions, Tavern Daniela offers excellent value for money. **Known for:** excellent steak tartare; many seafood options; friendly service. Ⓢ *Average main: 100 Kn* ⊠ *Veleniki 15a, Veleniki* ☎ *052/460–519* ⊕ *www.konobadaniela.com* ☉ *Closed mid-Feb.–mid-Mar.*

Pizzeria Nono
$$ | PIZZA | FAMILY | Right across the street from the main tourist office, the Nono is teeming with folks saying "yes, yes!" to scrumptious budget fare from pizzas and salads to such seafood standards as grilled squid. **Known for:** affordable prices; streetside terrace; summer crowds. Ⓢ *Average main: 65 Kn* ⊠ *Zagrebačka 4, Poreč* ☎ *052/453–088* ☉ *Closed Feb., Mon. Oct.–Apr., and 2 wks in Nov.*

Sv. Nikola Restaurant
$$$$ | CONTEMPORARY | Those with a discriminating palate and a not-so-discriminating pocketbook should try this sparkling, air-conditioned restaurant very close to the harbor. The menu offers such delicacies as fish filet in scampi and scallops sauce, cream soup with local mushrooms, and beefsteak with tartufi sauce, but it's the elegant seafront terrace that makes this the top fine dining spot in Poreč. **Known for:** special-occasion dining; harbor-facing terrace; delicious seafood food. Ⓢ *Average main: 150 Kn* ⊠ *Obala maršala Tita 23, Poreč* ☎ *052/423–018* ⊕ *www.svnikola.com.*

☕ Coffee and Quick Bites

★ Torre Rotonda Cocktail & Coffee Bar
$$ | CAFÉ | FAMILY | Do not be deterred by the cannon facing you as you enter the 15th-century stone tower that now houses the Torre Rotonda café and bar. Climb up the spiral staircase to a second floor with several intimate nooks, or go one more flight to the roof for an unbeatable, outstanding view of Poreč and its harbor. **Known for:** spectacular views over Old Town and the marina; delicious Aperol spritz; lively atmosphere at night. Ⓢ *Average main: 38 Kn* ⊠ *Narodni trg 3a, Poreč* ☎ *098/255–731* ⊕ *www.torrerotonda.com* ☉ *Closed Oct.–Apr.*

Hotels

BO Hotel Palazzo

$$$ | HOTEL | Its outstanding location on the head of a small peninsula in Poreč's Old Town sets this historic hotel apart; built in 1910, it housed the very first hotel in town. **Pros:** excellent location; historical building with character; outdoor pool and spa. **Cons:** smallish rooms; lacks its own beach; can be noisy at night. $ *Rooms from: 1855 Kn ⊠ Obala Maršala Tita 24, Poreč ☎ 052/858–800 ⊕ bohotel-porec. com* ⊗ *Closed Nov.–Mar.* ⇌ *74 rooms* ⦿ *Free breakfast.*

Hotel Park Plava Laguna

$$ | RESORT | FAMILY | The ideal family resort, the Park Plava allows each family member to choose what they most want to do: animation activities, beaches, sports, fine dining, or hanging out at the five on-property pools. **Pros:** many activities and programs for children; on the beach; close to Old Town. **Cons:** big and busy; not a romantic retreat; à la carte dining only for lunch. $ *Rooms from: 1440 Kn ⊠ Ul. Špadići 15b, Poreč ☎ 052/415–500 ⊕ www.plavalaguna. com* ⊗ *Closed Oct.–May* ⇌ *154 rooms* ⦿ *All-inclusive.*

Korta Gira Bed & Free breakfast

$$ | B&B/INN | FAMILY | Only 5 km (3 miles) from downtown Poreč, this small B&B on a family farm feels like a world apart. **Pros:** quiet and relaxing yet not far from Poreč; warm, friendly hosts; homemade products at breakfast. **Cons:** car is essential; outside town; not a full-service hotel. $ *Rooms from: 875 Kn ⊠ Buići 8, Poreč ☎ 091/427–0521 ⊕ www.bbkortagira. com* ⇌ *3 rooms* ⦿ *Free breakfast.*

Valamar Diamant Hotel & Residence

$$$ | HOTEL | FAMILY | Located a mile south of Old Town Poreč in the Brulo neighborhood, this large, fully renovated hotel is surrounded by pine forest but still close to the sea and a favorite for travelers looking for an activity-rich vacation. **Pros:** superlative sports facilities; excellent buffet food with all dietary needs; modern, bright and comfy rooms. **Cons:** 10-minute walk from Poreč; busy, active environment; caters to business travelers, too. $ *Rooms from: 1500 Kn ⊠ Brulo 1, Poreč ☎ 052/465–000 reservation center, 052/400–000 ⊕ www.valamar. com* ⊗ *Closed Nov.–Mar.* ⇌ *246 rooms* ⦿ *All-inclusive.*

Valamar Isabella Island Resort

$$$ | RESORT | FAMILY | Accommodations at this sprawling premium resort on car-free Sveti Nikola island (across the harbor from Old Town Porec), include apartments, villas, and hotels. **Pros:** wonderful location on car-free island; five-minute boat ride to downtown; stylish accommodations. **Cons:** large resort; hectic at dinner when full; different service level at different properties. $ *Rooms from: 2000 Kn ⊠ Island Sv. Nikola, Poreč ☎ 052/465–000 ⊕ www.valamar.com* ⊗ *Closed Oct.–May* ⇌ *334 rooms* ⦿ *Free breakfast.*

Valamar Riviera Hotel

$$ | HOTEL | On the seafront promenade, where Poreč's oldest hotels are found, the Valamar Riviera is an adults-only hotel with a chic restaurant and comfortable, traditionally appointed rooms, most of which have sea views and balconies. **Pros:** located right in Old Town; private sand beach served by shuttle boat; popular restaurant with outdoor dining. **Cons:** noise from the promenade reaches the rooms; off-site parking; occasional exhaust from yachts parked in front. $ *Rooms from: 1250 Kn ⊠ Obala M. Tita 15, Poreč ☎ 052/465–000 reservation center, 052/400–800 ⊕ www.valamar. com* ⊗ *Closed Oct.–Apr.* ⇌ *105 rooms* ⦿ *Free breakfast.*

Nightlife

Villa Club Porec

DANCE CLUBS | Located near the marina, right by the beach, the Villa Club is a popular hangout with lounge chairs, wicker canopy beds, and lounge music during the day. Night brings DJs, theme parties, live bands playing dance music, and go-go dancers until dawn. ⊠ *By the beach south of the marina, Poreč* ☎ *099/214–9004* ⊕ *www.villa-club.net.*

● Performing Arts

★ Poreč Open Air Festival of Life

FESTIVALS | Poreč celebrates life with a variety of shows, concerts, street performances, and special events daily from mid-June to mid-September. Town squares, streets, and the island of Sveti Nikola become open-air stages during the festival. Many activities are free. MTV Summerblast, a two-day festival event full of concerts and partying under the stars, happens at the end of August. ⊠ *Poreč* ⊕ *www.porecopenair.com.*

Street Art Festival

ARTS FESTIVALS | FAMILY | In the third week of August, Poreč's annual Street Art Festival enlivens the Old Town's streets and squares with musical, theatrical, art, multimedia, and acrobatic events and street performances. ⊠ *Poreč* ☎ *052/887–223* ⊕ *www.poup.hr.*

Activities

DIVING

Starfish Diving Center

SCUBA DIVING | This outfitter offers aspiring or advanced divers daily diving tours to local shipwrecks, reefs, and caves. A four-day certification course is also available. ⊠ *Autocamp Porto Sole, 10 km (6 miles) south of Poreč, Vrsar* ☎ *098/335–506, 098/334–816* ⊕ *www.starfish.hr.*

Novigrad

15 km (9½ miles) northwest of Poreč.

Imagine a mini Rovinj of sorts, not quite so well preserved, it's true, and without the hill. This is Novigrad—a pretty little peninsula town that was the seat of a bishopric for more than 1,300 years, from 520 to 1831, and, like Rovinj, was at one time an island (before being connected with the mainland in the 18th century). With its medieval structures still impressively intact, along with its Old Town wall, it merits a substantial visit and perhaps a one-night stay as you make your way up and down the coast or before heading inland toward the hilltop towns of Grožnjan and Motovun. At first glance, as you enter town on an uninspiring main road bordered by communist-era, concrete-box apartment buildings, you might wonder if it was worth coming this far. Continue on and you'll arrive at a little gem: to your right is a pint-size, protected harbor filled with boats, the Old Town is in front of you, and to your left is a peaceful park. The bustling harborside square has a few bars and restaurants. A nearby ice-cream stand is manned by enterprising, acrobatic young men who wow the crowds by hurling scoops 50 or more feet into the air to open-mouthed colleagues who then discreetly spit them into napkins, garnering much applause (and generating long lines). If you continue walking past the harbor on the left, you'll arrive at Vitriol, one of the most popular sunset bars in all of Istria.

GETTING HERE AND AROUND

There are daily buses from Pula to Novigrad. The town is also connected by bus with Zagreb, Rijeka, and Trieste. Novigrad is easily reachable by car, but the best way to get around town is on foot or by bicycle. The electric tourist train connects the resort complex to the south with Novigrad harbor from June to September.

Novigrad greets you with its charming harbor and colorful houses.

Sights

The 13th-century **Crkva svetog Pelagija** (Church of St. Pelagius), built on a 6th-century foundation and containing some elaborate Baroque artwork, stands near the tip of the peninsula with its towering late-19th-century campanile topped by a statue of St. Pelagius. As in Rovinj, the main church faces the sea.

On nearby Veliki trg is Novigrad's pale-red **city hall,** topped by a watchtower and contrasting sharply with the yellow building beside it. Here and there, Gothic elements are in evidence on the medieval architecture about town (e.g., two windows on a 15th-century building at Velika ulica 33).

Istralandia Waterpark
AMUSEMENT PARK/WATER PARK | **FAMILY** | The first water park in Istria opened in 2014, featuring 20 waterslides, including an almost 90-foot-high free-fall waterslide; family rafting in inflatable rafts; three pools, including a children's pool with water castle, pirate ship, and several smaller slides; sand volleyball; and a badminton court—a great place to spend a day! Direct buses from Poreč, Novigrad, and resort towns in between run throughout the day in July and August. ✉ *Nova Vas* ☎ *052/866–900* 🌐 *www.istralandia.hr* 🎟 *170 Kn–220 Kn* 🕒 *Closed Oct.–June.*

Restaurants

★ Damir e Ornella
$$$$ | **SEAFOOD** | Tucked away on a quiet side street, this superb (and pricey) little family-run establishment is a secret wonder you may want to share only with your fellow gourmands who appreciate raw-fish specialties. You can also enjoy grilled seafood and gnocchi, although you don't go here for a simple plate of pasta, but instead to indulge in a four-course meal. **Known for:** Mediterranean-style sashimi; intimate atmosphere; booking days in advance. [$] *Average main: 500 Kn* ✉ *Ul. Zidine 5* ☎ *052/758–134* 🌐 *www.damir-ornella.com* 🕒 *Closed Nov. and Feb. No lunch Sept.–May.*

Restaurant Marina

$$$$ | **CONTEMPORARY** | On the first floor of what looks like a typical family house, this seafood restaurant has a surprisingly elegant and stylish interior. Husband-and-wife duo Marina and Davor don't have a fixed menu; offerings are recited by the young owner. **Known for:** innovative seafood dishes; tasting menus; food and wine pairing. $ *Average main: 325 Kn* ✉ *Sv. Antona 38* ☎ *099/812–1267, 052/726–691* ⏱ *Closed Jan. and Feb., and Tues.*

★ Vecchio Mulino

$$ | **PIZZA** | **FAMILY** | The Old Mill pizzeria may look touristy—it is, after all, centrally located right by the harbor, and it is packed—but it's also good, and the raised terrace gives you the feeling of being a bit above the fray. This is the best place in town for pizza, spaghetti, salads, čevapčići (grilled Balkan sausages) and tiramisu. $ *Average main: 65 Kn* ✉ *Mlinska ulica 8* ☎ *052/647–451 , 052/726–300.*

Hotels

Hotel San Rocco

$$ | **HOTEL** | Nine km (6 miles) up the road from Novigrad in Brtonigla (on the road to Buje), the Hotel San Rocco is a real change of pace from the coast: among rolling hills surrounded by olive trees and vineyards, this upscale boutique hotel makes an impressive entrée to the Istrian interior. **Pros:** good (though pricey) restaurant on-site; magnificent views; elegant rural relaxation close to town. **Cons:** you'll need a car; terrace is within earshot of busy road; cute but simple local village to wander. $ *Rooms from: 1400 Kn* ✉ *Srednja ulica 2, Brtonigla–Verteneglio* ☎ *052/725–000* ⊕ *www.san-rocco.hr* ⤴ *14 rooms* ⦿ *Free breakfast.*

Rivalmare Boutique Hotel

$$$ | **HOTEL** | With just 13 spacious contemporary rooms—some with lovely sea views and balcony—this boutique hotel is popular for its chic minimalist look,

elegance, design furniture, and superb location right at the seafront. **Pros:** small and intimate; top location; on-site parking. **Cons:** no free parking; no swimming pool; extra charge for sun loungers at the beach. $ *Rooms from: 2000 Kn* ✉ *Rivarella 19* ☎ *052/555–600* ⊕ *www.rivalmare.hr* ⏱ *Closed Dec.–Mar.* ⤴ *13 rooms* ⦿ *Free breakfast.*

Olive Oil in Istria

As you head north to Umag or northeast toward the interior hilltop towns, remember that you're driving through some of Istria's most fertile olive-oil territory. The tourist offices in Novigrad, Buje, and Umag can give you a map outlining an olive oil (and wine) route with directions to several production facilities that offer tastings. Of course, farther south in and around Vodnjan you will also find a wonderful collection of award-winning olive oil producers' farms to visit.

Umag

15 km (9 miles) northwest of Novigrad.

Yet another onetime island, the peninsula town of Umag draws the fewest tourists of any of the major towns along Istria's western coast, even if it has more than its share of the usual beach resorts nearby. Perhaps it's the frustration with waiters who, while twiddling their thumbs in front of their restaurants, call out to every passing tourist, "Italiano? Deutsch? English?" and, less often, "Français?"

And yet Umag is a nice enough place to stroll for a couple of hours if you are passing this way, even if you might not be moved to stay for the night. Although the town grew up under the rule of Rome, practically none of its ancient roots are apparent in what remains of the historic core, which dates to the Middle Ages.

GETTING HERE AND AROUND

The best way to get to Umag is by car. This quaint historic town is best explored on foot.

Sights

Cuj Winery

WINERY/DISTILLERY | **FAMILY** | The Cuj olive oils (and wines) are a true labor of love and passion. Owner Danijel Kraljevic—Cuj—will infuse you with both when you visit his wine and olive oil estate in the village of Farnažine near Umag. A beautifully restored, old stone building houses an olive mill, wine cellar, and tasting room with an open fireplace. He produces three single-sort extra virgin olive oils—Buža, Črna, and Bjelica—and one multisort extra virgin olive oil—Selekcija. Call in advance to arrange a visit. ✉ *Farnažine BB* ☎ *098/219–277* 🌐 *www.cuj.hr.*

Kabola Winery

WINERY/DISTILLERY | Near the small medieval hill town of Momjan, the Kabola Winery is a must-visit for wine and olive-oil aficionados. This boutique winery offers tours of its wine cellar and small wine museum, as well as full tastings in its picturesque, traditional Istrian farmhouse. Vintners since 1891, the Markezic family produces only organic wines and extra virgin olive oil. Their wines are wonderful, with their Malvazija Unica, Teran, and Dolce some of the more popular. Their olive oil is a blend of three kinds of olives: indigenous Istarska Bjelica mixed with Leccino and Pendolino. Fresh, well-rounded, and balanced, it marries perfectly with seafood, cheese, and salads. Call in advance to arrange a visit. ✉ *Kanedolo 90, Momjan* ☎ *099/720–7106, 052/779–208* 🌐 *www.kabola.hr* 🕓 *Closed Sun.*

★ Kozlović Winery

WINERY/DISTILLERY | At the Kozlović family's stylish, modern winery, which blends perfectly with the scenic countryside, you can enjoy an extensive wine tasting indoors or on their outdoor terrace overlooking the vineyard. If you've called ahead you can enjoy a full tasting of wine and olive oil as you enjoy local cheeses and proscuitto. Next door is the Stari Podrum, one of the best taverns in Istria. ✉ *Vale 78, Momjan* ☎ *052/779–177* 🌐 *www.kozlovic.hr* 🕓 *Closed Sun.*

Moreno Coronica

WINERY/DISTILLERY | Moreno Coronica, in the northeast corner of the peninsula between Buje and Umag, produces some Croatia's most delicious wines. The Gran Teran, a local variety of red wine, has been a gold medal winner at international wine competitions for many years running. Call to schedule a tour and tasting. ✉ *Koreniki 86, Koreniki* ☎ *052/730–357* 🌐 *www.coronica.eu.*

Restaurants

Tavern Nono

$$$ | **VENETIAN** | **FAMILY** | Extremely popular and always busy, Tavern Nono is located in Petrovija, just a mile east of Umag. This family-run tavern offers hearty Istrian seafood, meat, and pasta dishes in a cozy and friendly atmosphere. **Known for:** traditional Istrian food; kid-friendly dining with a playground and a small farm behind the restaurant; popularity among locals and tourists. [$] *Average main: 130 Kn* ✉ *Umaška 35, Petrovija* ☎ *052/740–160* 🌐 *www.konoba-nono.com* 🕓 *Closed Mon. Oct.–May.*

Motovun

38 km (24 miles) southeast of Umag, 30 km (19 miles) northeast of Poreč.

It is an understatement to say that a day exploring the undulating green

Istria is filled with medieval hill towns, and Motovun is one of the most charming.

countryside and medieval hill towns of inland Istria makes a pleasant contrast to life on the coast. Motovun, for one, is a ravishing place. The king of Istria's medieval hilltop towns, with a double ring of defensive walls as well as towers and gates, may even evoke a scene straight from *Lord of the Rings.* If you opt to travel inland for only a day or two, Motovun is *the* place to visit. Be warned, though: the town sees lots of tour buses. That said, a walk around the ramparts offers views across the oak forests and vineyards of the Mirna Valley. On the town's main square stands a church built according to plans by Palladio. In late July the famed **Motovun Film Festival** transforms the town into one of Croatia's liveliest (and most crowded) destinations for about five days.

GETTING HERE AND AROUND

The best way to get to Motovun is by car, and traveling here by bus isn't a viable option. This small hilltop town is best explored on foot.

🍴 Restaurants

★ Konoba Tončić

$$$$ | VENETIAN | This rustic tavern with exposed stone walls, wooden beams, and a large open fireplace offers traditional hearty Istrian meat dishes. Located off the beaten path well past Oprtalj, the outdoor terrace has scenic views over the rolling hills, valley, and mountains in the background. **Known for:** delicious traditional Istrian food; charming but remote location; reservations are essential. [$] *Average main: 100 Kn* ✉ *Čabarnica 42, Zrenj* ☎ *052/644–146* 🌐 *www.agroturizam-toncic.com* 💳 *No credit cards* 🕒 *Closed weekdays. Closed Jul.*

Mondo

$$$ | VENETIAN | FAMILY | On a narrow cobblestone street just a few yards from the town's gate, this tavern is perhaps the best place to eat in town, with a truffle-centric menu and a breezy terrace perfect for alfresco dining. The pleasant rustic interior has roughly plastered stone walls. **Known for:** truffle-stuffed menu;

being featured on Anthony Bourdain's No Reservations and in the New York Times; charming location. $ *Average main: 140 Kn* ✉ *Barbacan 1* ☎ *052/681–791* ⊘ *Closed Jan.–Mar. Closed Tues.*

 ## Hotels

Boutique Hotel Kaštel

$$ | **HOTEL** | Nestled in a cloistered niche at the very top of the hilltop town sits this peaceful, old-fashioned boutique hotel that makes an ideal retreat if you prefer quaint streets and rolling green hills to sea views and island escapes. **Pros:** quiet location; indoor pool and spa facilities; nice views over the Mirna River Valley from some rooms. **Cons:** uphill walk to the hotel; no car access or parking at hotel; some smaller rooms. $ *Rooms from: 1060 Kn* ✉ *Trg Andrea Antico 7* ☎ *052/681–607, 052/681–735* ⊕ *www.hotel-kastel-motovun.hr* ⊘ *Closed Jan.–Apr.* 🛏 *33 rooms* ⦿ *Free breakfast.*

★ Roxanich Wine & Heritage Hotel

$$ | **HOTEL** | **FAMILY** | A communal wine cellar until 1990, this Hapsburg-era stone building today houses a sophisticated hotel and restaurant to complement the high-tech family-run winery below. **Pros:** attentive friendly staff; stylish design; amazing location with breathtaking views. **Cons:** not for those who don't like wine; high beds can be challenging; long walk up to Motovun Old Town. $ *Rooms from: 830 Kn* ✉ *Kanal 30* ☎ *052/205–700* ⊕ *www.roxanich.hr* 🛏 *32 rooms* ⦿ *Free breakfast.*

Grožnjan

18 km (11 miles) northeast of Motovun.

Close to Motovun and a reasonable drive from Poreč, Novigrad, Rovinj, or Umag, Grožnjan is among Istria's preeminent and most beautiful hilltop towns. A Renaissance loggia adjoining the ancient town gate are must-see historical sites,

Exploring Inland Istria

Istria's interior hilltop towns have been much celebrated in recent years, both for their stunning beauty as well as their gastronomical traditions. We recommend renting a car, even for one day, for a drive into the interior in the late afternoon, when fewer tour buses are likely to be on the road. Aside from Motovun and Grožnjan, you'll find that Oprtalj, Roč, Hum, Buzet, and Gračišće are all picturesque villages with their own medieval churches, old clock towers, culinary specialties, and small-town restaurants.

but wandering through the narrow rustic stone streets, perusing the many boutiques, galleries, and ateliers makes this town a favorite for locals and visitors In 1358, after at least 250 years in existence as a walled city, Grožnjan came under Venetian rule and remained so for more than 400 years. Though most of its population left after World War II, when decades of Italian rule came to an end and it officially became part of Yugoslavia, from the mid-1960s the government encouraged artists and musicians to settle here. This explains the number of art studios, painting and ceramic ateliers, and sculpture galleries you will encounter as well as charming cafés with views of the sea or Mirna River Valley. Many art, antique, and music festivals take place, including an international federation of young musicians that meets for training and workshops, presenting concerts beneath the stars throughout July and August.

Truffles in Istria

On November 2, 1999, in the village of Livade near Motovun, Giancarlo Zigante and his sharp-nosed dog unearthed a record-breaking, 1.31-kilogram (2.89-pound) white truffle. What he foraged was the most delicious fungus you are likely to find.

Truffles grow underground, in a symbiotic relationship with the roots of oaks and certain other trees. As such, they cannot readily be seen. It is their scent that gives them away—a swoon-inducing scent. Sows were once the truffle hunter's favored companion, as truffles smell a lot like male hogs. (To be fair, the earthy aroma and pungent taste of truffles, which has also been likened to garlic, is prized by gourmands the world over.) These days, dogs are the truffle hunter's best friend.

Truffles are extremely rare. Most efforts to cultivate them domestically have failed, not least because you first need to grow a forest full of trees whose roots are just right for truffles. Prices fluctuate, but the white truffle, prized for its superior scent—the "white diamond," it's often called—sells for up to $10,000 a pound. In addition to the white truffle, Istria is also home to three sorts of black truffle, which sell for a mere $1,500 a pound.

In Istria truffles have been extracted since ancient times. Even Roman emperors and Austro-Hungarian aristocrats had a taste for truffles, not least because of the aphrodisiac qualities attributed to them. Truffles were once consumed and gathered like potatoes—that's how plentiful they were. That was in the 1800s. No longer, of course. Still, their fine shavings impart an unforgettable, earthy aroma and an irresistibly pungent, vaguely garlicky taste to pastas, salads, omelets, beef specialties, sauces, and more.

Economics and truffle scarcity being what they are, the Istrian truffle has become a hot commodity indeed. These days, for example, much of what is sold by Italy as Italian white truffles actually comes from Croatia—not least from the moist woods around Motovun and Buzet, near the river Mirna.

Karlić Tartufi The Karlic family has been truffle hunting for over half a century, and a visit to their estate in Paladini near Buzet is a must for aficionados of this rare fungus. The family offers truffle-hunting tours followed by truffle-inspired meals, and their shop sells a variety of truffle products, such as fresh and frozen black and white truffles and truffle-infused olive oil, honey, and various tapenades. ⊠ *Paladini 14, Village Paladini, Buzet* ☎ *052/667–304* ⊕ *www. karlictartufi.hr* ⊠ *From 490 Kn.*

Istriana Travel If you'd like to join a truffle hunt, reserve a spot on a truffle-hunting excursion that departs from the village of Vrh from April to December. Accompanied by an English-speaking guide, you'll meet a truffle hunter and his trained truffle-sniffing dogs at the hunter's house, spend 45 minutes hunting in the woods, and enjoy a light lunch or dinner made with the truffles you unearthed. ⊠ *Vrh 46/3, Buzet* ☎ *052/667–022, 091/541–2099* ⊕ *www.trufflehuntingcroatia.com* ⊠ *From 415 Kn.*

GETTING HERE AND AROUND

The best way to get to Grožnjan is by car, as no buses connect it to Pula or other coastal towns. This small hilltop town is best explored on foot with plenty of time to sit and enjoy the view from one of the cafés perched on the outside ring of the city walls.

🍴 Restaurants

San Servolo Steakhouse, Resort & Beer Spa
$$$$ | **STEAKHOUSE** | It's always time for a cold one in this tavern and steakhouse tucked in the rolling hills between Buje and Grožnjan. The menu includes a tasty selection of six unfiltered and unpasteurized Istrian craft beers alongside an expansive menu of grilled meats and other hearty Istrian dishes. **Known for:** local craft beer; grilled meat; stunning views. [$] *Average main: 130 Kn* ✉ *Momjanska ulica 7, just outside Buje, 9 km (6 miles) northwest of Grožnjan, Momjan* ☎ *052/772–505* 🌐 *sanservoloresort.com* 🕒 *No lunch Mon.–Tues.*

🛏 Hotels

★ Bolara 60 Guesthouse
$ | **B&B/INN** | **FAMILY** | In a tiny village just below Grožnjan, you'll find Bolara 60, a lovingly restored 18th-century stone farmhouse within peaceful rolling hills, vineyards, and olive groves. **Pros:** Charming, welcoming hosts; incredible, homemade food; rooms in the main house and private 2-story house next door. **Cons:** shared bathrooms; 30-minute drive to the beach; healthy walk or ride uphill to town. [$] *Rooms from: 750 Kn* ✉ *Bolara 60* ☎ *052/894–5847* 🌐 *www.bolara60.com* 🛏 *6 rooms* 🍽 *Free breakfast.*

★ San Canzian Village & Hotel
$$$ | **HOTEL** | A luxurious boutique hotel has been created from several old houses found in the medieval village of Mužolini Donji, near Buje, Momjan, and Grožnjan. **Pros:** high-style interiors throughout; excellent restaurant with a knowledgeable sommelier; peaceful and restorative energy. **Cons:** more spa services needed; changing chefs; a drive to the beach. [$] *Rooms from: 2000 Kn* ✉ *Muzolini Donji 7* ☎ *052/302–0000* 🌐 *san-canzian.hr* 🕒 *Closed Jan.–Mar.* 🛏 *24 rooms* 🍽 *Free breakfast.*

Oprtalj and Završje 👁

As you near Grožnjan, you can take a small detour to the picturesque hilltop villages of Oprtalj and Završje. Take a stroll around Oprtalj's hushed little streets and central loggia, where the 15th-century church of Sveti Juraj and 16th-century bell tower still stand. Just a bit farther, halfway between Oprtalj and Grožnjan, mystical Završje is almost deserted today. Large houses covered in creeping ivy, as well as the town gate, a leaning tower, and the remains of defensive walls, were witnesses to Završje's past glory.

🛍 Shopping

Zigante Tartufi
FOOD/CANDY | Tourists visit the charming hilltop town of Grožnjan to enjoy its rustic beauty, art and crafts, and music programs. There's enough tourism, in fact, to merit yet another outlet of the family-owned Zigante Tartufi chain. The shop sells locally unearthed truffles and everything truffle-related you can possibly imagine, as well as other local products from aromatic herb brandies to honey, dried porcini mushrooms, wine, and olive oil. The gourmet boutique is near the town's loggia. Just follow your nose. ✉ *Ulica Gorjan 5* ☎ *052/776–099* 🌐 *www.zigantetartufi.hr* 🕒 *Closed Nov.–Mar.*

Labin-Rabac

Labin is 44 km (28 miles) northeast of Pula.

More travelers are taking time to explore Istria's newest must-stay tourist destination, Labin-Rabac. Located on the eastern coast, these sister towns offer the perfect combination of historic hilltop town (Labin) and beachfront resort town (Rabac) just four kilometers below. Beautiful blue flag beaches are surrounded by lush green mountains that lend themselves to hiking and biking.

GETTING HERE AND AROUND

There are nine buses daily from Pula to Labin, from which you can easily reach Rabac by bus or taxi. The best way to get around Rabac and Labin is on foot. Electric tourist trains in Rabac run from one end of the coastal town to the other; in other words, from Maslenica Hotel to Girandella Resort, from mid-June to mid-September. Of course, having your own car will allow you to move from town to town with ease.

◉ Sights

★ Labin

TOWN | FAMILY | Perched in all its compact medieval redolence atop a hill a short drive or walk from the sea, Labin is Croatia's former coal mining capital and the birthplace of Matthias Flacius Illyricus, a Reformation-era collaborator of Martin Luther. Its narrow, historic streets are well deserving of a good walk—followed, if time allows, by a dip in the sea at Rabac, the coastal beach town just 3 km (2 miles) below, filled with hotels, resorts, apartments, and villas to rent, and a vibrant promenade lined with cafés, restaurants, and family activities. From Labin's endearing little main square, **Titov trg,** with its 16th-century loggia and bastion, it's an easy stroll to **Šetalište San Marco**, a semicircular promenade

with a spectacular view of the sea. Walk to the end and take a sharp left up the cobblestone road. Once you reach the top of the hill, you can climb another 98½ feet up for an even better view from the town's onetime fortress, the **Fortica.** Making your way down the other side of the hill back toward the main square, you will pass the **Crkva Rođenja Blažene Djevice Marije** (Church of the Birth of the Virgin Mary). With a facade featuring a 14th-century rose window and a 17th-century Venetian lion of the sort you will encounter elsewhere in Istria, the church is a mix of architectural styles dating back to a late-16th-century renovation, though its foundations may date to the 11th century. Dotted throughout Old Town Labin are working art studios, souvenir shops, museums, and galleries. In July and August, the Labin Art Republika hosts art openings, live musical concerts and outdoor films. ⊠ *Labin ⊕ www.rabac-labin.com.*

★ Rabac

TOWN | FAMILY | With its beautiful aqua blue bay and splendid, natural surroundings down rocky cliffs that call to mind the Amalfi Coast, the seaside resort town of Rabac has transformed from a quiet, 17th-century fishermen's village into one of the most popular tourist destinations in Istria. Perfectly situated just 3 kms below Old Town Labin and equidistant from Opatija and Pula, Rabac offers an endless number of white pebble beaches and untouched nature ideal for hiking, biking, kayaking, windsurfing, fishing, diving, and exploring. Many hotels, resorts, boutique hotels, villas, apartments, and campgrounds host international tourists looking for family-friendly holiday experiences. Yet, despite its growing popularity, Rabac still manages to transmit the same casual coastal charm and welcoming spirit of that 17th-century village it once was. An added bonus is having the medieval hilltop town of Labin just 10 minutes up the road, where its numerous chic restaurants, live music programs, art galleries, and historical sites further enrich your holiday. ✉ *Rabac* 🌐 *www.rabac-labin.com.*

🍴 Restaurants

Burra Bistro & Pizzeria

$$ | **CAFÉ** | **FAMILY** | This casual, upbeat eatery in Old Town Plomin, just 12 km (8 miles) north of Labin, is worth a stop for a decadent burger, Asian stir-fry, spicy wings, steaming plate of pasta, or cheesy pizza. Better yet, order one of the many craft beers or sample a delicious homemade dessert (or three). **Known for:** cozy atmosphere; friendly staff; delicious international comfort food. [$] *Average main: 65 Kn* ✉ *Plomin 1, Labin* ☎ *052/204–330* 🕓 *Closed Mon.*

Due Fratelli

$$$$ | **MEDITERRANEAN** | **FAMILY** | When the family is not catching fish, they are preparing it at their well-regarded, folksy restaurant with a cool, grapevine-shaded, family-friendy terrace. The menu offers fresh, delicious seafood specialties like grilled squid, mussels alla buzzara, and a good selection of grilled steaks and poultry dishes. **Known for:** fresh fish; traditional Istrian dishes; relaxed atmosphere. [$] *Average main: 110 Kn* ✉ *Montozi 6, Labin* ☎ *052/853–577* 🌐 *www.due-fratelli.com* 🕓 *Closed Mon. Oct.–May. Closed Jan.*

★ Pizzeria Rumore

$$ | **ITALIAN** | **FAMILY** | Rumore, which means "noise" in Italian, is both lauded and popular. The terrace offers outstanding views of Rabac and the Kvarner Bay. **Known for:** traditional Neapolitan-style pizza; charming terrace on piazza with stunning views; fast, friendly service. [$] *Average main: 70 Kn* ✉ *Šetalište San Marco bb., Labin* ☎ *052/686–615* 🌐 *www.facebook.com/PizzeriaRumore/.*

Velo Kafe

$$$ | **INTERNATIONAL** | **FAMILY** | Whether it be a coffee, homemade cake, or hand-crafted gelato enjoyed on the shady ground-floor terrace, a gourmet dinner on the first-floor balcony, or hearty Istrian comfort food in the cozy lower-level tavern, it's all to be found at this popular restaurant located in the heart of Old Town Labin on Titov Trg, Labin's main square. The locally inspired menu is extensive and includes specialties like nettle gnocchi with salmon, steak in black-truffle sauce, branzino al forno, and hand-rolled pasta with foraged mushrooms. **Known for:** three floors, three experiences (café, restaurant, and tavern); great location with large outdoor spaces; homemade cakes and gelato. [$] *Average main: 120 Kn* ✉ *Titov Trg 12, Labin* ☎ *052/852–745* 🌐 *www.velokafe.com.*

Vorichi Osteria Mediteraneo

$$$ | **MEDITERRANEAN** | **FAMILY** | For those staying in or visiting Labin-Rabac, make sure to reserve a much-desired table at Vorichi Osteria in the little village of Orihi, between Barban and Svetivincenat, just 22 km (14 miles) from Old Town Labin as you head towards Rovinj. This hidden culinary gem is serving up modern Mediterranean food in an open-air garden setting, with orders for dinner taken by Tamara, the owner, as she joins you for a glass of Malvazija wine or Aperol spritz. **Known for:** relaxed, garden setting; freshest, local ingredients; incredible wine selection. [$] *Average main: 150* ✉ *Orihi bb, Svetvincenat* ☎ *099/229–4300* 🌐 *vorichi.com* 🕓 *Closed Nov.-Apr.*

🛏 Hotels

Girandella Valamar Collection Resort

$$$$ | **RESORT** | **FAMILY** | Offering three different sections (family hotel, adults-only hotel, and private villas) with shared facilities, this resort is 100 meters from the most beautiful blue-flag Istrian beaches. **Pros:** outstanding panoramic views of the

sea; six restaurants on-site; extensive kids' programs and on-site babysitting. **Cons:** rooms can be small; a large resort that can seem impersonal; lots of kids in all but the adults-only section. $ *Rooms from: 2195 Kn* ✉ *Ulica Girandella 7, Rabac* ☎ *052/465–000* ⊕ *www.valamar.com/en/hotels-rabac/valamar-girandella-resort* ☉ *Closed Nov.–Apr.* ⮐ *173 rooms* ⓧ *Free breakfast.*

Hotel Adoral

$$$ | HOTEL | This family-run hotel has an excellent location right across the seafront promenade just a few yards from the water, and its spacious, modern, and well-equipped rooms have balconies overlooking the sea. **Pros:** location right at the seafront; modern, stylish, and spacious rooms; great for business travelers. **Cons:** only street parking; needs more on-site options for bar or food service; ground-floor rooms have only partial sea views. $ *Rooms from: 1510 Kn* ✉ *Obala M. Tita 2a, Rabac* ☎ *052/535–840* ⊕ *www.adoral-hotel.com* ⮐ *15 rooms* ⓧ *Free breakfast.*

★ Hotel Peteani

$$ | HOTEL | On the main road leading up to Labin's Old Town, this stylish boutique hotel offers fresh and playful designer interiors in a beautifully renovated palazzo with throughtful facilities at the ready such as saunas, steambaths, bicycles, and one of the absolute best restaurants in town. **Pros:** small and friendly hotel; free parking; excellent on-site restaurant. **Cons:** some traffic noise in street-facing rooms; slightly apart from the main square; in-house family activities are minimal. $ *Rooms from: 1135 Kn* ✉ *Aldo Negri 9, Labin* ☎ *052/863–404* ⊕ *www.hotel-peteani.hr* ⮐ *14 rooms* ⓧ *Free breakfast.*

La Loggia Hotel

$ | HOTEL | FAMILY | Right on the main square (Titov trg) in the heart of Old Town Labin, La Loggia is a charming boutique hotel that offers both panoramic sea and picturesque city views. **Pros:** good sea or square views; breakfast on the terrace has great sea views; large modern bathrooms. **Cons:** some rooms hear street noise in the morning; no food other than breakfast; 10-minute drive to beaches. $ *Rooms from: 685 Kn* ✉ *Titov Trg 3/1, Labin* ☎ *052/431–492* ⊕ *www.laloggiahotel.com* ⮐ *9 rooms* ⓧ *Free breakfast.*

Terra Residence

$ | B&B/INN | For those desiring an apartment-like stay but also with maid service and a shared lounge, dining room, and garden, the sophisticated Terra Residenza is for you. **Pros:** sexy, romantic interiors; near restaurants and cafes in Old Town Labin; quiet, private location. **Cons:** no elevator, only stairs; rooms can seem dark; pets are not allowed. $ *Rooms from: 685 Kn* ✉ *Bože Štemberga 2, Labin* ☎ *091/882–5615* ⊕ *www.facebook.com/terraresidencelabin* ⮐ *8 rooms* ⓧ *Free breakfast.*

Chapter 8

ZAGREB AND
INLAND CROATIA

Updated by
Lara Rasin

⊙ Sights	🍴 Restaurants	🛏 Hotels	🛍 Shopping	🍸 Nightlife
★★★★★	★★★★☆	★★★☆☆	★★★☆☆	★★★★☆

WELCOME TO ZAGREB AND INLAND CROATIA

TOP REASONS TO GO

★ **Walkable Zagreb:** With lovely parks, squares, museums, and churches at every corner, exploring the compact Old Town of Croatia's capital is an unforgettable experience.

★ **Sparkling waterfalls:** Plitvice Lakes National Park, a UNESCO World Heritage site, is one of Croatia's most visited destinations, with over 16 crystal-clear turquoise lakes connected by waterfalls and cascades.

★ **Fairytale villages:** Idyllic countryside villages dot the expanse of inland Croatia, and each has charming farmlands, wooden architecture, and ever-smoking cooking chimneys.

★ **Baroque beauty:** Cities like Čakovec and Varaždin offer some of the most beautiful and well-preserved Baroque architecture in this corner of the continent.

★ **Unique cuisine:** This region is a historical crossroads of cultures with the cuisine to prove it. Here, you'll get everything from fresh seafood to hearty fare centering on meats and spices.

With the exception of the vast plains of Slavonia that stretch to the east, the rest of the inland region, with Zagreb as its approximate center, can be divided into two parts: north and south. To the north is the hilly, castle-rich Zagorje region; the smaller, often-overlooked Međimurje region; and, just a tram and bus ride from the city center, the hiking trails and ski slopes of Sljeme. To the south is the mountainous route to the coast that includes Karlovac, a regional center, as well as Croatia's most visited national park, Plitvice Lakes; and a second route along the less-traveled banks of the Sava River to Lonjsko Polje Nature Park, one of Europe's largest and best preserved wetlands.

1 Zagreb. Croatia's capital city.

2 Sljeme. Mt. Medvednica's peak.

3 Marija Bistrica. A Catholic pilgrimage site.

4 Veliki Tabor. A medieval hilltop castle dating to the 15th century.

5 Krapina. An idyllic village, home to the biggest Neanderthal archeological site in the world.

6 Trakošćan. A hilltop castle dating to the 13th century, surrounded by a lake and walking trails.

7 Varaždin. A charming Baroque town.

8 Čakovec and Međimurje. A beautiful town and small region with pretty landscapes and interesting architecture.

9 Samobor. A pretty town with 13-century castle ruins, also known for its delicious desserts.

10 Karlovac. An industrial city at the crossroads of three major rivers and home to one of Croatia's most popular brews.

11 Plitvice Lakes National Park. Croatia's first national park and a stunning collection of lakes and waterfalls.

12 Sisak. The biggest city in Sisak-Moslavina County, dotted with walkways, sculptures, and interesting architecture.

13 Čigoć. Home to a multitude of migrating storks and the beautiful Lonjsko Poje Nature Park.

14 Jasenovac. The site of Croatia's most notorious World War II labor camps.

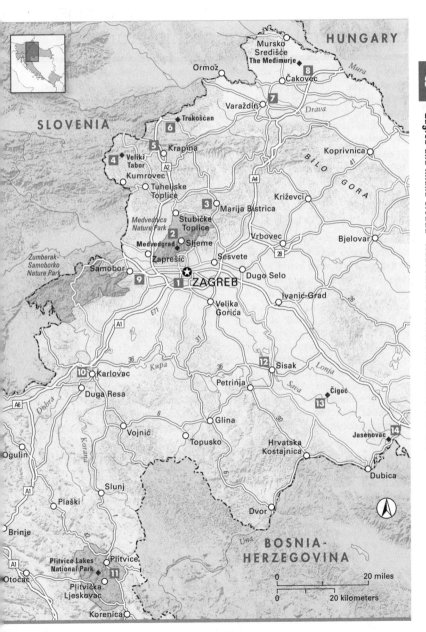

HUNGARY

Mursko
Središče
The Međimurje
Ormož
Mura
8
Čakovec
7
Varaždin
Drava
SLOVENIA
Trakošćan
6
Koprivnica
Krapina
5
Veliki
Tabor
4
A2
Kumrovec
A4
BILO
Tuheljske
Toplice
GORA
3
Marija Bistrica
Križevci
Medvednica
Nature Park
Stubičke
Toplice
2
Sljeme
Vrbovec
Bjelovar
Medvedgrad
Zaprešić
Sesvete
28
Žumberak-
Samoborko
Nature Park
Samobor
9
Dugo Selo
1
ZAGREB
Velika
Gorića
Ivanić-Grad
A1
E71
Kupa
Sisak
12
Karlovac
10
Lonja
Duga Resa
Petrinja
Sava
A6
Dobra
Čigoč
13
Glina
Vojnić
Topusko
Jasenovac
14
Ogulin
Hrvatska
Kostajnica
A1
Slunj
Dubica
Plaški
Dvor
Brinje
Una
BOSNIA-
HERZEGOVINA
Plitvice Lakes
National Park
Plitvice
Otočac
11
Plitvička
Ljeskovac
0   20 miles
0   20 kilometers
Korenica

Zagreb has become a full-fledged hot spot in tourism in recent years, thanks to its year-round festivals, world-class cuisine, and historic architecture.

Travelers who still make a beeline to the coast will miss out on the fact that much of the country's natural beauty and cultural heritage is rooted in places well inland from the sea. Unless you arrive overland from Slovenia, by boat from Italy, or by one of the air routes that deliver you straight to the coast, chances are that your first encounter with Croatia will be Zagreb, an eminently strollable capital city of attractive parks, squares, and museums.

Whether you're planning on hightailing it to the coast or staying inland, stay a few days here to explore the urban capital's historic center and pastoral environs. Even if you've already been lucky enough to explore the region, there are always more secret surprises waiting to be discovered. With its historic center on the northern bank of the Sava River, Zagreb has a fully walkable Old Town, inviting public spaces, grand architecture in a variety of historic styles, and a rich array of eateries, churches and museums that will lure you down small side streets.

kicks off hiking season, with plenty of treks and their blooming greenery waiting at the ready all throughout the region. Summertime in Zagreb is a special affair, when festivals pop up in almost every neighborhood, from big-name music fests to smaller-scale art and food events. Fall means foggy days made colorful by the foliage waiting to be explored around inland Croatia's hills, one of the prettiest areas being the Žumberak Mountains near Samobor.

No matter the time of year, there's never a shortage of things to do in Zagreb. Music, art, and food festivals take place across the city all year long. Outdoors activities, from hiking on Sljeme and jogging on the Sava riverbanks to kayaking on Jarun Lake are at your fingertips. Between that and a vibrant nightlife scene consisting of everything from buzzing clubs to underground live gigs, as well as hard-to-beat museums and cultural outings, this is a city you're not likely to be bored in, even if you're just sipping coffee in a café and people-watching.

Planning

When to Go

Zagreb and its environs are well worth a visit at any time of year, with each season bringing a different type of delight. Winter means skiing on Sljeme and enjoying the lively Zagreb Advent Market—continuously voted best or among the best Christmas markets in Europe. Spring

Getting Here and Around

AIR

Zagreb International Airport (ZAG) is actually located in the city of Velika Gorica, 17 km (10 miles) southeast of Zagreb's center.

There are no direct flights between the United States and Zagreb, but over 25 airlines, including Croatia Airlines and several major European carriers, connect Zagreb with the rest of the world. Croatia

Airlines usually operates at least two flights daily to Split (45 minutes), two flights daily to Dubrovnik (55 minutes), and two flights daily to Osijek (45 minutes). Internationally, there are usually regular flights to Frankfurt (1 hour, 25 minutes), Brussels (2 hours, 5 minutes), Paris (1 hour, 50 minutes), London (2 hours, 15 minutes), and more.

A regular shuttle bus runs from the airport to the main bus station, and vice versa, every 30 minutes to 1 hour, usually from 4:30 am to 8:30 pm, with some breaks in between. Check the timetables before you arrive. A one-way ticket costs 30 Kn, and the trip takes 30 minutes. By taxi, expect to pay 150 Kn to 250 Kn to make the same journey; the trip will be slightly faster and will take you directly to your destination.

AIRPORT CONTACTS Zagreb International Airport. (*Franjo Tuđman Airport Zagreb*) ⊠ *Rudolfa Fizira 21, Velika Gorica* ☎ *01/456–2222 general info, 060/320–320 within Croatia, 3851/456–2170 outside Croatia* ⊕ *www.zagreb-airport.hr/en.*

AIRPORT TRANSFER CONTACTS Pleso Transfer. (*Pleso Prijevoz*) ⊠ *Pleso prijevoz, Avenija Marina Držića 4, Zagreb* ☎ *01/633–1982* ⊕ *www.plesoprijevoz.hr.*

BUS

Frequent coach services to destinations all over mainland Croatia depart from the capital. The traveling time is around 6 hours from Zagreb to Split and between 9 and 12 hours from Zagreb to Dubrovnik. There are also daily international bus lines to Slovenia (Ljubljana), Serbia (Belgrade), Austria (Graz and Vienna), Germany (Munich, Stuttgart, Frankfurt, Dortmund, and Düsseldorf), Italy (Trieste, Verona, and Milan), and Switzerland (Zurich). Timetable information is available from the main bus station (Autobusni Kolodvor Zagreb), a 25-minute walk from the main square.

About 30 buses run daily between Zagreb and Karlovac in just under an hour and for a one-way fare of around 45 Kn.

Samobor is an hour bus ride from Zagreb; about 50 buses between Zagreb and Samobor run daily. The fare is around 30 Kn each way, and Samobor's small bus station is about 1 km (½ mile) north of the main square.

There are daily direct buses to Plitvice Lakes National Park. Some buses between Zagreb and Split will stop at both entrances to Plitvice Lakes National Park; the fare is around 95 Kn one-way between Zagreb and Plitvice.

About 20 buses depart daily from Zagreb to Sisak, with a travel time under 1 hour and an approximate 30 Kn cost for a one-way ticket.

There are around 15 buses from Zagreb to Varaždin daily, with a travel time of around 90 minutes, and a one-way ticket cost of 85 Kn. Just under 10 buses connect Zagreb with Čakovec, taking around 2 hours and costing about 100 Kn in one direction.

CONTACTS Varaždin Bus Station. (*Autobusni kolodvor Varaždin*) ⊠ *Zrinskih i Frankopana BB, Varaždin* ☎ *042/407–888.* **Zagreb Bus Station.** (*Autobusni kolodvor Zagreb*) ⊠ *Avenija Marina Držića 4, Zagreb* ☎ *072/500–400* ⊕ *www.akz.hr.*

BUS AND TRAM

An extensive network of city buses and trams—almost exclusively trams within the town center—runs 24 hours a day, with less frequent night service starting at approximately 11:30 pm and lasting until 5:30 am. Tickets for 4 Kn last in any direction for 30 minutes, 10 Kn for 90 minutes in any direction, and 15 Kn for a night-service ride. A full-day ticket (30 Kn), available at some kiosks, is valid until 4 am the next morning. As an alternative, you can buy the Zagreb Card for 98 Kn; this covers public transport within the city limits for 24 hours and offers substantial discounts at various museums and other cultural venues (for 72 hours, it's 135 Kn). After you board the bus or tram, you must validate your ticket with a time stamp (little yellow machines located only in the first and last cars of each tram). If you are caught without a valid ticket, you will be fined a minimum of 250 Kn, payable on the spot.

CONTACTS ZET. (*Zagreb Transit Authority*) ⊠ *Ozaljska 105, Zagreb* ☎ *13/651–555* ⊕ *www.zet.hr.*

CAR

Prices vary, and you will probably pay less if you rent from a local company that's not part of an international chain; it's best to shop around. You can find economy cars from 350 Kn per day, compact cars from 450 Kn per day, intermediate cars from 720 Kn per day, or standard cars from 850 Kn per day. If you can't drive a stick shift, be sure to double-check that the car you're renting has an automatic transmission. Prices usually include unlimited mileage, CDW (collision damage waiver), and TP (theft protection), but not PAI (personal accident insurance). If you drive one-way (say, from Zagreb to Dubrovnik), there is often an additional drop-off charge, but it depends on the type of car and the number of days you are renting. While staying in the capital you are better off without a car, but if you wish to venture out, for example, to visit the nearby hills of Zagorje, or go farther afield to the Međimurje region, a vehicle is helpful unless you want to take a bus to a different attraction each day.

TAXI

You can find taxi ranks in front of the bus and train stations, near the main square of Ban Jelačić, and often in front of large hotels. Several companies are available, including Radio Taxi, Eko Taxi, and Taxi Cammeo. It is also possible to order a taxi, or request your hotel order one for you. All drivers are bound by law to run a meter—but this doesn't necessarily mean they will unless you ask—and the price can vary from 10 Kn for a fixed start fee and from 3 Kn per km. You can also order Uber and Bolt within the city, and to and from the airport, as well. Most companies have the same prices for day and night riding, as well as for rides on Sundays and holidays. Most companies do not charge for luggage.

CONTACTS Eko Taxi. ⊠ *Vodovodna 20a, Zagreb* ☎ *01/549–9474* ⊕ *www.ekotaxi. hr.* **Radio Taxi.** ⊠ *Božidara Magovca 55* ☎ *16/600–671,* ⊕ *www.radiotaxizagreb. com/en.* **Taxi Cammeo.** ⊠ *Radnička cesta 27, Zagreb* ☎ *01/1212–211* ⊕ *www.cammeo.hr/en.*

TRAIN

Zagreb's main train station lies in the Lower Town, a 10-minute walk south from the main square of Ban Jelačić. There are regular international trains to and from Budapest (Hungary), Belgrade (Serbia), Ljubljana and Maribor (Slovenia), Munich (Germany), Vienna (Austria), Venice (Italy), Zürich (Switzerland), and beyond via easy connecting routes. From Zagreb there are multiple trains daily to Split in Dalmatia (6–8 hours) and to Rijeka in Kvarner (3½–4½ hours). The easiest way to get to Varaždin from Zagreb is by rail, with some 15 trains daily. Travel time is about 2½ hours and costs 65 Kn each way. About 15 trains run daily between Zagreb and Karlovac; you'll get there in just under an hour for a one-way fare of 37 Kn. If you don't have wheels, your best bet to reach Sisak is by rail for 34 Kn, with 15 trains daily from Zagreb that take just under an hour.

CONTACTS Čakovec Train Station. ⊠ *Kolodvorska 2, Cakovec* ☎ *040/384–333.* **Croatian Railways.** (*Hrvatske željeznice*) ⊠ *Strojarska 11, Donji Grad* ☎ *13/783–061* ⊕ *www.hzpp.hr/en.* **Karlovac Train Station.** ⊠ *Vilima Reinera 3, Karlovac* ☎ *060/333–444.* **Varaždin Train Station.** ⊠ *Kolodvorska 17, Varaždin* ☎ *060/333–444.* **Zagreb Train Station.** ⊠ *Trg kralja Tomislava 12, Donji Grad* ☎ *060/333–444.*

Restaurants

Due to Zagreb's proximity to the coast (under two hours at the closest point), fresh Adriatic fish fills up the city's marketplaces—and restaurants—daily. There are seafood restaurants in the other large inland towns too, though the offerings might be a bit less varied. Each inland region has its own delicious specialties, with many focused on roasted or fried meats accompanied by fresh salad and vegetable side dishes. For example, Zagorje is famous for duck with mlinci, while the Plitvice Lakes area is known for meaty dishes with wild game.

The influence of Austria to the northwest and Hungary to the northeast is evident in the form of hearty soups and stews like *varivo* (a thick broth with vegetables) and *gulaš* (the Croatian version of Hungarian goulash). Many restaurants also serve Italian-influenced pasta and pizza with added Croatian twists like Istrian truffles or Slavonian sausage. Other options include Turkish-influenced grilled meats such as *ćevapi* (seasoned minced meat links, often served with raw onions and pepper relish called *ajvar*), which are often lower in price than more elaborate main courses. Don't miss out on rich appetizers and desserts either. Doubling as both are the Zagorje region's famous *zagorski štrukli* (cheese dumplings)—served either baked or boiled, and salty or sweet. *Međimurska gibanica* (a triple-layer apple, sweet cheese, and poppyseed cake) is a must-try in Međimurje. Chocolate-, jam-, and sweet-cheese–filled *palačinke* (crepes) are on nearly every menu in the region too. If you head to Varaždin or a smaller town, prices will drop somewhat.

Hotels

With around 1.5 million tourists per year, Zagreb is Croatia's most-visited city, though it may not seem like it if you're wandering a crowded coastal town in mid-July. But Zagreb has the top-notch hotels and hostels to prove it, catering to any range of budgets. Rates of 1,100 Kn or (much) more for a double room are not uncommon, though there is a range of chic hostels and apartments available for rent that are comfortable, modern, and more budget-friendly. Smaller towns and the countryside, as a whole, do still offer cheaper options than the capital, with affordable private rooms and agritourism-style accommodations aplenty.

Restaurant and hotel reviews have been shortened. For full information, visit Fodors.com. Restaurant prices are the average cost of a main course at dinner or, if dinner is not served, at lunch. Hotel prices are the lowest cost of a standard double room in high season.

What It Costs in Croatian kuna (Kn)			
$	$$	$$$	$$$$
RESTAURANTS			
under 65 Kn	65 Kn–125 Kn	126 Kn–200 Kn	over 200 Kn
HOTELS			
under 800 Kn	800 Kn–1,450 Kn	1,451 Kn–2,000 Kn	over 2,000 Kn

Tours

The tourist information centers inside the Zagreb Train Station and on the main square (Trg bana Jelačića 11) give information on fun and informative guided tours of the city and surroundings.

Secret Zagreb

GUIDED TOURS | A tour with Secret Zagreb is one of the most unique ways to get to know Zagreb. Your personal tour guide will be Iva Silla, a passionate local who will show you around Zagreb while teaching and often engaging in games as you go. Secret Zagreb tours include the two-hour "Mysterious Zagreb: Ghosts & Dragons", the two-hour "Badass Women of Zagreb", and the "Zagreb Christmas Carol" (available only in December)". Each of these small group tours runs twice a week, and tickets can be booked online. ⊠ Zagreb ☎ 097/673–8738 ⊕ www. secret-zagreb.com.

Segway City Tour Zagreb

GUIDED TOURS | For a state-of-the-art experience, hop on a Segway City Tour year-round. The 50-minute "Basic Ride" costs 250 Kn per person, the 180-minute "Leisure Tour" costs 500 Kn per person, the 150-minute "Walk'n'Talk Tour" costs 480 Kn per person, and the 130-minute "All Around Tour" costs 400 Kn per person. Each one offers a unique look into the city. ⊠ Zagreb ☎ 095/903–4227 ⊕ www.segwaycitytourzagreb.com.

ZET City Tours

BUS TOURS | Zagreb's open-top buses operate along three routes (red, green, and yellow) throughout the city. The red line (1-hour tour) operates within the narrow city center with six stops along the route. The green line (1½-hour tour) includes the best-known green oases of Zagreb with seven stops along the route. The yellow line (1½-hour tour) includes New Zagreb, the Mirogoj Cemetery, and more. Tickets are valid for an entire day, which is plenty of time to see most of Zagreb's most famous landmarks. This service is provided by the Zagreb Electric Tram Company (ZET) in cooperation with the Zagreb Tourist Board. The departure point is from Bakačeva Street on Kaptol. The red line departs at 10, noon, 2, and 4; the green line departs at noon and 3; and the yellow line at noon and 2:45. The 24-hour tickets costs 70 Kn for adults and 35 Kn for children under 18. For children under 7, it's free. You can purchase tickets from the driver or at a ZET office in the city (keep in mind, offices are closed on Sundays). ⊠ Zagreb ☎ 072/500–400 ⊕ www.zet.hr.

Visitor Information

Zagreb's main tourist information center is right on the main square, Trg Bana Josipa Jelačića. Smaller city offices are located in the train station.

CONTACTS **Čakovec Tourist Board.** ⊠ Kralja Tomislava 1, Cakovec ☎ 040/313–319, 040/313–365 ⊕ www.visitcakovec.com/kontakt. **Croatian National Tourist Board.** ⊠ Iblerov trg 10/IV, Zagreb ☎ 01/469–9333 ⊕ croatia.hr. **Plitvice Lakes National Park Information Office.** ⊠ Entrance No. 1 to NP Plitvička Jezera, Velika Poljana ☎ 053/776–798 Tourist Board office, 053/751-014 Information office ⊕ www.tzplitvice.hr. **Samobor Tourist Board.** ⊠ Trg Krajla Tomislava 5, Samobor ☎ 01/336–004 ⊕ www.samobor.hr. **Varaždin Tourist Board.** ⊠ Ivana Padovca 3, Varaždin ☎ 042/210–987 ⊕ www.tourism-varazdin.hr. **Zagreb Tourist Board.** ⊠ Ban Josip Jelačić Square, Donji Grad ☎ 01/481–4051, 01/481–4052, 01/481–4054 ⊕ www.infozagreb.hr.

Zagreb

The capital of Croatia, Zagreb has a population of over 800,000 people and is situated at the extreme edge of the Pannonian Basin. The city straddles the north and south banks of the Sava River and is nestled below Mount Medvednica. The area's Stone Age history has not yet yielded signs of any settlements, but archeologists have found serpentine tools that point to the region first being an area of transit. Archeological finds have confirmed that the area was definitely settled from the Neolithic Age on, also being home to the intriguing Vučedol and Vinkovci cultures of the Bronze Age. The largest Neanderthal settlement in the world is located in Krapina; today, you can learn all about it at the on-site museum.

During the first millenium BC, the region saw a number of different inhabitants. First came the Hallstatt Culture (proto-Illyrian tribes) and the La Tène Culture (proto-Celtic tribes). The ancient Roman government captured much of present-day Croatia in the second century BC. Fourteen km (8½ miles) from the Zagreb center, you can visit Andautonia, an old Roman town that left well-preserved ruins. Slavic tribes descended into the area from the north, inhabiting it starting around the 7th century AD. In 925 AD, King Tomislav became Croatia's first monarch.

One of central Europe's oldest towns, the area of Zagreb was first documented as an official diocese in 1094 AD. Two separate but adjacent towns once stood on the area of the city, Gradec (today the Upper Town) and Kaptol (today the Lower Town). Gradec was designated a free royal city by Croatian-Hungarian King Bela IV following Tatar attacks in 1242.

The capital and ruling seat of Croatia changed throughout the centuries. Zagreb was first mentioned as being the capital in 1557, but Varaždin served as the main city from 1767 to 1776 until a fire moved the government seat from Varaždin back to Zagreb. Kaptol and Gradec were put under a single city administration in 1850, officially becoming the city of Zagreb. The legendary Orient Express flourished during the late 1800s and early 1900s, with Zagreb being a main stop for passengers on the Paris-Venice-Istanbul line. Beautiful public buildings began popping up across the city, including the National Theater, the university, and various museums. Built in a grand style and interspersed by wide, tree-lined boulevards, parks, and gardens, these old buildings adorn the entire city center today.

Throughout the 20th century, Zagreb saw increasing industrialization coupled with urban expansion, and the high-rise suburb of Novi Zagreb was constructed south of the Sava. Today, Novi Zagreb is a bustling residential area home to Bundek Park and and the Museum of Contemporary Art. From 1990 to 2000, Zagreb was, like the rest of the country, suffering and then recovering from the War of Independence. That also included a transition period from the communist government of the Socialist Federal Republic of Yugoslavia, to a free market economy and the parliamentary constitutional government of the Republic of Croatia.

Over the past couple decades, Zagreb has undergone an economic bloom, highlighted by Croatia's ascension to the European Union in 2013. Today, Zagreb is home to several international companies and an exciting local entrepeneurial scene.

Modern Zagreb is divided into 17 city districts which span almost 700 square km (270 square miles). Each has a number of neat attractions; for example, Novi Zagreb encompasses Bundek Park and the Museum of Contemporary Art, Trešnjevka is home to Jarun Lake and the Technical Museum Nikola Tesla, and Podsljeme includes the Mirogoj, often called the most beautiful cemetery in Europe. Zagreb's historic city center is divided into two distinct districts: Gornji grad (Upper Town) and Donji grad (Lower Town). Upper Gornji grad is made up of winding cobbled streets and terra-cotta rooftops among which are some of the city's most famous sites such as St. Mark's Church and Square, the Strossmayer Promenade, and the Stone Gate. Lower Donji grad is where you'll find some of the city's most important 19th-century cultural institutions, including the National Theater and a number of museums, all in a fairly walkable (or tramable) distance. Anywhere in the city, you'll find top-notch restaurants and cafés.

GETTING HERE AND AROUND

After arriving via any one of the numerous flights from Germany (Frankfurt, Munich), United Kingdom (London), France (Paris), Austria (Vienna), Hungary (Budapest), or elsewhere, the best way to get into the city is by taxi or the economical airport shuttle. The best way to get around the city is by the efficient tram system, for which you can buy multiuse and all-day tourist cards online and at many hotels and hostels.

Gornji Grad (Upper Town)

The romantic hilltop area of Gornji grad dates back to medieval times, and is undoubtedly one of the loveliest parts of Zagreb.

Sights

Ban Jelačić Square (*Trg bana Jelačića*)
PLAZA | Buildings lining the square date from 1827 onward and include several fine examples of Secessionist architecture. The centerpiece is an equestrian statue of Ban Josip Jelačić, the first Croatian viceroy, erected in 1866. Originally facing north toward Hungary, against which Jelačić waged war as a commander in the Austrian Imperial Army, the statue was dismantled after World War II by the communist government, only to be reinstalled in 1990, this time facing south. The square, which is Zagreb's main one, features the Manduševac fountain located to the east. ✉ *Between Ilica to the west, Praška to the south, and Jurišićeva to the east, Gornji Grad.*

★ Croatian Museum of Naïve Art (*Hrvatski muzej naivne umjetnosti*)
MUSEUM | The Naïve school of painting dates back to the 1930s, and the museum features more than 1,600 works of untutored peasant artists, primarily from the village of Hlebine in Koprivnica Križevci County. Canvases by the highly esteemed Ivan Generalić dominate

The Zagreb Card

Sold both online and in 16 venues around town, including several major hotels, the Zagreb Card offers unlimited travel on public transport in the city and discounts of up to 50% at more than 30 museums and galleries, as well as discounts at the zoo, on parking and car rentals, and 20% discounts at many shops, restaurants, theaters, and concert halls. Considering the cost of similar cards in other European capitals, this is truly a bargain. It's valid for 24 or 72 hours (from the date and time stamped on the card) and costs 98 or 135 Kn.

here, though there are also paintings, drawings, sculptures, and prints by other noted members of the movement, plus a section devoted to foreigners working along similar lines. The museum sits on the second floor of the Raffay Palace. ✉ *Sv. Ćirila i Metoda 3, Gornji Grad* 📞 01/485–1911 ⊕ www.hmnu.hr 💲 A25 Kn.

Crkva svete Katarine (*St. Catherine's Church*)
RELIGIOUS SITE | Built for the Jesuit order between 1620 and 1632, this church is the most beautiful Baroque church in Zagreb. It is a one-nave church with six side chapels and a shrine. The vaults and the walls are decorated with pink and white stucco from 1732 as well as 18th-century illusionist paintings. The altars are the work of Francesco Robba and 17th-century Croatian artists. The church was thoroughly reconstructed after the 1880 earthquake, based on the design of Hermann Bollé. ✉ *Katarinin trg bb, Gornji Grad* 📞 01/489–8555 💲 *Free.*

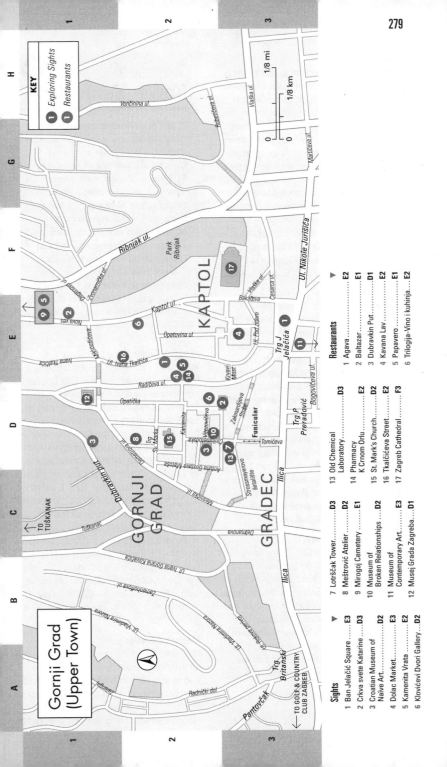

Gornji Grad (Upper Town)

KEY

- ① Exploring Sights
- ① Restaurants

GORNJI GRAD

GRADEC

KAPTOL

Sights ▶

1 Ban Jelačić Square	**E3**
2 Crkva svete Katarine	**D3**
3 Croatian Museum of Naïve Art	**D2**
4 Dolac Market	**E3**
5 Kamenita Vrata	**E2**
6 Klovićevi Dvori Gallery	**D2**
7 Lotršćak Tower	**D3**
8 Meštrović Atelier	**D2**
9 Mirogoj Cemetery	**E1**
10 Museum of Broken Relationships	**D2**
11 Museum of Contemporary Art	**E3**
12 Musej Grada Zagreba	**D1**
13 Old Chemical Laboratory	**D3**
14 Pharmacy K Crnom Orlu	**E2**
15 St. Mark's Church	**D2**
16 Tkalčićeva Street	**E2**
17 Zagreb Cathedral	**F3**

Restaurants ▶

1 Agava	**E2**
2 Baltazar	**E1**
3 Dubravkin Put	**D1**
4 Kavana Lav	**E2**
5 Papavero	**E1**
6 Trilogija-Vino i kuhinja	**E2**

Dolac Market

MARKET | Farmers from the surrounding countryside set up their stalls here daily, though the market is at its busiest on Saturday and Sunday mornings. On the upper level, fresh fruit and vegetables, along with flowers, traditional souvenirs, and artisan goods from honey to fresh juices, are displayed on an open-air piazza. Goods are sold under the protective shade of oversized umbrellas with a distinctive red color, known as *Šestinski kisobrani* (much smaller versions form part of the traditional garb of Zagreb's Šestine region). Dairy products and meats are sold in an indoor market below. ⊠ *Dolac 9, Gornji Grad* ⊕ *www.trznice-zg.hr.*

Kamenita Vrata (*Stone Gate*)

RELIGIOUS SITE | The original 13th-century city walls had four gates, of which only Kamenita Vrata remains. Deep inside the dark passageway, locals stop to pray before a small shrine adorned with flickering candles. In 1731 a devastating fire consumed all the wooden elements of the gate. Legend says that only a painting of the Virgin and Child, which was found in the ashes, remained remarkably undamaged. Kamenita Vrata has since become a pilgrimage site, as can be seen from the numerous stone plaques reading *Hvala Majko Božja* (Thank you, Mother of God). ⊠ *Kamenita Vrata, Gornji Grad* ⊕ *www.infozagreb.hr.*

Klovićevi Dvori Gallery

MUSEUM | Located off St. Catherine's Square, Klovićevi Dvori Gallery is Croatia's largest gallery institution. Among its three-floor exhibition space, international, local, classical, and modern exhibits are regularly held. Concerts are also often hosted in the gallery's beautiful atrium. Some of the city's best street art is hidden just behind the building as well. ⊠ *Jezuitski trg 4, Gornji Grad* ☎ *01/485–1926* ⊕ *www.gkd.hr.*

Lotrščak Tower Funicular 👁

If you're walking along Ilica from the main square, you might wonder about the best route up the hill to Lotrščak Tower and beyond to St. Mark's Church. Well, you can save yourself the steep hike up by catching the 66-meter (216-foot) funicular, which runs six times an hour, 6:30 am to 9:50 pm, from short Tomićeva ulica (just off Ilica) just a few hundred yards up the hillside. The cost is 5 Kn; you can buy the ticket when you board. Lasting just 64 seconds, this is the shortest funicular in the world.

Lotrščak Tower (*Kula Lotrščak*)

VIEWPOINT | Formerly the entrance to the fortified medieval Gradec, Kula Lotrščak now houses a multilevel gallery with occasional exhibits of contemporary art. Each day at noon a small cannon is fired from the top of the tower in memory of the times when it was used to warn of the possibility of an Ottoman attack. You can climb the tower partway, via a spiral wooden staircase, for a look into the gallery rooms (which occupy several floors), or you can ascend all the way to the observation deck for splendid views of Zagreb and its environs. You can also take the 66-meter (216-foot) Zagreb Funicular (the world's shortest) straight to the tower. ⊠ *Strossmayerovo šetalište, Gornji Grad* ☎ *01/485–1926* ⊕ *www.infozagreb.hr* ✉ *Observation deck 20 Kn; gallery free.*

Meštrović Atelier

MUSEUM | This 17th-century building, with its interior courtyard, served as home and studio to Ivan Meštrović from 1922 until his emigration to the United States in 1942. The building was extensively remodeled according to plans devised by the artist and was turned into a memorial museum with a permanent exhibition of his sculptures and drawings after his death in 1962. ✉ *Mletačka 8, Gornji Grad* ☎ *01/485–1123, 01/485–1124* ⊕ *www.mestrovic.hr* ✉ *40 Kn* ☾ *Closed Mon. and public holidays.*

Mirogoj Cemetery

CEMETERY | Designed by architect Herman Bollé and opened in 1872, Zagreb's most celebrated cemetery is set on a hillside north of downtown and features an imposing entrance: a long, massive brick wall topped by a row of striking green cupolas. This parklike cemetery, marked by paths lined with towering horse chestnut trees and by more black marble graves than you can count, is the final resting place for those of many creeds, from Roman Catholic and Serbian Orthodox to Jewish and Muslim. This satisfying if somber little outing can be had by catching Bus 106 or 226 on Kaptol, in front of the Zagreb Cathedral, and riding it about 10 minutes to the fifth stop, Arkade. ✉ *Aleja Hermanna Bollea 27* ⊕ *www.gradskagroblja.hr.*

★ Museum of Broken Relationships (*Muzej prekinutih veza*)

MUSEUM | The first museum of its kind in the world, this museum displays objects connected to love stories that didn't work out. The entire exhibition is made up of personal belongings donated by people from around the world who endured a failed relationship, and each exhibit is accompanied by a brief text, explaining the connection between the object and the relationship. Subtly illustrating the tragicomedy that is love, it is now one of Zagreb's most visited museums, and its collection has toured numerous locations in Asia, Africa, the U.S., and Europe. ✉ *Ćirilometodska 2, Gornji Grad* ☎ *01/485–1021* ⊕ *www.brokenships.com* ✉ *25 Kn.*

City Views

For sublime views east toward the Old Town, with its three prominent church steeples and many red-tile rooftops (including more than a few satellite dishes), stroll through the open wrought-iron gate just to the right of St. Catherine's Church. You'll find yourself on a spacious concrete plaza where you can take in the scene and then catch a flight of steps down past a lively café-bar toward Ilica.

Museum of Contemporary Art (*Muzej suvremene umjetnosti*)

MUSEUM | This long-awaited museum displays works created since 1950 by Croatian and foreign artists. It's well worth a visit for anyone interested in modern art—the vast collection includes paintings, sculptures, graphic design, films, and videos. It lies outside the city center. To get here, take Tram 6 from the Trg bana Jelačića (east direction); journey time is approximately 30 minutes. ✉ *Avenija Dubrovnik 17, Novi Zagreb* ☎ *01/605–2700* ⊕ *www.msu.hr* ✉ *30 Kn.*

Muzej Grada Zagreba (*Zagreb City Museum*)

MUSEUM | Well worth a visit for anyone interested in urban design, this museum traces the city's most important historical, economic, political, social, and cultural events from medieval times to the present day. Exhibits include detailed scale models of how the city has evolved, as well as sections devoted to the old trade guilds, domestic life, and sacred art. The museum also hosts a range of cool, temporary exhibits all year round; previous ones have included "Fashion and Clothing in Zagreb in the 1960s" and "Carnival Masks across the European Union". ✉ *Opatička 20, Gornji Grad* ☎ *01/485–1361, 01/485–1362*

The Museum of Broken Relationships contains artifacts donated from people around the world that tell the story of their failed love affairs.

🌐 *www.mgz.hr* ✉ *30 Kn* 🕐 *Closed Mon. and public holidays.*

Old Chemical Laboratory

HISTORIC SITE | Zagreb's bustling Strossmayer Promenade in Zagreb is best-known for hosting regular food and music festivals. But Stross also has a scientific secret up its sleeve. The Old Chemical Laboratory here was once used by two Croatian Nobel Prize-awarded chemists, Lavoslav Ružička and Vladimir Prelog. Visit for yourself to learn all about the lives and work of the scientists. ✉ *Strossmayerovo šetalište bb.*

Pharmacy K Crnom Orlu

HISTORIC SITE | Zagreb's oldest pharmacy is K Crnom Orlu (meaning "to the black eagle"), and it sits between the Stone Gate and St. Mark's Square. The pharmacy dates back to 1355. Local rumors say that pharmacist Nicolo Alighieri, great-grandson of Dante Alighieri, worked in K Crnom Orlu while he lived in Zagreb. ✉ *Kamenita 9, Gornji Grad.*

★ St. Mark's Church (*Crkva svetog Marka*)

RELIGIOUS SITE | The original building was erected in the 13th century and was once the parish church of Gradec. The Baroque bell tower was added in the 17th century, while the steeply pitched roof—decorated in brilliant, multicolored tiles arranged to depict the coats of arms of Zagreb on the right and the Kingdom of Croatia, Dalmatia, and Slavonia on the left—was added during reconstruction in the 19th century. It underwent another reconstruction in the first half of the 20th century. At that time, renowned painter Jozo Kljaković painted its walls, while the altar was decorated with works of famous sculptor Ivan Meštrović. ✉ *Trg Svetog Marka 5, Gornji Grad* ☎ *01/485–1611* 🎟 *Free.*

★ Tkalčićeva Street (*Tkalčićeva*)

PROMENADE | This street was once a stream until it was built over, but few people know that the water still flows beneath it. Today Tkalčićeva is a charming, well-maintained pedestrian zone lined with 19th-century town houses, many of which have been converted into popular café-bars at street level, attracting a huge cross section of locals and tourists from morning until late at night. ⊠ Tkalčićeva, Gornji Grad.

★ **Zagreb Cathedral** (Zagrebačka katedrala)
RELIGIOUS SITE | Dedicated to the Assumption of Mary and to the kings St. Stephen and St. Ladislaus, the Zagreb Cathedral was built on the site of a former 12th-century cathedral destroyed by the Tatars in 1242. The present structure was constructed between the 13th and 16th centuries. The striking neo-Gothic facade was added by architect Herman Bollé following the earthquake of 1880, its twin steeples being the identifying feature of the city's skyline. Behind the impressive main altar are crypts of Zagreb's archbishops and of Croatian national heroes. The interior is imposing and inspires silent reflection. Don't neglect the north wall, which bears an inscription of the Ten Commandments in 12th-century Glagolithic script. The cathedral's face is ever-changing, as its towers are being reconstructed again following the earthquake that hit Zagreb on March 22, 2020. ⊠ Kaptol 31, Gornji Grad ☎ 01/481–4727 ⊕ www.zg-nadbiskupija.hr ⌨ Free.

🍴 Restaurants

Croatia has seven Michelin-starred restaurants and countless recommended eateries, many of which are in Zagreb. There is an abundance of delicious, farm-to-table spots serving up authentic Croatian cuisine, as well as a number of international and fusion-oriented hotspots. For budget fare, traditional bakeries can be found on practically every street corner, offering sweet, savory, and salty pastries for as little as 5 Kn a piece.

Agava
$$$ | **MEDITERRANEAN** | Worth the steep walk up a flight of steps, in warm weather you can enjoy your meal sitting on the wooden terrace overlooking the street, or else bask in the homey elegance of the inside space, with its wood-beamed ceiling, parquet floor, and rattan furnishings. So sit back, relax, and enjoy almond croquant risotto (among a number of delicious risottos by head chef Belizar Miloš), pasta, seafood or interesting desserts, all in the style of Mediterranean haute cuisine. **Known for:** people-watching on the terrace; continental dishes; good value. $ Average main: 200 Kn ⊠ Tkalčićeva 39, Gornji Grad ☎ 01/482–9826 ⊕ www.restaurant-agava.hr.

Baltazar
$$$$ | **MEDITERRANEAN** | Nestled in a courtyard lying a 10-minute walk uphill beyond the cathedral, Baltazar is best known for barbecue classics of the region such as ražnjići (pork kebabs), čevapi (spiced ground-meat), and zapečeni grah (oven-baked beans). The interior is elegant, albeit slightly smoky, and the spacious courtyard has leaf-shaded seating. **Known for:** large barbecue platters; local wine list; expansive garden. $ Average main: 300 Kn ⊠ Nova ves 4, Gornji Grad ☎ 01/466–6999, 01/466–6824 ⊕ www.baltazar.hr.

★ Dubravkin Put
$$$ | **SEAFOOD** | Nestled in a verdant dale in Tuškanac Park, a 15-minute walk from the center in a low-rise building that might be mistaken for a ranch-style house, this prestigious fish restaurant specializes in creative Mediterranean fare, with the house favorites including buzara (stew prepared with shellfish and scampi and/or fish) and sea bass fillets in saffron and scampi sauce, as well as appetizers like avocado with scampi, not to mention a few meat delicacies. The dining room is light and airy, with candle-lit tables, a wooden floor, palmlike little trees, and colorful abstract art. **Known for:** location inside the park; excellent seafood; high-end service. $ Average main: 150 Kn ⊠ Dubravkin put 2 ☎ 01/483–4975 ⊕ www.dubravkin-put.com ⊗ Closed Sun., all of August.

★ Kavana Lav
$ | **CAFÉ** | Don't let the casual café fare fool you: this place, where you'll feel as if you were sitting in an art gallery or perhaps the living room of a wealthy, art-collecting uncle, is anything but standard. Located just up the hill (first right) from the Stone Gate, it is a perfect place to take a load off after the steep climb into Gornji Grad, before heading on to seeing the parliament, Museum of Broken Relationships, and St. Mark's Church. **Known for:** beautiful art collection; black and white modern decor; charming stone terrace. [$] *Average main: 35 Kn* ✉ *Opatička 2, Gornji Grad* ☎ *01/492–2108* 💳 *No credit cards.*

Papavero
$$ | **PIZZA** | This restaurant is the love child of married dynamic duo Ana, from Slavonia, and Pasquale, from Italy. Papavero uses fresh ingredients from both Italy and Croatia to make amazing pizza doughs and exciting topping combinations. **Known for:** great pizza; peaceful location; pet-friendly policy. [$] *Average main: 110 Kn* ✉ *Mlinovi 85A, Gornji Grad* ☎ *01/466-9328* 🌐 *www.papavero.hr.*

Trilogija-Vino i kuhinja
$$ | **MEDITERRANEAN** | This quaint, unpretentious restaurant offers superb food, an excellent wine list, and friendly, professional staff. The menu changes frequently depending on the seasons and what's fresh at the morning market, but you can expect creative dishes such as shrimp risotto with wild asparagus as well as a selection of wines including all of Croatia's best varieties. **Known for:** creative tapas; regular events; great wine list. [$] *Average main: 110 Kn* ✉ *Kaptol 10, Gornji Grad* ☎ *01/484–5336* 🌐 *www.facebook.com/trilogija.zagreb.*

Nightlife

Zagreb's bars, clubs, cinemas, and entertainment venues are occupied year-round. The city is also a hub for outdoor festivals throughout the year. For information about what's on, head to the Zagreb Tourist Board's website 🌐 *www.infozagreb.hr.*

Tuškanac
CULTURAL FESTIVALS | Located in a forested, hilly area, you would never think Tuškanac is part of Zagreb if you didn't know it. Over the summer, the 20th-century outdoor stage transforms into an open-air movie theater, airing a variety of flicks. The park is also home to a number of festivals, including the fun Pop-Up Summer Garden, which is centered around cool seating, food, and drink stands. The park also features a number of historic vacation villas once used by the city's artistocracy. ✉ *Dubravkin put bb, Gornji Grad* 🌐 *www.infozagreb.hr.*

Performing Arts

The Courtyards
CULTURAL FESTIVALS | At this annual summer event, some of Zagreb's most beautiful—and most secret—courtyards open their doors for guests. They include private historic villas, educational institutions such as the Institute of History, and government buildings. Each courtyard features live music (usually acoustic, jazz, or soft rock), finger food, and fun drinks. ✉ *Gornji Grad* 🌐 *www.facebook.com/dvorista.in.*

Kaptol Boutique Cinema and Bar
FILM | Sitting in the Centar Kaptol shopping complex, Kaptol Boutique Cinema and Bar is wedged in an area with a serene, parklike atmosphere a 10-minute walk north of the cathedral. Most foreign films (including those from the United States) are shown in their original language with Croatian subtitles. The cinema features a handful of showing rooms which are each uniquely desgined, and grabbing a coffee or drink in the establishment's designer bar before or after your movie is a must. ✉ *Nova Ves*

Tkalčićeva Street is a pedestrian-only area of Zagreb that appeals to visitors and locals alike.

17, Gornji Grad ☎ *01/639–6720* ⊕ *www. kaptolcinema.hr.*

★ Summer on Stross - Strossmartre

ARTS FESTIVALS | Embark on a journey toward the Strossmayer Promenade, next to the Lotrščak Tower, and you will see one of Zagreb's best entertainment projects. Strossmartre is arguably the most spirited spot in town, thanks to everything from the abundance of summer festivals to the much-awarded Advent in Zagreb offering concerts, exhibitions, art workshops, and great wine and beer deals all year-round. ⊠ *Strossmayerovo šetalište* ⊕ *www.infozagreb.hr.*

Zagreb Summer Tour

ARTS FESTIVALS | For the best free concerts in the park, street art, outdoor cinemas, and more, keep your eye out for the Zagreb Summer Tour. Highlights include performances by Croatian chamber orchestras, brass bands, and choirs, many of which take place at the music pavilion set amid the lovely plane trees and fountains of Zrinjevac Park. Taking place from June to September,

other must-sees are 19th-century-costume contests and displays, an antiques market, a play area and programs for children, pop-up art and design festivals, rides in horse-drawn carriages, and souvenir stands. Maksimir Park, east of the city center, also hosts a number of waltzes, polkas, chansons, and arias from operettas each summer. ⊠ *Zagreb* ⊕ *www.infozagreb.hr.*

👜 Shopping

A walk down the bustling Ilica or other nearby streets will take you past plenty of stores brimming with the latest fashions, as well as small-scale boutiques. Don't pass up the chance to stroll through the beautiful Oktogon shopping arcade, with its long, spacious yellow hall, elaborate wrought-iron gates at each end, and lovely glass ceilings from 1901. The arcade connects Ilica Street with Petar Preradović Square, and offers more than a few high-class shops along the way. In the center of the arcade, you'll find the elegant Croata, with its wide selection scarves, men's dress shirts, and, ...ably for the birthplace of the cravat, ...ountless variations on the classical necktie.

★ Bornstein Wine Bar (Vinoteka Bornstein)

SPECIALTY STORES | Housed in a tastefully arranged, vaulted brick cellar, Vinoteka Bornstein stocks a wide range of quality Croatian wines, olive oils, and truffle products. ⊠ Kaptol 19, Gornji Grad ☎ 01/481-2361 ⊕ www.bornstein.hr.

Donji Grad (Lower Town)

Part of the Lower Town's urban plan, which follows a grid pattern, was drawn up by Milan Lenuci. It combines a succession of squares and parks laid out in a horseshoe shape (hence its nickname, the Green Horseshoe), all overlooked by many of the city's stunning public buildings and cultural institutions.

Sights

Archaeological Museum (Arheološki muzej)

MUSEUM | Museum exhibits here range all the way from prehistoric times to the Middle Ages. Pride of place is given to the Vučedol Dove, a three-legged ceramic dove, dating back to the 4th millennium BC, and a piece of linen bearing the longest known text in ancient Etruscan writing. The courtyard features a collection of stone relics from Roman times. The museum also runs the Archaeological Park Andautonia, an ancient Roman town with well-preserved ruins located in the modern-day village of Ščitarjevo, just outside of Zagreb. ⊠ Trg Nikole Šubića Zrinskog 19, Donji Grad ☎ 01/487-3000 ⊕ www.amz.hr 🎟 30 Kn 🕙 Closed Mon. and public holidays.

Botanički Vrt (Botanical Garden)

GARDEN | Founded in 1889, Zagreb's Botanical Garden includes an arboretum with a regularly used exhibition space, a small artificial lake, and an ornamental bridge. Today, the museum has over 5,000 species of plants and is run by the prestigious Faculty of Science of the University of Zagreb. ⊠ Marulićev trg 9a, Donji Grad ☎ 01/489-8060 ⊕ hirc.botanic.hr/vrt/home.htm 🎟 Free.

★ Croatian National Theater in Zagreb (Hrvatsko narodno kazalište)

ARTS VENUE | The building dates from 1895, when it was designed by the Viennese firm Hellmer and Fellner as part of the preparations for a state visit by Emperor Franz Josef. In front of the theater, set deep in a round concrete basin, is Meštrović's little, eerily lifelike sculpture Zdenac Života (Fountain of Life), from 1912, which depicts four naked couples writhing uncomfortably in each other's arms around a small pool of water while one lone, likewise naked gentleman stares meditatively into the pool. The only way to see the impressive, stately interior of the theater is to attend a performance from its impressive show repetoire. Don your best clothes like the locals do and enjoy. ⊠ Trg maršala Tita 15, Donji Grad ☎ 01/488-8418 ⊕ www.hnk.hr.

★ Maksimir Park

BODY OF WATER | For a peaceful stroll in Zagreb's biggest and southeastern Europe's oldest public park, hop on a tram and head to Maksimir. A short ride east of the center of Zagreb (10 minutes on Tram 11 or 12 from Trg bana Jelačića or 15 minutes on Tram 4 or 7 from the train station), this 44½-acre expanse of vine-covered forests and several artificial lakes was a groundbreaker when it opened back in 1794. After getting off the tram, you walk forward a bit and enter on the left, through a prominent gate opposite the city's main soccer stadium, aptly named Stadion Maksimir. A long, wide promenade flanked by benches leads from here to Bellevue Pavilion (1843), perched atop a small hill and featuring a café. Be sure to check out the Echo Pavilion (Paviljon jeka), built in the late 19th century in honor of the Greek nymph Echo. Stand in the middle and you can hear the whispers of anyone standing within the pavilion, as if they were right next to you. To your right along the way are some small lakes and, beyond, the city's modest zoo, **Zoološki vrt Zagreb,** where admission is 30 Kn; it's open daily from 9 am to 5 pm (last tickets sold at 4 pm). To your left is a playground. ⊠ *Maksimir Park* ☎ *01/232–0460* ⊕ *www. park-maksimir.hr.*

Mimara Museum (*Muzej Mimara*)

MUSEUM | In a huge gray building that's dull compared to some of those nearby, this vast private collection, including paintings, sculptures, ceramics, textiles, and rugs, was donated by Ante Topić Mimara (1898–1987), a Croatian who spent many years abroad where he made his fortune, supposedly as a merchant. On display are canvases attributed to such old masters as Raphael, Rembrandt, and Rubens, as well as more modern works by the likes of Manet, Degas, and Renoir, and ancient artifacts including Egyptian glassware and Chinese porcelain. ⊠ *Rooseveltov trg 5, Donji Grad* ☎ *01/482–8100* ⊕ *www. mimara.hr* ⊠ *40 Kn* ⊗ *Closed Mon. and public holidays.*

Museum of Arts and Crafts (*Muzej za umjetnost i obrt*)

MUSEUM | Designed in 1888 by Herman Bollé, the architect responsible for the Zagreb Cathedral facade, this pleasant museum traces the development of the applied arts from the Baroque period to the 20th century. Exhibits are displayed in chronological order, and although furniture design predominates, there are also sections devoted to sacred art, clocks, and clothing. ⊠ *Trg maršala Tita 10, Donji Grad* ☎ *01/488–2111* ⊕ *www. muo.hr* ⊠ *40 Kn* ⊗ *Closed Mon. and public holidays.*

Strossmayer Gallery of Old Masters

(*Strossmayerova galerija starih majstora*)

MUSEUM | Now under the custody of the Croatian Academy of Sciences and Arts, this impressive gallery was founded in 1884 by Bishop Strossmayer and later expanded to include many private donations. Works by Venetian Renaissance and Baroque artists such as Bellini and Carpaccio predominate, but there are also masterpieces by Dutch painters Brueghel and Van Dyck, as well as a delightful Mary Magdalene by El Greco. ⊠ *Trg Nikole Šubića Zrinskog 11, Donji Grad* ☎ *01/489–5111* ⊕ *sgallery.hazu. hr* ⊠ *30 Kn* ⊗ *Closed Mon. and public holidays.*

Technical Museum Nikola Tesla (*Tehnički muzej Nikola Tesla*)

MUSEUM | FAMILY | Situated within an industrial building, this museum is guaranteed to appeal to both children and adults interested in science. Try to visit n the afternoon on a weekday or in the late morning on the weekend, when a series of guided visits are offered. The highlight here is the demonstration of some of Nikola Tesla's inventions, which takes place weekdays at 3:30 pm and weekends at 11:30 am, but there's also the tour of a lifelike reconstruction of a coal mine at 3 pm on weekdays and 11 am on weekends, and a planetarium visit at 4 pm on weekdays, noon on weekends. That's not to mention all the various vehicles on display, as well as a fascinating historical exhibit of firefighting equipment including trucks, ladders, and hoses aplenty. ⊠ *Savska cesta 18, Donji Grad* ☎ *01/484–4050* ⊕ *www.tmnt.hr* ⊠ *Museum 20 Kn, planetarium 15 Kn extra.*

🍴 Restaurants

★ Amélie

$ | CAFÉ | For a cake and coffee experience that the French namesake of this cute little café would be proud of, pop into Amélie just down the hill from the

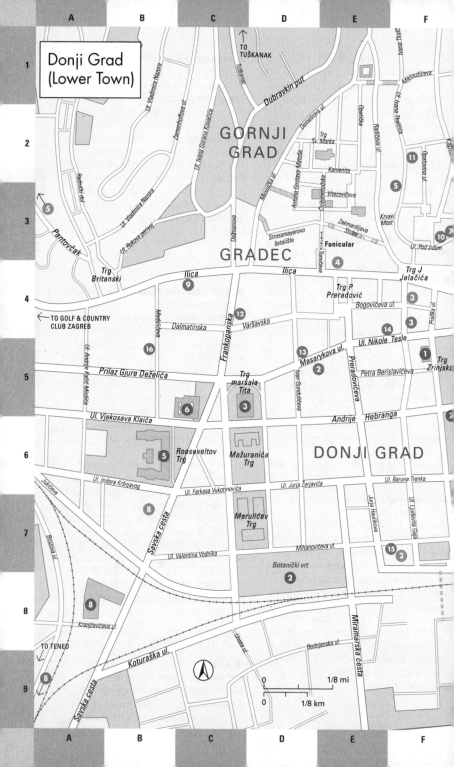

Donji Grad (Lower Town)

GORNJI GRAD

GRADEC

DONJI GRAD

TO TUŠKANAK

Dubravkin put

Trg Sv. Marka

Kamenita

Vitezovićeva

Strossmayerovo šetalište

Zakmardijeva Stube

Krvavi Most

Funicular

Trg Britanski

Ilica

Ilica

Trg J Jelačića

Trg P Preradović

Bogovićeva ul.

TO GOLF & COUNTRY CLUB ZAGREB

Dalmatinska

Varšavska

Ul. Nikole Tesle

Trg Zrinjsko

Prilaz Gjure Deželića

Trg maršala Tita

Petra Berislavićeva

Ul. Vjekosava Klaića

Andrije Hebranga

Rooseveltov Trg

Mažuranića Trg

Ul. Izidora Kršnjavog

Ul. Farkasa Vukotinovića

Ul. Jurja Žerjavića

Ul. Baruna Trenka

Marulićev Trg

Ul. Valentina Vodnika

Mihanovićeva ul.

Botanički vrt

TO TENEO

Kranjčevićeva ul.

Koturaška ul.

Savska cesta

Bednjanska ul.

0   1/8 mi

0   1/8 km

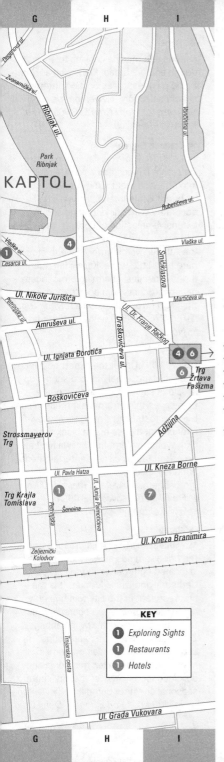

Sights ▼

1 Archaeological Museum F5
2 Botanički Vrt............. D8
3 Croatian National Theatre in Zagreb........C5
4 Maksimir Park.............I5
5 Mimara Museum B6
6 Museum of Arts and Crafts...........C5
7 Strossmayer Gallery of Old Masters F5
8 Technical Museum Nikola Tesla A8

Restaurants ▼

1 Amélie..................... G3
2 Beštija..................... D5
3 Boban F4
4 Bread Club............... G3
5 Cremme Zagreb.......... F3
6 El Toro...................... I5
7 Ficlek F3
8 Karibu Kaaawa........... A9
9 Pivnica Medvedgrad C4
10 Pod Zidom F3
11 Rocket Burger............ F2
12 Submarine................C4
13 Takenoko D5
14 Vinodol.................... E4
15 Zinfandel's Restaurant................ F7
16 Zrno Bio Bistro B5

Hotels ▼

1 Best Western Premier Hotel Astoria G6
2 Esplanade Zagreb F7
3 Hotel Dubrovnik.:......... F4
4 Hotel Jägerhorn E4
5 Hotel President Pantovcak A3
6 Le Premier.................I5
7 Sheraton Zagreb..........I6
8 The Westin Zagreb B7

Zagreb Cathedral. The wooden tables and cozy white interior give the place a charming, even slightly rustic feel, and the surprisingly varied selection of delectable cakes and pies will release all your caloric inhibitions. **Known for:** homemade everything; unique cakes; tasty quiches. $ *Average main: 35 Kn* ⊠ *Vlaška 6, Donji Grad* ☎ *01/558–3360* ⊕ *www.slasticeamelie.com.*

★ Beštija

$$ | EUROPEAN | Carnivores, pescatarians, and vegetarians will all find something to delight in at Beštija, which is located in a peaceful courtyard tucked away from the buzzing city center. Enjoy eating outside during the summer or head to the desinger interior, which features furniture procued by a local art dealer and a Picasso remake by academic painter Petra Potočnjak. **Known for:** fresh seafood from Dolac Market; modern interior design; house-made juices and desserts. $ *Average main: 110 Kn* ⊠ *Masarykova 11, Donji Grad* ☎ *091/324–0120* ⊕ *www.facebook.com/bestijazagreb.*

Boban

$$ | EUROPEAN | Just down the street from the Hotel Dubrovnik, Boban not only serves food at its street-level bar and dining room but also in its restaurant in the large vaulted cellar space below (with several tables outside for dining, chilling with a glass of Croatian wine, and people-watching). Specializing in pasta dishes, it is extremely popular with locals, so be prepared to line up for a table, since reservations are not accepted. **Known for:** popularity with locals; posh bar; hearty meals. $ *Average main: 95 Kn* ⊠ *Gajeva 9, Donji Grad* ☎ *01/481–1549* ⊕ *www.boban.hr.*

Bread Club

$ | BAKERY | Though it's nestled behind the Zagreb Cathedral, you'll still be able to smell the aromas of fresh-baked bread and warm pastries at the Bread Club from down the street. The bakery offers a range of baked goodies from PB&J cruffins and matcha cookies to sourdough and rye bread. **Known for:** all homemade pastries; great location; international food selection. $ *Average main: 35 Kn* ⊠ *Vlaška 27, Donji Grad* ☎ *01/655–1293* ⊕ *www.breadclub.eu.*

★ Cremme Zagreb

$ | CAFÉ | Think of your favorite bakery, ice cream parlor, and basic café rolled into one, and that's Cremme. With its bright white interior, its walls gaily decorated with quirky graffiti, and its extensive selection of cookies, brownies, and cakes hard to find on this side of the Atlantic, you'll simply have to stop here for a little while. **Known for:** mint fudge brownies; charming atmosphere; beauty products sold on-site. $ *Average main: 35 Kn* ⊠ *Tkalčićeva 21, Donji Grad* ☎ *091/276–0045* ⊕ *www.cremme.hr* ▭ *No credit cards.*

El Toro

$$$ | FUSION | Under the expert guidance of chef Mario Mihelj, El Toro serves up delicious Latin American fusion fare. Enjoy everything from roast meat to paella in the restaurant's romantically low-lit interior that blends matte black decor with wooden elements. **Known for:** Latin American fusion dishes; entertainment options including live music and DJs; chic atmosphere. $ *Average main: 140 Kn* ⊠ *Fra Filipa Grabovca 1* ☎ *099/613–2926* ⊕ *www.eltoro.hr.*

★ Ficlek

$$ | EUROPEAN | The latest creation behind the brilliant minds at Pod Zidom, Ficlek is located right between the Zagreb Cathedral and Dolac Market. It is the first resturant in the city to serve only authentic Zagreb fare prepared in traditional ways (think pasta with cabbage, Zagreb-style meat cuts, and soups cooked just like Croatian grandmas make them). **Known for:** traditional and delicious food; views of the city center; seasonal chestnut dumplings. $ *Average main: 100 Kn* ⊠ *Pod Zidom 5, Donji Grad*

Zagreb's stately Croatian National Theater dates from 1895.

☎ *099/495–8909* 🌐 *www.facebook.com/gostionicaficlek.*

Karibu Kaaawa

$ | **CAFÉ** | This is a gem of the Trešnjevka district, featuring a charming interior with wooden and geographic elements, as well as a small, tree-covered patio. Specialty coffee is offered, as well as a range of locally made sweet treats, such as vegan carrot cake. **Known for:** specialty coffee; proximity to the Trešnjevka Market; healthy desserts. [$] *Average main: 25 Kn* ✉ *Ozaljska 34* 🌐 *www.karibukaaawa.com* 💳 *No credit cards.*

Pivnica Medvedgrad

$$ | **EASTERN EUROPEAN** | Best known for its excellent beers brewed on the premises, all of the four Pivnica Medvedgrad locations serve up generous portions of roast meats, goulash, and beans and sausage, accompanied by a range of salads. The Ilica location and its the cavernous beer hall—replete with long wooden tables, high leather-backed chairs, and wood-beamed ceilings—is about a 10-minute walk west from the main square. **Known for:** local brews; hearty meals; beer-hall ambience. [$] *Average main: 85 Kn* ✉ *Ilica 49, Donji Grad* ☎ *01/484–6922* 🌐 *www.pivnica-medvedgrad.hr.*

★ **Pod Zidom**

$$$ | **EASTERN EUROPEAN** | Wedged between the cathedral and the Dolac farmer's market, jazzy bistro Pod Zidom offers a creative take on traditional Croatian dishes, making the most of fresh ingredients at its doorstep. The chef is renowned for his beef cheek, served up with a different sauce depending on the season and cooked for 12 hours before making it to your plate. **Known for:** farm-to-table fruits and vegetables; fresh organic meat; excellent selection of Croatian wines, including the restaurant's own. [$] *Average main: 130 Kn* ✉ *Pod Zidom 5* ☎ *099/325–3600.*

Rocket Burger

$$ | **AMERICAN** | This may well be the only place in Zagreb, if not the entire country, where you can get a relatively authentic American breakfast. Though

the establishment itself projects a limited dinner vibe, as it is forced to occupy a small closet-space of wire-rimmed tables and squat bar stools offering no room for a proper spread, the menu does the job quite nicely, with its bacon cheeseburgers, a monster called the "Double Double," and the Cheddar Bacon Supreme. **Known for:** American specialties; large breakfasts; late-night eats. $ *Average main: 70 Kn* ✉ *Tkalčićeva 50, Donji Grad* ☎ *01/484–5386* ⊕ *www.facebook.com/rocketburgerzagreb.*

Submarine

$$ | **BURGER** | This chain has a handful of locations around Zagreb, including on Frankopanska Street near the main square. The restaurant offers a range of all-natural burgers with locally procured toppings, including tasty choice of vegetarian options as well. **Known for:** all-natural burgers; great location; cool, modern interior. $ *Average main: 65 Kn* ✉ *Frankopanska 11, Donji Grad* ☎ *01/483–1500* ⊕ *www.submarineburger.com.*

Takenoko

$$ | **JAPANESE** | The menu of this utterly chic restaurant offers everything from sushi (both traditional Japanese rolls and American-style varieties) and teriyaki to wok dishes and specialties such as carrot and tofu soup or sea bass in jalapeño-wasabi sauce. Manned by head chefs Moto Mochizuki and Nenad Stošić, Takenoko gives meaning to the word *fusion,* merging Asian and European cuisine. **Known for:** upscale vibe; extensive drink list, including sakes; best sushi in town. $ *Average main: 120 Kn* ✉ *Masarykova 22, Donji Grad* ☎ *01/486–0530* ⊕ *www.takenoko.hr.*

★ Vinodol

$$ | **EASTERN EUROPEAN** | A few blocks southwest of the main square, Vinodol is an elegant spot both locals and tourists flock to when they hanker for traditional meaty fare such as veal and lamb, pork with plum sauce, or, for starters, *zagorska juha* (Zagorje-style potato soup with ham and mushrooms). Enjoy all this in a spacious, shaded courtyard or inside under brick-vaulted ceilings and amid low lighting that contrives to give you an elegant, wine-cellar sensation even though you're not in a cellar at all. **Known for:** meat-heavy dishes; large semi-outdoor garden; local hangout. $ *Average main: 120 Kn* ✉ *Nikole Tesle 10, Donji Grad* ☎ *01/481–1427* ⊕ *www.vinodol-zg.hr.*

Zinfandel's Restaurant

$$$$ | **EUROPEAN** | Just inside the luxurious Esplanade Hotel lies one of Zagreb's most elegant dining destinations known for its formal yet comfortable atmosphere and its history as a stop on the Orient Express. Order from the tasting menu, where wines are carefully selected by a sommelier to perfectly complement each dish. **Known for:** excellent tasting menu; stunning views from Oleander Terrace; catering to dietary restrictions. $ *Average main: 500 Kn* ✉ *Antuna Mihanovića 1* ☎ *01/456–6644* ⊕ *www.zinfandels.hr.*

Zrno Bio Bistro

$$ | **VEGETARIAN** | If you want to strengthen the body and nourish the spirit with seasonal, organic fresh fruits and vegetables, walk a few blocks west from the main square to Zrno, which offers fresh vegetables, tofu, seitan, warm sourdough bread, organic coffee, wine, tea, juice, smoothies, and shakes. All ingredients are delivered each day directly from Croatia's first 100% organic farm of the same name. **Known for:** vegan dishes; local produce; cheerful environment. $ *Average main: 75 Kn* ✉ *Medulićeva 20, Donji Grad* ☎ *01/484–7540* ⊕ *www.zrnobiobistro.hr.*

 Hotels

Best Western Premier Hotel Astoria

$$ | **HOTEL** | Less than five minutes by foot from the train station and 10 minutes from downtown, the hotel offers bright, modern rooms with the silky bedspreads and partly marble bathrooms that meet

the requirements of its Premier category. **Pros:** good location on a quiet side street midway between train station and main square; luxurious bathrooms with excellent amenities; top-notch 24-hour business center. **Cons:** smallish rooms; no health facilities or pool; shades that open when you enter the room may take some by surprise. $ *Rooms from: 800 Kn* ⊠ *Petrinjska 71* ☎ *01/480–8900* ⊕ *www.hotelastoria.hr* ⤴ *100 rooms* ⫪ *Free breakfast.*

★ Esplanade Zagreb

$$$ | **HOTEL** | This beautiful hotel, diagonally across from the train station, was built in 1925 for travelers on the original *Orient Express.* Louis Armstrong, Elizabeth Taylor, Charles Lindbergh, Orson Welles, Queen Elizabeth II, and Richard Nixon have all stayed here, among other famous names, many of whom left photos for the celebrity wall downstairs. **Pros:** unmitigated luxury and history; right by the train station; great fitness center. **Cons:** quite pricey; smallish lobby; formal atmosphere can be a bit stuffy. $ *Rooms from: 1,500 Kn* ⊠ *Mihanovićeva 1, Donji Grad* ☎ *01/456–6666* ⊕ *www.esplanade. hr* ⤴ *208 rooms.*

Hotel Dubrovnik

$$ | **HOTEL** | Claiming the most central location in the city, just off Trg bana Jelačića, Hotel Dubrovnik has been popular with business travelers and tourists since opening back in 1929. **Pros:** location right off the main square; numerous amenities; impressive history. **Cons:** lacking character; mediocre food; somewhat outdated decor. $ *Rooms from: 700 Kn* ⊠ *Gajeva 1, Donji Grad* ☎ *01/486–3555* ⊕ *www.hotel-dubrovnik.hr* ⤴ *222 rooms* ⫪ *Free breakfast.*

Hotel Jägerhorn

$$ | **HOTEL** | Located at the far end of a shop-filled courtyard off Zagreb's busiest shopping street and just a minute's walk from Ban Jelačić Square, this charming little hotel is the oldest in Zagreb (but fully updated) and a perfect base for

exploring the city. **Pros:** central location; excellent breakfast; historic café with great coffee. **Cons:** small, so often fully booked; not the trendiest hotel in town; somewhat outdated decor. $ *Rooms from: 900 Kn* ⊠ *Ilica 14, Donji Grad* ☎ *01/483–3877* ⊕ *www.hotel-jagerhorn. hr* ⤴ *18 rooms* ⫪ *Free breakfast.*

Hotel President Pantovcak

$$ | **HOTEL** | **FAMILY** | About a 20-minute walk from the city center and set in a quiet residential neighborhood, this stylish boutique hotel has a mix of antique furnishings, contemporary art, and floor-to-ceiling windows that flood with light year-round and are open in summer months. **Pros:** lovely garden; bottomless Champagne breakfast; beautiful decor. **Cons:** a walk to the city center; no pool; nightlife options a bit out of arm's reach. $ *Rooms from: 1,000 Kn* ⊠ *Pantovčak 52* ☎ *01/488–1480* ⊕ *www.president-zagreb. com* ⤴ *10* ⫪ *Free breakfast.*

Le Premier

$$ | **HOTEL** | Located on the doorstep of the Meštrović Pavilion, Le Premier sits in a former 20th-century palace and features elegantly decorated, modern rooms and a lobby with a crystal chandelier. **Pros:** modern and elegant rooms; high quality restaurant; proximity to Meštrović Pavilion. **Cons:** new brand as opposed to trusted option; a walk from the main square; can be pricey. $ *Rooms from: 1200 Kn* ⊠ *Kralja Držislava 5, Donji Grad* ☎ *01/440–0880* ⊕ *www.lepremier.hr* ⤴ *59 rooms* ⫪ *Free Free breakfast.*

Sheraton Zagreb

$$ | **HOTEL** | Located on a small side street in a somewhat nondescript part of town but only a 20-minute walk from the city center, the Sheraton Zagreb's high standards make this modern, six-story hotel a relative bargain. **Pros:** top-notch facilities and services; modern rooms; quality dining options. **Cons:** 20-minute walk from the main square; not exactly cozy; caters to business crowd. $ *Rooms from: 900 Kn* ⊠ *Kneza Borne 2, Donji*

Grad ☎ 01/455–9107 ⊕ www.hotel-sheratonzagreb.com ➥ 335 rooms ⎟○⎟ Free breakfast.

The Westin Zagreb

$$ | HOTEL | This colossal 17-story modern structure between the Mimara Museum and the Botanical Garden—previously the Opera Zagreb—still looks homely on the outside, but on the inside it's a sparkling affair. **Pros:** big, comfy rooms; excellent amenities and services; superb dining options. **Cons:** 15 minutes from main square; decor is somewhat outdated; neighborhood is not the most picturesque. $ Rooms from: 850 Kn ☒ Izidora Kršnjavoga 1, Donji Grad ☎ 01/489–2000 ⊕ www.marriott.com/hotels/travel/zagwi-the-westin-zagreb ➥ 296 rooms ⎟○⎟ Free breakfast.

Nightlife

Alcatraz

BARS/PUBS | With a lively combination of Zagreb students, partiers, and people looking for a chill night out, plus great drinks on the cheaper side and good music (usually rock), this location is a favorite among tourists seeking to make friends in the city. ☒ Preradovićeva 12 ☎ 091/521–3703 ⊕ www.alcatraz.pondi.hr.

Bulldog

BARS/PUBS | This popular split-level café-cum-wine-bar and bistro has a summer terrace. At night it becomes a club where you can enjoy live soul, rock, blues, and jazz performers. During the morning and day, enjoy sipping coffee and people-watching. ☒ Bogovićeva 6, Donji Grad ☎ 098/695–303 ⊕ www.bulldog-zagreb.hr.

Gallery

DANCE CLUBS | In a prime setting on the shore of Lake Jarun, known as the "Zagreb Sea," Gallery offers consistent party-driving music, and the dapper yet approachable crowd makes it a go-to spot for a night out to remember in Zagreb. If you're in need of a dance break, the beautiful terrace looking out over the lake is there to give you a chance to cool down and chat. Gallery is over two miles from the city center, so rather than chance your luck, you should call ahead to get on the guest list—especially if you wish to reserve a table. ☒ Aleja Matije Ljubeka 33 ☎ 91/531–3703 ⊕ www.facebook.com/gallery.club.

Katran

DANCE CLUBS | Croatian nightclubs are known for their lack of curfew, but this dance mecca takes that to the next level, bringing the party, and then the after party, and then the after-after party. The former warehouse factory sits on Radnička Street, located 15 minutes by car from the main square. The decor of exposed walls, graffiti, and pipe-lined ceilings testifies to its past. Four floors have different music, from rock and funk to rap and EDM. ☒ Radnička cesta 27 ⊕ www.facebook.com/MUSEUM.Katran.

Opera Club

DANCE CLUBS | A three-minute walk from the main square, Opera Club features a large dance floor, a stage, multiple bars, and a VIP area. Music choices range from techno and hip-hop to pop, while past line-ups have included Idris Elba and Fedde Le Grand. Reserve ahead if you'd like a table (and to skip the line). ☒ Petrinjska 4, Donji Grad ☎ 097/667–6666 ⊕ www.facebook.com/operaclubzagreb.

Swanky Monkey Garden

BARS/PUBS | A trendy vintage bar housed in an industrial space (a former dry cleaning and textile dye factory) with exposed brick and lofty ceilings, Swanky Monkey Garden also has outdoor seating on a beautiful terrace covered in lights. Parties and music events are common here, and the on-site hostel is rarely empty. ☒ Ilica 50 ☎ 01/400–4248 ⊕ www.swanky-hostel.com/swanky-monkey-garden.

Performing Arts

World Theatre Festival

FESTIVALS | For one week in mid-September, the World Theatre Festival brings to Zagreb theater companies from all over the world for one or more performances each evening at various theatrical venues about town. ☎ *01/487–4562* ⊕ *www. zagrebtheatrefestival.hr.*

🛍 Shopping

Croata

SPECIALTY STORES | Ties may not be the most original of gifts, but they are uniquely Croatian. During the 17th century, Croatian mercenaries who fought in France sported narrow, silk neck scarfs, which soon became known to the French as *cravat* (from the Croatian *hrvat*). At Croata you can buy "original Croatian ties" in presentation boxes, accompanied by a brief history of the tie. There, you can also find tasteful gifts for ladies, including scarves, shawls, and accessories. ⊠ *Ilica 5, within the Oktogon arcade, Donji Grad* ☎ *01/481–2726* ⊕ *www. croata.hr.*

Natura Croatica

SPECIALTY STORES | All manner of Croatian delicacies that use only natural ingredients are offered here from brandies and liqueurs to jams, olive oils, cheeses, truffles, soaps, wild-game jerkies, and pâtés. ⊠ *Preradovićeva 8, Donji Grad* ☎ *01/485–5076* ⊕ *www.naturacroatica. com.*

Sljeme

5 km (3 miles) north of Zagreb.

A favorite excursion on the outskirts of Zagreb is to the heights of Sljeme, the peak of Mt. Medvednica at 3,363 feet.

GETTING HERE AND AROUND

You can reach Sljeme by taking Tram 14 (direction: Mihaljevac) all the way to the terminal stop, where you should change to the bus, which goes to Sljeme (Tomislavov Dom).

👁 Sights

★ Sljeme

CASTLE/PALACE | The peak of Mt. Medvednica is an ideal place for picnicking, but you may wish to save your appetite for dinner at one of the excellent restaurants (located in large mountain cabins) on the road home. On the southwest flank of the summit of Mt. Medvednica is a reconstructed fortress called **Medvedgrad.** The original was built in the 13th century by Bishop Filip of Zagreb, and after a succession of distinguished owners over the next two centuries it was destroyed in an earthquake in 1590. You can wander around the outside (for free) and take in great views of Zagreb. It's a one-hour trek to the fortress from the cable car, or you can reach it more directly by taking Bus 102 from Britanski trg in central Zagreb (just off Ilica, a 20-minute walk west of Trg bana Josipa Jelačića) to the "Blue Church" in Šestine, and then hiking some 40 minutes uphill from there. Take trail No. 12, which is off the paved road past the church cemetery. ⊠ *Sljeme* ⊕ *www.sljeme.hr.*

Restaurants

Stari Puntijar

$$ | **EASTERN EUROPEAN** | On the road between Zagreb and Sljeme, Stari Puntijar is renowned for game and traditional Zagreb dishes such as *podolac* (ox medallions in cream and saffron), *orehnjača* (walnut roll cake), and *makovnjača* (poppy-seed roll cake). The wine list is excellent, and the interior design is marked by trophies, hunting weapons, old paintings, and big chandeliers. **Known for:** tasty game dishes; old-world vibe;

On Sljeme, you'll find a 13th-century fortress called Medvedgrad.

connection to museum hotel. *Average main: 80 Kn ✉ Gračanska cesta 65, Medveščak ☎ 01/467–5600 ⊕ www. hotelpuntijar.com.*

Marija Bistrica

40 km (25 miles) northeast of Zagreb.

Marija Bistrica and its famous pilgrimage site is the perfect destination for those looking for a peaceful, countryside getaway or day trip with few distractions. You can reach the village from the Zagreb Bus Station or via car (take the A2 highway). While there, you can sleep in a rural-style cabin or book a room at the Bluesun Hotel Kaj. Don't leave the town without trying some *zagorski štrukli* (cheese-filled and topped dumplings) and a glass of local wine.

◉ Sights

Pilgrimage Church of St. Mary of Bistrica (*Hodočasnička Crkva Majke Božje Bistričke*)

RELIGIOUS SITE | Croatia's preeminent religious pilgrimage site is home to the Blessed Virgin of Bistrica, a black, wooden, 15th-century Gothic statue of the Holy Mother associated with miraculous powers (per legend, having survived not only the Turkish invasion but a subsequent fire) and set in the main altar. The church, which was proclaimed a Croatian shrine by the nation's parliament in 1715, was rebuilt in neo-Renaissance style in the late 19th century by Hermann Bollé, who also designed the Zagreb Cathedral; the shrine complex adjacent to the church was enlarged in time for a 1998 visit by Pope John Paul II, who was in town to beatify Alojzije Stepinac, who became Archbishop of Zagreb in 1937 but was jailed and later placed under house arrest in Tito-led postwar Yugoslavia. Behind the church is a huge amphitheater that was built for the pope's visit, and from there you can climb up Kalvarija (Calvary Hill) to the stations of the cross, ornamented with sculptures by Croatian artists. ✉ *Župni ured, Trg pape Ivana Pavla II 32, Marija Bistrica* ☎ *049/469–156* 🌐 *www.svetiste-mbb.hr* 🎫 *Free.*

Pilgrimage Pathways
TRAIL | Marija Bistrica's surroundings (like much of Zagorje) are covered with beautiful hiking trails. Around the village, you'll find a number of interesting sights as you stroll. Check out the sculpture park located close to Marija Bistrica's main square, visit the Hudek Gallery with works by academic sculptor Pavao Hudek, and see a collection and information on UNESCO-protected *licitarstvo*, the art of decorating honey biscuits. ✉ *Marija Bistrica* ☎ *049/468–380* 🌐 *www.tz-marija-bistrica.hr.*

Veliki Tabor

52 km (32 miles) northwest of Marija Bistrica, 70 km (43 miles) north of Zagreb.

On a lofty hilltop stands the massive fortress of Veliki Tabor. The main pentagonal core of the building dates back to the 12th century, whereas the side towers were added in the 15th century as protection against Ottoman attacks.

GETTING HERE AND AROUND

Nine buses daily will get you here from Zagreb's main bus station in 2½ hours for 69 Kn one-way; but after getting off you have a 3-km (2-mile) walk still ahead of you. Hence, as is true more generally of site-hopping in the Zagorje region, a rental car may come in handy. Plus. that gives you the opportunity to stay longer in the countryside, which you can explore after taking in Veliki Tabor.

Sights

★ Veliki Tabor
CASTLE/PALACE | This is one of Croatia's best-preserved and most beautiful late Medieval-Renaissance buildings. Don't miss wandering around the interior of the impressive castle. The colonnaded galleries of the interior cast sublime shadows in moonlight.Outside, you'll find stretching vistas of the rolling hills surrounding you. To reach the site, you need to rent a car and make it part of a half-day tour of rural Zagorje. ✉ *Košnički Hum 1, Desinic* ☎ *049/374–970* 🌐 *www.veliki-tabor.hr/en* 🎫 *25 Kn.*

Restaurants

★ Grešna Gorica
$$ | EASTERN EUROPEAN | Visiting this rustic tavern is like stepping into a friend's home, although your friend's home is unlikely to have a stuffed fawn and a pair of *kuna* (a large, weasel-like creature), the national currency's namesake, on the wall. All produce used here is supplied by local farmers, and the menu features typical Zagorje dishes, including *zagorski štrukli* (baked pastry filled with cheese) and *pura s mlincima* (turkey with savory pastries). **Known for:** typical Zagorje dishes; regional štrukli; great views onto Veliki Tabor fortress. [$] *Average main: 80 Kn* ✉ *Taborgradska 35, Desinic* ☎ *049/343–001* 🌐 *www.gresna-gorica.com* 💳 *No credit cards.*

Hotels

★ Dvorac Bežanec
$$ | HOTEL | This lovely old manor house, just a 15-minute drive east of Veliki Tabor, offers spacious rooms with period furniture and breakfast. **Pros:** historic charm; period decor and Croatian artwork; reasonable rates. **Cons:** far from major tourist areas and towns; absolutely no drop-ins—need to call ahead to book and check availability; breakfast not included. [$] *Rooms from: 850 Kn* ✉ *Valentinovo 55, Pregrada* ☎ *049/376–800, 098/230–343* 🌐 *www.hotel-dvorac-bezanec.hr* 🛏 *25 rooms* 🍴 *No meals.*

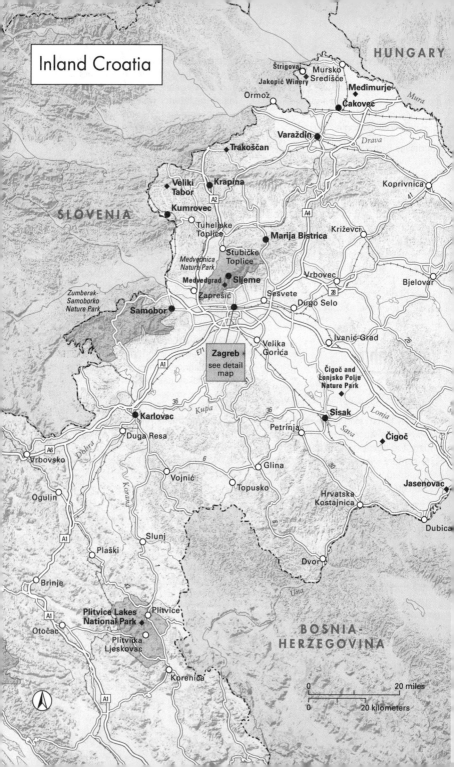

Inland Croatia

HUNGARY

Štrigova
Mursko
Jakopić Winery   Središće
Medimurje
Ormož   Čakovec

Varaždin

Trakošćan

Koprivnica

Veliki   Krapina
Tabor

Kumrovec   Križevci

Tuheljske   A4
Toplice
Marija Bistrica

Medvednica   Stubičke
Nature Park   Toplice

Medvedgrad   Sljeme   Vrbovec   Bjelovar

Zaprešić   Sesvete
Žumberak-
Samoborko   Dugo Selo
Nature Park   Samobor   A1

Velika   Ivanić-Grad
Gorića
Zagreb
see detail   Čigoč and
map   Lonjsko Polje
Nature Park

36   Kupa   36   Sisak
Karlovac
Petrinja   Čigoč

A6   Duga Resa   Sava
Dobra   Lonja
Vrbovsko   6   Glina
Vojnić   Jasenovac
Ogulin   Topusko
Hrvatska
Kostajnica   Dubica

Slunj
Plaški   Dvor

Brinje   Una

A1   BOSNIA-
Plitvice Lakes   Plitvice   HERZEGOVINA
National Park
Otočac   Plitvička
Ljeskovac

0   20 miles
Korenica
A1   0   20 kilometers

SLOVENIA

Krapina

20 km (12½ miles) east of Veliki Tabor, 66 km (41 miles) north of Zagreb.

Zagorje's quaint administrative and cultural center is on the tourism radar screen primarily as the home of *krapinski pračovjek* (Krapina Neanderthal). This is due to the 1899 discovery of a *homo Neanderthalensis* settlement (the world's largest), dating from 30,000-40,000 years ago, on a hillside a short walk from the town center. Indeed, this may be one of the few places in the world today where you can meet up with a family of such hominids and even a fearsome bear in the woods—that is, with life-size statues of Neanderthals going about their daily business (hunting, exploring, tending fire), at the same spot where the discovery was made. Leading its excavation was Croatian paleoanthropologist Dragutin Gorjanović-Kramberger.

 Sights

★ **Krapina Neanderthal Museum** (*Muzej krapinskih neandertalaca*)
MUSEUM | The Krapina Neanderthal Museum is located near the world-famous site of the Krapina Neanderthals "Hušnjakovo," and its architecture evokes the habitat of the prehistoric man. Displays at the museum provide insight into who these early Neanderthals were and how they lived, and more broadly into the region's geology and history. ⊠ *Šetalište Vilibalda Sluge BB* ☎ *049/371–491* ⊕ *www.mkn. mhz.hr* ⊠ *60 Kn.*

Trakošćan

41 km (25½ miles) west of Varaždin, 36 km (22½ miles) northeast of Veliki Tabor.

Perched resplendently several hundred feet above the parking lot where the tour buses come and go, the hilltop Trakošćan Castle is set amid beautifully landscaped grounds, and overlooks a lovely lake circled by a hiking trail.

 Sights

★ **Trakošćan Castle** (*Dvor Trakošćan*)
CASTLE/PALACE | Croatia's most visited castle took on its present neo-Gothic appearance during the mid-19th century, compliments of Juraj VI Drašković, whose family had already owned the castle for some 300 years and would go on to live there until 1944 (there has been a building here since the 14th century). The inside is as spectacular as the outside, with the wood-paneled rooms—a Baroque room, a rococo room, a neoclassical room, and so on—filled with period furnishings and family portraits, giving you some idea of how the wealthy local aristocracy once lived. A restaurant, café, and souvenir shop occupy the less extravagant Ministry of Culture–owned building at the foot of the hill. ⊠ *5 km (3 miles) northwest of the village of Bednja, Trakošćan 1, Bednja* ☎ *042/796–281, 042/796–422* ⊕ *www. trakoscan.hr* ⊠ *40 Kn.*

Varaždin

70 km (48 miles) northeast of Zagreb.

Situated on a plain just south of the Drava River, Varaždin (population around 50,000) is the most beautifully preserved Baroque town in this corner of the continent. A vibrant commercial and cultural center, still basking in the glow of its trade-town heyday in the 18th century, Varaždin is richly adorned with extraordinary churches and the palaces of the aristocratic families who once lived here. It was Croatia's capital from 1756 until a devastating fire in 1776 prompted a move to Zagreb. First mentioned under the name Garestin in a document by the Hungarian-Croatian king Bela III from 1181, it was declared a free royal town by King Andrew II of Hungary's

Trakošćan Castle is Croatia's most visited castle and is gorgeous inside and out.

Arpad dynasty in 1209 and went on to become an important economic, social, administrative, and military center. Near the heart of the city, in a park surrounded by grassy ramparts, the well-preserved castle is the main attraction. A short walk from the castle, on the outskirts of town, is one of Europe's loveliest cemeteries, with immense hedges trimmed and shaped around ornate memorials. Note that Varaždin's main churches are open only around an hour before and after mass, which is generally held several times daily, more often on weekends; the tourist information office can help you contact individual churches to arrange a look inside at other times.

GETTING HERE AND AROUND

After arriving in this charming city by bus from Zagreb, the best thing to do is to walk straight to the historical downtown, which will serve as your base for sightseeing and café-visiting.

Sights

City Museum Varaždin (*Gradski muzej Varaždin*)
MUSEUM | FAMILY | Varaždin's city museum is composed of multiple departments, including Archeology, History, Ethnography, and more. Housed in the Herzer Palace, the Entomološka (Entomology) Collection is one of the museum's highlights, with a fascinating presentation of some 50,000 different insect specimens. ✉ *Šetalište J. J. Strossmayera 1* ☎ *042/658–750* ⊕ *www.gmv.hr* ⊠ *25 Kn* ⊘ *Closed Mon. and public holidays.*

Franciscan Church (*Franjevačka crkva*)
RELIGIOUS SITE | Consecrated in 1650 on the site of a medieval predecessor, the pale yellow Franjevačka crkva has the highest tower in Varaždin, at almost 180 feet. In front is a statue of 10th-century Croatian bishop Grgur Ninski, a replica of the original, which is in Split; another such replica can be seen in Nin. ✉ *Franjevački trg 8* ☎ *042/213–166.*

Varaždin's Guitar Great

Although the global economic crisis forced Vladimir Šimunov Proskurnjak, Varaždin's most famous string instrument maker, to close his workshop on Krančevićeva 5, his legacy lives on. It's not by chance that he specialized in guitars. This particular instrument holds a special place in the hearts of the classical-music lovers of Varaždin and beyond. Indeed, there was a time when the guitar was among the most popular instruments in Croatia and elsewhere in Europe and earned the respect of the great music critics of the day. That time, in Croatia, peaked in the first half of the 19th century. The nation's greatest guitarist of the era, and one of the continent's best, was Varaždin's own Ivan Padovec. Born in 1800, Ivan was often ill as a child and extremely nearsighted. To make matters worse, at the age of 10 he was left half blind when a stone thrown at him by another boy hit his left eye. Since his physical limitations meant he could not become a priest, as his parents had hoped, Padovec trained to become a teacher. However, he chose quite another path.

By the age of 19 Ivan Padovec had not only taught himself to play the guitar, he was able to support himself by giving lessons to friends. Before long he decided to devote his life to music. Within five years, Padovec had a reputation not only as a virtuoso guitarist but also as a talented composer. By 1827 he was giving concerts from Zagreb and Varaždin to Zadar, Rijeka, and Trieste, and before long he'd earned the respect of even the court in Vienna. While living in the Austrian capital from 1829 to 1837, Padovec gave concerts throughout Europe, though weakening eyesight eventually forced a return to his native Varaždin. After a concert in Zagreb in 1840, one critic wrote, "[Padovec] showed that even on such an instrument it was possible to play tenderly and skillfully, thus surpassing everyone else." In addition to writing more than 200 compositions, he authored an influential book on guitar instruction and invented a 10-string guitar. Completely blind by 1848, Padovec retreated to his sister's house in Varaždin, unable to compose or teach. In 1871 he gave his final performance at the city theater. A life of music reaped little financial compensation for Padovec, and he died in poverty on November 4, 1873. His legacy lives on today, with the Varaždin Tourist Board now located in the house where he was born, at Ivana Padovca 3.

8

Zagreb and Inland Croatia VARAŽDIN

Gallery of Old and Contemporary Masters
(*Galerija starih i novih majstora*)
MUSEUM | Housed in the striking, 18th-century rococo Palača Sermage (Sermage Palace)—characterized by cinnamon-colored, black-framed geometric medallions decorating its facade and an impressive wrought-iron terrace—this gallery has a rich array of traditional paintings by Croatian and other European artists. ⊠ *Trg Miljenka Stančića 3* ☎ *042/658–754* ⊕ *www.gmv.hr* 🎟 *25 Kn.*

Gradska Vijećnica (*City Hall*)
GOVERNMENT BUILDING | This imposing landmark, one of Europe's oldest city halls, has been the seat of Varaždin's public administration since December 14, 1523. It was completely restored after the great fire of 1776. From May through October you can stop by on a Saturday

morning between 11 and noon to watch the changing of the guard called Purgari, a 250-year-old tradition that lives on. ✉ *Trg kralja Tomislava 1* ☎ *042/210–987* ⊕ *www.varazdin.hr.*

Lisakova Kula (*Lisak Tower*)

BUILDING | The 16th-century Lisakova kula is the only part of Varaždin's northern town wall that has been preserved. The wall formed part of the onetime city fortress, but most of it was razed in the early 19th century. It's from this spot that Ban led 50,000 soldiers across the Drava to Hungary in 1848. ✉ *Trg bana Jelačića* ⊕ *www.varazdin-online.com.*

Parish Church of St. Nicholas (*Župna crkva Sv. Nikole*)

RELIGIOUS SITE | Consecrated to Varaždin's patron saint in 1761 on the site of an older church, the Župna crkva Sv. Nikole is a Baroque structure that is more attractive on the outside than the inside. Note the false yet imposing white columns in the facade; the red-tiled, conical steeple; and the sculpture at the foot of the steeple of a firefighting St. Florian pouring a bucket of water onto a church, presumably an allusion to the fire that devastated Varaždin in 1776. ✉ *Trg slobode 11* ☎ *042/212–412* ⊕ *www.zupa-sv-nikole-varazdin.hr.*

★ Stari Grad (*Stari Grad Castle and Fortress*)

MUSEUM | Today a historical museum, Varaždin's main attraction is the massive Stari grad, which assumed its present form in the 16th century as a state-of-the-art defense fortification against the Turks, complete with moats, dikes, and bastions with low, round defense towers connected by galleries with openings for firearms. In the ensuing centuries it was often reconstructed by the families that owned it; for more than three centuries, until its 1925 purchase by the city, it belonged to the Erdödy clan. From the 12th century up until 1925, the castle served as the seat of the county prefect. You enter through the 16th-century tower gatehouse, which has a wooden drawbridge, to arrive in the internal courtyard with three levels of arcaded galleries. Indoors, there's an extensive display of antique furniture, with pieces laid out in chronological order and each room representing a specific period. Even if you don't go inside, do take a stroll around the perimeter, along a path that takes you between the outer wall and a ditch that used to be the moat. ✉ *Strossmayerovo Šetalište 7* ☎ *042/658–754* ⊕ *www.gmv.hr/en* 💰 *12 Kn* 🕐 *Closed Mon. and public holidays.*

Ursuline Church of the Birth of Christ (*Uršulinska crkva Rođenja Isusovog*)

RELIGIOUS SITE | This single-nave, pale-pink Baroque church with a particularly colorful, late-Baroque altar was consecrated in 1712 by the Ursuline sisters, who came to Varaždin from Bratislava nine years earlier at the invitation of the Drašković family. Its charming, strikingly slender tower was added in 1726. ✉ *Uršulinska 3* ⊕ *www.ursulinke.hr.*

★ Varaždin Cemetery (*Gradsko groblje*)

CEMETERY | Built in 1773 and thoroughly relandscaped in 1905 by Hermann Haller, a self-taught landscape architect who revolutionized traditional notions of what graveyards should look like, Varaždin's Gradsko groblje is as pleasant a place for a restful stroll as it may be, when the time comes, to be laid to rest in. Replete with flower beds and rows of tall cedars and linden trees flanking ornate memorials and laid out in geometric patterns, the cemetery sublimely manifests Haller's conviction that each plot should be a "serene, hidden place only hinting at its true purpose, with no clue as to whether its occupant is rich or poor, since all are tended equally, surrounded by every kind of flower…producing perfect harmony for the visitor." Haller himself, who ran the cemetery from 1905 to 1946, is buried here in a rather conspicuous mausoleum. You can reach the cemetery by walking about 10 minutes east of the castle along Hallerova aleja. ✉ *Hallerova aleja*

Varaždin's Stari Grad was created as a defense fortifcation, but today serves as a history museum.

☎ 042/210–987 ⊕ www.tourism-varazdin.hr/en.

Varaždin City Market (*Varaždinska Gradska tržnica*)

MARKET | Enjoy the smells of fresh fruits and vegetables, plus the friendly clamor of locals negotiating the best prices, with a stop at the City Market, which is open Monday through Saturday from 7 am to 2 pm. The open-air marketplace also features a number of bakeries and meat and fish stores. ✉ *Gradska tržnica, Augusta Šenoe 12* ☎ 042/320–956 ⊕ www.varazdinskiplac.hr.

Varaždin County Castle (*Palača Varaždinske županije*)

GOVERNMENT BUILDING | Palača Varaždinske županije rivals City Hall (on nearby Trg kralja Tomislava) in terms of sheer visual appeal, even if it is more than two centuries younger, what with its flamingo-pink facade and its location right across from the Franciscan Church. Opened in 1772, it boasted a late-Baroque pediment for four years only, until the fire of 1776 did away with that, and saw it bestowed with a triangular, neoclassical one. ✉ *Franjevački trg* ☎ 042/210–987 ⊕ www.tourism-varazdin.hr/en.

Restaurants

Palatin Restoran & Caffe Bar

$ | **EUROPEAN** | **FAMILY** | Set in the heart of Varaždin city, Palatin Restoran & Caffe Bar is a peaceful spot for a delicious meal of traditional Croatian dishes such as Istrian steak with truffles and venison medallions in "Lukarski" sauce. There is also a wide variety of vegan and vegetarian options to suit all diners. **Known for:** traditional Croatian dishes; complex flavors; signature Palatin cake for dessert. ⓢ *Average main: 60 Kn* ✉ *Ulica Brace Radic 1, Zagreb* ☎ 54/239–8300 ⊕ www.palatin.hr ▭ *No credit cards.*

Hotels

Hotel Istra

$$ | **HOTEL** | Varaždin's one and only centrally located accommodation, the Istra has 11 simply furnished but sleek rooms

with small windows that don't offer much of a view. **Pros:** near attractions, shops, and restaurants; all rooms have bathtubs; hotel has an elevator. **Cons:** hallways are hot in warm weather; small windows; few frills. $ *Rooms from: 900 Kn* ✉ *Ivana Kukuljevića 6* ☎ *042/659–659* ⊕ *www. istra-hotel.hr* ⇆ *11 rooms* ⦿ *Free breakfast.*

Pansion Garestin

$ | **B&B/INN** | A short walk from the town center, this small hotel has 13 simply furnished rooms, with ochre carpeting, sturdy if scratched desks, and small windows under a pitched roof. **Pros:** reasonably priced; comfy basic rooms; pleasant outdoor dining terrace. **Cons:** small bathrooms; few frills; no Internet access. $ *Rooms from: 400 Kn* ✉ *Zagrebačka 34* ☎ *042/214–314* ⊕ *www. gastrocom-ugostiteljstvo.com/en/restorani/garestin-restaurant-and-b-b.html* ⇆ *13 rooms* ⦿ *Free breakfast.*

Pansion Maltar

$ | **B&B/INN** | A short walk from the town center, this small guesthouse has clean, no-frills, but spacious rooms that are quite acceptable for a short stay. **Pros:** good value; friendly service; a five-minute walk to the town center. **Cons:** smoky café; modest decor; some rooms are twin beds only. $ *Rooms from: 500 Kn* ✉ *Franca prešerna 1* ☎ *042/311–100, 042/311–521* ⊕ *www.maltar.hr* ⇆ *28 rooms* ⦿ *Free breakfast.*

 Nightlife

Rock Art Café

CAFES—NIGHTLIFE | For a beer or two between walls adorned with pictures of famous revolutionaries from Elvis to Che Guevara, not to mention glass-encased electric guitars, stop by the Rock Art Café, which has frequent live-music evenings all year-long. ✉ *Petra Preradovića 24* ☎ *042/321–123* ⊕ *www.facebook. com/art.varazdin.*

 Performing Arts

Advent in Varaždin

FESTIVALS | Throughout the month of December, the town celebrates Advent in Varaždin, when the streets and squares come alive with the Christmas spirit. Ornaments and sweets are on sale, there's outdoor skating, and, yes, Santa Claus wanders about handing out gifts to kids. ⊕ *www.tourism-varazdin.hr.*

Špancirfest

FESTIVALS | For 10 days, usually in late August, Špancirfest (translated in tourist brochures as "Street Walkers' Festival") occupies various squares in the center of town. It features a colorful array of free, open-air theatrical and acrobatic performances, live music from classical to rock, traditional and modern dance, arts-and-crafts exhibits, and more. ⊕ *www. spancirfest.com.*

★ Varaždin Baroque Evenings

FESTIVALS | For three weeks, usually from September to October, the Varaždin Baroque Evenings take the form of classical-music concerts in various churches, palaces, and other venues throughout town. This is one of the most important cultural events in northern Croatia. ✉ *Varaždin* ☎ *042/212–907* ⊕ *www.vbv. hr.*

Čakovec and Međimurje

15 km (9½ miles) northeast of Varaždin.

At the northernmost tip of Croatia, between the Drava River to the south and the Mura River to the north, the Međimurje region looks small on the map, but it possesses a distinctive character that makes it ripe for at least a day's worth of exploration. Long off the radar screens of Croatia-bound visitors, Međimurje is also one of the country's newest up-and-coming inland tourist destinations: its largest town, Čakovec, is the most important cultural center between Varaždin and Hungary and Slovenia to the north (many Zagreb–Budapest trains stop there). Its many small villages are the home of rich wine-making and embroidery traditions, and there is even a locally cherished spa town, Toplice Sveti Martin, to the very north close to the Mura River.

Back in the 13th century, Count Dimitrius Chaky, court magistrate of the Croatian-Hungarian king Bela IV, had a wooden defense tower erected in the central part of the Međimurje that eventually became known as Čakov toranj (Chak's Tower). It was around this tower and other nearby fortifications that Čakovec saw a period of economic and cultural development under the influential Zrinski family, from the mid-16th century to the late 17th century. After a failed rebellion by the Zrinskis and the Frankopans against the Viennese court, the Viennese imperial army plundered the tower for building materials, and the last Zrinski died in 1691. A disastrous earthquake in 1738 saw the old, Gothic architecture give way to the Baroque. Međimurje's last feudal proprietors were the Feštetić counts, who lived here from 1791 to 1923—a period during which the region came under the administrative control of Hungary, then Croatia, then Hungary once again (until 1918). Toward the close of the 19th century the region was linked inextricably to the railroad network of the Austro-Hungarian Empire, setting the stage for intense economic development. Today, the region hosts a number of festivals, the largest being Porcijunkulovo, during which Čakovec turns to an open-air food, drink, wine-tasting, and music festival.

GETTING HERE AND AROUND

After arriving by bus from Zagreb, walk directly to the city center and begin experiencing the history all around you.

 Sights

Jakopić Winery

WINERY/DISTILLERY | Jakopić Winery, near the spa town of Sveti Martin in the Varaždin region, is operated by brothers Martin and Branimir Jakopić, who offer superb dining as well as scenic tours of the lush vineyards situated on the borders of Slovenia, Hungary, and Austria. The first wine here was produced in 1908, and the winery is especially renowned for its Pušipel, a notable white wine variety indigenous to Međimurje. ⊠ *Železna Gora 92, Štrigova* ☎ *040/851–300* ⊕ *www.vina-jakopic.hr.*

Štrigova

TOWN | Disregard the somewhat "lost in translation" sign outside this town's main church, one of Međimurje's most important ecclesiastical landmarks: "Saint Jerome's Church is a zero category monument of culture." In this case the "zero" means "top," for the church (plus a well-developed local wine industry) is what guarantees the otherwise sleepy, out-of-the-way village of Štrigova a place on the tourism map. In a bucolic hilly setting near the Slovenian border, 15 km (9½ miles) northwest of Čakovec, Štrigova is indeed best known for **Crkva Sv. Jeronima** and as the largest producer of Međimurje wines. Whether you arrive by bus (45-minute runs from Čakovec daily) or car, the first thing you are likely to notice is the striking yellow-and-white double steeple of the church, which is perched sublimely on a hillside just above the village center.

Completed in 1749 on the site of a 15th-century chapel that was destroyed in the region's 1738 earthquake, the church is dedicated to the village's most famous son: St. Jerome (340–420), known for translating the Bible from Greek and Hebrew into Latin. Note the painting of a bearded St. Jerome on the facade, framed by two little windows made to look like red hearts. The church is most famous, actually, for its lovely wall and ceiling frescoes by the famous Baroque artist, Ivan Ranger the Baptist (1700–1753). The main steeple was completed only in 1761, and the church also has two smaller steeples. The church is usually closed, but you can call the local parish to arrange a look inside. While you can get to Štrigova easily enough by one of several daily buses from Čakovec, it's good to have a car if you want to drop by the smaller village of Železna Gora, some 5 km (3 miles) south of Štrigova, along a country road to Čakovec. ⊠ *Štrigova* ☎ *040/851–325* ⊕ *www.strigova.info.*

Trgovački Kasino (*Commercial Casino*)
PLAZA | Čakovec's main square, Trg Republike, is a pretty, Baroque affair, with a clear stand out and major highlight being the Trgovački Kasino. Odd that the key gathering place of the town's early-20th-century rising bourgeois class should have survived the communist era intact, but here it has stood since 1903, wearing its Hungarian art nouveau style very much on its sleeve: red brick interspersed with a white stucco background, squares and circles across the bottom, curved lines formed by the brickwork working their way to the top. Back in its heyday, this was much more than a casino in the gambling sense of the word; in addition to a card room and a game parlor, it housed a ladies' salon, a reading room, and a dance hall. It was mostly a trade-union headquarters in the post–World War II era—and so it is today, rendering the inside off-limits to the public. Just off the main square, by the way, is Trg kralja Tomislava, the town's one and only major pedestrian shopping street. ⊠ *Trg Republike, Cakovec* ⊕ *www. visitcakovec.com.*

Zrinski Castle (*Stari grad Zrinskih*)
CASTLE/PALACE | Set in the middle of a large, shaded park right beside the main square is Čakovec's key landmark, the massive four-story Stari grad Zrinskih. Built over the course of a century from around 1550 by Nikola Šubic Zrinski, in an Italian-Renaissance style, it was the Zrinski family nest until the late 17th century. The fortress's foremost present-day attraction, the **Muzej Međimurja** (Museum of Međimurje), can be reached through the courtyard. Though it receives too few visitors to have regular opening hours, a staff member will be happy to let you in; just climb the steps to the hallway of offices on the second floor to find someone. If you kindly overlook the lack of English-language text, you will be treated on this floor to an intriguing, life-size look at a year in the life of a peasant family, from season to season as you proceed through the rooms. Move up a floor for a chronological display of the region's history, from the Stone Age to the recent past. Also on this floor are individual rooms dedicated to the Zrinski family (this one does have English text); lovely period furniture; displays of printing machinery; an old pharmacy; a fascinating collection of 19th- and 20th-century bric-a-brac; and, last but not least, a three-room gallery of impressive modern art by various painters. ⊠ *Trg Republike 5, Cakovec* ☎ *01/313–499* ⊕ *www.mmc. hr* 🖢 *20 Kn.*

Župna crkva sv. Nikole Biskupa i franjevački samostan (*Parish Church of St. Nicolas Bishop and the Franciscan Monastery*)
RELIGIOUS SITE | Čakovec's key ecclesiastical landmark was built between 1707 and 1728 on the site of a wooden monastery that burned down in 1699. The bell tower was added in the 1750s. Inside is a late-Baroque altar decorated with elaborate statues; on the outside is a facade from the turn of the 20th century (when Hungary ruled the region), with reliefs of several great Hungarian kings from ages past. ⊠ *Franjevački trg 1, Cakovec* ☎ *040/312–806* ⊕ *www.ofm.hr/ zupa_cakovec.*

🍴 Restaurants

★ Međimurski Dvori

$$ | EUROPEAN | FAMILY | Located in the heart of Međimurje County, in the picturesque town of Lopatinec, only 6 km (4 miles) away from Čakovec, Međimurski dvori is known across the region for its unique ambience, top gastronomic offerings, and friendly and professional staff. A seat anywhere near the beautiful wooden fireplace makes for an extra-special experience; you'll feel like you're in an upscale but extremely cozy Međimurje cabin. **Known for:** beautiful decor; traditional and locally procured food; idyllic countryside location. $ *Average main: 80 Kn* ⊠ *Vladimira Nazora 22* ☎ *040/856–333* ⊕ *www.medjimurski-dvori.hr.*

Terbotz (*Restoran Dvorac*)

$$ | EUROPEAN | FAMILY | In the village of Železna Gora some 5 km (3 miles) south of Štrigova, along a country road to Čakovec, stands the best restaurant in these parts where you can dine on everything from poultry to pork to wild game to seafood, in a lovely country house with wood-beam ceilings. A spacious terrace overlooks the area's sweeping vineyards, and on a breezy day you'll hear the clackety-clack of the windmill just outside. **Known for:** vineyard setting; unique flavors of Međimurje; locally sourced ingredients. $ *Average main: 70 Kn* ⊠ *Železna Gora 113, Štrigova* ☎ *040/857–444* ⊕ *www.terbotz.hr* ⊗ *Closed Mon.*

Hotels

Hotel Castellum

$ | HOTEL | A short walk from both the bus station and the main square (both of which are about a mile away), this is the best hotel in town, also featuring a rooftop bar with panoramic views and a wine cellar. **Pros:** close to the bus station and the main square; clean, modern rooms; good food and drink options. **Cons:** pricier than other spots in the area; along a bland road; a bit impersonal. $ *Rooms from: 480 Kn* ⊠ *Vladimira Nazora 16, Cakovec* ☎ *040/304–200* ⊕ *www.castellum-cakovec.com* ⤳ *9 rooms.*

Samobor

20 km (12½ miles) west of Zagreb.

That Samobor has been one of the capital's top weekend haunts since before the turn of the 20th century without really being on the way to anything else in Croatia testifies to its abundant cultural and natural charms. Close to the Slovenian border, this picturesque medieval town on the eastern slopes of the lushly forested Samoborsko gorje (Samobor Mountains) was chartered by the Hungarian-Croatian king Bela IV in 1242. The town and environs are popular with hikers, with trails leading into the hillside right from the center of town. Perched in those hills, just 30 minutes from town on foot, are the ruins of a 13th-century castle, which ennoble the main square from their sublime heights. And what would a visit to Samobor be without a stroll along Gradna, the peaceful stream that runs through town, and its Venice-like canals?

After an energetic hike, you may wish to fortify yourself with a glass of locally made *bermet,* a vermouth-like drink whose secret recipe was apparently brought here by French forces during their occupation from 1809 to 1813. Add the traditional pastry of *kremšnita,* a custard cake, and you've got yourself an authentic and tasty Samobor meal.

GETTING HERE AND AROUND

Take a 45-minute bus ride from the central bus station in Zagreb or travel for about 30 minutes by rental car to this charming getaway town where you can while away half a day leisurely strolling along the river and cobblestone streets and soak in the atmosphere from yesteryear.

Charming Samobor is a popular base for hikers who wish to explore the town's surrounding hills.

Sights

King Tomislav Square (*Trg Kralja Tomislava*)

PLAZA | The look of the city's rectangular main square is largely Baroque and positively lovely, all the more so because some building facades show art nouveau influences. In particular, the pharmacy building at No. 11 has two angels presiding, appropriately, on top. Also overlooking the square is a 17th-century parish church. Enjoy a coffee and a slice of kremšnita at one of the cafés dotting the square. ✉ *Samobor* ⊕ *www.samobor.hr.*

Museum Marton

MUSEUM | Croatia's first private museum is located on a quiet street just above Trg kralja Tomislava. Museum Marton was created to house a private collection of furniture, paintings, glass- and metalware, porcelain, and clocks previously on loan to the Zagreb Museum of Arts & Crafts. ✉ *Jurjevska 7* ☎ *01/336–4160, 01/483–8700* ⊕ *www.muzej-marton.hr* 🎟 *15 Kn.*

Samobor Museum

MUSEUM | Located in a lovely streamside park by the square, the Samobor Museum tells the story of the town's past. It sits in a manor in which members of the Illyrian movement once gathered. ✉ *Livadićeva 7* ☎ *01/336–1014* ⊕ *www.samobor.hr/muzej* 🎟 *8 Kn* ⊙ *Closed Mon. and public holidays.*

Samoborski Fašnik

FESTIVAL | By far Samobor's most famous event, this carnival draws thousands of visitors from across the world to town for several days beginning the weekend before Lent. Here, guests can take part in or simply enjoy the dazzling sight of the parades, featuring floats and masked revelers. Aside from the one in Rijeka, this is Croatia's most famous carnival. ✉ *Trg kralja Tomislava 5* ☎ *01/336–0044* ⊕ *www.fasnik.com.*

Restaurants

Pri Staroj Vuri

$$ | **EASTERN EUROPEAN** | **FAMILY** | Small yet ever so cozy, its walls decorated with old clocks and paintings by noted Croatian artists, this lovely old villa a few minutes' walk from the main square is the best place in town to try such meaty fare as *teleća koljenica* (knuckle of veal) and *češnjovke* (smoked sausage cooked in sour cabbage with potatoes). The latter is sometimes available only late in the year, after *kolinje* (the annual sausage-making period), when the hogs are butchered and the sausage smoked. **Known for:** hearty dishes; Croatian art; location surrounded by green space. $ *Average main: 70 Kn* ✉ *Giznik 2* ☎ *01/336–0548* ⊕ *www.staravura.pondi.hr.*

U prolazu

$ | **CAFÉ** | If you need a dose of sugar to perk you up, try some *samoborska kremšnita,* a mouthwatering block of vanilla custard between layers of flaky pastry served warm that can be tasted at its best at this otherwise small and smoky café with a large outdoor patio. It's one of the original spots in town to make the traditional dessert. **Known for:** central location; authentic Samobor pastries; views of the surrounding square and church. $ *Average main: 25 Kn* ✉ *Trg kralja Tomislava 5* ☎ *01/336–6420* ⊕ *www.tz-samobor.hr.*

Hotels

Hotel Livadic

$ | **HOTEL** | If you want to spend more than a half-day in Samobor, you could do much worse than this elegant and pleasant hotel right on the main square. **Pros:** centrally located; historical ambience; nice café. **Cons:** rooms vary in size; downstairs café is smoky; on the outdated side. $ *Rooms from: 530 Kn* ✉ *Trg kralja Tomislava 1* ☎ *01/336–5850* ⊕ *www.hotel-livadic.hr* ➪ *21 rooms* ❑ *Free breakfast.*

Karlovac

40 km (25 miles) southwest of Zagreb.

Many tourists taste the beer, but few stop by for a taste of the city. Karlovac is much more than home to one of Croatia's most popular brews, Karlovačko. Founded by the Austrians in 1579 as a fortress intended to ward off Ottoman attacks, Karlovac is today that big dot on the map between Zagreb and the coast. Visitors to the country, more often than not, simply pass it by, but anyone intrigued by the question of how a one-time fortress—still much in evidence—can develop into an urban center will want to stop here for at least a half-day and, perhaps, spend a night on the way to or from the coast. Once you pass through the city's industrial-looking suburbs, there is an inviting historical center awaiting you, one rendered more romantic because it is wedged between four rivers, the Kupa, the Korana, the Mrežnica, and the Dobra. Hence, the nickname "the city that sits on four rivers". The city's Renaissance-era urban nucleus is popularly known as the Zvijezda (Star), since its military planners were moved to shape it as a six-pointed star—evidenced in the surrounding moat, which is today a pleasant, if sunken, green space that is even home to a basketball court. Eventually, this center's military nature gave way to civilian life, and it took on the Baroque look more visible today. Though the town walls were razed in the 19th century, their shape is still discernible.

GETTING HERE AND AROUND

By far the best way to come here is by bus from Zagreb; it is along the route of countless buses from the capital. Once there, the best thing is to make a pedestrian beeline to the historical center.

Bloody Easter

Easter Sunday, March 31, 1991, has gone down in Croatian history as the day Croatia suffered its first casualties—and its first fatality—in its war of independence from the former Yugoslavia. And the unlikely setting was none other than one of Europe's most visited natural wonders, Plitvice Lakes National Park.

Before the deadly event, Croatian commando units—under the direction of General Josip Lucić, later to become head of the Croatian Armed Forces—were dispatched to Plitvice to restore order. This is because the region had been occupied by Serbian forces led by Milan Martić, who aimed to annex the park to Serbian Krajina. The Croatian commandos were ambushed en route, near the group of hotels at Entrance 2, and one member of the team, Josip Jović, was killed and seven of his fellow soldiers were wounded. As recorded in the annals of Croatian history, nine opposing soldiers were arrested, and order was restored, for a time.

The region, which had long been home to both Croats and Serbs, was occupied by Serbian forces for the next four years. The national park became a military encampment, and soldiers threatened to blow up the fragile travertine dams separating the lakes. UNESCO sent missions to prevent war from wreaking such havoc on a natural wonder. In the end, with the exception of the park's red-deer population, which fell dramatically during the occupation, the park's natural beauty pulled through intact. Only the human infrastructure was damaged, including the hotels. By 1999, four years after Croatian forces reoccupied the park and painstakingly cleared the area of mines, the last of the three hotels reopened, and the park was back in business.

Today a memorial in the park—behind the bus stop at Entrance 2 on the southbound side of the road—marks the life and death of Josip Jović, the first fatality in what was to be a long and bloody war.

Sights

Trg bana Josipa Jelačića

PLAZA | At the center of this old part of town, which you access over any of several bridges over the moat, is the main square, Trg bana Josipa Jelačića, one side of which, alas, features a great big empty building with some missing windows. At the center of this otherwise largely barren square is an old well dating to 1869; long filled in, it is ornamented with allegorical imagery. ✉ *Karlovac* 🌐 *www.visitkarlovac.hr.*

Restaurants

★ Bistro Kastel

$$$ | **EUROPEAN** | Climb the stone stairs onto the spacious terrace or dine inside the softly lit 13th-century manor, one of the most impressive examples of feudal architecture in Croatia. Kastel's offerings reflect its geographic location, representing both the Adriatic Sea and the continental plains with delicious detail. **Known for:** beautiful castle setting; lovely views of the town; craft beers and good wines. [$] *Average main: 160 Kn* ✉ *Dubovac Castle, Zagrad gaj 5* ☎ *047/658–922* 🌐 *www.bistrokastel.com.*

Hotels

Hotel Korana Srakovčić

$$ | HOTEL | Deep within a tree-shaded park a few minutes' walk from the Old Town, this luxury boutique hotel overlooks a peaceful stretch of its namesake, the Korana River. **Pros:** luxurious, spacious rooms; tranquil park setting; excellent amenities. **Cons:** 25-minute walk from the town center; pricey for the area; caters mostly to business travelers. *[$] Rooms from: 985 Kn ✉ Perivoj Josipa Vrbanića 8 ☎ 047/609–090 🌐 www.hotelkorana.hr 🛏 19 rooms 🍴 Free breakfast.*

Plitvice Lakes National Park

135 km (84 miles) southwest of Zagreb.

Triple America's five Great Lakes, shrink them each to manageable size (i.e., 536 acres in all), give them a good cleaning until they look virtually blue, envelop them in lush green forest with steep hillsides and cliffs all around, and link not just two but all of them with a pint-size Niagara Falls. The result? Nacionalni park Plitvička jezera, a UNESCO World Heritage site and Croatia's most-visited inland natural wonder.

GETTING HERE AND AROUND

The park is on the route of numerous cross-country buses starting from the coast (Zadar, Dubrovnik, Split) or from the capital, Zagreb. After arriving at the park, your feet are the only things you need to work your way around the wonders of this natural miracle.

Sights

★ **Plitvice Lakes National Park** (*Nacionalni park Plitvička jezera*)

NATIONAL/STATE PARK | This 8,000-acre park is home to 16 beautiful emerald lakes connected by a series of cascading waterfalls, stretching 8 km (5 miles) through a valley flanked by high, forested hills home to deer, bears, wolves, wild boar, and the Eurasian lynx. Thousands of years of sedimentation of calcium, magnesium carbonate, algae, and moss have yielded the natural barriers between the lakes, and since the process is ongoing, new barriers, curtains, stalactites, channels, and cascades are constantly forming and the existing ones changing. The deposited sedimentation, or tufa, also coats the beds and edges of the lakes, creating their sparkling, azure look.

Today a series of wooden bridges and waterside paths lead through the park. The only downside: because it's so lovely, the trails can get crowded from June through September. That said, there's no litter along the way—a testament to both respectful visitors and a conscientious park staff. There's also no camping, no bushwhacking, no picking plants, and absolutely no swimming. This is a place to look, to spend a day or two, but not to touch. It is, however, well worth the 200 Kn summertime entrance fee, and the lowered fees during the rest of the year. This is not just a summertime, but a year-round spectacle, with blooming flowers in the spring, sunset-colored foliage in the fall, and magical-looking frozen waterfalls in the winter.

The park is right on the main highway (E71) from Zagreb to Split, and it's certainly worth the three-hour trip from the capital. There are three entrances just off the main road about an hour's walk apart, creatively named Entrance 1, Entrance 2, and auxiliary Entrance Flora. The park's pricey hotels are near Entrance 2, the first entrance you'll encounter if arriving by bus from the coast. However, Entrance 1—the first entrance if you arrive from Zagreb—is typically the start of most one-day excursions, if only because it's within a 20-minute walk of Veliki slap, the 256-foot-high waterfall.

Did You Know?

Plitvice Lakes is Croatia's most popular national park, but despite seeing 1.8 million visitors a year, there's a wonderful sense of untouched tranquility. That's due to strict rules against camping, picking plants, and swimming in the lakes.

Hiking the entire loop that winds its way around the lakes takes six to eight hours, but there are other hikes, ranging from two to four hours. All involve a combination of hiking and being ferried across the larger of the park's lakes by national park service boats.

There are cafés near both entrances, but avoid them for anything but coffee, as the sandwiches and strudels don't offer the best value for your money. Instead, buy some of the huge, heavenly strudels sold by locals at nearby stands, where great big blocks of homemade cheese are also on sale. ■ TIP→ **At the boat landing near Entrance 2, you can rent gorgeous wooden rowboats for 50 Kn per hour.** ✉ *Plitvicka Jezera* ☎ *053/751–014, 053/751–015* ⊕ *www.np-plitvicka-jezera. hr* 💵 *July–Sept. 200 Kn; Apr.–June and Oct. 90 Kn; Nov.–Mar. 80 Kn.*

Restaurants

Although there's a restaurant near the hotels at Entrance 2, it has the same touristy, uninspiring look and feel as the hotels, and few people flock to it. You're much better off heading over to the excellent restaurant at Entrance 1—unless of course the food store near Entrance 2 provides you enough in the way of staples to fuel your hikes.

★ **Lička Kuća** (*Lika House Restaurant*)
$$ | EASTERN EUROPEAN | FAMILY | With unadorned log walls, wood-beam ceilings, white-curtained windows, lively Croatian folk music playing, and an open kitchen with an open hearth, this is exactly what a restaurant in a great national park should be. Fill up on hearty *lička juha* (a creamy soup of lamb, vegetables, and eggs), followed by boiled lamb with vegetables, suckling pig, or a "Lika Bundle" (renowned Lika lamb and potatoes—known as the best in Croatia—served with locally made plum rakija and veggies). **Known for:** proximity to national park; sausages, veal, and other hearty

fare; lots of tourists. $ *Average main: 85 Kn* ✉ *Rastovača bb, Across entrance 1, Plitvicka Jezera* ☎ *053/751–023.*

Hotels

The main advantage of staying in a rather bland, touristy park hotel near the park itself is that you'll be right in the center of all the hiking action. The hotels here are particularly convenient if you arrive without your own car, but other than that, they aren't much to write home about.

As an alternative, there are lots of private rooms in the immediate vicinity, where doubles go for around 240 Kn, a bargain compared to the hotels. Check out the tiny village of Mukinje, about a 15-minute hike south of Entrance 2. A bit farther south is the village of Jezerce, which also has rooms. (Note that the bus does not stop at either Mukinje or Jezerce, but it's a pleasant walk to both.) You can also get a private room in the rather faceless, one-road village of Rastovača, just off the main road a few hundred yards north of Entrance 1 (where the bus stops). Practically every one of the village's newish-looking houses has rooms for rent, and they're generally bright, clean, and modern.

A bit farther afield, the village of Rakovica, 12 km (7½ miles) north of the park, usually has more vacancies in high season and is a good option if you have a car. The tourist office in Rakovica (☎ *047/784–450*) can help with bookings. Last but not least, bear in mind that there's no place to store your bags in the park during the day if you arrive by bus and plan to head on to the coast or to Zagreb later in the day—so unless you're ready to cart your bags for hours along the park's steep trails or are traveling light, plan on an overnight stay.

Hotel Jezero
$ | HOTEL | Yards away from two other, lower-priced, fewer-frills hotels (the Plitvice and the Bellevue), this long,

three-story wood-paneled building looks almost like a U.S.-style motel. The rooms are simply furnished and a bit worn, but clean, and offer cheap plastic chairs on the unappealing terraces (not all rooms have terraces). **Pros:** centrally located; the best of the park's three hotel options; decent array of services and amenities. **Cons:** slightly worn rooms; pricey for what it is; filled with tourists. $ *Rooms from: 390 Kn* ⊠ *Nacionalni park Plitvička jezera, near Entrance 2, Plitvicka Jezera* ☎ *053/751–500* ⊕ *www.np-plitvicka-jezera.hr/en* ⇨ *229 rooms* ⦿ *Free breakfast.*

Sisak

75 km (47 miles) southeast of Zagreb via the Autocesta Expressway.

Sisak is historically one of the oldest continuously settled places in Europe since 400 BC, although human presence in the area has been revealed even prior. This unassuming little town was also the site of one of the more important battles in Croatia's history: a 1593 victory against Ottoman forces. More modern history saw the town converted into an industrial hub with life centered around its waterways (Sisak sits at the confluence of the Kupa and the Sava, and the Odra and the Kupa).

◉ Sights

Knightly Tournament (*Sisački viteški turnir*) **FESTIVAL** | Usually on a weekend in June, locals celebrate the historic victory over Ottoman forces with an annual Knightly Tournament. A whole lot of folks in medieval garb will entertain you with archery and equestrian contests, not to mention balloon rides, souvenirs, and plenty of food and drink. Check with the Sisak Tourist Board for details on this free event. ⊕ *www.tzg-sisak.hr.*

Sisak Fortress
MILITARY SITE | A bit to the south of the town center—3 km (2 miles) to be exact, where the rivers Kupa and Sava meet—stands the once-mighty Sisak Fortress (built 1544–50), with one prominent bastion at each point of its famously triangular form and a hugely significant past. It was here, on June 22, 1593, that the Habsburgs, in the company of Croats and Slovenes, pulled off a monumental victory over Ottoman armies, a triumph that figured prominently in halting the Ottoman advance toward Zagreb and farther into Western Europe. ⊠ *Sisak* ⊕ *www.tzg-sisak.hr.*

Čigoć

28 km (17½ miles) southeast of Sisak.

The charming village of Čigoć is officially known as the "European Village of Storks" because it draws so many of the migrating birds each spring, and a testament is its annual Stork Festival, usually held in late June. Several hundred of the birds while away much of the summer here before embarking on their long journey to southern Africa. That said, people live here, too, evidenced by the wooden, thatched-roof houses that are likewise a sight to behold.

It's also home to the headquarters of the beautiful Lonjsko polje Nature Park. The UNESCO-listed wetland is one of Europe's largest floodplains, and, as a protected area, it's home to diverse flora and fauna. Over 200 species of birds, 40 of fish, 10 of reptiles, and 15 of amphibians make this their home along with 550 plant species—notably, untouched forests of English oak. This is a place where you can take in the greenery around you as you watch drangonflies (almost 40 dragonfly types live in the park!) fly around you and wild boar run through the fields.

Sights

★ Čigoč Information Center

NATURE PRESERVE | In a traditional house of posavina oak, Čigoč Information Center is situated on the main road that runs through the village center. It is the top regional source for all you need to know about storks, the Stork Festival, and nearby Lonjsko polje Nature Park. It's open daily 8–4, and park maps are available for purchase. Be sure to find out about the park's educational programs or attractive boat trips (many options are available for an additional price). ⊠ *Čigoč 26* ☎ *044/715–115, 098/222–085 (ask for Davor Anzil)* ⊕ *www.pp-lonjsko-polje.hr.*

★ Lonjsko Polje Nature Park

NATURE PRESERVE | One of the largest floodplains in the Danubian basin, this unique ecological and cultural landscape of 20,506 acres along the Sava River was accorded park status in 1990 and is included on UNESCO's roster of World Heritage sites. It has numerous rare and endangered plant and animal species, from white-tailed eagles and saker falcons to otters and the Danube salmon—as well as storks, which are as easy to come by here as in Čigoč. Its 4,858 acres of pastureland is also home to Croatia's highest concentration of indigenous breeds of livestock. Traditional village architecture—in particular, houses made of posavina oak—further contributes to the region's appeal. The park office provides park maps and other information on where to go and what to see and also issues park entrance passes (40 Kn or more depending on the package you'd like). You can opt to take a solar-powered boat ride for 250 Kn, take a guided walking tour for 75 Kn, or do a group bird watching session for 250 Kn too. The easiest way to access the park is by car; if driving from Zagreb, exit the motorway at the pretty village of Popovača and take the road to the right through the villages of Potok and Stružec toward Sisak. ⊠ *Krapje 16, Krapje* ☎ *044/672–080, 044/611–190* ⊕ *www.pp-lonjsko-polje.hr* 🖼 *40 Kn.*

Jasenovac

35 km (22 miles) southeast of Čigoč.

Located where the Sava takes on the task of tracing Croatia's long east–west border with Bosnia and Herzegovina until taking a turn into Serbia more than 150 km (94 miles) away, Jasenovac is the site of Croatia's most notorious World War II labor camps. During the war, Croatia was largely a puppet state of Nazi Germany and Fascist Italy. Current estimates are that somewhere between 77,000 and 97,000 people—mostly Serbs, it is believed, along with Jews, Roma, and Croatian antifascists—perished at this string of five camps on the banks of the Sava River between 1941 and 1945 from exhaustion, illness, cold weather, and murder.

 Sights

Memorial Museum Jasenovac

MUSEUM | Although the camp was razed after the war, a memorial park was eventually established at the site, along with a museum featuring photographs and other exhibits related to the memorial. ⊠ *Braće Radić 147* ☎ *044/672–319* ⊕ *www.jusp-jasenovac.hr* 🖼 *Free.*

Chapter 9

SLAVONIA

Updated by
Andrea MacDonald

👁 **Sights**
★★★☆☆

🍴 **Restaurants**
★★☆☆☆

🛏 **Hotels**
★★☆☆☆

💼 **Shopping**
★☆☆☆☆

🍸 **Nightlife**
★☆☆☆☆

WELCOME TO SLAVONIA

TOP REASONS TO GO

★ **Charming towns:** Strolling around Osijek, Slavonia's largest town, packs a lot of charm into a compact space. Visit attractive churches and parks or explore Tvrđa, the Old Town redolent of ages past. There's also miles of bike lanes and riverside cafés.

★ **Bird-watching:** Head out with your binoculars to serenely beautiful Kopački Rit Nature Park, one of the last great wetlands on the continent.

★ **Tradition:** Discover a land lost in time in the unspoiled Baranja region, with its traditional Pannonian houses, rural restaurants, and extraordinary wine.

★ **Rebirth:** The Baroque town of Vukovar is a testament to the destruction wrought by the Homeland War and to the quiet strength of Croatia's rejuvenation.

★ **Wine country:** Cruise the wine roads of Slavonia, visiting 600-year-old cellars in Ilok or the region around Kutjevo that the Romans nicknamed the "Golden Valley."

Occupying the northeastern section of Croatia, Slavonia is wedged in between Serbia to the east, Hungary to the north, and Bosnia to the south.

1 Osijek. The capital of Slavonia and a true Croatian city.

2 The Baranja Region. An unspoiled area known for its wineries.

3 Vukovar. The site of one of the most tragic battles of the Croatia/Serbian war.

4 Ilok. A lovely town perched above the Danube.

5 Đakovo. A peaceful town famous for a traditional folk festival.

6 The Golden Valley. A charming wine region.

Somewhere beyond the sea, there is a region called Slavonia. There is no coastline here, which has always meant fewer tourists. What it offers instead is something increasingly rare: unspoiled culture and undiscovered treasures.

There are art galleries in Osijek, centuries-old wine cellars in Ilok, Baroque towns, natural parks, hot springs, and rural festivals. As the breadbasket of Croatia, it has miles of cornfields, vineyards, and, in the right season, towering sunflowers in bloom. There are even sandy beaches along the Danube. One thing is certain: Slavonia will not stay undiscovered for long. But for now, it's all yours. Welcome to the green heart of Croatia.

One of the four historical regions of Croatia, the sweeping agricultural plain of Slavonia has been inhabited and traversed through the ages by more ethnicities than practically any other region of Croatia; Croats, Serbs, Hungarians, Germans, Ottomans, and others have all left their mark on its culture. First settled by Slavic tribes in the 7th century and later an integral part of the Hungarian-Croat kingdom, Slavonia experienced a major change of culture with Sultan Suleiman the Magnificent's march toward Hungary and Austria in 1526. For almost 150 years much of the region became an Ottoman stronghold. Osijek and Požega flourished not as part of Christian Europe, but rather as full-fledged, mosque-filled Turkish towns. The Turkish retreat in the late 17th century ushered in an era of Austrian influence, with Osijek, now with a vastly different look, the region's economic cultural capital.

Long a vital transport route, particularly between Zagreb and Belgrade, the easternmost part of Slavonia was badly damaged during the Homeland War in the 1990s. The economy, which is based primarily on agriculture, is the slowest in the country and in recent decades, particularly since Croatia joined the European Union, many Slavonian residents left to find jobs elsewhere. You'll meet young people from Slavonia working all over Croatia, and if you tell them you've visited, or even heard of, their hometown you'll give them a very pleasant surprise. The region's sleepy towns and rural surroundings—from cornfields to forest-covered hills—have a distinctive low-key charm that can only be called Slavonian.

Planning

When to Go

Slavonia can be swelteringly hot in summer (which is considered the low season), when many establishments close because everyone, including the locals, has fled to the coast. The best time to visit is spring or early fall, which are conveniently the same months when hundreds of thousands of birds gather at the Kopački Rit Nature Park. Late August and September are harvest season, when there are plenty of local festivals throughout the region; it's a great time to visit a winery or farmhouse and maybe even lend a hand. It gets cold and snowy in Slavonia in winter, but there are traditional Christmas markets (including a fantastic Advent Market in Osijek, complete with a skating rink, live performances, and a Christmas tram), winter festivals, and local mulled wine to keep you warm.

Getting Here and Around

AIR

There are direct flights from Zagreb, Dubrovnik, Rijeka, Pula, and Split to Osijek with Croatia Airlines.

CONTACTS Osijek Airport. ⊠ *Vukovarska ulica 67, Klisa, Osijek* ☎ *031/284–611* ⊕ *www.osijek-airport.hr.*

BUS

Public transport in Slavonia is, to put it mildly, difficult. It is infrequent, particularly on weekends and holidays. Come summer, when kids aren't traveling to school, many routes are cancelled entirely. If you must use public transport, the bus is more reliable than the train. There are around ten daily buses between Zagreb and Osijek (4 hours, 125 Kn) and a couple of daily buses making the 45-minute trip from Osijek to Vukovar, or to Đakovo an hour away. A great resource for comparing routes is ⊕ *www.getbybus.com.*

CONTACTS Đakovo Bus Station. ⊠ *Splitska bb, Đakovo* ☎ *060/302–030.* **Osijek Bus Station.** ⊠ *Bartola Kašića 70, Osijek* ☎ *060/353–353.* **Vukovar Bus Station.** ⊠ *Ulica Kardinala Alojzija Stepinca 3, Vukovar* ☎ *060/337–799.*

CAR

Having your own wheels will make your life a whole lot easier in this region, particularly if you want to travel on weekends or visit wineries, parks, and small towns that are not served by public transport. Driving in Slavonia is pleasant as roads are quiet, flat, and well-maintained. You can find excellent deals on car rentals from Zagreb, which will make up for the high tolls you'll pay on the highway from Zagreb to Osijek; if you want to bypass the toll roads, it'll add a couple of hours to your trip.

CAR RENTAL CONTACTS Uni Rent. ⊠ *Osijek Downtown, Reisnerova 70, Osijek* ☎ *031/205–058* ⊕ *www.uni-rent.net.*

TRAIN

Train journeys between Zagreb and Osijek are quick and comfortable, with twelve trains daily (four hours, 120 Kn). Venturing farther afield is a different story, as train services have been reduced in recent years and many stations have fallen into disrepair. Once you actually get on the train, the experience is quite whimsical; it cuts right through the heart of Slavonia, giving you a real sense of the region's sweeping vistas. The most reliable source for train scheduling information is the German website ⊕ *www.bahn.de.*

CONTACTS Osijek Train Station. ⊠ *Trg Lavoslava Ružičke 2, Osijek* ☎ *060/333–444.*

Restaurants

Outside of Osijek, where you're spoiled for choice, there aren't a huge number of restaurants in Slavonia. In many towns, you'll find eating at hotels and wineries is your best (and sometimes only) opportunity to try hearty, spicy, and delicious Slavonian cuisine, considered by many Croatians to be the country's best. Slavonia's most popular dishes involve river fish, namely carp, pike, catfish, and pike-perch. With paprika-rich Hungary not far away, you'll often see dishes characterized by an unmistakable, bright-red zest, most evident in the region's most popular dish: the spicy-hot and extremely photogenic *fiš paprikaš*, a fish stew usually served in a bowl big enough for two. *Perkelt od soma* is another fish stew common in Baranja, often made with sliced catfish and accompanied by homemade noodles, cheese, and bacon.

Meat is a key part of the dining picture; regular menu staples include *čobanac*, a stew made with game meat, bathed in paprika sauce and usually served with spaetzle, and *kulen*, spicy, air-dried sausage similar to chorizo that is Slavonia's most beloved local product. Cabbage and cottage cheese are common side dishes, as are pepper, tomato, and cucumber salads straight from the garden. Of course no trip to Slavonia (Croatia's largest wine-producing area) would be complete without local wine. The region is best-known for its whites; look for varieties such as *Graševina* (known elsewhere as Welschriesling) and *Traminac*, a type of Gewürztraminer. Red wine lovers should try the delicious *frankovka*. Hearty meals, delicious wine, and extremely affordable prices all add up to one certainty: you are going to eat and drink far too much in Slavonia, and you'll love it.

Hotels

Slavonia offers fewer options than the rest of Croatia when it comes to accommodations. There are no five-star hotels in the region, and the few luxury hotels are quite expensive by Slavonian standards with fairly basic amenities. You'll find the best hotel options in Osijek and Ilok, while Baranja and Kutjevo offer lovely and unique rural stays where you can enjoy the countryside, taste homemade products, and even get your hands dirty helping out at harvest time.

Restaurant and hotel reviews have been shortened. For full information, visit Fodors.com. Restaurant prices are the average cost of a main course at dinner or, if dinner is not served, at lunch. Hotel prices are the lowest cost of a standard double room in high season.

What It Costs in Croatian kuna (Kn)

$	$$	$$$	$$$$
RESTAURANTS			
under 65 Kn	65 Kn–125 Kn	126 Kn–200 Kn	over 200 Kn
HOTELS			
under 800 Kn	800 Kn–1,450 Kn	1,451 Kn–2,000 Kn	over 2,000 Kn

Tours

The North Way Travel

SELF-GUIDED | This company can help you arrange self-guided itineraries throughout Slavonia with a focus on local experiences, local guides, food, and wine. They also operate a couple of fully guided tours through the year that depart from Zagreb, visiting Slavonia for 5 days before heading down the coast to Dalmatia. ⊕ *www.thenorthwaytravel.com.*

Tureta Travel

EXCURSIONS | This Zagreb-based boutique travel agency runs custom-made private tours around Croatia, including to Slavonia and Baranja. They organize everything based on the client's personal preferences, from transport to accommodation to wine tasting, and they specialize in local, off-the-beaten-track experiences. If you don't have your own transport but want to explore the region, Tureta should be your first call. ☎ *160/116–48* ⊕ *www. tureta-travel.com.*

Visitor Information

The websites of the tourist boards for **Osijek-Baranja County** (⊕ *www.tzos-barzup.hr*) and **Vukovar-Srijem County** (⊕ *www.tzvsz.hr*) have information on towns within the regions.

CONTACTS Đakovo Tourist Information. ✉ *Kralja Tomislava 3, Đakovo* ☎ *031/812–319* ⊕ *www.tzdjakovo.eu.* **Ilok Tourist**

Information. ✉ *Trg. Sv. Ivana Kapistrana 5, Ilok* ☏ *032/590–020, 032/592–966* ⊕ *www.turizamilok.hr.* **Osijek Tourist Information.** ✉ *Županijska 2, Osijek* ☏ *031/203–755* ⊕ *www.tzosijek.hr.* **Vukovar Tourist Information.** ✉ *J. J. Strossmayera 15, Vukovar* ☏ *032/442–889* ⊕ *turizamvukovar.hr.*

Osijek

280 km (175 miles) east of Zagreb.

Croatia's fourth-largest city is an often overlooked treasure trove of cultural and architectural attractions. There are music and food festivals, green markets, parties in the main square, miles of tree-lined streets and bike lanes, beach bars along the river, and no less than 17 parks. It rests on the south bank of the Drava River, which runs the length of the city and is a favorite recreational area for locals; you'll see them biking, rollerblading, walking dogs, or sitting at one of the many riverside terraces with a coffee. Taking a seat beside them is the best way to fully appreciate the city.

In the mid-12th century, Osijek was a prosperous market town in the Hungarian-Croatian kingdom, occupying the area of the present-day **Tvrđa** (Citadel). After more than 150 years of Ottoman occupation in the 16th and 17th centuries, it was a flourishing Turkish town. At 11 am on September 26, 1687, that era ended with the flight of the last Turkish soldier; as a continuing legacy of this watershed event, the church bells of Osijek undertake a celebratory ringing every Friday at 11 am. Osijek henceforth became a military garrison under the Austrians, who turned it into a walled fortress in the late 17th century. The city thrived economically and culturally during this period; its cathedral, national theater, and many other prominent buildings were built, the tram was introduced, and the city was redesigned in the Baroque style you see today. Tragically, Osijek was bombarded during the Homeland War between 1991–1992 in what is known as the Battle of Osijek. Some 800 people were killed, two-thirds of the population displaced, and the majority of those who remained were forced to live in bomb shelters. Most of the damage has since been repaired, but some scars remain in the building facades. Like Zagreb, which it resembles physically, Osijek today is a pleasant, easy-going city of parks, cafés, and locals enjoying a leisurely pace of life. It offers visitors a good chance to tap into a living and breathing Croatian city, and makes a perfect base for explorations farther into Slavonia and Baranja.

GETTING HERE AND AROUND

As the capital of Slavonia and its largest city, Osijek is also the easiest place to get to and from, with regular buses and trains from Zagreb and neighboring countries such as Austria, Serbia, and Hungary. You might consider basing yourself here and taking day trips to other destinations, many of which are just an hour or two away. The Osijek bus station and train station are near each other, both just a short walk from the city center. Although it is certainly possible to walk almost everywhere in the city, hopping aboard one of the trams will save you time. To get between Gornji grad and Tvrđa, take Tram No. 1; to get between the train station and Gornji grad, it's Tram No. 2.

Osijek also has miles of flat bike lanes, so one of the best ways to see the city is on two wheels, particularly with a ride along the river; bikes can be rented from Guesthouse Maksimilian. On the north side of the river, which can be crossed by a free local boat called *kompa* or by the pedestrian bridge *Pješački Most* (one of the main symbols of the city), you'll find Copacabana Beach Bar and the Osijek Zoo.

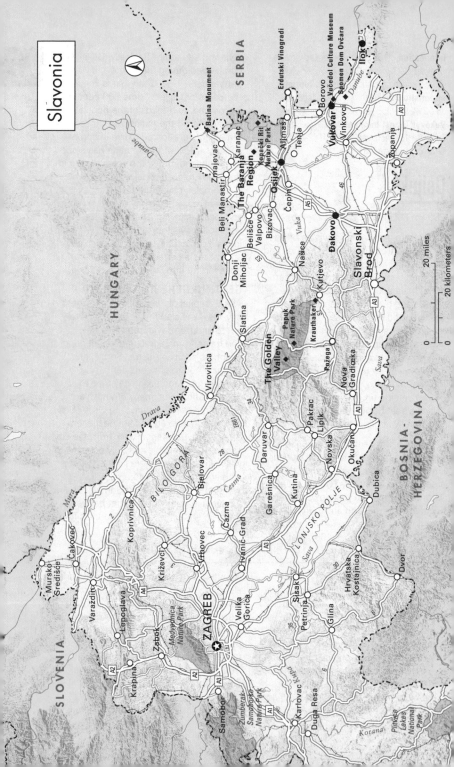

👁 Sights

Tvrđa (Citadel) is the city's historical Old Town, and while it's a bit sleepy during the day with just a couple of noteworthy sights, it comes to life at night with bars and terraces filling up the main square. **Gornji grad** (Upper Town) is the city's commercial and administrative center, where you will find the Cathedral, Hotel Waldinger, and Hotel Osijek, plus many shops and cafés. Europska Avenija is the broad avenue that connects the new and old towns. It is lined with late 19th- and early 20th-century neoclassical and art nouveau houses built as private residences, complete with gardens and cast-iron railings.

Arheološki Muzej (*Archeological Museum*)

MUSEUM | On Tvrđa's Holy Trinity Square, you'll find the spacious Archeological Museum in the renovated City Guardhouse. It has an impressive range of artifacts from Slavonia through the ages, from the neolithic Starčevo culture through to Celtic and Roman times. The building itself is modern and airy, with a glass dome over the arcaded courtyard, and the exhibitions are well laid out across several rooms. ✉ *Trg. Sv. Trojstva 2, Tvrda* ☎ *031/232–130* ☾ *Closed Sun. and Mon.*

★ **Konkatedrala Sv. Petra i Pavla** (*Co-cathedral of Saints Peter and Paul*)
RELIGIOUS SITE | This majestic single-nave church is the highlight of Osijek's downtown skyline. At 292 feet, its redbrick, neo-Gothic steeple is the second-highest structure in Croatia. Built between 1894 and 1898 on the initiative of the famous Đakovo-based bishop Josip Juraj Strossmayer, it has five altars and the walls are painted with colorful frescoes. ✉ *Trg Pape Ivana Pavla II, Gornji Grad* ☎ *031/310–020* ⊕ *www.svpetaripavao.hr.*

★ **Muzej Likovnih Umjetnosti** (*Museum of Fine Arts*)
MUSEUM | One of the mansions along Europska Avenija, formerly belonging to a prominent attorney, is now the home of the Museum of Fine Arts, with a focus on Croatian and Slavonian artists and a permanent collection of paintings, sculpture, and graphic arts from the 18th century to now. It is well worth a visit, particularly to check out its temporary exhibitions on the ground floor. ✉ *Europska avenija 9, Gornji Grad* ☎ *031/251–280* ⊕ *www.mlu.hr* ✉ *15 Kn* ☾ *Closed Mon.*

Muzej Slavonije (*Museum of Slavonia*)
MUSEUM | One of the largest museums in Croatia, the Museum of Slavonia is located in the city's former magistrate building, the oldest public building in Osijek that was once the city hall. It has myriad objects on display concerning the region's folklore, culture, and natural history, with everything from stuffed animals and old coins to pottery and swords. ✉ *Trg Sv. Trojstva 6, Tvrda* ☎ *031/250–731* ⊕ *www.mso.hr* ✉ *20 Kn* ☾ *Closed Sun. and Mon.*

Perivoj Krajla Tomislava (*King Tomislav Gardens*)
CITY PARK | **FAMILY** | With 17 around town, Osijek is known as a city of parks, and this is one of the nicest. The King Tomislav Gardens is a spacious, forested oasis that was laid out in the 18th century for the Austrian officers to take a breather from life in the citadel. It separates historic Tvrđa from Gornji grad, the more bustling, commercial heart of town. The park is home to playgrounds and a tennis club. ✉ *Europska avenija 2.*

★ **Tvrđa**
HISTORIC SITE | Now a somewhat sleepy Old Town that always seems to be under construction, this walled fortress has a history dating back to the mid-12th century when the site was a market town in the Hungarian-Croatian kingdom. It was later occupied by the Ottomans, and finally became a fortified military garrison

under the Austrians in the 17th century. It has one of the best-preserved ensembles of Baroque buildings in Croatia, with old barracks, churches, and monasteries. Facing the Drava River, the Water Gate is the only remaining gate in the original fortress wall, most of which was razed in the 1920s. **Trg Sv. Trojstva** (Holy Trinity Square) is Tvrđa's main square, and at its center is the Votive Pillar of the Holy Trinity, one of Osijek's finest baroque monuments. Erected in 1729-30 by the widow of General Maksimilijan Petraš, who died of the plague in 1728, it has an elaborate pinnacle and four pedestals at its base bearing the statues of various saints, including St. Sebastian. ✉ *Tvrda.*

ZOO-vrt Osijek (*Osijek Zoo*)
ZOO | FAMILY | Croatia's largest zoo is located on the north side of the Drava River. With about 80 animal species spread across 27 acres, including kangaroos, meerkats, lions, chimpanzees, giraffes, and zebras, plus 20 species in the aquarium and terrarium, it makes a great half-day out for the entire family. You can drive across the bridge to get there, or take a free kompa boat from the city side of the river. ✉ *Sjevernodravska obala 1, Gornji Grad* ☎ *031/285–234* 🌐 *www.zoo-osijek.hr* 🎟 *20 Kn.*

🍴 Restaurants

Gold by Waldinger
$ | CAFÉ | Offering old-world Viennese-style elegance, Gold by Waldinger is one of Osijek's finest cafés. Located on the main thoroughfare in Gornji Grad, just across the street from Hotel Waldinger, it is a stylish, popular place to relax over a cocktail, coffee, ice cream, or spectacularly indulgent cake. **Known for:** excellent but affordable cakes and pastries; best ice cream in Osijek; one of Osijek's most popular cafés. [$] *Average main: 12 Kn* ✉ *Županijska ulica 15, Gornji Grad* ☎ *031/623–057* 🌐 *gold.waldinger.hr.*

★ **Kompa**
$ | EASTERN EUROPEAN | On the bank of the Drava, just across the river from the Osijek Zoo, Kompa takes traditional dishes to another level. Their homemade sausages are perfectly spicy, the *koljenica* (pig's knuckle) is a firm favorite, and if you are around on a Sunday or holiday, join the locals for a big feast of *teleće pečenje* (roast veal). **Known for:** riverside location (be prepared for mosquitos); unique range of traditional food; excellent sunset views. [$] *Average main: 60 Kn* ✉ *Splavarska 1, Gornji Grad* ☎ *031/375–755* 🌐 *www.restorankompa.hr.*

Lumiere
$$ | MEDITERRANEAN | Under the glow of the Kino Urania sits Lumiere restaurant, a bright light in a city full of old-school restaurants. The menu is Italian-inspired, with a wide range of pasta, steaks, and seafood, and offers a modern take on Slavonian favorites such as *crna svinja* (black pig). **Known for:** sophisticated ambience; modern take on traditional favorites; romantic terrace. [$] *Average main: 120 Kn* ✉ *Šetaliste Kardinala Franje Šepera 8, Gornji Grad* ☎ *031/201–088* 🌐 *www.lumiere.com.*

Slavonska Kuća
$ | EASTERN EUROPEAN | Just a couple of blocks from Tvrđa's main square, this small one-room eatery is about as atmospheric as can be, with rustic wooden benches, walls adorned with bric-a-brac, and folksy background music. It's a local favorite and you won't find much English, but the waiters are friendly and will help you choose between regional fare like *fiš paprikaš, čobanac,* and *od divljači* (venison stew). **Known for:** traditional Slavonian food; longstanding Osijek favorite; central location in Tvrđa. [$] *Average main: 60 Kn* ✉ *Kamila Firingera 26, Tvrda* ☎ *031/369–955.*

The Co-cathedral of Saints Peter and Paul is the second-highest structure in Croatia.

Hotels

★ Guesthouse Maksimilian

$ | **B&B/INN** | Art, history, culture, and comfort come together in this 14-room guesthouse in Tvrđa, a one-of-a-kind accommodation option in Osijek. **Pros:** central location in Tvrđa; historical ambience; excursions of the region can be arranged. **Cons:** rooms can be noisy; kitchen off-limits for guest use; basic facilities. [$] *Rooms from: 450 Kn* ✉ *Franjevačka 12, Tvrđa* ☎ *031/497–567* 🌐 *maksimilian.hr* 🛏 *14 rooms* 🍴 *Free breakfast.*

Hotel Osijek

$ | **HOTEL** | This skyline-dominating glass edifice located right on the riverfront is the city's only luxury hotel; it has a Finnish sauna and Jacuzzi on the top floor with excellent views and a fantastic restaurant, Zimska Luka, right on the riverfront that is worth a visit even if you're not a hotel guest. **Pros:** central riverfront location; great on-site restaurant; rooftop wellness center and spa. **Cons:** large and rather impersonal; many rooms on the small side; lacking a distinctly Slavonian atmosphere. [$] *Rooms from: 720 Kn* ✉ *Šamačka 4, Gornji Grad* ☎ *031/230–333* 🌐 *www.hotelosijek.hr* 🛏 *147 rooms* 🍴 *Free breakfast.*

★ Hotel Waldinger

$ | **HOTEL** | Located in a 19th-century art nouveau building on the main street in Gornji Grad, the Waldinger—named after famous local painter Adolf Waldinger—offers luxury on a cozy scale with a period look and feel. **Pros:** old world luxury; excellent dining at restaurant and café; lavish decor. **Cons:** expensive by Slavonian standards; rooms on top floor have smallish windows; no elevator. [$] *Rooms from: 680 Kn* ✉ *Županijska 8, Gornji Grad* ☎ *031/250–450* 🌐 *www.waldinger.hr* 🛏 *16 rooms* 🍴 *Free breakfast.*

Nightlife

Osijek has a large student population so its bars and cafés are full day and night with people drinking coffee, eating ice cream, or enjoying a local Osječko. The promenade along the river (Zimska Luka) is lined with inviting café-bars and really comes alive on summer weekends with live music across the outdoor terraces. Much of the late-night action takes place in Tvrđa.

American Bar Dollar

BARS/PUBS | Located in the Upper Town, across the street from the tourist information center, American Bar Dollar is a hot spot that serves burgers, ribs, and craft beers in a space with kitschy, vintage Americana decor. It's a fun place to hang out with the local cool kids. ⊠ *Županijska 5, Gornji Grad* ☎ *031/284–625* ⊕ *www.americanbardollar.com.*

Gajba

BARS/PUBS | The first craft-beer bar in Croatia, this tiny establishment in the Upper Town is a great place to try Croatian and international craft brews. The staff are serious beer aficionados who also organize the very popular Osijek Craft Beer Festival. ⊠ *Sunčana 3, Gornji Grad* ⊕ *www.gajba.hr.*

Merlon

BARS/PUBS | This spacious, stylish pub with an outdoor terrace just off the main square in Tvrđa is a great option for a few drinks in the evening. They also have substantial American-style pub grub with excellent burgers and ribs, and a good selection of veggie burgers. ⊠ *Ul. Franje Markovića 3, Tvrđa* ☎ *031/283–240* ⊕ *www.merlon.hr.*

St. Patrick's Pub

BARS/PUBS | The main square in Tvrđa is lined with café-bars and terraces, distinguishable only by their different-colored umbrellas. St. Patrick's Pub, a paean to all things Irish, was the pioneer, and still one of the most popular. ⊠ *South side of Trg Svetog Trojstva, Franje Kuhača 15, Tvrđa* ☎ *031/205–202.*

Trica

CAFES—NIGHTLIFE | A popular student hangout on a side street beside Hotel Osijek with a lively soundtrack and quirky decor, Trica stretches over three rooms on split levels, with a few tables in the little garden out back. It's great for a coffee or cocktail any time of day. ⊠ *Lučki prilaz 2, Gornji Grad* ☎ *031/778–414.*

 Performing Arts

Hrvatsko Narodno Kazalište (*Croatian National Theater*)

THEATER | The Croatian National Theater is Osijek's venue for a broad array of Croatian and international plays. The building that has housed the theater since 1907 is an imposing ochre structure whose Venetian-Moorish style renders it the most striking of a string of classical facades along Županijska ulica. ⊠ *Županijska 9, Gornji Grad* ☎ *031/220–700* ⊕ *www.hnk-osijek.hr.*

Kino Urania (*Urania Cinema*)

FILM | This historic art nouveau cinema, which screened its first films back in 1912, was designed by famed Osijek architect Viktor Axmann. Movie buffs will love the old-school charm, particularly the vintage posters on the walls. Films are in English with subtitles. ⊠ *V. Hengla 1, Gornji Grad* ☎ *031/205–507* ⊕ *www.kinematografi-osijek.hr.*

Shopping

There are two big shopping malls in Osijek: Portanova and the Avenue Mall; a bus runs from the city center to both of them. Bustling Županijska street in Gornji Grad is similar to a smaller-scale version of Zagreb's Ilica Street with its independent boutiques, shops, and trams.

Green Market

OUTDOOR/FLEA/GREEN MARKETS | The outdoor green market is a super local and authentic place to buy Slavonian delicacies like cottage cheese with sour cream, bags of paprika and other spices, fresh produce, baked goods, and all manner of smoked meats, including the famous *kulen*. The market opens daily at 7 am. ✉ *5 Trg Ljudevita Gaja, Gornji Grad.*

 ## Activities

BEACHES

Copacabana

WATER SPORTS | FAMILY | Who says you need the Adriatic to have water fun in Croatia? On the north side of the Drava River, you'll find Copacabana, a complex of outdoor swimming pools, water slides, and a sandy beach where locals will jump straight into the river to cool down on hot summer days. There are also mini-golf facilities and bocce courts. It's a great place for the whole family to spend a sunny afternoon. ✉ *Tvrdavica bb* ⊕ *www. sportski-objekti.hr.*

The Baranja Region

314 km (195 miles) east of Zagreb.

The unspoiled Baranja region, whose name means "Mother of Wine" in Hungarian, is located in northeastern Croatia on the borders of Hungary and Serbia. It begins on the other side of the Drava River from Osijek, but seems a world away from city life. It is full of farmhouses and quaint villages with only a few thousand residents at most. Life is lived around the Danube, in vineyards and fertile fields, in Pannonian mud houses, and near the swamps of Kopački Rit. There are fish-stew cook-offs, harvest festivals, labyrinths of flowers, wine, goulash, and everything is sprinkled with paprika (just one aspect of the strong Hungarian influence here).

The best village to spend the evening is colorful, rural Karanac. You can have lunch or dinner at Baranjska Kuća, stay at Ivica i Marica for the night, and spend a few hours riding a bike around the gently sloping fields and vineyards. The entire region is quite compact, but it is tricky to get around Baranja by public transport. Arrange a day tour from Osijek if you don't have a car.

 ## Sights

Batina Monument

MEMORIAL | High on a hill above the border where Croatia meets Hungary and Serbia is this striking WWII monument, dedicated to the 2,000 members of the Red Army who died in the Battle of Batina. It was built in 1946, three years after the battle, by Croatian sculptor Antun Augustinčić. The monument itself, topped by a 89-foot-high obelisk, is quite impressive, but the views of the Danube, forests, and three countries below are the best part of the visit. ✉ *Batina.*

Erdutski Vinogradi

TOWN | The village of Erdut, with a medieval castle overlooking the Danube, is just 37 km (23 miles) east of Osijek. The Erdut Agreement, which brought a peaceful resolution to the war in 1995 in eastern Croatia, was signed here. There are several wineries to visit around the village, including Erdutski Vinogradi, which dates from 1450 and has produced wine since 1730. And there are lovely views from the winery, which is also home to one of the quirkiest sights in the Croatian wine world: the world's largest barrel still in use. Made of 150-year-old Slavonian oak, it can hold 75,000 liters of Graševina. Tastings can be arranged in the cellar beside the Great Barrel; call ahead to make a reservation. ✉ *Trg Branka Hercega 1, Erdut* ☎ *031/596–555* ⊕ *erdutski-vinogradi.hr.*

★ Josić Winery

WINERY/DISTILLERY | One of the best wineries in the country, the progressive Josić winery in the settlement of Zmajevac is a must-visit. Located on a narrow road alongside a few other small wineries, it's headed by the brilliant Damir Josić, who is both winemaker and head chef. Call ahead to arrange a free tour of the 1935 cellars and a wine tasting; those craving a glass of red wine in this land of whites will be happy to learn that Josić is renowned for its excellent Cabernet Sauvignon and cuvée (although 50% of its production is Graševina). The on-site restaurant, with a romantic indoor atmosphere and a lively local vibe on the terrace, is also deservedly popular for its traditional meals, including stews cooked on an open fire at the entrance. ✉ *Planina 194, Zmajevac* ☎ *031/734–410* 🌐 *www.josic.hr* 🕑 *Closed Mon.*

★ Kopački Rit Nature Park

NATIONAL/STATE PARK | One of the most popular sites in the region, Kopački Rit Nature Park is one of the largest remaining wetlands along the Danube and a place of serene beauty. Embracing more than 74,100 acres immediately north of the Drava, 10 km (6 miles) northeast of Osijek, the park is covered with immense reed beds, willow, poplar, and oak forests, and crisscrossed by ridges, ponds, shallow lakes, and marshes. More than 300 bird species, hundreds of varieties of plants, and dozens of species of butterflies, mammals, and fish live here, and it is also a breeding area for numerous endangered species, including the white-tailed sea eagle, the black stork, and the European otter. Egrets, herons, and cormorants are abundant, as are red deer, roe deer, and wild boar.

The best times of year to visit are during spring and autumn bird migrations, when there are often several hundred thousand birds in the park. There is an information office at the entrance in Kopač. A boardwalk leads to the landing where boat excursions set out daily into the marshy heart of the park, along a channel to Kopačevo Jezero, the largest lake.

There are different guided tours available, but the best is the Beaver's Trail, which includes entrance into the park and boardwalk, plus a small boat tour through the wetlands (1 hour). The best time to do the Beaver's Trail is during the morning when bird-spotting is best.

Getting to Kopački Rit from Osijek is simple if you have a car—just follow the signs once you're in Bilje. If you go by bus, get off in Bilje and follow the signs on foot for some 4 km (2½ miles) along rural roads to the entrance of the park, or ride a bike from Osijek. ✉ *Information Center near Kopačevo, Kopacevo* ☎ *031/445–445* 🌐 *www.pp-kopacki-rit.hr* 🎟 *150 Kn for Beaver's Trail.*

🍴 Restaurants

★ Baranjska Kuća

$$ | **EASTERN EUROPEAN** | **FAMILY** | With locals and visitors alike enjoying a meal at the large wooden tables, lots of space and antique toys for the kids, and the air scented with smoke from the outdoor firepits where cooks are making homemade *čvarci* (pork cracklings), the lively terrace at Baranjska Kuća is the best place to soak up the Baranja atmosphere. Considered one of the best restaurants in Slavonia, it is a great place to try typical Slavonian dishes such as čobanac and beans cooked in clay pots, or more unusual dishes such as snails in nettle sauce. **Known for:** traditional Slavonian food; interesting "Street of Forgotten Times" museum out back; lively local atmosphere. [$] *Average main: 110 Kn* ✉ *Kolodvorska 99, Karanac* ☎ *031/720–180* 🌐 *www.baranjska-kuca.com.*

Hotels

★ Ivica i Marica

$ | **B&B/INN** | The most welcoming and unique place to stay in Baranja is this beautifully restored, working farmhouse in the tiny village of Karanac. **Pros:** large outdoor space with horses and stables; excellent breakfast of local and home-made products; beautifully decorated rooms. **Cons:** difficult to reach by public transport; not many amenities within walking distance; rooms can get a little cold. [$] *Rooms from: 450 Kn* ✉ *Ive Lole Ribara 8A, Karanac* ☎ *091/137–3793* 🌐 *www.ivica-marica.com* 🛏 *25 rooms* 🍴 *Free breakfast.*

Shopping

Asztalos Kermaik

CERAMICS/GLASSWARE | Located in a renovated steam mill from 1911 and run by artist Daniel Asztalos, this quirky little ceramics shop sells lovely, original items, like spice pots, beer mugs, wine glasses, and olive-oil bottles, and also offers pottery workshops if you want to create your own keepsake. Find it in the settlement of Suza on the road between Karanac and Batina. ✉ *Maršala Tita 96, Suza* ☎ *098/945–5990.*

Vukovar

35 km (22 miles) southeast of Osijek.

There's no doubt that a visit to Vukovar hurts. As you visit the sights, the story of what happened here will slowly unfold, made even sadder by the glimpses of what a beautiful city of culture this once was. It's a place that holds a tender spot in the hearts of most Croatians, and it will earn a spot in yours too. Today, it is as much the scene of urban renewal as it is of destruction, and this is a good time to visit, as Vukovar recovers from its painful past and strives to regain its former vitality.

In 1991, Vukovar was a prosperous city. Located at the confluence of the Danube and Vuka rivers, it had a lovely ensemble of Baroque architecture, fine museums, and many restaurants. It was named after the ancient Vučedol culture that inhabited a site 5 km (3 miles) down-stream from the present-day city some 5,000 years ago. The area was later the site of a Roman settlement, and by the 11th century a community existed at the town's present location; this settlement became the seat of Vukovo County in the 13th century. After Turkish rule (1526–1687), almost all of Vukovar and environs was bought by the counts of Eltz, a German family that strongly influenced the development of the town for the next two centuries and whose palace is home to the town museum.

When Yugoslavia started to break apart in 1991 and Croatia declared independ-ence, the JNA (Yugoslav People's Army) and Serb militias began seizing control of areas with a large Serbian population. Vukovar, which at the time had a mixed population of 47% Croatians and 37% Serbians, was steadfastly claimed by both sides. A battle for the city ensued; it was up to lightly armed soldiers of the newly created Croatian National Guard, as well as 1,100 civilian volunteers, to defend it. During the 87-day siege, 12,000 shells and rockets were launched daily in the fiercest European battle since World War II. Those who had not fled Vukovar in the beginning became trapped inside, taking refuge in Cold War–era bomb shelters. On the 18th of Novem-ber, the defenders of the city, running out of ammunition, numbers, and strength, could hold on no longer and Vukovar fell. The once-lovely city was reduced to rubble. More than 30,000 Croatian residents were deported, thousands were killed, and thousands more are still reported as missing. Several military and political officials have since been indicted and jailed for war crimes, including those involved in the notorious Vukovar hospital massacre.

In 1998, Vukovar was peacefully reintegrated into Croatia and the slow recovery process began. Even ten years ago, it would have been unfathomable that a visit here could involve anything other than war, but today there are plenty of ways to pass your time. There are new modern shopping malls and cinemas, the Eltz Castle and the Franciscan Monastery have been rebuilt, and the ultra-modern Vučedol Culture Museum is the first step in a planned archaeological park. Vukovar is also a stop along the Danube bike path network, attracting cycling groups each summer, and its proximity to Ilok has made it a stop on many wine tours. The center is once again full of busy cafés and bustling markets, and there is a six-day Vukovar Film Festival every August.

Yet the memories are never far away. Next to brand-new structures are the burnt-out frames of old buildings. Walls are still pockmarked, houses remain empty, the population is now half of what it was pre-war, and although it is mixed, the two ethnic communities remain divided. There is hope in the air, but it's usually not long before a conversation with a local will, inevitably, turn to the past. In a poignant reminder, one cannot help but notice a steady, somber stream of pedestrian traffic to one of Vukovar's most conspicuous sites: a tall, simple white cross situated at the tip of a narrow causeway overlooking the Danube, with inscriptions in both Cyrillic and Roman letters, honoring victims on both sides. With memorials and sites all around town, Vukovar is a living war museum and an important and worthwhile stop on any Croatian itinerary.

GETTING HERE AND AROUND
Around five trains and buses make the daily 45-minute journey from Osijek to Vukovar, several of them continuing onward to Ilok farther south. Regular buses and trains also travel between Zagreb and Vukovar, stopping in Vinkovci along the way.

The main sights in Vukovar are spread out over an 8-km (5 mile) stretch of road that runs from one end of the city to the other. If you're coming from Osijek, you'll start with the Hospital Museum and end at the Vučedol Culture Museum. Many of the sights are within walking distance of each other in the center of town, but you'll need a car to get to those that are farther away. Ask at the tourist information office for assistance—they can arrange a tour guide to accompany you.

 # Sights

Ada
BEACH—SIGHT | FAMILY | Vukovar locals live their lives on the banks of the Danube, and when it gets hot outside, they hop right into it. Ada is the name of a sandy beach on Vukovar Island, in the middle of the river where locals go to swim, play volleyball, and suntan. There is a café on the island, but not many other facilities. It is a fun retreat, 10 minutes from the city, and can be reached by boats that leave regularly from near the Hotel Lav and Vrske restaurant. A return ticket costs 10 Kn. ⊠ *Island of Vukovar*.

Franjevački Samostan i Župa Sv. Filipa i Jakova (*Franciscan Monastery & Church of Sts. Philip and James*)
RELIGIOUS SITE | High on a hill southeast of the town center you'll find Vukovar's main ecclesiastical attraction, and one of the largest in Croatia. Construction on the Baroque monastery began in 1723, and it held one of the richest and most valuable libraries in the country, as well as prominent paintings and gold and silver vessels. Both have been restored to their former glory after being ravaged in the war. ⊠ *Samostanska 5* ☎ *032/441–381* ⊙ *Closed Sun.*

The Gradski Muzej Vukovar, the city's municipal museum, is housed in an 18th-century palace.

★ Gradski Muzej Vukovar (*Vukovar Municipal Museum*)

MUSEUM | The 18th-century palace Dvorac Eltz has housed the Gradski Muzej Vukovar since 1969. During the siege of Vukovar, the palace was severely damaged and the collection was moved to a Zagreb museum for safekeeping. After decades of reconstruction, the entire museum and all 2,000 of its pieces are once again open for viewing, a positive sign that Vukovar is back in business. Founded in 1946, the museum was originally housed in an old school and then a post office before the palace became its home. It has an excellent range of local archaeological artifacts, from the Vučedol culture that flourished around 3000 BC right up to the siege of Vukovar. ✉ *Županijska 2* ☎ *032/441–271* ⊕ *www. muzej-vukovar.hr* 🎫 *40 Kn (or free with Vuseum Pass)* 🕐 *Closed Mon.*

★ Mjesto Sjećanja–Vukovar Bolnica (*Place of Memory—Vukovar Hospital*)

HOSPITAL—SIGHT | You'll want to bring a steady set of nerves with you to this site: during the siege of Vukovar, the top four floors of the hospital were destroyed by consistent bombing, despite being designated an official safe zone; still, staff continued to work in the basement and bomb shelter, helping civilians and soldiers, operating even without running water. After Vukovar fell in 1991, and despite an agreement that the hospital must be safely evacuated, more than 200 people were removed from the hospital by a Serbian militia and brought to Ovčara farm, where they were beaten, tortured, and eventually executed. Others were sent to prisons or to refugee camps. Today, the structure has been rebuilt and functions as a regular hospital again, but the areas used during that time have been converted into a chilling multimedia museum-memorial. Opening hours are very sporadic, but in theory it is open from 8 am to 1 pm. Reach the memorial through the main gate of the hospital (under the Bolnica sign); ask at the small guard station on your right if it's open. You'll then find the memorial down the ramp to the right; the entrance is marked by a giant red cross, full of holes. ✉ *Županijska 35* 🌐 *www.ob-vukovar.hr* ⏲ *Closed weekends and afternoons.*

★ **Spomen Dom Ovčara** (*Ovčara Memorial*)
MEMORIAL | On November 20–21, 1991, more than 200 soldiers and civilians were brought from the hospital to this former agricultural hangar, 4 km (2½ miles) outside the city and surrounded by fields of crops, by a Serbian militia. They were beaten, tortured, and eventually executed at another site 1 km (½ mile) away. The mass grave was exhumed in 1996, and 194 bodies were identified; among the dead were men ranging from 16 to 77 years old, one woman, a prominent radio journalist, and a French volunteer. Ovčara Memorial is a somber, powerful site; it respectfully pays homage to the victims as well as conveys the horror that took place here. To get to the site, follow signs along the road to Ilok for 6 km (4 miles) past the Memorial Cemetery of Homeland War Victims, the largest mass grave in Europe since WWII—eventually turning right and driving another 4 km (2½ miles) down a country road. If you don't have wheels, check with the tourist information center about your transportation options. ✉ *Ovčara* ☎ *032/512–345* 🎫 *5 Kn.*

★ **Vučedol Culture Museum**
ARCHAEOLOGICAL SITE | Located 6 km (3.7 miles) from the center of Vukovar on the road to Ilok is the impressive Vučedol Culture Museum, a modern marvel celebrating the ancient Vučedol culture that once flourished in the vicinity. Exhibitions include the oldest Indo-European calendar, skulls demonstrating sacrificial practices, and the pit where the famous Vučedol Dove was discovered. This fascinating museum, spread across 19 rooms and built on a slope so that it almost seems part of the landscape, is the first step in a planned archaeological park. If this is the last sight you visit on your way out of town, you're left with a very encouraging sense of the city's future. ✉ *Vučedol 252* ☎ *032/373–930* 🌐 *www.vucedol.hr* 🎫 *40 Kn (free with Vuseum Pass)* ⏲ *Closed Mon.*

Water Tower
BUILDING | Visible from everywhere in Vukovar is its most famous symbol: the water tower. Rising 150 feet into the air, the imposing, redbrick structure once had a restaurant at the top with lovely views over the river and surrounding vineyards. Its sheer size made it a frequent target during the siege; it was hit with artillery more than 600 times. But it is still standing, with gaping holes on all sides, and although renovation is underway to restore the interior, the facade will remain that way as a constant reminder and a testament to the strength of the city. ✉ *1 Ulica Velika Skela.*

🍴 Restaurants

Stari Toranj
$ | **PIZZA** | **FAMILY** | This cozy family restaurant with a small patio and pleasant, down-to-earth staff is a local favorite. They serve up reliably good pizza and selection of simple, traditional meals. **Known for:** pretty good pizza; cozy space; local vibes. [$] *Average main: 50 Kn* ✉ *Trg Republike Hrvatske* ☎ *099/732–1255* 🌐 *www.restoranstaritoranj.com.hr.*

Vrške
$$ | **EASTERN EUROPEAN** | This apricot-color restaurant with a charming farmhouse look rests on an islet reached by a pedestrian bridge behind the Hotel Lav. Carp, catfish, pike-perch, and other freshwater fish are the favorites here, whether grilled, fried, or in a thick, vegetable-rich sauce. **Known for:** riverside location; river fish specialties; quaint atmosphere. [$] *Average main: 70 Kn* ✉ *Parobrodarska 3* ☎ *032/441–788* 🌐 *www.restoran-vrske.hr.*

Hotels

Hotel Lav

$$ | HOTEL | A sparkling white building with a glass front, Hotel Lav is the only luxury hotel in Vukovar. **Pros:** the only luxury hotel in town; centrally located; nice on-site restaurant. **Cons:** expensive by Slavonian standards; service is hit-and-miss; breakfast is disappointing. [$] *Rooms from: 830 Kn* ✉ *J. J. Strossmayera 18* ☎ *032/445–100* 🌐 *www.hotel-lav.hr* 🛏 *47 rooms* 🍴 *Free breakfast.*

Vukovarska Kuća

$ | B&B/INN | FAMILY | Located in the relaxing Adica forest just a short drive from the center of town, Vukovarska Kuća is a lovely, homey option with a great restaurant, walking trails nearby, a playground, and lots of space for the kids to run around. **Pros:** simple and sweet accommodations; great restaurant on-site; plenty of outdoor space in surrounding forest. **Cons:** services are basic; not in the center of Vukovar; Wi-Fi is spotty. [$] *Rooms from: 375 Kn* ✉ *Adica bb* ☎ *032/835–931* 🌐 *www.vukovarska-kuca.eatbu.com* 🛏 *6 rooms* 🍴 *Free breakfast.*

Ilok

37 km (22 miles) southeast of Vukovar, 74 km (45 miles) southeast of Osijek

Perched high on the western slopes of the Fruška Gora hills above the Danube and built around a medieval fortress, Ilok, Croatia's easternmost town, is one of the loveliest in Slavonia (although it is technically in the region of Syrmia, as the locals will proudly tell you). On a clear day, you can see all the way across the Vojvodina plain to Novi Sad in Serbia just 30 km (18 miles) away.

Ilok has been inhabited since the Neolithic era, but its golden age came in the 15th century when Nicholas of Ilok, the Ban of Croatia and King of Bosnia, built a fortification on a plateau overlooking the river and a castle within, turning Ilok into a fortified royal residence, and began the first construction of wine cellars. The last member of the Iločki family died in 1524; two years later, Ilok was occupied by the Ottomans, under whose rule it remained until 1697. There are still the remains of a hammam and a Turkish grave in the Old Town from this period. After defeating the Turks, the Habsburgs gave Ilok to the aristocratic Odescalchi family from Italy, who quickly set about rebuilding the town, particularly the castle, in Baroque style. They developed the wine cellars below the castle, and began production of the celebrated Traminac wine. There are now a dozen other vineyards around town producing award-winning wines, particularly Graševina and Traminac. All can be visited by appointment.

Ilok became part of Yugoslavia in 1918. At the beginning of the war in 1991, it was rapidly surrounded and occupied by Serb forces, sparing it the drawn-out devastation suffered by nearby Vukovar. Ilok was integrated into the Republic of Serb Krajina, and not reintegrated into Croatia until 1998.

Ilok is composed of two parts: the upper half is where the feudal families lived and where today you'll find the city's historical sights and the remains of the fortified walls, and the lower half where traditionally the townsfolk lived and worked, and where you'll find sandy beaches along the Danube.

GETTING HERE AND AROUND

There are frequent buses between Vukovar and Ilok (45 minutes, 35 Kn), many of which start or finish in Osijek; the bus will let you off in the center of the lower town. Ilok is best explored by foot as most of the main sites, hotels, and wineries are around the center of town. If you plan to visit a winery out of town, contact them or the helpful folks at the tourist information center and someone will usually come to pick you up.

The town of Ilok is located on the picturesque hills of Fruška Gora, perched above the Danube River.

⊙ Sights

★ Muzej Grada Iloka (*Town Museum of Ilok*)

MUSEUM | This impressive collection takes you through the ages of Ilok, from the Ottoman era to the Austrian Empire, the wars of the 20th century, right up to a modern art gallery. There are particularly interesting exhibits on the region's Jewish population pre-1945, relics from a 19th-century pharmacy, and an ethnological section on the top floor focusing on Ilok's large Slovak population. The museum is housed in the Odescalchi Castle, an imposing fortified structure overlooking the Danube, which was built on the foundations of the 15th-century castle of Nicholas of Ilok. Legend says that Suleiman the Magnificent once slept in this castle. The rooms themselves are exquisitely designed with period pieces, even mood music, in keeping with their original function, such as the hunting room and the drawing room. ⊠ *Šetalište o Mladena Barbarića 5* ☎ *032/827–410*

⊕ *www.mgi.hr* ✉ *20 Kn* ⊗ *Closed Sun. and Mon.*

★ Stari Podrum (*Old Cellar*)

WINERY/DISTILLERY | A wine cellar, restaurant, hotel, and history lesson all rolled into one, Stari Podrum is one of Croatia's most renowned wineries and a must-see when visiting Ilok. It is located next door to the Odescalchi Castle; in fact, the incredibly atmospheric, 100 meter-long cellars stretch underneath it. The Odescalchi family began producing high-class wines here in the 18th century, including the celebrated Traminac, which was served at the coronation of Queen Elizabeth II. A private tour will take you through the cool cellars, past Slavonian oak barrels, to the prestigious archive wines and old bottles, full of dust and cobwebs, that were hidden behind a wall for protection during the Homeland War. You can try all of the wines produced here, and buy souvenir bottles at very reasonable prices. The on-site restaurant serves delicious Slavonian dishes; you can eat inside surrounded by traditional embroidery and heavy wooden furniture, or outdoors in the sunny central courtyard. Accommodations can also be arranged in one of 18 on-site rooms. ✉ *4 Šetalište O. M. Barbarića* ☎ *032/590–088* 🌐 *www.ilocki-podrumi.hr.*

Župa Sv. Ivana Kapistrana (*Church of St. John of Capistrano*)
RELIGIOUS SITE | This Franciscan church and monastery overlooking the Danube, first constructed in 1349, holds the remains of St. John of Capistrano, a Franciscan friar and Catholic priest. In 1456, at age 70, he led a successful battle against the Ottomans, which earned him the nickname "Soldier Priest." He died three months later in Ilok of the bubonic plague but was said to have performed miracles even on his deathbed. The church—which also holds the remains of Nicholas and Lawrence of Ilok, both of whom made expansions to the monastery complex during their reign—was given a 20th-century neo-Gothic face-lift by Herman Bollé, the same architect who helped design the Cathedrals in Đakovo and Zagreb, as well as Zagreb's Mirogoj Cemetery. The tourist information center is next door; if the church is closed, contact them to arrange a visit. ✉ *Trg Sv. Ivana Kapistrana 3.*

🛏 Hotels

The best, and only, restaurants in Ilok are located in the hotels, so planning a visit to each of them for either lunch, wine-tasting, or dinner makes for a nice tour of Ilok.

Hotel Dunav
$ | **HOTEL** | **FAMILY** | Located right on the riverbank, this upscale family-run hotel makes a great base for exploring both parts of the town. **Pros:** riverside location; best restaurant in town; peaceful, quiet rooms. **Cons:** feels slightly empty in low season; some distance from wineries; far from the sights in the upper town. [$] *Rooms from: 530 Kn* ✉ *Julija Benešića 62* ☎ *032/596–500* 🌐 *www.hoteldunavilok.com* 🛏 *15 rooms* 🍴 *Free breakfast.*

Principovac Country Estate
$ | **HOTEL** | Located 1½ km (1 mile) from Ilok in the Baroque summer house of the Odescalchi family, this is an elegant retreat amid miles of rolling vineyards. **Pros:** beautifully designed premises; romantic escape; great for walking, biking, tennis, or golf. **Cons:** far from Ilok; no public transport; feels a little secluded. [$] *Rooms from: 720 Kn* ✉ *Principovac 1* ☎ *032/593–114* 🌐 *www.ilocki-podrumi.hr* 🛏 *6 rooms* 🍴 *Free breakfast.*

★ **Villa Iva**
$ | **HOTEL** | This peaceful boutique hotel and restaurant is located in the lower part of Ilok, at the base of the steps leading up to the Old Town. **Pros:** nicely decorated and spacious rooms; on-site wine cellar and restaurant; well-located in lower town. **Cons:** not in Old Town; far from main sights; basic amenities. [$] *Rooms from: 375 Kn* ✉ *S. Radića 23* ☎ *032/591–011* 🛏 *13 rooms* 🍴 *Free breakfast.*

Đakovo

38 km (24 miles) southeast of Osijek.

Đakovo is a peaceful little town, where the din of bicycles and the dribbling of basketballs on a Sunday afternoon outdo the roar of cars. The relatively bustling pedestrian main street is Ivana Pavla II, whose far end has a little parish church that was built rather cleverly from a former 16th-century mosque, one of the few remaining structures left in Slavonia from 150 years of Ottoman rule. The best time to be in town is the last weekend in September, during the annual Đakovački Vezovi (Đakovo Embroidery Festival), which sees a folklore show replete with traditional embroidered costumes, folk dancing, and folk singing, an array of song-and-dance performances, and an all-around party atmosphere—even a show by the famous Lipizzaner horses.

GETTING HERE AND AROUND

You can get to Đakovo from Osijek in about 40 minutes by one of several daily trains or buses for roughly 35 Kn one-way. The Đakovo train station is 1 km (½ mile) east of the center, at the opposite end of Kralja Tomislava, while the bus station is about 800 meters from the center of town.

Sights

Đakovačka Katedrala (*Đakovo Cathedral*)
RELIGIOUS SITE | Đakovo's centerpiece is its majestic, redbrick neo-Gothic cathedral, which towers above the city and is a stunning first sight as you arrive into town. Commissioned by the Bishop of Đakovo, Josip Juraj Strossmayer (1815–1905), and consecrated in 1882 after two decades of construction, the cathedral was called the "most beautiful church between Venice and Constantinople" by Pope John XXIII. ✉ *Trg Strossmayera.*

Lipizzan State Stud Farm
FARM/RANCH | **FAMILY** | The history of the Đakovo stud farm dates back to 1506, when one of the bishops kept 90 Arabic horses there. But perhaps the year that really put it on the map was 1972, when Queen Elizabeth II saw the famous Đakovo four-horse team perform at the opening ceremony of the Olympics and insisted on paying them a visit. The story goes that there was no paved road outside the stud farm at the time; by the time the queen arrived to take a carriage ride, one had been built. There are two locations in Đakovo where the prized white Lipizzaners are trained and bred; the Stallion Stable in the center of Đakovo, where a musical show is also held twice per month and plans are in place to build a museum; and Ivandvor, 6 km (4 miles) away, a pasture where the mares and offspring are kept in a peaceful, rural setting. It is possible to visit both farms to catch a glimpse of the horses and their stables, and a carriage ride through town can also be arranged. ✉ *Augusta Šenoe 45* ☎ *031/822–535* 🌐 *www.ergela-djakovo.hr* 🎫 *Guided tour of stud farm 30 Kn.*

Restaurants

Mon Ami
$ | **PIZZA** | Located in a big redbrick building around the corner from the Cathedral, this dark, publike restaurant specializes in grilled meat and pizza cooked in a giant wood oven. **Known for:** grilled meat; Slavonian breakfasts; cozy atmosphere. [$] *Average main: 50 Kn* ✉ *L. Botića 12* ☎ *031/821–477.*

Hotels

Hotel Đakovo
$ | **HOTEL** | With cheerful rooms, a big restaurant specializing in Slavonian food and wine, and a game room perfect for kids, this is your best hotel option in town. **Pros:** friendly service; nice on-site restaurant; spacious rooms. **Cons:** far from town and public transport; heavily focused on wedding parties; breakfast is disappointing. [$] *Rooms from: 450 Kn* ✉ *N. Tesle 52* ☎ *031/840–570* 🌐 *www.hotel-djakovo.hr* 🛏 *25 rooms* 🍴 *Free breakfast.*

The Golden Valley

150 km (94 miles) southeast of Zagreb, 96 km (60 miles) southwest of Osijek.

In the center of a fertile, vineyard-rich valley in Požega-Slavonia County (one of the smallest in Croatia), lies the area that the ancient Romans knew as "Vallis Aurea," or the Golden Valley. Going against Slavonia's reputation as one big, flat agricultural plain, this area is mountainous, with forested hills covered by the vineyards of more than 30 private wineries. It is a wonderful place to base yourself for a couple of days to sample great wine and explore nearby Papuk Nature Park.

The administrative and cultural center of the area is Požega (pop. 21,000). During the 150-year-long period of Ottoman rule that began in 1537, Požega became central Slavonia's most important administrative and military center. By the 19th century Požega's cultural dynamism had earned it a reputation as the "Athens of Slavonia," and in 1847 it became the first city to officially adopt the Croatian language. Today it is one of the prettiest towns in central Slavonia.

Just 23 km (14 miles) northeast of Požega is a small town called Kutjevo. It has a winemaking history dating back to the 13th century, and if there is any town where all of life is dedicated to viticulture, it is here. Nearly all 2,500 residents make a living from wine, and even the main square is named Trg Graševine after Slavonia's signature white wine; indeed, this is an excellent place to try it as 80% of Croatia's total Graševina production is here.

GETTING HERE AND AROUND

There are buses and trains from Osijek to Požega (three hours, 100 Kn), and only a couple of buses per day to Kutjevo from there.

Sights

★ Krauthaker

WINERY/DISTILLERY | If you only visit one winery on your trip, try to make it Krauthaker. Vlado Krauthaker was one of the first private wine producers to emerge after the fall of communism, opening the winery in 1992. He is still widely considered one of the best (and humble) winemakers in the country, producing over a dozen types of winery including award-winning Chardonnay. The location is lovely, with a terrace overlooking the town, a small pond and quaint bridge, and colorfully painted wine barrels scattered around the premises. Call ahead to arrange a visit. ✉ Ivana Jambrovića 6, Kutjevo ☎ 034/315–000 ⊕ www.

krauthaker.hr 🖾 40 Kn wine cellar tour and tasting ⊗ By appointment.

Kutjevačko Vinogorje

WINERY/DISTILLERY | There are 30 different wineries to choose from around Kutjevo; the biggest, and oldest, is Kutjevačko Vinogorje. The story of this winery is the story of the Kutjevo itself; its cellars date back to 1232 when the town was founded by Cistercian Monks from Hungary. Over the years, it passed into the hands of Ottomans, Jesuits, Habsburgs, and private families, and the stories of each of these eras and the influence they left on Kutjevo are etched chronologically onto the Slavonian oak barrels in the cellar. Ask your guide about the legend of Maria Theresa Habsburg and her dalliances on the circular stone table (where wine tastings are done). ✉ Kralja Tomislava 1, Kutjevo ☎ 034/255–002 ⊕ www.kutjevo.com 🖾 30 Kn wine cellar tour and tasting ⊗ By appointment.

★ Papuk Nature Park

NATIONAL/STATE PARK | Home to the largest mountain in Slavonia, this was the first geopark in Croatia to be recognized by UNESCO for its geological, biological and cultural diversity. Within its 336 square kilometers (129 square miles) are beech, oak, and fir forests, fresh rivers and waterfalls, the beautiful Jankovac Forest Park, and the large and inviting Lake Orahovica. There are hiking and biking trails and guided tours can be arranged. There are also archaeological sites from the Sopot and Starčevačka cultures (5500–3500 BC) as well as **Ružica Grad,** an abandoned medieval castle that was built in the 15th century during Hungarian rule. It can be reached by hiking 15 minutes uphill from Lake Orahovica; it's very much worth the effort if you're looking for a bit of solitude. The visitors center is located in Velika, but the lakes and Ružica Grad can be reached in a half hour from Kutjevo. ✉ Papuk Nature Park ⊕ pp-papuk.hr 🖾 10 Kn.

Požega

TOWN | One of the prettiest cities in central Slavonia, Požega is worth visiting for an afternoon. The striking **Holy Trinity Square** has a 19th-century Franciscan Monastery to one side and the massive Bishop's Palace at the other end. There is a plague column (built in memory of the nearly 800 citizens who died from the plague of 1739) in the middle of the square; an inscription explains that the pillar was sculpted by one Gabriel Granici at a cost of 2,000 eggs and 300 forints. He didn't eat the eggs or give them to his relatives; they were used to cement the pillar's marble sand. Tucked away in the corner of the main square is the **City Museum,** whose collection ranges from regional ethnography, history, art, and archaeology, from prehistoric times to the present day. ✉ *Požega* 🌐 *www.visit-pozega.com.*

Hotels

★ Sontacchi Boutique Winery Hotel

$ | **B&B/INN** | The only hotel in Kutjevo, but the only place you'd have wanted to stay anyway; the young Sontaki brothers, Anton and Kruno, will take care of everything you need, from arranging tastings at local wineries (including their own), to preparing organic dinner on their homemade BBQ (which you'll be grateful for, as there are few restaurants in the area). **Pros:** excellent full breakfast with local, organic products; small wellness center with sauna and jacuzzi on-site; walking distance to main sights around Kutjevo. **Cons:** some rooms are expensive by Slavonian standards; hard to reach by public transport; not many amenities nearby. [$] *Rooms from: 400 Kn* ✉ *Trg Grasevine 4, Kutjevo* ☎ *099/512–2312* 🌐 *www.sontacchi-vinarija.hr* 🛏 *5 rooms* 🍴 *Free breakfast.*

Chapter 10

MONTENEGRO

Updated by
John Bills

👁 Sights	🍽 Restaurants	🛏 Hotels	🛍 Shopping	🍸 Nightlife
★★★☆☆	★★★☆☆	★★★☆☆	★★☆☆☆	★☆☆☆☆

WELCOME TO MONTENEGRO

TOP REASONS TO GO

★ **Beautiful views:** In Kotor, climb to St. John's Fortress, following the medieval walls for postcard views.

★ **Luxurious getaways:** Indulge in a night (or if you can't afford it, a meal or a spa day pass) at the luxurious Sveti Stefan Aman resort. Once a village of old stone cottages, it's now a private island.

★ **The yachting life:** Charter a yacht for a private sailing trip round the Bay of Kotor.

★ **Floating churches:** Visit Gospa od Skrjelo (Our Lady of the Rocks), a lovely church perched on a tiny islet, opposite Perast, just outside Kotor.

★ **Mediterranean villages:** Zigzag down the mountain road above Kotor to get a full view of the bay including Kotor, Perast, and the other villages clustered around the sapphire water of this Mediterranean ria (a narrow inlet formed by the partial submergence of a river valley).

Of the small diamond-shaped stretch of mountainous terrain that makes up Montenegro, it is the southwestern face and coastal strip that gets most of the tourist attention. The most charming sights of this stretch of 100 km (60 miles)—as the crow flies—are at the northern end, though because of the short distances involved, more adventurous visitors can use any of the towns along the coast as a base to visit the inland towns and mountains. The coastline borders Croatia at its northern end and Albania to the south. Onward travel to the better-known towns and islands of Croatia is easily arranged by public transport or hired car, and the less discovered beaches and ancient sites of Albania are also accessible by regular buses across Montenegro's southern border. The UNESCO World Heritage sites and legendary hospitality of Bosnia-Herzegovina, Kosovo, and Serbia are also only a bus journey away as well.

1 **Kotor.** A historic city tucked into a magnificent bay.

2 **Perast.** A charming bayfront village.

3 **Sveti Stefan.** The opulent heart of Montenegro's coast.

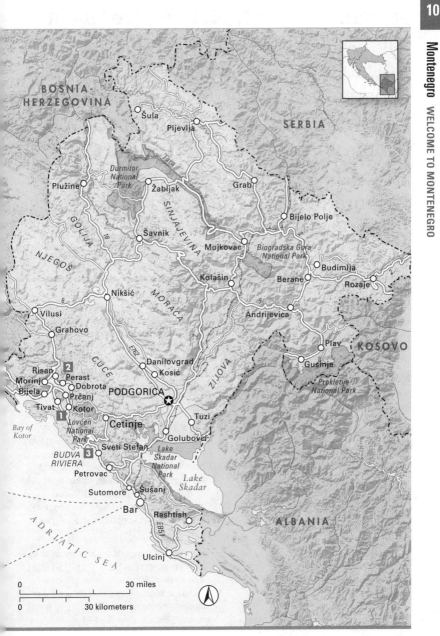

Officially independent since 2006 but with a long history of fierce self-sustainability, tiny Montenegro (about the size of Connecticut) lies on the Adriatic coast and is bordered by Croatia, Bosnia-Herzegovina, Serbia, Kosovo, and Albania. The 650,000 people who live here call it Crna Gora, which, like "Montenegro," means "black mountain"—a reminder of the pine-forested alpine terrain of most of the country.

Montenegro's main draw is its beautiful coastline, dotted with delightful Venetian-era fortified towns, home to excellent seafood restaurants, and set against the dramatic mountains of the interior.

Montenegro's first known inhabitants were the Illyrians, who were farmers and hunters, and also worked iron and traded with the ancient Greeks. Urbanization began in the 4th century BC when the Greeks founded Budva, on the coast. In AD 9, the Romans annexed the region into the province of Illyricum (which ran down the Adriatic coast from the Istrian peninsula to Albania), calling it Doclea after the dominant local Illyrian tribe. When the Roman Empire was divided between east and west in AD 395, the fault line passed right through Montenegro. Later, this was to be the dividing line between Eastern Orthodox and Roman Catholic lands.

In the 7th century, the Slavs arrived. They mixed with the descendants of the Romanized Illyrians and lived in the mountains, in clans, each ruled by a *župan* (chieftain). Originally pagan, they soon adopted Christianity. In 1077, their independent state of Duklja (the Slavicized version of the Roman name, Doclea) was recognized as a kingdom by the pope. Later, Duklja became known as Zeta (derived from the old Slavic word for harvest) and kept its freedom through paying off the Byzantine Empire, and fighting off the Ottoman Turks. Because of the constant threat of Ottoman invasion and fear of rival clans, courage in combat was emphasized as a major virtue in Zeta.

Meanwhile, most of what is today the Montenegrin coast was under Venetian rule from 1420 to 1797, though independent Montenegro had its capital at Cetinje, home of the first printing press in southern Europe in 1494.

Due to ties with Italy, Roman Catholicism was the dominant faith along the coast, whereas the Eastern Orthodox Church prevailed in Zeta. In fact, politics and religion became so intertwined in Zeta that from 1550 to 1696 it was governed by bishops. In 1697, the Petrović-Njegoš family took the helm as prince-bishops. The greatest of their rulers, still loved and revered in Montenegro today, was Petar II Petrović-Njegoš, who organized a 32-man band of traveling magistrates as well as a police force, paid for from a system of taxation that he organized. He was also an epic poet, and his work, *The Mountain Wreath,* is considered Montenegro's national poem.

King Nikola Petrović, who ruled from 1860, was another notable ruler, and father; six of his nine daughters married royal or aristocratic Europeans (including a grand duke of Russia and King Victor Emmanuel of Italy), which earned him the nickname "the father-in-law of Europe." King Nikola introduced free elementary education, an agricultural college, post and telegraph offices, and freedom of the press, although the messy end of his reign (which saw him deposed and sent into exile while Montenegro was annexed to Serbia) left a controversial legacy.

During both world wars, Montenegro sided with the Allies. In 1945, it became one of the six constituent republics that made up Yugoslavia, governed along communist lines by President Tito. Yugoslavia was not part of the Soviet Bloc, however, as Tito broke off relations with Stalin in 1948. The country was ruled under Tito's own form of communism—far more liberal than that in the former USSR.

During the breakup of Yugoslavia in the 1990s, no fighting took place on Montenegrin soil, though the region did suffer economic hardship and a degree of political isolation; a number of civilians were killed by NATO bombing in 1999.

When Croatia and Slovenia claimed independence from Yugoslavia in 1991, Montenegro remained loyal to Belgrade. However, by May 2006, when all that was left of Yugoslavia was the so-called Union of Serbia and Montenegro, Montenegro held a referendum and voted for independence (though it was close run, with only 55.5% of the votes in favor) and became its own democratic republic. Today, tourism is the main force behind the economy, and foreign investors (particularly Russian and British) keen to be in on the potential boom are buying up properties fast.

Planning

When to Go

May is a lovely time to visit coastal Montenegro, with temperatures running 14°C–22°C (56°F–72°F) but before the busiest crowds of summer. After that, temperatures rise to reach a peak in August with an average daily maximum of 29°C (84°F), although hotter temperatures aren't unusual. These are fine days for sun worshippers or anyone willing and able to laze under sunshades and admire the sparkle on the water, but if you want to explore the towns where sun glare bounces off the white stone, you may prefer to choose a different time of year (or at least plan your sightseeing for early in the days). By September, temperatures are cooling (17°C–26°C [62°F–78°F])—and the crowds in the most popular sights (notably Kotor) are thinning—while the sea is still as warm as in June or July (24°C [75°F]), so this is also a great time to visit. After this the season is properly over, and winter on the coast is a little bleak (temperatures in January run 5°C–12°C [40°F–53°F]) and many businesses shut down.

Montenegro

Budva Riviera

E80
2-3
Bečići
Rafailovici
Budva
Sveti Stefan
Jaz
Trsteno
Ostrvo
Sv Nikola
E65
A D R I A T I C   S E A
Petrovac

BOSNIA-
HERZEGOVINA

SERBIA

Šula
Pljevlja

Durmitor
National
Park

Tara

Plužine
Žabljak
Grab

Bijelo Polje

GOLIJA
18
Šavnik
SINJAJEVINA
Mojkovac

Biogradska Gora
National Park

Budimlja

NJEGOŠ
Kolašin
Berane
Rožaje

Nikšić
MORAČA
Andrijevica

Vilusi
6
9

Grahovo
Plav

CUCE
Danilovgrad
ZIJOVA
Gusinje

E762
Kosić
Prokletije
National Park

Risan
PODGORICA

Morinj
Perast
Dobrota

Bijela
Prčanj
Tivat
Kotor

Herceg
Novi
Lovćen
National
Park
Cetinje
Tuzi

*Bay of
Kotor*

**Budva
Riviera**
see inset

Sveti Stefan
Golubovci

Petrovac
Lake
Skadar
National
Park

Sutomore
Sušanj
*Lake
Skadar*

Bar
Rashtish

← TO
ANCONA

A D R I A T I C   S E A
E851

ALBANIA

← TO BARI

Ulcinj

KOSOVO

CROATIA

| 0 | | 30 miles |
| 0 | | 30 kilometers |

Getting Here and Around

AIR

Montenegro Airlines has service from both Tivat and Podgorica Airports to London and various other European capitals, with several budget airlines also traversing these routes. Well served by international airlines, Dubrovnik Airport, in Croatia, is a popular alternative gateway to Montenegro, but it's important to note that car-rental agencies may charge extra for taking the vehicle across borders.

AIRPORT CONTACTS Dubrovnik Airport. ✉ *Čilipi bb, Dubrovnik* ☎ *20/773–100 passenger services* ⊕ *www.air-port-dubrovnik.hr.* **Podgorica Airport.** ✉ *Podgorica Airport, Podgorica* ☎ *020/444–244* ⊕ *www.montenegroairports.com.* **Tivat Airport.** ✉ *Tivat Airport* ☎ *032/670–930* ⊕ *www.montenegroairports.com.*

BOAT

Montenegro Lines operates regular overnight car ferries year-round to the Montenegrin port of Bar, 38 km (24 miles) south of Budva, from Bari in Italy. The crossing can take anywhere between 8 and 10 hours and costs about €100 per person one-way (in a two-berth cabin with bathroom).

BUS

Buses are cheap (e.g., €7.50 for the two-hour journey from Kotor to Podgorica) and cover practically the entire country. They are generally clean and reliable. Numerous small bus lines operate regularly along the coast between Herceg Novi (in the north) and Ulcinj (in the south), stopping at most towns along the way. For other routes, inquire at the bus station of departure.

CONTACTS Kotor Bus Station. ✉ *Ul. Put prvoboraca bb, Kotor* ☎ *032/325–809* ⊕ *www.autobuskastanicakotor.me.*

CAR

Although Montenegro's buses have good service along the coast and can get you to most points in the country, renting a car gives you much more flexibility and makes life easier, especially when visiting the mountains.

Since the Old Town is compact and pedestrian-friendly, you do not need to rent a car in Kotor. It's easy to reach nearby Perast by bus or taxi.

CRUISE SHIP

Arriving at Kotor from the water via cruise ship is an impressive experience in itself, so be sure to be up on the deck in advance. Your ship will sail up a 28-km-long (18-mile-long) bay (often mistakenly referred to as a fjord), with rugged mountains rising in the background. Cruise ships dock on the quay, immediately in front of Kotor's medieval walled Old Town.

Restaurants

Along the Montenegrin coast, seafood predominates, with starters including *salata od hobotnice* (octopus salad) and *riblja čorba* (fish soup), followed by risotto dishes—most notably *crni rižot* (black risotto prepared with cuttlefish)—*lignje* (squid), or fresh fish from the Adriatic prepared on a barbecue. The quality is generally excellent, and the prices are slightly lower than in neighboring Croatia, although don't be surprised to see higher prices in Kotor, Perast, and (especially) Sveti Stefan. Note that on restaurant menus, fresh fish is priced by the kilogram. Inland, cheeses and meat dishes are more common. Cheeses to try include *sir iz ulje* (cheese preserved in olive oil) and *kožji sir* (goat's cheese), which are generally eaten at the beginning of the meal rather than at the end. Popular meat specialties are *pršut* (prosciutto), *Njeguški stek* (steak stuffed with prosciutto and cheese), and *jagnjece pečenje sa ražnja* (whole lamb roasted on a spit).

Montenegrins are also fond of the ubiquitous Balkan *Šopska salata* (a chopped salad of tomato, green peppers, cucumber, onion, olives, and strong white cheese). When it comes to local wines, Vranac is the most highly esteemed red, and Krstac a reliable white.

Hotels

The main delight of Montenegro's accommodation are the small, family-run establishments, many of which are centuries-old stone villas that have been converted into darling boutique hotels full of character and teeming with hospitality. However, many visitors still prefer to rent a private room or apartment, which can be arranged through local tourist information offices and travel agencies. The tourist season runs from Easter to late October and peaks in July and August, when prices rise significantly and it may be difficult to find a place to sleep if you have not booked in advance.

Restaurant and hotel reviews have been shortened. For full information, visit Fodors.com. Restaurant prices are the average cost of a main course at dinner or, if dinner is not served, at lunch. Hotel prices are the lowest cost of a standard double room in high season.

What It Costs in Euros (€)			
$	$$	$$$	$$$$
RESTAURANTS			
under €10	€10–€16	€17–€25	over €25
HOTELS			
under €100	€100–€200	€201–€300	over €300

Tours

Many private travel agencies offer tours, including hiking in the mountains, rafting on the Tara River, and visits to the towns of the interior, including the gorgeous former capital Cetinje and nearby Lovćen, as well as the other national parks, Lake Skadar (good for bird-watching), Biogradska Gora, and stunning Durmitor. Other companies will offer tours from Montenegro to other countries in the region, including through the Prokletije national park into Kosovo and Albania, or to Dubrovnik and other destinations in Croatia.

Visitor Information

CONTACTS National Tourism Organization of Montenegro. ✉ *Slobode 2, Podgorica* ☎ *032/08000–1300* ⊕ *www.montenegro. travel.*

Kotor

44 km (28 miles) from the border crossing between Croatia and Montenegro.

Backed by imposing mountains, tiny Kotor lies hidden from the open sea, tucked into the deepest channel of the Boka Kotorska (Kotor Bay), which is often mistakenly referred to as Europe's most southerly fjord, but is actually considered a ria. To many, this town is more charming than its sister UNESCO World Heritage Site, Dubrovnik, retaining more authenticity but with fewer tourists, and spared the war damage and subsequent rebuilding that has given Dubrovnik something of a Disney feel.

Kotor's medieval Stari Grad (Old Town) is enclosed within well-preserved defensive walls built between the 9th and 18th centuries and is presided over by a proud hilltop fortress. Within the walls, a labyrinth of winding cobbled streets leads through a series of splendid paved piazzas, rimmed by centuries-old stone buildings. The squares are increasingly packed with trendy cafés and chic boutiques, but directions are still given medieval-style by reference to the town's landmark churches.

In the Middle Ages, Kotor was an important economic and cultural center with its own highly regarded schools of stonemasonry and iconography. From 1391 to 1420 it was an independent city-republic, and later it spent periods under Venetian, Ottoman, Austrian, and French rule, though it was undoubtedly the Venetians who left the strongest impression on the city's architecture. Since the breakup of Yugoslavia, some 70% of the stone buildings in the romantic Old Town have been snapped up by foreigners, mostly Brits and Russians. Porto Montenegro, a marina designed to accommodate some of the world's largest superyachts, opened in nearby Tivat in 2011, and along the bay are other charming seaside villages, all with better views of the bay than the vista from Kotor itself, where the waterside is often congested with cruise ships and yachts. Try sleepy Muo or the settlement of Prčanj in one direction around the bay, or magical Perast and the Roman mosaics of Risan in the other direction.

GETTING HERE AND AROUND
AIR
Tivat Airport is 8 km (5 miles) from Kotor. Less convenient is the capital's Podgorica Airport, 90 km (56 miles) inland. Alternatively, some visitors fly in to Dubrovnik (Croatia) and drive 60 km (38 miles) down the coast to Kotor.

AIRPORTS AND TRANSFERS
Buses run regularly between Tivat Airport and Kotor; inquire at the airport information desks for schedule and fare information. There are frequent buses from Podgorica to Kotor, but you will need to take a taxi from Podgorica airport to the bus station (approximately €8). You can catch a taxi year-round from both Tivat and Podgorica airports.

BOAT
During the summer, private taxi boats operate from Kotor's harbor, taking passengers up the coast to the village of Perast.

VISITOR INFORMATION
Kotor's tourist information office gives out free maps and information and can help find private accommodation. You'll find the office in a kiosk just outside the Main Town Gate.

CONTACTS Kotor Tourist Board. (*Turistička Organizacija Kotora*) ✉ *Stari Grad 315* ☎ *032/322–886* ⊕ *www.tokotor. me.* **Tourist Info Biro-Kotor.** ✉ *Stari Grad* ☎ *032/325–950* ⊕ *www.tokotor.com.*

 # Sights

Kotor's Old Town takes approximately half a day to explore, although don't use that as an excuse to rush. Take your time, and you will be rewarded tenfold. Plan your visit for the morning, when the main sights are open to the public and the afternoon sun has yet to reach peak force.

Crkva Sv. Luke (*St. Luke's Church*)
RELIGIOUS SITE | Built in 1195, this delightful Romanesque church is the only building in the Old Town to have withstood all five major earthquakes that affected Kotor. Originally a Catholic church, the building later became an Orthodox place of worship. ✉ *Trg Sv. Luke.*

Crkva Sv. Nikole (*St. Nicholas' Church*)
RELIGIOUS SITE | Designed by a Russian architect and built in pseudo-Byzantine style between 1902 and 1909, this is Kotor's most important Orthodox church (the Cathedral, by definition, is Catholic). The gold used to gild the spires was a gift from Russia. ✉ *Trg sv. Luke.*

Kotor's Old Town is completely car-free and a designated UNESCO World Heritage Site.

Glavna Gradska Vrata

BUILDING | The Main Town Gate (also known as the Sea Gate because of its position on the coast), which accesses the Stari Grad via the western facade of the city walls, dates back to the 16th century, and comprises Renaissance and Baroque details. Originally, the outer gate bore a relief of the Venetian Lion, but in Tito's time this was replaced by the socialist star and dates, as well as a direct quote recording the liberation of Kotor on November 21, 1944, at the end of WWII. There are two other entrances to the Stari Grad: the Južna Vrata (South Gate) and the Sjeverna Vrata (North Gate). ⌧ *Jadranska Magistrala*.

Gradske Zidine (*Town Walls*)

BUILDING | Especially beautiful at night when they are illuminated, the well-preserved town walls were built between the 9th and 18th centuries. They measure almost 5 km (3 miles) in length, and reach up to 66 feet in height and 52 feet in width. They form a triangular defense system around the Old Town, then rise up the hill behind it to Tvrdjava Sv. Ivana (St. John's Fortress), 853 feet above sea level. You can walk up to the fortress along the walls; allow at least one hour to get up and back down, wear good hiking shoes, and don't forget to bring water. ⌧ *Stari Grad* 🖾 *€3; free Oct.–Apr.*

Katedrala Sv. Tripuna (*St. Tryphon's Cathedral*)

RELIGIOUS SITE | Undoubtedly Kotor's finest building, the Romanesque cathedral dates back to 1166, though excavation work shows that there was already a smaller church here in the 9th century. Due to damage caused by a succession of disastrous earthquakes, the cathedral has been rebuilt several times—the twin Baroque bell towers were added in the late 17th century. Inside, the most important feature is the 14th-century Romanesque Gothic ciborium above the main altar. Also look out for fragments of 14th-century frescoes, which would once have covered the entire interior. A collection of gold and silver reliquaries, encasing body parts of various saints and crafted by local masters between the 14th and 18th century, is on display in the treasury. ✉ *Trg Sv. Tripuna* ☎ *032/322–315* 🎟 *€3 for combined ticket to cathedral and treasury.*

Kneževa Palata (*Duke's Palace*)
CASTLE/PALACE | Built in the 18th century, the Duke's Palace comprises almost the entire west side of the Old Town. Originally it was the official seat of the Venetian governor, but it now forms part of the Hotel Cattaro. ✉ *Trg od Oružja, Stari Grad.*

Pomorski Muzej Crne Gore (*Montenegrin Maritime Museum*)
MUSEUM | In the 18th century, tiny Kotor had some 400 ships sailing the world's oceans. This museum, housed within the 18th-century Baroque Grgurina Palace, traces Montenegro's cultural and economic ties to the sea. The exhibition extends over three floors and includes model ships; paintings of ships, ship owners, and local naval commanders; navigation equipment; and uniforms worn by Montenegrin admirals and captains. Audio guides are available in a variety of languages. ✉ *Trg Bokeljske Mornarice 391, Stari Grad* ☎ *032/304–720* 🌐 *www.museummaritimum.com* 🎟 *€5.*

Toranj za sat (*Clock Tower*)
BUILDING | Built in the 17th century and considered a symbol of Kotor, the Clock Tower stands directly opposite the Main City Gate. In front of the Clock Tower, the "Pillar of Shame" was used to subject local criminals to public humiliation. ✉ *Trg od Oružja, Stari Grad.*

Trg od Oružja (*Square of Arms*)
PLAZA | The Main Town Gate leads directly into the Square of Arms, Kotor's main square, today a large paved space animated by popular open-air cafés. Under Venice, arms were repaired and stored here, hence the name. Notable buildings on the square include the 17th-century Toranj za Sat (Clock Tower), the 19th-century Napoleonovog Pozorišta (Napoléon Theatre), and the 18th-century Kneževa Palata (Duke's Palace), the latter two now forming part of the upmarket Hotel Cattaro. ✉ *Trg od Oružja, Stari Grad.*

★ **Tvrđava Sv. Ivana** (*St. John's Fortress*)
MILITARY SITE | On the hill behind Kotor, 853 feet above sea level, this fortress is approached via a series of bends and some 1,300 steps. The fantastic view from the top makes the climb worthwhile: the terra-cotta rooftops of the Old Town, the meandering ria, and the pine-clad mountains beyond. On the way up, you will pass the tiny Crkva Gospe od Zdravlja (Church of Our Lady of Health), built in the 16th century to protect Kotor against the plague. Be sure to wear good walking shoes and take plenty of water. The route up starts from behind the east side of the city walls. ✉ *Above Old Town.*

🍴 Restaurants

Galion
$$ | SEAFOOD | Serving creative twists on local food, such as beetroot risotto with sheep cheese or tuna ceviche, this sophisticated restaurant occupies an old stone building with a glass-and-steel winter terrace extension. It's a five-minute walk along the coast from the Old Town. **Known for:** great locale with views of both the Old Town and the sea; the signature mille-feuille cakes; creative takes on traditional dishes. [$] *Average main: €15* ✉ *Šuranj BB* ☎ *032/325–054* 🌐 *www.galion.me.*

Hotel Astoria Restaurant
$$ | ECLECTIC | The restaurant and bar housed in this 13th-century town house fuse ancient and modern, Montenegrin and international, in a setting dominated by a tree set within the main room, its branches spreading out across the ceiling. A light menu offers both Mediterranean and Asian dishes, and—a welcome opportunity for diners in Kotor who don't eat fish—some vegetarian and meat dishes. **Known for:** exuberant eclecticism

in decor and menu; great location; Mediterranean and Asian menu with veggie and meat options. $ *Average main: €15* ✉ *Trg od Brašna 322, Stari Grad* ⊕ *www. astoriamontenegro.com.*

★ Konoba Scala Santa

$$ | SEAFOOD | Believed to be the oldest restaurant in Kotor, this rustic eatery is one of the best places in town for lobster, mussels, and fresh fish, such as simple barbecued *zubatac* (dentex) drizzled with olive oil and served with a wedge of lemon. The candlelit dining room has exposed stone walls, a wood-beam ceiling hung with fishing equipment, and a big open fireplace. **Known for:** oldest tavern in the Old Town; great Montenegrin seafood dishes; big open fireplace and outdoor dining in the summer. $ *Average main: €12* ✉ *Trg od Salate* ☎ *067/393–458.*

Marenda Grill House

$$ | BARBECUE | Grillhouses and butcher shops go hand-in-hand, making Marenda Grill House a perfectly placed spot just outside Kotor's Old Town. The meat is about as locally sourced as you're going to get, cooked to perfection in a down-to-earth setting. **Known for:** succulent locally sourced meat; popularity with locals; lack of tourists. $ *Average main: €13* ✉ *Put Prvoboraca 232* ☎ *069/340–300.*

Pržun

$$ | SEAFOOD | This spot makes a great case as Kotor's most romantic restaurant. Settled in another of the city's hidden squares, Pržun straddles the fine line between private and popular, serving excellent seafood in a most professional manner. **Known for:** romantic atmosphere; legendary sea bass; locally crafted beer. $ *Average main: €16* ✉ *Stari Grad 397* ☎ *069/343–061.*

 Hotels

Hotel Astoria

$$ | HOTEL | In the heart of the Old Town the quirky Hotel Astoria and its restaurant, housed in a 13th-century town house, are a breath of fresh air amid the blander options available elsewhere in the center of Kotor. **Pros:** creative design; central location; good breakfast options. **Cons:** expensive for its category; the huge fleshy murals of Adam and Eve in the public restaurant may not be to everyone's taste; Wi-Fi isn't the best. $ *Rooms from: €195* ✉ *Kotor 322, Stari Grad* ⊕ *www.astoriamontenegro.com* ⤳ *9 rooms* ¶❍¶ *Free Breakfast.*

Hotel Cattaro

$$ | HOTEL | This solid old hotel is as magically central as it gets, occupying the 19th-century Napoléon Theatre, the 18th-century Duke's Palace, and other historic buildings on the Old Town's main square. **Pros:** located in Old Town; historic building; great views in all rooms. **Cons:** expensive; slightly lacking in charm; tends to book up. $ *Rooms from: €139* ✉ *Trg od Oružja bb, Stari Grad* ☎ *032/311–000* ⊕ *www.cattarohotel.com* ⤳ *19 rooms* ¶❍¶ *Free Breakfast.*

Hotel Monte Cristo

$$ | HOTEL | The family-run Hotel Monte Cristo, housed in a 13th-century building once the home of the first Bishop of Kotor, offers reasonably priced accommodation in the heart of the Old Town. **Pros:** prime location; great on-site restaurant; very informative staff. **Cons:** its position in the midst of Old Town café life can make it noisy at night; no elevator or step-free access; Wi-Fi is a struggle. $ *Rooms from: €120* ✉ *Stari Grad* ⤳ *12 rooms* ¶❍¶ *Free Breakfast.*

Hotel Vardar

$$ | HOTEL | Described as the only soundproofed place to stay in the Old Town, the Hotel Vardar is centrally located, some rooms having a view of the lovely main square where the hotel's restaurant offers a chance for people-watching in the shade of sun umbrellas. **Pros:** Old Town location; soundproofing; stylish bathrooms. **Cons:** even full soundproofing can't guarantee a night free of local bars' music; no twin rooms; breakfast area is in a dark separate restaurant from the terrace. [$] *Rooms from: €139* ✉ *Stari Grad 476* 🌐 *www.hotelvardar.com* 🛏 *25 rooms* 🍴 *Free Breakfast.*

★ Palazzo Radomiri

$$ | HOTEL | The owners of this family-run boutique hotel were inspired by local sea captains bringing back treasure from around the world and the rooms; suites in the hotel's three 18th-century stone buildings are named after ships in the fleet belonging to the original owners, and are furnished with antiques. **Pros:** lovely old building; tastefully furnished; great amenities, including outdoor pool and sauna. **Cons:** location outside Kotor; stairs and steps throughout make access difficult; often full in summer. [$] *Rooms from: €180* ✉ *Dobrota 221, 4 km (2 miles) from Kotor* ☎ *032/333–172* 🌐 *www.palazzoradomiri.com* ⏲ *Closed mid-Oct.–mid-Apr.* 🛏 *10 rooms* 🍴 *Free Breakfast.*

Royal House

$ | RENTAL | FAMILY | A family-run budget option right in the heart of Old Town, Royal House is a great base from which to explore the narrow streets of the Stari Grad. **Pros:** tremendous location; convivial hosts; value for money. **Cons:** street can be noisy at night; need to organize check-in and departure ahead of time; small bathrooms. [$] *Rooms from: €35* ✉ *Stari Grad 492* ☎ *069/049–981* 🛏 *2 apartments* 🍴 *No meals* 💳 *No credit cards.*

Shopping

Green Market

OUTDOOR/FLEA/GREEN MARKETS | Conversation and currency are king at Kotor's daily market, located just outside the main entrance of the city walls (on the main coastal road). It's filled with colorful, local, seasonal produce laid out on marble slabs: think artichokes, asparagus, and cherries in spring; tomatoes, eggplants, and figs in summer, alongside pots of tiny local mountain strawberries. It's also a great place to buy local dried porcini mushrooms. Best and busiest on Saturdays, the market takes place every day. ✉ *Gradska pijaca, Gradska Vrata* ✣ *When facing main entrance from outside City Walls, market is on the right.*

Activities

BEACHES

The small pebble Gradska Plaža (Town Beach), just outside the town walls, is fine for a quick dip after a hot day of sightseeing.

SAILING

Several charter companies are based in the protected waters of Kotor Bay. For a one-week trip in August, expect to pay €2,500 for a 40-foot sailboat sleeping six, plus €130 per day for a skipper; prices do not include food, fuel, or mooring fees. Early booking (e.g., by February for the summer) will offer worthwhile discounts. Montenegro Charter Company offers one-day sailing trips (with skipper) on a private yacht around Kotor Bay.

The former military shipyard in Tivat, 5 km (3 miles) away, has been totally renovated and reopened as Porto Montenegro, a luxury marina, able to accommodate some of the world's largest super-yachts.

Montenegro Charter Company

SAILING | ✉ *Porto Montenegro, Obala bb, Tivat, Podgorica* ☎ *067/201–655 (mobile)* 🌐 *www.montenegrocharter.com.*

Perast

15 km (9 miles) from Kotor.

Tiny Perast is a peaceful bayfront village of stone villas set in gardens filled with fig trees and oleander. It was built by wealthy local sea captains during the 17th and 18th centuries, at a time when it was prosperous enough to have some 100 merchant ships navigating the oceans. In fact, Perast's naval skills were so respected that in the early 18th century, the Russian czar, Peter the Great, sent his young officers to study at the Perast Maritime Academy.

In the bay in front of Perast lie its main attractions: Sveti Djordje (St. George) and Gospa od Skrpjela (Our Lady of the Rock), a pair of tiny, charming islets, each topped with a church. Perast has no beach to speak of, though swimming and sunbathing are possible from the jetties along the waterfront.

Each year on July 22, Perast celebrates the *fasinada,* a local festival honoring the folkloric origins of Our Lady of the Rock, with a ritual procession of boats carrying stones out to the island at sunset. The stones are dropped into the water around the island, protecting it from erosion by the sea for the coming year. The Fasinada Cup sailing regatta is held on the same day.

GETTING HERE AND AROUND
Perast can be reached by car or bus and can also be visited on an organized half-day boat trip from Kotor's harbor.

 ## Sights

Begin your exploration with a look in the Perast Town Museum, then take a taxi-boat from the quayside to visit the island church, Our Lady of the Rock. Head back to town for lunch at one of the area's charming rustic eateries.

★ The Islands of Gospa od Škrpjela (Our Lady of the Rocks) and Sveti Djordje (St. George)
ISLAND | St. George's is a natural island but its sibling, Our Lady of the Rocks, is man-made. Folklore has it that in 1452, local sailors found an icon depicting the Virgin and Child cast upon a rock jutting up from the water. Taking this as a sign from God, they began placing stones on and around the rock, slowly building an island over it. By 1630 they had erected a church upon the new island. The original icon, which has been attributed to the 15th-century local artist Lovro Dobričević, is displayed on the altar. Over the centuries, locals have paid their respects to it by donating silver votive offerings, some 2,500 of which are now on display. The church is also home to more than 60 paintings by local hero Tripo Kokolja, one of the three men honored in Perast's main square.

The other island, home to the Monastery of St. George and dating back to the 12th century, is closed to the public. In the 18th century the island became a favorite burial place for local sea captains, whose crypts remain today. ■TIP→ **Though closed to the public, you can snap photos from the shore or from neighboring Our Lady of the Rocks**.

To visit Our Lady of the Rocks, hop on a taxi-boat from Perast's waterfront (a five-minute trip that costs €5 round-trip); there is no shortage of options. ⌧ *Kotor Bay* ☎ *069/045–262 for Kotor tourist office.*

Muzej Grada Perasta
MUSEUM | In the 17th-century Renaissance-Baroque Bujović Palace, on the water's edge, Muzej Grada Perasta (Perast Town Museum) displays paintings of local sea captains and their ships, plus a horde of objects connected to Perast's maritime past. ⌧ *Obala Marka Martinovića bb* ☎ *069/313–999* 🗐 *€9 (combined ticket with Risan Mosaics).*

Roman Mosaics at Risan
ARCHAEOLOGICAL SITE | These beautiful mosaics are from a 2nd-century house in a small excavation site that is worth a brief stop if you are in the area. Particularly charming is the mosaic depicting Hypnos, the Roman god of sleep. Tour guides are available, as well as detailed information panels in many languages. ⌧ *Risan bb, Risan* ☎ *032/322–886* 🗐 *€9 (combined ticket with Perast City Museum)* 🕑 *Closed after 3 pm Dec.–Apr.*

The island known as Our Lady of the Rocks is man-made, but still has more than 350 years of history behind it.

🍴 Restaurants

★ Hotel Conte Restaurant
$$ | SEAFOOD | Widely regarded as one of the best restaurants on the coast, Hotel Conte's gastronomic offerings are proof of the benefits of culinary education and growth. The team of chefs have spent time at some of the finest restaurants in Europe, honing their craft and embracing new culinary trends in real time, leading directly to the food on your plate. **Known for:** romantic terrace; extravagant seafood dishes; convivial and professional service. [$] *Average main: €18* ✉ *Obala Kapetana Marka Martinovića bb* ☎ *067/257–387* 🌐 *www.hotelconte.me.*

Stari Mlini
$$ | MEDITERRANEAN | This rustic old mill on the Ljuta River, 7 km (4 miles) down the coastal road from Perast, dates back to 1670 and has been run by the current family for 40 years. The restaurant offers excellent food with an emphasis on fish (you can visit the restaurant's own trout ponds set in the attractive grounds). **Known for:** spectacular sea views; excellent local almond cake specialty; location in a historic mill. [$] *Average main: €16* ✉ *Ljuta bb, Kotor* ☎ *032/333–555* 🌐 *www.starimlini.com.*

🛏 Hotels

Hotel Conte
$$ | HOTEL | These four stone buildings dating from the 15th and 16th centuries have been tastefully converted into well-appointed apartments, some with kitchens and one with a Jacuzzi. **Pros:** lovely old building; tastefully furnished; good breakfast. **Cons:** Muzak in the restaurant not for everyone; steep steps up to some apartments; proximity to church means early morning bells. [$] *Rooms from: €125* ✉ *Obala Kapitana Martka Martinovica* ☎ *067/257–387* 🌐 *www.hotel-conte.me* 🛏 *18 rooms* 🍴 *Free Breakfast.*

Sveti Stefan

Often referred to as the "jewel of the Montenegrin coast," Sveti Stefan is a tiny island protected by 600-year-old defensive walls inside of which nestle several dozen limestone cottages and a small church. The island is actually joined to the mainland by a causeway, with a gravel beach on each side. Originally a fishing village, it was fortified with sturdy walls in the 15th century to protect it from the Turks and marauding pirates. By the late 19th century, however, many residents had emigrated abroad, due to the poor local economy. In 1955, the few remaining inhabitants were relocated so that the entire village could be renovated and turned into a unique luxury hotel. The resort opened with a splash in 1960, attracting over the years international jet-setters and celebrities, from Richard Burton and Elizabeth Taylor to Claudia Schiffer and Sylvester Stallone. But when the war hit in the 1990s, tourists stopped coming and the economy took a nose-dive, leading Sveti Stefan to fall into total disrepair. Now, after years of exhaustive renovation, it has reopened as the Aman Sveti Stefan, an exclusive resort of luxury suites.

GETTING HERE AND AROUND

Sveti Stefan is only about 9 km (5 miles) from Budva so accessible by taxi if Budva is your base. Buses between Petrovac and Budva run along the main road above the resort. A scramble down the steps that lead past the houses and private land owned by families in the village takes you—more directly than the winding road for cars—to the public beach with the picture-postcard view of the island.

🍴 Restaurants

Restaurant Drago

$$ | MEDITERRANEAN | This small family-run restaurant has been specializing in seafood since 1967. Set on the mainland hillside overlooking the sea, Restaurant Drago has a large terrace at the front, wonderful ocean views, and perfect sight lines to the fairy-tale island hotel, Aman Sveti Stefan. **Known for:** wonderful views; delicious local seafood; warm staff. $ *Average main: €10* ☒ *Slobode 32* ☎ *069/032–050* ⊕ *viladrago.com/restaurant* ◔ *Closed Nov.–Mar.*

🛏 Hotels

★ Aman Sveti Stefan

$$$$ | HOTEL | Connected to the mainland by a narrow causeway, the glamorous Aman Sveti Stefan is a small village of cobblestone lanes, quaint courtyards, and hand-restored medieval stone cottages with terra-cotta tile roofs, all within 15th-century defensive walls. **Pros:** historic buildings; stunning island location; modern interior design. **Cons:** some rooms have small windows and can be rather dark; very expensive; beaches are gravel. $ *Rooms from: €971* ☒ *Sveti Stefan Island, Budva* ☎ *033/420–000* ⊕ *www.amanresorts.com/aman-sveti-stefan* ◔ *Island closed mid-Oct.–Apr.* ⤴ *58 rooms* ⦿ *No meals.*

Vila Drago

$ | HOTEL | This friendly family-run hotel has an unbeatable location and thoughtful touches (a free bottle of wine in your room and beach towels), but the real draw here are the unbeatable views of the magical Sveti Stefan. **Pros:** great location; all but two rooms have views of Sveti Stefan; nice extra touches. **Cons:** gravel beaches; Aman Sveti Stefan dominates the cultural landscape; Wi-Fi very inconsistent. $ *Rooms from: €40* ☒ *Slobode 32* ☎ *068/514–874* ⊕ *viladrago.com* ⤴ *8 rooms* ⦿ *Free breakfast.*

Chapter 11

SLOVENIA

Updated by
John Bills

⊙ Sights	🍴 Restaurants	🏨 Hotels	🛍 Shopping	🍸 Nightlife
★★★★☆	★★★☆☆	★★★☆☆	★★★☆☆	★★★☆☆

WELCOME TO SLOVENIA

TOP REASONS TO GO

★ **Skiing and mountain adventures:** Explore the Julian Alps surrounding Lake Bled or hit the slopes at Kranjska Gora.

★ **Water sports:** Slovenia's small Adriatic coastline is lined with bays, inlets, and tiny, secluded beaches while the River Soča offers rafting and canyoning.

★ **An artsy city:** Capital Ljubljana is filled with a wide variety of excellent museums and a tremendously creative population.

★ **Food and drink:** As southern Europeans, Slovenians love simple pleasures like good food, wine, and coffee.

★ **Caving opportunities:** Slovenia's Karst region is filled with some amazing limestone caves.

★ **Lippizzaner horses:** The famed Spanish Riding School stallions in Vienna originally came from a farm in Lipica.

Ljubljana, the capital, takes its place in the geographical center of the country, magnetizing entrepreneurs, artists, students, and internationals into making it a funky modern city coated in Habsburg decor. An hour's drive from both the coast and the Alps, Ljubljana is well connected to the rest of the country by a modern highway system and decent rail connections. Just north of Ljubljana, the Julian Alps give way to the mesmerizing lakes of Bled and Bohinj, as well as some excellent skiing and hiking resorts such as Kranjska Gora. To the west of the lakes, the often turquoise yet always stunning river Soča starts its Adriatic-bound flow yielding sights that must be seen—or better, rafted—to be believed. The Soča offers adventure and excitement in equal measure, raising adrenaline levels with the promise of serenity waiting farther down on the short but memorable Adriatic coast. There, the intact Venetian jewel of Piran holds its own with more renowned cities in Italy and Croatia.

1 **Ljubljana.** Everything that is great about Europe in one pint-size capital city.

2 **Bled.** One of Europe's most stunning mountain resorts.

3 Bohinjsko Jezero. Slovenia's largest lake.

4 Kranjska Gora. The country's largest and most beloved ski resort.

5 Bovec. The gateway to water activities on the Soča River.

6 Postojnska Jama and Škocjanske Jama. Two of Europe's most impressive cave systems.

7 Lipica. Where the fabled white Lipizzaner horses were first bred.

8 Koper. The one-time capital of the Republic of Venice.

9 Piran. The jewel of the Slovenian coast.

Slovenia may be the best-kept secret in Europe. Just half the size of Switzerland, the country is often treated as fly-over— or drive-through—territory by travelers heading to better-known places in Croatia or Italy.

That's good news for anyone choosing Slovenia as a destination, either in its own right or as a highlight during a visit to the region. It means fewer crowds— even in the peak summer touring months—fewer hassles, and in many ways a more relaxed travel experience with a chance to get to know the friendly and sophisticated Slovenian people.

While Slovenia's beautiful artistic monuments and charming towns may lack the grandeur and historical importance found in neighboring Italy or Austria, they still cast a captivating spell. And when it comes to natural beauty, Slovenia easily competes with other European countries. The Julian Alps northwest of the capital are every bit as spectacular as their sister Alpine ranges in Austria, Italy, and Switzerland, while the magnificent countryside and the quietly elegant charm of Ljubljana await those with the imagination to choose a destination that is off the beaten path.

MAJOR REGIONS

Julian Alps and the Soča Valley. Northwest of Ljubljana lies an unspoiled region of breathtakingly beautiful mountains, alpine lakes, and fast-running rivers. Much of the region is part of the protected Triglavski Narodni Park (Triglav National Park), and it's the perfect jumping-off spot for adventure pursuits of all sorts. Superior skiing, hiking, rafting, biking,

and fly-fishing draw people here from around the world.

Each of the major towns and resorts in the region—Bled, Bohinj, Kranjska Gora, and Bovec—offers something a little different. At Bled, the focus is on comfort and excellent facilities, poised against a fairy-tale backdrop of an island church in a green-blue lake. Bohinj's charms are more rustic—a pristine deep-green alpine sea, bordered by mountains on three sides. Kranjska Gora and Bovec offer more immediate access to high-octane adventure. The former is Slovenia's leading ski resort. In summer, it opens its lifts to mountain bikers and free-riders seeking the adrenaline rush of a dash down the slopes. Bovec, on the Soča River, offers world-class rafting and canyoning—or gentler floats—down what must be one of the world's most beautiful mountain streams.

These regional centers can be approached individually or, in the summer, by car or bus as part of a large loop running northwest from Ljubljana. Proceed first to Bled and on to Bohinj, then push on farther north to Kranjska Gora, over the impossibly high Vršic pass, and down to Bovec.

The Karst Region. As you move south and west from Ljubljana toward the Adriatic, the breeze feels warmer, the air smells fresher, and the landscape looks less and less like Austria and more and more like Italy.

The word "karst," or in Slovenian *Kras,* is both a geological and geographic term referring to the large limestone plateau which stretches roughly from Nova Gorica in the north to well beyond Divača in the south. It is bordered on the west by the Italian frontier and on the east by the fertile, wine-growing Vipava valley. The Karst is typified by sinkholes, underground tunnels, and streams. The region is dotted with caves, most notably Postojna and Škocjan—which are jaw-dropping in beauty and size. Slovenia has more than 13,000 caves, but these two are undoubtedly king and queen of them all.

To most Slovenians, the word "karst," conjures up two things: *pršut* (air-dried ham) and blood-red Teran wine. The two pair beautifully, especially with a plate of cheese and a basket of homemade bread, taken at a traditional *osmica,* a small farmhouse restaurant. Teran is a strong wine made from the refošk grape that you will either love or loathe from the first sip. It takes its name from the *terra rossa,* or red soil, that typifies the Karst.

For visitors, the Karst is ideal for low-key exploration. The gentle terrain and numerous wine roads (look for the sign that reads *vinska cesta*) are perfect for leisurely walks or bike rides. Several wine roads can be found in the area around the town of Komen and along the main road from Komen to Dutovlje. The elegant towns—with their old stone churches and red-tile roofs—are a delight. The Lipica stud farm—the original breeding ground of the famed Lipizzaner horses of Vienna's Spanish Riding School—is an excellent base.

The Adriatic Coast. A little farther on, Slovenia's tiny piece of the Adriatic coast gives tourists a welcome opportunity to swim and sunbathe. Backed by hills

planted with olive groves and vineyards, the small strip is only 47 km (29 miles) long and dominated by the towns of Koper and Piran.

Following centuries of Venetian rule, the coast remains culturally and spiritually connected to Italy, and Italian is still widely spoken. The medieval port of Piran is a gem and a must-see. Its Venetian core is nearly perfectly preserved while Koper, Slovenia's largest port is a workaday town that nevertheless retains a lot of historical charm.

Piran and Koper are very different in character, but either can serve as an excellent base depending on what you plan to do. Choose Koper if you are searching for the bustle of a living city and the busy atmosphere of a working port surrounded by centuries of history. Or pick Piran if you're looking for something quainter, quieter, and more starkly beautiful. Whatever you choose, you can travel easily between the two. Buses make the 45-minute trip at least once an hour in season.

Planning

When to Go

The countryside is at its most beautiful in spring and fall, though the best period to visit depends on what you plan to do during your stay. Ljubljana is vibrant the whole year through. Many visitors want to head straight for the coast. Those in search of sea, sun, and all-night parties will find what they're looking for in peak season (July and August), including cultural events, open-air dancing, busy restaurants, and crowded beaches. If you want to avoid the crowds, hit the Adriatic in June or September, when it should be warm enough to swim and easier to find a place to put your beach towel.

In the mountains, there are two distinct seasons: winter is dedicated to skiing, summer to hiking and biking. Some hotels close in November and March to mark a break between the two periods. Conditions for more strenuous walking and biking are optimal in April, May, September, and October.

Lovers of fine food and wine should visit Slovenia during fall. The grape harvest concludes with the blessing of the season's young wine on St. Martin's Day, preceded by three weeks of festivities. In rural areas, autumn is the time to make provisions for the hard winter ahead: wild mushrooms are gathered, firewood is chopped, and koline (sausages and other pork products) are prepared by hand.

Getting Here and Around

AIR

There are no direct flights between North America and Slovenia. The Slovenian national carrier, Adria Airways, closed in 2019, but several low-cost airlines, such as EasyJet and Wizz Air, serve Ljubljana.

The Ljubljana Airport is at Brnik, 25 km (16 miles) north of the city. Public bus service runs regularly between the airport and Ljubljana's main bus station in the city center. Buses depart from the airport every hour on the hour weekdays and slightly less frequently on weekends. Tickets cost around €4. A private airport shuttle called GoOpti makes the same trip in slightly less time; departures average every 90 minutes or so. Tickets can cost as low as €9, but booking in advance is a must. A taxi costs approximately €30, and the ride takes about 30 minutes.

CONTACTS GoOpti. ☎ 1/320–4530 ⊕ goopti.com. **Ljubljana Airport.** ☎ 04/206–1000 ⊕ www.fraport-sloveni-ja.si. **Maribor Airport.** ☎ 02/629–1553 ⊕ www.mbx-airport.si.

BUS

International and domestic bus lines and the Ljubljana municipal bus service all operate conveniently from the city's main bus terminal, not far from the city center.

Private coach companies operate to and from Trieste in Italy and Zagreb in Croatia, as well as other European destinations farther afield. Domestic bus service is frequent from the capital to most Slovenian cities and towns. Outside of a car, the bus remains the only practical option to Bled and Bohinj and mountain destinations west and north of the capital. Except during peak travel periods, you can simply buy your ticket on the bus when you board. Otherwise, purchase tickets a day in advance. Many buses do not run on Sunday.

Hourly buses link Ljubljana to Bled, Bohinj, and Kranjska Gora. The resorts are linked by local buses; their frequency depends on the season. For schedules and fare information ask at a local tourist-information center. Six buses a day connect Kranjska Gora and Bovec during the summer via the jaw-dropping Vršič Pass, and there is one direct bus from Ljubljana to Bovec that takes a little over 4 hours.

Several buses a day connect Ljubljana to Koper and Piran, passing through Postojna and Divača on the way. There is also a daily service connecting the coastal towns to Trieste, Italy.

Within Ljubljana, the municipal bus network is extensive, and service is frequent during weekdays. Service continues but is less frequent on weekends and holidays. Buses on most lines stop running around 11 pm. To ride the bus you need an Urbana card, which can be purchased from any kiosk and is topped up using the green machines at bus stops. Simply swipe the card when you get on the bus and away you go.

CONTACTS Ljubljana Bus Station. ⊠ *Trg Osvobodilne fronte 4, Ljubljana* ☏ ⊕ *www.ap-ljubljana.si.*

CAR

From both Zagreb and Rijeka, the Slovenian border is about a 40-minute drive and about a 2½-hour drive from Zadar and the northern Dalmatian coast.

You don't need a car if you are not planning to leave Ljubljana; cars are, in fact, prohibited in the old city. However, traveling by car undoubtedly gives you the chance to reach remote areas of the country and will also allow you to appreciate the country's natural beauty. If you're bringing a car into Slovenia, be sure to buy a highway toll sticker, a vignette, at the border. It's required to drive on any highway, and fines are steep if you're caught without one. Short-term stickers are available at most gas stations and post offices. Any rental car hired in Slovenia should already have one.

From Ljubljana a four-lane highway (E61) runs northwest past Kranj and continues—occasionally reverting to a two-lane highway on some stretches—to the resorts of Bled and Kranjska Gora. Lake Bohinj lies 25 km (16 miles) southwest of Bled along local highway 209. The Vršič Pass, which connects Kranjska Gora and Bovec, is closed during the winter. If you want to go to Idrija, Kobarid, or Bovec from November to April, you will have to approach them via the south.

A car is advisable for touring the Karst region. However, parking can be a problem along the coast during summer, when town centers are closed to traffic. And parking in Piran, for example, is restricted to season ticket holders only. The E63 highway connects Ljubljana to the coast, passing through the Karst region en route.

TAXI

Private taxis operate 24 hours a day. Phone from your hotel or hail one in the street. Drivers are bound by law to display and run a meter.

TRAIN

Train travel is a pleasant way of getting around Slovenia, which is well-connected to neighboring countries and other European destinations, including Vienna (twice-daily; six hours) and Budapest (once-daily; eight hours). The Ljubljana train station is just north of the city center. Check the Slovenian Railways website for timetables and to buy tickets. A great weekend option is the Izletka ticket (€15), which allows unlimited travel on the entire Slovenian network on Saturdays and Sundays.

Four trains daily link Ljubljana and Koper, passing through Postojna and Divača en route. The capital also has a couple of direct links to Trieste (Italy) throughout the day, passing through Sežana, while three direct trains head daily to Zagreb (Croatia) via Zidani Most and Sevnica (Melania Trump's hometown). The journey takes two hours and 20 minutes.

CONTACTS Ljubljana Train Station. ⊠ *Trg Osvobodilne Fronte, Ljubljana* ☏ *386/1291–3332* ⊕ *www.slo-zeleznice. si.*

Restaurants

Slovenia's traditional dining institution is the *gostilna*, essentially an inn or tavern but cleaner, warmer, and more inviting than the English translation suggests. These are frequently family-run, especially in the smaller towns and villages, with Mom in the kitchen and Pop out front pouring beers and taking orders. The staff is usually happy to suggest local or regional specialties. Some of the better gostilnas are situated alongside vineyards or farms. In Ljubljana, these are usually on the outskirts of the city. Those in the city center tend to be oriented toward the tourist trade, since urban Ljubljaners usually prefer lighter, more modern fare.

Slovenian cuisine is highly regionalized, with offerings quite similar to dishes of neighboring countries and cultures. The Adriatic coast features Italian-influenced grilled fish and pasta, while the inland regions will offer cuisine very similar to that of Austria and Hungary. From the former Yugoslavia (and originally from Turkey), you'll find grilled meats and a popular street food called burek, a little pastry pocket stuffed with cheese or meat.

Mealtimes follow the Continental norm for lunch and dinner. Even if a restaurant posts earlier opening times, the kitchen won't normally start operating until noon. Dinners typically start around 7 pm. It can be tough to find a breakfast place, so it's best to take the standard hotel or pension offering of sliced meats and cheeses when available.

Restaurants usually close one day a week. In larger towns like Ljubljana that's likely to be Sunday. In resort areas that cater to a weekend crowd, Monday is the usual day off. When in doubt, phone ahead.

Hotels

Don't expect Slovenia to be an inexpensive option; lodging prices are similar to what you see in Western Europe at large. During peak season (July and August), many hotels—particularly those on the coast—are fully booked. Hotels are generally clean, smartly furnished, and well run. Establishments built under socialism are often equipped with extras such as saunas and sports facilities but tend to be gargantuan structures lacking in soul. Hotels dating from the turn of the 20th century are more romantic, as are the castle hotels. Over the few decades

many hotels have been refurbished and upgraded.

Private lodgings are a cheaper alternative to hotels, and standards are generally excellent. Prices vary depending on region and season. Look for signs proclaiming sobe (room to let) or apartma (apartments), alongside roads or in towns. Local tourist information centers, or in resorts like Bled or Piran private travel agencies, will often maintain lists of local rooms for rent.

Many hotels will offer better rates for stays of more than three days. Hotel rates frequently include breakfast— usually a mix of breads, cheeses, and cold cuts served buffet-style. Pensions and private rooms may include lunch or dinner—be sure to ask what's included in the price and whether you can opt out if you choose.

To really experience day-to-day life in the countryside, you should stay on a working farm. Agritourism is rapidly growing in popularity, and at most farms you can experience an idyllic rural setting, delicious home cooking, plus a warm family welcome. More information is available on the Slovenia tourist board's website.

Restaurant and hotel reviews have been shortened. For full information, visit Fodors.com. Restaurant prices are the average cost of a main course at dinner or, if dinner is not served, at lunch. Hotel prices are the lowest cost of a standard double room in high season.

What It Costs in Euros (€)			
$	$$	$$$	$$$$
RESTAURANTS			
under €12	€12–€20	€21–€30	over €30
HOTELS			
under €125	€125–€200	€201–€300	over €300

Visitor Information

Ljubljana's Turistično Informacijski Center (Tourist Information Center, or TIC) is next to the Triple Bridge on the Old Town side. Open weekdays and Saturday from 9-5 and Sunday 9 to 1, it's an excellent resource for maps, brochures, advice, and small souvenirs like postcards and T-shirts. If you are arriving by train, the TIC kiosk in the train station can help you find accommodations. It's open daily from 8 am to 9 pm from June through September and 10 to 6 from October through May.

Ljubljana

Slovenia's small but exceedingly charming capital is enjoying a tourism renaissance. Tourism officials now talk of Ljubljana proudly in the same breath as Prague or Budapest as one of the top urban destinations in Central Europe. That may be enthusiasm and excitement talking as opposed to reality, but there's no denying a sense of excitement as new hotels and restaurants open their doors, and each month seems to bring another admiring article in a prestigious newspaper or magazine abroad. Unfortunately, there is still no nonstop service from the United States.

The compact city center is immediately captivating. Part of the charm is doubtless the emerald green Llubljanica River that winds its way slowly through the Old Town, providing a focal point and the perfect backdrop to the cafés and restaurants that line the banks. Partly, too, it's the aesthetic tension between the stately Baroque houses along the river and the white neoclassical, modern, and Secessionist set pieces that dot the streets and bridges everywhere. Meticulously designed pillars, orbs, and obelisks lend the city an element of whimsy, a feeling of good cheer that's immediately

infectious. And part of the credit goes to the Ljubljaners themselves, who on a warm summer evening can be counted on to come out and party in force.

In truth, Ljubljana has always viewed itself as something special. Even when it was part of the former Yugoslavia, the city was considered a center of alternative music and arts. This was especially true during the 1980s, when it became the center of the Yugoslav punk movement. The band Laibach, noted for mocking nationalist sentiments, was the musical wing of the absurdist conceptual-art group Neue Slowenische Kunst (NSK), earning Ljubljana a reputation for pushing creative boundaries.

The romantic heart of the Old Town dates back centuries. The earliest settlement was founded by the Romans and called Emona. Much of it was destroyed by the Huns under Attila, though a section of the walls and a complex of foundations—complete with mosaics—can still be seen today. In the 12th century, a new settlement, Laibach, was built on the right bank of the river below Castle Hill by the dukes of Carniola. In 1335, the Habsburgs gained control of the region, and it was they who constructed the existing castle fortification system.

The 17th century saw a period of baroque building, strongly influenced by currents in Austria and Italy. Walk along the cobblestones of the *Mestni trg* (Town Square) and the *Stari trg* (Old Square) to see Ljubljana at its best, from the colored baroque town houses with their steeply pitched tile roofs to Francesco Robba's delightful *Fountain of the Three Carniolan Rivers*.

For a brief period, from 1809 to 1813, Ljubljana was the capital of Napoléon's Illyrian Provinces. In 1849, once again under the Habsburgs, Ljubljana was linked to Vienna and Trieste by rail. The city developed into a major center of commerce, industry, and culture, and the opera house, national theater, national museum, and the first hotels came into existence.

In 1895 much of the city was devastated by an earthquake. The reconstruction work that followed was carried out in florid Viennese Secessionist style. Many of the palatial four-story buildings that line Miklošičeva, such as the Grand Hotel Union, date from this period.

After World War I, with the birth of the Kingdom of Serbs, Croats, and Slovenes, Ljubljana became the administrative center of Slovenia. Various national cultural institutes were founded, and the University of Ljubljana opened in 1919. If you have been to Prague, you will already have seen some of the work of Jože Plečnik (1872–1957). Born in Ljubljana, Plečnik studied architecture in Vienna under Otto Wagner, then went on to lecture at the Prague School of Applied Arts and served as the chief architect for the renovation of Prague Castle. It was Plečnik who added many of the decorative touches to the city's parks, squares, and bridges. Some of his finest projects include the Triple Bridge, the open-air market on Vodnik Square, and the plans for the Križanke Summer Theater.

The city's years as part of Yugoslavia, under the leadership of Josip Broz Tito, saw increased industrialization. The population of Ljubljana tripled, and vast factory complexes, high-rise apartments, and modern office buildings extended into the suburbs.

PLANNING YOUR TIME

For short stays of two to three days, base yourself in Ljubljana. Spend at least one day taking in the attractions of the capital and the other day or two on day trips, such as to the Postojna or Škocjan Caves. If you have one other day to spend, you might consider dividing your time between Ljubljana and a town like Koper on the Adriatic coast.

GETTING HERE AND AROUND

Central Ljubljana is tiny and compact. You'll find yourself walking from place to place. Take taxis or city buses if you need to cover more ground. Taxis are ample and affordable, and the city bus route is extensive.

TOURS

For a private guided tour of the city, contact the Tourist Information Centre Ljubljana. Tours must be arranged in advance and are offered in several languages.

Tourist Information Centre Ljubljana

INFO CENTER | The general municipal tourist information office provides two-hour guided tours of the city and the castle. Book in advance in their office or on the website. The departure point is in front of the Town Hall. ⊠ *Adamič Lundrovo nabrežje 2* ☏ *1/306–1215* ⊕ *www.visitljubljana.com* ⌁ *Tours from €10.*

◉ Sights

Much of Ljubljana's architecture from the period between the two world wars is the work of Jože Plečnik (1872–1957). Born in Ljubljana, Plečnik studied architecture in Vienna under Otto Wagner and was an important member of the Viennese Secessionist School. It was Plečnik who added many of the decorative touches to the city's parks, squares, and bridges. Some of his finest projects include the Triple Bridge, the open-air market on Vodnik Square, the University Library, and the plans for the Križanke Summer Theater. Although Plečnik survived World War II, he fell out of favor with government officials, because his Roman Catholicism conflicted with the ideologies of the socialist state under Tito. Be on the lookout for his masterpieces. The city center is concentrated within a small area, so you can cover all the sights on foot.

Ljubljana has a picturesque Old Town bisected by the Ljubljanica River canal.

Cankarjevo Nabrežje

LOCAL INTEREST | An idyllic way to while away a day, Ljubljana's riverside is packed with cafes and restaurants that are perfect for people-watching. Prices have skyrocketed in recent years, but you're paying for location and atmosphere above all else. ⊠ *Between Tromostovje and Čevljarski most.*

Cathedral of St. Nicholas

RELIGIOUS SITE | FAMILY | This proud Baroque cathedral overlooking the daily market on Vodnikov trg is dedicated to St. Nicholas, the patron saint of fishermen and boatmen who created a powerful guild in medieval Ljubljana. Building took place between 1701 and 1708, under the Italian architect Andrea Pozzo, who modeled it after the church of Il Gesù in Rome. The magnificent frescoes on the ceiling of the nave are by the Lombard painter Giulio Qualglio and depict the transfiguration of St. Nicholas and the persecution of Christians under Diocletian and Nero. In honor of Pope John Paul II's visit in 1996, bronze doors were added to the church. The main door tells the story of Christianity in Slovenia, whereas the side door shows the history of the Ljubljana diocese. ⊠ *Dolničarjeva 1* ☎ *01/234–2690* ⊕ *lj-stolnica.rkc.si* ⌨ *Free.*

★ City Museum of Ljubljana

MUSEUM | FAMILY | Situated in the grand Auersberg Palace, this museum's beautifully designed exhibits trace the history of the city from pre-Roman times through the Austrian domination, the World Wars, the Tito years, and finally the establishment of independent Slovenia. In the basement, you can walk on a piece of the ancient Roman road or see a cross-sectioned excavation that shows the burning of Emona by Attila the Hun through a black, charred stratum. If you're interested, you can arrange for a museum guide to take you to other ancient Roman sites around the city. The city museum also houses the world's oldest wooden wheel, dating from 4000 BC. ⊠ *Gosposka 15* ☎ *01/241–2500* ⊕ *www.mgml.si* ⌨ *€6* ⊙ *Closed Mon.*

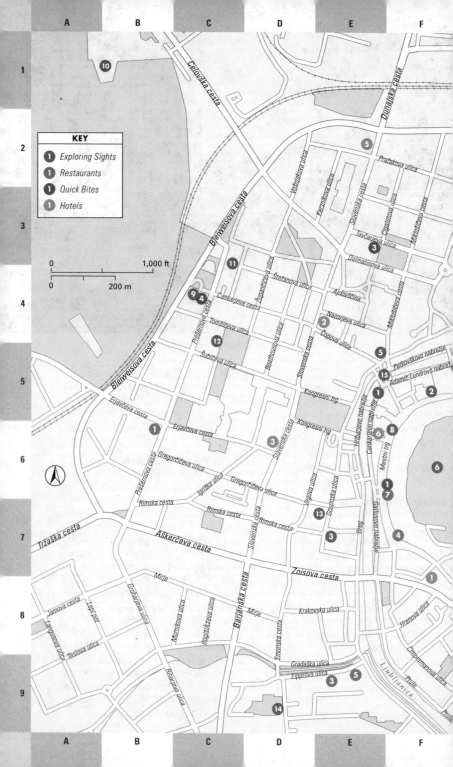

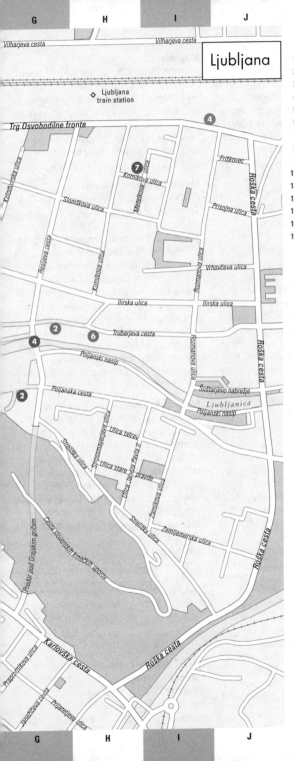

Ljubljana

Ljubljana train station

Sights ▼

1 Cankarjevo Nabrežje **E5**
2 Cathedral of St. Nicholas **F5**
3 City Museum of Ljubljana **E7**
4 Dragon Bridge **G5**
5 Franciskanska Cerkev **E5**
6 Ljubljanski Grad **F6**
7 Magistrat **H2**
8 Mestni Trg **F6**
9 Moderna Galerija **C4**
10 Muzej Novejše Zgodovine **B1**
11 Narodna Galerija **C3**
12 Narodni Muzej **C4**
13 National and University Library ... **E7**
14 Plečnik's House **D9**
15 Tromostovje **E5**

Restaurants ▼

1 Bazilika Bistro **B6**
2 Čompa **G4**
3 Dežela Okusov **E9**
4 Druga Violina **F7**
5 Manna **E9**
6 Skuhna **H4**
7 Valvas'or **E6**

Quick Bites ▼

1 Cafetino **E6**
2 Čokl **G5**
3 Kava Bar Tam Tam **E3**
4 Kavarna Moderna **C4**

Hotels ▼

1 Adora Hotel **F7**
2 Best Western Slon Hotel **E4**
3 Cubo **D6**
4 Hostel Celica **I2**
5 Intercontinental Ljubljana **E2**
6 Vander Urbani **E6**

Dragon Bridge

BRIDGE/TUNNEL | Four fire-breathing winged dragons crown the corners of this locally cherished concrete-and-iron structure. The dragons refer to the mythological origins of the city, when Jason, returning home from winning the Golden Fleece, killed a monster in a swamp on the present site of Ljubljana. It's undoubtedly one of the most photographed attractions in a city full of photogenic spots. ⊠ *Zmajski most.*

★ Franciskanska Cerkev (*Franciscan Church*)

RELIGIOUS SITE | Its color may now garner more attention than its history, but Ljubljana's famous Pink Church has plenty of stories waiting within. A High Baroque beauty built in the middle of the 17th century, the church flourished a century later under the watchful eye of the Franciscans, who made the decision to paint it red (hence the faded pink of today). The church's prime location on the city's main square makes it an obvious meeting point for people of all ages today. ⊠ *Prešernov trg 4* ☎ *01/242–9300* ⊕ *www.franciskani.si.*

★ Ljubljanski Grad (*Ljubljana Castle*)

CASTLE/PALACE | Ljubljana's hilltop castle affords views over the river and the Old Town's terracotta rooftops, spires, and green cupolas. On a clear day, the distant Julian Alps are a dramatic backdrop. The castle walls date from the early 16th century, although the tower was added in the mid-19th century. The surrounding park was landscaped by Plečnik in the 1930s. The castle also houses a virtual museum showcasing Slovenian history through digital technology. Take a step back through time and do the tour, it's a great introduction to Ljubljana. The castle is also home to the Museum of Puppetry, one of the most underrated museums in the city. ⊠ *Studentovska ul, uphill from Vodnikov trg, Grajska planota 1* ☎ *01/306–4293* ⊕ *www.ljubljanskigrad. si* 🎫 *€13 (including funicular).*

Magistrat (*Town Hall*)

GOVERNMENT BUILDING | The current town hall is the work of the Ljubliana architect Gregor Maček, who substantially renovated the 1484 original building from 1717 to 1719. The interior was completely reworked in the 19th and 20th centuries and now frequently hosts temporary art exhibits. ⊠ *Mestni trg 1* 🎫 *Free.*

Mestni Trg (*Town Square*)

PLAZA | Right up the street from the Old Town end of the Triple Bridge, this cobbled square extends into the oldest part of the city. Baroque town houses, now divided into functional apartments, present marvelously ornate facades: carved oak doors with great brass handles are framed within columns, and upper floors are decorated with balustrades, statuary, and intricate ironwork. Narrow passageways connect with inner courtyards in one direction and run to the riverfront in the other. The street-level floors contain boutiques, antiques shops, and art galleries. ⊠ *Ljubljana.*

Moderna Galerija (*Modern Gallery*)

MUSEUM | The strikingly modern one-story structure was designed by Plečnik student Edvard Ravnikar (1907–93) in the 1930s and finally finished in 1948. It contains a selection of paintings, sculptures, and prints by Slovenian and Eastern European 20th-century artists. In odd-number years, it also hosts the International Biennial of Graphic Art, an exhibition of prints and installations by artists from around the world. Works by Robert Rauschenberg, Susan Rothenburg, and Max Bill have been shown. The gallery also has a section of its permanent collection devoted to 20th century avant-gardes and the art of the Partisan Resistance. ⊠ *Cankarjeva 15* ☎ *01/241–6834* ⊕ *www. mg-lj.si* 🎫 *€5* 🕑 *Closed Mon.*

Muzej Novejše Zgodovine (*Museum of Modern History*)

MUSEUM | FAMILY | The permanent exhibition on Slovenes in the 20th century takes you from the days of

Austria-Hungary, through World War II, the victory of the Partisan liberation movement and the ensuing Tito period, and up to the present day. Relics and memorabilia are combined with a dramatic sound-and-video presentation (scenes from World War II are projected on the walls and ceiling, accompanied by thundering gunfire, screams, and singing). You'll find the museum in a pink-and-white Baroque villa in Tivoli Park. ⊠ Celovška 23 ☎ 01/300–9611 ⊕ muzej-nz.si ⊠ €5, free 1st Sun. every month ⊗ Closed Mon.

Narodna Galerija (*National Gallery*)
MUSEUM | FAMILY | This massive building houses a large collection of Slovenian art from the 13th through the early 20th century and a smaller but impressive collection of European paintings. It also houses the original of Francesco Robba's *Fountain of the Three Rivers.* ⊠ Prešernova 24 ☎ 01/241–5418 ⊕ www.ng-slo.si ⊠ €10 ⊗ Closed Mon.

Narodni Muzej (*National Museum*)
MUSEUM | The National Museum, home to more than 400,000 archaeological artifacts, rare books, historic documents, and artworks from the prehistoric era through modern times, is not to be missed. The centerpiece here is a bronze urn from the late 5th or 6th century BC known as the Vace Situle. Discovered in Vace, Slovenia, it is a striking example of Illyrian workmanship and is decorated with friezes depicting a procession of men, horses, and chariots. Extensive collections of classic artworks from Western and Northern Europe, Russia, and Japan complement the already impressive exhibit of Yugoslav pieces. ⊠ Muzejska ulica 1 ☎ 01/241–4400 ⊕ www.nms. si ⊠ €6 (€8.50 combined with Natural History Museum).

National and University Library
BUILDING | Built from 1936 to 1941, the National Library is architect Jože Plečnik's secular masterpiece. The external facades present a modernist version

of an Italian renaissance palazzo, using brick, stone, and even archaeological remains from excavations around Ljubljana. However, these are not arranged in registers as in a traditional palazzo, but rather are scattered haphazardly over the entire exterior, creating a dynamic and three-dimensional look that makes the massive building seem light and airy. Inside, there is a beautiful colonnaded black marble staircase and a reading room with huge windows at either end to let in light. The austere furniture in the reading room was also designed by Plečnik. Don't miss the beautiful horse-head door handles on the main entrance. ⊠ Turjaška ulica 1 ☎ 01/200–1209 ⊕ www.nuk.uni-lj.si ⊠ €5 for reading room ⊗ Closed Sun.

Plečnik's House
HOUSE | Architecture enthusiasts will enjoy a visit to architect Jože Plečnik's house, which is home to his preserved studio, living quarters, and garden. You'll be struck by the strange combination of refined aestheticism and severe, almost monastic, asceticism that pervades the residence of the man who played a large part in transforming Ljubljana between the two World Wars. Exploring the house itself is only possible on one of the hourly tours, but the gardens and exhibition are accessible with a ticket. ⊠ Karunova 4 ☎ 01/241–2506 ⊕ mgml.si/en/plecnik-house ⊠ €6 ⊗ Closed Mon.

Tromostovje (*Triple Bridge*)
BRIDGE/TUNNEL | This striking structure spans the River Ljubljanica from Prešernov trg to the Old Town. The three bridges started as a single span, and in 1931, the two graceful outer arched bridges, designed by Plečnik, were added. ⊠ Ljubljana.

🍴 Restaurants

Don't let the secret out, but Ljubljana is quietly becoming one of Europe's most engaging gastronomic experiences. The

Ljubljana Castle overlooks the Old Town and the river.

surrounding hills supply the capital with first-class meat and game, dairy produce, fruit, and vegetables. At some of the more modern restaurants, the menus may verge on nouvelle cuisine, featuring imaginative and beautifully presented dishes. The portions, however, are almost always more ample than their counterparts in other countries. Complement your meal with a bottle of good Slovenian wine; the waiter can help you choose an appropriate one.

Bazilika Bistro

$ | VEGETARIAN | The green-tinged leader of vegetarian and vegan eating in Ljubljana, the chefs at Bazilika Bistro are pros when it comes to marrying health with taste, pumping out beautiful lunches that tick all the nutritional boxes without skimping on the flavors. The ingredients are all locally sourced as well. **Known for:** colorful meals; health and taste in equal measure; locally sourced ingredients. [$] *Average main: €10* ✉ *Prešernova 15* ☎ *01/244–6275* 🌐 *www.bazilika.si* 🕒 *Closed weekends.*

Čompa

$$ | SLOVENIAN | Wonderful smells waft from the kitchen of this affordable little eatery, which is an absolute must-visit for meat lovers. With homemade beer to complement the savory menu, exposed stone interiors, and sturdy wooden tables, this cozy eatery makes for a welcome break. **Known for:** the best steak in town; grill-fried bread; romantic atmosphere. [$] *Average main: €20* ✉ *Trubarjeva cesta 40* ☎ *040/799–334* 🕒 *Closed Sun.*

Dežela Okusov

$$ | SLOVENIAN | All meat everything reigns supreme at this charming and cuts-fueled bistro on Eipprova. This is pub grub at an impeccably high standard: stacks of grilled and smoked meats mesh perfectly with any of Slovenia's impressive roster of craft beers. **Known for:** sumptuous smoked meat dishes; house-roasted coffee; lovely terrace. [$] *Average main: €13* ✉ *Eipprova 11* ☎ *01/283–9288* 🌐 *www.dezela-okusov.si.*

★ Druga Violina

$ | **SLOVENIAN** | **FAMILY** | The gorgeous Stari trg location and a hearty menu filled with Slovenian classics would be enough to justify a cheerful lunch at Druga Violina, but there is more to this spot than initially meets the eye. The restaurant doubles up as an initiative to help people with disabilities in the region, a talented group of people who help grow the ingredients on a nearby farm and work as the wait staff in the restaurant itself. **Known for:** fresh, locally grown produce; traditional Slovenian food; socially aware outlook. $ *Average main: €10* ✉ *Stari trg 21* ☎ *82/052–506* ⊗ *Closed Mon.*

Manna

$$ | **SLOVENIAN** | **FAMILY** | Expect exceptional food and excellent service at this pleasant, well-known eatery just three minutes from the city center. Every dish on the menu is sure to please, and there's a nice wine list. **Known for:** lots of outdoor seating; must-try manna strudel; central location. $ *Average main: €15* ✉ *Eipprova ulica 1a* ☎ *031/529–974* ⊕ *www.restaurant-manna.com.*

Skuhna

$ | **INTERNATIONAL** | **FAMILY** | Established by a Slovene non-profit organization with the aim of integrating the country's varied migrant communities, all corners of the world are touched with life and love at this small restaurant on Trubarjeva. You'll find dishes from Zimbabwe, Nigeria, Iran, and more, right in the heart of Ljubljana. **Known for:** the most varied menu in the city; socially aware ambitions; packed events calendar. $ *Average main: €7* ✉ *Trubarjeva 56* ☎ *41/339–978* ⊕ *www.skuhna.si.*

Valvas'or

$$ | **EUROPEAN** | An ode to modern design and inventive tastes, Valvas'or will first woo you with their stylish remodel of an old, arched tavern and then amaze you with little pleasures like sorbet between courses. Between ample and excellently prepared dishes, take note of the gold perforated metal wall that details the city plan. **Known for:** food to match the beautiful atmosphere; tasting menus available; professional waitstaff. $ *Average main: €19* ✉ *Stari trg 7* ☎ *01/425–0455* ⊕ *www.valvasor.net* ⊗ *Closed Sun.*

☕ Coffee and Quick Bites

The coffee revolution that has swept through Europe has made it to the Slovenian capital. There has never been a better time to enjoy a cup of hot coffee in Ljubljana, with a great selection of cafés on the riverside and farther afield.

Cafetino

$ | **CAFÉ** | **FAMILY** | A longtime favorite with coffee lovers across Ljubljana, Cafetino is a friendly place to stop for that all important first cup of the day. The interior is tiny and getting a seat can be difficult, so it's best to stroll up early and start the day in the right way. **Known for:** picturesque location; conversation-filled setting; wide range of coffee beans. $ *Average main: €2* ✉ *Stari trg 5* ☎ *04/222–950* ⊕ *www.cafetino.si.*

★ Čokl

$ | **CAFÉ** | Ljubljana's caffeine-mecca, Čokl is a postage stamp-sized café that serves up the best coffee in the city, at least according to those in the know. The terrace is a lovely spot to spend an afternoon, especially taking into account how small the interior is. **Known for:** impressive coffee expertise; teeny-tiny interior; Ljubljana's best espresso. $ *Average main: €2* ✉ *Krekov trg 8* ☎ *041/837–556.*

★ Kava Bar Tam Tam

$ | **CAFÉ** | **FAMILY** | A hugely personable café, Tam Tam is focused on flavor while refusing to skimp on extras, serving snacks along with its coffees, beers, and wines. It has a tranquil, authentic atmosphere that comes from an inherent serenity and a seriously good selection of beverages. **Known for:** great food selection; modernist vibes; serene parkside setting. $ *Average main: €2* ✉ *Cigaletova* *ulica 3* ☎ *040/566–044* 🌐 *www.facebook.com/KavaBarTamTam.*

Kavarna Moderna

$ | **CAFÉ** | Located in the basement of the Museum of Modern Art, Kavarna Moderna is great place to reflect on the creativity upstairs or to simply enjoy a quality cup of coffee. An obvious hangout for Ljubljana's artistic types, the café also serves up some seriously good breakfast and brunch options. **Known for:** digital nomad-friendly atmosphere; wide range of bites; art gallery cool. [$] *Average main: €2* ✉ *Cankarjeva 15* ☎ *041/336–927* 🌐 *www.facebook.com/kavarnamoderna.*

Hotels

Hotel rates in Ljubljana continue to creep towards Western European numbers with each passing year. The standards here are usually high, but rooms, even in older historic hotels, tend to be modern and somewhat devoid of charm. In summer, you can get good deals through private accommodations or university dorms. Ask about these options at the tourist information kiosk in the town center.

Adora Hotel

$ | **B&B/INN** | This is one of the few outstanding family-run boutique hotels around the city center; it is reasonably priced, very central, and boasts a wonderful courtyard in the back. **Pros:** private courtyard; peaceful atmosphere; bike rental available. **Cons:** a walk or bike ride to the city center; no 24-hour concierge; parking not available on-site. [$] *Rooms from: €93* ✉ *Rožna ulica 7* ☎ *386/820–57240* 🌐 *www.adorahotel.si* 🛏 *10 rooms* 🍴 *Free Breakfast.*

Best Western Slon Hotel

$ | **HOTEL** | Close to the city's historic center, this high-rise hotel stands on the site of a famous 16th-century inn and maintains an atmosphere of traditional hospitality. **Pros:** great buffet breakfast; comfortable beds; centrally located. **Cons:** not very personable; decor is outdated; street noise is loud in some rooms. [$] *Rooms from: €70* ✉ *Slovenska cesta 34* ☎ *01/470–1100* 🌐 *www.hotelslon.com* 🛏 *170 rooms* 🍴 *Free Breakfast.*

★ Cubo

$$ | **HOTEL** | In addition to its central position next to the National Drama Theater and a mere five-minute walk from the old city, this top-rated hotel also boasts excellent service, boutique design, and a very good restaurant. **Pros:** central location; excellent staff; stylish boutique decor. **Cons:** busy lobby; some rooms feel small; on the more expensive side. [$] *Rooms from: €175* ✉ *Slovenska Cesta 15* ☎ *01/425–6000* 🌐 *www.hotelcubo.com* 🛏 *26 rooms* 🍴 *Free Breakfast.*

Hostel Celica

$ | **HOTEL** | Celica, which translates to a cell, is just that: a reconstructed prison that has become one of the most interesting hostels in the region. **Pros:** energetic and involved staff; fascinating venue set-up; fun and convenient location. **Cons:** small bag lockers; inconsistent opening times for café; very basic breakfast. [$] *Rooms from: €21* ✉ *Metelkova 8* ☎ *01/230-9700* 🌐 *www.hostelcelica.com* 🛏 *20 rooms, from double en-suite cells to 12-bed dorms* 🍴 *Free breakfast.*

Intercontinental Ljubljana

$$ | **HOTEL** | **Pros:** city center location; five-star luxury; gorgeous views from rooms. **Cons:** close to main road; modern building feels out of place; not that much of a local feel. [$] *Rooms from: €175* ✉ *Slovenska cesta 59* ☎ *059/128–000* 🌐 *www.ihg.com/intercontinental/hotels/gb/en/ljubljana/ljuha/hoteldetail* 🛏 *165 rooms* 🍴 *No meals.*

Vander Urbani

$$ | **HOTEL** | Arguably the most central hotel in Ljubljana, Vander Urbani was born of architectural creativity; several 18th-century town houses in the old city were joined to form this trendy hotel right beneath the Ljubljana castle. **Pros:**

stylish design; ideal location; beautiful pool with a fantastic view. **Cons:** some flats feel crammed, though they've done their best to utilize space; hotel might feel like a nightclub to some; breakfast area gets a little too crowded. $ *Rooms from: €160* ✉ *Krojaska ulica 6–8* ☎ *01/200–9000* ⊕ *www.vanderhotel.com* ⇨ *20 rooms* ⦿ *Free Breakfast.*

▼ Nightlife

It might not get the hype showered upon other European capitals, but don't sleep on Ljubljana as a nightlife destination. The city is full of bars, pubs, and clubs that know how to turn it on when need be, with fun-filled nights fueled by an ever-growing roster of independent breweries and vineyards.

BARS

Almost in the blink of an eye, Ljubljana's city center has blossomed as a nightlife destination. Stylish bars, charming pubs, and elegant wine bars abound—all you need to do is pick your spot.

Daktari

CAFES—NIGHTLIFE | With its hodge-podge of furniture and an undeniable artistic streak running through the walls, Daktari is a veritable Ljubljana institution. A wide range of patrons regularly enjoy the packed schedule of events here or simply an evening of drinks and discussion, from early in the morning until late at night. You won't find a more eclectic crowd anywhere else in the city. ✉ *Krekov trg 7* ☎ *64/166–212* ⊕ *www.daktari.si.*

Godec Rock Pub

BARS/PUBS | An intimate rock music-friendly pub just outside the city center, Godec is a great option for anyone looking for good beer and music, thanks to its selection of classic tunes and a beer list covering Slovenia and beyond. Godec is a favorite with locals, making it a tremendous option for anyone looking for something a little more Ljubljanan. ✉ *Knezova ulica 3*

☎ *68/146–261* ⊕ *www.facebook.com/godecrockpub.*

The Human Fish Taproom

BREWPUBS/BEER GARDENS | Slovenia's original craft beer is best enjoyed at its brewery, located in Vrhnika, an easy 25-minute journey from Ljubljana. The selection of beers is extensive (including a no-alcohol Respectable Fish), and the terrace is a great spot for a quiet afternoon drink with great conversation. It's closed Monday and Tuesday. ✉ *Tržaška cesta 27* ☎ *030/381–473* ⊕ *www.facebook.com/taproomvrhnika.*

Patrick's Irish Pub

BARS/PUBS | Everything that makes Irish pubs great can be found at Patrick's, a down-to-earth home away from home in the center of town. The beer list is the envy of all other pubs in town, while the monthly pub quizzes are heavily contested and always enjoyed. It's your best bet for live sports and pub grub in the heart of Ljubljana. ✉ *Prečna 6* ☎ *041/581–333* ⊕ *www.irishpub-ljubljana.si.*

★ Pritličje

CAFES—NIGHTLIFE | With two fingers on the cultural pulse of the country, Pritličje is fast-becoming an iconic ground zero for all things social in Ljubljana. The cooler-than-cool vibe is more than just aesthetics at this people-friendly bar with open doors and open minds. Located directly next to the Town Hall, Pritličje is a beacon of positivity, all night long. ✉ *Mestni trg 2* ☎ *08/058–742* ⊕ *www.facebook.com/pritlicje.*

MUSIC
Čin Čin

BARS/PUBS | Ljubljana's old tobacco factory is now a prime spot for all-night partying, thanks to the cheerfully monikered Čin Čin. Live music and the best DJs in the region fill the schedule as party-goers toast with impeccably prepared cocktails and more. ✉ *Tržaška 2* ☎ *051/130–949* ⊕ *www.facebook.com/cincintobacna.*

Cirkus Klub

DANCE CLUBS | A mature and eclectic clubbing scene congregates in this former movie theater turned night club near the city center. Considered one of the top nightlife venues in the capital, Cirkus attracts DJs and bands that bring dance, R&B, hip-hop, house, pop, and rock to its multiple floors. It's open Wednesday, Friday, and Saturday. ☒ *Trg Mladinskih delovskih brigad 7* ☏ *051/631–631* ⊕ *www.cirkusklub.si.*

★ Kino Šiška

MUSIC CLUBS | A major player in Ljubljana nightlife since forever, Kino Šiška contiues to be the capital's best source of live entertainment and partying. The schedule is as packed as Ljubljana schedules get, and the whole place is dripping in modern cool. ☒ *Trg prekomorskih brigad 3* ☏ *01/500–3000* ⊕ *www.kinosiska.si/en.*

Metelkova

BARS/PUBS | Formerly an army barracks, Metelkova has been transformed into a multipurpose venue for shows and happenings. Today, it is the center of the Slovenian alternative culture scene, full of street art, unique galleries, and music of every genre in its various clubs. Check the website for schedules of openings and performances. ☒ *Metelkova, Tabor* ⊕ *www.metelkovamesto.org.*

🎭 Performing Arts

One in 10 of the capital's inhabitants is a student, hence the proliferation of trendy cafés and small art galleries. In addition, each summer is filled with creative events that breathe new life into the Ljubljana cultural scene, sparking off a lively program of concerts and experimental theater.

ANNUAL EVENTS

In summer, Ljubljana comes alive with live music, with renowned festivals including the Ljubljana Festival and the International Jazz Festival attracting both homegrown and international artists.

Ljubljana Festival

ARTS FESTIVALS | The Ljubljana Festival is held annually from June to August in the open-air Križanke Summer Theater. Musical, theatrical and dance performances attract acclaimed artists from all over the world. Check the website for schedules and reservations. ☒ *Trg Francoske Revolucije 1–2* ☏ *01/241–6000* ⊕ *www. ljubljanafestival.si.*

CLASSICAL MUSIC

Ljubljana has plenty of events for classical-music lovers. The season, which runs from September through June, includes weekly concerts by the Slovenian Philharmonic Orchestra and the RTV Slovenia Orchestra, as well as performances by guest soloists, chamber musicians, and foreign symphony orchestras.

Slovenska Filharmonija (*Slovenian Philharmonic*)

CONCERTS | The 19th-century performance hall houses concerts by the Slovenian Philharmonic. This hall was built in 1891 for one of the oldest music societies in the world, established in 1701. Haydn, Brahms, Beethoven, and Paganini were honorary members of the orchestra, and Mahler was resident conductor for the 1881–82 season. Check the website for a schedule of performances and to make reservations. ☒ *Kongresni trg 10* ☏ *01/241–0800* ⊕ *www.filharmonija.si.*

THEATER, DANCE, AND OPERA

Ljubljana has a long tradition of experimental and alternative theater, frequently incorporating dance as well. Contemporary dance plays by the internationally recognized choreographers Matjaz Faric and Iztok Kovac and performances by the dance troupes Betontanc and En Knap are ideal for those who don't understand Slovenian.

SNG Opera in Balet (*Slovene National Opera & Ballet Theater*)

DANCE | FAMILY | This neo-Renaissance palace, with an ornate facade topped by an allegorical sculpture group, was erected in 1892. When visiting ballet and opera companies visit Ljubljana, they perform here. The opera house fell into disrepair during the Yugoslav years but has been carefully and lovingly restored since Slovenian independence. From September through June, the SNG Opera in Balet stages productions ranging in style, from classical to modern and alternative. ⊠ *1 Župančičeva St* ☎ *01/241–5900* ⊕ *www. opera.si.*

🛍 Shopping

Shopping isn't huge in Ljubljana like it is in other European cities, but there are still plenty of places to scope out the latest fashions or pick up a traditional Slovenian souvenir.

Anappurna

SPORTING GOODS | This store has a good selection of mountaineering equipment for those looking to enjoy hiking. ⊠ *Krakovski Nasip 4* ☎ *01/426–3428* ⊕ *www. annapurna.si.*

Ljubljana Flea Market

ANTIQUES/COLLECTIBLES | FAMILY | Held on the Breg Embankment each Sunday morning, the Ljubljana Flea Market offers a good selection of antiques and memorabilia. ⊠ *Breg Embankment.*

Piranske Soline

LOCAL SPECIALTIES | FAMILY | Beloved worldwide, the salt harvested at the Sečovlje Salina Nature Park is available in various shapes and sizes at this friendly shop on Mestni trg. ⊠ *Mestni trg 8* ☎ *01/425–0190* ⊕ *www.soline.si.*

Trgovina IKA

GIFTS/SOUVENIRS | FAMILY | Ljubljana has no shortage of options when it comes to buying souvenirs, but the creative style of those on offer at Trgovina IKA makes it stand out from the pack. ⊠ *Ciril-Metodov trg 13* ☎ *01/232–1743* ⊕ *www.trgovinaika. si.*

Bled

50 km (31 miles) northwest of Ljubljana on the E61.

Bled is among the most magnificently situated mountain resorts in Europe. The healing powers of its thermal springs were known during the 17th century, and in the early 19th century, the aristocracy arrived to bask in Bled's tranquil alpine setting. Even today—when Bled can swell to overflowing in the high season of July and August—it retains something of the refined feel of a fin de siècle spa town.

Recent years have brought a string of improvements to Bled's tourist facilities to cope with the ever-increasing number of visitors. Resorts and wellness centers, arguably the country's best golf course, and a clutch of adventure-oriented travel agencies mean there is now much more to do than simply stroll the banks of the lake. Bled is also an excellent base for hikes into the eastern half of Triglav National Park.

VISITOR INFORMATION

CONTACTS Bled Tourist Information. ⊠ *C. Svobode 10* ☎ *04/574–1122* ⊕ *www.bled. si.*

👁 Sights

★ Blejski Grad (*Bled Castle*)

CASTLE/PALACE | FAMILY | The stately Bled Castle perches above the lake on the summit of a steep cliff, against a backdrop of the Julian Alps and Triglav Peak. You can climb up to the castle for fine views of the lake, the resort, and the surrounding countryside. An exhibition traces the development of the castle through the centuries, with archeological artifacts to period furniture on display,

In the middle of Lake Bled, you'll find a small island with the charming St. Martin's Pilgrimage Church located on it.

but it is the view that steals the show. ✉ *Bled* ☎ *04/572–9770* 💳 *€9.*

★ Blejsko Jezero (*Lake Bled*)

BODY OF WATER | Bled's famed lake is nestled within a rim of mountains and surrounded by forests, with a castle on one side and a promenade beneath stately chestnut trees on the other. Horse-drawn carriages clip-clop along the promenade while swans glide on the water, creating the ultimate romantic scene. On a minuscule island in the middle of the lake, the lovely **Cerkov svetega Martina** (St. Martin's Pilgrimage Church) stands within a circle of trees. Take a ride over to the island on a *pletna*, a traditional covered boat. ✉ *Bled.*

Čebelarski Muzej (*Beekeeping Museum*)

MUSEUM | Radovljica is an adorable town not far from Bled, and its intriguing Čebelarski muzej may well be its cultural highlight. Located within the 17th-century town hall in the center, the museum gives a charming exploration of the humble bee, through a variety of interactive exhibitions. The museum also houses its own hive, a buzzing colony of some 5,000 bees, working away behind the safety of a glass cabinet. ✉ *Linhartov trg 1, Radovljica* ☎ *04/532–0520* ⊕ *cebelarski-muzej.si* ⊘ *Closed Mon.*

Soteska Vintgar (*Vintgar Gorge*)

CANYON | FAMILY | This gorge was cut between precipitous cliffs by the clear Radovna River, which flows down numerous waterfalls and through pools and rapids. The marked trail through the gorge leads over bridges and along wooden walkways and galleries. ✉ *Zgornje Gorje Rd., Podhom 80, 5 km (3 miles) northwest of Bled* ⊕ *www.vintgar.si.*

🍴 Restaurants

Cafe Belvedere

$ | SLOVENIAN | FAMILY | Once a waiting hall for those hoping for an audience with the king (and designed by Plečnik no less), Cafe Belvedere is now a gorgeous café offering the most exquisite views of Bled Island. The prices reflect that (expect to pay upwards of €2.60 for an espresso), but finding a better view of the beauty below is downright impossible. **Known for:** important history; gorgeous vistas; pricey coffees. $ *Average main: €10* ✉ *Cesta svobode 18* ☎ *04/575–3721* ⊕ *www.brdo.si/en/vila-bled/cafe-belvedere* ⊗ *Closed Oct.–Apr.*

Gostilna Lectar

$$$ | SLOVENIAN | FAMILY | This warm country-style inn serves an impressive selection of traditional dishes. For a cross section of the local cuisine, try the pumpkin soup, the Peasant's Plate (buckwheat dumplings, mixed smoked meats, potatoes, and fresh steamed vegetables), and the apple strudel. **Known for:** hearty meals for omnivores and vegetarians; big garden soups; desserts from grandma's kitchen. $ *Average main: €25* ✉ *Linhartov trg 2, Radovljica* ☎ *04/537–4800* ⊕ *www.lectar.com/.*

Gostilna pri Planincu

$$ | SLOVENIAN | With large portions at modest prices, this friendly spot is busy year-round. Rowdy farmers take advantage of the cheap beer at front bar and everyone loves the menu "for people who work all day": roast chicken and fries, steak and mushrooms, black pudding, and turnips. **Known for:** big helpings of local pub food; sweet walnut štrukli; cheap beer. $ *Average main: €12* ✉ *Grajska 8* ☎ *04/574–1613* ⊕ *www.pri-planincu.com.*

Julijana

$$$ | SLOVENIAN | If you happen to be a celebrity looking for a bite to eat in Bled, Julijana is where you will likely end up. This is a restaurant perched very much at the top table of the region's gastronomic scene, a high-class experience that combines stunning food with equally stunning views of the lake and the castle. **Known for:** world-class tasting menu; stunning views; quality over quantity. $ *Average main: €70* ✉ *Cesta svobode 12* ☎ *031/758–371* ⊕ *www.sava-hotels-resorts.com/en/sava-hoteli-bled/*

gastronomy/the-julijana-restaurant ⊗ *Closed Sun - Thurs.*

★ 1906

$$$ | SLOVENIAN | Meticulously prepared meals, perfectly paired wine, and homemade ice cream are all offered at a premium price for these parts, although the setting and experience makes that great value for your money. The head chef specializes in reviving traditional dishes with modern flair but will adapt any dishes to any customer's request. **Known for:** elegant yet down-to-earth atmosphere; impressive views; organized events like cooking classes. $ *Average main: €30* ✉ *Kolodvorska Cesta 33* ☎ *04/575–2610* ⊕ *www.hoteltriglavbled.si.*

Hotels

Garden Village Bled

$$ | ALL-INCLUSIVE | FAMILY | This collection of unique lodging options offers innovative new ways to accommodate travelers that are looking for a completely luxurious retreat that takes them back to nature. **Pros:** wellness offer includes massage and sauna; sophisticated dining on premises; bikes for rent. **Cons:** some tent locations better than others; no a/c in treehouse; Wi-Fi can be iffy in certain spots. $ *Rooms from: €200* ✉ *Cesta Gorenjskega odreda 16* ☎ *0/8389–9220* ⊕ *gardenvillagebled.com* ⊗ *Closed Nov.– Apr.* ⊐ *25 rooms* ⦿ *Free breakfast.*

Vila Bled

$$ | HOTEL | Late Yugoslav president Tito was the gracious host to numerous 20th-century statesmen at this former royal residence amid 13 acres of gardens overlooking the lake. **Pros:** unforgettable lake views; old-school elegance; free Wi-Fi in rooms. **Cons:** rooms can seem a bit dated if you're not a fan of retro style; café and restaurant on the expensive side; hard to get to without private transport. $ *Rooms from: €130* ✉ *C. Svobode 26* ☎ *04/575–3710* ⊕ *www.brdo.si/vila-bled* ⊐ *31 rooms* ⦿ *Free breakfast.*

Vila Prešeren

$$ | B&B/INN | This tastefully renovated 19th-century lakeside villa, named after Slovenia's foremost poet who was a frequent guest, is a step away from many of the Alpine accommodations in the area and feels more intimate than some of the lodgings located near the town center. **Pros:** lakeside location; bold furnishings; romantic ambience. **Cons:** restaurant is popular with tour buses; reception is located in the restaurant and staff are usually busy; nearby church bells seem to ring constantly. $ *Rooms from: €140 ⊠ Veslaška Promenada 14 ☎ 04/575–2510 ⊕ www.villa-preseren. com ⇨ 8 rooms ⊚ No meals.*

Activities

During summer, the lake turns into a family playground, with swimming, rowing, sailing, and windsurfing. The main swimming area lies below the castle along the northern shore. In the winter, you can ski day and night on Straža Hill, immediately above town, thanks to floodlighting. Just 10 km (6 miles) west of Bled, a larger ski area, Zatrnik, has 7 km (4½ miles) of alpine trails. The area's two golf courses—the 18-hole "Kings" course and the 9-hole "Lake" course—are located 4 km (2½ miles) outside of town at the Golf & Country Club Bled. For information on winter and summer sports, contact Bled's tourist-information center or one of the many private travel and activity agencies around town.

Royal Bled Golf

GOLF | King's Course (18 holes) and Lake's Course (9 holes) are both run by Royal Bled. Clubs, caddies, and carts are available for rent; the club also provides instruction and sanctions golf events. ⊠ *Kidričeva 10c ☎ 04/537–7711 ⊕ www. golfbled.com ⊠ King's Course: €150, golf cart €40; Lake's Course: €55, golf cart €25 ⥱ 18 holes, 6666 yards, par 72; 9 holes, 3089 yards, par 36.*

3glav Adventures

TOUR—SPORTS | FAMILY | 3glav Adventures puts together hiking and rafting outings and, for thrill seekers, organizes more extreme activities like parachuting and paragliding. ⊠ *Ljubljanska 1 ☎ 041/683–184 ⊕ www.3glav.com.*

Bohinjsko Jezero

When talking to locals about Lake Bled, don't be surprised to hear them say that they prefer Bohinj. Lake Bohinj, the largest permanent lake in Slovenia, sits within Triglav National Park and is a popular spot for swimming, boating, and other water sports. It's a refreshing, tranquil alternative to its more famous sibling.

VISITOR INFORMATION

CONTACTS Bohinj Tourist Information.
⊠ *Ribčev Laz 48 ☎ 04/574–6010 ⊕ www. bohinj.si.*

Sights

★ Bohinjsko Jezero

BODY OF WATER | Lake Bohinj is the quieter, wilder, and prettier sister of Bled and lies entirely within the Triglav National Park. The entire length of the north shore is wild and accessible only by foot. The lake, at an altitude of 1,715 feet, is surrounded on three sides by the steep walls of the Julian Alps. The altitude means the temperature of the water—even in August—rarely rises above a brisk but still swimmable 74°F. The small village of Ribčev Laz, on the eastern end of the lake functions as the de facto town center, where you'll find a grocery store, post office, currency exchange, an ATM, and the tourist information center. On the western shore lies the remote village of Ukanc, anchored by the Hotel Zlatorog, a campsite, and a few small shops. Just to the north and east of Ribčev Laz are the tiny hamlets of Stara Fužina, Studor, and Srednja Vas. ⊠ *Triglav National Park.*

Slovenia's only national park, Triglav is one of its most popular camping destinations.

Mt. Vogel

MOUNTAIN—SIGHT | At the west end of Lake Bohinj (near Ukanc) a cable car leads up Mt. Vogel to a height of 5,035 feet. From here, you have spectacular views of the Julian Alps massif and the Bohinj valley and lake. From the cable-car base, the road continues 5 km (3 miles) beyond the lake to the point where the Savica River makes a tremendous leap over a 194-foot waterfall. The cable car runs every half hour from 8 am to 6 pm. A round-trip ticket costs €24. ⊠ *Žičnice Vogel Bohinj, Ukanc 6* ⊕ *www.vogel.si.*

Sveti Janez (*St. John*)

RELIGIOUS SITE | FAMILY | On the eastern bank of Lake Bohinj in Ribčev Laz, you'll find the 15th-century Gothic church of Sveti Janez. The small church has a fine bell tower and contains a number of notable 15th- and 16th-century frescoes. ⊠ *Ribčev Laz.*

★ Triglav National Park

NATIONAL/STATE PARK | FAMILY | Covering some 4% of Slovenia's entire landmass, it can be argued that Triglav National Park is the ideological and spiritual heart of the country. The iconic three peaks of Triglav (the highest point in the country) are found on Slovenia's coat of arms and its flag, placing this dreamland of gorges, caves, waterfalls, rivers, and forests front and center for the nation. Winter sees locals and visitors alike head here in search of skiing and other snow-based activities, while the warmer months are perfect for both amateur and experienced climbers and hikers. Mountain huts dot the landscape offering affordable accommodations for those looking to wander the meadows. Slovenia's only national park, Triglav contains everything that makes Slovenian nature magnificent, all within 840 square km (324 square miles) of magic. ⊠ *Triglav National Park* ☎ *04/578–0200* ⊕ *www.tnp.si.*

Turistična Ladja (*Tourist Boat*)

TRANSPORTATION SITE (AIRPORT/BUS/FERRY/ TRAIN) | Because gasoline-powered engines are not allowed on Lake Bohinj, the super-quiet Turistična Ladjas runs on electrical power. The boats make hourly runs during daylight hours from June to mid-September from the boat dock just below Ribčev Laz to Camp Zlatorog on the western side of the lake and back. A ticket costs €9 one-way, €12 round-trip. 🌐 *www.bohinj.si.*

🍴 Restaurants

Most of the hotels and pensions in the area offer full or least half-board, reducing the number of independent restaurants. However, that is not to say there aren't places worth searching out, as pension food may become monotonous and there may be afternoons or evenings when you will want to explore on your own.

Gostilna Danica

$$ | **SLOVENIAN** | **FAMILY** | Don't be deceived by this restaurant's casual appearance at the Danica campsite: it tries much harder to add variety to the average Slovenian fare than most. Economically priced while still delivering a full plate, a good portion of the menu changes seasonally. **Known for:** three-course meal for under €15; distinctively better than most campsite restaurants; full regional wine menu. [$] *Average main: €13* ✉ *Triglavska cesta 60, Bohinjska Bistrica* ☎ *04/575–1610* 🌐 *www.camp-danica.si.*

★ Strud'l

$ | **SLOVENIAN** | **FAMILY** | This spot offers a quaint backdrop for a menu of alluring local food, offered at a reasonable price. The staff are attentive, and the atmosphere is warm, as are most of the dishes. **Known for:** foraged mushroom soup with homemade bread; traditional Slovenian mountain delights; cash-only policy. [$] *Average main: €8* ✉ *Triglavska cesta 23,, Bohinjska Bistrica* ☎ *041/541–877* 🌐 *www.strudl.si* 💳 *No credit cards.*

🛏 Hotels

The Bohinj area is the perfect place to opt for a stay in a private home or pension. The tourist information center in Ribčev Laz maintains an extensive list of options. Pensions are usually priced per person and often include lunch or dinner. Many of the nicest properties are in the outlying villages of Ukanc, Stara Fužina, and Srednja Vas—so you will need your own transportation (bike or car) to get there.

Apartments Alpik

$$ | **B&B/INN** | **FAMILY** | Located a stone's throw from Lake Bohinj, the Vogal ski resort contains a handful of restaurants. **Pros:** good for families or groups; self-contained kitchen; shoe- or ski-drying hallway setup. **Cons:** a walk into town; best to organize arrivial and departure times beforehand; kitchen sometimes lacks basic ingredients. [$] *Rooms from: €160* ✉ *Ukanc 85* ☎ *041/435–555* 🌐 *www.alpik.com* 🛏 *6 rooms* 🍴 *No meals.*

★ Bohinj Park ECO Hotel

$$ | **HOTEL** | **FAMILY** | As the first ecological hotel in Slovenia, Park ECO has won a litany of awards, all for good reason. **Pros:** furnishings made from all-natural materials; vegetarian options; entertainment for all ages and skill levels. **Cons:** large, full hotel; conferences can seemingly take over the hotel; a little on the pricey side of things. [$] *Rooms from: €170* ✉ *Triglavska cesta 17* ☎ *08/200–4140* 🌐 *www.bohinj-eco-hotel.si* 🛏 *102 rooms* 🍴 *Free breakfast.*

Hotel Gasperin

$ | **B&B/INN** | Showcasing no notable frills but all of the clean, basic amenities, Hotel Gasperin is organized and set up for easy vacationing. **Pros:** good for families or groups; lots of nearby hiking options; beautiful location by the lake. **Cons:** a walk to the nearest restaurant; nothing more than basic amenities; outside noise can be heard from rooms. [$] *Rooms from: €100* ✉ *Ribčev Laz 36a* ☎ *041/540–805* 🌐 *www.gasperin-bohinj.com* 🛏 *24 rooms* 🍴 *Free breakfast.*

Vila Park

$ | B&B/INN | A luxurious little A-frame pension sits astride an impossibly gorgeous alpine meadow and just beside the bright-green Savica stream that feeds Lake Bohinj. **Pros:** good for families or groups; lovely location near stream; excellent breakfast. **Cons:** remote from major area sights; walk to nearest restaurant; decor a bit dated. $ *Rooms from: €55 ⊠ Ukanc 129 ☎ 04/572–3300 ⊕ www.vila-park.si ⇨ 10 rooms ⥁ Free breakfast.*

🏃 Activities

Bohinj is a natural base for exploring the trails of the Triglav National Park. Before heading out, pick up a good trail map from the tourist information center. The cable car to Vogel is an excellent starting point for many of the walks. Just remember to start early, wear proper hiking boots, take plenty of water, and protect yourself against the sun. Other popular warm-weather pursuits include swimming, biking, rafting, canyoning, and horseback riding. In winter you can ski at the ski areas of Vogel and Kobla.

Alpinsport

TOUR—SPORTS | FAMILY | In the village of Studor, Alpinsport rents mountain bikes and organizes raft, kayak, hydrospeed (a small board for bodysurfing rapids), and canyoning trips. ⊠ *Ribčev Laz 53* ☎ *041/918–803* ⊕ *www.alpinsport.si.*

Mrcina Ranč

HORSEBACK RIDING | FAMILY | This company organizes horseback rides in and around Bohinj and the Triglav National Park to suit all skill levels. ⊠ *Studor* ☎ *041/790–297* ⊕ *www.ranc-mrcina.com.*

Perfect Adventure Choice/PAC Sports

WATER SPORTS | This is another local outfitter offering a slew of water sports, including paragliding, caving expeditions, and ice climbing. ⊠ *Ribčev Laz 60* ☎ *040/864–202* ⊕ *www.pac.si.*

Kranjska Gora

39 km (24 miles) northwest of Bled, 85 km (53 miles) from Ljubljana.

Kranjska Gora, amid Slovenia's highest and most dramatic peaks, is the country's largest ski resort. In summer, the area attracts hiking and mountaineering enthusiasts. It's a pleasant town in any season. The resorts spread out along the perimeter, leaving the surprisingly charming core intact.

VISITOR INFORMATION

CONTACTS Kranjska Gora Tourist Information. ⊠ *Kolodvorska ulica 1c* ☎ *04/580– 9440* ⊕ *www.kranjska-gora.si.*

🍴 Restaurants

Bar Pristavec

$ | ECLECTIC | This cute, laid-back place is just off the main square, and it's perfect for a morning coffee and a light roll or sandwich. **Known for:** early morning conversation; pet-friendly policies; quick bites. $ *Average main: €5 ⊠ Borovška 77* ☎ *04/588–2111* ▭ *No credit cards.*

Gostilna pri Martinu

$$ | SLOVENIAN | This traditional Slovene gostilna is known for their down home good cooking. Try the homemade sausages or a local favorite, *telecja obara* (veal stew). **Known for:** local wedding receptions and large parties; traditional cooking; homemade sausages. $ *Average main: €13 ⊠ Borovška 61* ☎ *04/582–0300* ⊕ *www.gostilnamartin.si.*

Penzion Lipa

$$ | SLOVENIAN | This pension is primarily a hotel but also has a decent restaurant. The pizza is undoubtedly worth the money, but if you're in the mood for some local food, opt for the *ješprenj* (pronounced "yesh-preny"), an old-school Slovenian farmers' dish centered around barley and smoked meat. **Known for:** idylic mountain setting; classic Slovenian fare; elegant dining room. $ *Average main:*

€15 ✉ *Koroška str. 14* ☎ *45/820–000*
⊕ *www.hotel-lipa.si.*

★ Slaščičarna Kala

$ | SLOVENIAN | Tucked away near the
bus station, this little patisserie is easy
to miss, yet worth every effort to find.
Specializing in homemade ice cream and
desserts from the Prekmurje region, this
charming café will tempt you and keep
you coming back for more. **Known for:**
homemade ice cream and cakes; krem
snita (typical Balkan pastry); good coffee.
$ *Average main: €3* ✉ *Koroška ulica 13B*
☎ *04/588–5544* ⊕ *www.sobe-kala.si*
▭ *No credit cards.*

 ## Hotels

Most of Kranjska Gora's hotels are
relatively large and were built during
the 1970s and '80s to accommodate ski
groups. The tourist information center
can help you find smaller properties, pensions, and private rooms if you are looking for something simpler and cheaper.

★ Kronau Chalet Resort

$ | RESORT | FAMILY | Considered one of
the best mountain lodges in Slovenia and
situated near the famed Kranjska Gora
World Cup giant-slalom slopes, this a truly relaxing place to stay. **Pros:** paradise for
skiers; tastefully decorated; eco-friendly
policies. **Cons:** no coffeemakers in rooms;
best to arrange arrival and departure
beforehand; a little pricey. $ *Rooms
from: €100* ✉ *Bezje 19* ☎ *51/356–179*
⊕ *www.kronau.si* ⇄ *6 chalets (36 beds)*
▯◯▮ *No meals.*

Skipass Hotel

$$ | HOTEL | FAMILY | Family-run and
family-friendly, this small hotel of eight
spacious rooms and two deluxe suites
is affordable yet generous and accom-
modates guests with indulgent details
such as heated bathroom floors and
generous breakfasts. **Pros:** excellent
restaurant; good location; community
feel. **Cons:** must book amply in advance;
decor is not exceptional; no free parking.

$ *Rooms from: €140* ✉ *Koroška ulica 14c*
☎ *04/582–1000* ⊕ *www.skipasshotel.si*
⇄ *10 rooms* ▯◯▮ *Free breakfast.*

 ## Activities

Skiing is the number-one sport in Kranjska Gora, and Kranjska Gora is the number-one skiing spot in Slovenia. There are
more than 30 km (19 miles) of downhill
runs, 20 ski lifts, and 40 km (25 miles) of
groomed cross-country trails open during
the winter ski season, which typically
runs from mid-December through mid-
March. During summer, from late May
through mid-September, mountain biking
is big, and you'll find plenty of places to
rent bikes, as well as 12 marked trails
covering 150 km (93 miles) to take you
through scented pine forests and spectacular alpine scenery. An unused railway
track, tracing the south edge of the Kar-
avanke Alps, brings hikers and bikers all
the way to the village of Jesenice, about
20 km (12 miles) away. The Kranjska
Gora Bike Park is oriented more toward
experienced free-riders and thrill seek-
ers—those who like to take their bikes to
the top of the hill and careen back down.
There are also numerous hiking trails; you
can pick up a good local trail map from
the tourist information center or at kiosks
around town.

Dom Trenta

MOUNTAIN—SIGHT | FAMILY | In Trenta, you'll
find the Triglav National Park Information
Center at Dom Trenta. Here, you can
watch a presentation about the history
and geography of the region and tour
the small museum. It's also a good
access point to the 20-km (12-mile) Soča
Trail that winds its way along the river's
banks. The center is open from April
through October, daily from 10 to 6. ✉ *Na
Logu v Trenti, Trenta* ☎ *05/388–9330*
⊕ *www.tnp.si.*

Fun Bike Park Kranjska Gora

BICYCLING | This company rents full- and
front-suspension mountain bikes for use

along downhill mountain and forest trails. The emphasis here is on fast, adrenaline-filled rides. Lifts are open from May through the third week of September. ✉ *Borovška 107* ☎ *041/706–786* 🌐 *www.bike-park.si.*

Kranjska Gora Recreational Ski Center
SKIING/SNOWBOARDING | This center runs the lifts and is the main place for skiing information. The website lists prices in English and has a live webcam so that you can see the conditions on the mountain. ✉ *Borovška 103a* ☎ *04/580–9400* 🌐 *www.kr-gora.si.*

Sport Bernik
TOUR—SPORTS | A full-service sports-equipment rental center, Sport Bernik rents both skis and mountain bikes in their respective seasons. It's located close to the ski center. ✉ *Borovška 88a* ☎ *04/588–4783* 🌐 *www.intersport-bernik.com.*

Vršič Pass
MOUNTAIN—SIGHT | From Kranjska Gora, head south over the breathtaking Vršič Pass, some 5,253 feet above sea level. You'll then descend into the beautiful Soča Valley, winding through the foothills to the west of Triglav Peak and passing truly magnificent scenery in the process. From Trenta, continue west for about 20 km (12 miles) to reach the mountain adventure resort of Bovec.

Bovec

35 km (22 miles) south of Kranjska Gora, 124 km (77 miles) from Ljubljana.

Bovec is a friendly, relaxed, youth-oriented town that owes its modern existence largely to the adventure tourism afforded by the Soča River. The center is filled with private travel agencies, all offering a similar array of white-water rafting, kayaking, canoeing, hydrospeeding, and canyoning trips. The Soča—by the time it reaches Bovec—is a world-class river that regularly plays host to international rafting events. The main tour operators are experienced, and the rafting trips are aimed at all levels of experience. The river is at its best in spring, swelled by the melting snowcaps, but it is raftable throughout the summer. Even if you don't decide to ride, plan a walk along the Soča's banks—the emerald green or electric blue (depending on the glint of the sun) color of the water is not to be missed.

🍴 Restaurants

With its emphasis on sports, Bovec is not exactly teeming with great places to eat. Nevertheless, several central gostilnas that serve basic food, and the hotel restaurants offer acceptable options as well.

Gostišče Sovdat
$$ | **SLOVENIAN** | This family-run inn serves grill specialties and pasta entrées. There is attractive garden seating in the back and the lively bar is known for sing-alongs toward the end of the day. **Known for:** burgers with home-made fries; fresh fish; good selection of best Slovenian wines. [$] *Average main: €12* ✉ *Trg Golobarskih Žrtev 24* ☎ *40/202–366* 🌐 *www.gostilna-sovdat.si* 🕒 *Closed Wed.*

Pristava Lepena
$$ | **SLOVENIAN** | **FAMILY** | Attention to healthy, local food and vegetarian cuisine will quickly win over any traveler who has had their fill of pizza or mediocre meat-and-potato dishes. The picnic area is a lovely place to enjoy the main specialty, local river fish, and the barbecue is set up for children to help prepare their own meals over a campfire. **Known for:** log cabins in picturesque setting; lots of open space; horses and archery. [$] *Average main: €18* ✉ *Lepena 2* ☎ *041/671–981* 🌐 *www.pristava-lepena.com.*

Hotels

Hotel Dobra Vila
$$ | HOTEL | FAMILY | A welcome high-end addition to the local lodging scene, Hotel Dobra Vila is located is a restored, early-20th-century telephone exchange building. **Pros:** excellent restaurant; many quiet nooks; books everywhere. **Cons:** could feel too remote if planning a long stay; need a car to get most places; formal atmosphere. [$] *Rooms from: €160* ✉ *Mala vas 112* ☎ *05/389–6400* 🌐 *www.dobra-vila-bovec.com* 🛏 *12 rooms* 🍴 *Free breakfast.*

★ Hotel Sanje Ob Soči
$ | HOTEL | FAMILY | Family-friendly to the point of featuring full-time babysitters and a mini cinema, Hotel Sanje has positioned itself well as a bright and modern, fully equipped nature lodge for groups or individuals seeking group interaction. **Pros:** stunning views; many services; tremendous breakfast. **Cons:** difficult to find; no coat racks in rooms; inconsistent showers. [$] *Rooms from: €120* ✉ *Mala vas 105a* ☎ *05/389–6000* 🌐 *www.sanjeobsoci.com* 🛏 *19 rooms* 🍴 *Free breakfast.*

Nightlife

★ Thirsty River Brewing Bar and Rooms
BREWPUBS/BEER GARDENS | In addition to the comfortable and affordable accommodations it offers in the heart of Bovec, Thirsty River lives up to its name with some of the best beer in town. The staff are convivial and informative, friendly whlle the range of beers is fantastic. It's the perfect combination of a comfy bed and a refreshing pint. ✉ *Trg golobarskih žrtev 46* ☎ *040/530–171.*

Activities

White-water rafting is not the only game in town. Bovec is a great base for leisurely cycling trips or more aggressive mountain-bike climbs. Private bike outfitters or the tourist information center can provide maps and advice. It's also a great base for hiking the western regions of the Triglav National Park. The map *Bovec z Okolico* is available at the tourist information center and kiosks around town; it marks out several good walks and bike trips of varying degrees of difficulty.

Soča Rafting
TOUR—SPORTS | This is one of the better-known rafting and kayaking outfitters. They are also well connected to the biggest zipline park in Slovenia. Zipping between trees and over canyons is another way to quickly see this region's nature on the fly. ✉ *Trg Golobarskih Žrtev 14* ☎ *05/389–6200* 🌐 *www.socarafting.si.*

Sportmix
TOUR—SPORTS | This company offers excellent adrenaline-inducing activities on the Soča river tributaries. From canyoning to rafting via kayaking, the professional and meticulous Sportmix team will help get your excitement boosted and your blood pumping. ✉ *Trg Golobarskih žrtev 18* ☎ *031/871–991* 🌐 *www.sportmix.si.*

Postojnska Jama and Škocjanske Jama

44 km (27 miles) southwest of Ljubljana.

The so-called "Queen of Caves", Postojnska Jama has been wowing visitors since it was discovered in 1818, ahead of a visit by the first Emperor of Austria-Hungary. One of the country's most visited tourist attractions along with nearby Škocjanske Jama, the caves are home to the famous *olm*, the delightfully monikered "human fish", a species of amphibians who live in total darkness.

Sights

Postojnska Jama (*Postojna Cave*)
CAVE | FAMILY | This is one of the largest networks of caves in the world, with 23

km (14 miles) of underground passageways. A miniature train takes you through the first 7 km (4½ miles) to reveal a succession of well-lighted rock formations. This strange underground world is home to the snakelike "human fish" on view in an aquarium in the Great Hall. Eyeless and colorless because of countless millennia of life in total darkness, these amphibians can live for up to 60 years. Temperatures average 8°C (46°F) year-round, so bring a sweater, even in summer. Tours leave every hour on the hour May through October and three to four times a day November to April. ✉ *Jamska 30, Postojna* ☎ *05/700–0100* 🌐 *www.postojnska-jama.eu* 🎟 *€27.50.*

★ **Škocjan Jama** (*Škocjanske Caves*)
CAVE | FAMILY | The 11 interconnected chambers that compose the Škocjan Jama stretch for almost 6 km (about 4 miles) through a dramatic, subterranean landscape so unique that UNESCO has named them a World Heritage Site. The 90-minute walking tour of the two chilly main chambers—the Silent Cave and the Murmuring Cave—is otherworldly as winds swirl around the dripstone sculptures, massive sinkholes, and stalactites and stalagmites that resemble the horns of a mythic creature. The highlight is Europe's largest cave hall, a gorge 479 feet high, 404 feet wide, and 984 feet long, spanned by a narrow bridge lighted with footlights. Far below, the brilliant jade waters of the Reka River rush by on their underground journey. The view is nothing short of mesmerizing. ✉ *Škocjan 2, Divaca* ☎ *05/7082–110* 🌐 *www.park-skocjanske-jame.si* 🎟 *€24.*

Lipica

5 km (3 miles) west of Divača, 30 km (19 miles) south of Stanjel, 80 km (50 miles) from Ljubljana.

Lipica is best known as the home of the Kobilarna Lipica, the Lipica Stud farm, where the fabled white Lipizzaner horses were first bred. The horse farm is still the primary reason most people come here, though the area has developed into a modern sports complex, with two hotels, a popular casino, an indoor pool, tennis courts, and an excellent 9-hole golf course. It makes a pleasant, hassle-free base for exploring the nearby Škocjan caves and Karst region. The horses, the large areas of green, and the facilities of the Hotel Maestoso—including a pool—are all great for families with children.

Sights

Kobilarna Lipica (*Lipica Stud Farm*)
FARM/RANCH | FAMILY | Founded in 1580 by the Austrian archduke Karl II, the Kobilarna Lipica was where the white Lipizzaners—the majestic horses of the famed Spanish Riding School in Vienna—originated. Today, the farm no longer sends its horses to Vienna, but rather breeds them for its own performances and riding instruction. The impressive stables and grounds are open to the public. Riding classes are available, but lessons are geared toward experienced riders and must be booked in advance. ✉ *Lipica 5, Sežana* ☎ *05/739–1696* 🌐 *www.lipica.org* 🎟 *€16.*

Restaurants

Gostilna Muha
$$ | SLOVENIAN | A friendly, family-run tavern in the village of Lokev is about 4 km (2 miles) from the Lipica stud farm. This is a great place to try traditional dishes and wine from the Karst region; a good starter is *jota* (bean and sauerkraut soup) followed by slow-roasted pork and a green salad topped with a spoonful of beans. **Known for:** friendly atmosphere; no menu, just the daily specials; hearty dishes. [$] *Average main: €15* ✉ *Lokev 138, Lokev* ☎ *05/767–0055* 🌐 *www.gostilna-muha.com* 💳 *No credit cards* 🕒 *Closed Thurs. and Fri.*

Gostilna Prunk

$$ | SLOVENIAN | Cavernous dining rooms and excellently prepared beef dishes provide authentic ambience at Gostilna Prunk, a delightful surprise in the backwoods of Slovenia. The menu is simple and meat-centric (the family-owned butcher shop is attached) but enhanced by fresh ingredients and well-chosen spices. **Known for:** family-owned butcher shop attached; overflowing meat platters; reasonable prices. $ *Average main: €12* ✉ *Lokev 166 b, Lokev* ☎ *05/767–1102* ⊕ *www.mesarija-prunk.si.*

Koper

50 km (31 miles) southwest of Divača (Lipica), 105 km (65 miles) southwest of Ljubljana.

Today a port town surrounded by industrial suburbs, Koper is criminally underrated by visitors and locals alike. The Republic of Venice made Koper the regional capital during the 15th and 16th centuries, and the magnificent architecture of the Old Town bears witness to the spirit of those times.

The most important buildings are clustered around **Titov trg**, the central town square. Here stands the **Cathedral**, with its fine Venetian Gothic facade and bell tower dating back to 1664. Across the square the splendid **Praetor's Palace**, formerly the seat of the Venetian Grand Council, combines Gothic and Renaissance styles. From the west side of Titov trg, the narrow, cobbled **Kidriceva ulica** brings you down to the seafront.

VISITOR INFORMATION

CONTACTS Koper Tourist Information. ✉ *Titov Trg 3* ☎ *05/664–6403* ⊕ *www.koper.si.*

Sights

Hrastovlje Church of the Holy Trinity

RELIGIOUS SITE | Hidden behind the 16th-century defensive walls of this small town is the tiny Romanesque **Cerkev sveti Trojice** (Church of the Holy Trinity). The interior is decorated with a remarkable series of frescoes, including the bizarre *Dance Macabre,* completed in 1490. The church is locked, but if you ask in the village, the locals will be glad to open it for you. Alternatively, you can make arrangements to visit at the tourism booth in Koper beforehand. From Koper take the main road toward Ljubljana; then follow the signs for Hrastovlje (22 km [14 miles] from Koper).

Restaurants

Istrska Klet Slavček

$$ | MEDITERRANEAN | FAMILY | Creating a homey atmosphere in the center of town isn't the easiest task, but Istrska Klet Slavček more than pulls it off. All things Istrian are embraced on the menu, highlighted by a tremendous seafood selection straight from the port to your plate. **Known for:** local seafood specialties ; traditional Istrian atmosphere; family-friendly feel. $ *Average main: €12* ✉ *Župan);čiceva ulica 39* ☎ *5/627–6229.*

Nightlife

★ Bar Cameral

CAFES—NIGHTLIFE | Just about as down-to-earth as you could hope to find on the coast, this homage to all things independent serves delicious coffees and teas by day and a fine range of Slovenian craft beers by night. Cafés in Koper can lean on the uncreative side of things, but Cameral stands out from the pack. ✉ *Čevljarska ulica 14* ☎ *70/543–919.*

Piran is the most popular spot on Slovenia's Adriatic coast.

Piran

3 km (2 miles) from Portorož, 126 km (78 miles) from Ljubljana.

The Slovenian coast's most popular spot, the medieval walled Venetian town of Piran stands compact on a small peninsula, capped by a neo-Gothic lighthouse and presided over by a hilltop Romanesque cathedral. Narrow, winding, cobbled streets lead to the main square, Trg Tartini, which in turn opens out onto a charming harbor. Historically, Piran's wealth was based on salt making. Culturally, the town is known as the birthplace of the 17th-century violinist and composer Giuseppe Tartini.

If you are arriving by car, avoid the tiny lanes around the harbor and instead leave the car in the lot outside of town. The lot farthest out has the cheapest long-term rates, and a shuttle bus will then take you into town.

Piran fills to capacity in July and August, so try to arrange accommodation in advance. If you show up without a room, inquire at one of the privately run travel agencies. Along the coast, these are likely to be more helpful than the local tourist-information centers.

VISITOR INFORMATION

CONTACTS Piran Tourist Information.
⊠ *Trg Tartini 2* ☎ *05/673–4440* ⊕ *www. portoroz.si.*

Sights

Sergej Mašera Pomorski muzej (*Sergej Mašera Maritime Museum*)
MUSEUM | FAMILY | This museum tells the story of Piran's connection to the sea. On display is a beautiful collection of model ships, sailors' uniforms, and shipping instruments, and a fascinating historical section on the town's changing affiliations over the centuries. ⊠ *Cankarjevo nabrežje 3* ☎ *05/671–0040* ⊕ *www. pomorskimuzej.si* ⊠ *€4* ⊗ *Closed Mon.*

🍴 Restaurants

Piran's waterfront is filled with romantic, open-air restaurants. The quality of the food and the relatively high prices are mostly uniform. Stroll the walk and see which one appeals. Restaurants with better food at better prices can be found away from the shore, though they will not offer the same charming view.

Caffe Neptun

$ | CAFÉ | FAMILY | Not to be confused with the restaurant of the same name, Caffe Neptun is a delightful little café located directly next to the bus station. It's a friendly spot that focuses as much on sustainability and ethics as it does on good coffee and a warm atmosphere. **Known for:** best coffee on the coast; gorgeous sea views; great selection of beers. $ *Average main: €5* ✉ *Dantejeva ulica 4* ☎ *05/901–5633* ⊕ *caffeneptun.net.*

Neptun

$$ | SEAFOOD | Highly regarded by the locals, this tiny, family-run place focuses on all manner of local fish, grilled or fried; don't miss the grilled shrimp or calamari. Less touristy and more affordable than the restaurants along the sea front, Neptun only serves local catches rather than the imported farmed fish from Italy and Greece, like so many of their neighboring establishments. **Known for:** tasty grilled shrimp and calamari; authentic and low-key atmosphere; outdoor dining in summer. $ *Average main: €20* ✉ *Županćiĉeva 7* ☎ *05/673–4111.*

Pri Mari

$$ | SEAFOOD | Leave the throngs of central Piran behind and take a ride to this mom-and-pop restaurant. A 10-minute walk out of town leads you to this unique fusion of Italian and Slovenian cuisine. **Known for:** top-quality fish at a fair price; cozy, family-run atmosphere; apartments also available to rent. $ *Average main: €18* ✉ *Dantejeva ulica 17* ☎ *05/673–4735* ⊕ *www.primari-piran.com* ⊗ *Closed Mon. and Jan.*

🛏 Hotels

Hotel Piran

$$ | HOTEL | Located on a quiet patch of coastline close to the seaside restaurants, Hotel Piran is the best place to stay for an enchanting sea view. **Pros:** great views; historic atmosphere; next to the public beach. **Cons:** rooms aren't elegantly furnished; air conditioning in only the more expensive rooms; proximity to square means evening noise. $ *Rooms from: €140* ✉ *Kidriĉevo nab 4* ☎ *08/201-0420* ⊕ *www.hoteli-piran.si* ⇄ *103 rooms* ❑ *Free breakfast.*

Hotel Tartini

$ | HOTEL | Overlooking Trg Tartini is a modern hotel with a historic exterioir and a spacious central atrium in this convenient location. **Pros:** central and pleasant location; the cocktail bar has the best view in Piran; very relaxing rooms. **Cons:** rooms are rather dully decorated; expensive for what you get; can be noisy at night. $ *Rooms from: €95* ✉ *Trg Tartini 15* ☎ *05/671–1000* ⊕ *www.hotel-tartini-piran.com* ⇄ *45 rooms* ❑ *Free breakfast.*

Vila Piranesi

$$ | B&B/INN | FAMILY | At the center of Piran's old town, Vila Piranesi occupies a few floors of a renovated high school and offers well-priced, modern apartments with fully functional kitchenettes. **Pros:** good for families and groups; modern but not flashy; free parking. **Cons:** lacks basic amenities; entrance is a bit hard to find; horrible Wi-Fi. $ *Rooms from: €90* ✉ *Stjenkova 1* ☎ *040/779–935* ⊕ *www.piranesi.si* ⇄ *17 rooms* ❑ *No meals.*

🎭 Performing Arts

Piran Musical Evenings are held in the cloisters of the Minorite Monastery every Friday in July and August. The **Primorski Summer Festival** of open-air theater and dance is staged in Piran, Koper, Portorož, and Izola.

Index

Photo Credits

Front Cover: Ana Jovanic / EyeEm [Description: High Angle View Of Lake By Trees]. Back cover, from left to right: Dreamer4787/Shutterstock, lukaszimilena/Shutterstock, S-F/Shutterstock. Spine: Dreamer4787/iStockphoto. Interior, from left to right: Ivica Drusany / Shutterstock (1). xbrchx/Shutterstock (2-3). **Chapter 1:** Experience Croatia: Xbrchx/Dreamstime (6-7). Anton_Ivanov / Shutterstock (8). Alexey Stiop / Shutterstock (9). Dziewul/Dreamstime (9). stjepann / Shutterstock (10). joyfull/Shutterstock (10). Ken Gillham / age fotostock (10). K13 ART / Shutterstock (10). Liane Matrisch / age fotostock (11). Funkystock / age fotostock (11). DeymosHR/Shuttertock (12). parkerphotography / Alamy (12). DavorLovincic/iStockphoto (12). Ilijaaa/Dreamstime (12). xbrchx/Shutterstock (13). Ilijaaa/Dreamstime (14). RomanBabakin/iStockphoto (14). Croatian National Tourist Board / Ivo-biocina (14). Travelpeter/Dreamstime (14). xbrchx/Shutterstock (15). Littleaom/Shutterstock (15). zeleno/iStockphoto (20). phant/iStockphoto (21). Mark Marcec/Shutterstock (22). Pag Tourist Board (22). Nkooume/Dreamstime (22). Ivan Tibor Grujić/Samobor Tourist Board (23). Zvonimir Atletic/Shutterstock (23). goran_safarek/Shutterstock (24). Aleksandar Gospic/Croatian National Tourist Board (24). Visit Brac (24). xbrchx/Shutterstock (24). steve estvanik/Shutterstock (24). Xbrchx/Dreamstime (25). Harald Voglhuber/Rab Tourist Board (25). City of Krk Tourist Bord (25). Jakša Kuzmičić/Hvar Tourist Board (25). Ihor Pasternak/Shutterstock (25). **Chapter 3:** Dubrovnik and Southern Dalmatia: cge2010/Shhutterstock (59). Indos82 Dreamstime (70). Ihor Pasternak/Shutterstock (73). Birute/iStockphoto (74). RomanBabakin/iStockphoto (77). Rndmst/Dreamstime (78). xbrchx/Shutterstock (89). Donyanedomam/Dreamstime (94). Stjepan Tafra/Shutterstock (99). novak.elcic/Shutterstock (103). **Chapter 4:** Split and Central Dalmatia: emicristea/iStockphoto (105). xbrchx/iStockphoto (117). Ilija Ascic/Shutterstock (128). Mail2355/Dreamstime (132). Xbrch/ Dreamstime (137). xbrchx/iStockphoto (144). xbrchx/iStockphoto (148). **Chapter 5:** Zadar and Northern Dalmatia: xbrchx/iStockphoto (153). Borisb17/iStockphoto (160). Steveheap/Dreamstime (165). Mareticd/Dreamstime (170). Ilija Ascic/Shutterstock (173). Happy window/Shutterstock (181). **Chapter 6:** Kvarner Bay and the Northern Adriatic Islands: Ilijaaa/Dreamstime (183). iascic/iStockphoto (191). Joppi/Shutterstock (195). Ivica Pavicic/iStockphoto (200). xbrchx/iStockphoto (204). mislaw/Shutterstock (207). I love takeing photos and i think that is a really great opportunity for me to share them/iStockphoto (208). Sebestyenzoltan/Dreamstime (211). Xbrchx/Dreamstime (216). Deymos/Dreamstime (221). **Chapter 7:** Istria: Xbrchx/Dreamstime.com (225). Electropower/Dreamstime.com (235). xbrchx/Shutterstock (237). Epolischuk/Dreamstime (243). Goran234/ Dreamstime (245). Janoka82/iStockphoto (251). Sjankauskas/Dreamstime (254). xbrchx/Shutterstock (259). xbrchx/Shutterstock (262). **Chapter 8:** Zagreb and Inland Croatia: Dreamer4787/iStockphoto (269). Paulprescott/Dreamstime (282). Zdravko Troha/iStockphoto (285). Zdravko Troha/iStockphoto (291). Davor Djopar/shutterstock (296). mislaw/Shutterstock (300). Erix2005/Dreamstime (303). Ilija Ascic/Shutterstock (308). Rognar/Dreamstime (312-313). **Chapter 9:** Slavonia: Ilijaaa/Dreamstime (317). Tcerovski/Dreamstime (327). Ilija Ascic/Shutterstock (333). tokar/Shutterstock (336). **Chapter 10:** Montenegro: Olga355/iStockphoto (341). MichałBogacz/iStockphoto (350). Nightman1965/Shutterstock (355). **Chapter 11:** Slovenia: Bhirling/Dreamstime (357). Georgios Tsichlis/Shutterstock (367). S-F/Shutterstock (372). Gasparij/Dreamstime (378). Renedreuse/Dreamstime (381). RAndrei/Shutterstock (389). About Our Writers: All photos are courtesy of the writers.

Every effort has been made to trace the copyright holders, and we apologize in advance for any errors. We would be happy to apply the corrections in the following edition of this publication.

Fodor's ESSENTIAL CROATIA

Publisher: Stephen Horowitz, *General Manager*

Editorial: Douglas Stallings, *Editorial Director*; Jill Fergus, Jacinta O'Halloran, Amanda Sadlowski, *Senior Editors*; Kayla Becker, Alexis Kelly, *Editors*

Design: Tina Malaney, *Director of Design and Production*; Jessica Gonzalez, *Graphic Designer*; Mariana Tabares, *Design and Production Intern*

Production: Jennifer DePrima, *Editorial Production Manager*; Elyse Rozelle, *Senior Production Editor*; Monica White, *Production Editor*

Maps: Rebecca Baer, *Senior Map Editor*; David Lindroth, Mark Stroud (Moon Street Cartography), *Cartographers*

Photography: Viviane Teles, *Senior Photo Editor*; Namrata Aggarwal, Ashok Kumar, Carl Yu, *Photo Editors*; Rebecca Rimmer, *Photo Intern*

Business and Operations: Chuck Hoover, *Chief Marketing Officer*; Robert Ames, *Group General Manager*; Devin Duckworth, *Director of Print Publishing*; Victor Bernal, *Business Analyst*

Public Relations and Marketing: Joe Ewaskiw, *Senior Director Communications and Public Relations*

Fodors.com Jeremy Tarr, *Editorial Director*; Rachael Levitt, *Managing Editor*

Technology: Jon Atkinson, *Director of Technology*; Rudresh Teotia, *Lead Developer*; Jacob Ashpis, *Content Operations Manager*

Writers: John Bills, Andrea MacDonald, Melissa Paul, Lara Rasin

Editors: Amanda Sadlowski, Douglas Stallings

Production Editor: Jennifer DePrima

2nd Edition

ISBN 978-1-64097-368-8

ISSN 2574-352X

All details in this book are based on information supplied to us at press time. Always confirm information when it matters, especially if you're making a detour to visit a specific place. Fodor's expressly disclaims any liability, loss, or risk, personal or otherwise, that is incurred as a consequence of the use of any of the contents of this book.

SPECIAL SALES
This book is available at special discounts for bulk purchases for sales promotions or premiums. For more information, e-mail SpecialMarkets@fodors.com.

PRINTED IN CANADA

10 9 8 7 6 5 4 3 2

400

About Our Writers

 John Bills is an independent author, travel writer, and amateur darts player from the small nation of Wales. The majority of his adult life has been spent traipsing across the former Yugoslavia, writing doe-eyed love letters to everywhere from Belgrade to Bloke. He has written a variety of decidedly non-academic books about the region, covering history, travel, and more, all of which are available at ⊕ *www.johnbills. com*. He updated the Zadar and Northern Dalmatia, Montenegro, and Slovenia chapters this edition.

 Within ten minutes of her first arrival in Croatia **Andrea MacDonald**, mesmerized by the stunning old architecture and gorgeous locals, decided to rip up her return ticket and stay. She has since worked at a hostel in Istria learning the proper way to fold bed sheets, spent two summers guiding boat tours around the Dalmatian islands, and wrote a master's thesis about her travels around this wonderfully surprising country. These days, she divides her time between Croatia and her native Canada, leading tour groups around Europe and searching the rest of the world for a sea as beautiful as the Adriatic. For this edition, she updated the Experience, Travel Smart, Dubrovnik and Southern Dalmatia, and Slavonia chapters.

 Raised in Southern California, **Melissa Paul** was born craving adventure and kept traveling east to find it. From the mountains of Arizona to the big cities of New York and Philadelphia, Melissa finally managed to get all the way to Croatia, first landing on the island of Krk before falling in love with the hilltop artist town of Labin in Istria. In the six years she's called Croatia home, Melissa has renovated a 500-year-old stone house, jumped off cliffs into the aqua blue waters of the Adriatic Sea, and learned the benefits of slowing down to enjoy the beauty and simplicity of everyday life in Croatia. For this edition, she updated the Istria and Kvarner Bay chapters.

An international business graduate and former project manager who chose a passion-driven career change, **Lara Rasin** is currently a writer, editor, translator, and aspiring anthropologist as well as a project volunteer for the United Nations International Organization for Migration. Her work has appeared in *Time Out*, *Norway Today*, Croatia Honestly, Culture Trip, and more. Lara was born and raised in the United States and now divides her time between Croatia and Massachusetts. She's lived in Maryland, Massachusetts, North Carolina, Italy, and Croatia. A few of her favorite things are human rights, traveling, rock music, dessert, writing, places where nature is vast, freedom of speech, morning coffee, reading in bed, and old-school Star Trek. She updated the Split and Central Dalmatia and Zagreb and Inner Croatia chapters this edition.